A PRACTICAL APPROACH TO

CRIMINAL PROCEDURE

A PRACTICAL APPROACH TO
CRIMINAL
PROCEDURE

TWELFTH EDITION

John Sprack

BA, LLB, BARRISTER

Formerly Reader, Inns of Court School of Law

OXFORD
UNIVERSITY PRESS

OXFORD

UNIVERSITY PRESS

Great Clarendon Street, Oxford OX2 6DP

Oxford University Press is a department of the University of Oxford.
It furthers the University's objective of excellence in research, scholarship,
and education by publishing worldwide in

Oxford New York

Auckland Cape Town Dar es Salaam Hong Kong Karachi
Kuala Lumpur Madrid Melbourne Mexico City Nairobi
New Delhi Shanghai Taipei Toronto

With offices in

Argentina Austria Brazil Chile Czech Republic France Greece
Guatemala Hungary Italy Japan Poland Portugal Singapore
South Korea Switzerland Thailand Turkey Ukraine Vietnam

Oxford is a registered trade mark of Oxford University Press
in the UK and in certain other countries

Published in the United States
by Oxford University Press Inc., New York

© John Sprack and Christopher J Emmins 2008

First published by Blackstone Press 1981
Twelfth edition published 2008

British Library Cataloguing in Publication Data

Data available

Library of Congress Cataloging in Publication Data

Sprack, John.
A practical approach to criminal procedure / John Sprack.—12th ed.
   p. cm.
Includes bibliographical references and index.
   ISBN–13: 978–0–19–953539–2 (pbk.: alk. paper)   1. Criminal procedure—
England.   2. Criminal procedure—Wales.   I. Title: Criminal procedure.
II. Title.
   KD8329.E46 2008
   345.42'05—dc22   2008016303

Typeset by Newgen Imaging Systems (P) Ltd., Chennai, India
Printed in Great Britain
on acid-free paper by
CPI Antony Rowe, Chippenham, Wiltshire

ISBN 978–0–19–953539–2

5 7 9 10 8 6

PREFACE

The influence of the Criminal Justice Act 2003 continued to cast its shadow over the preparation of this edition. That is due, in part, to the staggered manner of its implementation (with the withdrawal of some target dates, so that important reforms such as the new procedure for mode of trial and sending to the Crown Court are left in limbo). It is also due to the need for the appellate courts to interpret some of its provisions, particularly the sometimes baffling measures in relation to sentencing.

The other area in which there has been considerable activity since the production of the last edition is the appearance of a range of sentencing guidelines. The Sentencing Guidelines Council, acting with input from the Sentencing Advisory Panel, has produced a series of comprehensive documents which are increasingly important in practice, with the result that more space is devoted in this edition to this development, together with the burgeoning case law in connection with dangerous offenders.

There are two other areas which have been given increased attention in this edition. The first is abuse of process, an important area for practitioners. Previous editions have covered the topic, but in a rather piecemeal fashion, and I have attempted to provide a clearer focus on the principles involved in this edition. The second is the inevitable tension between the growing emphasis which is placed by the judiciary on case management, and the desire of defence practitioners to protect the rights of their clients. This tension, which surfaces in areas such as defence disclosure, is exemplified by cases such as *R (Kelly) v Warley Magistrates Court* and *R (DPP) v Chorley Justices*.

As far as format is concerned, I have taken the opportunity in this edition to set out some of the more complex procedures in flowchart form, for example determining mode of trial and dealing with dangerous offenders, in the hope that this will make the verbal explanation clearer.

Finally, my thanks are due to my publishers, and in particular to Faye Judges and Jodi Towler for their hard work and professionalism.

I have endeavoured to state the law as at 15 April 2008.

John Sprack
April 2008

PREFACE TO THE FIRST EDITION

In writing this book I have tried to avoid the two main pitfalls which are present in many of the more traditional books on procedure. On the one hand there are those so filled with detail that it is almost impossible for the reader to keep sight of the main outlines of the subject. On the other hand it is tempting, for the sake of clarity, to deal with the main elements of court procedure only, but in so doing, omit many points which are necessary detail for the serious student of the subject.

I believe that this book steers a middle course between these two extremes and I am grateful to my publishers who have presented the book in such a way as to highlight the more important parts of the text. Matters of detail or interest, not essential to a broad understanding of the subject, have been printed in small type, slightly indented from the remainder of the text. The reader may therefore make use of the book at either of two levels. He may gain an overall view of the subject just by reading those parts of the book which are in large type; or he may acquire more detailed knowledge through reading in addition the paragraphs in small type. I have also used examples of the documents most commonly used in connection with criminal procedure either at the appropriate point in the text or in an imaginary Brief to Counsel on the case of John Smith. This further ensures that the book fully justifies its title as *A Practical Approach* to Criminal Procedure.

My thanks are due to my colleague at the Inns of Court School of Law, Miss Lynn Slater, BA, LLM, who has not only prepared the case and statute indexes, but also read the book as it was in the course of composition and made many invaluable suggestions for its improvement. My thanks also go to my publishers for their kindness and helpfulness, and, above all, to my parents for their unstinted support during the time the pages which follow were being written.

Walthamstow
17 September 1981

CONTENTS—SUMMARY

CONTENTS

SGS1

SGS3

PART 3 TRIAL ON INDICTMENT

Contents   XV

86519

TABLE OF CASES

European Union

TABLE OF STATUTORY INSTRUMENTS AND CODES OF PRACTICE

TABLE OF STATUTES

THE CLIENT

A INTRODUCTION

This Chapter attempts to give some guidance to the practitioner in dealing with a client in a **IN.01** criminal matter. It is not geared particularly to either barristers or solicitors, but takes certain situations where the tasks to be performed and the instructions to be sought are common to both branches of the profession. For ease of presentation it is presented from the point of view of the defence lawyer, but the points made are easily transferable to those who are representing the prosecution.

B PRELIMINARY MATTERS

A client charged with a criminal matter may well be frightened, bewildered and disorientated. **IN.02** Quite apart from the particular situation in which he finds himself, he may suffer from particular problems e.g., drug addiction, alcohol abuse, or mental health problems. Or he may be someone who has led a relatively sheltered life, and is completely thrown by the situation in which he finds himself. He may be resentful of authority and suspicious of lawyers, or may look upon you with gratitude and relief. The crucial point is that your client is someone who is in trouble, and that you are able to help. It is important to avoid stereotyping the person who is in front of you, and remember that he needs your advice and help (whether he knows it or not!).

A frequent feature of the interview with a client in a criminal matter is that it is conducted **IN.03** in conditions which are not conducive to careful thought or exploration of the issues.

At its most extreme, this can involve getting instructions for a bail application in a few minutes through the grille in a cell door at the police station. Yet the information and instructions which are sought may be crucial to the success or otherwise of the proceedings. As a result, it is vital that the lawyer is prepared, in the sense of being aware of as much of the legal and factual background as is possible in the circumstances, and has an agenda for the conduct of the interview. While there is no template which is going to fit all situations, the remainder of this Introduction attempts to help provide checklists for four of the commonest situations where the practitioner comes in contact with the client.

C   INITIAL INTERVIEW

IN.04   In the first interview with the client:

- Obtain the crucial information while the events are as fresh as possible in the client's mind.
- Ascertain personal details: name, address, date of birth, financial circumstances including both income and assets.
- Get as much detail as you can about any previous convictions: date, offence and circumstances, plea, sentence.
- Try to get hold of the charge sheet or summons for the present case.
- Get full details of any possible defence witnesses.
- Assist in completing the representation order for public funding.
- Give only general advice as to plea/mode of trial/sentence.
- Ascertain the position on bail (see IN.05).
- Tell the client that you await details of the prosecution case before giving firmer advice.

D   BAIL APPLICATION

IN.05   The application for bail is frequently the most important single task the advocate can perform for the client on a criminal charge. It is certainly the way in which many clients are persuaded of the merits of a particular lawyer. In taking instructions for the bail application, bear in mind the commonest grounds for objection to bail, i.e.,

(a) fear of absconding
(b) fear of further offences
(c) fear of interference with witnesses.

(See Chapter 7 for detail).

Instructions should cover:

- What previous convictions does the client have, if any?
- In particular, are there any instances of failure to surrender to bail?
- If so, what are the client's instructions?
- Was the failure to surrender deliberate, or due to an honest (even if unreasonable) mistake?

- Did the client surrender himself, or was he arrested for failure to answer his bail?
- If there are no convictions for failure to surrender despite a substantial record, this may help to show that he will not abscond. But check that the absence of convictions was not because he was in custody while awaiting trial on previous occasions!
- What are his community ties, e.g., job, family, house/flat, qualifications, prospects?
- Ask the client why the court should believe that he will answer to his bail—there may be reasons which do not appear on any checklist!
- What is the strength of the evidence against him? (If it is a weak case, the chances of his absconding are reduced).
- What is his plea? (If not guilty, he may be anxious to clear his name; if guilty, the credit which he should receive may make a custodial sentence less likely).
- What conditions will the client be prepared to accept if he is granted bail? (Assuming that in your judgement these may be necessary to ensure bail).
- Does he need his passport?
- Is there an address at which he could reside?
- Does he have any means to provide security?
- Does he know of a suitable surety?
- Is he prepared to keep his distance from the alleged victim and/or prosecution witnesses?
- Examine his record: if there is a pattern of offences, can it be explained?
- Have circumstances changed since the offences were committed?
- Is there a break since the last offence?
- Were any of the offences committed while he was on bail?

E   ADVICE ON PLEA

The consequences of the client's decision on how to plead are particularly far-reaching. **IN.06** The following matters ought to be canvassed:

- What are the client's instructions about the facts of the alleged offence, and (if relevant) his state of mind (intention/recklessness/self-defence etc.)?
- Does he wish to plead guilty or not guilty?
- Assuming for the present that the instructions and the proposed plea are consistent, proceed to advise on plea.
- The advice should be given with clarity and courtesy, and the reasons should be explained.
- If a not guilty plea has been indicated, the strengths and weaknesses of the prosecution and defence cases should be highlighted.
- The consequences of the client giving (or failing to give) evidence in his own defence should be explained.
- The likely position in regard to any previous convictions should be explored.
- The principle of credit for a guilty plea (particularly if early) should be dealt with.
- But the client should be told that if he is not guilty, your advice is that he should plead not guilty.
- It should be emphasized that the decision on plea is his own decision, and you can only advise.

- The above points deal with the relatively straightforward situation where instructions and proposed plea coincide, but that is not always the case, so consider the position where there is a conflict between his proposed plea and his instructions.
- If his instructions show that he is not guilty and he wishes to plead guilty, explore his motives.
- Is he aware of the consequences of a criminal conviction?
- Does he know that any plea in mitigation will have to be on the same basis as if he were guilty?
- Ensure that his intention as to plea, together with your advice, is reduced to writing, and signed in proper form to certify that he pleads of his own free will and despite advice.
- Assume on the other hand that the client confesses his guilt, but wishes to plead not guilty and have you represent him. Bear in mind the ethical position in which this puts you, and explain it.
- The burden of proof remains on the prosecution, and you can make sure that any defects in their case are exposed.
- But you cannot assert as true that which is false, and he should be aware of that.

F   ADVICE ON MODE OF TRIAL

IN.07   Where the offence is triable-either-way, and the client is pleading not guilty, the decision on mode of trial is of great importance. The factors at play are dealt with in detail in Chapter 8, but the main points to deal with are these:

- Explain the relevant differences between the way in which cases are tried in each court, e.g., who are the members of the jury, and what is their role and that of the judge.
- Point out that proceedings in the magistrates' court are somewhat less formal.
- Explain that, almost invariably, a case will be dealt with more quickly in the magistrates' court—both in the sense that it will be listed more quickly, and also that it will not take as long to hear.
- Deal with the costs implications in each court: the magistrates' court will be cheaper.
- Point out that the magistrates' powers of sentencing are limited, although they can commit to the Crown Court for sentence (bear in mind that the position will change in relation to the limit and the power of committal when the CJA 2003, Sch 3 is implemented).
- If the admissibility of any evidence (e.g., a confession) is challenged, then the jury in the Crown Court will not hear it unless the judge decides that they should. It is inevitable that the magistrates would hear the evidence, even if they decided that it was inadmissible.
- The same point may apply to previous convictions which may or may not be admissible (although in many magistrates' courts, this question is decided before trial, e.g., by a district judge).
- The most weighty factor in the decision-making process, however, may well depend on the answer to the question: 'where will I stand the best chance of acquittal?' Almost invariably, this is in front of a jury, although for particular types of offence the answer may be different, and this is one area where knowledge of local conditions may be crucial. And bear in mind that some clients will stand little or no chance of acquittal whatever the forum.
- Give your advice on mode of trial, explaining the reasons.
- Tell the client that it is his decision in the last analysis.

PART 1
INTRODUCTION

1

SETTING THE SCENE

Criminal trials in England and Wales take one of two forms. They are either trials on indict- **1.01** ment or summary trials. Trial in the youth court, which might at first sight appear to be a third distinct form of trial, is in fact a special form of summary trial. Parts 2 and 3 of this book will deal in detail with, respectively, summary trial and trial on indictment. The following two Paragraphs will give an indication of the salient characteristics of the two methods of trial.

A TRIAL ON INDICTMENT

Trial on indictment is the method used for trying the more serious offences. The trial takes **1.02** place before judge and jury in the Crown Court (subject to the exception mentioned in 1.05). The name 'trial on indictment' originates from the formal written statement of charges, and it is to the 'counts' contained in this indictment that the accused pleads 'Guilty' or 'Not guilty' at the beginning of his trial.

The trial is presided over by a paid professional judge, who is or was a practising barrister or **1.03** solicitor. The judge controls the course of the trial, adjudicates on all matters of the admissibility of evidence, and is the sole arbiter of matters of law in the case.

Matters of fact are decided by the jury, which consists of lay men and women, drawn at ran- **1.04** dom from a broad cross-section of the community, who are summoned for a period usually of two weeks. It is by no means unusual for this to be their only experience of the judicial system. They must accept and apply the law as it is explained to them by the judge in his summing-up at the end of the case, but they alone decide questions of fact. Should the judge, when summing-up, comment on the weight of the evidence or indicate what facts he thinks have been proved thereby, the jury may—and indeed, should—ignore the judge's views entirely unless they happen to coincide with their own. Having heard the evidence, the speeches of counsel and the judge's summing-up, it is then the duty of the jury to bring in the verdict. Thus the general principle may be stated that at trial on indictment, 'the law is for the judge, and the facts are for the jury'.

1.05 Exceptionally certain trials on indictment may be held in front of a judge, sitting without a jury (see Chapter 19).

B   SUMMARY TRIAL

1.06 Summary trial takes place in the magistrates' courts. At the commencement of the trial the accused pleads guilty or not guilty to a charge contained in a document called an information. The case is heard and determined by magistrates (also known as justices of the peace) who are the judges of both law and fact. The great majority of magistrates are lay men and women, but since most magistrates serve as such for many years, and will normally sit in court at least twice a month, they become familiar with summary proceedings and are not 'complete amateurs' like the average juror. In practice, too, magistrates tend to be drawn from a narrower social and age range than jurors (for details on appointment of magistrates see Chapter 6). A minority of magistrates are district judges, i.e., full-time, paid magistrates appointed from amongst barristers and solicitors of at least seven years' standing. One major difference between district judges and lay magistrates is that the former may, and normally do, sit alone to try cases, whereas at least two lay magistrates are required to try a case, and it is normal for them to sit in benches of three. Magistrates are entitled to seek advice from their clerk on matters of law, admissibility of evidence and procedure, but the decision on these matters remains solely for the magistrates. Clerks are qualified lawyers (for details on appointment see Chapter 6), and, in addition to their duties in advising magistrates, they play an important role in the smooth functioning of the court, both in court (e.g., putting the information to the accused) and behind the scenes (e.g., working on the issue of summonses). The merits and demerits of trial on indictment as opposed to summary trial are much debated. Some of the arguments are mentioned in Chapter 8.

C   CLASSES OF OFFENCES

1.07 For purposes of mode of trial, offences are divided into three major classes, namely: those triable only on indictment, those triable only summarily, and those triable either way. Chapter 8 explains in detail how to decide into which class a particular offence falls, but the broad principle is that the most serious offences (e.g., murder, manslaughter, robbery, rape, incest, and causing grievous bodily harm with intent to do so) are triable only on indictment. Offences of medium gravity, especially those whose gravity varies greatly depending upon the facts of the particular case, are triable either way (e.g., theft, handling stolen goods, obtaining property by deception, most forms of burglary, non-aggravated criminal damage, assault occasioning actual bodily harm, unlawful wounding, and indecent assault). The least grave offences are triable only summarily. Most of them are very trivial and are not even punishable with imprisonment. They do, however, include some relatively serious matters such as assaulting a police officer in the execution of his duty, interfering with a motor vehicle, drink-driving offences, using threatening words or behaviour, taking a motor vehicle without the owner's consent, and driving while disqualified. Finally, it should be noted that special rules govern the trial of juveniles (i.e., those under 18). The effect of these rules is that many offences which are triable only on indictment or triable either way in the case of an adult must be tried summarily in a youth court if the accused is under 18.

Linked to the three-fold classification of offences described above is a simpler division   **1.08** between 'indictable offences' and 'summary offences'. Those terms are defined by Schedule 1 to the Interpretation Act 1978 as follows:

(a)   'Indictable offence' means an offence which, if committed by an adult, is triable on indictment, whether it is exclusively so triable or triable either way;

(b)   'Summary offence' means an offence which, if committed by an adult, is triable only summarily.

Also, the Interpretation Act, defines, not surprisingly, 'offence triable either way' as an offence which in the case of an adult, may be tried either on indictment or summarily.

The major point to note from the above definitions is that, when the term 'indictable offence'   **1.09** is used in a statute without further qualification, it encompasses not only offences that must be tried on indictment but also the numerous offences which, depending on the circumstances, may either be tried on indictment or tried summarily.

2

THE ROLE OF THE CRIMINAL PROCEDURE RULES

The procedural framework for the criminal courts is governed by various sets of rules. Of **2.01** course, these rules do not always provide a clear description of what actually happens on the ground. In order to get an overall picture of the workings of the courts in practice, it is necessary to have some idea of the context in which the rules operate, the way in which they interact with the underlying principles of substantive criminal law and evidence, and the conventions which are adopted by the judges and practitioners who implement them. This book is an attempt to provide that context. But the rules themselves play an important part in setting out the duties of the parties and the court in relation to the case and the various transactions which it involves. They set deadlines, prescribe methods of performing tasks, and lay down the powers of the courts to deal with a variety of situations. They constitute the bricks with which the edifice of criminal procedure is constructed.

Given the central role of the rules in describing criminal procedure, it is important that they **2.02** should be accessible and readily understandable. Until 2005, however, there was no one place in which one could expect to find them. There were some 50 separate sets of rules, to be found in a variety of places, and sometimes with difficulty. The judiciary and the legal profession saw this as a significant barrier to an efficient and effective system of criminal justice, and as a result, a committee of judges, magistrates, legal practitioners and representatives of users of the criminal justice system was set up—the Criminal Procedure Rules Committee. It embarked upon a major project to consolidate the various sets of rules, operating across the different criminal courts. The result is the Criminal Procedure Rules 2005 (CrimPR), which are set out in a statutory instrument (SI 2005 No 384).

This Chapter begins by looking at the scope of the CrimPR and likely future developments **2.03** (2.04. to 2.07). It then goes on to consider the linch-pin of the CrimPR, the 'overriding objective' which lays down the purpose of the courts in dealing with a case, and the duties of the parties which flow from that purpose (2.08 to 2.13). It then looks at the very considerable case management powers conferred upon the court—which have caused some controversy, and are seen by some as an unwelcome innovation, by others as a crucial necessity for the modern criminal justice system (2.14 to 2.17). It then considers the way in which the CrimPR deal with two areas of evidence which were radically altered by the Criminal Justice Act 2003 (CJA 2003): the procedure relating to hearsay evidence (2.18 to 2.20) and the procedure relating to evidence of bad character (2.21 to 2.24). These have been singled out both because of their day-to-day importance, and because they constitute major areas of new procedural law. Many of the remaining parts of the CrimPR, and individual rules, are dealt with in the relevant sections of this work.

A   THE SCOPE OF THE CRIMINAL PROCEDURE RULES

2.04   In the main, the rules are a massive exercise in consolidation. They bring together under one umbrella a number of sets of rules, and arrange them in structured form. In the process, rules pertaining to the magistrates' court and Crown Court have in a number of instances been unified, with a view to consistency. The rules can be downloaded from the website of the Ministry of Justice <http://www.justice.gov.uk/criminal/procrules_fin/index.htm> (see also the various related websites listed at the end of this Chapter). They are divided into ten main subject divisions, which essentially follow a chronological order in accordance with the progress of a criminal case, as follows:

(a) General matters (Parts 1 to 6)
(b) Preliminary proceedings (Parts 7 to 17)
(c) Custody and bail (Parts 18 to 20)
(d) Disclosure (Parts 21 to 26)
(e) Evidence (Parts 27 to 36)
(f) Trial (Parts 37 to 41)
(g) Sentencing (Parts 42 to 55)
(h) Confiscation and related proceedings (Parts 56 to 62)
(i) Appeal (Parts 63 to 75)
(j) Costs (Parts 76 to 78)

2.05   Some sections of the CrimPR were not completed prior to initial commencement in April 2005, and were published at a later date, or are still due to be published. The Criminal Procedure Rule Committee has indicated that other sections are likely to be simplified, e.g., those dealing with custody and bail, and that yet others will change as new procedures are introduced, e.g., those dealing with the allocation of cases between the magistrates' court and Crown Court. It is part of the aim of the CrimPR to ensure that the new rules are written in plain modern English, so as to be accessible to the lay reader. As the project is not complete, a glossary is provided at the end of the rules, to explain words used in those of the old rules which have been adopted by the CrimPR prior to the process of simplification.

B CONSOLIDATION AND CODIFICATION

Generally, the content of the CrimPR replicates the rules which are being replaced (drawn in **2.06** particular from the Crown Court Rules (SI 1982 No 1109), the Magistrates' Courts Rules (SI 1981 No 552), and the Criminal Appeal Rules (SI 1968 No 1262)). The process of consolidation has, of course, resulted in certain drafting amendments, for example to cope with the fact that there is now one set of rules for the various courts in question. Nevertheless, it is still best described, in the main, as a consolidation process. But it is not intended to end there. Quite apart from filling in the gaps, the CrimPR are seen as 'an essential first step towards the creation of a comprehensive criminal procedural code—something that was recommended in the *Review of the Criminal Courts of England and Wales* by Lord Justice Auld' (Explanatory Summary from the Criminal Procedure Rule Committee Secretariat, spring 2005). One of the attractions of a Criminal Procedure Code is that it would set out the law relating to any particular procedural topic in one place. To take an example, Part 19 of the CrimPR contains the rules relating to bail in the magistrates' court and Crown Court. It sets out the manner in which applications should be made, the duties of the parties and the court in relation to notification, the various deadlines and the like. What it does not do, however, is set out

(a) what legal criteria will be applied in deciding whether to grant bail upon an application or an appeal; nor
(b) what will actually happen in court.

As far as (a) is concerned, the answer is to be found in the Bail Act and the case law upon it, and there is a commentary in Chapter 7 of this book. As far as (b) is concerned, the answer depends upon the practices adopted in the courts in question, which are seldom set out in either statute or case law. However, both (a) and (b) fall clearly within the scope of 'criminal procedure'. Arguably, then, a Criminal Procedure Code would cover such topics as this, so that they were readily accessible, understandable, and could be found in the same place as other procedural topics.

Broadly, then, the CrimPR has thus far been a project of consolidation. There are two Parts of **2.07** it which cannot be accurately described as consolidation, however, although each builds to some extent upon the current practice of the courts of first instance, and the decisions of the appellate courts. Those parts are:

(a) Part 1: the Overriding Objective; and
(b) Part 3: Case Management.

These Parts are dealt with respectively in 2.08 to 2.13 and 2.14 to 2.17.

C THE OVERRIDING OBJECTIVE

Part 1 of the CPR deals with the overriding objective, and reads: **2.08**

1.1 **The overriding objective**
 (1) The overriding objective of this new code is that criminal cases be dealt with justly.

(2) Dealing with a criminal case justly includes—

    (a) Acquitting the innocent and convicting the guilty;

    (b) dealing with the prosecution and the defence fairly;

    (c) recognising the rights of a defendant, particularly those under Article 6 of the European Convention on Human Rights;

    (d) respecting the interests of witnesses, victims and jurors and keeping them informed of the progress of the case;

    (e) dealing with the case efficiently and expeditiously;

    (f) ensuring that appropriate information is available to the court when bail and sentence are considered; and

    (g) dealing with the case in ways that take into account—

        (i) the gravity of the offence alleged,

        (ii) the complexity of what is in issue,

        (iii) the severity of the consequences for the defendant and others affected, and

        (iv) the needs of other cases.

1.2 The duty of the participants in a criminal case

(1) Each participant, in the conduct of each case, must—

    (a) prepare and conduct the case in accordance with the overriding objective;

    (b) comply with these Rules, practice directions and directions made by the court; and

    (c) at once inform the court and all parties of any significant failure (whether or not that participant is responsible for that failure) to take any procedural step required by these Rules, any practice direction or any direction of the court. A failure is significant if it might hinder the court in furthering the overriding objective.

(2) Anyone involved in any way with a criminal case is a participant in its conduct for the purposes of this rule.

1.3 The application by the court of the overriding objective

The court must further the overriding objective in particular when—

(a) exercising any power given to it by legislation (including these Rules);

(b) applying any practice direction; or

(c) interpreting any rule or practice direction.

In its brief form, then, the overriding objective is (rather unsurprisingly) 'that cases be dealt with justly' (r 1.1(1)). The rule then goes on to specify a number of elements which are included within the ambit of dealing justly with a criminal case. Again, they are by and large uncontroversial, and together form the aims which the courts ought to have at the centre of their function. The fact that 'acquitting the innocent and convicting the guilty' are mentioned with apparent equivalence did cause some criminal practitioners concern. It was felt by some that this did not emphasize sufficiently the fundamental principle that it is the prosecution which brings the case, and must prove it beyond reasonable doubt. But the formulation of the overriding objective does not in any sense undermine the burden and standard of proof. The Lord Chief Justice, in his note to the Lord Chancellor which accompanied and introduced the CPR, stated that: 'The presumption of innocence and a robust adversarial process are essential features of English legal tradition and of the defendant's right to a fair trial. The overriding objective acknowledges those rights. It must not be read as detracting from a defendant's right to silence or from the confidentiality properly attaching to what passes between a lawyer and his client.'

Similarly, r 1.1(2)(b) with its inclusion of 'dealing with the prosecution and the defence **2.09** fairly' must inevitably be taken to incorporate the reality of the situation—that the prosecution, as representative of the state, has access to investigatory resources which are not generally available to the defence. The jurisprudence of the European Court of Human Rights in emphasizing the principle of equality of arms (see, for example, *Kaufman v Belgium* (1986) 50 DR 98 at 115) has an important part to play in interpreting what the formal equivalence of defence and prosecution ought to mean in practice.

There is a notable contrast between the formulae in r 1.1(2)(c) and (d), which properly **2.10** reflects the longstanding basis of the English legal tradition, and the European Convention on Human Rights (ECHR). Whereas the rights of the defendant (particularly those under Art 6 of the ECHR) have to be recognized, there is a different formula—'respecting the interests' in relation to other parties in the case, e.g., victims and witnesses. The terms in which these propositions are expressed give proper weight to the two sets of considerations, and make it clear that proposition (c) takes precedence over proposition (d) where there is any clash between the two (which, of course, there will not be in the great majority of instances).

Rule 1.1(2)(e)—'dealing with the case efficiently and expeditiously'—is closely related to the **2.11** new provisions on case management which are dealt with in 2.14 to 2.17. Rule 1.1(2)(f) will apply particularly to agencies which may have information relating to the defendant's criminal record, or be responsible for reports, and underlines their duty to assist the court by ensuring that the relevant information is available at the crucial time when decisions as to bail and sentence are considered. It is submitted that the use of the word 'appropriate' makes it clear that there is no change to the duty of confidentiality which is owed by lawyer to client (see also the quote from the Lord Chief Justice in 2.8).

As to r 1.1(2)(g), the courts ought to be astute to ensure that cases are dealt with justly, even if **2.12** the offence in question is a relatively minor one. Any criminal conviction carries some sort of stigma, has the potential for life-altering adverse consequences, and is of great importance to the individual directly affected. Nevertheless, it would be unrealistic to expect equivalent resources to be devoted to a case which ought to be tried in the magistrates' court and one which was indictable only. Again, the factors to be taken into account under this element of 'dealing justly' must be fleshed out by the approach of the courts to case management (see 2.14 to 2.17).

After the concept of 'dealing justly' has been elaborated in r 1.1(2), the remaining rules in Part **2.13** 1 deal with the duty of the participants in the case to prepare and conduct the case in accordance with the overriding objective, and to comply with the rules and directions which the court makes. They are also expected to notify the court and all parties 'at once . . . of any significant failure' to comply with the rules or directions. A failure is 'significant' if it might hinder the court in furthering the overriding objective. This duty holds whether the participant in question is responsible for the failure or not. This provision, familiarly known as the 'grassing up' rule, means that a party who does not inform the court of the shortcomings of another party will itself be liable to sanctions. The court, for its part, is fixed with a duty to implement the overriding objective by r 1.3. As to the manner in which it does so, that is a matter for the case management provisions (see 2.14 to 2.17).

D CASE MANAGEMENT

2.14 Part 3 of the CrimPR applies to the management of all cases in the magistrates' court and Crown Court, including the Crown Court acting in its appellate capacity with respect to the magistrates' court (r 3.1). Rule 3.2(1) lays down that the court must further the overriding objective (see 2.08 to 2.13) by 'actively managing the case'. Rule 3.2(2) then sets out a list of elements of active case management, based upon early identification of the issues and including the setting of a timetable. The court must give directions appropriate to the needs of the case as early as possible. Rule 3.2 has been bolstered by Rule 3.3, which puts the parties under a duty to assist the court in achieving the overriding objective. This means, in particular, that the defence is fixed with a duty to identify the issues which are in dispute in a criminal trial. The position was stated with clarity by Thomas LJ in *R (DPP) v Chorley Justices* [2006] EWCA 1795 (Admin):

> If a defendant refuses to identify what the issues are, one thing is clear: he can derive no advantage from that or seek, as appears to have happened in this case, to attempt an ambush at trial. The days of ambushing and taking last-minute technical points are gone. They are not consistent with the overriding objective of deciding cases justly, acquitting the innocent and convicting the guilty.

There are, however, limits to the obligations of the defence to assist the court by revealing its case in advance, as was made clear in *R (Kelly) v Warley Magistrates' Court* [2007] EWHC 1836 (Admin). In that case, the defence advocate was ordered by the district judge to disclose the names, addresses, and dates of birth of defence witnesses, the order being based upon supposed powers within the CrimPR. The case was taken on judicial review, and it was held on appeal that such an order was outside the power of the magistrates, as it would contravene legal professional privilege and litigation privilege (see para 9.24).

2.15 The need for active case management is a theme which the Court of Appeal has emphasized in various cases, particularly in the recent past, and perhaps most notably in *Jisl* [2004] All ER (D) 31 (Apr), where Judge LJ stated (paras 114–118):

> The starting point is simple. Justice must be done. The defendant is entitled to a fair trial: and, which is sometimes overlooked, the prosecution is equally entitled to a reasonable opportunity to present the evidence against the defendant. It is not however a concomitant of the entitlement to a fair trial that either or both sides are further entitled to take as much time as they like, or for that matter, as long as counsel and solicitors or the defendants themselves think appropriate. Resources are limited. The funding for courts and judges, for prosecuting and the vast majority of defence lawyers is dependent on public money, for which there are many competing demands. Time itself is a resource. Every day unnecessarily used, while the trial meanders sluggishly to its eventual conclusion, represents another day's stressful waiting for the remaining witnesses and the jurors in that particular trial, and no less important, continuing and increasing tension and worry for another defendant or defendants, some of whom are remanded in custody, and the witness in trials which are waiting their turn to be listed. It follows that the sensible use of time requires judicial management and control. . . .

> The principle therefore is not in doubt. This appeal enables us to reemphasise that its practical application depends on the determination of trial judges and the co-operation of the legal profession. Active, hands on, case management, both pre-trial and throughout the trial itself, is now regarded as an essential part of the judge's duty. The profession must understand that this has

become and will remain part of the normal trial process, and that cases must be prepared and conducted accordingly.

The issues in this particular trial were identified at a very early stage, indeed during the course of the previous trial itself. In relation to each of the defendants, in a single word, the issue was knowledge. And indeed, the issue in most trials is equally readily identified.

B [2006] Crim LR 54 deals with the way in which the judge ought to exercise his powers of case **2.16** management, with particular emphasis on time limits. The trial judge intervened on several occasions during cross-examination by defence counsel of the complainant in a rape trial, but the cross-examination continued at some length. In due course, the judge said 'You will finish your cross-examination within ten minutes.' Counsel continued until the judge told her that she had three more minutes. Eventually, she was told to bring matters to an end, and asked for it to be recorded that she was being told to stop her cross-examination. The defendant was convicted and appealed on the ground that the judge had prevented his counsel from exercising her right to cross-examine the witness properly. The Court of Appeal dismissed the appeal. Although it should not become a routine feature of trial management that judges should impose time limits for evidence in chief or cross-examination of witnesses, where counsel indulged in prolix or repetitious questioning, judges were fully entitled, and indeed obliged to impose reasonable time limits. A fair trial was not inconsistent with proper judicial control over the use of court time. The Court of Appeal would not interfere with a decision made by a judge when exercising a case management function unless it was plain that it had resulted in unfairness. In this case, the judge's decision to impose a time limit was entirely justified and did not result in any unfairness to the appellant.

There is now, in addition to Part 3 of the CrimPR, a case management Practice Direction, **2.17** which forms Part IV.41 of the *Consolidated Criminal Practice Direction* (see <http://www. hmcourts-service.gov.uk/cms/pds.htm>). The Consolidated Practice Direction also contains an annex (Annex E) which sets out the forms to be used for case management purposes (r 3. 11(1) of the CrimPR). These forms may be amended from time to time under the authority of the Lord Chief Justice, to take account of changes in the law.

E   HEARSAY EVIDENCE

Part 34 of the CrimPR sets out the procedural rules relating to hearsay evidence. These rules **2.18** were introduced in the wake of the new provisions relating to such evidence in the CJA 2003. They lay down the framework within which the court can consider the admission of hearsay evidence. The main points are:

(a) the rules apply both to the magistrates' court and the Crown Court;
(b) where the prosecutor wishes to introduce certain types of hearsay evidence at a hearing in the magistrates' court, he must give notice of it at the same time as prosecution disclosure (see Chapter 9);
(c) where the prosecutor wishes to introduce such hearsay evidence at a hearing in the Crown Court, he must give notice of it not more than 14 days after committal or the equivalent event (see Chapter 13);

(d) where the defendant wishes to introduce such hearsay evidence (in whatever court), he must do so not more than 14 days after prosecution disclosure;

(e) a party who receives notice of hearsay evidence may oppose it by giving notice within 14 days;

(f) any notice must be given in the form set out in the Practice Direction (see 2.17);

(g) the court may dispense with the requirement for notice, allow it to be given in a different form or orally, and shorten a time limit or extend it even after it has expired.

2.19 It is only certain categories of hearsay evidence which fall subject to the notice regime set out in the preceding paragraph. The categories in question are:

(a) hearsay evidence admissible because the witness is unavailable in accordance with the conditions laid down in s 116 of the CJA 2003;

(b) hearsay evidence admissible because it complies with the business documents exemption (see s 117 of the 2003 Act);

(c) multiple hearsay (see s 121 of the 2003 Act);

(d) evidence sought to be admitted at the discretion of the court or the judge, on the basis that it is in the interests of justice to admit it (see s 114 (1)(d) of the 2003 Act).

In addition, the court's power to vary the deadlines and allow oral notification or opposition is crucial, given the fact that the need for the introduction of hearsay evidence (or the fact that a particular piece of evidence is hearsay) may only become apparent during the course of a trial.

2.20 The CrimPR do not deal with the bases on which hearsay evidence may be admitted, nor the factors which the court will take into account in deciding whether to admit it. Those are matters which are dealt with in the CJA 2003, ss 114 to 136. As they are clearly part of the law of evidence, they are also beyond the scope of this book.

F   EVIDENCE OF BAD CHARACTER

2.21 The CJA 2003 also introduced radical changes to the law of evidence insofar as it related to admissibility of evidence of bad character of the defendant and others. Evidence of bad character in this sense is usually about previous convictions, but may be broader than that. The evidential changes are contained in CJA ss 98 to 113, and the CrimPR set out the procedural rules in Part 35. Similar comments to those contained in 2.20 can be made in relation to this area.

2.22 Part 35 of the CrimPR deals first with the introduction of a non-defendant's bad character (rr 35.1 to 35.3) and can be summarized as follows:

(a) the rules apply both to the magistrates' court and the Crown Court;

(b) a party wanting to introduce evidence or cross-examine about a non-defendant's bad character in the magistrates' court must apply to the court with copies to all other parties not more than 14 days after prosecution disclosure (Chapter 9);

(c) such an application should be made as soon reasonably practicable where it concerns a non-defendant who is giving evidence for the defence;

(d) the application may be opposed by notice in writing to the court and all other parties.

Part 35 then goes on to deal with the introduction of evidence of the defendant's bad charac- **2.23**
ter (rr 35.4 to 35.6), and may be summarized as follows:

(a) a prosecutor who wishes to adduce evidence or cross-examine about the defendant's bad
    character in the magistrates' court must give notice to the court and all other parties at the
    time of production disclosure (Chapter 9);
(b) in a Crown Court case, the prosecution must give notice not more than 14 days after com-
    mittal or the equivalent event (Chapter 13);
(c) a co-defendant who wants to adduce evidence or cross-examine about a defendant's bad
    character must give notice not more than 14 days after prosecution disclosure;
(d) a defendant applying to exclude evidence of his own bad character must do so not more
    than 14 days after receiving notice from the prosecutor or the co-defendant of their inten-
    tion to introduce or cross-examine about such evidence.

All the notices and applications about evidence of bad character, whether of a defendant or **2.24**
someone else must be given on the relevant form contained in the Practice Direction (see
2.17). The court has a discretion (r 35.8) to allow notice to be given in a different form or orally.
Further, it may shorten a time limit or extend it even after it has expired. As pointed out in
relation to hearsay evidence, such flexibility is crucial to the trial process, where an issue as
to the admissibility of evidence may arise suddenly, e.g., because of something which a
witness has said.

KEY DOCUMENTS

Criminal Procedure Rules 2005, available on the website of the Ministry of Justice:
    <http://www.justice.gov.uk/criminal/procrules_fin/index.htm>.
Practice Direction (Criminal Proceedings: Consolidation) [2002] 1 WLR 2870. The updated
    version is available at <http://www.hmcourts-service.gov.uk/cms/pds.htm>.

3

PRELIMINARIES TO COURT APPEARANCE

3.01 This Chapter aims to deal with what happens to a suspect between his initially being questioned by a police officer about an offence and his making his first court appearance. The subject is a wide-ranging one, involving evidence and constitutional law as well as procedure proper. The aim is to give an overall impression of what happens to a suspect, concentrating especially on police procedure and practice. For those aspects of the subject which are more properly the province of constitutional law or evidence (e.g., powers of arrest and search or the exclusion of inadmissible confessions), the reader is referred for details to *Blackstone's Criminal Practice 2008*, especially sections D1 and F17.

A   'PACE' AND CODES OF PRACTICE

3.02 For most of the areas of law dealt with in this Chapter, the prime source of authority is the Police and Criminal Evidence Act 1984 and the Codes of Practice promulgated under s 67 thereof.

PACE

3.03 The Police and Criminal Evidence Act 1984, generally known as 'PACE', was passed as a result of the wide-ranging report of the Royal Commission on Criminal Procedure (the Philips Commission). To a large measure, the Act reflects the recommendations of the Report, although inevitably the Government departed from the Commission on points of detail. It brought about a sea-change in several significant aspects of police procedure. Parts of the legislation were completely new (e.g., those sections dealing with the periods of time for which a suspect may be held at a police station without being charged); other parts built upon the pre-existing statute and common law (e.g., the provisions as to powers of arrest). Thus, to understand the Act, it is sometimes necessary to know a little of what preceded it. The Act is supplemented by the Codes of Practice, the importance of which is explained in the next Paragraph.

Codes of Practice

The provisions of PACE are principally concerned with police powers—e.g., to stop and search **3.04**
a member of the public, to search premises in order to find evidence of crime, to arrest a suspect, to detain him at the police station and to question him both before and after arrest.
However, an Act would become unwieldy if it tried to do more than lay down a framework for
the exercise of such powers. Detailed advice and regulations to cover even a representative
sample of the vast range of different problems encountered by the police in the course of their
investigations cannot be put into primary legislation. On the other hand, such detailed rules
are desirable so that the police and public will know with reasonable certainty how an investigation ought to be conducted and what their respective rights and duties are. The solution
adopted by PACE was to empower the Home Secretary to issue Codes of Practice covering certain aspects of police powers and procedure. The Codes are something of a constitutional
oddity in that they are not statutory instruments (i.e., they have no legislative effect), but
they were brought into operation by a statutory instrument, namely an order made by the
Home Secretary which had to be approved by a resolution of each House of Parliament (see
PACE, s 67(1)–(7)). Before the order was approved, draft Codes were laid before Parliament.
There are eight Codes presently in operation, entitled as follows: Code A (Code of Practice for
the Exercise by Police Officers of Statutory Powers of Stop and Search), Code B (Code of
Practice for the Searching of Premises by Police Officers and the Seizure of Property found by
Police Officers on Persons or Premises), Code C (Code of Practice for the Detention, Treatment
and Questioning of Persons by Police Officers), Code D (Code of Practice for the Identification
of Persons by Police Officers), Code E (Code of Practice on Tape Recording), Code F (Code of
Practice on Video Recording), and Code G (Code of Practice for the Statutory Power of Arrest
by Police Officers). Code H, which is beyond the scope of this book, deals with detention
under the Terrorism Act. They will hereafter be called the 'Stop and Search Code', the 'Search
of Premises Code', the 'Detention, Treatment and Questioning Code', the 'Identification
Code', the 'Tape Recording Code', the 'Video Recording Code' and the 'Power of Arrest Code'.
The Codes are published by and are obtainable from The Stationery Office. Copies are kept at
police stations, and are made available to detained suspects on request. Code C is the most
important, and a reference simply to 'the Code' should be understood as referring to Code C.

As a result of the CJA 2003, orders revising the Codes may either be laid before Parliament or **3.05**
be subject to the draft affirmative procedure. During the passage of the 2003 Act the
Government undertook to be bound by the advice of the Home Affairs Select Committee as to
the appropriate procedure to be followed for future proposed changes. However, it is clear that
amendments to existing Codes will in future be easier to effect. Any new Code, by contrast, will
have to be laid before Parliament and approved by each House.

The Codes are seen by the Home Office as a concise guide to the proper conduct of criminal **3.06**
investigations. Each Code commences with a paragraph which says that it must be 'readily
available at all police stations for consultation by police officers, detained persons and members of the public'. Some of the material is a repetition in less formal language of what is also
in PACE itself. Other parts of the Codes are an amplification and explanation of the Act, while
yet other parts deal with subjects not directly covered by the primary legislation (e.g., the cautioning of suspects and the holding of identification parades). Any breach of a provision of a
Code is not of itself a criminal offence or civil wrong, although in both civil and criminal proceedings the courts are obliged to take into account any provision of a Code which appears to

be relevant to a question arising in the proceedings (s 67(10) and (11)). Thus, if evidence against an accused was obtained through breach of a Code, that is a matter which the defence can pray in aid when objecting to the admissibility of the evidence.

3.07   The Codes of Practice had no precise equivalent in the pre-1986 law. They are, however, roughly related to the Judges' Rules. Those were rules of practice, formulated by the judges for the guidance of police officers. They dealt with the cautioning of suspects (Rule II), the charging of suspects (Rule III), the taking of written statements under caution (Rule IV), and the showing of statements made by others to persons who had already been charged (Rule V). In addition, there was a Preamble which affirmed certain general principles relating to the questioning of suspects, whilst appended to the Rules were administrative directions (e.g., about giving refreshment to suspects at the police station) which were issued by the Home Office without the direct approval of the judiciary. Evidence obtained through breach of the Judges' Rules, notably confessions, might be excluded at the discretion of the trial judge. In practice, it was rare for that to happen, although a departure from the Rules provided a useful additional ground for the defence to rely upon when their basic argument was that the accused's confession was inadmissible because it had been made involuntarily as a result of police oppression.

Enforcing PACE and the Codes

3.08   The proper conduct of criminal investigations is not ensured merely by carefully defining police powers and offering wise guidance on how they should be exercised. It is essential that the police both stay within the powers given to them by PACE and observe the provisions of the Codes of Practice. This obvious truth was not lost upon the Philips Commission. They considered two basic methods of ensuring that such of their proposals as found favour with the legislature would be obeyed by the police. These were (a) to rely on the police to discipline themselves through bringing disciplinary charges against officers who breached PACE or the Codes, and (b) to enable the courts to exclude evidence which had been obtained illegally or unfairly. The Commission came down firmly on the side of the first method, almost to the exclusion of the second. They did not think that the rules on admissibility of evidence at criminal trials should be used as an indirect means of controlling the way the police gather evidence. The one exception to this was in respect of confessions obtained through actual or threatened violence which the Commission wanted automatically excluded so as to mark society's absolute disapproval of the use of force against suspects. Otherwise, they saw the recording of when and why police powers were exercised and the threat of disciplinary charges in cases of apparent excess as the best means of controlling police conduct. The original Police and Criminal Evidence Bill followed the Commission's recommendations, but at a late stage of the progress of the second Bill through Parliament Lord Scarman proposed an amendment which would have placed on the courts a duty to exclude illegally obtained evidence. The Government responded by bringing forward an amendment of its own, which was enacted as s 78 of PACE. As a result, there are now five main sanctions to discourage contravention of the Act and the Codes:

(a)   If the contravention amounts to a criminal offence, the officer can be prosecuted in the normal way. For example, the carrying out of an unlawful search of premises might entail damage to the premises and hence a charge of criminal damage, or a prosecution for assault might result from either the effecting of an unlawful arrest or the use of violence to obtain a confession. In other words, being a member of the police confers no immunity against the operation of the criminal law. If the Crown Prosecution Service (CPS) are reluctant to prosecute, it is open to the victim to begin proceedings privately. The disadvantage with criminal proceedings is that proving a case beyond reasonable doubt against a police officer is difficult, especially if there is no independent evidence of what occurred, and anyway a successful prosecution will not directly benefit the victim.

(b) If the contravention of the Act or Codes amounts to a civil tort (e.g., assault, false imprisonment or malicious prosecution), the victim can sue the officers responsible. He may also join as a co-defendant the Chief Officer of Police for the force concerned, who is vicariously liable for the tortious conduct of his officers in the performance or purported performance of their duties.

(c) Whether or not it is also against the criminal or civil law, any contravention of a Code of Practice may be a disciplinary offence, covered by the police discipline regulations. The penalty can be as severe as dismissal from the force.

(d) A contravention of PACE or the Codes (or any other illegal or unfair conduct) may result in the evidence which was thereby obtained being ruled inadmissible. This is the effect of s 78 of PACE, which provides that the court may exclude evidence on which the prosecution proposes to rely if 'having regard to all the circumstances, including the circumstances in which the evidence was obtained, the admission of the evidence would have such an adverse effect on the fairness of the proceedings that the court ought not to admit it'.

(e) If a contravention of PACE or the Codes leads to the accused making a confession, the contravention may, depending on its precise nature, either be sufficient of itself to make the confession inadmissible or be a contributory factor which—taken in conjunction with other circumstances—will have the same result. Thus, the general rule discussed in (d) is reinforced and extended in the particular case of irregularities leading to confessions (see 3.49 for details).

In relation to both (d) and (e) above, judges at first instance and the Court of Appeal have, **3.09** since the passing of PACE, shown a readiness to exercise the discretion in favour of the defence (see 3.52 to 3.63 and 3.66 to 3.67 in particular). This contrasts with the attitude which prevailed in the days of the Judges' Rules (see above).

B   COMMENCING A PROSECUTION: THE TWO BASIC METHODS

There are two basic methods of commencing a prosecution. One is for the police to arrest the **3.10** suspect without a warrant; take him to the police station, and then (probably after a period of questioning at the station) have him charged formally with the offence. The other is for a prosecutor to lay an information before a magistrate or a magistrates' clerk, alleging that the accused has committed the offence specified in the information. On the basis of the information, a summons is issued and served on the accused. The summons requires the accused to attend at the magistrates' court on a specified day to answer the allegation.

Commencing a prosecution with a charge is an option available only to the police, in liaison **3.11** with public prosecutors. The police, and other public prosecuting agencies (in some areas— see 3.12) and private individuals may all make use of summonses. Where the police prosecute by summons, they will almost certainly have first talked to the suspect about the offence and warned him that he might be prosecuted. There are a number of variations on the two basic procedures. For example, a private citizen may arrest a suspect without warrant and then hand him over to the police with a view to their preferring a charge. Or the police sometimes arrest a person, take him to the station, and then decide that the case is more conveniently dealt with by way of summons. They therefore release him without charge, informing him that consideration is still being given to the question of prosecuting him. Yet another possibility is for a magistrate before whom an information has been laid to issue a warrant for the arrest of the person named in the information. This is much less likely than the issue of a summons because, if the allegation is serious enough to justify the issue of a warrant by a magistrate, the probability is that it will carry a power of arrest without warrant, thus rendering application for a warrant superfluous.

3.12 A very significant change will take place once the CJA 2003, ss 29–30 come fully into effect. These sections provide for a new method of instituting criminal proceedings which are available to a public prosecutor (primarily the CPS). In July 2007, these provisions came into force in 18 locations of the magistrates' court. The person to be prosecuted will be issued with a written charge at the instance of the prosecutor, and must appear in court to answer it (see 3.45 to 3.47). This procedure is only available in a limited number of areas, but will be extended to other areas, for the use of public prosecutors. However, the new procedure will not be extended to private prosecutors, who must continue to make use of the summons and information process. (These matters are dealt with in more detail in 3.33 to 3.47).

C   ARREST WITHOUT WARRANT AND CHARGE

3.13 The pre-court stages in a police prosecution by way of arrest and charge are described in the Paragraphs below.

The arrest

3.14 The main power of arrest without warrant is contained in ss 24 and 24A of PACE, which provide that a police officer may arrest any person whom he has reasonable grounds to suspect of having committed, committing, or being about to commit an offence. The section gives slightly less extensive powers to private citizens, who may arrest on reasonable suspicion that a person is committing an indictable offence, but have no power to arrest on the basis that an offence is about to be committed and, if they arrest on reasonable suspicion that the arrestee has committed an indictable offence, must show, in order to justify their actions, that somebody (not necessarily the arrestee) actually committed the offence suspected (s 24A and see also *Walters v W.H. Smith and Son Ltd* [1914] 1 KB 595 which established at common law the aforementioned limitation on the private citizen's powers of arrest).

3.15 Powers of arrest were reshaped by the CJA 2003, which made radical amendments to PACE, doing away with the former distinction between arrestable and non-arrestable offences. All offences are now, in effect, arrestable, provided that certain conditions are fulfilled. Police officers have the power to arrest in the following situations:

(a) they can arrest a person who is about to commit an offence, or whom they have reasonable grounds to suspect is about to commit an offence;
(b) they can arrest a person who is in the act of committing an offence, or whom they have reasonable grounds to suspect is committing an offence;
(c) where they have reasonable grounds for suspecting that an offence has been committed, they can arrest a person whom they have reasonable grounds to suspect is guilty of it.

In any of the situations (a) to (c) above, however, the arrest must be necessary in accordance with the criteria in s 24(5) of PACE. Hence the arrest must be necessary:

(a) to enable the person's name to be obtained;
(b) to enable the person's address to be obtained;
(c) to prevent physical injury, loss of or damage to property, an offence against public decency or the unlawful obstruction of the highway;
(d) to protect a child or other vulnerable person from the arrestee;
(e) to allow prompt and effective investigation of the offence or of the conduct of the person in question;
(f) to prevent any hindrance of prosecution for the offence by the person's disappearance.

Criteria (a) and (b) only apply where the officer cannot readily ascertain the name and address, or has reasonable grounds for suspecting that the name and address given by the person are not real. Criterion (c), insofar as it applies to the prevention of an offence against public decency, applies only where members of the public going about their normal business cannot reasonably be expected to avoid the person in question.

The legislation on powers of arrest repeatedly refers to the arrester reasonably suspecting the **3.16** arrestee of committing or having committed an offence. Lord Devlin in *Hussien v Chong Fook Kam* [1970] AC 942 at p. 948 described suspicion as 'a state of conjecture or surmise where proof is lacking [which arises] at or near the starting point of an investigation'. It may be contrasted with a mere intuitive hunch based on no ground that could be rationally evaluated by a third party. In deciding whether he has grounds to arrest, an officer may take into consideration information which could not be used at any subsequent prosecution (e.g., knowledge that the arrestee has convictions for roughly similar offences, or an underworld 'tip-off' that he committed the offence). Thus, an arrest is very often made while there is still insufficient evidence to charge the suspect with any offence, for a charge is not appropriate until the police have evidence admissible in court on the basis of which a conviction would be more likely than not. The mere fact that a police officer would be entitled to arrest somebody does not, of course, mean that he definitely ought to go ahead and do so. He should consider, as a matter of discretion, whether an arrest is really necessary or desirable. The officer is, however, entitled to take into consideration the fact that, by arresting the suspect, he gains the advantage of being able to question him at the police station where he may, perhaps, be more likely to confess than in the security of his own home (see *Holgate-Mohammed v Duke* [1983] AC 437). The Power of Arrest Code (Code G) states that the necessity criteria set out in s 24(5) of PACE and summarized in 2.15 are 'exhaustive'. It does not provide any guidance as to how they should be interpreted, stating merely that 'the circumstances that may satisfy those criteria remain a matter for the operational discretion of individual officers' (Code G, para 2.7). It does say, however, that 'it is essential that [an arrest power] is exercised in a non-discriminatory and proportionate manner' (Code G, para 1.3). As far as the question of proportionality is concerned, it would seem important that the officer should take into account the seriousness of the suspected offence, together with a consideration of whether some less intrusive method of proceeding would be sensible.

Action on and after arrest

3.17   The arrest is effected *either* by using a form of words that makes it clear to the arrestee that he is no longer free to come and go as he chooses, or by physically seizing or touching his person and telling him as soon as practicable thereafter that he is under arrest: *Alderson v Booth* [1969] 2 QB 216 and PACE, s 28(1). The arrestee must also be told the reason for the arrest, even if it is obvious: s 28(3) and (4). The reason given need not, however, be in precise technical language (*Abbassy v Metropolitan Police Commissioner* [1990] 1 WLR 385). If a reason for arrest is given that is inadequate in law (e.g., because the offence mentioned does not carry a power of arrest), the fact that the arrester had other suspicions which would have justified him in detaining the suspect does not validate the arrest: *Christie v Leachinsky* [1947] AC 573.

3.18   Often an arrest follows some conversation between the officer and a suspect during which the officer asks questions with a view to establishing whether an arrest is in fact called for. In such cases, the officer ought to have cautioned the suspect immediately he had grounds to suspect him of an offence (see para 10.1 of Code C and 3.50). The caution was formerly to the effect that the suspect did not have to say anything unless he wished to do so, but anything he said may be given in evidence. The Criminal Justice and Public Order Act 1994, s 34, which provides that in certain circumstances the court may draw inferences from the accused's silence, necessitated a radical change in the nature of the caution. The caution now reads:

> You do not have to say anything. But it may harm your defence if you do not mention when questioned something which you later rely on in court. Anything you do say may be given in evidence.

If no caution was administered before arrest, it must be given upon arrest (unless rendered impracticable by the arrestee's behaviour) (Code C, para 10.4).

3.19   Once the arrest has been made, the arrestee should normally be taken to the police station forthwith: s 30(1). The reason for insisting that, in general, the officer and his suspect go straight to the police station is that the various procedures prescribed by the Act and Code C to protect suspects can only operate effectively at a station. 'Taking the scenic route' there thus creates an opportunity for improper pressure to be brought on the arrestee but evidence obtained in such circumstances is now likely to be excluded under s 78 of PACE. The first exception to the rule reflects the common law (see *Dallison v Caffery* [1965] 1 QB 348 where taking the arrestee first to his home—which was searched with his permission—and then to his place of work to check out an alibi was held to be a justifiable detour on the way to the station). The second exception relates to what is generally termed 'street bail' and is governed by s 30A, which was inserted in PACE in 2004. It allows the arresting officer to release the suspect on bail with a requirement to attend a police station, but no other requirement. The suspect must be given a notice informing him of the offence for which he was arrested, the grounds of arrest, the police station which he is required to attend, and the time of attendance. The aim is to give the officer discretion to avoid wasting time away from the streets where the suspect was arrested, particularly in the case of relatively minor offences.

Initial action at the station

Upon arrival at the police station the arresting officers and their arrestee report to the *custody* **3.20**
officer (who is often called the custody sergeant). He is an officer of at least the rank of sergeant
who must be unconnected with the investigation (see PACE, s 36 for details of appointment,
etc. of custody officers). His role is to ensure that, while the arrestee (henceforward referred to
as the 'detainee') is in detention at the police station, he is properly treated in accordance with
the Codes of Practice and the Act: s 39(1). Since the custody officer is not personally involved
in the enquiry, he can take a more detached view of proceedings than the investigating officers
and will not be tempted to bend the rules in the way the latter might. Should there be a conflict between him and a more senior investigating officer as to how the detainee should be
dealt with (e.g., should he be released or detained for further questioning?), the dispute must
be referred to the station superintendent: PACE, s 39(6). Otherwise the custody officer always
has the last word in such matters. Chief police officers have been given the power to appoint
civilian custody officers (Serious Organised Crime and Police Act 2005, ss 120 and 121, amending s 38 of the Police Reform Act 2002 and ss 36 and 39 of PACE). The civilians will be subject
to the PACE Codes and to the complaints process of the Independent Police Complaints
Commission. Nevertheless, the proposal is highly controversial, as the custody officer is the
linch-pin of the regulatory regime brought into being by PACE, and needs to have the necessary credibility and authority to hold his own within the police station. The statutory power to
appoint civilian custody officers can only be exercised in police areas specifically covered by an
order bringing it into effect. At the time of writing, the proposal had not been implemented.

At the outset of his time at the police station the detainee must be told by the custody officer **3.21**
of his rights to free, independent and private legal advice, to have somebody named by him
informed of his arrest, and to read the Codes of Practice (Code C, para 3.1). In addition he
should be given a written notice repeating those rights and also setting out the words of the
caution. Next the custody officer should open a *custody record*. This, as the name implies, is a
standard-form document recording the essential details of what happens to the detainee at
the station. He is entitled to a copy on request, and such a copy may well prove useful to his
lawyers in, for example, seeking to exclude a confession made at the station. Amongst the
items that should go into the record are: the reason why the arrestee is being detained; an
acknowledgement, signed by him, that he has received the written statement of his rights; an
indication (again signed) of whether he wants legal advice; details of all visits he receives; the
times at which meals are served to him; the time and place of any caution; the times at which
he is handed over to the investigating officers for questioning; the time of his being charged
and anything he says in response; and any complaints made by him about improper
treatment. Other matters to be recorded will be mentioned in the course of the succeeding
Paragraphs. Section 2 of the Code deals with the custody record.

The custody officer has a duty to ascertain the possessions which a detainee has brought to the **3.22**
police station (s 54(1)). Whether to record such possessions is at the custody officer's discretion. In order to ascertain what property he has, the custody officer may order that he be
searched: s 54(6). In addition, there is a general discretion to seize and retain anything found as
a result of the search, save that clothing and personal effects may be seized only if *either* the custody officer believes that the detainee might use them to injure himself or others, to damage
property, to interfere with evidence or to assist in an escape, *or* there are reasonable grounds for

believing that they might be evidence of an offence: s 54(3) and (4). A search should not be regarded as the automatic result of being taken to the police station under arrest, but the custody officer will usually order at least a perfunctory turning out of the pockets. If it seems justified by the circumstances, however, he may order anything up to a full strip search, but not an intimate body search (see 3.88 to 3.89). Property taken from the detainee should be restored to him on his release from the station unless it is required for use as evidence.

Consideration of the evidence

3.23   Once the initial formalities are completed, the custody officer has to consider the evidence against the detainee: PACE, s 37(1). If it appears that he should never have been arrested in the first place, he will order his immediate release. Otherwise, the question is whether there is already enough evidence to charge him with an offence—i.e., evidence on which a conviction is more likely than not. If there is, the custody officer should require the investigating officers to choose between preferring a charge (which would be the usual course to adopt) and releasing the detainee without charge. The latter course might be taken when, for the kind of discretionary reasons discussed in Chapter 5, the police or CPS feel that it is not in the public interest to commence a prosecution even though the evidence amply warrants it. A half-way house is to utilize the power given to the police by s 47(3)(b) of PACE to bail the detainee on condition he return to the station on a stated day. During the interim, a decision can be taken as to the desirability of a prosecution, and, if need be, the detainee can be charged when he answers to his bail. Alternatively, the detainee can be released unconditionally from the police station, with a warning that consideration will be given to the question of whether to prosecute him. Once a suspect has been charged, he may not, in general, be asked any further questions about the offence (see 3.50 to 3.51). It follows that a decision by the custody officer as to whether there is enough evidence to charge a detainee effectively prevents the investigating officers interrogating him at the police station, since he then either has to be charged (with the effect on questioning just noted) or has to be released.

3.24   If, however, there is sufficient material to justify the arrest but not enough evidence to found a charge, the custody officer may sanction *detention without charge*, provided he has reasonable grounds for believing such detention to be necessary:

(i)   to secure or preserve evidence relating to the offence for which the detainee is under arrest, *or*

(ii)   to obtain such evidence by questioning him.

Thus, s 37(2) sanctions detention without charge for questioning at the discretion of the custody officer. The custody officer's reasons should be entered in the custody record and also given to the detainee orally: s 37(4) and (5).

Detention without charge

3.25   Sections 40–44 of PACE set out a complicated timetable for detention without charge, only an outline of which will be attempted here. The timetable represents a compromise between the principled argument that any statement a suspect makes against his own interests should be totally voluntary, and the pragmatic view that—unless some pressure is brought to bear through skilled questioning in the hostile environment of a police station—hardly anybody would ever confess, with dire consequences for the criminal justice system. The main stages in detention without charge are as follows:

(i) **Within six hours.** Within six hours of the custody officer's decision to allow detention without charge, a *review officer* must consider whether it is still proper so to hold the detainee. Essentially he goes through the same sequence of questions as did the custody sergeant, asking whether there is by now enough evidence to charge the detainee and, if not, whether further detention without charge is justified on either of the two grounds mentioned in s 37(2) (see 3.24 for s 37(2)). The review officer must be of at least the rank of inspector and, like the custody officer, may not be directly involved in the investigation. He should give the detainee and/or his legal representative an opportunity to make representations about the validity of continued detention. If the decision goes against the detainee, the reasons for it must be given to him orally and also entered in the custody record.

(ii) **Within fifteen hours.** Within nine hours of the holding of the first one, a second review must be held. Thereafter reviews are required at no more than nine-hourly intervals. This applies even if detention without charge has been authorized by the station superintendent and/or magistrates under (iii)–(v) below. It also applies if the detainee has been charged but still not released, although at that stage the custody officer himself can act as reviewing officer.

(iii) **Within twenty-four hours.** Within twenty-four hours a detainee must be released or charged unless his continued detention without charge has been authorized by the *station superintendent*. The twenty-four hours runs from the 'relevant time'—i.e., the time the detainee arrived at the station or (if he initially attended voluntarily but was arrested at the station—see 3.31), the time he was told he was no longer free to leave. In order to authorize continued detention, the superintendent must be satisfied that at least one of the matters of which the detainee is suspected is an indictable offence (see 1.08 and 1.09). In addition, the superintendent must have reasonable grounds for believing that (a) one or other of the grounds for detention without charge mentioned in s 37(2) still applies (see 3.24), and (b) the investigation is being conducted diligently and expeditiously. Again there are provisions for allowing the detainee or his solicitor to make representations and for noting the reasons for continued detention in the custody record. If the detainee has not yet exercised his rights to consult a solicitor and/or have somebody informed of his arrest, the superintendent must remind him of the rights and decide whether he should be permitted to exercise them.

(iv) **Within thirty-six hours.** Within thirty-six hours of the relevant time, the detainee must be released or charged unless a magistrates' court has issued a *warrant of further detention.* The hearing is in camera before at least two magistrates. The detainee is entitled to free legal representation. In order to grant a warrant, the magistrates must be satisfied:

(a) that the detainee is being held for an indictable offence;

(b) that his continued detention is necessary to secure or preserve evidence of the offence or to obtain such evidence by questioning him; and

(c) that the investigation is being conducted diligently and expeditiously.

If a warrant is granted, it may be for a period not exceeding thirty-six hours. The Magistrates' Association have indicated that, within reason, their members are prepared to consider applications for warrants of further detention on any day and outside normal court hours. However, should it not be possible for a court to sit at the time the thirty-six hour period expires, the police may hold the detainee for a further six hours, although they then run the risk of having the warrant refused if they acted unreasonably in not applying for a warrant earlier. It would, it is submitted, be unreasonable to hold a detainee for forty-two hours without charge if— although a court could not sit at literally the moment the thirty-six hours expired—one was sitting at the thirty-fifth hour.

(v) **After seventy-two hours.** Although the period specified in a warrant of further detention is limited to thirty-six hours, the magistrates may subsequently extend the period. Precisely the same rules apply to an application for extension as apply to the original application for a warrant. Although more than one extension may be made, the extended period must not be such as to expire more than ninety-six hours from the relevant time.

(vi) **After ninety-six hours.** It follows from (v) above that the maximum period a detainee can be held without charge is ninety-six hours running from the relevant time. At the end of that period he must either be released or charged.

3.26 As mentioned at 3.20, the custody officer has the primary responsibility for ensuring that a person in police detention is properly treated in accordance with PACE and the Codes. Paras 8.1 to 8.11 of Code C are headed 'Conditions of Detention' and deal with matters such as the state of the cells; the visiting of the detainee at no more than hourly intervals; the provision of food (two light meals and one main meal per day); the provision of exercise if practicable and access to toilet and washing facilities. If the investigating officers wish to question the detainee, they must persuade the custody officer to release him into their custody (see para 12.1 of Code C). If he agrees to do so, they become responsible for the detainee's treatment, and must report on how they have discharged that responsibility when they return him to the custody officer's charge: PACE, s 39(2) and (3). The rules governing the questioning of a suspect in detention are considered at 3.50 to 3.51.

Charging the detainee

3.27 As soon as the investigating officers consider that there is enough evidence for a successful prosecution, and that the detainee has said all that he wishes to say about the offence, they must take him before the custody officer, who is then responsible for deciding whether to charge him. Assuming that the custody officer decides to charge him, the procedure outlined in paras 16.1 to 16.3 of the Code has to be followed. The detainee is cautioned in terms identical to those laid out at 3.18. The charge is then written down on the charge sheet and read over to him. Any reply he makes is recorded, and he is supplied with a written notice repeating the charge and caution, and also stating the name of the officer in the case and the case's police reference number. Once a detainee or other suspect has been charged, it is more appropriate to refer to him as 'the accused'.

3.28 Under s 37A of PACE, inserted by s 28 of the CJA 2003, the DPP has issued guidance for police officers on when to charge or otherwise deal with a suspect without reference to the CPS. This includes minor cases, such as most road traffic offences, cases where the suspect has admitted an offence which could be disposed of by the magistrates, and cases where there is a need to bring the suspect before the court because a remand in custody should be sought. In other cases, it may be appropriate for the police to release the suspect without charge, but on bail, while the case is referred to the CPS (see 3.45 to 3.47 for the procedure followed by the CPS in charging a suspect).

Release or detention after charge

Once a detainee has been charged with an offence, the custody officer must order his release **3.29** from the station unless either:

(a)   the detainee has refused to give his name and address; *or*
(b)   there are reasonable grounds for the custody officer to believe any of the following:
    (i)   the name and address furnished are not genuine; or
    (ii)   the detainee will not answer bail; or
    (iii)   (where the offence charged is imprisonable) his detention is necessary to prevent him committing a further offence; or
    (iv)   (where the offence charged is non-imprisonable) his detention is necessary to prevent him causing injury to another or loss of or damage to property; or
    (v)   his detention is necessary to prevent him from interfering with the administration of justice or the investigation of an offence; or
    (vi)   his detention is necessary for his own protection (PACE, s 38(1)).

Should the custody officer decide further to detain a charged detainee, and it is intended that the proceedings against him shall be in the local magistrates' court, he must be brought before the court 'as soon as is practicable', and in any event not later than its first scheduled sitting after the charge: PACE, s 46(2). If no sitting is arranged for the day after the day of the charge, the clerk of court must be notified that the police have a detainee who ought to come before the court, and the clerk then arranges for a special sitting: s 46(3) and (6)–(8). A detainee charged on Saturday may be held over until the following Monday.

Most detainees are bailed once they have been charged, if only because of lack of space to keep **3.30** them at the station. One condition of bail is that they attend at the appropriate magistrates' court on a certain day to answer the charge that has been preferred against them.

'Helping police with their enquiries'

So far this account of the procedure for arrest without warrant and charge has proceeded on **3.31** the assumption that there are just two classes of person for these purposes, namely those who have been arrested and may therefore be detained at the station for the periods prescribed by PACE, and those who are not under arrest. As a matter of pure law, that assumption is entirely correct. It always was so at common law and it has been confirmed by s 29 of PACE. In real life, though, there is a third category of person, namely those who are 'helping police with their enquiries'. Such a person has not formally been arrested—the police have merely invited him to come to the station where he may be questioned more conveniently, and he has agreed to their request. Rightly or wrongly, though, the suspect probably thinks that, if he does not voluntarily accompany the police, they will simply arrest him. At the station, he may well feel under as much pressure and be as much in need of protection as an arrestee. Therefore, to protect this category of suspect, para 10.2 of Code C states that, when he is initially cautioned at the police station (or other premises, which presumably would include his home), he must be told that he is not under arrest and is not obliged to remain with the officer. Moreover, if he does choose to remain, he may obtain legal advice. Should the police decide that somebody who has come to the station voluntarily ought to be arrested, they simply inform him that he is no longer free to leave. The timetable for detention without charge then runs from the moment of their so informing him.

Uncooperative detainees

3.32   Several parts of the arrest and charge procedure depend on the arrestee/detainee affording the police officers at least a minimum degree of cooperation. It would obviously be absurd if the police were to be blamed for not complying with the provisions of PACE and the Codes if the only reason for their not doing so was the recalcitrance of the subject of their attentions. Accordingly, s 28 (which deals with the information to be given to a person on arrest) only places upon the arrester a duty to tell the arrestee the grounds of the arrest 'as soon as is practicable', which means that if the arrestee behaves in such a way that communication with him is impossible he cannot subsequently claim that the arrest was unlawful because he was not immediately informed of the grounds. Similarly, the custody officer's duty to explain to an arrestee why he is authorizing his detention (see 3.24) does not apply if he is incapable of understanding what is said to him, violent or likely to become violent, or in need of urgent medical attention (see PACE, ss 37(6) and 38(5)). Where the proper procedure for keeping the custody record requires the detainee to sign something (e.g., an acknowledgement that he has received the notice setting out his rights at the station) but he refuses to do so, the custody officer should simply record the refusal (see para 2.7 of Code C). Lastly, if the custody officer considers that there is enough evidence to prefer a charge but the detainee is not in a fit state for that to be done (e.g., he is drunk), he may be held until he has recovered: s 37(9). The special provisions which govern the treatment of juveniles and other vulnerable groups are summarized at 3.101 to 3.107.

D   SUMMONS AND INFORMATION

3.33   It is intended that, in due course, all prosecutions brought by the CPS and other public authorities will be dealt with by the charge and requisition procedure. This is the procedure set out in s 29 of the CJA 2003, and is detailed in 3.45 to 3.47. At the time of writing, the charge and requisition procedure had been brought into effect in some 18 locations of the magistrates' court. In the majority of the country, public prosecutors did not have the option of using the charge and requisition procedure. Further, even once that procedure is fully implemented, it will not be available for private prosecutors. The current position, therefore, is that a substantial number of prosecutions (both public and private) are begun by the laying of an information and the issue of process—i.e., the issue of a summons or a warrant for arrest.

Paragraph 3.34 gives a brief outline of the main stages in a typical police prosecution by way of summons. Various aspects of the procedure are then looked at in more detail at 3.35 to 3.44.

The main stages

It will be convenient to relate this description of the information and summons procedure to **3.34** an imaginary prosecution for careless driving. Of course, it must not be thought that summonses are only used in road traffic cases. An offence may be prosecuted by summons whatever its nature and however grave. Nevertheless, the typical use of a summons is in respect of minor offences in general and road traffic matters in particular.

(a) **Speaking to the suspect**. PC Smith on foot patrol in Casterbridge High Street sees a car pass him at a speed he estimates at 50 m.p.h. A short distance down the street, the car brakes sharply and pulls partly on to the wrong side of the road to pass vehicles parked on its own side. In doing so, it scrapes the side of a van coming in the opposite direction. What the officer has himself observed is sufficient to give him grounds for suspecting that the car driver (a Mr Speedy) has committed one or more driving offences. The officer must therefore caution him—the obligation to caution a suspect is as applicable to minor cases as it is to serious ones.

(b) **Warning of prosecution**. PC Smith considers that the evidence against Speedy is sufficient to justify criminal proceedings. The officer warns him that he will be reported and that consideration will be given to prosecuting him for dangerous driving, careless driving and speeding. It is always good practice for the police to warn a suspect if they are considering proceeding against him by way of summons, but in the case of certain road traffic offences it is a pre-condition of a conviction that the accused was given notice of intended prosecution either orally at the time of the alleged offence or in writing within 14 days (see ss 1 and 2 of the Road Traffic Act 1988). Speedy is then allowed to go on his way and the officer returns to the police station.

(c) **Decision to prosecute**. PC Smith makes a report of the incident to the police process department. As well as the report, they have a written statement from the van driver, who says he is willing to testify against Speedy. In the light of the evidence and the factors discussed in Chapter 5, they decide to prosecute. Their view is that there is clear evidence of carelessness, but that dangerous driving would be difficult to establish and that a prosecution for speeding would fail because the only evidence of Speedy having been over the limit is PC Smith's uncorroborated opinion.

(d) **Preparing an information**. Next an information is prepared. A busy police station will deal with literally thousands of prosecutions by way of summons during the course of a year. If they laid oral informations in each case (i.e., went to the local magistrates' court and told a magistrate on oath what the accused did), the work of both the court and the station would grind to a halt. So, the standard procedure is to use a written information (see 10.12 to 10.25 for the wording of an information). Omitting the formal parts, the information against Speedy might be as follows:

Date: 1 August 2008
Accused: James Arthur SPEEDY
Address: 10 The Esplanade, SANDITON, Hardyshire.

Alleged offence: On the 28th day of July 2008 did drive a motor vehicle, namely a Vauxhall Cavalier motor car registration number F999 XYZ, on a road, namely the High Street, Casterbridge, without due care and attention, contrary to s 3 of the Road Traffic Act 1988.

The information of: John Smith PC 50B.

Address: Casterbridge Police Station, Law Street, CASTERBRIDGE.

(e) **Laying the information.** The written information is delivered to the appropriate magistrates' court. The information is treated as having been laid as soon as it is received in the clerk's office at the magistrates' court: *Manchester Stipendiary Magistrate ex parte Hill* [1983] 1 AC 328. This is important because of the rule that an information for a summary matter must be laid within six months of commission of the offence (Magistrates' Courts Act 1980, s 127, and see 10.19). Provided the information is received in the office within the six months, it does not matter that nobody considers it until after that time.

(f) **Issuing a summons.** The information is put before a magistrate or magistrates' clerk—more probably the latter. He checks that it is prima facie a valid information. If it is, he issues a summons by signing the draft summons which has been delivered with the information. In theory, the magistrate or clerk issuing a summons should consider each information judicially to ensure that the issue of process is justified. In practice, at least where public prosecutions are concerned, the examination of informations is perfunctory in the extreme. The summons sets out the information against the accused and also states the date on which he is to attend court to answer it.

(g) **Serving the summons.** The court and/or the police serve the summons on the accused. As well as being sent the summons, Speedy is likely, for an offence such as careless driving, to be given a brief statement of the facts and a notice explaining how he can plead guilty by post. In any event, he will be asked to indicate if he intends to plead not guilty, and advised that, if he does, he should not attend court on the date stated in the summons but wait until he has been notified of a day when there will be time for a contested hearing. If he does not plead guilty by post and fails to attend court on the day fixed by the summons (or later day notified to him), the case may be proved in his absence (see 10.34 to 10.39). This is subject to the prosecution being able to prove due service of the summons and of any adjournment notices. Having convicted him in his absence, the magistrates would then have to adjourn before sentence for Speedy to attend court and produce his licence. At this stage—though not before—they could issue a warrant for his arrest (see 10.44). If Speedy does attend court in answer to the summons, the information will be put to him, and the trial proceeds.

Jurisdiction to issue a summons

3.35 Magistrates and magistrates' clerks have power to issue a summons upon an information being laid before them: Magistrates' Courts Act 1980, s 1 and Justices' Clerks Rules 2005 (SI 2005 No 545). By virtue of s 43 of the Courts Act 2003, magistrates have national jurisdiction. They have the power to deal with cases no matter where the offence was committed. Consequently, magistrates and their clerks have jurisdiction to issue a summons or warrant in respect of the whole of England and Wales. As is set out in 3.47, however, the issue of a summons following an information will no longer be available to public prosecutors once s 29 of the CJA 2003 comes fully into force.

Laying an information

Issue of a summons depends upon an information first being laid before a magistrate or a mag- **3.36** istrates' clerk. An information may be laid orally or in writing. The laying of a written infor- mation has been sufficiently described under subheadings (d) and (e) of 3.34. As explained there, in those areas where they are still able to use this procedure, the police and other prose- cuting agencies almost invariably use written informations to save both themselves and the courts a great deal of time. Further, where an accused has been charged, it is usual for the charge sheet to be used as the information (see 3.27). However, a private prosecutor might well choose to lay his information orally. In essence, he tells either an individual magistrate, or a magistrates' clerk or a bench of magistrates sitting as an 'applications court' the nature of the allegation and the name and address of the accused. The substance of his information is taken down in writing and put into the appropriate terminology. He may be asked to sign it, and the magistrate or clerk will also sign that the information was taken before him. The information may, but need not be, substantiated on oath. Only magistrates (not magistrates' clerks) can take informations on oath.

The decision to issue a summons

The decision to issue a summons is a judicial, not an administrative one—that is why it can- **3.37** not be delegated to an official in the clerk's office, however well qualified he might be. The magistrate or clerk must look at each information laid before him, and ask himself whether it justifies a summons: *Gateshead Justices ex parte Tesco Stores Ltd* [1981] QB 470. He must not issue a summons if either:

(a) the offence alleged in the information is unknown to law; or
(b) the information was laid out of time; or
(c) any consent necessary to the bringing of a prosecution has not been obtained; or
(d) he lacks jurisdiction in the matter because the offence was committed outside the county etc.

Of course, in most cases none of these impediments to the issue of a summons will apply. Nevertheless, there is still a residual discretion not to issue a summons if the prosecution appears frivolous or vexatious (see *Bros* (1901) 66 JP 54—proposed prosecution of a Jew for Sunday trad- ing) or if the evidence is clearly inadequate (*Mead* (1916) 80 JP 382) or even if the prosecutor has been inexplicably slow in laying the information (*Clerk to the Medway Justices ex parte DHSS* [1986] Crim LR 686). However, it is not in general the duty of the magistrate/clerk to enter upon a preliminary survey of the evidence, and in the case of a police prosecution he is likely to assume that it is neither frivolous nor unsupported by evidence. Indeed, much as the Divisional Court might deplore it, there is reason to suppose that the issue of a summons is often more or less auto- matic. As the Philips Report said—'Where a summons is applied for by the police or other recog- nised prosecution agencies no consideration is given as to whether or not a summons should be issued'. The Commission did, however, find a different attitude prevailing towards private pros- ecutors, with the magistrate or clerk in such cases seeking to 'ensure the propriety of the prose- cution and the technical correctness of the information'. That might involve asking the informant to outline the evidence he has available, or even giving the proposed defendant an opportunity to attend and argue against issue of a summons (see *West London Metropolitan Stipendiary Magistrate ex parte Klahn* [1979] 1 WLR 933 for an example of that happening).

3.38 In *Bradford Justices ex parte Sykes* (1999) 163 JP 224, the Divisional Court considered whether a clerk or a magistrate had to make enquiries into the basis of the information laid before him in making the decision whether to grant it. It was held that the magistrate or clerk was entitled to enquire further, but had no duty to do so. In *Horseferry Road Magistrates' Court ex parte Bennett* [1993] 3 WLR 90, the House of Lords had shown that there were limits to the extent to which the magistrates' court should be expected to ignore the history of the accused's production before it. B had been forcibly brought back to the UK in disregard of proper extradition procedures. Their lordships held that, where the police, prosecution, or other executive authorities in this country had been a knowing party to such irregularity, the courts should stay the prosecution as an abuse of process (see 10.26 to 10.31 for abuse of process).

Contents and service of a summons

3.39 A summons should contain the following details:

(a)   the name and address of the accused;
(b)   the address of the court before which he is to appear;
(c)   the day on and time at which he is to appear;
(d)   the contents of the information or informations he is to answer; and
(e)   the name and address of the informant (in the case of a police information the address of the police station will be given).

3.40 Once the summons has been issued and signed it must be served on the accused. That may be done by delivering it personally to him or posting it to his last known or usual address: Magistrates' Courts Rules 1981, r 99. However, a magistrates' court may not treat service by post as proved unless *either* they are satisfied that the summons came to the knowledge of the accused, *or* the summons was issued in respect of a summary offence and it was sent by registered letter or recorded delivery service. The usual sequence of events is to send the summons by ordinary post, then (if there is no response from the accused) to send it by recorded delivery, and finally, if the Post Office cannot get anyone to sign for it, to ask the police to try to effect personal service by going to the address where the accused is believed to reside.

3.41 The options open to the magistrates if the accused fails to appear in answer to a summons for a summary offence are set out at 10.34 to 10.39. They can either adjourn and notify him of the new hearing date, or they can issue a warrant for his arrest, or they can proceed in his absence. The latter two options are dependent upon proof of service of the summons; issuing a warrant for his arrest is dependent in addition upon the information being substantiated on oath and the offence being imprisonable. If the summons is for an indictable offence, the magistrates cannot proceed with committal proceedings or with proceedings to determine the mode of trial unless the accused is personally present or (in limited circumstances) is absent but represented by counsel or solicitor (see MCA, ss 4(3) and (4) and 18(2) which deal with the need for the accused to be present for committal proceedings and mode-of-trial proceedings, and draw no distinction between prosecutions begun by summons and prosecutions begun by arrest and charge). Thus, the magistrates' only options upon failure to appear in response to a summons for an indictable offence are to adjourn with or without the issue of a warrant for arrest.

Issue of a warrant for arrest

Where a magistrate has jurisdiction to issue a summons in respect of the offence alleged in an information laid before him, he may, instead of issuing a summons, issue a warrant for the arrest of the accused provided: **3.42**

(a)   the information is in writing, and

(b)   either the accused is a juvenile, or his address cannot be sufficiently established for a summons to be served on him, or the offence alleged in the information is indictable: MCA, s 1(3) and (4).

A warrant for arrest is a document commanding the constables of the police force for the area in which it is issued to arrest the accused and bring him before the magistrates' court named in it. It must contain particulars of the offence alleged in the information which led to its being issued, and must be signed by the magistrate who issued it. Its effect is to order and empower police officers to arrest the person named, and bring him before a magistrates' court. **3.43**

As a compromise between issuing a summons and issuing an unconditional warrant for arrest, a magistrate may issue a warrant but endorse it with a direction that, having been arrested, the accused shall be released on bail subject to a duty to appear at the magistrates' court at a time specified in the endorsement: MCA, s 117. This is known as 'backing the warrant for bail'. The bail may be made subject to conditions—e.g., providing sureties or reporting to the police station at specified intervals or living at a certain address. If the accused cannot comply with those conditions (e.g., he is unable to find a surety), he is brought before the magistrates who will either vary the terms of bail or remand him in custody. Whenever a magistrate or a magistrates' court has jurisdiction to issue a warrant for arrest, it may be backed for bail. The power is particularly useful when an accused fails to appear in answer to a summons or fails to answer to his bail, but the magistrates feel that this is due to inadvertence rather than design. The shock of being arrested should ensure that he attends for the adjourned hearing, while the endorsement for bail saves him from an unnecessary period of custody. **3.44**

E   CHARGE AND REQUISITION

The CJA 2003, ss 28 to 30 introduced a radical new departure in the procedure to be adopted for charging suspects. The CPS and other public prosecutors have been given a central role in determining whether a charge is to be brought, and the nature of that charge. Section 28 of the CJA 2003 amended s 37 of PACE, and introduced s 37A to 37D. Under s 37A, the DPP (as head of the CPS) was given power to issue guidance setting out the circumstances in which it is appropriate for the police to charge or otherwise deal with a suspect without reference to the CPS. This includes most summary-only and triable-either-way offences, where a guilty **3.45** plea is anticipated which the magistrates could deal with. Certain offences which satisfy these conditions are, however, classified as offences where the CPS must make the charge decision, e.g. offences triable only on indictment, assault occasioning actual or grievous bodily harm, domestic violence, certain public order offences, deception, and handling stolen goods. (Full details of the offences where the CPS, rather than a custody officer, must make the charge decision are to be found in the DPP's *Guidance on Charging*, issued under PACE 1984, s 37A and obtainable on the website (see Key Documents at the end of this Chapter)).

3.46   In other cases, the suspect should be released without charge, but on bail. It is then for the CPS to determine, if they agree that the evidence is sufficient, whether the suspect should be charged, and if so with what offence, or whether he should be given a caution and if so in respect of what offence. The suspect must then be charged, cautioned, or informed in writing that he is not to be prosecuted (s 37B of PACE).

3.47   Section 29 of the CJA 2003 goes on to set out a new method of instituting criminal proceedings which is available to a public prosecutor as set out in s 29(5). These are:

(a)   a police force;
(b)   the Director of the Serious Fraud Office;
(c)   the DPP (hence covering all CPS prosecutions);
(d)   the Director of Revenue and Customs Prosecutions;
(e)   the Director General of the Serious Organized Crime Agency;
(f)   the Attorney-General;
(g)   a Secretary of State.

The new method consists in the issue to the defendant of a written charge, together with a written requirement ('requisition') to appear before a magistrates' court to answer to the charge. It follows that the prosecutor, rather than the court, will notify the accused of the requirement to attend court. Further, public prosecutors will no longer be able to lay an information in order to obtain the issue of a summons, although this will still be the way to commence a private prosecution (ss 29(4) and 30(4) of the CJA 2003). In July 2007, these provisions came into force in 18 locations of the magistrates' court. The written charge and requisition procedure is not intended for use by prosecutors other than those set out above, who will be obliged to continue to use the summons and information procedure described in 3.34 to 3.44.

F   POLICE QUESTIONING OF A SUSPECT

3.48   A major part of the evidence at most criminal trials concerns the answers the accused made in interview with the police and any written statement he may have signed under caution.

The overall framework

3.49   Until 1986, police questioning of suspects was conducted within the framework of the common law on involuntary confessions and the rules of practice for police officers set out in the

Judges' Rules (see 3.07 for a brief description of the Rules). The Judges' Rules have been replaced by the Detention, Treatment and Questioning Code of Practice (Code C). The Code, although developing from the Judges' Rules, is far more detailed than they ever were. The description of the questioning of suspects which follows is based upon the Code. It should, however, be remembered that the police must conform not only with the Code directed specifically at them but also with the general law of evidence on involuntary confessions. That is now contained in s 76(2) of PACE, which states that an alleged confession must be excluded (even if it appears to be true) if *either* it was obtained by oppression, *or* it was obtained as a result of words or conduct which—given the circumstances then obtaining— were likely to render unreliable any confession the suspect might make in consequence thereof. Oppression is statutorily defined to include any actual or threatened violence (s 76(8)), but otherwise it is restricted to really serious and deliberate abuse of power by a person in authority (see Lord Lane CJ's judgment in *Fulling* [1987] QB 426). For details about inadmissible confessions, the reader is referred to *Blackstone's Criminal Practice 2008*, section F17 in particular. As already explained in 3.08, breaches of the Code of Practice may lead to a confession being excluded *either* because, with other factors, they lead to the conclusion that any confession the accused might have made is likely to be unreliable, *or* because the judge exercises the discretion given him by s 78 of PACE to exclude unfairly obtained evidence.

The conduct of questioning by the police

Code C controls the conduct of police questioning. One of the Code's main purposes is **3.50** to ensure as far as possible that interrogations are conducted in such a way that the defence will not subsequently be able to claim with any plausibility that the accused's confession was obtained by oppression or in breach of the reliability principle. Another purpose is to facilitate the accurate recording of what an interviewee says. In considering the main provisions of the Code, it is helpful to divide the questioning process into a number of stages:

(a) **Gathering information.** The Code states that 'all citizens have a duty to help police officers to prevent crime and discover offenders' (see note 1K). Consequently, an officer is entitled to question any person from whom he thinks useful information can be obtained. Even if the person concerned states that he is unwilling to answer, that does not affect the officer's entitlement to put the questions. The duty to help the police is, however, merely a civic and moral one. There is no legally enforceable obligation to answer their questions (see *Rice v Connelly* [1966] 2 QB 414). False answers might, of course, lead to prosecution for wasting police time or even for assisting an offender. Also, if someone who is ultimately charged with an offence failed or refused to answer a question put to him by an officer at the information-gathering stage, it is possible that his silence might be evidence against him.

(b) **The cautioning stage.** A person whom there are grounds to suspect of an offence must be cautioned before any questions about it are put to him for the purpose of obtaining evidence which may be given to a court in a prosecution (see para 10.1 of the Code). If it is the person's unsatisfactory answers to previous questions which have provided grounds for suspicion, he must be cautioned before any further questions are put. The terms of the caution are set out in the Code, para 10.5:

You do not have to say anything. But it may harm your defence if you do not mention when questioned something which you later rely on in court. Anything you do say may be given in evidence.

Minor deviations from the formula do not matter, provided that the general sense is preserved. This form of the caution was introduced as a result of s 34 of the Criminal Justice and Public Order Act 1994, which permits certain inferences to be drawn at trial where the accused has failed to mention after caution any fact which he relies on in his defence (see *Blackstone's Criminal Practice 2008* F19.4 et seq and also *Argent* [1997] 2 Cr App R 27). There are, in addition, special warnings laid down in paras 10.10 and 10.11 of the Code which must be administered where s 36 and/or s 37 of the 1994 Act apply (a suspect's refusal to answer questions about objects, marks or substances found on him, or about his presence at the place where he was arrested). For an inference to be drawn from the suspect's failure or refusal satisfactorily to answer a question on one of these matters, the interviewing officer must first tell him the offence which is being investigated, the fact which the suspect is being asked to account for, the officer's belief that this fact is connected to the suspect's participation in the offence, the power of the court to draw an inference from a failure or refusal to account for the fact, and that a record of the interview may later be given in evidence at trial.

The obligation to caution does not arise until there are grounds to suspect the interviewee of an offence (see above). Suspicion has been described as 'a state of conjecture or surmise where proof is lacking'. The grounds for conjecture do not have to be matters which the officer could or would want to put before a court as evidence (e.g., they might be his knowledge of the suspect's criminal record or something he has been told by an underworld informer). Thus, para 10.1 of Code C requires a caution to be given at a very early stage of the investigative process—an earlier stage, in fact, than was required by the Judges' Rules prior to 1986. However, no caution is needed if the officer's purpose in questioning is other than to obtain evidence which might be used in the prosecution of the interviewee—e.g., if he is seeking to establish the latter's identity or the ownership of a vehicle.

Para. 10.4 of the Code supplements para 10.1 by providing that an arrestee must be cautioned upon his arrest, unless either that has been done immediately before in pursuance of para 10.1 or his conduct makes the administering of a caution impracticable. When there is a break in the questioning of a cautioned suspect, the officer must ensure on its resumption that the suspect is aware that he is still under caution. If there is any doubt, the caution should be given again in full (para 10.8). A suspect who attends voluntarily at a police station must, on being cautioned (or, if he was cautioned before going to the police station, on being reminded of the caution), be informed also that he is not under arrest, need not stay with the officer and has a right to free legal advice (paras 10.2 and 3.21).

(c) **Questioning away from the police station.** One of the aims of the Code is to reduce the frequency of allegations that the suspect was 'verballed' prior to arrival at the police station, e.g., in the police car on the way to the station via the 'scenic route'. Para. 11.1 states that, once a suspect has been arrested he must not usually be interviewed about the offence until he is at the station (and hence subject to the protection of the custody regime there). The prohibition on interviews outside the station is relaxed only where the consequent delay is likely to lead to interference with evidence, harm to other persons, the alerting of other suspects, or damage to property.

The restriction applies only to interviews, and the definition of 'interview' in para 11.1A of the Code is:

An interview is the questioning of a person regarding their involvement or suspected involvement in a criminal offence or offences which, under para 10.1 must be carried out under caution Whenever a person is interviewed they must be informed of the nature of the offence or futher offence—procedures undertaken under section 7 of the Road Traffic Act 1988 . . . do not constitute interviewing for the purpose of this code.

(Section 7 of the 1988 Act deals with the provision of specimens of breath, blood, or urine by those suspected of drink-driving offences.)

(d) **Questioning at the police station.** Para. 11.5 of the Code states that no interviewer may seek to elicit answers by the use of oppression. Interrogation at the police station is covered in paras 12.1 to 12.14. Such questioning may occur either when a person has attended voluntarily to 'help police with their inquiries' (see 3.21), or when a suspect has been arrested, taken to the station and detained without charge on the authority of the custody officer (see 3.23 to 3.26). In the latter case, the questioning will inevitably be under caution because of the rule that a person must be cautioned on arrest if not before. In the former case, the probability is that the police officers will already suspect the interviewee of an offence, and therefore should caution him, but that will not necessarily be so. Much of paras 11 and 12 are directly related to detainees, rather than those who are merely helping with enquiries. However, 'those there voluntarily to assist with an investigation should be treated with no less consideration' than is given to detainees (note 1A).

When an investigating officer wishes to interview a detainee, he must first obtain the custody officer's permission in the sense that the detainee has to be 'delivered' from the custody officer's custody into that of the investigating officer (para 12.1). In any 24-hour period, he should be given at least eight hours' continuous rest from questioning, normally at night (para 12.2). However, the rest period may be interrupted if there are good reasons for doing so (e.g., the need to obtain quick answers so as to prevent harm to other persons or serious damage to property). If practicable, questioning should take place in an interview room, which is adequately heated, lit and ventilated (para 12.4). The detainee must not be required to stand (para 12.6). At the beginning of the interview, the interviewing officers must identify themselves (para 12.7). Breaks in an interview should occur at approximately two-hour intervals and at regular mealtimes subject to the discretion to delay on reasonable grounds (e.g., risk of harm to others or serious damage to property) (para 12.8). Any complaints by the detainee must be recorded and reported to the custody officer (para 12.9). If the detainee asks what will happen if he stays silent or answers questions or signs a written statement, the officers may tell him the action they propose to take in any of those events (para 11.5). But they may not give this information unless they have first been directly asked. In any event, they must be careful not to phrase their answers in such a way that the admissibility of any subsequent confession could be challenged by suggesting that what the police said makes it likely to be unreliable. However, para 11.5 seems to sanction an officer telling a detainee in response to a question that, for example, once he has made a statement he will be charged and then, in all probability, released on bail. (Contrast the pre-1986 position as established by *Zaveckas* [1970] 1 WLR 516 which was that any promise of bail, even in response to a question from the suspect, made a confession inadmissible.) The maximum periods for which a suspect may be detained for questioning without being charged have already been considered at 3.25 to 3.26.

(e) **The charging stage**. Immediately a police officer questioning a suspect believes that a prosecution should be brought against him and that there is enough evidence for the prosecution to succeed, he must ask him if he has anything further to say and (if he has nothing more to say) stop questioning him (para 11.6). The evidence against the suspect is then considered by the custody officer, who either supervises the making of a charge or, if it is a case where the police in their discretion decide that it is better not to prosecute, releases the suspect without charge. The terms of para 11.6 (see above), combined with the 'realistic prospect of conviction' test laid down in the Code for Crown Prosecutors (see 5.22 to 5.23), suggest that the correct time for a charge is as soon as the police have evidence on the basis of which a prosecution would be more likely than not to succeed. Applied rigidly, however, such an approach to charging would have inconvenient results, bearing in mind that after an accused has been charged he cannot normally be further questioned about the offence. For example, if a housebreaker is arrested climbing out of a window with his pockets full of the householder's jewellery, the evidence of his being caught in the act would be ample to sustain a successful prosecution for burglary. It could therefore be argued that he ought not to be asked any questions about the offence but should be charged immediately upon his arrival at the station. That, however, would hardly be fair to the housebreaker himself, in that he should be given an opportunity to make a statement, in which he might frankly admit his guilt, express contrition, and thus hope to secure a lighter sentence. Nor would it be fair to the police, who understandably like to complete their case with admissions from the suspect, however strong the rest of the evidence may be. So, the Code should be understood as requiring a suspect to be charged (or released) as soon as the police (i) have evidence making his conviction more likely than not, and (ii) have had a reasonable opportunity to question him with a view to his making a statement about the offence. Point (ii) is reflected in the wording of para 11.6 of the Code. What is impermissible is delaying a charge when there is the evidence for it and the suspect has made it plain that he has said all he intends to say. In such cases, the only purpose of delay would be the improper one of breaking down the suspect by continued detention without charge, hoping that he will eventually confess and thus make a conviction not merely the probable but the almost certain outcome of a prosecution. The procedure for charging has already been described at 3.27 to 3.28. It will be recalled that the caution must again be given when charging.

(f) **The post-charge stage**. Once a person has been charged he may not, as a general rule, be asked any further questions about the offence. The exceptions are when (i) the questions are necessary to prevent or minimize harm or loss to others, *or* (ii) they are necessary to clear up an ambiguity in a previous answer or statement, *or* (iii) it is in the interests of justice that he should be given the opportunity of commenting on information which has come to light since he was charged (para 16.5 of the Code). If the police wish him to look at a statement made by some other person (e.g., another suspect who has implicated him), a copy of the statement should be handed to him but no reply or comment is to be invited (para 16.4). Both before asking post-charge questions and before giving the chargee a copy of another's statement, the police must caution him.

The above has been written on the assumption that the offence under investigation is a fairly **3.51** serious one. If it is a less serious matter, the rules on cautioning still apply and again the officer should not ask any more questions once he has the evidence to prosecute. But, there is unlikely to be any questioning at the station and, instead of being charged, the suspect is told that he may be prosecuted. Once he has been told that, the rules on further questioning are the same as apply after a charge.

Right to consult a solicitor

Suspects questioned by the police are frequently at a disadvantage in that they have little or **3.52** no knowledge of the law or police powers. Thus, although cautioned, they do not appreciate the arguments for and against staying silent, or realize that, by answering, they may supply the police with vital admissions without which there would not even be a case to answer or the possibility of a prosecution. Similarly, a detainee at the police station is naturally anxious to be released as soon as possible. If he does not know for how long the police can lawfully hold him, he may in desperation give the investigating officers the answers he thinks they want in the hope that they will then bail him, not realizing that they would in any event be obliged to let him go (or charge him) after 24 or at most 96 hours. To redress the inequality between suspect and police and ensure that the former understands his rights, PACE provides that, save in limited and well-defined circumstances, he must be allowed to consult a solicitor. Moreover, having been consulted, the solicitor is then in a position to check that any interrogation is conducted fairly and in accordance with the Code.

Section 58(1) of PACE provides that a person arrested and held in custody at a police station **3.53** (a detainee) shall be entitled, if he so requests, to consult an independent solicitor privately at any time free of charge. He must be told of this right by the custody officer when he arrives at the station (para 3.1 of the Code), and should be invited to sign the custody record to indicate whether—at that stage—he wants legal advice (para 3.5). Indeed, any request to see a solicitor, whenever made, should be noted in the custody record: s 58(2). Once a request has been made, the detainee must be allowed to consult a solicitor as soon as practicable unless (i) he is suspected of an indictable offence (see 1.08 to 1.09), and (ii) delay is authorized by an officer of at least the rank of superintendent: s 58(6). Moreover, the senior officer may authorize delay if, and only if, he has reasonable grounds for believing that immediate consultation with a solicitor would have any of the following consequences:

(i) interference with or harm to evidence connected with an indictable offence, or interference with or physical injury to other persons; *or*
(ii) the alerting of other persons suspected of having committed an indictable offence; *or*
(iii) hindrance to the recovery of the proceeds of an indictable offence (s 58(8)).

It is clear that the suspect must not be refused access to a solicitor merely because the police fear that the solicitor will advise the suspect not to answer questions (*Alladice* (1988) 87 Cr App R 380, and Code C, annex B, para 4). In *Samuel* [1988] 1 WLR 920, the Court of Appeal gave guidance on the circumstances in which delay could be authorized. The essential facts were that S was arrested on 6 August 1986 on suspicion of armed robbery from a building society and arrived at the police station at 2 p.m. He first asked to see a solicitor at 8 p.m. during a second interview with investigating officers when the questioning turned to masks and other items discovered in a search of his home. That request and subsequent requests were refused. S was then interviewed a further three times without having had the benefit of legal advice, the last interview being at around 5.30 p.m. on 7 August 1986 when he at last confessed to the robbery. Prior to that he had already confessed to and been charged with two unconnected burglaries. Throughout the afternoon of the 7th, Mr W, a highly respected local solicitor, had been unavailingly seeking access to S. The trial judge was invited to exercise his discretion under s 78 of the Act and exclude the confession on the basis that there had been a breach of s 58 (and also of the Code). In the Court of Appeal, Hodgson J said that the senior officer authorizing delay in access must have a subjective belief that, in the event of immediate consultation with a solicitor, one or other of the three harmful consequences mentioned in s 58(8) 'will very probably happen'. That in turn implies a belief that the solicitor would either deliberately interfere with evidence, warn other suspects etc., or would inadvertently do so. As to the first possibility (i.e., deliberate misconduct by the legal adviser), the number of occasions on which fear of it could be genuinely advanced would be rare, and would have to relate to the particular solicitor whom the detainee wished to consult, not to solicitors in general. As to the inadvertent disclosures (e.g., through the solicitor passing on a coded message), that implies a naivety on the part of the solicitor and a sophistication on the part of the detainee which is most unlikely to occur in practice. The task of satisfying the court that a senior officer delaying access genuinely and reasonably believed such a disclosure might occur would be a 'formidable one'. In S's case, the superintendent might just have been entitled to authorize delay when S first asked for a solicitor (since at that stage he did not know who the solicitor would be), but once it was appreciated that it would be the highly respected Mr W, any possible justification for his decision was removed. Accordingly, there had been a clear breach of s 58.

3.54   The rights may also be delayed where the officer reasonably believes their exercise will hinder recovery of property constituting the benefit from criminal conduct (Code C, annex B, para 2).

3.55   The detainee must be told why he is being refused access to a solicitor, and that reason must be entered on the custody record: s 58(9). As soon as the reason ceases to exist, access must be allowed: s 58(11). It must in any event be allowed once the detainee has been held for 36 hours, which is the stage at which the police have to go before a magistrates' court to obtain a warrant for further detention if they want to hold and question the detainee further: s 58(5).

3.56   Section 58 does not in terms say that the police cannot interview a detainee until he has consulted a solicitor—it merely says that, unless delay has been duly authorized by a senior officer, they must not actively prevent consultation taking place. This raises the question of how feasible it is for the average detainee actually to get a solicitor to come to the station to advise him. Where a detainee is prepared to pay for advice himself then he must be given the opportunity to consult a specific solicitor or another solicitor from the same firm, and if a solicitor is unavailable by these means, up to two alternatives. If the detainee requires publicly funded legal advice, then the officer telephones a call centre authorized by the Legal Services Commission. That centre determines whether legal advice should be dispensed by telephone, or whether a solicitor should attend (Code C, guidance notes 6B1 and 6B2). Whether a solicitor is authorized to attend will depend upon matters such as whether the arrest was for an offence which is non-imprisonable, or results from a bench warrant or driving with excess alcohol (in which case attendance will not be approved). If a solicitor is authorised to attend, the costs are paid out of the public funds. The scheme operates on a round-the-clock basis.

The statutory rights contained in s 58 have been buttressed by the provisions of the Code. **3.57** Para. 6 deals in detail with the right to legal advice. In summary, the Code lays down certain rules which relate to all situations other than those to which exceptions (i) to (iii) in 3.53 apply, or where the suspect is detained under the Terrorism Act 2000 (see Code H under PACE, which is summarized in *Blackstone's Criminal Practice 2008*, Appendix 2). In summary, these rules of general application are:

(a) Detainees must be informed of their right to communicate privately with a solicitor, and that independent legal advice is available free of charge from the duty solicitor (para 6.1).
(b) A poster advertising the right should be displayed prominently in the charge room (para 6.3).
(c) No police officer should do or say anything with the intention of dissuading a detainee from obtaining legal advice (para 6.4).
(d) When a solicitor arrives at the station to see the suspect (presumably at the invitation of a friend or relative), then the suspect must be informed of the solicitor's arrival and asked if he would like to see him. This is so even if he has earlier declined legal advice (para 6.15).
(e) Where the suspect is allowed access to legal advice, he must be allowed to have his solicitor present for interview once the latter is present at the station, or on his way, or easily contactable by telephone (para 6.8).
(f) If the solicitor requested is on his way to the station or about to set off, an interview should not normally be started until he arrives (note 6A).
(g) The solicitor may be required to leave the interview only if his conduct stops the officer from properly questioning the suspect, e.g., by answering questions for his client. He can, however, challenge improper questions or advise his client not to answer certain questions (para 6.9 and note 6D).

Quite apart from the cases where consequences (i) to (iii) in 3.53 apply, there are three limit- **3.58** ed sets of circumstances where a suspect can be interviewed without a solicitor despite his request for legal advice. The first is if the solicitor cannot be contacted or refuses to attend, and the suspect refuses to make use of any duty solicitor scheme. The second is where awaiting the arrival of a solicitor would cause unreasonable delay to the investigative process which might lead to interference with evidence, or with other people, serious damage to property, alerting other suspects, or hindering the recovery of property obtained by an offence. The third is if the suspect changes his mind about wanting legal advice, and agrees in writing or on tape to being interviewed without a solicitor. In each of these sets of circumstances, authority for the interview to proceed must be received from an officer of senior rank (see para 6.6 for details).

The rules in the Code apply to 'solicitors', but the term is defined so as to include trainee solici- **3.59** tors, duty solicitor representatives, and accredited representatives on the register maintained by the Legal Services Commission. Where a solicitor sends a non-accredited representative to provide advice to the suspect, the police have greater powers to refuse access. The representative must still be admitted unless an officer of the rank of inspector or above considers admission 'will hinder the investigation and directs otherwise' (para 6.12A). The officer is advised to have regard to whether the representative's identity and status have been satisfactorily established, and whether he is of suitable character to provide legal advice (e.g., a criminal record of any recency and/or substance is likely to prove a bar). If the representative is allowed access, then he is in much the same position as a solicitor (para 6.12). If access is refused, the solicitor and the suspect must be told and the custody record noted (para 6.14).

3.60   The suspect is entitled to be notified of his right to free legal advice on arrival at the police station (para 3.1). In addition, he must be reminded of the right prior to each interview, including the restart of an interview (para 11.2). Further, the review officer must, when reviewing the suspect's detention in police custody, remind him of his right (para 15.4). In *Beycan* [1990] Crim LR 185, the trial judge held that there had been a failure properly to inform B of his rights when taken to the station, but that those breaches were cured when he was offered a solicitor at the outset of the challenged interview. The Court of Appeal held, bearing in mind that B was a Turkish Cypriot with no previous experience of the police, that this offer did not cure the previous breaches.

3.61   The right is to *private* consultation and communication with the solicitor (s 58 and Code C, para 6.1). The interview must take place outside the hearing of third persons. In particular, it must not be capable of being overheard by a police officer (*Brennan v United Kingdom* (2002) 34 EHRR 507) applying Art 6(3) of the European Convention on Human Rights).

3.62   Although s 58 itself is silent as to the consequences of non-compliance with it, the courts have been robust in their attitude to denials of the right given by the section. The leading case is *Samuel*, the facts of which are set out above. Once the Court of Appeal had decided that there had been a clear breach of s 58, the prosecution's contention that breach of the section should lead to exclusion of a confession only in cases of police 'impropriety' was unhesitatingly rejected. The court did not, however, hold that the trial judge definitely ought to have excluded the confession—merely that, in the circumstances, he had a discretion to do so under s 78 of PACE and had failed to take into consideration the major factor relevant to the exercise of that discretion, namely that the superintendent had had no good reason for preventing S consulting Mr W. The case thus stops short of saying that breach of s 58 will definitely, or even probably, deprive the prosecution of the evidence obtained thereby. Where, however, the police do permit consultation with a solicitor but deliberately trick him into believing that their evidence against his client is stronger than it is, the deceit practised on the officer of the court ought to lead to any subsequent confession being excluded (see *Mason* [1987] 1 WLR 139).

3.63   *Walsh* (1989) 91 Cr App R 161 puts forward three propositions which clarify the way in which the Court of Appeal is likely to deal with substantial breaches of the Code insofar as they relate to access to legal advice. First, if there were significant and substantial breaches of s 58 of PACE or provisions of the Code, prima facie the necessary standard of fairness had not been met. Second, the court must nonetheless (under s 78 of PACE) consider whether the effect would be so adverse that justice required the exclusion of the evidence. Third, breaches which were inherently serious could not be rendered insubstantial by the good faith of the officers.

Other rights at the police station

PACE and the Code give detainees at a police station two further rights in addition to the right **3.64** to consult a solicitor. The first is simply a right to consult the Codes themselves. Each of the Codes begins with a paragraph stating that it must be 'readily available at all police stations for consultation by police officers, *detained persons* and members of the public'. The second right is contained in s 56 of the Act. It is the right to have one relative, friend, or other person likely to take an interest in one's welfare informed of the fact of one's arrest and of the station where one is being held. This is sometimes loosely referred to as the right to a phone call, although in fact the detainee himself is not entitled to make the call—it is the police who have the duty of passing on the information to the person named by the detainee. Exercise of the right may be delayed in the same circumstances as exercise of the right to consult a solicitor may be delayed. To some extent the rights dovetail with each other in that the person informed of the detainee's arrest may well choose to contact a solicitor on his behalf, irrespective of whether the detainee himself has asked for the duty solicitor to come to the station. Over and above the basic right contained in s 56, a detainee is allowed to make a phone call and/or write letters, but any such communication (unless it is with a solicitor) is liable to be listened to or read by the police (see paras 5.6 and 5.7 of the Code). Again, it is subject to delay in the same way as the right to consult a solicitor (see 3.52 to 3.63).

Recording what the suspect says

The rules discussed so far about cautioning a suspect, about the periods for which and condi- **3.65** tions in which he may be questioned, and about access to legal advice are all designed to ensure that what he says to the police, whether or not it amounts to an admission, is reliable. It is equally important, though, to ensure that the record of anything he may say is reliable. Before PACE was introduced the police used simply to note an interviewee's answers to questions in their pocket books after the interview had concluded. He was not asked to sign the note. The result was that trials were disfigured by endless arguments over what was or was not said in interview, the accused complaining that he had been 'verballed' by the police. Code C has introduced rules that have attempted to address these problems (see paras 11.7 to 11.14 and 12.10 to 12.14).

The system now is that any interview with a suspect, whether it takes place at the station or **3.66** not, must be accurately recorded by the police. Moreover, if the interview is at the station, it must be recorded (i.e., noted down) *contemporaneously* on forms specially provided for the purpose or in the officer's pocket book (para 11.7). Subject to the possibility of tape recording (see below), the only exceptions to contemporaneous noting are if the investigating officer considers it would not be practicable or if it would interfere with the conduct of the interview. At the end of the interview, the suspect should be invited to read the record through (or have it read to him), and be asked to sign it to indicate that it is accurate. If he refuses to sign, a senior officer is told what has happened and certifies to that effect on the record. The record should be signed by the suspect, and may subsequently be used as an exhibit at his trial, either as containing admissions or as being consistent with his defence and therefore of assistance to him. Where the interview record is not made contemporaneously, the reason must be recorded in the interview record (para 11.10), and the record must be made as soon as practicable after the completion of the interview (para 11.8).

3.67 Failure to comply with the above rules may lead to evidence of the suspect's answers being excluded at trial. In Delaney (1988) 88 Cr App R 338, the Court of Appeal held that failure to compile a contemporaneous record of the bulk of a 90-minute interview with D was a 'flagrant breach' of the Code. Although the breach did not automatically render evidence of the confession D eventually made inadmissible, in the circumstances of the particular case admission was unfair because, had the whole interview been properly recorded, facts might well have emerged to show that the confession was inadmissible as a matter of law under s 76. In Canale (1990) 91 Cr App R 1, the Court of Appeal quashed C's conviction because the trial judge should have acted under s 78 to exclude admissions which had not been contemporaneously recorded. In so doing, their lordships stated that 'the importance of the rules relating to contemporaneous noting of interviews could not be over-emphasised'. Their purpose was to ensure accurate records of suspects' remarks and to protect the police. In Keenan [1990] 2 QB 54, the Court of Appeal said that the 'verballing' provisions of the Code should be 'strictly complied with' and that the courts would not be slow to exclude evidence obtained following 'substantial breaches' of the Code.

3.68 The obvious alternative to written records of interviews is to tape record them. A detailed Code of Practice now governs the procedure for recording interviews (Code E), and the *Consolidated Criminal Practice Direction* [2002] 1 WLR 2870, para IV.43 deals with their use in court, and the provision of summaries or transcripts. According to Code E, para 3.1, tape-recording is to be used at police stations:

(a) for suspects cautioned in respect of an indictable offence (including an offence triable either way);

(b) for further questions put to a suspect after charge for such an offence (note that this can only be done in exceptional circumstances—see 3.50 to 3.51); or

(c) for an interview taking place after a suspect charged with such an offence has been shown a statement by, or an interview with, another person (e.g., an alleged accomplice).

3.69 The usual system is that the interview is taped on a double-deck machine, with two tapes being used and a time-coding device to deter subsequent tampering. After the interview, one tape is sealed and kept as a potential exhibit. The other tape is used as a working copy. From it, the officers prepare a summary of the interview, the defence being given a copy. Upon request, they are also entitled to a copy of the tape itself and can thus check the accuracy of the summary. If there is a dispute, a transcript of the tape may be ordered, which can then be used as an administrative convenience at the trial. The tape itself will also be produced and, if necessary, played to the jury, while the interviewing officers should be called to identify who spoke the words on the tape and to deal with any suggestion that it has subsequently been falsified. Whether the audio-typist's transcript should also be read to the jury and/or given to them when they retire is a matter for the trial judge's discretion—the actual evidence is the tape itself, not the transcript.

3.70 A final possibility, which has largely died out as a result of contemporaneous interview notes and tape recording, is for a suspect to write or dictate a statement under caution. Statements under caution are dealt with in annex D to Code C.

G POWERS OF SEARCH

Police powers to search for evidence divide into three main types, namely powers to search the persons of members of the public who are merely under suspicion, powers to search premises, and powers to search the person and/or premises of an arrestee. **3.71**

Powers of stop and search

Sections 1 to 3 of PACE provide the police with a general power to detain a member of the public without arresting him for the purpose of carrying out a search of his person. The Stop and Search Code, Code A, indicates that it governs the power to search a person without first arresting him. Past police practice in the use of similar powers has been to stop and search where suspicions about the proposed subject are too vague to amount to reasonable grounds for an arrest. The object of the search is to dispel or confirm those vague suspicions. In the latter event, an arrest will no doubt follow. **3.72**

A police officer may search a person or vehicle if he has reasonable grounds for suspecting that he will find stolen or prohibited articles: PACE, s 1(2) and (3). 'Prohibited articles' comprise (a) offensive weapons and (b) articles made or intended by the persons carrying them for use in connection with burglary, theft, taking vehicles, obtaining property by deception, or criminal damage: s 1(7) to (9). Para 2 of the Stop and Search Code gives quite full guidance on what amounts to reasonable suspicion justifying a stop and search. The main point is that there must be a concrete basis in fact for the suspicion, as opposed to a mere 'hunch' or instinct. Such a basis may be found in the nature of the property which the member of the public is seen or thought to be carrying, coupled with facts such as the time and place and his general behaviour. But para 2.2 of Code A states: **3.73**

> Reasonable suspicion can never be supported on the basis of personal factors alone without reliable supporting intelligence or information or some specific behaviour by the person concerned. For example, a person's race, age, appearance, or the fact that the person is known to have a previous conviction, cannot be used alone or in combination with each other as the reason for searching that person. Reasonable suspicion cannot be based on generalisations or stereotypical images of certain groups or categories of people as more likely to be involved in criminal activity. A person's religion cannot be considered as reasonable grounds for suspicion and should never be considered as a reason to stop or stop and search an individual.

The power to stop and search may be exercised only in a place to which the public have access: s 1(1). Broadly speaking, this means any public place; any place to which the public (or a section thereof) have access by permission whether with or without payment, and any place to which the public do in fact have 'regular access' even though they might not be entitled to go there. Within the last-mentioned category are car-parks, forecourts, the common parts of blocks of flats, and even private yards or gardens adjoining the road. However, a person may not be stopped and searched in his own garden or yard; nor may somebody who is there by his permission. But, if a stranger jumps over the garden fence to hide behind a hedge, the police have power to search him where he is. The period for which a person may be detained by virtue of the s 1 power is that necessary to carry out the search either at the place where he was stopped or nearby: s 2(8). The most that the officer carrying out the search can require the **3.74** subject to do in public is to remove an outer coat, jacket, or gloves: s 2(9)(a). However, there is nothing to stop the officer taking the subject to a nearby van or police station where a more thorough examination can take place out of the public view (para 3.6 of the Code). Reasonable force may be used both for purposes of detaining the person to be searched and then for actually searching him, but it should be employed as a last resort where the subject is not willing to cooperate (para 3.2). Every effort should be made to spare the subject embarrassment, and not to extend the search beyond what is strictly necessary. Before commencing the search, the officer must tell the subject his name and the name of the police station to which he is attached; the object of the proposed search; the grounds on which it is being made; and the right of the subject to have a copy of the record of the search: s 2(2) and (3). If the officer is not in uniform, he must produce his warrant card (para 3.9). The officer may also ask some preliminary questions. The subject is not obliged to answer, nor is the officer entitled to detain him for the purpose of asking questions—it is a power to stop and search, not a power to stop and question. However, if answers are forthcoming, they may dispel the suspicions which led to the original decision to stop, and thus avoid the need for a search (see s 2(1)). Although a vehicle may be stopped in order to search it, this may only be done by a constable in uniform: s 2(9)(b). Where an unattended vehicle is searched, a notice must be left on it, stating what has happened and giving the information about the officer's name etc. which would have been given to the driver in person had he been there: s 2(6).

3.75   The powers to stop and search contained in ss 1 to 3 of PACE are among the most controversial of its provisions. There is, plainly, room for abuse, in that individuals or groups could be harassed by over-enthusiastic use of the powers. This is acknowledged in guidance given by the Stop and Search Code. The Code says that the powers are to be employed 'responsibly' and without 'unlawful discrimination' (para 1.1)—for example on grounds of race. The Philips Commission's answer to such anxieties was to require the police to make adequate records of when and why they exercise the stop and search power. This is dealt with in s 3 of PACE. The record is to be made on the spot or as soon as is practicable after the carrying out of the search. It must give the name of the officer concerned and, if known, that of the subject, otherwise a description of him. The object, grounds, date, time, and place of the search are all to be specified, together with what was found and details of any injury to a person or damage to property apparently caused. The subject is entitled to a copy of the record: s 3(7) and (9). That might assist him, for example, in suing the police if the search appears to have been unjustified or in making a complaint about their conduct.

3.76   The Criminal Justice and Public Order Act 1994, s 60, introduced a new police power to stop vehicles or pedestrians and search for offensive weapons or dangerous instruments. The power can be exercised only in a particular locality where written authorization has been signed by a police officer of the rank of superintendent or above. If no more senior officer is available, an inspector may sign the authority. In any event, authority may be issued only where serious violence may occur. It is then valid for up to 24 hours, but can be extended for a further six hours. Once authority has been issued under s 60, it gives a constable the right to make such search as he sees fit 'whether or not he has any grounds for suspecting that the person or vehicle is carrying weapons or articles of that kind': s 60(5). This is in stark contrast to the exercise of the power under s 1 of PACE, which is restricted to cases where the officer has 'reasonable grounds for suspecting that he will find stolen or prohibited articles'.

There are also powers (the list is not exhaustive): **3.77**

(a) to stop and search vehicles for the prevention of acts of terrorism (Terrorism Act 2000, s 44(1));
(b) to stop and search pedestrians for prevention of acts of terrorism (Terrorism Act 2000, s 44(2));
(c) to search for controlled drugs under the Misuse of Drugs Act 1971, s 23;
(d) to search for firearms under the Firearms Act 1968, s 47.

Powers to search premises

Prior to PACE, a wide variety of statutory provisions gave the police power to enter premises   **3.78** and search for evidence relating to a criminal offence. Usually, a warrant had to be obtained from a magistrate to authorize the search. In other cases it could be authorized by a senior police officer. However, there were some strange gaps in the law, the best known of which was that there was no power to enter premises to search for evidence of murder (see *Ghani v Jones* [1970] 1 QB 693). Sections 8 to 14 of PACE are designed to fill these lacunae. Most of the pre-existing powers to authorize searches are retained, so the Act supplements the earlier law, rather than changing it. Sections 15 to 22 contain general provisions relating to the obtaining and executing of search warrants both under PACE and under any other legislation.

Section 8 of PACE provides that a magistrate may issue a warrant authorizing a police officer   **3.79** to enter and search premises if there are reasonable grounds for believing that:

(a) an *indictable offence* has been committed; and
(b) there is material on the premises in question which is likely to be both of *substantial value* to the investigation of the offence, and ultimately admissible as evidence should there be a prosecution; and
(c) the aforementioned does not consist of or include *legally privileged* items, *excluded material* or *special procedure material*; and
(d) it is either not practicable to obtain permission to enter the premises without a warrant (e.g., because the person entitled to grant permission would refuse it or cannot be contacted) or the purpose of the search would be frustrated (e.g., by destruction of the evidence) if the officers arriving to make it could not insist upon immediate entry.

In short, the offence suspected must be serious; the evidence likely to be found must be cogent; and the alternatives to entering with a warrant must be unsatisfactory. The three categories of material mentioned in (c) above and the special provisions relating to them are described below.

There are two different types of warrant: **3.80**

(a) a specific premises warrant; and
(b) an all premises warrant.

The specific premises warrant is confined to the set(s) of premises specified. An all premises warrant covers any premises occupied or controlled by a specified person. Either species of warrant may authorize multiple entries and searches of premises if a magistrate is satisfied that such authorization is necessary (PACE, s 8(1A)to (1C)).

3.81   Of the still effective pre-1986 legislation dealing with the issue of search warrants by far the most important is s 26(1) of the Theft Act 1968. This provides that a magistrate who has reasonable cause to believe that a person has 'in his custody or possession or on his premises any stolen goods' may 'grant [a police officer] a warrant to search for and seize the same'. 'Stolen goods' are defined so as to include those obtained by deception or blackmail. There is an overlap between s 8 of PACE and s 26 of the Theft Act in that the stolen goods might be evidence of an indictable offence. However, under s 26, there is no express requirement that the magistrate must be satisfied that gaining entry otherwise than by a warrant would be unsatisfactory or impracticable. Thus, in cases where it seems on the face of it that a warrant could be granted under either section, it will be simpler to make the application under s 26 of the Theft Act.

3.82   The proposal in the Police and Criminal Evidence Bill that there should be a general power to issue warrants to search for evidence caused great concern to various groups of professional and business people, who felt that their relationships with clients would be jeopardized if they could be forced to surrender to the police documents or other material that had been entrusted to them in confidence. In deference to these concerns, the Act was eventually passed with complicated safeguards to protect the following three classes of material:

(i)   **Items subject to legal privilege** (s 10). These are essentially any communications between a legal adviser and his client; communications between a legal adviser or the client and a third party made in contemplation of legal proceedings; and items enclosed with such communications (provided they are lawfully in the possession of whoever has them and are not, for example, stolen). The concept of documents which attract legal professional privilege is, of course, familiar in evidence and civil procedure, and s 10 should be regarded as a statutory adoption of the common law definition (see dicta in *Central Criminal Court ex parte Francis and Francis* [1989] AC 346). Again following the common law, s 10(2) provides that items held with the purpose of furthering a criminal purpose cannot enjoy legal privilege. This applies even if the person actually in possession of the items (e.g., the solicitor of a person being investigated by the police) was entirely unaware of anything improper (*Ex parte Francis and Francis*, in which case files held by the respondent solicitors concerning a client's business transactions were not items subject to legal privilege because it was contended that the transactions were a means by which the client 'laundered' and distributed the proceeds of drug trafficking). Where the police seek material which is prima facie covered by legal privilege, it will be rare for the judge to issue a blanket order granting a search warrant in respect of wide categories of documents held by a firm of solicitors. In certain circumstances, however, such an order may be proper. Hence, in *Leeds Crown Court ex parte Switalski* [1991] Crim LR 559, the Divisional Court upheld the circuit judge in granting such a blanket order where the firm in question was the subject of an enquiry into fraud on the legal aid fund and conspiracy to pervert the course of justice.

(ii) **Excluded material** (ss 11–12). This consists of 'personal records' held in confidence by the person who created them. Personal records are defined as medical records, records of spiritual counselling, and files kept on their clients by social workers, probation officers, and the like. Thus, the category of excluded material is a narrow one.

(iii) **Special procedure material** (s 14). This is a rather wider category than excluded material, covering anything that a person acquired in the course of his trade, business, or employment, and which he holds subject to an express or implied undertaking to keep it confidential. It also covers 'journalistic material' (unless it was acquired and has always been held in confidence, in which case it comes within the category of excluded material).

The scheme of the Act is that legally privileged items are totally protected from seizure under **3.83** a search warrant. Access to excluded material or special procedure material may be obtained, if at all, only by application to a circuit judge, not through a warrant issued by a magistrate or authorization given by a senior police officer: s 9(1). The procedure for obtaining excluded or special procedure material is contained in Sch 1 to PACE. Essentially, a police officer must apply to a circuit judge for an order that the person in possession of the material (the respondent) shall, within a week or longer period specified by the judge, hand the material over to the police or allow them to take copies of it. Notice of the application must be given to the respondent, and should specify the documents or other material sought (see *Central Criminal Court ex parte Adegbesan and others* [1986] 1 WLR 1293). The defendant, on the other hand, has no right to be made a party to, or be given notice of, the application. The applicant must tell the judge of anything known which might weigh against making the order (*Lewes Crown Court ex parte Hill* (1990) 93 Cr App R 60). If the material is excluded material, a production order may be made only if, prior to the enactment of s 9(2) of PACE, a warrant to search for the material could have been issued under provisions such as s 26(1) of the Theft Act. If it is special procedure material, the judge may make an order if he considers that what is sought would be of substantial value in the investigation of an indictable offence; that other methods of obtaining access to the material would clearly not succeed, and that it is in the public interest to make the order. Deciding where the 'public interest' lies will involve balancing the benefits to be gained from the successful investigation of a serious crime against the harm done by damaging confidential relationships. Having been served with notice of intention to apply for a production order, the respondent is under a duty not to hide, destroy, damage, etc. the subject matter of the proposed order. Where the police think that he cannot be trusted not to do those things, they may apply without notice for a search warrant, which the judge may grant if he considers that (i) he would be entitled to make a production order, but (ii) an application on notice for such an order would indeed have entailed undue risks to the preservation of the evidence. Failure to comply with a production order is contempt of court, and may sometimes also result in the issue of a search warrant.

The scheme of the legislation means that it can never be right for a magistrate to issue a s 8 warrant **3.84** to search for documents which are prima facie legally privileged. If they turn out to be privileged, they will be covered by s 10. If they are excluded from the scope of legal privilege because of a criminal purpose, they are pushed into the ambit of special procedure material. Hence s 14 would come into play, and application must be made to a judge, not a magistrate.

If a party is aggrieved by the decision of the judge, it is not appropriate to apply to him to **3.85** rescind his order. The proper course is to apply to the Divisional Court for judicial review (*Liverpool Crown Court ex parte Wimpey plc* [1991] Crim LR 635).

3.86 Sections 15 and 16 of PACE and the Search of Premises Code contain numerous detailed safe-guards relating to the obtaining and execution of search warrants. For example, the application for a warrant should be made *ex parte* without notice, for the obvious reason that, if notice were given, the items sought might vanish. The application should be supported by a written information, specifying *inter alia* the premises to be searched, the items it is hoped to find, and how those items relate to the investigation on which the police are engaged. The officer should attend and be prepared to answer questions on oath—e.g., as to the general nature of the information which leads him to want to search the premises, although he should not be expected to reveal the name of an individual informant.

3.87 When executing the warrant, the police should have it with them to show to the occupier of the premises. Normally they should seek his permission to enter, but they need not do so if that might frustrate the object of the search or endanger the officers. A warrant should not be used as an excuse to ransack the entire premises—i.e., the police should look in those places where the items they are authorized by the warrant to search for are most likely to be. If, however, they come across other items which appear to be the proceeds or evidence of crime, they may seize them, even though they are not mentioned in the warrant (s 19). The officer conducting the search must endorse the warrant with a statement of whether the property mentioned therein and/or anything else was found. Anything taken by the police may be retained 'for so long as is necessary in all the circumstances' (s 22)—e.g., until after the trial at which the item is to be used as evidence. A record of what has been seized must be given to the occupier of the premises, who then has certain limited rights to see, photograph, and take copies of the items concerned.

Searches arising out of arrests

3.88 The following are the main powers of search connected with the exercise of a power of arrest:

(a) **Search of person on arrest**. An officer who arrests a suspect otherwise than at the police station may search him if he has reasonable grounds to suspect that he has anything which might *either* be used for purposes of an escape *or* might be evidence of an offence (not necessarily the offence for which the arrest was made): PACE, s 32(2)(a). This mere-ly reflects the common law (see *Dillon v O'Brien and Davis* (1887) 16 Cox CC 245). Anything found which comes within the two stated categories may be seized and retained by the officer. The search should not extend beyond what is reasonably required to discover whether the arrestee has anything on him which might be so seized: s 32(3). He may not, in any event, be required to remove any clothing in public, other than an outer coat, jacket, or gloves: s 32(4).

(b) **Search of arrestee at police station**. One of the custody officer's initial duties in respect of an arrestee brought to the police station is to record what he has with him. For this pur-pose, he may and normally would authorize a search. The extent of the search is in the custody officer's discretion. It may extend to a strip search, in which case it must be car-ried out by an officer of the same sex. Nobody of the opposite sex (other than a doctor or nurse) may be present. Nor may anybody whose presence is unnecessary (see annex A to Code C, which defines a strip search as one involving more than the removal of the outer clothing). Searches at the police station are dealt with in s 54 of PACE. For further details, see 3.22.

(c) **Intimate searches**. A strip search is not necessarily an intimate search as defined by PACE. The latter is 'a search which consists of the physical examination of a person's body orifices other than the mouth': s 65 and Code C, annex A, para 1. Clearly, such searches should be subject to strict controls because they might be used to humiliate or intimidate the subject. If inexpertly carried out, they could cause physical harm. So, the custody officer, although entitled to order a strip search under s 54 to ascertain what an arrestee has with him, may not sanction an intimate search: s 54(7). Section 55 deals with intimate searches. They must be authorized by an officer of at least the rank of inspector but only if he reasonably believes that an arrestee in detention at the station has concealed on him *either* anything which he could and might use to cause physical injury to himself or others while in police detention or at court, *or* a Class A drug which, prior to his arrest, he had in his possession for purposes of supply or illegal exportation. Class A drugs are the drugs such as cocaine, heroin, and Ecstasy (but not cannabis). If the superintendent believes that the detainee might have, say, heroin concealed in his body but that he is simply a user (not a supplier or exporter) of the drug, an intimate search should not be authorized. Neither should it be authorized if the object of the search might be found by other means (e.g., by waiting for it to be passed through the natural bodily functions). A search for drugs *must* be carried out by a doctor or nurse at a hospital or doctor's surgery, not at the police station. If possible, a search for items capable of causing injury should also be by a doctor or nurse, although they may be asked to come to the station for the purpose rather than the detainee having to be taken to hospital. However, in an emergency the senior officer may authorize another officer to make the search (e.g., if the police doctor called to the station refuses to search without the detainee's consent and that consent is not forthcoming, or if it is likely to be a long time before the doctor arrives).

(d) **Search of premises where arrested**. Section 17 of PACE, which is basically a codification of the common law, provides *inter alia* that a police officer may enter and search premises in order to execute a warrant for arrest or to make an arrest without warrant for an arrestable offence. He must have reasonable grounds for believing that the person he seeks is on the premises. Reasonable force may be used to effect an entry. The power to search given by s 17 is limited in the sense that the officer may only do whatever is reasonably required to ascertain whether his quarry is on the premises—he is not entitled to search for evidence. However, s 32(2)(b) supplements s 17 by empowering the police to search premises in which an arrestee was at the time of or immediately before his arrest for evidence relating to the offence in respect of which the arrest was made. The subsection applies even if the arrest was for a non-arrestable offence. If, in making a search under either s 17 or s 32(2)(b), the officer discovers evidence of other offences he may seize that too (see s 19 of PACE).

(e) **Search of arrestee's home etc**. The premises searched under s 17 or s 32(2)(b) could be the arrestee's own home, but that will not necessarily be so. For many years, the police assumed that, if they arrested a person away from his home, they had the same right to search it as if he had been arrested at his home. This was confirmed in *Jeffrey v Black* [1978] 1 QB 490, subject to the important qualification that the property which the police hoped to find as a result of the search had to have some connection with the matter for which the arrestee had been detained. PACE, s 18 enables an officer of at least the rank of inspector to give written authorization for 'any premises occupied or controlled by a person under arrest for an arrestable offence' to be searched by the investigating officers. In addition to a search of the arrestee's home, a search of his shop or other business premises might be authorized. Authorization may only be given if the inspector reasonably suspects that there is evidence on the premises relating either to the offence in respect of which the arrest was made, or to another connected or similar arrestable offence. The facts of *Jeffrey v Black* provide a good example of when authorization for a search would *not* be justified. Cannabis was found in B's lodgings when they were searched without his consent following his arrest for stealing a sandwich from a public house. The Divisional Court held that the search was unlawful because the officers could have had no reason to suppose that it would yield evidence relating either to the theft for which B was under arrest, or to other 'sandwich thefts', or even to other offences of dishonesty. Precisely the same reasoning would apply under s 18. Having authorized a search, the inspector should note his reasons and the nature of the evidence sought in the arrestee's custody record. The only situation in which a s 18 search may be made without prior authorization is when the arresting officer decides that it is appropriate to delay taking the arrestee to the station so that they can go together to the premises in question, with a view to carrying out the search in the arrestee's presence (see s 30(10)). The officer should then inform the inspector as soon as practicable of what has occurred.

3.89 Finally, three general points about police searches remain to be made. First, in cases where the police do not have the power to carry out a search against the will of the occupier of the premises concerned, they may, of course, ask him for his consent. Para 5 of Code B (the Search of Premises code) deals with what the occupier should be told when his permission for a search is sought and also provides that any consent should be given in writing if practicable. Secondly, where any provision of PACE gives the police power to perform a certain act and does not make that power dependent upon the consent of the person affected by it, reasonable force may be used in the exercise of the power: PACE, s 117. Thus, reasonable force may be used *inter alia* to effect an arrest under s 24, to enter premises to effect an arrest under s 17, to search an arrestee both upon arrest and at the police station under ss 32 and 54, to make an intimate search under s 55 and to enter and search an arrestee's premises under s 18. Lastly, evidence discovered as a result of unlawful searches may well be admissible at an accused's trial, irrespective of whether he or some third party was the victim of the illegality. As explained at the beginning of the Chapter, there is merely a discretion to exclude unlawfully obtained evidence if its effect on the fairness of the proceedings would be so marked that it ought not to be admitted (see s 78). There clearly is a discretion under s 78 of PACE to exclude the fruits of an illegal search (see, for example, *Wright* [1994] Crim LR 55). But the courts have traditionally been slow to disallow evidence on this basis, and the Court of Appeal will be reluctant to interfere with the trial judge's discretion (*Christou* [1992] QB 979).

H   EVIDENCE OF IDENTITY

3.90 The methods by which the police gather evidence to establish that their suspect was indeed the person who committed the *actus reus* of the offence in question are too many and various for a comprehensive survey. However, two particular ones call for comment, since they are dealt with in PACE and the Codes. They are identification procedure evidence and fingerprint evidence.

Identification procedures

The simplest means of identifying the accused as the person who perpetrated or took part **3.91** with others in the perpetration of the offence charged is to call an eye-witness of the crime, and ask him whether the person he saw committing the offence is present in court. The witness will almost certainly say, 'Yes, there he is, standing in the dock'. Such evidence is, however, far from satisfactory. A witness knows perfectly well that whoever is in the dock is the man the police believe committed the offence. He is therefore likely to identify him, not because of the resemblance between him and whoever he saw committing the offence, but simply because he is where he is—i.e., in the dock. Therefore, unless there has been some prior identification of the accused by the witness (e.g., at an identification parade), the courts will not normally permit a 'dock identification'. This general principle may be departed from if the accused refused to go on a parade, or if it was not practicable to hold one because the witness did not recover from the injuries he received through the alleged offence until shortly before the trial, or the accused was of such unusual looks that not enough people even roughly resembling him could be found to go on a parade with him (see *John* [1973] Crim LR 113, *Caird* (⁊70) 54 Cr App R 499, and *Hunter* [1969] Crim LR 262). However, the basic rule is that, if there is any possibility of a dispute arising at a suspect's future trial about his being the person who was seen in a certain place or committing certain acts, the police should give him the chance of an identification procedure at which the witness(es) can try to pick him out. If he is not given that option, any evidence of identity from the witnesses will probably be ruled inadmissible.

The procedure relating to identification, including the holding of parades, is contained in **3.92** Code D. Para 3.1 states that a written record should be made of the description of a suspect first given by a potential witness. The aim is to ensure that it is clear whether the witness's description is a good 'fit' for the actual appearance of the suspect. This record may form part of a witness statement, or may be in the form of an immediate record, such as a police control room log. (Note 3A makes it clear that as a general rule a police officer who is a witness is subject to the same principles and procedures as a civilian witness.) The written record must be made available to the suspect or his solicitor as soon as practicable and, if available, before any identification procedure takes place (para 3.1). Where a potential witness is shown photographs of possible suspects, the officer supervising the showing of the photographs must ensure that the first description is recorded before the photographs are shown (annex E).

Where there is a witness whose identification of the suspect is in issue, then an identification **3.93** procedure should be arranged as soon as possible. The arrangements for such procedures are under the control of an officer of the rank of inspector or above, who is styled the 'identification officer'. He must not be involved in the investigation other than in this capacity (para 3.11).

An identification procedure need not, however, be held if it is not practicable or would serve **3.94** no useful purpose, e.g., where the suspect is already well known to the identifying witness, or the witness would not be able to make an identification at all (Code D, para 3.12).

3.95 Set out in Code D are the four identification procedures which put a suspect before witnesses to ascertain whether they can identify him. They are:

(a) video identification (when the witness is shown moving images of a known suspect, together with similar images of others who resemble the suspect);

(b) identification parade (when the witness sees the suspect in a line of others who resemble him);

(c) group identification (when the witness sees the suspect in an informal group of people);

(d) confrontation of the suspect by the witness, normally in the police station.

Until 2002, Code D laid down that the identification parade was the preferred procedure, provided that the suspect was prepared to take part. This has now been altered, and the position is that the video identification is the usual procedure of choice. An identification parade is offered by the identification officer and the investigating officer where is it more practicable and suitable than a video identification (para 3.14). The third choice procedure is the group identification. It may, however, be used where it is considered more suitable than a video identification or an identity parade (para 3.16). The last resort is a confrontation between witness and suspect, which is only to be used if the other procedures prove impracticable (para 3.23). Where a suspect refuses to consent to the identification procedure suggested by the police, he may make representations as to why another procedure should be used. The identification officer may then offer him an alternative 'if appropriate' (para 3.15).

The rules for the procedures are set out in the annexes to Code D as follows:

Annex A: video identification;

Annex B: identification parades;

Annex C: group identification;

Annex D: confrontation by a witness;

Annex E: showing photographs;

Annex F: fingerprints, footwear impressions and samples—destruction and speculative searches.

For details of the various procedures, reference should be made to the Code itself; and for the treatment of identification evidence at trial, see *Blackstone's Criminal Practice 2008* F18.2 to 18.26 (the Code is printed as Appendix 2 in *Blackstone's Criminal Practice 2008*).

3.96 As is well known, the police keep a 'rogues' gallery' of pictures of convicted criminals. If the officers investigating a crime do not have information which would justify them arresting a particular suspect but there are eye witnesses to what happened, they may show those witnesses photographs from the rogues' gallery (Code D, annex E). A witness looking at photographs should be given as much privacy as possible, and not be allowed to communicate with other witnesses. He should be shown at least 12 photographs at a time, being told that the person he is looking for may or may not be amongst those photographed. No prompting or guidance is permissible. If the police already have suspicions of a certain person (but nothing to justify an arrest), they should ensure that his picture is shown with pictures of others who as far as possible resemble him. Once a positive identification has been made from photographs, then— unless it was plainly wrong—neither the witness making the identification nor any other witness should be shown further pictures, but they should be asked to attend an identification procedure. The defence should be told if a witness who attended an identification procedure had previously been shown photographs (or an Identikit likeness) of the suspect. The defence could then argue that an identification at the parade should be discounted because the witness was picking out the person whose photograph he had seen, rather than picking out the person he saw committing the offence. Unfortunately, this inevitably reveals to the jury that the accused has previous convictions, for otherwise the police would not have a photograph of him.

Fingerprints

The National Identification Bureau at Scotland Yard keeps records of convictions and the fin- **3.97** gerprints of those convicted. Broadly speaking, only offences punishable with imprisonment are 'recordable offences', conviction for which will result in the offender's fingerprints being added to the national collection if they are not already there. Section 61 of PACE and paras 4.1 to 4.9 of Code D deal with the taking of fingerprints. The police are always at liberty to fingerprint somebody with his consent (e.g., the occupiers of burgled premises might be asked for their prints so as to distinguish them from any left behind by the burglars). Consent given at the police station should be in writing: PACE, s 61(2). Fingerprinting of detainees at police stations otherwise than by consent is allowed if an officer of at least the rank of inspector authorizes it on the grounds that it will tend to confirm or disprove the detainee's involvement in the offence of which he is suspected: s 61(3)(b) and (4). The authorization should be in writing or confirmed in writing as soon as practicable: s 61(5). The reasons should be explained to the detainee and noted on his custody record: s 61(7) and (8). The inspector's authorization may be given even if the offence suspected is non-recordable. The fingerprints of someone who has been arrested for a recordable offence, and who is detained in a police station, may be taken without his consent. Once a detainee has been charged, his prints may be taken without his consent and without authorization, provided the offence concerned is a recordable one: s 61(3)(b). And, having been convicted of a recordable offence, an offender is again liable to fingerprinting: s 61(6). Thus, if it did not seem necessary to fingerprint the offender when he was charged with a recordable offence, his prints may be taken from him at court immediately after he is found guilty. Whenever there is a right to fingerprint without the subject's consent, reasonable force may be used to accomplish the task if he does not co-operate. Fingerprints taken from a non-suspect or from a suspect who is cleared of the offence must be destroyed as soon as is practicable after the conclusion of the proceedings. He is entitled to be present when they are destroyed (see PACE, s 64).

Section 61 represents a significant change from the pre-1986 law, under which a suspect's **3.98** fingerprints could be taken against his will only if the police obtained an order from the magistrates permitting that to be done. PACE also deals with the taking of other samples from a suspect which are of potential use for forensic purposes. *Intimate samples* (e.g., blood, urine, semen, a swab taken from the genitals) may only be taken from someone in police detention if (a) the taking has been authorized by an officer of at least the rank of inspector, and (b) the detainee gives his written consent. The senior officer's authorization is dependent upon his reasonably believing that the sample will tend to disprove or confirm the detainee's involvement in a recordable offence (this includes all imprisonable offences, and a few non-imprisonable ones). If the detainee refuses consent, inferences can be drawn from that refusal in subsequent proceedings: s 62(10). When asked for his consent, the detainee must be warned of the possible evidential consequences of refusing it. *Non-intimate samples* (e.g., hair other than pubic hair, scrapings from under a nail, footprints, saliva) may be taken with the written consent of the person concerned whatever the nature of the offence under consideration and without the authorization of a senior officer. Since there is no statutory provision allowing the prosecution to adduce evidence of refusal of a non-intimate sample, the person concerned is not under the same pressure to give the sample as he is when intimate samples are requested. However, in the case of non-intimate samples, an inspector can authorize their being taken against the suspect's will, provided a recordable offence is suspected, and the officer reasonably believes that the sample will assist in proving or disproving the case against the suspect. An intimate sample, other than one of urine, must be taken by a doctor or registered nurse. There are no express requirements about the taking of non-intimate samples. Sections 62 and 63 deal respectively with intimate samples and non-intimate ones. Section 62 contains a saving subsection making it clear that it does not affect the provisions of the drink-driving laws relating to samples of blood or urine.

3.99   In addition, by PACE, s 63(3A), a non-intimate sample can be taken without consent where the person has been arrested or charged with a recordable offence or told he will be reported for one, and he has not given a non-intimate sample suitable for analysis. A similar power exists where an offender has been convicted of a recordable offence (s 63(3B)) or acquitted on grounds of insanity or found unfit to plead (s 63(3C)).

3.100   Police officers have the power to take footwear impressions with or without the suspect's consent. Apparently, footwear impressions are recovered from about 20 to 30 per cent of crime scenes. The power was introduced by the Serious Organised Crime and Police Act 2005, which inserted a new s 61A in PACE. Normally, the impression should be taken with the suspect's consent, but it may be taken without consent where he has been arrested for, charged with, or informed that he will be reported for a recordable offence.

I   SPECIAL GROUPS

3.101   So far police powers and procedures have been considered on the assumption that the suspect is an adult of normal intelligence and with all his faculties. Some extra protections for the suspect are necessary if he is a juvenile or a member of another vulnerable group. At the other end of the scale, those arrested for terrorist offences are denied some of the rights that other suspects have.

Juveniles

3.102   The various powers of arrest without warrant described at 3.14 may be exercised in respect of a juvenile just as they may be exercised in respect of an adult—the relevant legislation, in particular s 24 of PACE, makes no mention of the age of the arrestee. Similarly, the powers of a magistrate to issue a warrant for arrest (e.g., under ss 1 and 13 of the MCA) are in no way restricted by the accused's youth. In practice, of course, both a police officer and a magistrate considering, respectively, the making of an arrest without warrant and the issuing of a warrant will bear in mind the undesirability of taking a juvenile to the police station, and might refrain from exercising their powers when, in an equivalent case involving an adult, they would unhesitatingly do so. Any person who arrests a juvenile must take all reasonable steps to inform his parents of what has occurred: s 34 of the Children and Young Persons Act 1933.

Having arrived under arrest at the police station, a juvenile's continued detention there **3.103** depends, just like an adult's, on whether the custody officer considers there is enough evidence to charge him and whether—if there is not—detention without charge is necessary to secure or preserve evidence relating to the offence suspected or to obtain such evidence by questioning him. One major difference, however, between an adult and a juvenile is that neither before nor after charge should a juvenile be put in a police cell unless that is the only secure accommodation available and he could not safely be left in a non-secure room. Nor should he be placed in a cell with an adult (para 8.8 of Code C).

The questioning of juveniles is dealt with in paras 11.15 to 11.20 of Code C. Save in excep- **3.104** tional circumstances (see below), a juvenile should not be interviewed or asked to provide a statement under caution unless an 'appropriate adult' is also present. This applies whether or not the juvenile is himself suspected of an offence. An appropriate adult is defined as either his parent/guardian or a social worker or (in default of either of those) some other responsible adult unconnected with the police (para 1.7). Note 1B points out that a parent or guardian will *not* be the appropriate adult if he is the victim, a witness or a suspected accomplice, or has received admissions. Similarly, where a child in care admits the offence to a social worker, another social worker should be the appropriate adult. Further, if juvenile and parent are 'estranged', and the juvenile objects, then the parent should not be called as the appropriate adult (following *DPP v Blake* [1989] 1 WLR 432). The appropriate adult's role, according to para 11.17 of the Code, is not merely to act as an observer, but also to advise the juvenile and, if necessary, to 'facilitate communication with him'. A decision to exercise the right under s 58 to consult a solicitor may be taken on the juvenile's behalf by the appropriate adult. The reasons for taking extra care in questioning juveniles are fairly obvious, but the Code reminds investigating officers of them. They are that, without necessarily meaning to do so, juveniles are particularly prone to give information which is 'unreliable, misleading or [falsely] self-incriminating' (Note 11C). Even so, in an emergency, it may be necessary to question a juvenile without the safeguard of an appropriate adult being present. This may only be done if an officer of at least the rank of superintendent considers that delay will lead to physical harm to other people or harm to evidence connected with an offence, or alert other suspects not yet arrested for the offence, or hinder the recovery of property obtained from an offence (see para 11.1 and annex B of Code C). What if the police cannot obtain an appropriate adult from one of the above categories, and an interview cannot be justified on these emergency grounds? The juvenile cannot then be interviewed, and must be charged or released (para 11.18).

Reference has been made to a juvenile being charged. However, the more appropriate course **3.105** usually is to release him from the station without charging him, so that the police and the other interested agencies can consider at their leisure whether it is an appropriate case for prosecution or can better be dealt with by way of a caution (see 5.06 to 5.11 for the practice of giving a formal caution).

Mentally vulnerable people

Code C gives special consideration to those who are 'mentally disordered or otherwise men- **3.106** tally vulnerable' (hereafter referred to as 'mentally vulnerable'). Annex E to Code C, in particular, deals with the way in which they should be treated. The provisions in question are framed so as to include not only those with a specific mental illness but also those whose low intelligence etc. make them incapable of understanding the significance of questions put to them by an officer and/or the significance of their replies. Moreover, if the officer has a suspicion or is told in good faith that somebody is mentally vulnerable, he should treat him as such. Broadly speaking, the mentally vulnerable are regarded as a group and are equated with juveniles. Thus, like juveniles, they should normally have an appropriate adult present when they are questioned. Furthermore, if a mentally vulnerable accused is prosecuted substantially on the basis of a confession which he made in the absence of an appropriate adult, the judge must warn the jury of the special need for caution before convicting: PACE, s 77. It might seem surprising that Parliament thought it necessary to have a specific provision to that effect—surely, any judge in the circumstances predicated by s 77 would be expected to emphasize the unsatisfactory nature of the prosecution evidence without being told to do so by statute. In *Lamont* [1989] Crim LR 813, however, L was charged with the attempted murder of his baby. He was mentally subnormal, with an IQ of 73 and a reading age of eight. He confessed after 18 hours at the police station. He was very emotional in interview and cried. There was no other adult present. The judge allowed the confession in. He omitted any direction along the lines of s 77 and stated that the absence of the appropriate adult from the interview was of little importance. The Court of Appeal quashed the conviction, commenting adversely on both the failure to give a direction under s 77 and the statement about the absence of an appropriate adult. The 'appropriate adult' in respect of a mentally vulnerable person is *either* a relative, guardian or other person responsible for his welfare, *or* a person who has had experience in dealing with mental problems (e.g., a specialist social worker), *or* (in default of either of the above) any other responsible adult unconnected with the police. This is slightly different from the definition of appropriate adult *vis-à-vis* a juvenile. As regards identification parades, although an appropriate adult must be present both when the mentally vulnerable person gives his consent to standing on one and when it is held, there is no requirement that the appropriate adult should himself agree to the holding of the parade.

Interpreters

3.107 A person who appears to be deaf may not be interviewed in the absence of an interpreter (i.e., somebody who can communicate with him by sign language) unless he agrees or a senior officer considers that waiting for an interpreter would involve the risk of injury to third persons or serious damage to property. When an interpreter is present, he should take a note of the interview for possible future use if he is called as a witness at the interviewee's trial. The services of an interpreter will also be needed if the interviewee has difficulty in speaking English. Again the interpreter should take a note of the interview. He should also take down in the relevant foreign language any written statement the suspect wishes to make, the statement then being signed by the suspect. An official English translation is made in due course. Interpreters are provided at the public expense (Code C, paras 13.1 to 13.11).

Suspected terrorists

3.108 Some of the provisions of PACE and of Code C do not apply to those detained for examination under the Terrorism Act 2000. For example, the maximum period for which terrorism suspects can be held without charge was increased from 7 days to 14 days by the CJA 2003, s 306, and has since been the subject of fierce debate as government ministers have sought to increase it further. There is a separate Code of Practice (Code H) issued under the Terrorism Act, and its provisions are beyond the scope of this book.

J   DRUG TESTING

There is a power to test a suspect for Class A drugs (PACE ss 63B and 63C, Code C, section 17).   **3.109** These powers are aimed at those suspected of offences which are related to, or caused by, certain specified drug offences. They have been introduced in certain parts of England and Wales, with conditions which vary according to the location, and the age of the suspect. Details are beyond the scope of this work, but are to be found in *Blackstone's Criminal Practice 2008*, D1.70 to 1.75. In outline, the legislation provides that a non-intimate sample, or a sample of urine, can be taken from a suspect who meets the conditions in question. He can be detained for up to 24 hours in order for such a sample to be taken, and failure to provide one is a summary offence. Where a suspect aged 18 or over tests positive for one of the specified Class A drugs, the police may impose a requirement that he attend for an assessment of his drug misuse. Again, failure to comply is a summary offence. The sample obtained may only be used for certain specified purposes, including:

(a)   informing a decision as to bail;
(b)   informing a decision as to the imposition of a conditional caution;
(c)   informing a decision as to sentence;
(d)   providing advice and treatment.

KEY DOCUMENTS

Police and Criminal Evidence Act 1984, as amended.

Codes of Practice under the Police and Criminal Evidence Act 1984

Guidance on Charging issued by the DPP is available at <http://cps.gov.uk/publications/ directors_guidance/dpp_guidance.html>.

4

PROSECUTORS

The English constitutional system has traditionally avoided a centralized ministry of justice on the continental model. Responsibility for investigating crime, commencing prosecutions and presenting the case at court has been shared amongst a large number of different agencies. In October 1986, however, a major change was made to the system by the introduction of the Crown Prosecution Service (the CPS). The CPS has assumed a dominant role in the prosecution (but not the investigation) of crime. This Chapter will summarize the roles of the police, the CPS, other prosecuting authorities, and the private individual in the prosecution process. The subject is complex, but, for purposes of understanding criminal procedure in court, it is only necessary to deal with it in outline. **4.01**

A   THE POLICE

Historically, the great majority of the prosecutions in England and Wales have been com- **4.02** menced by the police in the sense that the accused is either charged at a police station or an information is laid against him by a police officer in the course of his duty (see 5.02 to 5.04 for explanation of charging and laying an information). Prior to commencing a prosecution, the police will, of course, have been responsible for investigating and obtaining evidence about the alleged offence. Under the pre-Crown Prosecution Service system, they were also responsible for the presentation of the case at court in the sense that they employed solicitors who appeared for the prosecution in the magistrates' court and instructed counsel for the Crown Court. Most police forces had salaried 'in-house' solicitors' departments. A minority simply instructed firms of solicitors in private practice. Either way, the police had the last word on, for example, the charges which should be proceeded with as the relationship between them and their solicitors was, in the final analysis, one of client and lawyer.

4.03   Since October 1986, the police have been stripped of their responsibility for actually prosecuting crime. The CPS now takes over the prosecution of all cases initiated by the police. Further, the statutory charging arrangements introduced by s 28 of the CJA 2003 mean that the CPS determines the charges in all but minor cases. By the beginning of 2006, statutory charging was in force in 15 CPS areas out of 42 (basically, in all the metropolitan areas of the CPS). It was scheduled to be in place in the remaining areas by March 2007. In any event, the police and CPS obviously need to act in close cooperation, since it will be necessary for police officers to attend court as witnesses, to warn private witnesses as to when they will be required, and to gather any further evidence that the CPS wants. However, the CPS is independent of the police, not their agent in prosecuting offences.

4.04   In common speech, one refers to 'the police' as if they were a unified force. In fact, however, there are a number of separate police forces, each acting within its own geographical area. Each force has a chief officer, called the 'Commissioner' in the City of London and Metropolitan forces, the 'Chief Constable' in other forces. The chief officer is answerable for the general efficiency of his force to a police authority made up of local authority members and magistrates from the areas served by the force, save that the Home Secretary is the police authority for the two London forces. It is generally accepted that the police authority should not interfere in operational matters—i.e., the day-to-day running of the force. In particular, they should not interfere with the police discretion on whether or not to commence prosecutions, either by seeking to influence general policy on the kinds of cases in which prosecutions are appropriate or by ordering a prosecution in a particular case. Such decisions are for the chief officer and his men, not the police authority. Even the courts lack power to intervene, save in extreme cases where a policy adopted by the chief officer amounts to a dereliction of his duty to uphold the law. As Lord Denning put it in *Metropolitan Police Commissioner ex parte Blackburn (No 1)* [1968] 2 QB 118:

> I hold it to be the duty of the Commissioner of the Police of the Metropolis, as it is of every chief constable, to enforce the law of the land . . . . He must decide whether or not suspected persons are to be prosecuted . . . . But [in this] he is not the servant of anyone, save of the law itself. No Minister of the Crown can tell him that he must or must not prosecute this man or that one. Nor can any police authority tell him so. The responsibility for law enforcement lies on him. He is answerable to the law and to the law alone.

Thus, police policy on prosecuting suspects can only be challenged in the unlikely event of the chief officer laying down a manifestly unreasonable policy, such as never commencing proceedings for theft if the amount involved is under £100. If that were to happen, any person with sufficient locus standi could apply for a mandatory order to compel the chief officer to fulfil his duty of enforcing the law. The considerations taken into account in deciding whether or not to prosecute are discussed in Chapter 5.

B   THE CROWN PROSECUTION SERVICE

4.05   The Crown Prosecution Service was created by s 1 of the Prosecution of Offences Act 1985. It consists of the Director of Public Prosecutions, who is its head; the Chief Crown Prosecutors, each of whom is responsible to the Director for supervising the operation of the service in a particular area, and some 7,800 other staff (including Crown Prosecutors and non-legally qualified support staff) who are appointed by the DPP with Treasury approval (see s 1(1) of the 1985 Act).

The Director of Public Prosecutions

The office of Director of Public Prosecutions was created in 1879. For over a century, despite the all-embracing nature of the title, the DPP's role in the prosecution system was relatively limited. However, the Prosecution of Offences Act 1985 transformed the position by requiring the DPP to take over the conduct of *all* criminal proceedings instituted by the police (s 3(2)(a)). Section 3(2) lists the duties of the DPP. The major ones are as follows:
4.06

(i)   to take over the conduct of all criminal proceedings commenced by the police;

(ii) to commence proceedings himself in any case where that appears appropriate (e.g., because of its importance or difficulty);

(iii) to take over the conduct of all proceedings under s 3 of the Obscene Publications Act 1959 for the forfeiture of obscene articles;

(iv) to give advice to police forces on all matters relating to criminal offences;

(v)   to appear for the prosecution, if so directed by the court, on appeals from the Crown Court to the Court of Appeal, from the Court of Appeal to the House of Lords and from the High Court to the House of Lords;

(vi) to discharge any other functions assigned to him by the Attorney-General.

In addition, s 6(2) enables the DPP to take over any prosecution begun by a person or authority other than the police, while miscellaneous legislation other than the 1985 Act imposes further duties on him (e.g., consenting to the institution of certain types of prosecution).

The DPP is appointed by and acts under the general 'superintendence' of the Attorney-General (ss 2 and 3(1) and see 4.22 for the role of the Attorney). Since the DPP is responsible to the Attorney and the Attorney is responsible to Parliament, there is an indirect sense in which the DPP can be called to account by Parliament for the way he discharges his functions. Before the 1985 Act, the DPP had a fairly small department of lawyers and other staff. However, the massive extension of duties entailed in assuming responsibility for all police prosecutions meant that the old DPP's department would no longer be remotely adequate. Hence, the Crown Prosecution Service was brought into being.
4.07

Structure of the Crown Prosecution Service

Below the DPP at the head of the Crown Prosecution Service are *Chief Crown Prosecutors*, each of whom is responsible for the operation of the CPS in a particular geographical area (see Prosecution of Offences Act 1985, s 1(1)(b)). Within each of the 42 areas there are one or more local branches, each of which is responsible for handling prosecutions at a group of magistrates' courts. The personnel at a branch office will consist of CPS lawyers, known as *Crown Prosecutors*, plus non-legally qualified executive officers and general support staff. The office will be headed by a *Branch Crown Prosecutor* and the area by a *Chief Crown Prosecutor*. All Crown Prosecutors must be designated as such by the DPP, and must be either barristers or solicitors (s 1(3)). They
4.08

have 'all the powers of the Director as to the institution and conduct of proceedings' (s 1(6)). In particular, they may authorize the commencement of proceedings in those cases where the DPP's consent to a prosecution is required (s 1(7)). Although a Crown Prosecutor must exercise his powers under the direction of the Director, it is not necessary for him to obtain specific authority for every action he takes on the DPP's behalf. The point is well-illustrated by *Liverpool Crown Court ex parte Bray* [1987] Crim LR 51 where it was held that an application by a Crown Prosecutor for a voluntary bill of indictment (see 13.75 to 13.77) had been made 'by or on behalf of' the DPP and therefore, according to the relevant rules of court, did not require an affidavit in support, even though the Crown Prosecutor had acted entirely on his own initiative. Watkins LJ described the defence contention that s 1(6) of the Prosecution of Offences Act conferred powers on Crown Prosecutors only when they acted on the DPP's express instructions as 'absurd'. It follows that, when legislation such as the Prosecution of Offences Act gives powers to or imposes duties upon the DPP, it is more realistic to read the enactment as empowering or burdening the CPS.

4.09   Crown Prosecutors, whether they are barristers or solicitors, have the same rights of audience as practising solicitors (s 4). In other words, they may appear in magistrates' courts but not in the Crown Court unless they have been granted rights of advocacy in the higher courts. The original intention when the Crown Prosecution Service was being planned was that the bulk of the advocacy required to be done on its behalf in the magistrates' courts would be undertaken by internal staff—i.e., Crown Prosecutors. In practice, difficulty in recruiting staff and the sheer volume of work have meant that some of the advocacy is still delegated to solicitors or barristers in private practice who act as agents for the CPS (see 4.12). As to representation of the CPS at the Crown Court (e.g., for trials on indictment), that usually has to be by barristers briefed by the CPS. However, there are now some 838 prosecutors working for the CPS who have the right to present cases in the Crown Court, and the CPS is determined to increase that number (CPS Annual Report for 2006/7).

4.10   Details of the way the CPS functions are a matter of internal administration and beyond the scope of this book. However, in broad outline, the system is that, once a person has been charged or an information has been laid against him, the papers in the case are dealt with by the appropriate branch office of the CPS. There the evidence is reviewed by a CPS lawyer who decides whether or not the charges are justified. If he considers that no prosecution should have been brought, then he has power to discontinue the proceedings (see 4.14). If he considers that additional or alternative charges are needed, he can have them put to the accused when he appears in court. The great majority of cases, even serious and/or complex ones, will be handled throughout at branch office level. The more difficult the case, however, the more likely it is that the branch Crown Prosecutors will liaise and seek advice from lawyers at the area office and/or refer the case to the CPS headquarters staff. A handful of offences must always be referred to headquarters (e.g., those where the Attorney-General's consent to a prosecution is required; large scale drugs and immigration conspiracies, and most prosecutions of police officers). On the other hand, even murder and rape are handled at branch office level unless it is thought there that exceptional factors require the file to be sent higher. Besides taking direct responsibility for a small minority of prosecutions as described above, CPS headquarters staff formulate general prosecutions policy, conduct relevant research, and generally support the area and offices of the Service. However, the offices are permitted a considerable degree of autonomy so that, although the CPS is a national service with certain operational guidelines laid down at national level, each office develops its own particular approach to prosecuting in a way that reflects local conditions.

Perhaps the single most important feature to notice about the CPS is that it does not investi- **4.11**
gate crime. In taking decisions about a case, the CPS lawyer will obviously liaise closely with the police but he should be independent of them and, in the last resort, must act on his own view of what should be done, not on the police's.

Agents

The DPP (i.e., Crown Prosecutors acting on his behalf) may assign the conduct of cases to barris- **4.12**
ters or solicitors in private practice (Prosecution of Offences Act 1985, s 5). Any agent thus acting for the CPS has the powers of a Crown Prosecutor but must exercise those powers in accordance with any instructions given him by an actual Crown Prosecutor. The usual system is for a CPS agent to be engaged for a day (or perhaps a morning or afternoon) in a particular magistrates' court. He then handles all the CPS cases appearing in the list for that day, the files having (hope-fully) been sent to him the day before. The position of an agent in the magistrates' court is subtly different from that of counsel briefed to appear for the prosecution in the Crown Court. Whereas the latter has the final word about how the case should be conducted, the former is, at least in theory, obliged to abide by the wishes of the CPS. Thus, agents are normally forbidden to drop cases except with the authority of a CPS lawyer, whereas counsel in the Crown Court may—and indeed should—exercise his own judgement on whether there is sufficient evidence to proceed and/ or whether a proposed set of pleas would be an acceptable way of disposing of the case.

Taking over prosecutions

The commencement of prosecutions is not, of course, the exclusive prerogative of the police or **4.13**
the CPS. Indeed, in strict constitutional theory, they are merely paid to do what any private citizen or organization may do as a matter of civic duty. Paragraphs 4.19 to 4.21 mention some of the organizations, other than the police and CPS, which are commonly involved in prosecuting crime. On occasion, however, the institution of a prosecution by a private individual or non-police body may be considered against the public interest. Alternatively, the prosecution may be considered so much in the public interest that it ought to be handled by the state rather than the individual. To cater for such situations, s 6(2) gives the DPP (which, in practice, of course means the CPS) an unfettered discretion to take over the conduct of any non-police prosecution. Having taken over a prosecution, the CPS may carry it to its conclusion or discontinue it as it sees fit.

Discontinuing prosecutions

A major reason for creating the CPS was to provide an independent check on whether police **4.14**
prosecutions were justified and, if not, to halt them at an early stage. To help the CPS fulfil this role, s 23 of the Prosecution of Offences Act provides that, where the CPS has the conduct of proceedings for an offence, they may give notice to the clerk of the magistrates' court that they do not want them to continue (s 23(3)). The notice must be given before the prosecution

start calling their evidence for purposes of a summary trial or, if there is going to be a trial on indictment, before the accused is actually committed for trial (s 23(2)).

4.15   In the case of an indictable-only offence sent for trial in the Crown Court, the prosecution may serve the notice at any time before the indictment is preferred. The CPS must include in the notice their reasons for discontinuing (s 23(5)). The effect of the notice is automatically to halt the proceedings, although the accused is not technically acquitted so it would be possible to commence fresh proceedings at a later date if, for example, further evidence came to light (s 23(9)). However, the accused must be served with a copy of the notice of discontinuance (though not the reasons for discontinuing), and he may insist on the prosecution going ahead (s 23(7)). The great majority of accused persons will be only too happy to receive a notice of dis-continuance, but very occasionally an individual may want his day in court either to proclaim publicly that the charges against him were totally unfounded or to preclude any possibility of a fresh prosecution by obtaining a formal acquittal (once someone has been acquitted, he may not again be prosecuted for the same offence, subject to the exceptions described in 17.4 to 17.61).

4.16   The number of cases discontinued by the CPS in the magistrates' courts is quite substantial: 10.8 per cent of all completed cases in the year 2006/7.

4.17   Quite apart from serving notice of discontinuance, the CPS can always in effect ensure that a prosecution does not go ahead by offering no evidence at court. If there is no prosecution evidence, the court has no option but to acquit. The CPS would seem to have an unfettered dis-cretion to offer no evidence in the magistrates' court (dicta in *Canterbury and St Augustine Justices ex parte Klisiak* [1982] QB 398). For the position in the Crown Court see 17.29 to 17.32.

Other powers of the DPP in connection with the CPS

4.18   The Prosecution of Offences Act places upon the DPP (and also the Attorney-General) a num-ber of powers and duties in relation to the CPS in addition to those already mentioned above:

   (i)   By s 8 the Attorney-General may make regulations requiring the police to inform the DPP whenever there is a prima facie case that offences falling into certain defined categories have been committed within their police area. This is a re-enactment of provisions contained in earlier Prosecution of Offences Acts. The list of reportable offences was formerly quite long, but it was greatly reduced in 1985 and now only includes a few highly important or politi-cally sensitive types of crime (e.g., large-scale drugs offences, large-scale conspiracy to con-travene immigration laws, criminal libel, and obscenity cases). By and large, the DPP and the CPS do not need to know that there is evidence of an offence unless and until the police act upon that evidence and charge somebody or hand the matter over to the CPS for them to decide on charges. If a charge is preferred, the papers have to go to the CPS in any event, as described above. However, in the few categories of offence covered by the regulations, it is presumably thought that the police should not be left to decide by themselves whether to bring charges. Therefore, the DPP has to be informed as soon as there is prima facie evidence which might justify a prosecution, and he can then advise on how to proceed.

   (ii) By s 9, the DPP has to make an annual report to the Attorney-General dealing with how he has discharged his functions in the preceding 12 months. The AG is required to lay the report before Parliament. Also, the report is published and obtainable from TSO. In addi-tion, the Attorney may request the DPP to report to him on any other matters.

(iii) By s 10, the DPP is required to issue a Code for Crown Prosecutors, giving guidance on (a) when a prosecution should be discontinued; (b) charging policy in general, and (c) the factors which make an offence triable either way suitable for summary trial or, as the case may be, trial on indictment. The current code is considered in 5.21 to 5.28.

C   OTHER PROSECUTORS

The 25 per cent or so of prosecutions not commenced by the police or the CPS are brought by   **4.19** a wide variety of prosecutors. For example, the Revenue and Customs Prosecutions Office prosecutes for tax offences, VAT offences, and also for illegal import or export of drugs; the Department of Social Security for fraudulent benefit claims; and local authorities for breach of food and health regulations. Big stores used to prosecute for shoplifting offences but the almost invariable practice now is to hand such cases over to the police and CPS. The Criminal Justice Act 1987 created a new investigative and prosecuting authority, namely the Serious Fraud Office. This was done in response to fears about the increase in major fraud. The Office consists of a small number of specialists in anti-fraud work. As well as lawyers, there are accountants and investigators. The function of the SFO is to assume responsibility for the investigation and prosecution of a small minority of extremely serious suspected frauds (perhaps less than 100 a year). The Office works in conjunction with the police fraud squads, directing them to relevant lines of inquiry. It also has extensive powers to compel those who might have information about a fraud under investigation to answer questions and/or supply documentary evidence. Unlike the CPS, the SFO both investigates suspected major fraud and then, if the evidence is forthcoming, commences and conducts the prosecution.

As will be apparent, most non-police prosecutions are commenced by a government or quasi-   **4.20** governmental authority. However, a minority are still brought by individuals acting in a purely private capacity. Thus, it is not unusual for trouble between neighbours to result in the parties cross-summoning each other for assault. Occasionally, too, an individual will feel so outraged at the decision of the police not to prosecute that he will take the initiative and commence proceedings himself. A famous example was the case of *Whitehouse v Lemon* [1979] AC 617 where Mrs Mary Whitehouse successfully prosecuted the defendants for blasphemous libel, that being the first recorded prosecution for the offence since 1922. More recently, the parents of a young man who had died through injecting a certain drug both gathered the evidence and then initiated proceedings for manslaughter against a person who had assisted their son in making the injection. The DPP had originally advised the police against any action, and he only took over the prosecution after there had been a committal for trial. The ultimate result was a conviction for manslaughter.

Section 6 of the Prosecution of Offences Act 1985 gives the DPP a discretionary power to take   **4.21** over the conduct of any non-police prosecution. He may then, again at his discretion, either continue the prosecution in the normal way, or discontinue the proceedings under s 23, or simply offer no evidence. Provided he is not acting completely unreasonably, his conduct in taking over a prosecution and then discontinuing it will not be open to judicial review by the High Court. In *DPP ex parte Duckenfield* [2000] 1 WLR 55, the Divisional Court considered the basis upon which the DPP ought to take over private prosecutions in order to stop them. It was held that the DPP acted quite properly in not adopting the same test for stopping a prosecution as for starting one. The policy of the DPP was that he would only intervene to stop a private prosecution on evidential grounds where there was clearly no case to answer, and the Divisional Court made it clear that such a policy was in accordance with s 6(1) of the 1985 Act. It follows that, provided there is evidence to support a private prosecution, the DPP will not intervene to stop it, even though he would not have commenced proceedings himself.

D THE LAW OFFICERS OF THE CROWN

4.22 A discussion of prosecuting authorities would be incomplete without mention of the Law Officers of the Crown—i.e., the Attorney-General and the Solicitor General. The Attorney-General is a barrister member of the Government who, *inter alia*, advises his government colleagues on questions of law; takes proceedings for contempt of court (e.g., against newspapers for breach of the *sub judice* rules), and seeks injunctions against public bodies which have acted unlawfully. In the realm of criminal procedure, as already mentioned, he supervises the work of the DPP, and thus is accountable to Parliament for the operation of the Crown Prosecution Service. There are also certain categories of prosecution which may only be commenced with the Attorney's consent (see 5.38 to 5.39). A further power of the Attorney is to enter a *nolle prosequi*, the effect of which is to halt a trial on indictment. The power is completely discretionary but is normally used only on compassionate grounds where an accused has become seriously ill during the course of his trial. Alternatively, the Attorney could take over the conduct of the prosecution and offer no evidence, although this power now seems superfluous in view of the DPP's similar power.

The second Law Officer of the Crown is the Solicitor General. He is a kind of deputy Attorney-General who may discharge the latter's functions when authorised to do so or when the Attorney is absent or sick (Law Officers Act 1944, s 1).

KEY DOCUMENTS

Prosecution of Offences Act 1985.
Annual Report of the Crown Prosecution Service, obtainable from: <http://www.cps.gov.uk>.
   It contains the Code for Crown Prosecutors as an annex.

5

THE DECISION TO PROSECUTE

This Chapter is mainly concerned with the considerations taken into account by the police **5.01** and the Crown Prosecution Service in deciding whether they should commence a prosecution and (in the case of the CPS) whether they should discontinue a prosecution already begun. First, however, it is necessary to describe briefly the way in which criminal proceedings commence. A more detailed account will be found in Chapter 3.

A   METHODS OF COMMENCING A PROSECUTION

There are two main methods of commencing a prosecution. One, which is open to the **5.02** police, other prosecuting authorities and private citizens alike, is to *lay an information* before a magistrate. If the information appears prima facie correct, the magistrate will then issue a *summons* requiring the accused to appear before the magistrates' court to answer the allegation contained in the information. When the CJA 2003, s 29 is fully in force, all public prosecutions will commence by the prosecution issuing a written charge, and a requisition requiring the recipient to appear before the magistrates to answer it. Public prosecutors who will have to use the new procedure will include the police, CPS and various government agencies.

5.03 The second way of commencing a prosecution is used only by the police and the CPS and it is to *charge* a suspect with an offence. Laying an information, charging a suspect and procedures for arrest and questioning at the police station are considered in detail in Chapter 3.

5.04 While there is no hard and fast rule as to when proceeding by way of a charge is appropriate rather than proceeding by information and summons, the police generally use a summons for less serious offences, especially summary ones, whereas most prosecutions for indictable offences are commenced by charging.

B   ALTERNATIVES TO PROSECUTION

5.05 Apart from the obvious alternative of doing absolutely nothing, there are two alternatives to a prosecution which, depending on the nature of the suspected offence, the police might consider. They are (i) administering a formal caution, and (ii) issuing a fixed penalty notice.

Cautions

5.06 The police have a discretion to issue a formal caution. This practice was initially developed as a means of keeping juveniles out of the machinery of the criminal justice system. It can now only be used for adults, in view of the system of reprimands and warnings introduced for juveniles by the Crime and Disorder Act 1998. A caution is normally administered in the police station by an officer of the rank of inspector or above. Although a caution does not rank as a conviction, records are kept of them for at least five years and they may be cited in court as evidence of the offender's character. Cautioning practice is dealt with by a Home Office Circular on the subject (30/2005), which incorporates revised National Standards for Cautioning.

5.07 The Crime and Disorder Act 1998 introduced major changes to the system of alternatives to prosecution in the case of juveniles, abolishing the formal caution and replacing it with a scheme of reprimands and warnings. Details of this new scheme are set out at 5.12 to 5.14. In addition, the CJA 2003, ss 22 to 27, introduced a scheme of conditional cautions which is described in 5.15 to 5.17.

5.08 The major conditions for issuing a caution are, first, that the evidence should be strong enough to justify a prosecution (see 5.22 to 5.23). Cautioning should not be used as a way of saving the police's face when they do not really have a case that would stand up in court. Secondly, the offender must admit the offence. If he does not, the police are thrown back on the stark choice between prosecuting and doing nothing. This aspect of the cautioning system is perhaps open to criticism in that it can unfairly pressurize a suspect into admitting something he has not done so as to avoid all risk of a prosecution.

Where these conditions are satisfied, consideration must then be given to whether a caution **5.09** is in the public interest. Home Office Circular 30/2005 makes the following points about the factors involved:

(a) The police should take into account the public interest principles in the Code for Crown Prosecutors (see 5.24 to 5.28).

(b) Cautions should not be used for offences which are triable on indictment only, other than in the most exceptional circumstances.

(c) Other offences may also be too serious for a caution. In deciding on this, factors to be considered include, for example, the harm resulting from the offence, whether it was racially motivated, whether it involved a breach of trust, and whether it was carried out in an organised way.

(d) The victim's view of the offence, and whether a caution is appropriate, should be sought and considered, but is not conclusive.

(e) Only in the following circumstances should an offender be cautioned for the second time:
   (i) where the subsequent offence is trivial; or
   (ii) where there has been a sufficient lapse of time since the first caution to suggest that it had some effect.

(f) There should be a presumption in favour of cautioning rather than prosecuting certain categories of offender, such as the elderly, and those who suffer from mental illness or impairment or a severe physical illness. Membership of these groups does not, of course, afford absolute protection against prosecution.

(g) The offender's attitude to the offence must be considered—in particular the wilfulness with which it was committed, and his subsequent attitude. An apology and/or an offer to put matters right may support the use of a caution.

(h) Each offender must be separately considered, even in the case of a group offence. Different disposals may be justified in the light of different degrees of involvement and personal circumstances.

The police may in some cases issue an oral warning (sometimes misleadingly referred to as 'an **5.10** informal caution'). Such a warning has no official status, and may not be cited in subsequent court proceedings, whereas a formal caution may be. In *Jones v Whalley* [2006] Crim LR 67, the Divisional Court considered the legal effect of a formal caution. The respondent was alleged to have assaulted the appellant, who was a railway conductor. The respondent admitted the offence, and accepted a formal caution. The appellant refused to accept this way of dealing with the matter, and brought a private prosecution. The magistrates ruled that such a prosecution was an abuse of process, and stayed the proceedings (see 20.14 to 20.20 for the principles relating to abuse of process). The appellant appealed on the basis that he had a legal right to prosecute which could not be taken away from him by the police decision to caution. The Divisional Court allowed the appeal, holding that there was no abuse of process. However, the House of Lords stressed that allowing the prosecution to proceed in such circumstances would undermine the various schemes which exist for cautions to be administered. They made it clear that it was an abuse of process.

The police decision whether to caution or not is closely related to the CPS decision whether to **5.11** prosecute or not (see 5.20 to 5.28). In *Chief Constable of Kent ex parte L; R v DPP ex parte B* [1993] 1 All ER 756, the Divisional Court considered the availability of judicial review in relation to the question of whether a juvenile should be cautioned or prosecuted. It was held that any judicial review could only lie against the body which had 'the last and decisive word, the CPS' (Watkins LJ at p. 767), and not the police. Watkins LJ went on to say:

> I have come to the conclusion that, in respect of juveniles, the discretion of the CPS to continue or discontinue criminal proceedings is reviewable by this court but only where it can be demonstrated that the decision was made regardless of or clearly contrary to a settled policy of the Director of Public Prosecutions evolved in the public interest, for example the policy of cautioning juveniles.... But I envisage that it will be only rarely that a defendant could succeed in showing that a decision was fatally flawed in such a manner as that.

Reprimands and warnings

5.12 The policy of cautioning, as an alternative to prosecution, was radically altered as far as juveniles are concerned by the Crime and Disorder Act 1998. Sections 65 and 66 of the CDA replaced cautions for juveniles with a scheme of reprimands and warnings. The aim was to set out a series of stages, under which the juvenile may expect to be reprimanded for a first offence, warned for a second, and prosecuted for a third.

5.13 A juvenile suspect who has not previously been reprimanded or warned may be reprimanded, provided that certain conditions are met. Those conditions are set out in s 65(1) of the CDA, and may be summarized as follows:

(a)   a police officer must have evidence that the juvenile has committed an offence;
(b)   the officer must consider that there would be a realistic prospect of conviction;
(c)   the juvenile must admit the offence to the officer;
(d)   the juvenile must not previously have been convicted of any offence; and
(e)   the officer must be satisfied that it would not be in the public interest for the suspect to be prosecuted.

As can be seen, the fact that the suspect must not previously have been reprimanded or warned means that a second reprimand is ruled out. In addition, a prior conviction for any offence, no matter how trivial or unrelated to the one under consideration, shuts out the prospect of a warning or reprimand.

5.14 The officer must decide whether there would be sufficient evidence, and a realistic prospect of conviction, if the suspect were to be prosecuted. The officer has also to decide that it would not be in the public interest to prosecute the suspect. These questions are also posed by the CPS in deciding whether a prosecution should proceed (see 5.20 to 5.26).

Conditional cautions

5.15 The CJA 2003, ss 22 to 27, introduced a new scheme of conditional cautions for adult offenders (those aged 18 and over). Unlike the cautions dealt with in 5.06 to 5.14, which are matters for the police, conditional cautions may only be decided upon by a public prosecutor. The conditional caution is not meant to be part of a hierarchy of cautions. Generally, if the offender has previously been given a simple caution, a conditional caution will not be appropriate unless, exceptionally, it is believed that it will prevent re-offending. It has been described as a 'caution with a sting in the tail', as it involves carrying out a condition, with the threat of prosecution in the event of failure to do so.

For a conditional caution to be administered, the following conditions must be met: **5.16**

(a) An authorized person (police officer or other person authorized by a public prosecutor) must have evidence that the offender committed the offence.
(b) A relevant prosecutor (defined to include the main public authorities) must decide that there is sufficient evidence to charge, but that a conditional caution should be given.
(c) The offender must admit to the authorized person that he committed the offence.
(d) The effect of the conditional caution must be explained by the authorized person, including a warning that failure to carry out the condition may result in prosecution.
(e) The offender must sign a document containing details of the offence, an admission that he committed it, consent to the conditional caution, and details of the conditions.

As far as the conditions are concerned, they should be applied to the caution in order to facil- **5.17** itate the rehabilitation of the offender, and/or to make sure that he makes reparation for the offence (CJA 2003, s 22). If he fails without reasonable excuse to comply with any of the conditions, proceedings may be instituted, and the signed document will be admissible in evidence (s 24). The conditional caution system has largely been used for offences of criminal damage, theft and common assault. Conditions which prosecutors have imposed include the payment of compensation by instalments, painting out graffiti, writing a letter of apology to the victim, and taking drug treatment.

Fixed penalty notices

Fixed penalty notices have for some time been relevant to certain road traffic offences. Parking **5.18** tickets are the fixed penalty notices with which the public are perhaps most familiar. However, Part III of the Transport Act 1982 extended the fixed penalty system from parking infringements (where, of course, the great bulk of the enforcement is done by traffic wardens) to some of the commonest non-parking offences, including a few which carry endorsement of the driving licence as part of the penalty (see now, the Road Traffic Offenders Act 1988, Sch 3). Thus, notices can now be given for, *inter alia*, speeding, going through a red light, failing to stop when required to do so by a constable, breach of the construction and use regulations regarding the condition of a vehicle, breach of pedestrian crossing regulations, not wearing a seat-belt and not wearing a crash helmet. Importantly, the fixed penalty system has been greatly extended in recent years by the Criminal Justice and Police Act 2001 (CJPA) and the Anti-social Behaviour Act 2003 (ASBA). The CJPA makes provision for fixed penalty notices in respect of offences such as theft, behaviour likely to cause harassment, alarm or distress, and criminal damage. The ASBA deals with various offences relating to graffiti and fly-posting.

The advantage of the fixed penalty system to the police and courts is that the consequences **5.19** for the offender are virtually the same as if he had gone through the prosecution system in the normal way, but court time is saved in that there is no hearing. There is merely the administrative task of collecting the fixed penalty and (in some motoring cases) sending the licence to Swansea to be endorsed. To tempt the offender to cooperate with the procedure, the fixed penalties are pitched deliberately low. But, it is a matter for the police officer's discretion whether he issues a fixed penalty notice or takes alternative action (or takes no action at all).

C   FACTORS TO CONSIDER IN DECIDING WHETHER TO PROSECUTE

5.20   As was explained in Chapter 3, taking the decision on whether to prosecute is, as far as police prosecutions are concerned, a two-stage process. First, the police themselves decide whether to initiate proceedings. Secondly, if the police decision is for prosecution, the papers go to the CPS where a lawyer reviews the case and may discontinue the proceedings if he considers that the police were wrong to start them. As a result of the charge and requisition procedure introduced by the CJA 2003, in a wide range of cases it is now the sole responsibility of the CPS to determine whether a suspect should be charged and, if so, with what offence (see 3.45 to 3.47 for details).

5.21   As regards the approach of CPS lawyers when reviewing papers with a view to discontinuance, guidance for them is contained in the Code for Crown Prosecutors that the DPP issues under s 10 of the Prosecution of Offences Act 1985 (see 4.18). For their part, the police are encouraged to follow the criteria laid down in the Code, for example when deciding whether to caution or prosecute an offender (see Home Office Circular 30/2005).

Sufficiency of evidence

5.22   The first essential precondition for the commencement of a prosecution is the availability of sufficient evidence. The approach for Crown Prosecutors is laid down in paras 5.2 to 5.5 of their Code. They must be satisfied that there is enough evidence for a 'realistic prospect of conviction' in respect of each charge against each defendant. In their consideration, they must take into account the likely defence case. The test of a 'realistic prospect of conviction' is objective. The question is: Would a jury or a bench of magistrates, properly directed in accordance with the law, be more likely than not to convict the defendant of the charge alleged? In attempting to answer this question, the Crown Prosecutor should consider whether there is sufficient evidence, whether it can be used, and whether it is reliable. Hence, the Prosecutor should consider:

(a)   The likelihood that evidence will be excluded by the court, e.g., because of an impropriety in the way that it was gathered. If a piece of evidence may be excluded, is there enough other evidence?

(b)   The reliability of the evidence, e.g., whether identification evidence is likely to be excluded on the basis of the guidelines in *Turnbull* [1977] QB 224.

5.23   Using this approach, a legally trained and relatively detached Crown Prosecutor may well take a different view of the strength of the case from that taken by the investigating officers who commenced the proceedings. It is submitted that such an approach is in accordance with the interests of justice and efficiency. It is wrong that someone should be punished if he is innocent, and prosecution often involves serious consequences for the person accused. It is at the least a source of inconvenience and worry, and it may well entail considerable expense. In some cases, the very fact that the accused has been prosecuted may lead to a stigma, with the suspicion that there is 'no smoke without fire'. In addition to these ethical considerations, there are questions of resources. It is a waste of time and money for the various parts of the criminal justice system to deal with a case which is going to result in an acquittal. It was largely to weed out weak cases, in fact, that the CPS was set up. (For a perceptive analysis of this and other ethical questions in the criminal justice system, see A. Ashworth, *The Criminal Process* (Oxford University Press, 2005).

Public interest factors

Lord Shawcross, the former Attorney-General, in a House of Commons debate of 1951, stated that:

5.24

> It has never been the rule of this country—I hope it never will be—that suspected criminal offences must automatically be the subject of prosecution. Indeed, the very first regulations under which the Director of Public Prosecutions worked provided that he should prosecute 'wherever it appears that the offence or the circumstances of its commission are of such a character that a prosecution in respect thereof is required in the public interest'.

In other words, the availability of sufficient evidence should not automatically result in a prosecution. Before bringing a case to court, first the police and then the CPS must consider, as a matter of discretion whether a prosecution is really in the public interest. If it is not, the suspect should either have no action taken against him or be 'let off' with a caution. The approach adopted by the Code for Crown Prosecutors in calculating the public interest is to list first the factors which tend towards a decision to prosecute, and then those factors which militate against bringing a prosecution. The aim is that once the factors in each list have been considered, it can be decided whether the prosecution is in the public interest or not. The factors favouring the commencement of a prosecution are listed in para 5.9 of the Code:

(a) a conviction is likely to result in a significant sentence;

(b) a conviction is likely to result in a confiscation or any other order;

(c) a weapon was used or violence was threatened during the commission of the offence;

(d) the offence was committed against a person serving the public (for example, a police or prison officer, or a nurse);

(e) the defendant was in a position of authority or trust;

(f) the evidence shows that the defendant was a ringleader or an organiser of the offence;

(g) there is evidence that the offence was premeditated;

(h) there is evidence that the offence was carried out by a group;

(i) the victim of the offence was vulnerable, has been put in considerable fear, or suffered personal attack, damage or disturbance;

(j) the offence was committed in the presence of, or in close proximity to, a child;

(k) the offence was motivated by any form of discrimination against the victim's ethnic or national origin, sex, religious beliefs, political views or sexual orientation; or the suspect demonstrated hostility to the victim based on any of those characteristics;

(l) there is a marked difference between the actual or mental ages of the defendant and the victim, or there is any element of corruption;

(m) the defendant's previous convictions or cautions are relevant to the present offence;

(n) the defendant is alleged to have committed the offence whilst under an order of the court;

(o) there are grounds for believing that the offence is likely to be continued or repeated, for example, by a history of recurring conduct;

(p) the offence, although not serious in itself, is widespread in the area where it was committed; or

(q) a prosecution would have a significant positive impact on maintaining community confidence.

The factors which tend against a prosecution are set out in para 5.10 of the Code as follows:

(a) the court is likely to impose a nominal penalty;

(b) the defendant has already been made the subject of a sentence and any further conviction would be unlikely to result in the imposition of an additional sentence or order, unless the nature of the particular offence requires a prosecution or the defendant withdraws consent to have an offence taken into consideration during sentencing;

(c) the offence was committed as a result of a genuine mistake or misunderstanding (these factors must be balanced against the seriousness of the offence);

(d) the loss or harm can be described as minor and was the result of a single incident, particularly if it was caused by a misjudgement;

(e) there has been a long delay between the offence taking place and the date of the trial, unless:

    (i) the offence is serious;

    (ii) the delay has been caused in part by the defendant;

    (iii) the offence has only recently come to light; or

    (iv) the complexity of the offence has meant that there has been a long investigation;

(f) a prosecution is likely to have a bad effect on the victim's physical or mental health, always bearing in mind the seriousness of the offence;

(g) the defendant is elderly or is, or was at the time of the offence, suffering from significant mental or physical ill health, unless the offence is serious or there is a real possibility that it may be repeated (the CPS, where necessary, applies Home Office guidelines about how to deal with mentally disordered offenders and Crown Prosecutors must balance the desirability of diverting a defendant who is suffering from significant mental or physical ill health with the need to safeguard the general public);

(h) the defendant has put right the loss or harm that was caused (but defendants must not avoid prosecution simply because they can pay compensation); or

(i) details may be made public that could harm sources of information, international relations or national security.

5.25 The Code then makes the obvious point in para 5.11 that the decision on the public interest is not simply a matter of adding up the number of factors on each side. The Crown Prosecutor must decide how important each factor is in the case under consideration, and go on to make an overall assessment. In doing so, the interests of the victim must be very carefully considered, even though the CPS act in the interests of the public as a whole rather than any particular individual (para 5.12).

5.26 There are particular considerations in deciding whether to proceed with the trial of a juvenile. Although young offenders can sometimes be dealt with outside the court system, Crown Prosecutors are told that they should not decline to prosecute simply because of the defendant's age. The seriousness of the offence and previous behaviour may make prosecution necessary (para 8.8).

Clearly, the most common alternative to a prosecution, in the case of an adult, is a simple or **5.27**
conditional caution. The Code states that Crown Prosecutors should apply the same guidelines
as the police in deciding whether a caution is appropriate (see 5.06 to 5.11 above). The caution
will, however, be administered by the police rather than the CPS. The Crown Prosecutor should
therefore inform the police when deciding that a caution is more suitable than a prosecution
(para 8.7).

In addition to the decision whether to prosecute or not, there is also the question of the **5.28**
appropriate offence to charge. A series of Charging Standards has now been agreed by the
police and the CPS. Their purpose 'is to make sure that the most appropriate charge is selected at the earliest opportunity'.

D   SPECIAL FACTORS RELEVANT TO THE DECISION TO PROSECUTE

Whether there is sufficient evidence and, if so, whether there are none the less discretionary **5.29**
reasons for not prosecuting are questions which fall to be considered whenever criminal
proceedings are proposed. In a minority of cases, however, a potential prosecutor will also
have to answer the following questions:

Do the English courts have jurisdiction?

The jurisdiction of the English courts is essentially territorial. In other words, they accept **5.30**
jurisdiction over offences committed in England or Wales irrespective of the nationality of
the accused, but, generally speaking, they refuse jurisdiction over offences committed abroad
even if the accused is a British subject. There are, however, several examples of 'foreign'
offences being triable in England if the accused is a British subject, and very occasional
examples of such offences being triable here irrespective of the accused's nationality. In this
context, 'abroad' should be understood to mean outside England and Wales, and 'British
subject' includes not only citizens of the United Kingdom but also, for example, citizens of
Commonwealth countries: British Nationality Act 1981, s 51.

Exceptions to the general rule that the English courts only try offences committed in England **5.31**
or Wales include:

(a) Offences of murder, manslaughter, bigamy or perjury, which are triable in England wher-
     ever committed, provided the accused is a British subject: Offences against the Person Act
     1861, ss 9 and 57, and Perjury Act 1911, s 8. The same applies to offences under the
     Official Secrets Acts (see s 10 of the 1911 Act).
(b) *Any* offence committed by a British subject abroad is triable here if, at the time of the
     offence, he was a servant of the Crown, and was acting (or purporting to act) in the course
     of his employment: Criminal Justice Act 1948, s 31.
(c) *Any* offence committed abroad is triable here if, at the time of the offence or within the
     three months preceding it, the accused was a member of the crew of a British merchant
     ship: Merchant Shipping Act 1995, s 282.
(d) By s 4 of the Suppression of Terrorism Act 1978, the English courts may try both British
     subjects and foreigners for terrorist offences committed in any country which is a party
     to the European Convention on the Suppression of Terrorism 1977. However, unless the

courts would have jurisdiction apart from s 4, prosecutions may only be brought with the consent of the Attorney-General, and in most cases extraditing the accused to the country where the offence occurred might seem preferable to sanctioning proceedings here.

(e) Offences committed on a British ship on the high seas are triable here whether or not the accused is a British subject: Merchant Shipping Act 1995, s 281.

(f) Offences committed on board British-controlled aircraft while they are in flight are triable here even if the plane was outside United Kingdom airspace at the relevant time: Civil Aviation Act 1982, s 92.

(g) Piracy and aircraft hijacking are triable here wherever they occurred, and whatever the nationality of the ship, aircraft or accused involved. Piracy is an ancient example of an offence against the law of nations, and hijacking is dealt with in s 1 of the Aviation Security Act 1982.

(h) The Sexual Offences Act 2003, s 72, confers jurisdiction on British courts over certain sexual offences against infants (aged under 16) committed abroad, where the act in question constitutes an offence in the country in which it is committed, and also in this country. The statute, together with the Sexual Offences (Conspiracy and Incitement) Act 1996, is aimed at 'child sex tourism', and attempts to penalize the exploitation of children for sexual purposes, wherever it occurs. Details of the offences involved and the procedural conditions are dealt with in *Blackstone's Criminal Practice 2008*, B3.268.

(i) A number of offences of fraud and dishonesty are now dealt with under rules contained in the Criminal Justice Act 1993, ss 1 to 4 and 6. Among the most important of these offences are theft, obtaining property by deception, false accounting, blackmail, handling stolen goods, and forgery. If any act or omission, proof of which is required for conviction of the offence in question, occurs in England or Wales, the offence is triable in our courts (Criminal Justice Act 1993, s 2(1)) (see *Blackstone's Criminal Practice 2008*, A8.4).

(j) The Sexual Offences Act 2003, s 60, confers extensive jurisdiction in relation to a number of offences of sexual trafficking where the offender is connected with the United Kingdom as a British citizen, subject, protected person or the equivalent. The offences in question need not be committed in the United Kingdom.

Is the offender entitled to immunity?

5.32 A second special question the prosecutor may have to consider is whether the accused is entitled to immunity. The Queen is immune from criminal jurisdiction. The same applies to foreign sovereigns or heads of state, together with their families and private servants: State Immunity Act 1978, s 20. Diplomatic agents, members of the administrative and technical staff of a diplomatic mission, and the families of such agents or staff are similarly immune: Diplomatic Privileges Act 1964, s 2(1). Members of the service staff of a diplomatic mission have immunity in respect of acts performed in the course of their duties, and some consular officials also enjoy a limited immunity: Consular Relations Act 1968. Immunity may always be waived by the state sending the diplomat, etc., but unless there has been an express waiver a conviction obtained against a person entitled to immunity will be quashed. The above rules are subject to some modification where the person claiming immunity is a citizen of, or permanently resident in, the United Kingdom.

5.33 Although the phrase is not usually employed in the context, children under ten are also immune from prosecution. This follows from it being conclusively presumed that no child under that age can be guilty of any offence: Children and Young Persons Act 1933, s 50, as amended.

Can the prosecution be commenced in time?

The fact that an offence is stale is, as explained at 5.24, a reason for deciding, as a matter of discretion, not to prosecute. In addition, there are some statutory provisions which, as a matter of law, require proceedings to be commenced within a certain time-limit. **5.34**

Of these provisions, the only one of general importance is s 127 of the Magistrates' Courts Act 1980, which lays down the blanket rule that an information for a summary offence must be laid within six months of its commission. The obvious purpose of the rule is to ensure that summary matters, being relatively trivial, are tried quickly before memory of what occurred has faded from the minds of the witnesses. Prosecutions for indictable offences may, in general, be commenced at any time, although there are some exceptions to that rule. The time-limit (or lack of time-limit) for an indictable offence is unaffected by the fact that the offence is triable either way and the accused has elected summary trial. **5.35**

One notable example of a statutory time limit for indictable offences is the Trades Description Act 1968. Section 19(1) of that Act provides that a prosecution under it must commence within three years of the offence, or within one year of its discovery, whichever is the earlier. **5.36**

Finally, in connection with time limits, it should be noted that the courts do have a very limited discretion to halt proceedings if they consider that, although no statutory limit has been breached, delay in bringing the case to court is such as to amount to an abuse of proper process. For details, see 10.26 to 10.31 and 20.14 to 20.20. **5.37**

Is any consent required?

The consent of, in some cases, the Attorney-General and, in other cases, the Director of Public Prosecutions is a pre-condition of the bringing of prosecutions for certain offences. Although there is no clearly defined practice, Parliament tends to stipulate the Attorney's consent (or fiat) where prosecution for an offence might raise considerations of public policy, national security, or relations with other countries. The DPP's consent is required in areas where a rigid application of the letter of the law is likely to be oppressive to the individual or offensive to public opinion. As regards the DPP's consent, it can be given on his behalf by a Crown Prosecutor (see Prosecution of Offences Act 1985, s 1(7) and 4.08). Thus, what is now required is, effectively, the consent of the CPS rather than the consent of the DPP personally. The level at which consent to a proposed prosecution is given is a matter of internal CPS administration. As regards some offences requiring consent, the papers must always be sent to CPS headquarters where, presumably, they are considered either by the DPP personally or a very senior CPS lawyer. In other cases the question of consent can be handled at local level. Papers in a case requiring the Attorney's consent are automatically sent to CPS headquarters for transmission to the Attorney. **5.38**

Examples of the Attorney's consent being necessary for a prosecution are: **5.39**

(a) offences of bribery under the Public Bodies Corrupt Practices Act 1889 and the Prevention of Corruption Act 1906 (s 4 of the 1889 Act and s 2 of the 1906 Act);

(b) offences under the Official Secrets Act 1911 (s 8 of the Act);

(c) offences of stirring up racial hatred, possessing racially inflammatory material, etc. contrary to Part III of the Public Order Act 1986 (s 27 of the Act);

(d) offences of belonging to a proscribed organization and other offences under the Prevention of Terrorism (Temporary Provisions) Act 1989 (s 19 of the Act), and

(e) offences under the Explosive Substances Act 1883 (s 7 of the Act).

5.40 The DPP's consent is necessary for prosecutions for *inter alia*:

(a) offences of theft or criminal damage where the property in question belongs to the spouse of the accused (s 30(4) of the Theft Act 1968);

(b) offences of assisting offenders and wasting police time contrary to ss 4(4) and 5(3) of the Criminal Law Act 1967;

(c) homosexual offences where either or both of the parties are under 16 (s 8 of the Sexual Offences Act 1967);

(d) offences of incest (Sch 2 to the Sexual Offences Act 1956);

(e) offences of aiding and abetting suicide (s 2 of the Suicide Act 1961); and

(f) riot contrary to s 1 of the Public Order Act 1986 (s 7 of the Act);

(g) terrorism offences;

(h) offences under the War Crimes Act 1991.

5.41 The necessity for the Attorney's or DPP's consent to prosecution does not prevent a suspect being arrested, charged at the police station and thereafter remanded by a court (in custody or on bail) prior to consent having been obtained (Prosecution of Offences Act 1985, s 25). However, it is submitted that no effective stage in the proceedings (such as determination of mode of trial or committal) should be embarked upon until the consent is forthcoming, and the prosecutor should in any event use his best endeavours to obtain a decision from the Attorney or, as the case may be, DPP as soon as possible. In *Whale* [1991] Crim LR 692, it was held that the consent of the Attorney-General, as required under the Explosive Substances Act 1883, could be obtained validly up to the time that the defendant appeared in court for the purpose of committal. It should be noted, however, that a magistrate will not issue a summons in respect of an offence requiring consent to prosecution unless satisfied that consent has been granted (see *Gateshead Justices ex parte Tesco Stores Ltd* [1981] QB 470). It follows that non-police prosecutors (who, or course, do not have the option of proceeding by way of charge but are forced to use a summons) must apply for consent before taking any steps whatsoever against their suspect.

KEY DOCUMENTS

The Code for Crown Prosecutors, obtainable from: <http://www.cps.gov.uk>. The Code for Crown Prosecutors is published as an annex to the Annual Report of the Crown Prosecution Service.

PART 2

THE MAGISTRATES' COURT

6

MAGISTRATES AND THEIR COURTS

The office of justice of the peace, or magistrate, is an ancient one first mentioned in 1264. As **6.01** early as 1361 the Justices of the Peace Act provided for the appointment in each county of 'one lord and three or four of the most worthy in the county with some learned in the law' whose duty it would be to 'pursue, arrest . . . and chastise' offenders and rioters, and take surety of good behaviour 'towards the King and his people' from those who were not 'of good fame'. The magistrates retain their original function of assisting in the keeping of the peace, and, to further that end, can still bind a person over to keep the peace or be of good behaviour even though no offence has been proved against him.

Over the centuries the work of the magistrates widened in scope. By the eighteenth century **6.02** they had extensive judicial and administrative powers. Administratively, they were responsible for, *inter alia*, the licensing of ale houses, the appointment of overseers of the poor and surveyors of highways, the levying of rates in their counties, and the transaction of important county business. Judicially, they not only tried minor cases summarily but, at quarter sessions, benches of two to nine magistrates presided over trials by jury. Only the most serious of indictable offences were excluded from the jurisdiction of quarter sessions and reserved for the assize courts. However, in the late nineteenth and early twentieth centuries the magistrates' powers were reduced. Their administrative functions were transferred to elected local authorities, although traces of the old system can still be seen in, for example, the work of the licensing justices who control the granting of licences to sell alcohol. Their judicial functions were not expressly reduced, but the introduction of a rule that at quarter sessions the bench must always have a legally qualified chairman (usually the sort of person who today would be appointed a circuit judge or recorder) meant that lay magistrates had much less influence than formerly. The role of the magistrates at quarter sessions is reflected today in the requirement that two of them be present at appeals in the Crown Court: Supreme Court Act 1981, s 74 and see 14.17 to 14.19.

6.03 Although the powers of magistrates are not as great as they were, they still play a very important part in the administration of the criminal law. In summary, their work is as follows:

(a) They can issue either a warrant for the arrest of a person against whom an offence is alleged or a summons requiring him to attend at a magistrates' court to answer the allegation (see Chapter 3). In practice, this does not form a major part of their work as proceedings against a person for a serious offence normally begin with an arrest without warrant by a police officer, while the issuing of a summons can be and usually is done by a magistrates' clerk rather than the magistrate himself.

(b) They sit as examining justices for the hearing of committal proceedings (see Chapter 13).

(c) They try cases summarily in the adult magistrates' courts (see Chapter 10).

(d) They try in the youth courts cases brought against those under 18. Only magistrates who have been appointed by their colleagues to the youth court panel are eligible to sit in the youth court (see Chapter 11).

(e) They have a minor role to play in the work of the Crown Court (see 14.17 to 14.19).

6.04 In addition, magistrates have a wide-ranging civil jurisdiction. For example, they make maintenance orders as between the parties to a marriage and custody orders in respect of the children of the family; they rule upon the paternity of children in affiliation proceedings; they put children into care on grounds such as neglect or ill-treatment of the child; the licensing justices, as already mentioned, grant licences to sell alcohol; Betting Licensing Committees perform a similar function in granting permits to bookmakers and licensing premises for gaming—in short, the administration of justice in England and Wales depends to a greater extent than many people realize on the work of the magistrates.

A   LAY MAGISTRATES

6.05 There are about 30,000 active lay magistrates in England and Wales. Lay magistrates are so called because their work is unpaid, although they can claim allowances for travelling, subsistence and loss of earnings: Courts Act 2003, s 12. Most lay magistrates are also 'lay' in the sense that they have no legal qualifications, but there is no bar to lawyers or, indeed, holders of high judicial office becoming magistrates. Academic lawyers may find work as lay magistrates a suitable way in which to serve the community.

Appointment of lay magistrates

6.06 Lay magistrates are appointed by the Lord Chancellor 'on behalf and in the name of Her Majesty': Courts Act 2003, s 10. Appointments are made each year to replace magistrates who die or whose names are placed on the supplemental list (see 6.10), or to cope with an increase in the amount of work to be done. It is said that the number of suitable candidates for appointment considerably exceeds the vacancies to be filled. In deciding whom to appoint, the Lord Chancellor is principally concerned that the appointee will, by character and ability, be suited for the work of a magistrate, and that he will be recognized by his fellows as being so suited. Certain categories of persons will not, in practice, be considered (e.g., those aged 60 or over, members of the armed forces or the police, and those with convictions for serious crime). Although political affiliations are ignored in deciding whether a person is suited to be a magistrate, many magistrates are or were involved in local politics. Magistrates in a particular area should not be heavily weighted in favour of one party. As well as trying to maintain a political balance, the Lord Chancellor tries to maintain a balance between the sexes (in fact, there are roughly three male to every two female magistrates), and to introduce younger people in their thirties or early forties to the magistracy. Criticism of the approach to appointing magistrates is usually based on an assertion that magistrates do not represent a sufficiently broad cross-section of the local community. Too often, it is said, they are drawn from what, for want of a better term, may be described as the upper social classes. Further, adverse comment is frequently made about the under-representation of ethnic minorities among magistrates. A high proportion of the magistracy comprises people who have retired from full-time employment, and those falling within this category are in addition able to sit more frequently than those who are in work. The magistracy is balanced according to gender, by contrast with the overwhelmingly male ranks of professional judges. There have been concerns, however, about the extent to which members of ethnic minorities are adequately represented. It appears that in 2000 about 2 per cent of magistrates were black, and about 2 per cent of Asian origin—figures which were beginning to approach the proportions in the population at large (see the Auld Report, p. 119).

Training and court attendance of lay magistrates

Before appointment magistrates undertake to complete, within one year of appointment, a **6.07** course of basic instruction in the duties which they will be carrying out. It is the responsibility of Magistrates' Courts Committees to administer training schemes for the areas for which they are responsible. The aim of the training is to impress upon the new magistrate the necessity of acting judicially, to give him a grounding in law and evidence which will enable him to follow intelligently the types of case he will normally encounter, to inform him of the nature of the sentences he will be able to pass, and to help him understand the role of others who work in the courts (e.g., the clerk, court staff, and legal representatives). The training should include, in addition to formal lecturing, visits to courts and penal institutions, and group discussions of the problems magistrates frequently face.

Magistrates are expected to sit in court at least 26 times during a year. No doubt, the frequency **6.08** with which they actually do sit varies greatly, but the average attendance is around 40 times a year. The significance of this is that through their initial training and through their regular attendance at court, often over many years, magistrates become knowledgeable about the work of their courts. Although the adjective 'lay' is used to describe them, they are far from being ignorant of the ways of the law. This was recognized by Lord Bridge of Harwich in a handsome tribute which he paid to magistrates in the course of giving the House of Lords' judgment in *Re McC (A Minor)* [1985] AC 528. He was discussing, *obiter dicta*, the rule that a judge of a court of record is not liable civilly for wrongs he may do when exercising his jurisdiction, even if he acts in bad faith, whereas in earlier centuries magistrates acting *intra vires* were held liable for acts done maliciously and without reasonable or probable cause. His

Lordship doubted whether this still applied because the rule:

> had its origins in society's view of the justice, reflected in Shakespeare's plays, as an ignorant buffoon. How long this view persisted and how long there was any justification for it, I am not a good enough legal or social historian to say. But it clearly has no application in today's world either to stipendiary magistrates or to lay benches. The former are competent professional judges, the latter citizens from all walks of life chosen for their intelligence and integrity, required to undergo some training before they sit and advised by legally qualified clerks. They give unstinting voluntary service to the community and conduct the major part of the criminal business of the courts. Without them the system of criminal justice in this country would grind to a halt.

6.09 No doubt many lawyers, not to mention defendants, would regard Lord Bridge's compliments as exaggerated, but it remains true—as his Lordship said—that the modern magistrate is far removed from the buffoon of Shakespeare's day.

Removal and 'retirement' of magistrates

6.10 Lay magistrates can be removed from office by the Lord Chancellor: Courts Act 2003, s 11. This can be done for incapacity or misbehaviour, persistent failure to meet prescribed standards of competence, or for declining or neglecting to take a proper part in the exercise of their functions as a magistrate. If a magistrate is infirm or it is expedient for any other reason that he should cease to exercise judicial functions, or if he fails to attend court as often as he ought, the Lord Chancellor can order that his name be placed on the supplemental list: Courts Act 2003, s 12. A magistrate on the supplemental list retains the status of justice of the peace but the only powers he can exercise are trivial ones in connection with the witnessing of documents—he cannot sit in court or even issue a summons or warrant. At the age of 70 (75 in the case of one who holds or has held high judicial office) a magistrate is automatically placed on the supplemental list. In effect, therefore, lay magistrates retire at the age of 70.

B   DISTRICT JUDGES (MAGISTRATES' COURT)

6.11 District judges (magistrates' courts) are professional salaried members of the judiciary who were formerly known as stipendiary magistrates. They are appointed by the Queen upon the recommendation of the Lord Chancellor from among barristers and solicitors of at least seven years' standing: Courts Act 2003. There are about 140 of them, supported by a larger number of deputy district judges, who sit part-time as a precursor to full-time appointment. Although district judges are assigned to a particular centre or magistrates' courts committee area, they may be required to sit anywhere as the work demands. About half of the full-time appointees sit in London, and half in the provinces. A district judge may be removed from office by the Lord Chancellor for inability or misbehaviour. Otherwise he can continue in office until the retirement age, which is 70 (subject to the Lord Chancellor's power to extend for a limited period).

6.12 A district judge can try a case sitting alone, whereas at least two magistrates must sit together for the purposes of a summary trial (see Chapter 11 for the position in the youth court). This fact, together with his legal knowledge and experience, enables the district judge to be significantly faster than lay magistrates, who need to confer among themselves and take the advice of their clerk. The district judge is characteristically more interventionist than a lay bench, and there is some evidence that the typical district judge sentences more heavily, and is more likely to remand in custody than the lay magistracy (Auld Report, p. 95). There is some controversy over the respective roles of the professional district judge and the lay magistrates. Supporters of the lay magistracy rely upon the wide experience of life which they bring to the bench, and the greater chance that a decision reached by several people will be more considered, and consequently fairer, because of the interaction between the members of the bench. Those favouring a greater role for the district judges focus upon their greater speed and efficiency in dealing with a day's list, and their ability to take hold of longer and more complex cases.

Apart from the power of the district judge to sit alone, there is at present no rigid distinction between their powers and those of the lay magistracy. However, district judges tend to be allocated cases involving complex points of law or evidence, long and/or inter-linked cases, those involving considerations of public safety, public interest immunity applications, and extradition cases. **6.13**

C   MAGISTRATES' CLERKS

Justices' clerks are appointed by the Lord Chancellor, and must: **6.14**

(a) have had a right of audience in the magistrates' court for at least five years; or
(b) be a barrister or solicitor who has served for not less than five years as an assistant to a justices' clerk; or
(c) have previously been a justices' clerk.

The Lord Chancellor may also appoint assistant justices' clerks who have a five year magistrates' court qualification.

The nature of the work done by the magistrates' clerk and his assistants is described in later Chapters. Briefly, they play a major part in the behind the scenes administration of the court (e.g., issuing summonses and processing legal aid applications), and, in court, they advise the magistrates on the law. The primary duty of the justices' clerk is to his bench or benches, as a legal adviser, and in that role he is not accountable to the justices' chief executive. **6.15**

7

BAIL AND REMANDS

7.01   The principal subject-matter of this Chapter is bail, which may be defined as the release of a person subject to a duty to surrender to custody at an appointed time and place. The time when a person bailed is to surrender to custody may be fixed when bail is granted or, in the case of a person sent on bail to the Crown Court for trial or sentence, it may be notified to him subsequently. The place where he is to surrender is either a court or a police station, usually the former. The granting of bail in criminal proceedings is governed by the Bail Act 1976.

A   REMANDS AND ADJOURNMENTS

7.02   The power of courts (especially magistrates' courts) to remand an accused person is closely bound up with the power to grant bail. A remand occurs when a court adjourns a case and either bails the accused for the period of the adjournment or commits him to custody to be brought before the court on the adjournment date. As the above implies, remands are either on bail or in custody, by contrast with a simple adjournment, which does not entail the same restrictions. A magistrates' court has a general discretion to adjourn a case at any stage prior to or during committal proceedings or summary trial (see Magistrates' Courts Act 1980, ss 5 and 10). It also has power to adjourn after summary conviction for the preparation of reports.

7.03   In fact, it is rare for a case of any gravity or complexity to be totally disposed of on the occasion of the accused's first appearance. Either the prosecution will need time to prepare statements for committal, or serve advance information, or ensure that their witnesses are present for summary trial; or the accused will want an adjournment to apply for publicly funded representation, see a solicitor and generally put his case in order. The only type of case likely to need only one appearance is where the accused pleads guilty to a relatively minor offence and the court does not consider it needs reports before passing sentence.

7.04   Assuming the magistrates do have to adjourn, they are always entitled to remand the accused. However, if the offence is summary and it is an adjournment prior to trial, they have a discretion simply to adjourn without remanding. Similarly, if the offence is triable either way and the accused has not been remanded before and appears in answer to a summons (as opposed to having been charged and bailed from the police station), there is a discretion not to remand upon adjourning. In all other cases (e.g., offences triable only on indictment, those triable either way where the prosecution was commenced by way of charge, and all adjournments after conviction for reports), the magistrates must remand—i.e., grant the accused bail or remand him in custody. The difference between, on the one hand, simply adjourning and, on the other, adjourning and granting bail is that, in the former case, no adverse consequences flow from the accused failing to appear on the adjournment date, save that the offence will very likely be proved against him in his absence, whereas in the latter case he is under a duty to appear and commits an offence by not doing so. Normally, magistrates only adjourn without remanding in trivial cases, especially road traffic matters. The next Section deals especially with the periods for which magistrates may remand an accused; the remainder of the Chapter deals with bail.

Periods of remand

7.05   Subject to what follows, when magistrates remand an accused in custody prior to committal proceedings or summary trial, the period of the remand must not exceed eight clear days:

MCA, s 128(6). Usually it is simpler to make the adjournment and remand for a week, rather than using the full period allowed. The limitation on remands in custody is inconvenient when a period of several weeks or months is bound to elapse before the committal or summary trial can take place. Again, subject to what follows, the accused has to be brought before the court each week, even though the virtually foregone conclusion of his appearance is that he will be remanded in custody for another week. The pointlessness of his appearing in the dock just to be told that his case is further adjourned until such and such a date is accentuated by the fact that, since the decision of the Divisional Court in *Nottingham Justices ex parte Davies* [1981] QB 38, the defence have basically only been allowed one, or at most two, fully argued bail applications. Once they have exhausted those applications, they can only re-open the question of bail if fresh considerations have arisen which were not placed before the bench that originally refused bail. Obviously, if the defence are prevented from arguing for bail, the remand hearing turns into a charade. The decision in *Ex parte Davies* has been statutorily confirmed by the insertion in 1988 of Pt IIA in Sch 1 to the Bail Act 1976 (see 7.38 to 7.41).

7.06 In recognition of the unsatisfactoriness of successive remands in custody and the necessity for the accused's presence at each remand, the Criminal Justice Act 1982 introduced several new subsections into s 128 of the MCA, the basic effect of which is to allow the accused to consent to being remanded in custody for up to a 28 days without attending court. The system is that, on the first or any subsequent occasion when magistrates propose to adjourn prior to committal or summary trial and remand the accused in custody, they must, if he is legally represented in court, inform him of the possibility of further remands being made in his absence. If, and only if, he consents, they may then remand him thrice without his being brought to court. On the fourth occasion he must attend whether he wishes or not. The possibility of custodial remand in absence does not arise if the accused is unrepresented or if he is a juvenile.

7.07 Although probably the bulk of defendants who will have to be remanded in custody for substantial periods do sooner or later agree to remands in absence, the Government apparently came to think that, given the pressures under which the prison service is currently working, it was unsatisfactory to burden the service with the task of bringing remandees to court when no useful purpose could possibly be served by that being done. Accordingly the Criminal Justice Act 1988 inserted a new section (s 128A) into the Magistrates' Courts Act which allows a magistrates' court to remand an accused in custody for up to 28 clear days, whether or not he consents. It enables a magistrates' court, once it has set a date for the next stage of the proceedings to take place, to remand an accused in custody for a period ending on that date, or for a period of 28 clear days, whichever is the less. Importantly, it does not apply on the occasion of a first remand in custody but only if at a second or any subsequent remand the court again decides to refuse bail. Section 128A thus dovetails with the statutory provisions about argued bail applications, because the defence has a right to make an argued bail application both on the occasion of the accused's first appearance in connection with the charge and (if bail is then refused) at the next hearing. Thus, it is only when the ration of argued applications has been used up that the court may remand in custody for up to 28 days. If they are considering an extended remand under s 128A, magistrates should have regard to the total period of time the accused would spend in custody if they were so to remand him (see para 9B, added to Pt 1 of Sch 1 to the Bail Act 1976).

7.08   Where magistrates remand an accused after conviction for the purpose of preparing reports on him, the period of the remand must not exceed three weeks if it is in custody; four weeks if it is on bail: MCA, ss 10(3) and 30(1). Remands on bail prior to summary trial or committal proceedings may be for any convenient period. There is also a power in addition to s 128A to remand in custody for up to 28 days if the accused is already serving a custodial sentence for some other offence (see MCA, s 131(1)).

B   OCCASIONS ON WHICH A PERSON MAY BE GRANTED BAIL

7.09   The occasions on which a court or magistrate or police officer is faced with the decision to grant or refuse bail are as follows:

(a)   During the arrest and charge procedure at the police station, the question of bail can arise either as a result of the police charging the arrestee or as a result of their deciding that he should be released from the station without being charged. In the last resort, the decision on whether or not the arrestee should be bailed rests with the custody officer, although he will no doubt be much influenced by the views of the investigating officers. For details, see 3.29 to 3.30 and ss 37 to 38 of the Police and Criminal Evidence Act 1984.

(b)   A magistrate issuing a warrant for the arrest of the person named in a written information which has been laid before him should consider whether to endorse the warrant for bail: MCA, s 117—see 3.42 to 3.44. Similarly, a magistrates' court or the Crown Court on issuing a warrant may back it for bail: s 117 and Supreme Court Act 1981, s 81(4).

(c)   A magistrates' court has jurisdiction to grant bail when:

   (i)   it remands an accused for the period of an adjournment prior to committal proceedings or summary trial: MCA, ss 5, 10(4) and 18(4)—see 7.09; or

   (ii) it remands an offender after conviction for the period of an adjournment for reports under MCA, ss 10(3) or 30—see 7.09; or

   (iii) it commits or sends an accused to the Crown Court for trial on indictment or for sentence (MCA, ss 6(3) and 38 which provide respectively that committals for trial and sentence may be in custody or on bail); or

   (iv) a person in custody is appealing to the Crown Court or the Divisional Court against one of its (the magistrates' court's) decisions: MCA, s 113—see 27.03 to 27.11 and 27.18 to 27.23.

   The maximum periods for remands in custody prior to committal proceedings or summary trial have been explained at 7.05 to 7.08. A remand for preparation of reports following summary conviction may be for a maximum of three or four weeks depending on whether the offender is or is not in custody (see MCA, ss 10(3) and 30). Committals for trial or sentence in custody will be for whatever period may elapse until the case can be heard in the Crown Court. Because that period will certainly be one of several weeks and may extend to several months, the decision to grant or refuse bail on committal is a particularly important one.

(d)   The Crown Court has jurisdiction to grant bail when:

(i) a magistrates' court has remanded an accused in custody and has issued a certificate to the effect that it heard full argument before taking the decision to refuse bail (see 7.45 for details); or

(ii) a person has been committed or sent to it for trial or sentence in custody or is appealing to it against conviction or sentence by the magistrates; or

(iii) a person is appealing from it by case stated to the Divisional Court or is seeking judicial review of its decision; or

(iv) the appropriate Crown Court judge has certified that a case is fit for appeal to the Court of Appeal against conviction or sentence (see also 26.10 to 26.11).

The above powers to grant bail are contained in s 81(1) of the Supreme Court Act 1981. The Crown Court also has inherent jurisdiction to grant bail during the course of a trial on indictment and for the period of an adjournment for reports following conviction. If the accused was on bail prior to the commencement of the trial and surrenders to custody at the appointed time, it is normal practice to renew his bail for any overnight adjournments. Bail may be withdrawn, however, where there is a real danger that he might abscond (e.g., because the case is going badly for him), or interfere with witnesses or jurors. When a custodial sentence would be the likely result of conviction and the prosecution case seems strong, bail is often withdrawn once the judge has commenced his summing-up. The *Practice Direction* (*Criminal Proceedings: Consolidation*) [2002] 1 WLR 2870, para III.25 deals with the principles governing bail during the course of a trial.

(e) The High Court has jurisdiction to grant bail when a person is appealing to it by way of case stated or seeking to quash a decision of the magistrates' court or the Crown Court.

(f) The Court of Appeal (acting through a single judge) has jurisdiction to grant bail both to a person appealing to it against conviction or sentence in the Crown Court, and to a person who, after an unsuccessful appeal to it, is further appealing to the House of Lords: Criminal Appeal Act 1968, ss 19 and 36.

C   PRINCIPLES ON WHICH THE DECISION TO GRANT OR REFUSE BAIL IS TAKEN

Section 4 of the Bail Act 1976 gives to an accused person what may usefully, if slightly inaccurately, be described as a right to bail. The section does not apply at all stages of the criminal process, and, even if it does apply, the accused may be refused bail if the circumstances of his case fall within one of a number of sets of circumstances defined in Schedule 1 to the Act. Nevertheless, the right to bail is of value to an accused because it emphasizes that it is for the prosecution to show a good reason why bail should be withheld, not for the defence to plead for bail as a favour to which the accused is not prima facie entitled.   **7.10**

There is a group of defendants who may be granted bail only if there are 'exceptional circumstances which justify it'. This is the category covered by s 25 of the Criminal Justice and Public Order Act 1994. That provision covers any person charged with murder, attempted murder, manslaughter, rape, attempted rape, or one of the serious sexual offences added by the Sexual Offences Act 2003, Sch 6, para 32, if he has previously been convicted in the   **7.11**

United Kingdom of one of those offences, or of culpable homicide. Where the prior conviction was manslaughter or culpable homicide, however, the provision applies only if the sentence imposed on that occasion was imprisonment or long-term detention. The current offence with which the accused is charged does not need to be the same as that for which he was convicted previously. The restriction on bail for accused in this category applies also on appeal against conviction.

7.12   In *R(O) v Harrow Crown Court* [2007] 1 AC 247, the House of Lords considered that s 25 is compatible with Art 5 of the ECHR, which guarantees the right to liberty. It did not cast a formal burden of proof upon a defendant to make out the exceptional circumstances allowing bail. In so far as s 25 appeared to do so, it should be 'read down' in accordance with s 3 of the HRA 1998, so as to ensure that it was consistent with Art 5 (see 28.07).

Occasions on which there is a 'right to bail'

7.13   Section 4 provides that a person to whom it applies 'shall be granted bail except as provided in Schedule 1'. The section applies whenever a person accused of an offence appears or is brought before a magistrates' court or the Crown Court in the course of or in connection with proceedings for the offence. Thus, at his first court appearance before the magistrates and at all subsequent appearances before the magistrates or the Crown Court up to the occasion on which he is convicted or acquitted, the accused has a right to bail. Even following conviction, he still has a right to bail if his case is adjourned for reports prior to sentencing. He can also rely on the right to bail if, during these stages of the proceedings, he applies to the Crown Court for bail following a refusal of bail by the magistrates. There is no right to bail when:

(a)   the custody officer is considering bailing an arrestee from the police station after he has been charged; or

(b)   the magistrates, having summarily convicted an offender, commit him to the Crown Court for sentence; or

(c)   a person who has been convicted and sentenced, whether by the magistrates or in the Crown Court, is appealing against conviction or sentence.

Of course, in all three of the above cases the police officer or court has power to grant bail, but there is no statutory presumption in its favour by virtue of s 4. In case (a), s 38(1) of the PACE gives the accused something very similar to the Bail Act 'right to bail'. The subsection provides that a person who has been charged *shall* be released from the police station (either on bail or unconditionally) unless the custody officer reasonably fears that that would have one or more of a number of undesirable consequences (e.g., the arrestee absconding or interfering with witnesses—3.29 to 3.30).

Refusing bail for a defendant charged with an imprisonable offence

7.14   Schedule 1 to the Bail Act 1976 sets out the circumstances in which a person to whom s 4 applies (i.e., a person with a right to bail) may be refused bail. Schedule 1 refers to a person with a right to bail as 'the defendant'.

7.15   Part I of Sch 1 applies when the defendant stands accused or convicted of at least one offence punishable with imprisonment. He need not be granted bail if:

(a) the court is satisfied that there are substantial grounds for believing that, if released on
     bail, he would:
     (i)   fail to surrender to custody; or
     (ii) commit an offence while on bail; or
     (iii) interfere with witnesses or otherwise obstruct the course of justice whether in relation
           to himself or some other person; or
(b) he was already on bail at the time of the charged offence; or
(c) the court is satisfied that he should be kept in custody for his own protection or, if he is a
     juvenile, for his own welfare; or
(d) he is already serving a custodial sentence; or
(e) the court is satisfied that lack of time since the commencement of the proceedings has
     made it impracticable to obtain the information needed to decide properly the questions
     raised in (a) to (c) above; or
(f) he has already been bailed during the course of the proceedings, and has been arrested
     under s 7 of the Act (arrest of absconders etc.—see 7.60 to 7.63).
(g) he is aged 18 or over, there is drug test evidence of a specified Class A drug in his body, the
     offence is a Class A drug offence (or was caused or contributed to by a Class A drug) and
     he does not agree to undergo an assessment or a follow-up programme as to drug misuse
     or dependency.

Exception (b) above deals with the general position where the defendant is alleged to have **7.16**
committed an offence on bail. Section 14(1) of the CJA 2003 introduced a new test where the
offence for which bail is being considered carries a maximum sentence of life imprisonment.
In circumstances where the offence appears to have been committed on bail and the defendant is aged 18 or over, he may not be granted bail unless there is no significant risk of his
committing an offence while on bail. Section 14(2) states that in the case of a defendant aged
under 18 who was on bail when the alleged offence was committed, the court can give particular weight to this fact when deciding whether he will be likely to re-offend if released on
bail. Exception (f) above deals with the general position where the defendant has absconded
during the course of current proceedings. Section 15 of the CJA 2003 again introduced a new
test where the offence for which bail is being considered carries a maximum sentence of life
imprisonment. In the case of an adult offender who has absconded during the current proceedings, he may not be granted bail unless there is no significant risk of his failing to surrender to custody. If he is under 18, the court shall give particular weight to the fact that he has
previously absconded in the proceedings when deciding on bail.

The above reasons for refusing bail are listed in paras 2 to 6 of Pt I of Sch 1. The one most **7.17**
commonly relied upon is that set out in (a). It will be noticed that the wording of the reason
is very precise. The court must be 'satisfied that there are substantial grounds for believing'
that, if bail were granted, one or other of the undesirable consequences specified would
ensue. A subjective belief that that is what would happen is not enough if it is based on flim-
sy or irrational grounds. On the other hand, the prosecution are not required to prove beyond
reasonable doubt that the defendant would jump bail etc., or even to produce formal evidence to that effect. The question for the court is essentially a speculative one, not amenable
to proof according to the rules by which disputed issues are normally resolved in a court of
law. Thus, a prosecutor objecting to bail may state his opinion that it would lead to the
accused absconding, or he may even, with a view to showing that there is a risk of interference

with witnesses, recount to the court what a police officer has been told by a potential witness of threats the latter has received (*Re Moles* [1981] Crim LR 170). This was confirmed by *Mansfield Justices ex parte Sharkey* [1985] QB 613, where the Divisional Court accepted counsel's proposition that 'a bail application is an informal inquiry and no strict rules of evidence are to be applied'. However, para 9 of Pt I of Sch 1 does give the courts some guidance on how this informal inquiry should be approached by listing a number of considerations to be taken into account; para 9 only applies when the objection to bail is one of those presently being discussed—i.e., that the defendant would abscond, commit further offences or interfere with witnesses. The factors which it lists are described in 7.18.

7.18 First, there is 'the nature and seriousness of the offence and the probable method of dealing with the defendant for it'. The more serious the charge the more likely it is that he will abscond because he will realize that conviction would result in a lengthy prison sentence. Secondly, the 'character, antecedents, associations and community ties' of the defendant are relevant. Under the heading of 'community ties' the court will be assessing how much the defendant has to lose by absconding. If he is a married man with a family living in his own house, he is less likely to abscond than a teenager with a room in a hostel. However, a person should not be refused bail simply because he is living in the latter type of accommodation— it is merely one factor which goes to indicate a lack of roots in the local community and therefore a greater risk of jumping bail (see Home Office Circular, No 155 of 1975). The defendant's character and previous convictions are important in two ways. They may show that he is untrustworthy, and they may also show that, even though the offence charged is not intrinsically in the first rank of gravity, he is likely if convicted to receive a custodial sentence because, for example, he will be in breach of a suspended sentence. Thirdly, the court may look at the defendant's past record for answering bail and/or committing offences while on bail. If he has previously been bailed and has not abused the trust placed in him, that is some reason for saying that he can be trusted on bail on the present occasion. Lastly, the court should consider the strength of the prosecution case—the weaker the evidence seems, the stronger is the argument for bail. Unfortunately, the strength or weakness of the case will probably not emerge until later in the proceedings, by which time the defendant may have spent a considerable period in custody. The list of relevant considerations in para 9 is not intended as an exhaustive one. One obviously important factor not mentioned in the paragraph is whether the defence can put forward sureties.

7.19 Reason (b) in 7.15 for refusing bail was added to the list by s 26 of the Criminal Justice and Public Order Act 1994 and amended by CJA 2003. It covers the position of the offender who is alleged to have committed a further offence while on bail. An accused who is in due course found guilty of that further offence can expect a harsher sentence as a result (see 23.22). But his bail prospects will also be affected. The court still has a discretion whether to grant him bail or not. In exercising that discretion, however, they need not regard him as having the right to bail. As a result, the refusal of bail will be easier, for in cases where there is a right to bail there must be substantial grounds for believing that one of the exceptions applies before bail can be withheld. In this context, 'substantial' means more than a subjective perception (*Ex parte Sharkey* at p. 625).

7.20 The other justifications in Sch 1 for refusing to bail a defendant with a right to bail call for little comment. Keeping somebody in custody for his own protection might be necessary where the offence charged has raised a great deal of local anger, as where it is alleged that the defendant sexually assaulted young children. If the defendant is a juvenile, bail can be refused in his own best interests even though he would not be physically endangered through being released (e.g., if he has run away from home, remanding him into the care of the local authority may be preferable to leaving him to fend for himself). Where the defendant is already serving a custodial sentence which will last until well after his next court appearance on the present charge, there is little point in going through the motions of considering a bail application. Lack of information on which to base a proper decision about bail is a problem when the defendant makes his first court appearance before the magistrates after being arrested without warrant, charged at the police station and thereafter kept in police detention. He may not have been able to consult with a solicitor or to arrange for one to be at court to make a bail application for him. Although the duty solicitor will no doubt be asked to assist, there will be little time for him to be given proper instructions (e.g., as to who might be prepared to stand surety). From the police viewpoint, they may not have been able to check on matters such as the defendant's address, identity and previous convictions. The magistrates are therefore allowed to 'play safe' by remanding in custody for a week or so, at the end of which the arguments for and against bail can be properly presented on both sides. Lastly, if the defendant has already been bailed in connection with the present proceedings against him and has had to be arrested for absconding or otherwise failing to comply with the conditions of his bail, the court is entitled to say the legal equivalent of 'once bitten twice shy' and refuse to set him at liberty again.

7.21 At the stage of an adjournment for reports following the defendant's conviction, there is one additional possible reason for refusing bail, namely that the court believes it will not be practicable to complete the report without the defendant being in custody. For example, the court may have ordered medical reports, but the mental condition of the defendant may make it obvious that he will not voluntarily attend at a hospital so as to be examined. The court should therefore remand him in custody (or it may now have the additional option of remanding him to a mental hospital—see 10.72 to 10.74).

Refusing bail for a defendant charged with a non-imprisonable offence

7.22 Part II of Sch 1 applies when none of the offences of which the defendant stands accused or convicted is punishable with imprisonment. He need not be granted bail if reasons (c) or (d) for refusing to grant bail to a defendant accused of an imprisonable offence apply in his case (i.e., he should be kept in custody for his own protection, or he is already serving a custodial sentence). Further, where he is arrested under s 7 of the Bail Act, bail may be refused only if there are substantial grounds for believing that, if released on bail (whether subject to conditions or not) he would fail to surrender to custody, commit an offence while on bail, or interfere with witnesses or otherwise obstruct the course of justice (Sch 1, Part 2, para 5 of the Bail Act, as amended by CJA 2003, s 13(4)). There is no general power to refuse bail on the grounds that he might abscond, but, if he failed to surrender to custody after being bailed in previous criminal proceedings and the court therefore believes that, if now granted bail, he would again fail to surrender, bail may be refused. It is very rare for a court to refuse bail if the offences are non-imprisonable.

Custody time-limits

7.23 Under a s 22 of the Prosecution of Offences Act 1985, there are regulations which lay down custody time-limits (i.e., maximum periods during which the accused can be kept in custody before trial). The regulations were originally in force in certain areas only, but have now been extended to all parts of the country. They fix the following maximum periods for which an accused may be held:

(a) 70 days between his first appearance in the magistrates' court and committal proceedings;

(b) 70 days between first appearance and summary trial for an offence which is triable either way (reduced to 56 days if the decision for summary trial is taken within 56 days);

(c) 56 days between first appearance and trial for a summary offence;

(d) 112 days between committal for trial and arraignment; and

(e) 182 days between the date sent for trial under s 51 of the Crime and Disorder Act 1998 (indictable-only offences), and the start of trial.

7.24 Special rules apply to the accused's right to bail when the prosecution fails to comply with a custody time-limit. When the limit has expired, the exceptions to the right to bail listed in Sch 1 to the Bail Act 1976 no longer apply (reg 8 of the Prosecution of Offences (Custody Time-Limits) Regulations 1987: SI 1987 No 299). The effect is to give the accused an absolute right to bail. (other than in cases governed by s 25 of the CJPOA 1994 – see 7.11 and *R(O) v Harrow Crown Court* [2007] 1 AC 247). Further, the court is prevented, when bailing an accused entitled to bail by reason of the expiry of a custody time-limit, from imposing a requirement of a surety or deposit of security or any other condition which must be complied with *before* release on bail. It may impose a condition such as a curfew, or a condition of residence or reporting, which has to be complied with *after* release. The prosecution can, of course, avoid these consequences by ensuring that the case is dealt with quickly, so as to avoid the expiry of the custody time-limit. Failing that, it can apply for an extension of the time-limit.

7.25 The application for an extension must be made before the custody time limit expires. In considering whether to grant an extension, the criteria laid down in s 22(3) of the Prosecution of Offences Act 1985 are applied. The court must be satisfied:

(a) that the need for the extension is due to:
   (i) the illness or absence of the accused, a necessary witness, a judge or a magistrate;
   (ii) the ordering by the court of separate trials in the case of two or more accused or two or more offences; or
   (iii) some other good or sufficient cause; and
(b) that the Crown has acted with all due expedition.

(For a detailed analysis of the case law on custody time limits, see *Blackstone's Criminal Practice 2008*, D14.6 to 14.35.)

D   REQUIREMENTS IMPOSED WHEN GRANTING BAIL

7.26 A defendant may be granted bail unconditionally, in which case he is not required to provide sureties before being released and, having been released, the only obligation he is under is that of surrendering to custody at the appointed place and time. Alternatively, s 3 of the Bail Act allows the police or the courts to attach requirements to a grant of bail.

One of the common requirements attached to bail is that of providing one or more sureties. **7.27** Both the police when bailing an arrestee from the station and the courts may require sureties, but they should only do so if it is necessary to ensure that the defendant surrenders to custody (see s 3(4)). A surety is a person who undertakes to pay the court a specified sum of money in the event of the defendant failing to surrender to custody as he ought. The undertaking into which the surety enters is called a recognizance. If the defendant absconds the surety may be ordered to pay part or all of the sum in which he stood surety. This is known as forfeiting or estreating the recognizance. A surety whose recognizance has been estreated is dealt with as if he had been fined, so if he fails to pay the sum forfeited a means inquiry is held and, ultimately, he could be committed to prison. The possibly serious consequences of being a surety mean that no person proffered as a surety should be accepted as such unless he apparently has the means to satisfy his potential liability under the recognizance. On granting bail, the police officer or court fixes the number and amount of the sureties which will be required, and the defendant must remain in custody until suitable sureties in the stated sums have entered into their recognizances. If the sureties are not forthcoming the defendant, at his next appearance before the court or on an application to the Crown Court, may argue that the requirement for sureties should be varied or dispensed with all together.

Note that a surety for an adult accused is responsible only for ensuring that the accused **7.28** attends court. He is not obliged to ensure that other conditions of bail (e.g., not to commit further offences) are met. Some magistrates' courts have been in the practice of asking for 'sureties for good behaviour'. There is no power to do this under the Bail Act 1976, so they attempt to remedy the deficiency by using their general powers to bind over under the Justices of the Peace Act 1361 and the Justices of the Peace Act 1968. There are two problems with this practice:

(a) Binding over to keep the peace is only of relevance where the court fears repetition, for example, of an offence of violence. It can hardly be properly invoked in relation, say, to an offence of dishonesty.

(b) A court requiring a surety for good behaviour appears to be contravening the Bail Act 1976, s 3(3)(c) of which provides: 'Except as provided *by this section* . . . no other requirement shall be imposed [on the accused] as a condition of bail' (emphasis added).

The position as far as sureties for juveniles is concerned is different. By s 3(7) of the Bail Act **7.29** 1976, where the accused is a juvenile and his parent or guardian stands surety for him, the court may require that surety to ensure that the juvenile complies with any condition of bail imposed by virtue of s 6. Hence, the court can quite properly require the parent or guardian to be a surety for good behaviour. The recognizance under s 3(7) is, however, limited to £50.

A requirement for sureties does not involve the sureties or the defendant himself paying **7.30** money to the court as a pre-condition of his release on bail. The position is different, however, where the court requires that the defendant supply *security* for his surrender to custody (s 3(5)). Giving security means that the defendant or somebody on his behalf deposits money or other property with the court, which will be forfeited if he absconds.

7.31   Instead of or in addition to imposing a requirement for sureties or, where appropriate, a requirement for the giving of security, a court may require the defendant to comply with such other conditions as appear necessary to ensure that he does not abscond, commit offences while on bail or interfere with witnesses: (s 3(6)(a) to (c)). The court may impose conditions to protect the accused, or (if he is a child or young person) for his own welfare or in his own interests (BA 1976, s 3(6)(ca) added by the CJA 2003, s 13(1)). A condition may also be imposed to ensure that the defendant attends an interview with his legal representative (s 3(6)(e)). By virtue of s 3(6), the defendant may be required, for example, to report to the police station once a week or even once a day, to surrender his passport, to live at a certain address (e.g., his home address or, if he is of no fixed abode, a bail hostel run by the probation service), to report any change of address, or to be indoors by a certain time each night. Negatively, he could be ordered not to contact potential prosecution witnesses or not to go within a certain distance of where the victim of the alleged offence lives. More controversially, in *Mansfield Justices ex parte Sharkey* [1985] QB 613, a number of miners from Yorkshire involved in the strike of 1984–5 were required as a condition of bail not to picket otherwise than at their own pits, which were solidly for the strike anyway. They were awaiting trial on threatening behaviour charges, the alleged offences having occurred when they were taking part in the mass picketing of working pits in the East Midlands. The Divisional Court upheld the requirements on the basis that the defendants would otherwise have returned to the picket lines which, given that the picketing was 'by intimidation and threat' (per the Lord Chief Justice at p. 627), might have resulted in their committing further offences. *Ex parte Sharkey* was of interest not only for its political implications and the impact it had on the course of the miners' strike, but also for the Lord Chief Justice's comments on how probable the commission of further offences must appear if that is to be used as a justification for imposing conditions of bail. The court must perceive a real, as opposed to a fanciful, risk of unconditional bail resulting in offences being committed while on bail, but it need not have the 'substantial grounds' for its belief which it would have to have if it were minded to refuse bail completely for the same reason. Thus, the justices were entitled to impose the conditions even though the defendants were of previous good character and the only grounds for supposing they would commit offences if allowed to picket again was the justices' local knowledge of how the picketing was in general being conducted. The implication of Lord Lane's judgment was that those grounds would not have been substantial enough for a total refusal of bail.

7.32   *Ex parte Sharkey* was a case where the accused were charged with an imprisonable offence. In *Bournemouth Magistrates' Court ex parte Cross* (1989) 89 Cr App R 90, the point at issue was whether conditions could be imposed on bail for non-imprisonable offences. C was a hunt protester who was arrested for an offence under s 5 of the Public Order Act 1986 (non-imprisonable). He was bailed on condition he did not attend another hunt meeting before his next court appearance. He was arrested for alleged breach of this condition, and remanded in custody by the magistrates. On application for judicial review, the Divisional Court held that the condition had been validly imposed. The justices had been of the view that it was necessary to prevent the commission of further offences, and they were entitled to impose it by s 3(6) of the Bail Act 1976.

7.33   When a convicted defendant is remanded on bail for the preparation of reports on his physical or mental condition prior to sentencing the Crown Court may and a magistrates' court must require him to make himself available for the necessary medical examinations (see Bail

Act 1976, s 3(6), and s 30(2) of the Magistrates' Courts Act 1980). When a juvenile has conditions attached to his bail, his parents (provided they consent) may be required to secure his compliance with the conditions, on pain of forfeiting a recognisance of not more than £50 (Bail Act 1976, s 3(7)). Otherwise sureties have no responsibility for ensuring that the defendant complies with any conditions of bail, other than the basic one of surrendering to custody at the appropriate time.

E   PROCEDURE AT AN APPLICATION FOR BAIL IN A MAGISTRATES' COURT

Most bail applications are made in the magistrates' courts. Essentially the procedure is that the   **7.34**
court asks the defence whether there is an application for bail and the prosecutor whether there are any objections. Strictly speaking, the granting or withholding of bail is always a matter for the court, not for tacit agreement between the parties, but obviously if a bail application is unopposed the court is unlikely to raise objections, whereas if no application is made it will need little convincing that there are sufficient reasons for remanding in custody. Assuming, however, that there is an opposed bail application, the prosecutor outlines his objections. It is rare for the police officer in the case actually to attend court, but he should have completed a form contained in the CPS file stating why (in his view) bail is undesirable. Reasons commonly given are that the gravity of the offence charged and/or the accused's previous record make it likely that he will receive a custodial sentence if convicted; that he is currently appearing in other courts for other matters and that the present offences were committed while on bail; that he has past convictions for failing to appear after being granted bail; and that he knows the chief prosecution witnesses and, if at liberty, would be in a position to influence them. A list of previous convictions may be handed into the court and commented on in general terms but it is not normally read out in full (see *Dyson* (1943) 29 Cr App R 104). Following the prosecution objections to bail, the defence representative makes a speech countering those objections as best he can. He may, for example, stress that the accused has a permanent address and strong community ties and so is unlikely to abscond, even though the charges are serious. If there are sureties available, it is sometimes helpful to call them so that the bench can appreciate the quality of the persons who are prepared to put money at risk on behalf of the accused. The more impressive the surety, the more likely it is that bail will be granted. On the other side of the argument, while it is unusual for a police officer to be called by the prosecution at the outset, the court may occasionally ask that a responsible investigating officer attend to elucidate the nature and strength of the case against the accused and—if one of the objections to bail is that enquiries are still being undertaken which may result in more serious charges against the accused or others—to explain the nature of those enquiries in general terms. Having heard the arguments for and against bail, and having considered the evidence of any witnesses called, the magistrates announce their decision.

Bail hearings have been much criticized for what is perceived as their cursory nature. One   **7.35**
study of two busy London magistrates' courts put the average length of bail proceedings at six minutes, leading to a recommendation from Lord Justice Auld that 'magistrates and judges in all courts should take more time to consider matters of bail' (Auld Report, pp. 428–430).

7.36   In addition, the form taken by hearings related to bail has been questioned in the light of the Human Rights Act 1998, and the safeguards contained in Art 6 of the European Convention on Human Rights. The question may be posed in this way: to what extent should the safeguards in Art 6 apply in reviews of pre-trial detention guaranteed by Art 5 (see 28.15 to 28.33 for the terms of the Articles). The question was examined in *DPP v Havering* [2001] 1 WLR 805. In that case, the need for formal evidence and procedures was rejected, in favour of a focus upon the quality of the material, with the accused given a right to cross-examine if oral evidence is presented. In *R (Malik) v Central Criminal Court* [2006] 4 All ER 1141, the Divisional Court considered that Art 6 may apply at bail hearings, and that they should take place in public.

7.37   Whenever magistrates (or any court) refuse bail to an accused with a prima facie right to bail, they must state the reasons for their so doing (see 7.45 for details). In addition, para 9A was inserted into Pt I of Sch 1 to the Bail Act by the Criminal Justice Act 1988, requiring a court which grants bail to an accused charged with certain offences to give reasons and cause those reasons to be entered into the record of the court proceeding. The offences to which para 9A applies are murder, manslaughter, rape and attempts to commit the same. The duty to state reasons where one of these grave offences is alleged is distinct from the restrictions on the grant of bail for a person who is charged with such an offence and has a previous conviction for a similar crime (see 7.11 to 7.12).

Successive bail applications

7.38   The rule that a remand in custody prior to committal proceedings or summary trial could not exceed eight clear days led in the past to defendants using each weekly appearance before the magistrates to renew a bail application. The same arguments for bail that had been presented at perhaps numerous previous hearings would be re-presented, the magistrates would listen with as much patience as they could muster, and the result would almost inevitably be a further remand in custody. Eventually the courts devised a way of preventing these time-consuming charades. In *Nottingham Justices ex parte Davies* [1981] QB 38 the Divisional Court held that a decision by one bench of magistrates that bail should be refused was a finding to which *res judicata* or something akin to it applied, and the defence could not therefore re-open the question of bail unless they had some fresh argument to put forward which had not been before the magistrates who originally remanded in custody. Most courts interpreted this decision fairly liberally so as to allow the accused two bail applications, one on his first appearance after being arrested without warrant and charged, and a second when, perhaps a week later, the defence solicitors had had more time to consider the case, find potential sureties and generally marshal the arguments for bail. The Criminal Justice Act 1988 confirmed and clarified the decision in *Ex parte Davies* by inserting a new part (Pt IIA) into Sch 1 to the Bail Act.

7.39   First, Pt IIA states that it is the court's duty, having refused bail, to consider at each subsequent hearing while the accused remains in custody whether the decision ought to be reversed (para 1). But there is an element of unreality about this statement of principle because paras 2 and 3 then provide that, although the accused at the first hearing after that at which the court decided not to grant him bail may as of right 'support an application for bail with any argument as to fact or law whether or not he has advanced that argument previously', at subsequent hearings 'the court need not … hear arguments which it has heard previously'. Of course, although it is not expressly stated in Pt IIA of Sch 1, the accused may on his first appearance support a bail application with any relevant argument. The defence (perhaps through the duty solicitor) may argue for bail on the occasion when the accused is first brought before the magistrates in custody by the police, secure in the knowledge that—should their arguments fail—a second argued application may be presented a week later. However, should that second application also fail, any further argued application will be at the court's discretion unless the defence can point to some fresh argument (whether of fact or law) that has not previously been aired. In *Blyth Juvenile Court ex parte G* [1991] Crim LR 693, the Divisional Court gave consideration to the question of what constitutes a fresh argument such as to trigger off the right to make a further bail application. The situation was that G, aged 11, was charged with the murder of the 18-month-old child whom she was baby-sitting. She was remanded into the care of the local authority for the protection of her own welfare, and it was ordered that she be held in secure accommodation. Various unsuccessful bail applications were made on her behalf, but an appeal against the secure accommodation order was successful. The justices were asked to hear a further bail application on her behalf, and refused on the ground that there were no changed circumstances. The fresh arguments put forward on G's behalf were that the passage of time had meant that feelings against her no longer ran so high; that there had been a change from secure to non-secure accommodation; that the move to some 46 miles from her home meant it was difficult for her mother to visit her; and that G had been assaulted by three other inmates. The Divisional Court allowed the application, and directed the justices to hear a further application for bail. The necessary change in circumstances need not be major, and it was sufficient in this case.

Once the defence have used up their argued applications, further remand hearings become **7.40** meaningless exercises. Although in theory the magistrates consider whether a remand in custody is necessary, in fact the decision is a foregone conclusion, and the 'hearing' consists in the chairman saying that the case of Z is adjourned to such and such a date, he being remanded in custody. In recognition of the pointlessness of the accused being present to hear the above take place, Parliament amended the Magistrates' Courts Act 1980 first to allow three successive remands in custody to take place in the accused's absence provided he consents and then to allow remands in custody for up to 28 days whether or not he consents so long as he has already been remanded in custody once (see 7.05 to 7.08).

What is the position if the accused consents to being remanded in his absence? In *Dover & East* **7.41** *Kent Justices ex parte Dean* [1992] Crim LR 33, D made no bail application on his first appearance, and consented to be remanded in his absence for three weeks. He appeared before the justices at the end of the three-week period, and wished to make a bail application. The justices decided that the hearing at which he had the right to do so was the first date on which he was remanded in his absence. Not surprisingly, the Divisional Court held that D had a right to make a bail application when he came before the justices at the end of the period of remand by consent.

Taking sureties

If the magistrates grant bail subject to the provision of sureties, and the necessary sureties **7.42** are present at court, they may enter into their undertakings before the magistrates. Section 8(2) of the Bail Act 1976 provides that, in considering the suitability of a proposed surety, regard may be had to his financial resources, character and previous convictions, and connection with the defendant (e.g., is he a relative, friend, neighbour etc?). Before he formally agrees to be a surety, it is normal practice to explain to him the nature of his obligations and the possible consequences to him of the defendant absconding. He is also asked whether he is worth the sum involved after all his debts are paid. If the sureties are not at court when bail is granted, they may enter into their recognizances subsequently before a magistrate, magistrates' clerk, police officer not below the rank of inspector, or (if the defendant has already been taken to a prison or remand centre) the governor of that establishment. Until they have done so, the defendant must remain in custody. If a surety attempts to enter into a recognizance before one of the persons mentioned above, but he declines to take the recognizance because he considers the surety unsuitable, the surety may apply to the court to take the recognizance.

7.43 To avoid the inconvenience to the sureties of their having to enter into recognizances every time the defendant's case is adjourned, the magistrates may make the sureties continuous. This means that on the occasion when bail is first granted the surety undertakes to pay the specified sum if the defendant fails to appear on any of the occasions to which his case is adjourned. If the offence charged is indictable the recognizance may be further extended to secure the defendant's appearance before the Crown Court should he be committed for trial: MCA, s 128(4).

7.44 Similar provisions to those described above apply when the Crown Court, Divisional Court or Court of Appeal grants bail subject to sureties. Continuous bail is particularly useful where, following the defendant's surrender to custody on the first day of his trial on indictment, he is granted bail for the overnight adjournments. If bail is made continuous the sureties only need to be present to enter into their recognizances on the occasion of the first adjournment.

Recording and giving reasons for decisions on bail

7.45 Section 5 of the Bail Act 1976 sets out some administrative procedures which must be followed when decisions on bail are taken. They are that:

(a) Whenever bail is granted (whether by a court or by the police) and whenever a court withholds bail from a defendant with a right to bail under s 4, a *record* must be made of the decision. A copy of the record should be given to the defendant on request.

(b) When a magistrates' court or the Crown Court withholds bail from a defendant with a right to bail (or grants bail but subject to conditions), it must give *reasons* for its decision. The reasons should be such as to help the defendant decide whether it is worth making an application for bail to another court (see 7.49 to 7.54). A note must be made of the reasons and a copy given to the defendant (unless the decision was taken by the Crown Court and the defendant is represented by counsel or solicitor who does not request a copy). As a result of the Criminal Justice Act 1988 it is now also necessary for the court to give its reasons for granting bail to defendants charged with certain offences (see 7.37).

(c) If a magistrates' court withholds bail from an unrepresented defendant, they must tell him of his right to make a bail application to the Crown Court.

(d) If a magistrates' court remands a defendant in custody after a fully argued bail application, they must *issue a* certificate confirming that they did hear argument. Where it was not the first or second argued bail application, the certificate must state the change in circumstances which persuaded the court to listen to renewed argument. A copy of the certificate must be given to the defendant. Its significance will emerge at 7.49). However, no certificate is required if the defendant was committed for trial or sentence in custody or had an application for bail pending determination of an appeal from the magistrates turned down.

Variations in the conditions of bail etc.

Where a court has granted bail either the prosecution or the defence may apply to it for a variation in the conditions of bail, or, if bail was granted unconditionally, the prosecution may apply for conditions to be imposed: Bail Act 1976, s 3(8). If the defendant has been committed on bail to the Crown Court for trial or sentence, an application for variation may be made to either the Crown Court or the magistrates' court. Should the court decide to vary or impose conditions a record must be made of its decision. If the defendant has a right to bail, reasons for the decision are required, and the defendant is entitled to a copy of the note of the reasons: s 5.   **7.46**

A magistrates' court which has remanded a defendant on bail to appear before it on a certain date may, if it is convenient, appoint a later date for the defendant to appear and amend the recognizances of any sureties accordingly: MCA, s 129(3). This power to 'enlarge bail' is useful if, for example, the court will not have time to deal with the defendant's case on the day originally fixed. Where a defendant who has been remanded in custody or on bail cannot be brought or appear before the magistrates on the day appointed because of illness or accident, the magistrates may further remand him in his absence, and a remand in custody may exceed eight clear days: MCA, s 129(1).   **7.47**

Reviewing bail on new information

What if the court grants bail, and information later comes to light which throws light on the correctness of that decision? Under s 5B of the Bail Act 1976 (inserted by the Criminal Justice and Public Order Act 1994), the court may then reconsider the whole question of bail on the application of the prosecution. This power is only available if the offence is indictable-only or triable-either-way. The application must be based on information not available to the court (or to the police officer) who made the grant of bail which is now under review. If invoked, it enables the court to vary bail conditions, impose conditions for the first time, or remand in custody. The application can be heard in the defendant's absence, provided he has been notified of the prosecution's application for review.   **7.48**

F APPLICATIONS TO THE CROWN COURT AND HIGH COURT CONCERNING BAIL

The Crown Court may grant bail to a defendant refused it by the magistrates if either: **7.49**

(a) they remanded the defendant in custody (whether prior to committal proceedings or summary trial or after summary conviction and before sentence), and heard a fully argued bail application before deciding on the remand in custody; or

(b)   they committed the defendant in custody to the Crown Court for trial or sentence; or

(c)   they convicted him summarily, imposed a custodial sentence and refused to bail him pending determination of his appeal to the Crown Court: Supreme Court Act 1981, s 81.

Thus, in most cases a defendant whose bail application to the magistrates fails will have the option of making a further application to the Crown Court. So that there will be no disputes as to whether there has been an argued bail application, the magistrates must issue a certificate stating, if it be the case, that they refused bail after hearing argument (see 7.47).

Applications to the High Court for bail

7.50   An application to the High Court for bail is made to a judge in chambers. The procedure is set out in Ord 79, r 9 of the Civil Procedure Rules 1998. It is to be followed when the High Court has jurisdiction under s 37 of the Criminal Justice Act 1948 to grant bail to a person who has applied to the Crown Court to state a case or who is applying to quash a Crown Court or a magistrates' court decision (see 7.09). The jurisdiction of the High Court to deal with appeals from the magistrates on bail matters was abolished by the CJA 2003, s 17 with effect from April 2004.

Applications to the Crown Court for bail

7.51   A defendant refused bail by the magistrates is usually able to make a further application to the Crown Court (see above). If, as will usually be the case, the defendant has been granted legal representation for the proceedings as a whole (or even if he was just granted it for the purpose of making a bail application to the magistrates) it will cover a Crown Court bail application. The application, which may be heard in chambers, is normally listed for hearing by a circuit judge or recorder.

7.52   Prior to April 2004, the position was that any appeal against *conditions* of bail imposed by the magistrates had to be made to the High Court and not to the Crown Court. Section 16 of the CJA 2003 created a new right of appeal to the Crown Court against the imposition of certain conditions of bail. The conditions which may be challenged in this way are requirements relating to the provision of a surety or giving a security, curfew, electronic monitoring, residence, or contact. Section 17 removed the power which the High Court had up until then to deal with such appeals, abolishing the jurisdiction of the High Court in respect of bail where it duplicated that of the Crown Court.

7.53   The procedure for applying to the Crown Court for bail is to serve written notice on the prosecutor of intention to make the application (Criminal Procedure Rules 2005, r 19.18). The notice must be served at least 24 hours before the application. The prosecutor must then do one of three things. He may either notify the appropriate officer of the Crown Court and the defendant that he wishes to be represented at the hearing of the application, or he may give notice that he does not oppose the application, or he may give to the appropriate officer, for the consideration of the Crown Court, a written statement of his reasons for opposing the application. A copy of the written statement must be sent to the defendant. Although he may be given leave to attend the hearing of the application, the defendant has no right to be present. If bail is granted subject to the provision of sureties, they may enter into their recognizances before an appropriate officer of the Crown Court or before any of the persons who may take a surety following a grant of bail by magistrates (see 7.42 to 7.44).

The above procedure is not applicable where a bail application is made during the course of **7.54** the Crown Court proceedings (e.g. for bail during the period of an overnight adjournment). Such applications are made without notice to the judge trying the case. As a matter of practice, counsel waits for the jury to leave court before making the application.

Prosecution appeals against bail   *See 8AQ*

The Bail (Amendment) Act 1993 confers upon the prosecution the right to appeal to the **7.55** Crown Court against a decision by magistrates to grant bail. It is limited cases where:

(a) the offence is imprisonable; and

(b) the prosecution is conducted by the CPS, or by certain designated public prosecutors prescribed by statutory instrument; and

(c) the prosecution made representations against bail before it was granted.

The 1993 Act lays down procedural requirements with which the prosecution must comply in **7.56** order to exercise their right. They must give oral notice of appeal at the conclusion of the proceedings in which bail was granted, and before the defendant is released from custody. This notice must be confirmed in writing within two hours after proceedings end; otherwise the appeal is deemed to be disposed of. Pending appeal, the magistrates must remand the defendant in custody. The Crown Court, for its part, must hear the appeal within 48 hours (excluding weekends and public holidays). The appeal takes place by way of rehearing in the usual way and the judge may then remand the defendant in custody or grant bail with or without conditions.

This right to appeal against the grant of bail is distinct from the review of bail at the instance **7.57** of the prosecution (see 7.48). It is triggered off immediately after the magistrates have decided to grant bail (whereas the power to review may take place some considerable time thereafter). The conditions for the exercise of the right to appeal are also somewhat different. Crucially, moreover, where the procedure under the Bail (Amendment) Act 1993 is used, the accused is kept in custody until the appeal is heard (whereas with the review procedure the accused will typically be at large).

G   CONSEQUENCES OF A DEFENDANT ABSCONDING

If a defendant who has been granted bail fails to surrender to custody at the appointed time **7.58** and place, three questions arise for the court's consideration. There is the immediate question of how to secure the defendant's attendance before the court, and there are the further questions of how to deal with him for his breach of bail and how to deal with any sureties for breach of their recognizances.

Prior to discussing these questions, it is necessary to consider just what is meant by 'failing to **7.59** surrender to custody'. According to *DPP v Richards* [1988] QB 701, it means complying with whatever procedure the court prescribes for those answering to their bail. If the court operates a procedure whereby persons bailed are required to report to an usher, and are then allowed to wait in the court precincts until their case is called, a person who so reports has surrendered to custody. If he then goes away before the court calls his case, he has not absconded within the meaning of s 6 of the Bail Act 1976. (Note, however, that in these circumstances the court is entitled to issue a warrant under s 7(2) of the Act—see 7.60 to 7.62.)

Powers in respect of an absconder

7.60 Section 7(1) of the Bail Act 1976 provides that if a defendant has been bailed to appear before a court and fails to do so, the court before which he should have appeared may issue a warrant for his arrest. This is known as a bench warrant. Although it could be endorsed for bail, it is unlikely that the court would want to take the risk of the defendant again absconding.

7.61 In the circumstances which arose in *DPP v Richards* [1988] QB 701, s 7(2) can be invoked. This provides that, where a person on bail absents himself at any time after he has surrendered to custody but before the court is ready to hear the case, then the court may issue a warrant for his arrest. Where a person was arrested without warrant and bailed by the police to appear back at the police station, s 7 does not apply, but should the person fail to answer to his bail, the police will have power to arrest him without warrant (s 46A of PACE).

7.62 In order to prevent possible breaches of bail, a police officer may arrest without warrant a defendant whom he reasonably believes is unlikely to surrender to custody: s 7(3). The power only applies if the defendant was bailed to surrender to the custody of a court. A police officer also has power to arrest a defendant whom he reasonably suspects of having broken, or reasonably believes will break, a condition of his bail. Thus, if it was a condition of bail that the defendant report to a police station, and he fails to report, he may forthwith be arrested without warrant. Similarly, if a surety notifies the police in writing that the defendant is unlikely to surrender to custody and that he (the surety) therefore wishes to be relieved of his obligations, the defendant may be arrested. A defendant who is arrested for suspected or anticipated breach of bail must be brought before a magistrate as soon as practicable and, in any event, within 24 hours of arrest (unless he was to have surrendered to custody within 24 hours in which case he is brought before the appropriate court). If the magistrate is of the opinion that the defendant has broken or is likely to break any condition of his bail, or is not likely to surrender to custody, he may remand him in or commit him to custody, or impose more stringent conditions of bail. Otherwise, he must release him on bail on the same conditions, if any, as were originally imposed.

7.63 The CJA 2003, s 15(1) and (2) apply to cases where the offence carries a maximum sentence of life imprisonment and lay down that the court must refuse bail to an adult defendant who failed without reasonable cause to surrender to custody in answer to bail in the same proceedings, unless it is satisfied that there is no significant risk that he would so fail if released. In the case of a defendant under 18, the court must give particular weight to the fact that they have failed to surrender to bail in assessing the risk of future absconding.

The offence of absconding

7.64 In 1976 the Bail Act created a new offence of *absconding*. Section 6(1) provides that:

if a person who has been released on bail in criminal proceedings fails without reasonable cause to surrender to custody he shall be guilty of an offence.

Similarly, an offence is committed if, having had reasonable cause for not surrendering at the time he should have done, the accused then fails to surrender as soon thereafter as is reasonably practicable (s 6(2)). An offence may be committed under s 6 even though the accused is acquitted of the offences that formed the subject matter of the proceedings in respect of which bail was granted. Moreover, it is always for him to prove, on a balance of probabilities, that he had reasonable cause for not surrendering when he ought.

7.65 Section 6 prescribes three methods by which an accused may be prosecuted and sentenced for an offence of absconding. First, he may be tried summarily for the offence and sentenced by the magistrates to up to three months' imprisonment and/or a £5,000 fine. Although the Act appears to contemplate summary trial as a possibility even when the offence consisted in failure to surrender to the custody of the Crown Court, judicial interpretation of s 6 has subsequently decreed that magistrates should deal only with failure to attend at their own court.

7.66 Secondly, following summary conviction for a s 6 offence, the magistrates may commit the offender to the Crown Court to be sentenced if *either:*

(i) they consider their own powers of punishment to be inadequate; *or*
(ii) they are committing the offender for trial in respect of an indictable offence and they consider it preferable that the Crown Court should sentence him both for the absconding and (should he be convicted) the other offence.

The Crown Court's powers of sentence upon such a committal are 12 months' imprisonment and/or an unlimited fine.

7.67 Thirdly, failure to answer bail at the Crown Court can and should be dealt with by that court as if it were a criminal contempt. This means that the Crown Court judge 'tries' the accused without empanelling a jury. The enquiry is semi-informal with the judge adopting whatever rules of procedure or evidence appear to him appropriate for giving the accused a fair hearing. If convicted, the accused is liable to the same penalties as if he had been committed for sentence for the offence following summary conviction (see above).

7.68 Whether an alleged offence of absconding is tried summarily or dealt with as if it were a criminal contempt, the only issue likely to be in dispute is whether the accused had reasonable cause for failure to surrender. The actual non-appearance can be established from the court records which are virtually incontrovertible.

7.69 The nature of the offence of absconding and the correct procedure for dealing with it were analyzed in some depth by Watkins LJ in *Schiavo v Anderton* [1987] QB 20. Some minor clarifications of the judgment are contained in Practice Direction (*Criminal Proceedings: Consolidation*) [2002] 1 WLR 2870, part 1, para 13). The effect of the judgment and Direction are summarized in the following propositions, which apply to bail granted by a court, rather than police bail.

(i) The offence of absconding is *sui generis* in the sense that it is neither summary nor triable either way, and the normal rules about commencing prosecutions by the laying of an information do not apply.

(ii) The offence should *invariably* be tried in the court at which the substantive proceedings in respect of which bail was granted have been or are to be heard. Thus, if an accused was remanded on bail prior to committal proceedings or summary trial, any alleged failure to answer to bail should be heard by the magistrates as the substantive proceedings (i.e., the committal or trial) are in their court. If, on the other hand, there was a committal for trial on bail, the Crown Court is obliged to deal with non-appearance as a criminal contempt. Contrary to earlier suggestions, it would never be right for the Crown Court to remit such a case to the magistrates for summary trial. The rule that magistrates should try summarily allegations of failing to appear before their court is, of course, without prejudice to their power to convict and then commit for sentence in the circumstances already described.

(iii) Since absconding is 'tantamount to the defiance of a court order', it is normally more appropriate for the court to initiate proceedings on its own motion without waiting for any formal information or charge to be preferred. However, the court should not act except upon the invitation of the prosecutor, who should consider whether proceedings are necessary or desirable in the light of factors such as the seriousness of the failure to appear and any explanations advanced by the accused. However, in practice in the magistrates' court the bench often asks the absconder why he did not appear. If his answer is satisfactory, no further action is taken. If it is not, the charge is put to the accused by the clerk.

(iv) According to the *Practice Direction* (para I.13.5) the courts should no longer automatically defer dealing with the offender for failing to surrender until the conclusion of the proceedings in respect of which bail was granted. Instead, they should deal with him as soon as practicable, taking into account the seriousness of the original offence, the likely penalty for breach of bail, and any other relevant factors. If the disposal of the bail offence is deferred, it is necessary, in the event that the accused is found guilty, to consider imposing a separate penalty, which will normally be custodial and consecutive to any other custodial sentence. In addition, bail will usually (but not invariably) be revoked in the meantime. If the original offence is unlikely to result in a custodial sentence, then trial in the absence of the defendant may be the pragmatic solution.

(v) If the accused denies absconding, the prosecution should conduct the proceedings and call the evidence in the normal way, notwithstanding that the proceedings are, in a sense, initiated by the court (see (iii) above). But, since proof of the actual failure to surrender to custody will come from the court's own records, the role of the prosecution representatives is likely to be confined to cross-examining the accused about any reason for non-appearance which he puts forward.

7.70 As far as police bail is concerned, the failure to surrender cannot be said to be in defiance of a court order. There is therefore no compelling reason for the court to act of its own motion, and any failure to surrender should be dealt with by charging the accused or laying an information.

7.71 The CJA 2003, s 15(3), which came into effect in April 2004, disapplied s 127 of the MCA 1980 (which prevents summary proceedings from being instituted more than six months after the commission of an offence) in respect of offences under s 6 of the Bail Act. It provides that such an offence may not be tried unless an information is laid either within six months of the commission of the offence, or within three months of the defendant's surrender to custody, arrest, or court appearance in respect of that offence. This will ensure that a defendant does not evade prosecution for absconding merely by keeping out of the way for more than six months.

Estreating a surety's recognizance

Where bail was granted subject to a surety being provided, and the defendant absconds, the **7.72** court before which he was due to appear must:

(a) order that the recognizance of the surety be estreated (i.e., that he has to pay the sum in which he stood surety); and

(b) issue a summons to the surety requiring him to appear before the court to show cause why he should not be ordered to pay the sum promised

(MCA, s 120, as amended by the Crime and Disorder Act, s 55). The court should then consider the means of the surety, and the extent to which he was to blame for the defendant absconding—e.g., did he, on first having reason to suspect that the defendant would abscond, give written notice to the police and ask to be relieved of his obligations as a surety? Failure to consider these matters may lead to the quashing of a decision by magistrates to forfeit a recognizance: *Southampton Justices ex parte Green* [1976] QB 11. However, the presumption is that the defendant's absconding will lead to the surety having to pay the whole sum in which he stood surety. As it was put in *Horseferry Road Magistrates' Court ex parte Pearson* [1976] 2 All ER 264:

> The surety has seriously entered into a serious obligation and ought to pay the amount which he or she has promised unless there are circumstances in the case, relating either to means or culpability, which make it fair and just to pay a smaller sum.

The above principles have been confirmed in numerous more recent cases, including *Uxbridge* **7.73** *Justices ex parte Heward-Mills* [1983] 1 WLR 56 and *Warwick Crown Court ex parte Smalley* [1987] 1 WLR 237. *York Crown Court ex parte Coleman and How* [1987] Crim LR 761 provides an example of the kind of exceptional case in which it is unfair to forfeit the whole recognizance. C and H stood surety for C's son who had been committed for trial at York Crown Court. They telephoned him at regular intervals to remind him of the trial; they arranged for other relatives to accompany him to court on the actual day; and they received a message that he had arrived. Unfortunately, the case could not commence until the afternoon and, during the wait, the accused's nerve broke and he absconded. The Divisional Court held that C and H had done everything they practically could to secure proper surrender to custody and so should not have lost the entire amount of their recognizances. However, May LJ stressed what had earlier been said by McCullough J in *Ex parte Heward-Mills* (above), namely that 'the burden of satisfying the court that the full sum should not be forfeited rests on the surety *and is a heavy one*'.

The point was underlined in *Maidstone Crown Court ex parte Lever* (1994) *The Times*, 7 November **7.74** 1994, where the remarks of Lord Widgery CJ in *Southampton Justices ex parte Corker* (1976) 120 SJ 214 were quoted with approval:

> The real pull of bail ... is that it may cause the offender to attend his trial rather than subject his nearest and dearest who had gone surety for him to pain and discomfort.

The surety's obligation is extinguished once the defendant surrenders to the court. After such **7.75** surrender, the surety is no longer at any risk of being estreated (unless, of course, the surety is renewed). In *Central Criminal Court ex parte Guney* [1996] AC 616, the House of Lords held that, where a defendant was formally arraigned, the arraignment amounted to a surrender to the custody of the court, so as to extinguish the liability of the surety. Neither the agreement of the parties nor the order of the judge could deprive arraignment of its legal effect.

H   DETENTION OF A DEFENDANT WHEN BAIL IS REFUSED

7.76   The arrangements for detaining a defendant who is refused bail are as follows:

(a) If he has attained the age of 21, he is committed to prison.

(b) If he is aged 17 to 20 inclusive he is committed to a remand centre, provided that one is available 'for the reception from the court of persons of his class or description': Criminal Justice Act 1948, s 27. If a remand centre is not available he is committed to prison.

(c) If he is under 17 he is committed to the care of a local authority: Children and Young Persons Act 1969, s 23.

(d) By the Children and Young Persons Act 1969 (CYPA), s 23, courts have additional powers to remand children between 12 and 16, to local authority secure accommodation. For remand to secure accommodation, the following conditions must be satisfied:

> (a) the juvenile must be charged with, or have been convicted of:
>
> > (i)   a violent or sexual offence, or
> >
> > (ii) an offence punishable in the case of an adult with 14 or more years in prison, or
> >
> > (iii) one or more imprisonable offences amounting to a 'recent history of repeatedly committing imprisonable offences while remanded on bail or to local authority accommodation';
>
> and
>
> (b) the court must be of the opinion that only a remand to secure accommodation would be adequate to protect the public from serious harm from him, or to prevent the commission by him of imprisonable offences.

7.77   When a magistrates' court has power to remand a defendant in custody it may instead commit him to police detention for a period not exceeding three days (24 hours in the case of a juvenile: CYPA, s 23(14)), provided that is necessary for the purpose of inquiries into offences other than the one charged: MCA 1980, s 128(7). As soon as the inquiries have been completed the defendant must be brought back before the magistrates, who will either bail him or, more probably, remand him in custody to prison or remand centre. Whilst in police detention, he is entitled to the same safeguards as is an ordinary arrestee (e.g., there must be periodic reviews of the propriety of continuing to detain him). Presumably, if the offences to which the inquiries relate are not serious arrestable ones, he should be charged or brought back before the magistrates within 24 hours, since an ordinary arrestee suspected of a non-serious offence would have to be released or charged within that period (see 3.25). However, s 128 is not clear on the point.

KEY DOCUMENTS

Bail Act 1976, as amended.

Forms relating to Bail, contained in annex D of the *Practice Direction* (*Criminal Proceedings: Consolidation*) [2002] 1 WLR 2870 and available at: <http://www.hmcourts-service.gov.uk>.

Part 19 of the Criminal Procedure Rules 2005, available on the website of the Ministry of Justice: <http://www.justice.gov.uk/criminal/procrules_fin/index.htm>.

8

MODE OF TRIAL

A CLASSIFICATION OF OFFENCES

An offence is either summary or indictable (see 1.07 to 1.09). An indictable offence is one   **8.01**
for which an adult either must or may be tried on indictment; a summary offence is one
which must be tried summarily: Interpretation Act 1978, Sch 1. As the definition of indictable
offence implies, some are only triable on indictment and some may be tried either on indictment or summarily. The latter are known as offences triable either way.

Summary offences

Summary offences are all statutory. The statute creating a summary offence shows that it is   **8.02**
summary by specifying a maximum penalty which may be imposed on summary conviction

without specifying a second greater penalty for offenders convicted on indictment. For example, s 89(1) of the Police Act 1996, as amended, provides that:

> any person who assaults a constable in the execution of his duty…shall be guilty of an offence and liable on *summary* conviction to imprisonment for a term not exceeding six months or to a fine not exceeding the amount at level 5 on the standard scale, or to both.

Since s 89(1) does not mention a penalty imposable following conviction on indictment, the offence of assaulting a constable in the execution of his duty is summary.

8.03   A vast number of minor and occasionally not so minor offences are summary. They include dropping litter, not paying the TV licence fee, offences under the Food and Drugs Act 1955 (e.g., selling food that is unfit for human consumption), offences under the Factories Act 1961 (e.g., not maintaining machinery in a safe condition), travelling on the railway without a ticket and almost all road traffic offences (e.g., careless driving, speeding, going through red lights, defective brakes, tyres, etc., failing to report an accident, no insurance and many more). Among the most serious summary offences are using threatening words or behaviour contrary to s 4 of the Public Order Act 1986, drink/driving offences contrary to ss 4 to 7 of the Road Traffic Act 1988, interference with a motor vehicle contrary to s 9 of the Criminal Attempts Act 1981, and assaulting a constable in the execution of his duty. In addition, ss 37 and 39 of the Criminal Justice Act 1988 made summary three offences which were formerly triable either way, namely taking a motor vehicle without the owner's consent, driving while disqualified, and common assault. All the offences mentioned in the last two sentences carry six months' imprisonment, except motor vehicle interference which carries only three.

8.04   When the provisions in Sch 26 of the CJA 2003 are brought into effect, the maximum sentence for a number of summary offences and offences triable either way, tried summarily, will be raised to 51 weeks. This is to fit in with the introduction of the new sentence of 'custody plus' (see Chapter 24). At the time of writing, these changes had not been implemented.

Indictable offences

8.05   All common law offences (e.g., murder, manslaughter, and conspiracy to defraud or corrupt public morals) are indictable. Statutory offences are indictable if the statute creating the offence specifies a penalty to be imposed following conviction on indictment. For example, the Theft Act 1968 shows that robbery is an indictable offence by providing, in s 8(2), that 'a person guilty of robbery…shall on *conviction on indictment* be liable to imprisonment for life'. Where a statute creating an offence provides for two separate penalties, one to be imposed on summary conviction and the other on conviction on indictment, the offence created is indictable but triable either way. An example is dangerous driving which is punishable on summary conviction with six months' imprisonment and a £5,000 fine and punishable on conviction on indictment with two years' imprisonment and an unlimited fine. It should be noted, however, that many offences are triable either way even though the statute creating them does not itself provide for a penalty on summary conviction (see below). Theft, for example, may be tried summarily, but there is no indication to that effect in s 7 of the Theft Act.

Offences triable either way

Offences triable either way fall into two groups. They are either, like dangerous driving, made **8.06** triable either way by the statute creating them, or they are included in Sch 1 to the Magistrates' Courts Act 1980, s 17 of which provides that 'the offences listed in Schedule 1 . . . shall be triable either way'. *look up the schedule*

As one would expect, the most serious offences are triable only on indictment. Offences triable **8.07** either way tend to be those which, although serious enough to be indictable, are never, even at worst, very grave (e.g. dangerous driving or taking a motor vehicle without consent), and those which vary greatly in gravity depending upon the facts of the particular case (e.g. criminal damage or theft). The table below lists some of the most common indictable offences according to whether they are triable only on indictment or triable either way.

Nature of offence	Triable only on indictment	Triable either way
Offences against the person	Murder, manslaughter, child destruction, attempt to procure abortion, causing grievous bodily harm with intent to do so.	Inflicting grievous bodily harm, unlawful wounding, assault occasioning actual bodily harm, assault with intent to resist arrest.
Sexual offences	Rape, assault by penetration	Sexual assault, controlling prostitution for gain.
Offences under the Theft Acts 1968 and 1978	Robbery, aggravated burglary, blackmail, assault with intent to rob, burglary in a dwelling if any person therein was subjected to violence or the threat of it.	All offences under the Acts apart from those which are triable only on indictment and taking a motor vehicle or pedal cycle which are summary. They include theft, handling stolen goods, obtaining property by deception, most forms of burglary, going equipped, obtaining services by deception.
Criminal damage	Arson or damage charged under s 1(2) of the Criminal Damage Act 1971 (offence committed with intent to endanger life or being reckless as to the endangering of life).	Criminal damage offences where no intent etc. to endanger life is alleged.

(Continued)

Nature of offence	Triable only on indictment	Triable either way
Road traffic offences	Causing death by dangerous driving.	Dangerous driving.
Miscellaneous offences	Perjury in judicial proceedings contrary to s 1 of the Perjury Act 1911; attempt to pervert the course of justice; collecting, communicating etc. information intended to be useful to an enemy contrary to s 1 of the Official Secrets Act 1911; possessing firearm with intent to endanger life, using firearm to resist arrest, and carrying firearm to commit indictable offence; riot contrary to s 1 of the Public Order Act 1986; assisting an offender contrary to s 4 of the Criminal Law Act 1967 if the offence of the person assisted was triable only on indictment.	Making false statements on oath otherwise than in a judicial proceeding and making certain other false statements or declarations contrary to ss 2–6 of the Perjury Act 1911; having an offensive weapon in a public place; violent disorder, affray and stirring up racial hatred contrary to ss 2, 3, and 18 of the Public Order Act 1986; all offences of possessing, supplying, cultivating, etc. controlled drugs contrary controlled drugs contrary Act 1971 (apart from a few minor ones which are summary).

Attempts and incitement to commit offences triable either way are themselves triable either way, but conspiracy is only triable on indictment.

8.08 Leaving aside road traffic offences and minor summary offences carrying no real social stigma, the offences which occur most frequently are triable either way. Therefore, how one decides the mode of trial for these offences is a question of major importance.

B   ADVANCE INFORMATION

8.09 The accused plays an important part in determining the mode of trial process, with the right to elect Crown Court trial for an offence which is triable either way. In order to exercise that election on an informed basis, it is necessary that the accused should be aware of the evidence which the prosecution relies upon. One of the reasons why this awareness is important is that the prosecution is obliged to reveal information about its evidence prior to committal for trial in the the Crown Court. If the accused does not know the strength of the prosecution case, there will be a temptation to elect Crown Court trial, in order to discover it. As a result, rules were introduced in 1985 to allow the defence the right to a measure of advance information about the prosecution case. It is important to distinguish this right to advance information (which is set out in the remainder of this Section) from the rules relating to disclosure of unused information by the prosecution (which are detailed in Chapter 9). We are here dealing with information about evidence which the prosecution *intend* to call. The prosecution's duty of disclosure relates to evidence which they do *not intend* to call.

The rules relating to advance information are now set out in the Criminal Procedure Rules **8.10** 2005, Part 21. They provide that, if the accused is charged with an offence triable either way, the prosecution must upon request provide the defence *either* with copies of the prosecution witnesses' written statements *or* with a summary of the facts and matters about which evidence will be adduced during the course of the prosecution case (r 21.3(1)). A request for advance information should be made before the proceedings to determine the mode of trial (see 8.16) and should be complied with as soon as practicable. Knowledge of the prosecution case is intended to assist the defence in deciding where the case should be dealt with, and to remove the temptation (which formerly existed) to elect trial on indictment as a tactical ploy to get a sight of the prosecution evidence, after which the court was asked to allow the election to be withdrawn. So that the accused will know of his rights, a notice explaining the advance information rules has to be given to him as soon as possible after he has been charged with/summoned for an either-way matter (r 21.2). In addition, the magistrates must satisfy themselves that the accused is aware that he can request advance information before they go on to consider mode of trial (r 21.5). The only situation where the prosecution may properly refuse such a request is if they fear that complying with it might lead to the intimidation of witnesses or other attempts to interfere with the course of justice (r 21.4). Except when r 21.4 applies, failure to comply with such a request will necessitate the adjournment of the proceedings (unless the court is satisfied that the defence will not be prejudiced by the non-compliance: r 21.6).

The prosecutor ought to be able to comply with any request for advance information **8.11** either before or at the first hearing where an accused is charged with an either way offence (para 1.4 of the Protocol for the Provision of Advance Information, Prosecution Evidence and Disclosure of Unused Material in the Magistrates' Courts—May 2006). Defence advocates are then expected to go through that material with the accused and advise on plea and venue at that hearing. The court can then proceed to deal with mode of trial. Where the case is a complex one or the documents substantial, then the case can either be put back in the list to be dealt with later on the same day or an adjournment can be granted.

What the prosecution give by way of advance information varies considerably from one area **8.12** of the CPS to another. Some serve typed copies of the prosecution witnesses' statements, which are virtually the same as would be served for purposes of a committal under s 6(2) of the Magistrates' Courts Act 1980; others give photocopies of handwritten statements and of the police officers' notebooks; yet others serve a copy of the summary of the case that is sent to the CPS by the police, together with copies of the notes of any interview with the accused at the police station. Where the defence consider the advance information to be inadequate, they can apply to the justices to rectify the situation. The justices have no power under the Magistrates' Courts (Advance Information) Rules 1985 to order that the prosecution provide further information, but they can have recourse to their power to adjourn under the Magistrates' Courts Act 1980, s 10, if they agree that the information has been inadequate (*Dunmow Justices ex parte Nash* (1993) *The Times*, 17 May 1993).

The Advance Information Rules apply only to either-way offences. As regards summary **8.13** offences, the defence still have no legal right to know the prosecution case prior to trial although defence solicitors frequently request it. Of course, some summary offences both carry imprisonment and are quite likely in practice to be dealt with by a custodial sentence (e.g. assaulting a police officer, taking a motor vehicle without the owner's consent, and driving while disqualified). Guidelines issued by the Attorney-General therefore require advance provision to the defence of all proposed prosecution evidence 'in sufficient time' to allow proper consideration of it before it is called (*Attorney-General's Guidelines. Disclosure of Information in Criminal Proceedings*, para 57). This is likely to ensure that the hearing concentrates upon the issues, and that the court's time is not wasted while the defence representative obtains instructions from the accused. It also appears to be within the spirit of the prosecutor's general duty not to 'attempt to obtain a conviction by all means at his command' nor to 'regard himself as appearing for a party' (see the Code of Conduct of the Bar, annexe F, standards applicable to criminal cases, para 11.1).

8.14   In *Stratford Justices ex parte Imbert* [1999] 2 Cr App R 276, the Divisional Court considered whether this lack of a legal obligation upon the prosecution is a violation of Art 6(3)(a) of the European Convention on Human Rights (ECHR) 'to be informed promptly...and in detail, of the nature and cause of the accusation against him...'. The Divisional Court held that it was not, although their lordships recognized that their decision was clearly obiter.

8.15   It is submitted that the absence of advance information might in certain circumstances be a violation of Art 6(3)(b), which lays down the right 'to have adequate time and facilities for his defence', as well as a violation of Art 6(3)(a). In order that the trial should be fair, it is necessary that the defence should be able to consider the prosecution evidence, and prepare upon the basis of knowledge rather than guesswork. Sometimes the nature of that evidence will be predictable, and the defence advocate will be able to respond with the necessary agility of thought. But in other instances, the defence may be ambushed by an unexpected line of evidence. Overall, it may be that what is generally recognized as good practice (the provision of the statements of prosecution witnesses in summary trials) should also be regarded as part of the rights provided by the European Convention on Human Rights.

C   DETERMINING MODE OF TRIAL

8.16   The procedure for determining whether an adult charged with an offence triable either way shall be tried on indictment or summarily is contained in ss 18–21 and 23 of the Magistrates' Courts Act 1980. It must be carried out before any evidence is called for purposes of committal proceedings or summary trial: s 18(2). It may take place before a single magistrate (s 18(5)), but it is more usual for the court to consist of at least two lay justices (or, of course, a district judge). Depending on the outcome of the procedure, the court may, upon its completion, have to adjourn either for preparation of the prosecution statements for committal to the Crown Court or for the attendance of witnesses for a summary trial. If, however, the accused pleads guilty, the magistrates may be able to proceed to sentence forthwith. When s 41 and Sch 3 of the CJA 2003 are brought into effect (no date had been set at the time of writing) the procedure described below will be substantially altered. The changes are summarized at 8.48 below. The following are the main steps in the procedure for determining mode of trial (they are set out in flowchart form on page 126):

(a)   The clerk to the justices reads the charge to the accused;

(b)   The clerk then explains that the accused may indicate whether he would plead guilty if the case proceeded to trial. The clerk should further explain that, if the accused pleads guilty, the proceedings will be treated as a summary trial at which a guilty plea has been tendered. The clerk must also explain that the accused will be committed to the Crown Court for sentence if the magistrates regard their powers of punishment as inadequate.

(c)   The clerk asks the accused if he would plead guilty or not guilty if the offence went to trial.

Steps (a) to (c), taken together, constitute the 'plea before venue' procedure. If the accused has indicated a plea of guilty, then the court proceeds as if he had pleaded guilty at summary trial. If, on the other hand, the accused indicated a plea of not guilty, then the court proceeds to determine the mode of trial, as follows:

(i)   First the prosecution and then the defence are given the opportunity to make representations as to whether trial on indictment or summary trial would be the more suitable method of trial: s 19(2)(b). The factors relevant to that question, to which the prosecution or defence might refer in their representations, are indicated in (ii) below.

(ii)   The magistrates consider which of the two methods of trial is the more suitable. They must bear in mind the representations, if any, made by the prosecution and defence, and they must have regard to the nature of the case, whether the circumstances make the offence one of serious character, whether the punishment which a magistrates' court would have power to inflict for it would be adequate, and any other circumstances which make the case more suitable for one method of trial rather than the other: s 19(3).

(iii)   If the magistrates consider that the offence is more suitable for summary trial, the court clerk tells the accused that the magistrates have taken that view. He then informs him that he may, if he consents, be tried by the magistrates, but that if he wishes he can choose to be tried by a jury instead. However, if he is tried by the magistrates and found guilty and if the magistrates consider that greater punishment should be imposed than they have power to inflict, they may send him to the Crown Court to be sentenced. The clerk then puts the accused to his election—he asks 'Do you wish to be tried by this court or do you wish to be tried by a jury?' If, and only if, the accused consents, the magistrates proceed to summary trial with the accused pleading guilty or not guilty to the charge against him. If the accused does not consent to summary trial, committal proceedings must be held: s 20.

(iv)   If the magistrates consider that trial on indictment is more appropriate, the accused is told of their decision, and the case will be sent to the Crown Court: s 21.

The essence of the procedure laid down in ss 18–21 is that there can be a summary trial for an   **8.17**
offence triable either way only if both the magistrates and the accused agree to it. Of the matters mentioned in s 19(3) to which the magistrates must pay regard in considering the more suitable method of trial by far the most important is whether, in the event of a conviction, they would be able to inflict adequate punishment. In brief, the maximum penalties they can impose are: six months' imprisonment and/or a fine of £5,000 for any one offence triable either way; for two or more such offences, an aggregate prison term of 12 months and/or fines of £5,000 per offence. In deciding whether those powers would be sufficient to deal with the accused should he be convicted, the magistrates will look first at what the wording of the charge itself reveals about the gravity of the offence. For example, a charge of theft will list the

items stolen; that will give a rough idea of the value involved in the offence, which, in turn, is a very rough guide to the appropriate level of penalty. Other charges are worded less informatively. Thus, a charge of unlawful wounding will not specify whether the victim suffered merely a slight graze or a deep stab-wound. In such cases, the magistrates should seek extra information from the parties (especially the prosecution) about the nature of the allegations. Of course, the parties may volunteer such information unasked in the representations they make about the more suitable method of trial. Magistrates should also be aware that a charge which, on the face of it, seems fairly minor may be rendered far more serious by the circumstances surrounding the offence (e.g., a charge of theft of £100 seems prima facie well within the magistrates' proper jurisdiction, but if the offence was committed by an employee stealing in the course of his employment, the aggravating element of a breach of trust might make the matter more suitable for the Crown Court). It is open to the prosecution to mention any such aggravating features to the magistrates—indeed, they might properly be criticized for failing to do so. One aggravating feature of which the magistrates must, however, remain unaware is the bad character of the accused. Where he has previous convictions, that must *not* be revealed to

Figure 8.1 Mode of Trial

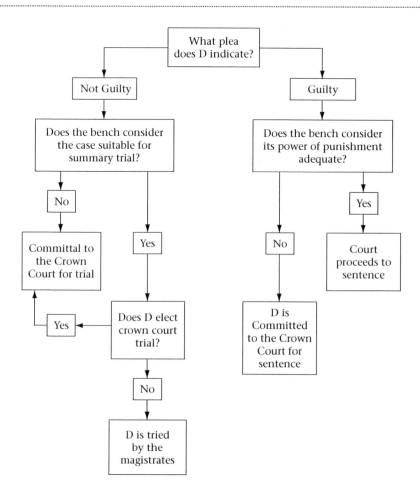

the court at the stage of determining the mode of trial (*Colchester Justices ex parte North East Essex Building Co Ltd* [1977] 1 WLR 1109—but this is set to change when s 41 and Sch 3 of the CJA 2003 come into force). Thus, the question the magistrates have to answer may be reduced to this: assuming the accused to be of good character, and bearing in mind what we know about the gravity of the offence from (a) the wording of the charge and (b) any additional information about the prosecution case and the circumstances of the crime given to us in the course of the parties' representations, would six months' imprisonment and a £5,000 fine be a sufficiently severe punishment should we agree to summary trial and convict? If the answer to that question is no, the magistrates ought to opt for Crown Court trial, however strongly one or both parties may argue in favour of summary trial. If the answer is yes, then summary trial will normally be the more suitable method, but occasionally other factors (e.g., the potential complexity of the legal issues involved or the fact that the accused is a well-known public figure who would suffer greatly from conviction even for a minor crime) may still tip the scales in favour of trial on indictment.

The decision which the magistrates make has an important bearing on the efficient administration of justice. If they accept jurisdiction in respect of a case which really ought to go to the Crown Court, then, because of the limits on their powers, there is a danger that the sentence passed will be inadequate. On the other hand, if they err on the side of caution by committing too many cases to the Crown Court, it will lead to delays, both in the cases referred, and in the others with which the Crown Court has to deal. The potential extent of the problem is considerable. In the year 2004/5, of the cases which went to the Crown Court for trial, some 54 per cent went on the magistrates' direction, 40 per cent were indictable only, and only 6 per cent went on the accused's election (*Annual Report of the Crown Prosecution Service*, TSO). The proportion sent on the magistrates' direction has been increasing over the past few years. Further, an influential Home Office study has shown that, in the sample analysed, in some 60 per cent of the cases committed by magistrates to the Crown Court for trial, the sentence eventually imposed by the Crown Court would have been within the powers of the magistrates. **8.18**

Guidance to magistrates is now contained in the *Practice Direction (Criminal Proceedings: Consolidation)* [2002] 1 WLR 2870 para 51, which is reproduced in Appendix 1. **8.19**

It states the general principles and it then goes on to enumerate certain of the common either-way offences, indicating the factors which will make them more appropriate for the Crown Court. In view of the importance of the Guidelines, they are reproduced in full as Appendix 1. **8.20**

One of the stated principles deals with the problem which arises where two or more accused are jointly charged and one (or more) wants summary trial, while the other(s) want trial on indictment. Frequently co-defendants differ in their intentions in this way, with one wanting summary trial (usually prior to pleading guilty) and the other seeking jury trial with a view to contesting the matter fully. In this situation, are the magistrates entitled, when deciding whether to accept jurisdiction, to take into account the fact that, in respect of one accused at least, the case will have to go to the Crown Court? In *Brentwood Justices ex parte Nicholls* [1992] 1 AC 1, the House of Lords held, in effect, that, in these circumstances, the court should not be influenced by the fact that one of the accused was electing Crown Court trial. Hence, they should proceed to try summarily the accused who elected summary trial, and should hold committal proceedings in respect of the accused who elected trial on **8.21** indictment. The reason is that s 20(3) gives the right of election as to mode of trial to each accused individually, and not to all accused collectively. As a result, point 51.3(e) in the Guidance states: 'where two or more defendants are jointly charged with an offence each has an individual right to elect his mode of trial'.

8.22 Except as mentioned below, the prosecution cannot insist upon trial on indictment. Their views on the appropriate method of trial are, however, given great weight by the magistrates, who may feel that the police are the people in the best position to know how serious the alleged offence is. Therefore, if the prosecution are content with summary trial, and the defence indicate that the accused wishes to opt for summary trial, the magistrates may, in practice, agree without enquiring minutely into whether their sentencing powers will be adequate. Conversely, if the prosecution wish to go for trial on indictment, the defence may have a difficult task in persuading the magistrates that the matter is suitable for them to deal with. Moreover, if the prosecution is being carried on by the Attorney-General, Solicitor General, or Director of Public Prosecutions, and he applies for trial on indictment, the magistrates *must* comply with his wishes and hold committal proceedings: s 19(4). This is subject to the proviso that the DPP may make such an application only if he has the consent of the AG: s 19(5). There would have to be something very unusual about a case for the DPP to think it right to bother the Attorney with a request that he (the DPP) be allowed to make a binding application for trial on indictment.

8.23 Where the prosecution are aggrieved by the magistrates' decision to try the defendant summarily, it is open to them to seek judicial review of that decision in the Divisional Court. They will have an uphill struggle, since the Divisional Court will refuse an application for a quashing order unless the magistrates' decision is so wrong that no reasonable bench could have arrived at it (*McLean ex parte Metropolitan Police Commissioner* [1975] Crim LR 289). Occasionally, however, the Divisional Court will overrule the magistrates, as they did in *Northampton Magistrates' Court ex parte Commissioners of Customs and Excise* [1994] Crim LR 598. In that case, the defendant was charged with a VAT fraud causing loss of over £193,000. The Divisional Court held that the decision to try him summarily measured up to the yardstick which they had to apply in deciding whether to overrule it, in that it was 'truly astonishing'. The unrecovered property was of very high value, the offence was of a serious character, and in the absence of mitigating features a sentence of more than six months could be expected. The Divisional Court allowed the application, and remitted the case to the magistrates to deal with as examining justices.

8.24 In the majority of cases the procedure for determining the mode of trial will not take nearly as long to carry out as it has taken to describe. The prosecutor is asked whether the prosecution desire summary trial. If he says that they do, the defence advocate is invited to comment. He may indicate that the accused also wants the case dealt with summarily. If so, the magistrates will probably agree to summary trial without more ado. Should the charge seem more serious than is normally tried summarily, they may enquire further into how grave the case really is before accepting jurisdiction (e.g., they may ask whether all the property allegedly stolen has been recovered, or whether the victim of an assault has suffered any permanent injury, or whether the accused abused a position of trust in order to commit the offence). Immediately the magistrates have said that they consider summary trial appropriate, the clerk informs the accused of his right to be tried by a jury etc. (see stage (d) of the procedure), and the accused elects summary trial.

Where the prosecution ask for summary trial, but the defence wish the case to go for trial on **8.25** indictment, there is little point in making lengthy representations to show that the case is one fit for the Crown Court, as it cannot in any event be tried by the magistrates unless the accused consents. Accordingly, the defence may make no representations, the magistrates say that they consider summary trial appropriate, and the clerk proceeds to put the accused to his election. Having asked for summary trial, the prosecution cannot be criticized for having inflicted on the public the extra expense of a judge and jury trial. The only situations in which determining the mode of trial is likely to lead to any real argument are where the prosecution say that trial on indictment is appropriate but the defence are anxious that the case stay in the magistrates' court, and where both prosecution and defence are content with summary trial but the magistrates have doubts about the adequacy of their sentencing powers.

Failure to comply with the procedure

The magistrates' jurisdiction to deal with offences triable either way derives solely from ss 18–20 **8.26** of the Magistrates' Courts Act 1980. Therefore, if the procedure set out in those sections is not strictly complied with but the court nevertheless proceeds to try an accused for an offence triable either way, the magistrates act in excess of jurisdiction, and any conviction they pronounce is liable to be quashed by the Divisional Court: *Kent Justices ex parte Machin* [1952] 2 QB 355. In *Machin*, the justices—purporting to act under legislation then in force which was similar in effect to the present ss 18–20—convicted M of larceny and obtaining credit by fraud, and committed him to Quarter Sessions to be sentenced. M's solicitor had said to the magistrates, 'My client wishes you to deal with the case', so there was no doubt that M wanted summary trial. However, the clerk had failed to warn him of the possibility of his being committed for sentence, and for that reason the High Court held that both the conviction and the subsequent committal were nullities which had to be quashed. In *Ashton* [2007] 1 WLR 181, the correctness of the decision in *ex parte Machin* was doubted, the court stating that, where there was a procedural failure as in that case, the appellate court should consider whether Parliament intended subsequent proceedings to be invalid. If they concluded that that was not the intention of Parliament, then they should go on to consider whether there was a real possibility that either party would suffer prejudice. The court concluded that, in the light of the application of this new test, a number of authorities, including *ex parte Machin*, would have to be reconsidered.

Lord Goddard's uncompromising insistence on the need to follow the statutory procedure **8.27** was echoed by Donaldson LJ in *Horseferry Road Justices ex parte Constable* [1981] Crim LR 504, a case where failure to ask C for his representations as to the more appropriate method of trial meant that his original election for summary trial was not binding on him, even though one might have thought that—as he then wanted summary trial—any representations he might have made would only have reinforced the magistrates' opinion that the case was fit for them to deal with. There has also been one instance of non-compliance with the procedure leading to the quashing of a summary *acquittal* (see *Cardiff Magistrates' Court ex parte Cardiff City Council* (1987) *The Times*, 24 February 1987).

Presence of the accused

The accused should normally be present for proceedings under ss 18–21 to determine the **8.28** mode of trial. His presence can be dispensed with, however, in certain circumstances. The court can proceed in his absence if his disorderly conduct makes it impracticable to continue the proceedings in his presence: s 18(3). It can also proceed in his absence if there is a good reason for so doing, and he is represented by counsel or solicitor who states that he (the accused) consents to the proceedings being conducted without him: s 23(1). The 'good reasons' for proceeding without the accused are not limited to reasons of health, but might include the accused having an important prior engagement for the day in question. If the magistrates consider that summary trial is more appropriate, the accused's consent to their dealing with the case can be signified by counsel or solicitor on his behalf. The magistrates could then deal with the case immediately (e.g., if the defence representative has been further authorized to enter a guilty plea) or adjourn to give the accused an opportunity to attend.

Changing the original decisions

8.29   The decision in favour of summary trial or, as the case may be, trial on indictment is not irreversible. If the original decision is for summary trial, the court may, at any stage before the close of the prosecution evidence, discontinue the trial and hold committal proceedings instead: MCA, s 25(2). The evident purpose of the subsection is to allow the magistrates to revise their original affirmative opinion as to the adequacy of their sentencing powers in the light of extra information about the offence emerging during the course of the prosecution case. Once the prosecution have closed their case, the full gravity of what the accused allegedly did will have been revealed, and the magistrates are from that point irretrievably committed to a summary trial. Although s 25(2) does not expressly say so, it applies only when the accused pleads not guilty. This is implied in its referring to the conclusion of the prosecution evidence, since it is only when the accused denies the offence that there will be any such evidence: *Dudley Justices ex parte Gillard* [1986] AC 442. Thus, if the accused agrees to summary trial and pleads guilty, the magistrates are precluded from switching to committal proceedings even if some further development in the case makes them wish they could. A further consequence of the wording of s 25(2) is that, even where the accused has pleaded not guilty to an either-way offence, the magistrates must usually wait until they have actually heard some evidence before withdrawing their acceptance of jurisdiction. The point is illustrated by *St Helens Magistrates' Court ex parte Critchley* [1988] Crim LR 311 where, after C had elected summary trial on two charges and pleaded not guilty, he was further charged with five more offences arising out of the same series of events, and the magistrates at the resumed hearing forthwith decided that he should go to the Crown Court on all seven matters. The High Court held that their decision as regards the original two charges was *ultra vires* since it was only s 25(2) that gave them power to decide to send the case to the Crown Court, and that subsection required them to commence the summary trial. In certain circumstances, however, the power to switch to committal proceedings may commence before the court has begun to hear evidence (e.g., where it has heard submissions on a point of law which has a direct and immediate bearing upon the process of determining the accused's guilt or innocence, such as the availability or otherwise of the defence of insanity in the magistrates' court: *Horseferry Road Magistrates' Court ex parte K* [1996] 3 WLR 68).

8.30   Where the original decision is for trial on indictment, the magistrates may decide that the charge is not as grave as they at first thought, and give the accused the opportunity of having it tried summarily: s 25(3). They must first ask the prosecution and defence for their views on the proposed change, and—if he has not already done so—the clerk must explain to the accused the possibility of his being committed for sentence. Any switch to summary trial is, of course, dependent upon the accused's consent. The magistrates' court can only change its decision from trial on indictment to summary trial *after* it has begun the committal proceedings. In *Liverpool Justices ex parte Crown Prosecution Service, Liverpool* (1989) 90 Cr App R 261, D was charged with reckless driving and a number of other offences. The justices decided on trial on indictment. At a later hearing, a differently constituted bench heard an application from D's solicitor for summary trial. The application was made before committal proceedings began. The justices acceded to the request and accepted pleas of guilty to all matters charged. The prosecution applied for judicial review of their decision, on the ground that they had no jurisdiction to change the mode of trial. The Divisional Court held that there was no power to vary the decision for trial on indictment except that contained in the Magistrates' Courts Act 1980, s 25. Since D's submissions had been made before the justices began committal proceedings, the provisions of s 25(3) had not been complied with. Thus the decision to change to summary trial was a nullity. The case was remitted to the magistrates to continue the committal proceedings, bearing in mind that D's admission of guilt in open court was a compelling reason for changing to summary trial.

A probably unintended consequence of the wording of s 25(3) is that, if the only charge against the accused is one triable only on indictment (e.g., wounding with intent to cause grievous bodily harm contrary to s 18 of the Offences against the Person Act 1861) but the magistrates decide on a submission that there is a case to answer only in respect of an offence triable either way (e.g., unlawful wounding contrary to s 20 of the 1861 Act), they may not hold a summary trial in respect of the latter offence however much they and the parties might desire them to do so: *Cambridgeshire Justices ex parte Fraser* [1984] 1 WLR 1391.   **8.31**

The magistrates have a discretion to allow an accused who has elected summary trial to withdraw his election. The question most often arises when he is initially unrepresented, agrees to summary trial at that stage, and then obtains legal advice during an adjournment prior to the hearing of the case. The central factor in the magistrates' decision should be the accused's state of mind at the time of his election. 'Did he properly understand the nature and significance of the choice which was put to him?' (see McCullough J's judgment in *Birmingham Justices ex parte Hodgson* [1985] QB 1131). Whether one intends to plead guilty or not guilty always has a major influence on where one would prefer to be tried (see 8.45 to 8.47). Therefore, if the accused elects summary trial and pleads guilty under the misapprehension that he has no defence to the charge, but he is subsequently advised that he might have a defence, and the magistrates in consequence allow the plea of guilty to be withdrawn, then it follows almost automatically that they should also allow the election for summary trial to be withdrawn (see *Ex parte Hodgson* and especially Watkins LJ's judgment in *West London Metropolitan Stipendiary Magistrate ex parte Keane* (1985) *The Times*, 9 March 1985). Where the accused has intended to plead not guilty throughout, but claims that his original willingness to be tried summarily was due to his not realizing the seriousness of the charge and/or the advantages of trial on indictment from a defendant's point of view, the exercise of the magistrates' discretion will depend upon matters such as the accused's age, intelligence and apparent understanding of court proceedings. These criteria were applied in *Highbury Corner Metropolitan Stipendiary Magistrate ex parte Weekes* [1985] QB 1147. W (aged 17) was arrested on a Saturday evening on a charge of unlawful wounding. He was bailed to attend at the magistrates' court on the Monday morning, and did so in   **8.32** company only with his mother. He had not had any opportunity to obtain legal advice, nor had he ever been in a magistrates' court before. Upon his agreeing to summary trial and pleading not guilty, the case was adjourned. At a subsequent unsuccessful application for the election to be withdrawn, it was conceded that W had not even understood what the Crown Court was, so obviously he could not have appreciated 'the nature and significance' of the choice between modes of trial that he was making. The High Court accordingly held that the magistrate had erred in refusing the defence application. The magistrate's mistake perhaps arose from his view that 'this court can grapple with the difficulties in this case'. No doubt it could have done, but that was not a consideration relevant to the application with which he was dealing. Even in a case eminently suitable for summary trial, the accused has the right to be tried on indictment if the offence charged is indictable, and he should not be deprived of that right by an election made at a time when he does not really know what he is doing. McCullough J's judgment in *Weekes* shows that he was unhappy that the question of method of trial had been dealt with on a first appearance by a young and unrepresented accused. However, His Lordship was not prepared to lay down any general principle to the effect that the court should always wait until the accused has had the opportunity of obtaining legal advice before putting him to his election.

8.33 The power that magistrates have to switch from summary trial or to allow an accused to withdraw his consent to summary trial should not be confused with the power to commit for sentence, described in Chapter 12. Committal for sentence occurs where the accused pleads or is found guilty by the magistrates and they then consider that their powers of punishment are insufficient. The Crown Court's only function is then to sentence the offender. In the event of the case being sent for trial in the Crown Court, on the other hand, there is no completed summary trial and questions of guilt or innocence are determined in the Crown Court. Moreover, as already explained, s 25(2) only applies where the accused pleads not guilty, whereas powers to commit for sentence are not dependent on the plea.

Adjusting the charges

8.34 As explained at 8.16 to 8.25, the prosecution, for all practical purposes, have no direct veto on an offence triable either way being tried summarily. Conversely, they cannot prevent the accused insisting on trial on indictment. Indirectly, however, they can control the mode of trial through the almost unfettered discretion they enjoy in relation to charging a suspect. Thus, if they choose to regard the conduct alleged as giving rise only to a summary offence, the accused cannot ask to be charged with something triable either way. Since either-way offences are generally more serious than summary offences, it might be thought inconceivable that anybody would prefer to be charged with the former rather than the latter. In practice, however, there is an overlap between the most serious summary matters and the least serious either-way ones, so that, in certain situations where the facts alleged would fit either, the sentence an offender will actually receive (as opposed to the legal maximum theoretically imposable) is likely to be the same whether he is convicted of the summary offence or the either-way alternative. The prosecution can then ensure that he is tried in the magistrates' court by the simple expedient of charging only the former. (As to the reason why the prosecution might wish to avoid jury trial, see 8.45 to 8.47).

8.35 The further question arises of whether the prosecution can have the best of both worlds by first charging an either-way offence and then, if the accused elects trial on indictment, reducing the charge to one that is summary only. The answer, basically, is 'yes, they can, as a matter of strict law'. In *Canterbury & St Augustine Justices ex parte Klisiak* [1982] QB 398 four defendants were charged with assault occasioning actual bodily harm ('ABH') plus a variety of minor public order offences, all arising out of disturbances on the seafront one Bank Holiday. They elected trial on indictment for the assault and the remaining charges (being summary) were adjourned *sine die*. During an adjournment prior to committal proceedings, further charges of assaulting a police officer in the execution of his duty (a summary offence) were preferred. Subsequently, no evidence was offered at what would have been the committal proceedings for 'ABH', but a date was fixed for summary trial of both the public order charges and the assault on police. The Divisional Court held that the prosecution was entitled to choose what offence to charge. The court could not prevent them from acting in this way, unless it resulted in blatant injustice (but see 8.37 for the position in practice).

The principles in *Ex parte Klisiak* do not apply to the reverse situation where the prosecution   **8.36**
feel aggrieved by the magistrates' decision to accept jurisdiction in respect of an either-way charge. Thus, in *Brooks* [1985] Crim LR 385, where B was convicted of causing grievous bodily harm to his lover's husband by striking him over the head with a hammer, the Court of Appeal heavily criticized the prosecution for adding the GBH charge (which is triable only on indictment) after the magistrates had held that the original either-way charge of unlawful wounding was suitable for summary trial. Given the timing of the additional charge, it looked very much like a refusal to accept the ruling of the bench. Largely because of the procedural irregularity, their lordships reduced B's sentence from 15 to 9 months.

Whatever the strictly legal position may be with regard to the adjustment of charges, CPS pros-   **8.37**
ecutors are now put under ethical constraints by the Code for Crown Prosecutors. Para. 7.3 of the Code addresses the fundamental issue raised by the cases discussed above when it states: 'Crown Prosecutors should not change the charge simply because of the decision made by the court or the defendant about where the case will be heard'. The introduction of charging standards provides further limits within which the discretion of the prosecution will in practice be exercised (see 5.28).

D   THE SPECIAL PROCEDURE FOR CRIMINAL DAMAGE CHARGES

The Criminal Law Act 1977 contained many provisions, now repealed and re-enacted in the   **8.38**
Magistrates' Courts Act 1980, for simplifying the law on the mode of trial of offences, and also for redistributing the work of the criminal courts so that a greater proportion of cases would be heard in the magistrates' courts than had been so previously. Offences such as driving with excess alcohol in the blood and assaulting a police constable in the execution of his duty, which had formerly been triable either way, became summary, and offences ranging from bigamy to failing to provide one's apprentice with sufficient food, which had before been triable only on indictment, became triable either way. However, the most controversial proposal for shifting work to the magistrates only reached the statute book in an attenuated form. The Criminal Law Bill contained provisions which would have made minor offences of theft, obtaining property by deception and criminal damage triable only summarily, but the outcry at this restriction on the right to jury trial was such that only the provisions in respect of

criminal damage offences became law. The present legislation is contained in the Magistrates' Courts Act 1980, s 22.

8.39   If the accused is charged with criminal damage contrary to the Criminal Damage Act 1971, s 1(1), or an attempt to commit such an offence, then, unless the offence involved damage or attempted damage by fire, the magistrates must proceed as follows:

(a)   They consider, having regard to any representations made by the prosecution or defence, the value involved in the offence—i.e., the cost, in a case where property was allegedly destroyed or damaged beyond repair, of replacing the property, or, in other cases, the cost of repair. 'Representations' normally entail merely arguments and assertions of fact by counsel, perhaps accompanied by the production of documents such as a bill for repairs that have been carried out on the damaged property. There is no need to call evidence at this point (see *Canterbury & St Augustine Justices ex parte Klisiak* [1982] QB 398).

(b)   In *R (on the application of Abbott) v Colchester Magistrates' Court* [2001] Crim LR 564, the Divisional Court made it clear that the value on which the magistrates must focus is the value of the damage to the property itself. They should not concern themselves with any consequential losses which might have been sustained as a result of the damage.

(c)   If the value involved is clearly £5,000 or less, the magistrates proceed as if the offence were triable only summarily. They do not follow the procedure in ss 19 to 21 of MCA (see 8.16), and the accused has no right to a trial on indictment.

(d)   If the value involved is clearly over £5,000, the charge is dealt with like any other offence triable either way. The magistrates hear any representations as to the more suitable mode of trial, and, if they consider that summary trial is appropriate, the clerk asks the accused if he consents to the magistrates dealing with the case.

(e)   Where the case is tried summarily under (c) above, the maximum sentence the magistrates can impose is three months imprisonment or a £2,500 fine. They cannot commit for sentence to the Crown Court although, in appropriate circumstances, they could exercise one of the other primary powers of committal mentioned in 12.21.

(f)   Where the case is tried summarily under (d) above, the maximum sentence is that which can be imposed for any other of the offences triable either way listed in Sch 1 to the 1980 Act—i.e., six months imprisonment and a £5,000 fine. In addition, the magistrates may commit for sentence under PCC(S)A 2000, ss 3 and 4.

(g)   If the magistrates are not sure whether the value involved is more or less than £5,000, the clerk asks the accused if he consents to summary trial. If he does so and is convicted, the maximum penalty is as in (d) above and, again, he cannot be committed for sentence to the Crown Court. The clerk explains the maximum penalty to the accused before asking for his consent to summary trial. If he does not want to be tried summarily, the normal ss 19–21 procedure for determining the mode of trial comes into operation.

8.40   Where an accused is charged on the same occasion with two or more offences of criminal damage that appear to the court to form a series of the same or similar character, the relevant consideration in determining mode of trial is the *aggregate* value involved in all the offences—i.e., if the aggregate is more than £5,000 the accused retains his right to jury trial even though the value of each individual offence is less than that amount (see Magistrates' Courts Act 1980, s 22(11)).

Prior to the amendment made by the CJA 1988, there was an arbitrary rule that, if the accused **8.41**
faced a series of criminal damage charges, he was entitled to elect Crown Court trial however
small the values (see, for example, *St Helens Justices ex parte McClorie* [1983] 1 WLR 1332 where
magistrates were compelled to hold committal proceedings in respect of (i) damaging a pad-
lock in breaking into a yard, and (ii) damaging a watch belonging to a police officer trying to
arrest the accused for being in the yard, the total aggregate value involved being a mere £20).
The figure at or beneath which the special procedure applies has increased massively in real
terms over the years. When it was introduced in 1977, it was £200. It was then increased to
£400 in 1984, £2,000 in 1988, and £5,000 in 1994. It is rare for an accused to do more than
£5,000 worth of damage (other than by arson, which is excluded from the procedure anyway). The great majority of criminal damage charges have therefore been excluded from the
ambit of jury trial.

It should be noted that even where the special procedure applies and the value involved in the **8.42**
offence is £5,000 or less, s 22(2) merely requires the *magistrates* to proceed as if the offence
charged were triable only summarily—it does not provide that the offence shall be deemed to
be summary for all purposes (*Considine* (1980) 70 Cr App R 239).

It is submitted that an accused in a case such as *Considine* (where the charge was criminal **8.43**
damage valued at £34) would be entitled to advance information from the prosecution (see 8.09
to 8.15 for details of advance information). This is so since the entitlement to advance information is triggered off by the nature of the offence. The offence is criminal damage, and it is triable either way, notwithstanding that the magistrates are obliged to deal with it summarily in
certain circumstances. Similarly, whether an offence is indictable is important in other con-
texts, e.g., in relation to powers of detention for questioning (see 3.25), withholding the right
to legal advice (see 3.53), and the issue of warrants to search premises (see 3.79). In each of
these cases, criminal damage must be regarded as an indictable offence, whatever the value
involved.

E LINKED SUMMARY AND INDICTABLE CHARGES

Subject to what is explained in this Section, a fundamental principle of classification of **8.44**
offences is that summary offences must be tried in a magistrates' court. The only way the
Crown Court can become involved in dealing with a summary matter (other than on appeal)
is if the accused has pleaded or been found guilty in the lower court and is then committed
for sentence under s 6 of the PCC(S)A 2000. Until the passing of the Criminal Justice Act
1988 there were no exceptions to the above principle. However, ss 40 and 41 of that Act
introduced two new procedures, one of which enables a limited range of summary offences
actually to be tried on indictment and the other of which allows the accused, having been
convicted on indictment of an either-way offence, to be sentenced at the same time for a
summary offence. But, both these procedures apply only if the accused is charged with an
indictable offence and a linked summary matter. It remains true that a summary charge
standing by itself must always and without exception be tried summarily. Since the use of
s 40 and/or 41 is dependent on the accused having been sent to the Crown Court for trial on

an indictable charge, it makes more sense to deal with this topic in detail later (see 13.78 to 13.83).

F TRIAL ON INDICTMENT OR SUMMARY TRIAL?

8.45 Where the accused has a choice of trial on indictment by judge and jury, or summary trial by magistrates, the following points should be borne in mind as to the advantages and disadvantages of each method.

8.46 Summary trial is less expensive and less time-consuming than trial on indictment. If the accused elects to be tried by the magistrates and is found guilty, any order to pay some of the prosecution's costs will almost certainly reflect the fact that he has chosen the less costly form of trial. In addition, the sentence itself may well be less severe than if he had been tried at the Crown Court. If he cannot be committed for sentence (see Chapter 12), the punishment will not exceed six months' imprisonment and a £5,000 fine (twelve months if convicted of two or more offences triable either way). Even if the magistrates have power to commit for sentence, they may well deal with the offender themselves in cases where, had he been convicted on indictment, the Crown Court judge would have passed a sentence in excess of that which the magistrates may pass. As a result of the plea before venue procedure, of course, a defendant who intends to plead guilty will be dealt with in any event by the magistrates' court (subject to the possibility of committal for sentence—see Chapter 12). However, the constraints upon sentencing powers in the magistrates' court will be borne in mind by the astute legal adviser who is aware that the defendant will plead not guilty, but knows there is a chance that he will nevertheless be convicted.

8.47 However, the general view is that trial by a jury offers a better prospect of an acquittal. Three reasons may be advanced in support of this view. First, at a trial on indictment, the defence know exactly what evidence the prosecution propose to adduce because that will have been disclosed by the committal proceedings and any notices of additional evidence. It is true that advance information of the prosecution case must be provided whenever the offence charged is triable either way (see 8.09 to 8.15), and the Attorney-General's Guidelines do tell prosecutors to provide all evidence upon which they propose to rely in summary trial (8.13). However, the rules do not in terms require the prosecution to give the defence copies of the statements made by prosecution witnesses—it is sufficient to provide 'a summary of the facts and matters about which the prosecutor proposes to adduce evidence in the proceedings'. Thus, knowledge of evidence prior to summary trial may still not be as satisfactory from the defence point of view as the information which they enjoy prior to trial on indictment. Secondly, as explained at 10.57, it is difficult to object effectively to inadmissible evidence at summary trials, because the magistrates learn what the evidence is in the course of ruling on its admissibility, and are inevitably influenced even by material which they ultimately decide should be excluded. At a trial on indictment, the judge decides whether evidence is admissible in the absence of the jury. Finally, it is suggested that jurors are more likely to believe the accused than are magistrates, especially in cases where there is a conflict between police evidence and defence evidence. Some would say that this is because magistrates are less gullible than juries, others that through often sitting in court magistrates become 'case-hardened' and suspend their critical faculties in relation to police evidence. Whatever the reason, statistics appear to support professional opinion on this point. In the year 2006/7, 40 per cent of Crown Court trials ended in acquittal and 60 per cent in conviction. In the magistrates' court, by contrast, only 32 per cent of defendants were acquitted, whereas 68 per cent were found guilty after trial (*Annual Report of the Crown Prosecution Service*, TSO).

G   THE NEW ALLOCATION PROCEDURE UNDER THE CJA 2003

When s 41 and Sch 3 of the CJA 2003 are brought into effect (no date was in prospect at the time of writing), a number of changes will be made to the procedure for allocation of offences (deciding on mode of trial). These can be summarized as follows (references are to paragraphs in Sch 3):   **8.48**

(1)   It is to be made clear that the plea before venue and allocation procedures can take place before a single justice (paras 3 and 4).
(2)   The court is to be informed about, and take account of, any previous convictions of the defendant in deciding whether its sentencing powers are adequate.
(3)   The court must have regard both to the representations made by defence and prosecution, and to allocation guidelines issued by the Sentencing Guidelines Council under s 170 of the CJA 2003 (para 5).
(4)   The defendant will be told before he is put to his election that he may request an indication from the magistrates whether, if he pleaded guilty before jurisdiction is determined, the sentence would be custodial or not (para 6).
(5)   The magistrates will have a discretion whether or not to give such an indication to a defendant who seeks one. Where an indication is given, the defendant will be given an opportunity to reconsider his original indication as to plea.
(6)   Where a defendant then decides to plead guilty, the magistrates' court will proceed to sentence. A custodial sentence will be available only if it was indicated.
(7)   The option of committal for sentence to the Crown Court under s 3 of the PCC(S)A 2000 will not be available, if the defendant pleads not guilty, and the magistrates accept jurisdiction and try him. However, if the defendant pleads guilty and the magistrates do not accept jurisdiction, they may commit to the Crown Court. In any event, committal for sentence under s 3A of the 2000 Act will be available where the criteria for an extended sentence or a sentence for public protection appear to be met.
(8)   Committal for trial will disappear, and where the court decides that trial on indictment is suitable it will send the case to the Crown Court under s 51 of the CDA 1998 (see Chapter 13).
(9)   Consequently, the power to switch between summary trial and committal will also disappear, and in its place there will be a new power for the prosecution to apply for a triable-either-way case which has been allocated for summary trial to be tried on indictment instead (para 11).

This substantially altered procedure for allocation is linked to changes in mode of trial for juveniles (see Chapter 11), committal for sentence (see Chapter 12) and the way in which cases are to be sent to the Crown Court (see Chapter 13). Reference should be made to those chapters for more details of the changes in question.

KEY DOCUMENTS

Magistrates' Court Act 1980, ss 18 to 25, as amended.

Criminal Justice Act 2003, Schedule 3 (when in force).

Protocol for the Provision of Advance Information, Prosecution Evidence and Disclosure of
Unused Material in the Magistrates Courts, available at <www.judiciary.gov.uk> click 'judgments and guidance' and then 'protocols and guidance on criminal cases'.

9

DISCLOSURE

One crucial feature of the criminal trial in England and Wales has always been the duty of the **9.01**
prosecution to disclose the evidence which is at its disposal to the defence. The rationale for
this duty is the disparity of resources between the Crown on the one hand (with its access to
the investigative facilities of the police and specialist services such as those of forensic scien-
tists), and the individual accused of an offence on the other hand. In an effort to ensure a fair
trial for the accused, and to achieve 'equality of arms' as far as possible between the Crown
and the accused, there developed a common law duty owed by the prosecution to the
defence. This duty had two aspects:

(a) The obligation to notify the defence of the evidence upon which the prosecution
intend to rely. This can conveniently be referred to as the 'duty to provide advance
information'. As far as trial on indictment is concerned, this is met in part by the
papers served upon the defence prior to committal to the Crown Court, or after a case
is sent to the Crown Court under the indictable-only procedure (see Chapter 13). Any
further evidence which the prosecution later decide to adduce as part of their case
must be brought to the defence's attention by way of a notice of additional evidence
(see 20.32 to 20.33). The duty in respect of summary trial is less comprehensive, and is
dealt with in 8.09 to 8.15.

(b) The duty to make available to the defence any material of relevance to the case upon
which they do *not* intend to rely—'unused material'. It is upon this aspect of the

prosecution's obligations (known as the 'duty of disclosure') that most of the remainder of this Chapter concentrates, but it will also deal with the duty placed upon the defence to make disclosure of the case upon which it will rely at trial.

9.02 Although the prosecution duty of disclosure was evolved by the judges at common law, in an effort to ensure a fair trial for the accused, it has now been made subject to the statutory regime set out in the Criminal Procedure and Investigations Act 1996 (CPIA), as supplemented by a Code of Practice issued under that Act. The disclosure provisions of the CPIA came into effect on 1 April 1997. Their application is set out in s 1(3), which states that part I (containing the disclosure provisions) applies in relation to alleged offences into which no criminal investigation has begun before the appointed day (1 April 1997). 'Criminal investigation' is defined in s 1(4) as 'an investigation which police officers or other persons have a duty to conduct with a view to it being ascertained (a) whether a person should be charged with an offence, or (b) whether a person charged with an offence is guilty of it'. The Act is supplemented by the Code of Practice and a series of rules and regulations which came into effect on the same day (on the statutory rules as to disclosure, see Sprack, *The Criminal Procedure and Investigations Act 1996: (1) The Duty of Disclosure* [1997] Crim LR 308. A series of important amendments to the CPIA came into force in 2005 as a result of the CJA 2003.

9.03 The scheme of the legislation is as follows:

  (a) There is a statutory duty upon the police officer investigating an offence to record and retain information and material gathered or generated during the investigation (see 9.07).
  (b) The prosecution should inform the defence of certain categories of that material which they *do not* intend to use at trial (see 9.13 to 9.15)—as stated, there are separate obligations to inform the defence of material which they *do* intend to use.
  (c) The defence then inform the prosecution of the case which they intend to present at trial (see 9.16 to 9.29).

9.04 The legislation makes provision for applications to be made to the court in certain circumstances where there is a dispute about whether the prosecution should disclose certain material (see 9.30); and there are sanctions laid down for defence failure to disclose, or disclosure which is false or inconsistent (9.41 to 9.53).

9.05 The cases to which this legislative scheme applies are laid down in s 1. In brief, it is compulsory in relation to cases sent to the Crown Court to be tried on indictment. It may also apply on a voluntary basis to any summary trial, including those in the youth court, whether the charges in question are summary, triable either way, or even (in the case of the youth court) indictable only (see 9.54 to 9.56 for the application of the statutory provisions to summary trial).

A   THE INVESTIGATOR'S DUTY

9.06 Section 23 of the CPIA requires the Secretary of State to prepare a Code of Practice which will govern investigations carried out by police officers. By s 26, those other than police officers (e.g., customs officers and trading standards officers) charged with the duty of conducting criminal investigations must have regard to the Code's provisions.

The Code of Practice (see Key Documents at the end of the Chapter) makes the investigator **9.07** responsible for ensuring that any information relevant to the investigation is recorded and retained, whether it is gathered in the course of the investigation (e.g., documents seized in the course of searching premises) or generated by the investigation (e.g., interview records). Where there is any doubt about the relevance of material, the investigator should retain it. The duty to retain material includes in particular the following categories:

(a) crime reports, including crime report forms, relevant parts of incident report books, and police officers' notebooks;
(b) final versions of witness statements;
(c) draft versions of witness statements where their content differs from the final version;
(d) interview records (written or taped);
(e) expert reports and schedules;
(f) any material casting doubt upon the reliability of a confession;
(g) any material casting doubt on the reliability of a witness.

But the duty to retain material does not extend to items purely ancillary to that in the above categories which possess no independent significance, such as duplicate copies of documents. The material must be retained at least until criminal proceedings are concluded. Where the accused has been convicted, the material must be retained for at least six months after conviction, or until he is released from custody (whichever is the later).

Where the investigator believes that the person charged with an offence is likely to plead not **9.08** guilty at a summary trial, or that the offence will be tried in the Crown Court, he or she must prepare a schedule listing material which has been retained and which does not form part of the case against the accused. If the investigator has obtained any sensitive material, this should be listed in a separate schedule. Sensitive material is material which the investigator believes it is not in the public interest to disclose. The Code gives a number of examples, which range from material relating to national security to material given in confidence, and include material relating to informants, under-cover police officers, premises used for police surveillance, techniques used in the detection of crime, and material relating to a child witness generated, e.g., by a local authority social services department (see 9.33 to 9.40).

The investigator should draw the prosecutor's attention to any material which might **9.09** undermine the prosecution case. The disclosure officer (defined as the person responsible for examining the records created during the investigation and criminal proceedings and disclosing material as required to the prosecutor or the accused) must certify that to the best of his knowledge and belief the duties imposed under the Code have been complied with.

If a defence statement is given (see 9.16), the investigator must look again at the material **9.10** retained, and draw the prosecutor's attention to any material which might reasonably be expected to assist the defence disclosed. Again the disclosure officer must certify compliance with the duties imposed by the Code. If the investigator comes into possession of any new material after complying with the duties described above, then this must be treated in the same way.

9.11 If the prosecutor so requests, the investigator must disclose to the accused:

(a)   material which might undermine the prosecution case;

(b)   where the accused has given the prosecutor a defence statement (see 9.16), material which might reasonably be expected to assist the defence which the accused has disclosed;

(c)   any material which the court orders be disclosed.

9.12 The statute has therefore placed the police disclosure officer at the centre of the obligation to disclose material in the possession of the prosecution. This role is controversial, and the way in which it is carried out has led to fierce criticism by the legal profession. As was noted in a major study carried out for the Home Office, most police forces regard the training which they receive on disclosure as inadequate—its average length is less than one day. Officers frequently provide to prosecutors documentation which is late, inaccurate or incomplete. Frequently, prosecutors disagree with the assessment of disclosure officers as to whether material should be disclosed or not (Auld Report, pp. 449–451, relying in part on Plotnikoff and Woolfson, *A Fair Balance? Evaluation of the Operation of Disclosure Law*, Home Office, 2001).

B   PROSECUTION DISCLOSURE

9.13 The main duty of the prosecution to disclose unused material is contained within the CPIA, within the framework set out in 9.03. Before this statutory obligation arises, however, the prosecution may be under a common law duty to disclose such material to the defence at an earlier stage, e.g., because it might help the defence in a bail application, or to prepare for trial: *DPP ex parte Lee* [1999] 1 WLR 1950.

9.14 However, the main duty of the prosecution arises as a result of the scheme set out in the CPIA. Section 3 requires the prosecutor to disclose previously undisclosed material to the accused if it 'might reasonably be considered capable of undermining the case for the prosecution against the accused, or of assisting the case for the accused' (CPIA, s 3(1)(a), as amended by the CJA 2003, s 32). If there is no such material, then the accused must be given a written statement to that effect. Prosecution material includes material which the prosecutor possesses or has been allowed to inspect under the provisions of the Code (see 9.06 to 9.12). It may be disclosed either by giving it to the defence, or allowing them to inspect it at a reasonable time and place. Prosecution disclosure must be carried out as soon as reasonably practicable (s 13). Material must not, however, be disclosed under this provision if a court has concluded that it is not in the public interest that it be disclosed (s 3(6), dealt with at 9.33 to 9.40). By s 4, if the prosecutor has been given a document indicating any non-sensitive material which has not been given to the accused, that document must be given to the accused at the same time as primary prosecution disclosure takes place.

9.15 It will be the prosecutor who will judge, then, whether material should be disclosed to the defence. On what basis will that judgement be exercised? The common law position prior to the CPIA was encapsulated in the test laid down in *Keane* [1994] 1 WLR 746, which held that material fell to be disclosed (unless subject to immunity) if it could:

be seen on a sensible appraisal by the prosecution: (a) to be relevant or possibly relevant to an issue in the case; (b) to raise or possibly raise a new issue whose existence is not apparent from the evidence the prosecution proposes to use; (c) to hold out a real (as opposed to a fanciful) prospect of providing a lead on evidence which goes to (a) or (b).

When the government introduced the new statutory disclosure scheme contained in the CPIA they aimed, by the use of the word 'undermine', to narrow the test of relevance as defined in *Keane* (*Hansard*, Lords, 18 December 1995, cols 1436–47; and see Leng and Taylor, *Blackstone's Criminal Procedure and Investigations Act 1996*, pp. 13–14). Parliamentary attempts by amendment to incorporate the relevance test as laid down in that case were resisted. Nevertheless, it was also made clear during the passage of the Bill that material which might undermine the prosecution case would include more than evidence which was *fatal* to the prosecution case. The test was, for example, described as follows by the Home Office Minister, Mr David McLean:

> The test for primary disclosure is designed to ensure that the prosecutor discloses at the first stage material that, generally speaking, has an adverse effect on the strength of the prosecution case. It is not confined to material raising a fundamental question about the prosecution.... The disclosure scheme is aimed at undisclosed material that might help the accused, notwithstanding the fact that there is enough evidence to provide a realistic prospect of conviction (*Hansard*, House of Commons Standing Committee B, 14 May 1996, col 34).

One category of material which 'might undermine' the prosecution case is notification of the previous convictions of prosecution witnesses. In *Vasiliou* [2000] Crim LR 845, the Court of Appeal held that the appellant's conviction had been rendered unsafe because the prosecution had failed to reveal the previous convictions of their witnesses. This had meant that the appellant was deprived of the chance to challenge those witnesses as to their character. Lack of knowledge had resulted in the appellant being unable to pursue a different strategy at trial from that which had been taken. The conviction was quashed and a retrial ordered.

C   DEFENCE DISCLOSURE

By s 5, once primary prosecution disclosure has taken place, and the case is committed or sent to the Crown Court, the accused must give a defence statement to the prosecutor and the court. The position is different if the matter is to be dealt with in the magistrates' court, where the defence statement is voluntary, rather than compulsory (see 9.54 to 9.56). Where a defence statement is served, whether in the magistrates' court or the Crown Court, its contents are prescribed by CPIA, s 6A, which says that it is a written statement which: **9.16**

(a)   sets out the nature of the accused's defence, including any particular defences on which he intends to rely;
(b)   indicates the matters of fact on which he takes issue with the prosecution;
(c)   sets out why he does so; and
(d)   indicates any point of law (including those as to the admissibility of evidence or abuse of process) which he wishes to take, and any authority relied on.

If the defence statement discloses an alibi, particulars of alibi must be given, including the name, address, and date of birth of any alibi witness, or information which might be of use in finding the witness if his or her name or address is not known. The definition of alibi evidence is 'evidence tending to show that by reason of the presence of the accused at a particular place or in a particular area at a particular time he was not, or was unlikely to have been, at the place **9.17**

where the offence is alleged to have been committed at the time of its alleged commission'
(see 20.61 to 20.63 for examples of the way in which this definition has been applied).

9.18   The duty which the CPIA places upon the defence is a novel one as, with certain limited exceptions such as the revelation of a defence of alibi discussed in the preceding paragraph, there
has historically been no obligation for the defence to reveal their case in advance of trial. The
argument against placing the defence under such a duty has traditionally been that it erodes
two fundamental principles: that the prosecution have the burden of proof, and that the
accused is entitled to protection against self-incrimination. As soon as any pressure is placed
on the accused to reveal his defence, so the argument runs, then he may in effect be con-
scripted to help fill in the gaps in the prosecution case against him. Notwithstanding these
arguments, the CPIA introduced the duty of defence disclosure (at least in the Crown Court).
It does place the defence lawyers in a difficult tactical quandary. They must weigh up the
advantages and drawbacks of a detailed defence statement. An appropriate degree of detail can
trigger off the release of further prosecution material (see 9.31), whereas non-disclosure can
result in the drawing of inferences potentially unfavourable to the defendant (see 9.41 to
9.53). On the other hand, if the defence are bound by a detailed statement which later proves
to be inaccurate, there is the danger of adverse inferences being drawn for that reason.

9.19   A tight time-limit for defence disclosure has been laid down by regulations which came into
effect at the same time as the statutory provisions (Criminal Procedure and Investigations Act
1996 (Defence Disclosure Time Limits) Regulations 1997: SI 1997 No 684). The defence statement must be served within 14 days of the prosecution's compliance (or purported compliance) with the duty of primary disclosure (reg 2). Whilst the defence may apply for an
extension, specifying their belief, on reasonable grounds, that it is not possible to meet the
deadline, the application must be made before the deadline expires (reg 3). The court may
grant an extension 'entirely at [its] discretion', and may order further extensions on the same
basis. The rules of court (the Crown Court (Criminal Procedure and Investigations Act 1996)
(Disclosure) Rules 1997 (SI 1997 No 698), r 8; and the Magistrates' Court (Criminal Procedure
and Investigations Act 1996) (Disclosure) Rules 1997 (SI 1997 No 703), r 8), which also came
into force at the same time as the statutory provisions, envisage the application being heard
at least 14 days after it has been received, to give the prosecutor an opportunity to make representations on whether an extension should be granted. It is therefore envisaged that the
defence will have to make application before the deadline expires, but will not be aware of the
fate of the application until after its expiry.

9.20   It should be stressed that the duty of disclosure imposed on the defence is of a different kind
from what is normally meant when one talks about 'the prosecution duty of disclosure'. The
prosecution duty is to disclose *unused material,* i.e., material which they do not intend to
introduce at trial. As far as defence disclosure is concerned, the duty is to reveal the case which
will be presented at trial. There is no obligation on the *defence,* either at common law or under
the statutory scheme of the CPIA, to reveal material which is *not* to be used at trial.

9.21   While that much is clear, it is less certain just how detailed the defence statement needs to be.
Does it have to provide the prosecution with an account of the evidence which will be produced at trial? Should it include the lines upon which it is intended to cross-examine prosecution witnesses? The question is an important one, because of the inference which the court
may draw if the defence statement is inconsistent with the defence which is run at trial.

In addressing this question, one needs to consider what the defence will have received by the **9.22**
time their duty to serve a defence statement is triggered off, and what they will not have
received. The prosecution must have served the committal papers, or their equivalent in cases
sent to the Crown Court under the indictable-only procedure or by notice of transfer or voluntary bill of indictment (see Chapter 13 for an account of the process of committal for trial
and the alternative procedures). The prosecution must also have complied, or purported to
comply, with the duty to make primary disclosure (s 5(1)(b)). What the prosecution will not
have done is to serve a statement of the way in which they intend to put the case. The prosecution case, in this latter sense, consists of the inferences and conclusions to be drawn from
the evidence upon which it relies. Whilst in some cases the evidence relied on by the prosecution will be self-explanatory, in others it may be impossible for the defence to say in what
way they take issue with the prosecution case, or the reasons (see the contribution of Lord
Ackner during the debate on the Bill: *Hansard*, Lords, 18 December 1995, cols 1458–9).

The degree of detail in which the defence statement must now be set out (see 9.16) results **9.23**
from a perception among some prosecutors and members of the judiciary that defence
lawyers were providing defence statements which were couched in the most general way. One
extreme example was commented on in *Bryant* [2005] EWCA Crim 2079 by the Court of
Appeal as 'woefully inadequate' because it consisted merely of a general denial of the charges,
accompanied by a statement that the defendant took issue with any witness purporting to
give evidence contrary to his denial. Such a document, said their Lordships, did not meet the
purposes of a defence statement. The central purpose of the defence statement is its role in
helping to define the issues in the case, in the hope that benefits in terms of improved case
management will result. Whatever the reason for the expanded duty, it clearly puts a greater
burden on defence representatives to embark on detailed preparation, at an earlier stage.
Further, given the early notification which the defence must now give of its legal arguments,
which include those in relation to any alleged abuse of process and admissibility of evidence,
there would seem to be a strong case for the prosecution to be compelled to give advance
notice of its arguments and authorities on such points, if sought. Any failure to do so would
seem to offend against the requirement that a fair trial should be based upon the principle of
equality of arms. Similar reasoning might be advanced in appropriate circumstances for the
prosecution to spell out the inferences which it will be asking the trier of fact to draw from the
primary facts adduced in its evidence, given that the defence is obliged to set out the reasoning surrounding the anticipated factual disputes. It follows that the scope of the defence statement should be viewed in the context of what might reasonably be required of the defence at
a stage when they may not be clear about the way in which the prosecution put their case.

Section 34 of the CJA 2003 amends s 6C of the CPIA 1996 so as to introduce an expanded **9.24**
duty for the defence to notify the court and the prosecutor of any witnesses. This duty,
which had not been implemented at the time of writing, involves notification of witnesses
other than alibi witnesses (as to alibi witnesses, see 9.17). The duty is separate from that
attaching to the defence statement, with the result that it will apply to the defence in the
magistrates' court as well as the Crown Court, on a compulsory basis. The accused will be
required to give to the court and the prosecutor a notice indicating whether he intends to
call any witnesses at trial, other than himself and any alibi witnesses already notified. Again,
as in the case of alibi witnesses, the defence will have to provide names, addresses, dates of
birth or other identifying information if any such details are not known. Any change in the

plans to call witnesses (including a decision not to call a previously notified witness, or to call a witness not previously notified) will have to be dealt with by way of an amended notice to the court and the prosecutor. One interesting point is that, while there are sanctions in relation to a failure to notify the court and prosecution of prospective witnesses (see 9.44 to 9.47), there are none in respect of a failure to call a witness who has been so notified.

9.25 Section 21A of the CPIA 1996 (inserted by CJA 2003, s 40) envisages a Code of Practice for police interviews of witnesses notified by the accused (either to support an alibi or otherwise). It is to deal with such matters as the attendance of solicitors on behalf of the accused and the interviewee. It will come into force by statutory instrument after approval by affirmative resolutions of both Houses of Parliament. The Code was not available at the time of writing.

9.26 Section 6D of the CPIA 1996, inserted by the CJA 2003, s 35 (not in force at the time of writing), deals with any expert report commissioned by the accused. If he instructs a person with a view to providing any expert opinion for possible use at trial, he must give the court and the prosecutor the name and address of the expert in question. The aim is presumably to stop 'expert shopping' on the part of the defence. However, the innovation appears to offend against the principle that the defence has never been subject to an obligation to disclose material which it does not intend to use, as opposed to notifying the case which it intends to run at trial (see 9.20). Potentially, such notification might open the door to the prosecution seeking evidence from the expert, as there is no property in a witness (subject to any considerations of legal professional privilege: see *Blackstone's Criminal Practice 2008*, F9.32).

9.27 The CJA 2003, s 33, introduced an amendment relating to defence statements in multi-defendant cases, inserting s 5(5A), (5B), and (5D) in the CPIA 1996. The court will be able to order each defendant to give copies of his defence statement to his co-accused. The court may take the initiative in the matter, or respond to an application by any party. The usual practice will no doubt be to order simultaneous exchange of statements by co-defendants, to avoid any advantage being gained by a defendant who exchanges his statement late.

9.28 Section 6B of the CPIA, inserted by the CJA 2003, s 33(3), applies where the accused has given a defence statement before prosecution disclosure. It requires the accused to provide an 'updated defence statement', or alternatively a statement that he has no changes to make to his initial defence statement (not in force at the time of writing).

9.29 The question of the authorship of the defence statement (or an updating statement, or a statement that no updating is necessary) is dealt with in s 6E(1) of the CPIA, inserted by the CJA 2003, s 36. It deems that where an accused's solicitor purports to give such a statement on behalf of the accused, it is given on behalf of the accused, unless the contrary is proved. Of course, evidence can be adduced to show that it was not given with the accused's authority, but that may have adverse consequences where legal professional privilege is waived as a result (as to legal privilege, see *Blackstone's Criminal Practice 2008*, F9.29 to F9.37).

D   APPLICATIONS TO THE COURT

9.30 The prosecutor may make application to the court that material should not be disclosed, either at the primary or the secondary stage, on the basis that it is not in the public interest to disclose it. For its part, the defence can under s 8 apply to the court for an order that the prosecutor should disclose material. This applies to material held or inspected by the prosecutor (s 8(3)), but also to any material which the disclosure officer must either supply to the prosecutor, or allow the prosecutor to inspect if requested (s 8(4)). Such an application may only be made, however, after the defence have served a defence statement (s 8(1)). In practice, the defence may find it difficult to mount a successful challenge to prosecution disclosure. First, the scope of any such challenge is limited to matters which were raised in the defence statement. The failure to include matters in a defence statement may not, of course, mean that the defence in question is invalid, let alone that the accused is inevitably guilty. What about the case of the defendant who is mentally ill, too drunk to remember events with any clarity, or prone to confess to crimes which he has not committed? (Judith Ward is perhaps the most memorable instance of a victim of a miscarriage of justice falling into the latter category: see *Ward* [1993] 1 WLR 619.) Second, there is the problem of identifying the material which has not been disclosed. In doing this, the defence will be reliant on the good faith and efficiency of the investigator, who is charged with bringing to the prosecutor's attention the material which ought to form the basis of secondary disclosure. The investigation will in most cases be long closed, and the case passed over to the Crown Prosecution Service, so that any incentive to ferret out relevant material will be negligible. The investigator will almost inevitably have formed a firm view of the accused's guilt, and will be sceptical (at any rate at a sub-conscious level) about whether any material really does assist the defence. And the investigator is unlikely to have the legal skills (let alone the defence perspective) to be able to identify material which an advocate could turn to advantage at trial. Third, the defence will have to satisfy the court that it has 'reasonable cause to believe':

(a) that 'there is prosecution material which might be reasonably expected to assist' the defence as notified; and
(b) that the material has not been disclosed to the accused.

The operation of s 8 is crucial to the whole disclosure scheme, for it provides the means whereby the court can monitor its operation. It is therefore important, if there is to be some corrective to the disparity of resources between prosecution and defence, that the courts should recognize the practical difficulties faced by the defence in mounting a successful challenge to what is suspected to be inadequate disclosure, and reflect that recognition in deciding upon applications for review. It is submitted that an order for disclosure should follow where there is a reasonable chance that it might assist the defence.

E   CONTINUOUS REVIEW

The prosecutor remains under a continuing duty to review questions of disclosure (s 7A). If he   **9.31** at any time before the accused is acquitted or convicted forms the opinion that there is material which might undermine the prosecution case, or be reasonably expected to assist the accused's defence, then it must be disclosed to the accused as soon as reasonably practicable (provided that the court has not ruled against disclosure in respect of that material). This duty of continuous review would come into play, for example, where a prosecution witness gives evidence which is materially inconsistent with a statement made earlier to the police. If the defence are unaware of the statement, prosecuting counsel should disclose it to his opposite number so that he can use it in cross-examination to discredit the witness' testimony (*Clarke* (1931) 22 Cr App R 58—although the case was many years before the CPIA, it is submitted that the principle still holds).

9.32   For its part, the court must keep under review the question of whether it is still not in the public interest to disclose material affected by its order (s 15).

F   PUBLIC INTEREST IMMUNITY

9.33   The prosecution duty of disclosure is subject to immunity where the public interest so dictates. There will be some cases where the prosecution take the view that the material should be withheld, for example, because it is so sensitive that it is subject to public interest immunity. This would be the case if the material disclosed the identity of an informer (*Marks v Beyfus* (1890) 25 QBD 494). The obvious reason for the rule is to prevent retaliation against informers, and the fear that revelation of their identity would lead to the drying up of sources of information for the police. *Marks v Beyfus* made it clear, however, that the rule may be departed from if the judge is of the opinion that the informer's name should be disclosed in order to show the defendant's innocence. The rule about police informers has been extended to observation posts used by the police (*Rankine* [1986] QB 861). The reasoning is that those members of the public who make premises available for the police to observe suspected criminals might be subject to retaliation in the same way that informers are.

9.34   Even if the Crown believes that the unused materials should be immune from disclosure, at common law that did not end the matter. The case of *Ward* [1993] 1 WLR 619 makes it clear that it is for the court, and not the prosecution, to make the final decision as to whether immunity from disclosure should be granted. Judith Ward had been convicted of multiple murder and explosives offences. The prosecution failed to disclose material relevant to her alleged confessions and certain scientific evidence. The Court of Appeal held that, if the prosecution claimed that they were entitled to withhold material documents on the basis of public interest immunity, the court must be asked to rule on the legitimacy of their claim. If the prosecution were not prepared to have the issue determined by a court, they would have to abandon the case.

9.35   Although the CPIA generally disapplies the rules of common law in relation to the prosecution duty of disclosure (s 21(1)), it preserves 'the rules of common law as to whether disclosure is in the public interest' (s 21(2)).

9.36   Public interest immunity (PII) is a thread which runs through the provisions of the CPIA. By s 3(6), prosecution disclosure is made subject to PII. Section 8(5) prohibits the court from ordering disclosure where it would be contrary to the public interest. Section 7A(8) places a similar limitation on the prosecution's continuing duty of review.

9.37   In addition, the Code of Practice has bearing on the question of PII, in that it compels the disclosure officer to 'list on a sensitive schedule any material the disclosure of which would give a real risk of serious prejudice to an important public interest, and the reason for that belief' (para 6.12). The Code gives examples of such sensitive material, which include material:

(a)   relating to national security;

(b)   given in confidence;

(c)   relating to the identity or activities of informants or under-cover police officers;

(d)   revealing the location of premises used for police surveillance;

(e)   revealing surveillance techniques and other methods of detecting crime;

(f)   relating to a child or young person and generated e.g., by a local authority social services department.

Crucially, inclusion on a 'sensitive' schedule is in no way conclusive of the question whether disclosure is in the public interest. That question is quite clearly one to be answered by the court, both in terms of the statutory provisions referred to above, and the common law rules which the statute preserves. The principle in *Ward* [1993] 1 WLR 619 therefore remains intact: the court, rather than the prosecutor (let alone the investigator) is the final arbiter as to whether disclosure can be avoided on the basis of PII. Further, it is clear that the categories of 'sensitive material' as spelt out in the Code are wider than the types of material which the courts have been prepared to shield behind public interest immunity. The Code gives as an example of sensitive material, 'material given in confidence'. But the fact that material has been given in confidence is not sufficient of itself to ensure that it attracts public interest immunity, so as to enable the prosecution to avoid disclosing it. It is submitted that the courts will be alive to the dangers of a category such as this. If 'sensitivity' was sufficient to attract PII, then all that a police officer would have to do in order to ensure non-disclosure would be to state that material would be treated in confidence, and such an assurance could be given even if it was not sought by the informant. In *H and C* [2004] 2 AC 134, the House of Lords dealt with the questions which the judge must address in making a decision on PII, and reference should be made to the report for a detailed analysis.

There may be certain circumstances in which the prosecution want to make an application for non-disclosure, but believe that revealing the arguments in favour of PII (or even the fact that they are making the application) would 'let the cat out of the bag', e.g., by revealing the existence of an informer and hence allowing the defendant to guess who that informant might be. The CrimPR, Part 25 follow the procedure set out in *Davis* [1993] 1 WLR 613 governing the circumstances in which the defence must be informed of applications made for non-disclosure. The hearing can be either *inter partes* or *ex parte*, and notified to the defence or not notified, depending on the type of application made by the prosecutor. The problem with an *ex parte* hearing is, of course, that there is no opportunity for the defence to argue in favour of disclosure. The court will hear only arguments from the prosecution. As a result, the *ex parte* procedure was challenged in the European Court of Human Rights in *Rowe and Davis v UK* (2000) 30 EHRR 1 (for details, see 28.23 to 28.28). **9.38**

In *Jasper v United Kingdom* (2000) 30 EHRR 441, the European Court of Human Rights held (by a majority of nine to eight) that, in the particular circumstances of the case under consideration, there was no violation of Art 6(1). The application for an order permitting non-disclosure had been heard on an *ex parte* basis. However, the defence were notified that the application had been made, the trial judge gave them as much information regarding the nature of the withheld evidence as possible without revealing what it was, and the defence were permitted to outline their case to the judge. **9.39**

The question of protection for defendants in proceedings to determine disclosure issues came before the European Court of Human Rights again in *Edwards v United Kingdom* (2003) **9.40**

The Times, 29 July 2003. In that case, the tribunal of fact was the trial judge, who had to decide whether to exclude evidence because the accused had been entrapped. Material was produced to the trial judge in *ex parte* hearings. The defence was not aware of the material, and was unable to put forward an argument on it. The material included evidence that the accused had been involved in the supply of heroin before the start of the undercover operation. The case of *Jasper* was distinguished by the court because the evidence subject to public interest immunity in that case had not been put to the tribunal of fact (the jury). Here the tribunal of fact was the judge, and he saw the undisclosed evidence. The defence should have been given the opportunity to counter the evidence and show the judge that it was mistaken or unreliable. The court held that the right of the accused to a fair trial under Art 6(1) had been violated.

G   SANCTIONS RELATING TO DEFENCE DISCLOSURE

9.41   One disadvantage that the defence faces if it has not served a defence statement is that it is unable to make an application for specific disclosure under s 8 of the CPIA.

9.42   In addition, the failure to serve a defence statement may mean that the attention of the prosecution is not directed to a particular line of defence, with the result that it does not identify material which might be expected to assist that defence.

9.43   Section 11 of the CPIA lays down additional sanctions to which the defence will be liable if they are deficient in the duty of disclosure. They apply if the defendant:
(a)   fails to give the initial defence statement required under CPIA 1996, s 5;
(b)   fails to provide an updated statement required under s 6B(1) or a statement that no updating is necessary under s 6B(4);
(c)   fails to give notice of defence witnesses, as required by s 6C;
(d)   supplies any of the above outside the applicable time limit;
(e)   sets out inconsistent defences in the defence statement;
(f)   puts forward a defence at trial which was not mentioned in the defence statement;
(g)   relies on a matter which should have been mentioned in his defence statement to comply with s 6A, but was not;
(h)   gives evidence of alibi or calls a witness to give evidence in support of alibi without having complied with the provisions relating to notification of alibi witnesses;
(i)   calls a witness not included or adequately identified in his notice of defence witnesses.

(The sanctions relating to (b), (c), and (i) were not yet in force at the time of writing).

9.44   By the CPIA 1996, s 6E(2), inserted by CJA 2003, s 36, if it appears to the judge at a pre-trial hearing (see Chapter 16) that the accused has failed to serve a defence statement so that there may be comment made or inferences drawn under the CPIA 1996, s 11(5), he should warn the accused of that possibility. Once the relevant duties are in force, a similar duty is imposed in respect of a failure to update the defence statement when required to do so, or to serve notice of intention to call defence witnesses, The implication is that the defendant may be in a position to remedy the defect at this stage, with the result that the comment or inferences might be avoided.

9.45   At trial, the judge may, if any of the conditions listed in 9.43 apply, ensure that the jury receives a copy of any defence statement (whether initial or updated), edited to exclude any reference to inadmissible evidence. This can be done of the judge's own motion or on application, but only if it would help the jury to understand the case or resolve any issue in it (s 6E(4), (5) and (6)).

In the event that any of the listed conditions is met, then the court may comment upon the **9.46** failure in question. Further, the court or jury may draw such inferences as appear proper in deciding whether the accused is guilty of the offence in question. The accused may not, however, be convicted solely on the basis of such an inference (CPIA 1996, s 11(10)). Other parties (the prosecution and co-accused) may also comment upon the defect, but in certain circumstances such comment requires the leave of the court. Those circumstances are where the defect which triggers off the sanction is:

(a) a failure to mention a point of law or legal authority to be relied on;
(b) a failure to mention a point about admissibility of evidence or abuse or process; or
(c) a failure to give notice of or adequately identify a witness, or failure to give such notice in time (this latter duty was not in force at the time of writing).

Guidance is given about the making of comments and drawing of inferences in three **9.47** situations:

(a) where the defect in question is that the accused put forward a defence different from that set out in his defence statement, the court shall have regard to the extent of any difference, and whether there is any justification for it (s 11(8));
(b) where the defect concerns failure to give notice of, or identify adequately a defence witness the court shall have regard to whether there is any justification for the failure (CPIA 1996, s 11(9));
(c) where the defect is that the accused issued a notice indicating that no updating is required to the defence statement, the question whether there has been a breach of the requirements for the contents of the defence statement or of the duty to supply particulars of alibi must be determined at the time when the statement under s 6B(4) was made and as if the original defence statement had been made at that time.

The duties set out in (b) and (c) were not in force at the time of writing.

In a trial on indictment, where the judge decides to allow the jury to draw an inference, this **9.48** may trigger off the need for a direction in accordance with *Lucas* [1981] QB 720 (see *Burge* [1996] 1 Cr App R 163 as to the circumstances in which a *Lucas* direction ought to be given). The judge would need to direct the jury to consider whether the defence statement constituted a deliberate lie, on a material issue, which was due to the realization of guilt and the fear of the truth. As far as the final point is concerned, the admonition in *Lucas* that a lie did not equate with guilt, but might originate from a variety of causes, including the wish to bolster a just cause, is perhaps particularly apposite in the case of a defence statement which makes exaggerated claims. It is difficult to predict what inference could be drawn where the accused might have lied in order to gain a tactical advantage, let alone where the accused alleges that the falsehood originates in faulty legal advice, or an administrative error on the part of his solicitor.

In *Wheeler* (2000) 164 JP 565, the Court of Appeal gave important guidance on the **9.49** consequences where there is inconsistent defence disclosure. The defendant was charged with knowingly importing cocaine from Jamaica. He had been arrested at Gatwick when 'swallower' packages of the drug were found in his briefcase. Four further packages were found in the room where he was detained, and a further 17 packages were later excreted from his body. When interviewed he said that he did not know how many of the packages he had swallowed. He had brought them into the country out of desperation because he was being threatened by drug suppliers, to whom he owed money.

9.50   The issue at trial was whether he knew that he had been carrying the drugs. He gave evidence that he had been given the drugs to swallow at the airport in Jamaica, but had later vomited, and thought that he had vomited all the packages. He stated that he was not aware that any drugs remained in his stomach when he was stopped at Gatwick, and did not realize that he had drugs with him until the customs officers had found the drugs in his luggage. That version of events was at odds with the defence statement served by his solicitors prior to the trial, which indicated that he was aware that he was carrying drugs, but had done so under duress. When that statement was put to the defendant in cross-examination, he said that the statement was a mistake. Prosecuting counsel then suggested that he had knowingly lied about his defence. In summing up, the judge mentioned that the defendant had said that his defence statement was mistaken, but gave no specific direction to the jury about the inconsistency between it and the defendant's evidence. The defendant was convicted, and appealed. It was the appellant's case, and was accepted by his solicitors, that the defence statement did not reflect his instructions, and had not been approved by him.

9.51   The appeal was allowed. In cases where there was a conflict between the defence statement and the defendant's evidence at trial, the judge ought to give the jury a specific direction on how to approach that inconsistency. The defendant's credibility had been crucial to his case, and the conviction was unsafe in all the circumstances. A retrial was ordered.

9.52   The court made it clear that it was undesirable for solicitors to serve a defence statement without obtaining the defendant's signature as acknowledgement of its accuracy.

9.53   It seems right that the Court of Appeal should insist on clear guidance to the jury in cases where there is apparent inconsistency between the defence statement and the case run by the defence at trial. The judge needs first to make a decision as to whether the jury should be permitted to draw an inference from the inconsistency, in accordance with s 11(3)(b) of the CPIA 1996. Even where it is likely that the defendant has lied, either in the defence statement or in his evidence, then there should be a direction in accordance with *Lucas* [1981] QB 720. In the instant case, it seems that the fault did in fact lie with the solicitors in any event. The Court of Appeal made the point that it would have been wise for the judge to have accepted that, given that the conduct of the defence at trial was in accordance with the version of events given in interview.

H   SUMMARY TRIAL

9.54   The account in the preceding paragraphs relates to trial on indictment. As far as summary trial is concerned, the CPIA partially incorporates such proceedings into the statutory disclosure scheme, by virtue of s 1(1). The prosecution's duty of primary disclosure applies whenever the accused pleads not guilty and the court proceeds to summary trial. Once the prosecutor has complied (or purported to comply) with that duty, the accused *may* give the prosecutor and the court a defence statement (s 6). If he does so, that means that the court may allow comment or draw inferences from disclosure which is late, defective or inconsistent, in much the same circumstances as it may do so in a jury trial (s 11(2) and see 9.41 to 9.53). These sanctions for the defence apply also to the notification of alibi evidence (which until the CPIA had no formal role in summary proceedings). The voluntary regime applies to summary trial, whether it is of a summary or an either-way offence or even (in the case of a juvenile) of an indictable-only offence (s 1(1)).

Few defendants in summary proceedings have in any event volunteered to enter the scheme. **9.55** Most defence lawyers see the balance of advantage as lying in remaining firmly outside the statutory scheme where that is an available option. The obligation to notify the court and the prosecution of witnesses whom the defence intends to call (see 9.24 and 9.25) is one which falls outside the defence statement, which is voluntary as far as the magistrates' court is concerned. It follows that the defence must send notification about the witnesses whom it intends to call, regardless of whether it chooses to serve a defence statement or not. Once this provision is in force, it will introduce an important compulsory element to defence disclosure in the magistrates' court. If the defence fails to fulfil this duty, it will be open to the sanctions described in 9.41 to 9.47.

The question of public interest immunity (PII) in summary trial is dealt with in s 14. Where **9.56** the court has made an order that material should not be disclosed because it is not in the public interest, the accused may apply at any time for the ruling to be reviewed. Section 14 does not impose upon the court an obligation to keep under continuous review any decision not to disclose on PII grounds in summary trial, however, despite the fact that s 15 does impose such an obligation upon the Crown Court in respect of trial on indictment. The difference would appear to stem from the dual role of the magistrates as triers of both fact and law, which was encountered in *South Worcester Magistrates' Court ex parte Lilley* [1995] 1 WLR 1595 (and see the commentary at [1995] Crim LR 954). The problem is that, when the magistrates (in their role as triers of law) conduct a review of documents for which PII is claimed, it may appear to prejudice them in their role as triers of fact; the problem is compounded when the review is conducted *ex parte*, in the absence of the defendant and the defence lawyer. As a result, a new bench may be needed to try the case, after the old bench rules against disclosure. If that new bench were under a duty of continuous review, it would mean that it would be impossible ever to recruit a bench proof against the contamination which results from looking at the material. Hence the onus is put on the defendant to make the application, presumably inhibited by knowledge of the consequences.

I THIRD PARTY DISCLOSURE

Sometimes the information which the accused needs for his defence will be in the hands of **9.57** someone other than the prosecution—a 'third party' as far as the criminal case is concerned. This would be so, for example, if an alleged victim in a child abuse case had files which were in the possession of the local authority, and which the accused alleged were relevant. In such a case, the local authority would be likely to oppose disclosure in any event, on the basis of public interest immunity. But how could the accused apply for disclosure?

9.58   In some cases, the documents would have come into the possession of the police, and possibly the prosecution as well, in the course of the investigation. If so, the documents in question must be retained by the police, and fall within the CPIA disclosure regime (Code, para 5.1).

9.59   If the material remains in the hands of the third party, then the accused is obviously entitled to request it. If the third party is not prepared to hand it over, the procedure available to the accused (or anyone else seeking disclosure from a third party, but it is usually the accused who is in this position) is laid down by s 2(1) of the Criminal Procedure (Attendance of Witnesses) Act 1965, as far as Crown Court trial is concerned. In the magistrates' court, the procedure is governed by the MCA 1980, s 97. The procedure involves seeking a witness summons to compel the third party to attend with the document(s) to give evidence, and/or to produce the document(s) in advance. The person seeking the witness summons must satisfy the court that the third party:

(a)   is likely to be able to give or produce material evidence in the case; and

(b)   will not voluntarily attend or produce the evidence.

9.60   The application will usually be heard on notice to the person to whom the summons is directed (the third party), who may appear or be represented at the hearing. The application should be supported by an affidavit, setting out the charges, identifying the evidence or document sought, stating the grounds for believing that the third party is able to give or produce it, and the grounds for believing that it is material. At the hearing, the third party would be able to argue, for example, that there is no evidence held, or that it is not material, or that it should not be disclosed on grounds of public interest immunity (PII).

9.61   In *Alibhai* [2004] All ER (D) 573 (Mar), Longmore LJ pointed out various unsatisfactory features of the procedure for disclosure of material held by third parties:

(i)   It is not possible to issue a witness summons to a person outside the jurisdiction.

(ii)   A witness summons to produce a 'document or thing' will not elicit information.

(iii)   The 'document or thing' must itself be likely to be material evidence, and a witness summons will not be issued for documents which will not themselves constitute evidence in the case but merely give rise to a line of enquiry which might result in evidence being obtained, still less for documents merely capable of use in cross-examination as to credit.

(iv)   There is no provision for the prosecution or defence, unless they so agree, to examine the documents before they are produced to the court as a result of the witness summons.

9.62   In *Brushett* [2001] Crim LR 471, the Court of Appeal considered a case where disclosure of reports held by social services departments was sought by the accused in a case of alleged sexual abuse of children. Their lordships characterized the principles governing disclosure by third parties as 'narrower' than those where the prosecution held such material. They indicated that disclosure should nevertheless be granted, for example, where there had been false accusations by the subject of the report in the past, or where there had been sexual activity with another adult.

KEY DOCUMENTS

Criminal Procedure and Investigations Act 1996, as amended.

Code of Practice on Disclosure (reproduced as Appendix 5 in *Blackstone's Criminal Practice 2008*).

Part 25 of the Criminal Procedure Rules 2005, available on the website of the Ministry of Justice: <http://www.justice.gov.uk/criminal/procrules_fin/index.htm>.

The Attorney-General's Guidelines on Disclosure of Information in Criminal Proceedings (reproduced as Appendix 5 in *Blackstone's Criminal Practice 2008*).

CPS/Police Disclosure Manual: available at <www.cps.gov.uk/legal/section20/chapter_a.html>. It contains links to many of the other documents referred to in this list.

Protocol for the Provision of Advance Information, Prosecution Evidence and Disclosure of Unused Material in the Magistrates' Courts—available at <www.judiciary.gov.uk>, click 'judgments and guidance' and then 'protocols and guidance on criminal cases'.

Protocol for the Control and Management of Unused Material in the Crown Court—available as above.

10

COURSE OF A SUMMARY TRIAL

10.01 Subject to a limited exception introduced by the Criminal Justice Act 1988 (see 8.44), all summary offences are tried in a magistrates' court. Offences which are indictable but triable either way (see 1.07 to 1.09) are tried in a magistrates' court if, essentially, both the magistrates and the accused agree. Because the most commonly committed offences (e.g., those under the Road Traffic Act 1988) are summary, and because many accused charged with a triable either way matter elect, if given the option, to stay in the lower court, over 95 per cent of criminal cases are disposed of by the magistrates. The course of a summary trial is the same whether the offence charged is summary or triable either way. In the latter case, however, the procedure set out in the Magistrates' Courts Act 1980, ss 19–22 for determining the mode of trial must be complied with before the start of the hearing (see Chapter 8).

10.02 The conduct of a summary trial is governed principally by the Magistrates' Courts Act 1980 (MCA). Note that the terms 'summary trial' and 'trial by the magistrates' may be used interchangeably.

A   JURISDICTION OF A MAGISTRATES' COURT

10.03 A magistrates' court has jurisdiction to try an offence triable either way wherever it was allegedly committed: MCA, s 2(3) and (4). This is subject (a) to its being an offence in respect of which the English courts claim jurisdiction (see 5.29 to 5.31), and (b) to the accused consenting to summary trial following the procedure for determining the mode of trial described in Chapter 8. Assuming those two conditions are met, the magistrates' jurisdiction simply depends upon the accused appearing or being brought before their court. An accused will come to court either in answer to a summons, or in answer to his bail, or in the custody of the police or of the prison authorities (see Chapter 7 for details). Even if the accused's attendance is secured by unlawful means (e.g., through the execution of a wrongfully issued warrant for arrest) the magistrates' jurisdiction is unaffected, at least if no objection is made at the time to the illegality: *Hughes* (1879) 4 QBD 614. In most cases, the prosecutor—who, in effect, takes the initial decision as to which court the proceedings shall be held in—will opt to have the accused come before the magistrates' court for the petty sessional division where the offence allegedly occurred. In addition, a magistrates' court has jurisdiction to try any summary offence.

B   THE BENCH

10.04 'A magistrates' court shall not try an information summarily...except when composed of at least 2 justices...' MCA, s 121(1). The maximum number who may sit is three. Usually the bench consists of three in order to avoid the risk of being equally divided as to the verdict. Except in the youth court, a district judge may and normally does sit alone. Where, exceptionally, a district judge sits with lay justices, he acts as their chairman. The chairman of an all lay bench will be one of the chairmen chosen at the annual elections held by the bench, unless none is present in which case it will simply be the most senior magistrate.

10.05 During the course of a trial, the bench has a discretion to hear representations in chambers, i.e., in private: *Nottingham Magistrates' Court ex parte K* (1996) 160 JP 201. However, the discretion must be exercised with even greater caution than applies to the equivalent procedure when seeing a judge in a trial on indictment (for the details of which, see 20.13). All parties should be made aware of the hearing and be represented in chambers (except where there is an issue of public interest immunity to be heard on an *ex parte* basis: see 9.33 to 9.47).

A contemporaneous note of proceedings should be taken, normally by the clerk, so as to have a record in the event of any future dispute.

A magistrate is disqualified from adjudicating in a particular case if *either* he has any direct **10.06** pecuniary interest (however small) in the outcome *or* he has a non-pecuniary interest substantial enough to lead to a real danger of bias (*Gough* [1993] AC 646). This is one aspect of the rule of natural justice that 'nobody shall be a judge in his own cause'. The rule applies equally to civil and criminal cases, and to the Crown Court and Court of Appeal as well as to the magistrates' courts. However, it is of special importance in the context of summary proceedings as magistrates, by reason of the local nature of their involvement, are far more likely to have an interest in a case than, say, a High Court judge sitting in the Crown Court. The strictness of the rule against a judge or magistrate having a pecuniary interest in the matter before the court is illustrated by the old case of *Dimes v Grand Junction Canal* (1852) 3 HL Cas 759, where decrees granted by the then Lord Chancellor in favour of a canal company were set aside when it was discovered that he owned shares therein. Nobody could seriously have suspected that the Lord Chancellor would be swayed by the thought that his shares might have risen marginally in value were he to hold in favour of the company, but even that minimal pecuniary interest disqualified him from hearing the case. As regards non-pecuniary interests, the test is: would a fair-minded and informed observer conclude that there was a real danger that the bench was biased (see *Porter v Magill* [2002] 2 AC 357 and 18.55).

In *Altrincham Justices ex parte Pennington* [1975] 1 QB 549 a conviction for delivering less **10.07** than the contracted weight of carrots to two state schools was quashed by the High Court because the chairman of the convicting magistrates was a co-opted member of the county council's education committee and thus had a general interest in the good running of local schools. By contrast, in *Camborne Justices ex parte Pearce* [1955] 1 QB 41, a magistrates' clerk was held to be under no duty to withdraw from a case where a trader was being proceeded against by the local authority under food and drugs legislation since, even though the clerk was a local councillor, he was not a member of the health committee that had advised the prosecution.

It quite often happens that a magistrate realizes (perhaps after the case has started) that he **10.08** knows a witness or a party, or is aware of information detrimental to the accused. In such cases, the test of whether the magistrate should sit or continue to sit is again whether a fair-minded and informed observer would conclude that there is a real danger of bias. Where the charge sheets informing the magistrates of the day's business indicate that an accused is appearing in court for several unconnected matters, and he then pleads not guilty to the first charge, the knowledge that there are other charges may be sufficient to disqualify the bench from hearing the not guilty plea, but it will depend on the facts of the individual case. Thus, in *Liverpool Justices ex parte Topping* [1983] 1 WLR 119 the charge sheets showed that T was appearing to be sentenced for one offence and had also been charged with a second offence. The High Court held that the magistrates should not have tried T's not guilty plea to the second matter. On the other hand, in *Weston-super-Mare Justices ex parte Shaw* [1987] QB 640, where S was listed as appearing on seven charges, one of wasting police time and the remainder arising out of a quite separate 'escapade' with a motor cycle, the bench were entitled to try the first information (to which S pleaded not guilty) even though they knew of the six other allegations (which he ultimately admitted after being convicted of the first). Perhaps the vital distinction between the two cases is that in *Ex parte Topping* the magistrates knew that T had already been convicted by their court of something else, whereas in *Ex parte Shaw* they merely knew that S faced several charges. As a matter of administration, the clerk's office at a magistrates' court usually tries to prevent the occurrence of problems such as arose in *Ex parte Topping* and *Ex parte Shaw* by concealing from the magistrates due to try an accused for one offence any other charge sheets relating to unconnected offences. After the trial of the not guilty plea, the bench can be given the additional charge sheets. If the accused pleads guilty to them, he can be sentenced both for those offences and (if he was convicted) for the offence he denied. If he pleads not guilty, the magistrates would probably be well advised to avoid any suspicion of unfairness, and would therefore adjourn for a hearing by different magistrates. Ultimately, though, it is a matter for the justices' discretion, applying the test set out above.

10.09   Decided cases also deal with the position of a magistrate who happens to know that the accused has previous convictions (e.g., because he was a member of the court which previously convicted and sentenced him). It has been stated that it is desirable that the magistrate should withdraw but there is no rule of law to that effect: *McElligott ex parte Gallagher* [1972] Crim LR 332. Indeed, in the case of a recidivist offender from a small community, it might be difficult to find a magistrate who does not know that the accused is, so to speak, a regular client. In *Downham Market Magistrates' Court ex parte Nudd* [1989] RTR 169, N was convicted of various motoring offences, including failure to provide a specimen of breath. A month before, the chairman of the convicting magistrates had imposed a suspended sentence on him for threatening to kill his wife, and had seen his record, which included a conviction for drink-driving. He applied to have his conviction quashed. The Divisional Court accepted that the justices would sometimes be called on to deal with defendants whom they had dealt with before. This was inevitable where the bench was small (Downham Market's was 11 strong at the time). In view of the fact that N's solicitor had sent a letter to the clerk well before the hearing, however, he should have considered whether it was in the interests of justice for the chairman to sit. The convictions were quashed. Where knowledge about previous convictions has been gained as a result of adjudicating upon a bail application by the accused in the same proceedings, there is an absolute statutory rule that the magistrate must not sit for a summary trial: MCA, s 42. When the repeals contained in Part 4 of Sch 37 of the CJA 2003 come into force, s 42 of the MCA will be repealed. As a result, there will no longer be a bar on a magistrate who has acquired knowledge of previous convictions in such circumstances sitting on the trial.

10.10   Failure by a magistrate to withdraw from a case if he has a disqualifying interest will render any decision the court arrives at liable to be quashed through an application for judicial review.

10.11   The rule that magistrates must not sit if they have a disqualifying interest entails the corollary that their names should not unnecessarily be kept secret—otherwise it may be impossible for the parties, the press or the public at large to discover that somebody was on the bench who ought not to have been. For that reason, and also on account of general considerations of the desirability of open justice, it was held in *Felixstowe Justices ex parte Leigh* [1987] QB 582 that the respondent justices' practice of withholding their names from the press and even the parties was unlawful. While it may not be practicable to print the names of the adjudicating magistrates on the court lists for the day, any bona fide enquirer ought to be able to ascertain from a court clerk who they are or were. If the clerk reasonably thinks that the information is wanted for improper purposes (e.g., to threaten or harass the magistrate), he has a discretion to withhold it.

C THE INFORMATION

The information plays a dual role in criminal procedure. It is the charge to which the accused **10.12** pleads guilty or not guilty at the beginning of a summary trial, and also, at a much earlier stage of the proceedings, it is the justification for the issue of a summons in a case where the accused's first appearance before the magistrates is secured by that means. This Section is concerned with the information's first-mentioned role, but to put the discussion into context it is necessary to recapitulate on how the information comes into being (see also 3.36 and 5.04).

An information may be likened to a count in an indictment. Like a count it must not charge **10.13** more than one offence. The form of the information is governed by CrimPR, r 7.3, which states that a magistrates' court may not try an information which charges more than one offence, although two or more informations may be set out in the same document. In addition, two or more separate criminal acts may be alleged in one information if the accused's conduct comprised a single activity (see *Jemmison v Priddle* [1972] 1 QB 489 and *Horrix v Malam* [1984] RTR 112 where the High Court approved single informations for, respectively, shooting two deer one after the other, and for careless driving on three different roads, the driving complained of being divided into two incidents separated by about ten minutes in time and two miles in distance and observed by two different police officers). An information which includes allegations in the alternative is valid if it is alleging different ways of committing what, on a true construction of the relevant statutory provision, is a single offence. It is invalid if it is alleging two different offences in the alternative, even if those offences are created by a single provision (see *Thompson v Knights* [1947] KB 336, where a conviction on an information for driving under the influence of drink *or* drugs contrary to what is now s 4 of the Road Traffic Act 1988 was upheld because the section creates one offence of driving when unfit which can be committed either in a drunken or a drugged condition. Contrast *Surrey Justices ex parte Witherick* [1932] 1 KB 450 in which an information for driving without due care and attention or without reasonable consideration contrary to what is now s 3 of the Road Traffic Act 1988 was held invalid since under s 3 there are two separate offences, one of careless driving and a second of driving without reasonable consideration). Although the above principles are relatively easy to state, applying them to informations seems to cause even more difficulty than applying them to counts in an indictment. The High Court is asked surprisingly frequently to quash a summary conviction on the ground that the information was bad for duplicity, and in such cases their Lordships tend to draw distinctions which are so fine as to be almost invisible. Thus, in *Bristol Crown Court ex parte Willets* [1985] Crim LR 219 it was held that a single information for possessing for publication for gain five different obscene video tapes contrary to s 2(1) of the Obscene Publications Act 1959 was valid since it alleged a single activity—there was no need to have a separate information for each tape. In *Ward* [1988] Crim LR 57, on the other hand, an information for possessing by way of trade 15 videotaped films in breach of copyright contrary to s 24(1) of the Copyright Act 1956 was held duplicitous. In both cases, the articles wrongfully in the accused's possession were found as a result of a single search of his premises, so it is difficult to see why in the one case the conduct amounted to a single activity and in the other it did not. Trying to reconcile all the decisions in this area of procedure is a fruitless task.

10.14 An information which is bad for duplicity can, however, be rescued even after the trial has commenced. CrimPR, r 7.3 provides that, if the fact that the information charges more than one offence is spotted at any stage in the trial, the court shall call on the prosecutor to elect on which offence he desires the court to proceed. The other offences are then struck out, and the court proceeds to try the information afresh. Failing an election by the prosecution, the information will be dismissed. Where the accused requests an adjournment to deal with the amended information, the court must grant his request if it appears he has been unfairly prejudiced.

10.15 The contents of an information are similar to the contents of a count. Using, as far as possible, non-technical language, it must give reasonable particulars of the nature of the charge, but it need not state every element of the offence alleged. Where the offence is statutory it must refer to the statute and section contravened. It is not necessary, however, to allege specifically that the accused falls outside the ambit of any defence provided by the statute creating the offence (see r 6 of the Indictment Rules 1971 for a similar rule in relation to counts in an indictment). The main difference between an information and a count is that the former, unlike the latter, is not split into a Statement of Offence and Particulars of Offence. Below are three examples of informations:

> John Smith on the 1st day of January 2008 did assault Richard Brown, a constable of the county of Barsetshire, in the execution of his duty contrary to s 89(1) of the Police Act 1996.

> John Smith on the 1st day of January 2008 interfered with a motor vehicle, namely a Ford Mondeo number W123 ABC, with intent to steal the said motor vehicle or take it for his own use without lawful authority or steal property within the said motor vehicle, contrary to s 9(1) of the Criminal Attempts Act 1981.

> John Smith on the 1st day of January 2008 drove a motor vehicle, namely a Rolls-Royce number V100 CJE, on a road, namely Acacia Avenue, London W30, without due care and attention, contrary to s 3 of the Road Traffic Act 1988.

The CrimPR, rr 7.2 and 7.3 govern the drafting of informations.

10.16 Two or more accused may be charged in one information with having committed an offence jointly. If so, they will nearly always be tried together, irrespective of their wishes in the matter.

10.17 Where there are two or more informations against one accused or where two or more accused are charged in separate informations, the magistrates may try the informations together if none of the parties objects. Should there be an objection (albeit only from one of several accused) there must be separate trials, unless the magistrates decide that the informations are so related to each other by time or other factors that the interests of justice will best be served by a single hearing. The interests of justice include the convenient presentation of the prosecution case as well as the minimizing of any risk of injustice to the accused (see *Re Clayton* [1983] 2 AC 473, which abolished the previous inconvenient rule that a single trial of separate informations was always conditional upon all the parties agreeing, however unreasonable any objection might appear to be). Where magistrates hear submissions as to whether several informations against one accused should be tried together, and they decide against that course, they will further have to consider whether, in the light of the principles set out in *Porter v Magill* [2002] 2 AC 357 (see 10.06), it is appropriate for them to deal with any part of the case. They may well decide that, knowing that the accused faces other charges, there is a real danger of bias if they accept jurisdiction even in respect of one matter. They would therefore have to adjourn for all the informations to be heard in sequence by differently constituted benches.

The court may not try an information for a *summary* offence unless it was laid within six months **10.18** of the offence being committed: MCA, s 127. The rule does not apply to summary trials of either-way offences, which may take place at any time, subject only to the few exceptional cases in which the statute creating an indictable offence lays down a time-limit for commencing prosecutions (see 5.35 to 5.36). Such time-limits apply regardless of whether the proposed mode of trial would be summary or on indictment. The purpose of s 127 was succinctly expressed by May J in *Newcastle upon Tyne Justices ex parte Bryce (Contractors) Ltd* [1976] 1 WLR 517, where he said that the section existed:

> To ensure that summary offences are charged and tried as soon as reasonably possible after their alleged commission, so that the recollection of witnesses may still be reasonably clear, and so that there shall be no unnecessary delay in the disposal by magistrates' courts of the summary offences brought before them to be tried.

It could be argued that those considerations apply equally to summary trial of either-way offences, but Parliament no doubt considered that the graver nature of either-way offences and the fact that witnesses are likely to remember such crimes more vividly than they remember less serious summary infractions made it undesirable to extend s 127 beyond summary offences. Where the aims of the section are indirectly thwarted by tardiness between the laying of an information and the bringing of the case to court the magistrates have a discretion to prevent the prosecution calling their evidence (see 10.26 to 10.31). It has even been held that there is a discretion not to issue a summons if the information, although technically within time, has been laid tardily and no explanation for the delay is given (see *Clerk to the Medway Justices ex parte DHSS* [1986] Crim LR 686 where the High Court refused to order the clerk to issue a summons against X for fraud on the DHSS, the relevant facts being that, although the information was laid within the period of 12 months prescribed by s 147(3) of the Social Security Act 1973, officials of the Department had simply sat on the papers relating to X for about four months before bothering to ask for a summons).

Since the information must be laid within six months of the commission of the offence, it is **10.19** necessary to pinpoint:

(i) the date on which the offence was committed; and
(ii) the date when the information is laid.

As far as (i) is concerned, the case of *Lawrence v Ministry of Agriculture, Fisheries and Food* (1992) *The Times*, 26 February 1992 illustrates the problem which may occasionally arise. L was charged with making a false statement to obtain a farm capital grant. He completed the form on 6 December 1989, it was received by the appropriate office on 15 December, and the information was laid on 12 June 1990. The justices held that the information was laid in time.

On appeal, the Divisional Court upheld their decision: the offence was committed when the statement was made, and it was made when the person to whom it was made received it.

10.20   As to (ii), the question of when an information is laid arose in *Kennet Justices ex parte Humphrey* [1993] Crim LR 787. H and W were charged with affray; W also faced a charge of reckless driving. The CPS decided to reduce the charges to breach of the peace and driving without due care, and wrote to the clerk to the justices to that effect, attaching copies of the reduced charges. The letter arrived at the magistrates' court within six months of the date of the alleged offences. H and W did not appear in court until after the six months had expired. The original charges were then dismissed, and the new ones preferred. H and W objected that the new informations had not been laid within six months. The Divisional Court disagreed, and dismissed their appeal. Section 127 of the MCA merely imposed a time-limit for the laying of informations— not for the first appearance of a defendant to answer a charge. The informations were laid when the prosecution informed the clerk by letter of the intention to charge H and W at a later date.

10.21   The magistrates have a discretion to allow, at any stage of the hearing, an amendment to the information. In addition, MCA, s 123 provides that defects in the form or substance of an information and variations between the allegations in it and the evidence adduced by the prosecution at the trial are not grounds for objecting to the information. Where, however, the accused has been misled by a variance between the information and the prosecution evidence he must, on application, be granted an adjournment.

10.22   Section 123 is so widely worded that, if read literally, it would enable the prosecution to support a conviction however grossly inadequate or misleading the information was. In fact, numerous cases have given a restricted meaning to the section. The cases establish that where the defect in the information, or variation between it and the evidence, is trivial, so that the accused is not prejudiced or misled by it, any conviction upon the information will stand even though the information is not amended. Misspellings of the accused's name or of place names provide examples of such trivial errors. In *Sandwell Justices ex parte West Midland Passenger Transport Board* [1979] Crim LR 56 a variation between the evidence (that the Board had put on the road a bus with a defective rear off side tyre) and the information (which alleged that the defective tyre was the rear near side one) was stated by the High Court to be so slight that, even in the absence of the amendment which was in fact made, the conviction would have stood. The Board had always been aware of which tyre was the subject of complaint, and, indeed, brought it to court for examination. The position of the tyre on the bus was a matter of no consequence.

10.23   Where the variation between the information and the evidence is substantial, the prosecution should apply for an amendment. If they allow the amendment, the magistrates should consider whether the accused has been misled by the original information, and, if he has, they must grant him an adjournment. Failure to obtain an amendment, or failure by the magistrates to allow the accused an adjournment when he is entitled to one, will lead to any conviction being quashed. In *Wright v Nicholson* [1970] 1 WLR 142, for example, the High Court quashed W's conviction for inciting a child to commit an act of gross indecency contrary to the Indecency with Children Act 1960, s 2. The information, which was not amended, alleged that the offence occurred on 17 August 1967. The evidence of the child was vague as to when the incident happened—it could have been any time in August. W, who had called alibi evidence in respect of August 17, was convicted on the basis that he committed the offence some time in August. The information misled W, it was not amended, and it may have caused him grave injustice because, in the absence of an adjournment, he was unable to call alibi evidence for other days in August.

Amendment of the information and, if appropriate, the granting of an adjournment can **10.24** remedy almost any defect in it. In *Wyllie v CPS* [1989] Crim LR 753, the Divisional Court upheld the bench's decision to allow amendment of an information from failing to supply a specimen of urine to failing to supply blood. The evidence in that case would have been the same regardless of which offence was proceeded with. Further, the Divisional Court found it significant that, faced with the amendment, the defence had not asked for an adjournment. That suggested that they had not been prejudiced. Where, however, the information is laid against the wrong person (e.g., a company secretary and not the company itself) the defect is so fundamental that even an amendment will not assist the prosecution: *City of Oxford Tramway Co. v Sankey* (1890) 54 JP 564.

Where an information is laid within the time limit, the magistrates may allow the information **10.25** to be amended after the expiry of the time limit, provided that:

(i) the proposed amendment arises out of substantially the same facts as gave rise to the original offence; and

(ii) the interests of justice favour the amendment (*Scunthorpe Justices ex parte M* (1998) *The Times*, 10 March 1998).

D ABUSE OF PROCESS

The magistrates are under a general statutory duty, imposed by MCA, s 9(2), to hear the available **10.26** evidence first, and then decide whether to convict or acquit. *Birmingham Justices ex parte Lamb* [1983] 1 WLR 339. However, the bench does have a limited discretion to dismiss a case on the grounds that it constitutes an abuse of process. The issues relating to applications for dismissal on the grounds of abuse of process are broadly similar to those in the Crown Court, and reference should be made to 20.14 to 20.20 where the principles are set out. The paragraphs which follow concentrate upon the position in the magistrates' court.

There is a statutory rule that an information for a summary offence must be laid within six **10.27** months of its commission (see MCA, s 127 and 10.18(e)). Clearly, the purpose of this provision is to ensure that trials for summary offences, which by and large are relatively minor matters unlikely to remain for long in the minds of witnesses, shall take place speedily before memories have completely faded. There is, however, no statutory prohibition on the prosecution laying an information just within time, and then—whether by accident or design—being very slow in serving the summons and bringing the case to court. To prevent Parliament's intentions being thus indirectly thwarted, the High Court has recognized that magistrates do have a discretion to acquit without hearing evidence if *either* the prosecution have abused correct court procedure by deliberate delay, *or* their inefficiency has led to extreme delay which might prejudice the accused if the trial were to be allowed to proceed. The first-mentioned type of case is illustrated by *Brentford Justices ex parte Wong* [1981] QB 445. Having laid an information just within the six-month period, the police prosecutor then took a further four months to serve the summons on W. Apparently, he laid the information without having decided whether or not to proceed with a prosecution, and it was only after the additional four months that he made up his mind. This amounted to a deliberate abuse of the criminal process, in that an information should be laid with the intention of serving the resultant summons on the accused as soon as reasonably possible. Therefore, the justices were entitled to dismiss the information without a hearing. An example of the second type of case—i.e., inefficiency but no deliberate abuse—is *Oxford City Justices ex parte Smith* (1982) 75 Cr App R 200. The offence, driving with excess alcohol in the blood, was allegedly committed during S's last term at university, but, by the time the information was laid, he had gone down. However, he had sensibly given the police both the address of his 'digs' and his home address. Unfortunately, the prosecutions department failed to realize until some two years later that they had the home address, and it was only then that they managed to serve the summons. Since S's recollection of relevant matters might have been affected by a delay for which he was not to blame, the High Court held that the magistrates should not have allowed the prosecution to proceed. The police had been 'inefficient, unobservant or both', and the delay was so long as to be 'unconscionable'.

10.28 The case law on abuse of process is not confined to circumstances where there has been lengthy and/or prejudicial delay (see 20.14 to 20.20) and the magistrates may protect the court's process from abuse on various grounds. It has been made clear by the appellate courts, however, that the magistrates' power ought only to be utilised in exceptional circumstances. In *R(CPS) v City of London Magistrates' Court* [2006] EWHC 1153, the Divisional Court stated that the magistrates' power to restrain abuse of process should usually be invoked only where the court decided either (a) that the defendant could not receive a fair trial or (b) that it would be unfair for him to be tried.

10.29 Certainly it is possible, in appropriate circumstances, for the magistrates to decide that apparent bad faith on the part of the prosecutor is sufficient to justify dismissal without hearing. In *Sherwood v Ross* [1989] Crim LR 576 it was held that private prosecutions for theft, assault, and threatening words or behaviour arising out of an incident at the prosecutor's business premises were properly stayed because, after the police had declined to prosecute, a period of six months elapsed during which there was correspondence between the solicitors for the parties mentioning only the possibility of civil proceedings. In all the circumstances, it seemed that the prosecutor had decided to institute criminal proceedings merely as a bargaining counter in the negotiations over a civil settlement.

10.30 On the other hand, in *Dorchester Justices ex parte DPP* [1990] RTR 369, the circumstances fell short of what was necessary for the bench to refuse properly to try the information. In that case, an ambulance driver attended court as a defence witness. He was seen talking to police officers, who were witnesses for the prosecution. The defence solicitor submitted that the police officers' evidence could have been tainted. Without hearing any evidence, the bench dismissed the information. The Crown applied for judicial review. The Divisional Court allowed the application, remitting the case to be heard by a different bench. No decision as to whether testimony would be tainted could be reached properly without hearing evidence.

10.31 It was made clear in *Crawley Justices ex parte DPP* (1991) *The Times*, 5 April 1991, that before dismissing an information as an abuse of process, the justices should hear from both prosecution and defence. In that case, the justices had not heard from the prosecution before making their decision, but similar principles apply were the bench refuses to hear from the defence: *Clerkenwell Stipendiary Magistrate, ex parte Bell* (1991) 155 JP 669.

E   APPEARANCE OF THE ACCUSED AND THE PROSECUTOR

A major difference between summary trial and trial on indictment is that in the latter case the **10.32** accused must be present to plead to the indictment, and should normally be in court throughout his trial (see 20.71 to 20.73). Summary trials, on the other hand, may and often do take place in the accused's absence. Section 12 of the MCA permits the accused to plead guilty by post, ss 11 and 13 set out the options open to the magistrates when an accused, who has not intimated under s 12 that he wishes to plead guilty, fails to appear at the time appointed for trial.

Where the accused does appear in court, he should not be in handcuffs, unless there are **10.33** reasonable grounds for apprehending violence or an attempt to escape (*Cambridge Justices ex parte Peacock* [1993] Crim LR 219).

Proceeding in the accused's absence under s 11

If the accused does not appear at the time and place fixed for summary trial, the magistrates **10.34** have a discretion to proceed in his absence: s 11(1). If they do so, a plea of not guilty to the information is entered on behalf of the accused, and the prosecution proceed to call their evidence. In the circumstances, they are unlikely to have much difficulty in proving their case, but should the evidence for any reason prove insufficient (e.g., an essential witness fails to give the evidence which was expected of him) the magistrates would be obliged to find the accused not guilty. The position is different where the accused pleads guilty by post under s 12 (see the next Section). If there are several informations against an absent accused, or if several absent accused are charged in separate informations, the magistrates can dispose of the informations together if that is in the interests of justice (see *Re Clayton* [1983] 2 AC 473 and 9.19(d)).

It would obviously be unfair to proceed without the accused if he did not know of the proceed- **10.35** ings against him. Accordingly, if the proceedings began with the laying of an information and the issue of a summons requiring the accused to appear at court, the magistrates may not begin to try the case without him unless it is proved that the summons was served on him a reasonable time before the hearing date, or he appeared on a previous occasion in answer to the summons when the case was adjourned: s 11(2). A summons can be served by sending it through the post to the accused's last known address. Where that method of service is adopted, and the offence charged is indictable, the prosecution in order to prove service must prove that the summons actually came to the knowledge of the accused. If the offence charged is summary, proof that the summons was sent to the last known address is sufficient proof of service: CrimPR, r 4.1. That gives rise to the possibility that the prosecution may be able to prove service when the accused is, in fact, totally unaware of the summons (e.g., because the letter containing it was received by somebody else at the same address, and that person failed to pass it on to the accused). Section 14 accordingly provides that where proceedings commence with the issue of a summons, and the accused is tried in his absence, he may deliver to the magistrates' clerk a statutory declaration to the effect that he did not know of the summons or the proceedings until a date after the trial's commencement. The declaration should normally be delivered within 21 days of the date on which the declarant found out about the proceedings. A timeously delivered declaration makes void the summons and all subsequent proceedings, but the information remains valid so the prosecution can restart the prosecution process.

10.36 Where proceedings begin, not with the issue of a summons, but with the accused being arrested, either with or without warrant, the fact of the arrest alerts him to the charge against him. Accordingly, if he is bailed from the police station to appear at the magistrates' court but fails to do so, the magistrates can try him in his absence without any formal proof that he knows of the hearing. In fact, if the offence charged is serious enough to justify an arrest, the magistrates might be reluctant to deal with it without the accused.

10.37 *Bolton Justices ex parte Merna* (1991) 155 JP 612 considered the position where the accused is absent, and seeks an adjournment. After M's case had been adjourned on a number of occasions, it was set down for trial, the justices indicating that if he failed to attend, they would proceed in his absence. He did not attend, but provided a medical certificate and a doctor's letter stating that he was suffering from acute anxiety and depression and was not fit to attend court. The justices refused to adjourn, and proceeded to try and convict him. M sought judicial review, which was granted, and the conviction quashed. The Divisional Court said that the magistrates should have exercised their discretion judicially. If an accused claimed to be ill with apparently responsible professional support for his claim, the court should not reject that claim without satisfying itself that it was proper to do so.

10.38 Two final points should be noticed about proceeding in the absence of the accused. First, although he can be tried summarily in his absence for an offence triable either way, he must normally be present for the hearing at which it is decided to deal with the case summarily (see Chapter 8). Second, if the magistrates, as often happens, do not try the case on the first occasion it comes into their list but adjourn it to another day, the adjourned hearing cannot proceed unless all parties have had adequate notice of the date to which the case was adjourned: s 10(2).

10.39 Even if the magistrates have power to try the information without the accused they may choose not to do so if for example the offence alleged seems fairly serious. The court ought generally to be more reluctant to try in his absence an offender who is young, has not been placed on bail, and/or has no record of failing to appear on previous occasions (*Dewsbury Magistrates' Court ex parte K* (1994) *The Times*, 16 March 1994). If there is apparently a good reason for the accused's non-appearance (e.g., the police officer in the case says that he is in hospital) the magistrates may simply adjourn, and trust that on the date the hearing is to resume the accused will be present. Should there be no satisfactory explanation for his absence, the magistrates will want to issue a warrant for his arrest. Where the accused was on bail and has failed to surrender to custody in answer to his bail, the court can issue a bench warrant: Bail Act 1976, s 7. If he is not on bail but has merely failed to appear in answer to a summons, s 13 provides that a warrant for arrest can only be issued if there is proof of service of the summons, or the case has been adjourned from a previous occasion and the accused appeared on that occasion. In the case of an accused aged 18 or over, there are additional requirements that the offence charged must be punishable with imprisonment, or that the court must propose to impose a disqualification upon the accused. In the case of a juvenile, there is a condition that the court proposes to impose a disqualification upon the accused.

Pleas of guilty by post

Proceeding in the absence of the accused under MCA, s 11 has at least three disadvantages. **10.40** The court's time is wasted hearing evidence which nobody is present to challenge, the prosecution witnesses are inconvenienced, and the accused has no opportunity to tell the magistrates about any mitigating circumstances which ought to reduce the penalty imposed upon him. These disadvantages are overcome by the s 12 procedure for pleading guilty by post. The procedure can only be used where the accused is summoned to appear before a magistrates' court to answer an information alleging a summary offence. The procedure is as follows:

(a) The prosecutor serves on the accused, together with the summons, a notice explaining how he can plead guilty by post and what will happen if he does so. In addition, the prosecutor serves a brief statement of the facts of the alleged offence. The statement of facts is necessary because the accused may admit that he committed the offence alleged in the information set out in the summons but be unwilling to forgo attending court unless he knows what the prosecution will say about the manner in which he committed the offence. In place of a statement of facts, the prosecution may supply witness statement(s).

(b) The prosecutor notifies the magistrates' clerk that the documents referred to in (a) have been served.

(c) The accused, if he so wishes, notifies the clerk in writing that he wants to plead guilty without appearing before the court. With the notification, he can send a statement of any mitigating facts which he would like to be brought to the court's attention.

(d) On the day of the 'hearing', neither the defence nor the prosecution witnesses attend court. All that happens is that the clerk states that a plea of guilty by post has been received; the prosecution representative (or the clerk) recites the brief statement of facts; and the clerk reads out the letter in mitigation. The magistrates may then proceed to sentence. So that an accused pleading guilty by post can know with confidence what will and what will not be said against him, it is a strict rule that the only facts about the offence given to the court are those set out in the brief statement served with the summons.

(e) If, having given notice that he wished to plead guilty, the accused changes his mind, he may notify the clerk in writing that he wants his original notification to be withdrawn. The case is not dealt with under s 12, and the accused is entitled to attend court and plead not guilty in the usual way.

(f) The magistrates always have a discretion not to accept a plea of guilty by post. If the accused's statement of mitigating circumstances should allege facts which, if accepted, would amount to a defence to the charge it would clearly be wrong to proceed on the guilty plea. Instead, the court should adjourn the case. Notice is then given to the accused of the adjournment and the reason for it, and the case proceeds as if no notification of a guilty plea had ever been given.

Section 12 can still apply, by virtue of s 12A, even when the defendant does make an appearance **10.41** in court. If the defendant has indicated that he wants to plead guilty by post but then appears, the court may with his consent proceed under s 12, just as if he were absent. The court is given a similar power even where the defendant has never notified it of an intention to plead guilty by post. In either event, if the s 12 procedure is used but the defendant is present, the court must give him the option of making a statement in mitigation.

10.42 A great many minor summary offences are disposed of through pleas of guilty by post. The procedure is especially well-suited to road traffic offences.

10.43 The system of fixed penalty fines for offences such as speeding and jumping the lights (see 5.18 to 5.19) has to some extent replaced pleas of guilty by post. However, whether or not to deal with a road traffic matter by means of a fixed penalty notice is within the discretion of the police, and officers still frequently opt for proceeding by summons (but with the option of a plea by post) if they consider that a fixed penalty would be inadequate having regard to the speed the vehicle was doing.

Sentencing an offender in his absence

10.44 Magistrates may not pass a custodial sentence in the absence of the offender (MCA, s 11(3)). Nor may they disqualify from driving unless *either* the offender is present *or* the case was previously adjourned for him to attend and show cause why he should not be disqualified, notice to that effect having been served on him (s 11(4)). Following conviction in the accused's absence under s 11(1), magistrates may issue a warrant for his arrest provided (i) the offence is punishable with imprisonment or they are considering disqualification, and (ii) they think it undesirable to continue in his absence having regard to the gravity of the offence (s 13(3) and (4)).

Non-appearance of the prosecution

10.45 If the prosecution fail to appear at the time and place fixed for summary trial, the magistrates have a discretion either to dismiss the information or adjourn the case: MCA, s 15. If the case has been adjourned part-heard from a previous occasion, and the prosecution do not appear for the adjourned hearing, the magistrates have the additional option of proceeding in the absence of the prosecution. The evidence given for the prosecution on the previous occasion will then be the case against the accused, and in meeting that case he has the obvious advantage of not facing any prosecution challenge to his evidence or arguments.

F   LEGAL REPRESENTATION

10.46 Both barristers and solicitors have the right of audience in the magistrates' courts. In addition, in certain circumstances, the CPS may be represented by a designated member of staff who is not a solicitor or barrister. The prosecution need not be legally represented so, for example, a private prosecutor alleging an assault by his neighbour could present the case himself. The accused may, of course, defend himself if he so wishes. Where he is not legally aided and the consequences of a conviction are unlikely to be serious, he would be well advised to save money by doing so. The clerk may assist him in presenting his case (e.g., by indicating the sort of questions he should ask in cross-examination), and an unrepresented accused sometimes seems to attract the sympathy of the bench in a way a represented one would not.

It is not the practice for the magistrates to grant persons other than the parties or their   **10.47**
counsel or solicitor the right of audience. Occasionally, however, a party may wish to have
a friend to sit by him and advise him. Traditionally such a person has been referred to as a
'*McKenzie* friend' (after *McKenzie v McKenzie* [1971] P 33) although, as will be seen, that
phrase has provoked judicial irritation. The status of this 'friend' was examined by the
Court of Appeal in *Leicester City Justices ex parte Barrow* [1991] 2 QB 260. The justices refused
to allow the applicants to have the assistance of their adviser in court, during proceedings
for recovery of the community charge or poll tax. The justices made liability orders against
the applicants, who then sought judicial review. Their application was refused by the
Divisional Court and they appealed to the Court of Appeal. The Court of Appeal emphasized that what was at issue was a party's right to reasonable assistance. The applicants had
wanted their friend to assist them in court by taking notes, quietly making suggestions, and
giving advice. A litigant had the right to present his own case and, in doing so, to arm himself with such assistance as he thought necessary, subject to the right of the court to intervene. It was misleading to refer in this context to a '*McKenzie* friend', since that implied a
special status and a right akin to a right of audience. The right at issue here was that of a
party to the case to arm himself with assistance. He did not have to seek the leave of the
court to exercise that right. Nevertheless, the court should be informed of the fact that the
party would have his adviser with him. Further, if the assistance was unreasonable in manner or degree, or was provided for an improper purpose or in a way inimical to the administration of justice, the court could restrict him in the use of that assistance. The justices here
had erred. Their error created apparent unfairness and the potential for actual unfairness.
Their order was quashed.

Where an accused (or, indeed, any party) does not physically attend at a magistrates' court, but   **10.48**
he is legally represented for the hearing, he is for most purposes deemed to be present: MCA,
s 122(2). Thus, solicitor or counsel for an absent accused may cross-examine the prosecution
witnesses, call defence witnesses and, in the event of a conviction, present mitigation on behalf
of his client, just as if the latter were present. Further, the presence of the legal representative
prevents the issue of a warrant for arrest under s 13 of the MCA (warrant where the accused does
not appear for the trial of an information—see 10.39 and 10.44). However, the deeming provision does not apply if the accused's personal presence is required either by statute or by the
terms of his bail: s 122(3). Thus, the accused must normally be at court for committal proceedings and proceedings to determine the mode of trial for an offence triable either way (MCA,
ss 4(3) and 18(2)). Also, if he has been bailed to appear and does not do so, a bench warrant may
be issued for his arrest and he may subsequently be prosecuted for absconding (see Chapter 7),
irrespective of whether he had a lawyer at court. It is not clear whether, in theory at least, magistrates could pass a sentence of imprisonment on an offender merely deemed to be present—
in practice, it is very doubtful whether they would want to do so.

G   PRE-TRIAL HEARING

Where a guilty plea is expected in the magistrates' court, an 'Early First Hearing' will be set   **10.49**
down. It will be conducted by a single justice who will either deal with the matter there and
then, or remand the accused on bail or in custody. In the case of anticipated not guilty
plea, an 'Early Administrative Hearing' may be scheduled, conducted by a justices' clerk or

authorized assistant clerk, who can adjourn the case to another day, remanding the accused on bail (he will have no power to remand the accused in custody).

Section 45 and Sch 3 of the Courts Act 2003 make provision for binding rulings to be made at a pre-trial hearing in a case which is due to be heard in the magistrates' court. At such a hearing, the magistrates are empowered to make binding rulings and directions where it is in the interests of justice to do so, provided that the accused has pleaded not guilty. The rulings can be made on questions of law and admissibility of evidence. Before they can be made, the parties must be given an opportunity to be heard, and the magistrates must consider whether an accused who is not represented, but wishes to be so, should be granted legal representation at public expense. Once made, such a ruling will remain binding until the case is disposed of, or sent to the Crown Court. However, the magistrates may discharge or vary a ruling on application (where there has been a change of circumstances) or of their own motion (where it is in the interests of justice to do so). There is no prospect of appeal against a binding ruling, the reasoning being that if the accused is convicted, he has the right of appeal to the Crown Court is any event. There are standard directions which apply in cases to be tried in the magistrates' court unless they are varied. These allow the parties eight weeks in which to prepare for trial (14 weeks where there is to be expert evidence). The standard directions can be accessed on the Criminal Procedure Rules website (see Key Documents). At the pre-trial review, the court will go through the standard directions, determining whether to vary them and making orders on the steps to be taken for trial, including:

(a) applications for special measures in relation to witnesses;
(b) disclosure;
(c) notices relating to hearsay and bad character evidence;
(d) expert evidence;
(e) points of law;
(f) certificates of trial readiness;
(g) appointment of case progression officers for the court, the prosecution and the defence.

H   COURSE OF THE TRIAL

10.50   The course of a summary trial is, to a large extent, identical to the course of a trial on indictment (described fully in Chapters 17 to 21). The following Sections will concentrate upon such differences as do exist. There is also one general distinction to be borne in mind, namely that the magistrates are judges both of questions of law and of questions of fact, whereas in the Crown Court the professional judge rules on the law and the jury decide the facts. As to the law, however, the magistrates are advised by their clerk (see 10.75 to 10.76) and, in practice, usually do what he tells them with regard to legal matters.

The plea

10.51   A summary trial begins with the clerk putting the information to the accused. He must either plead guilty or plead not guilty. The various alternatives to a straightforward guilty or not guilty response, which are available to the defence at trials on indictment, do not apply in summary trials. In particular, it is not open to the accused to plead not guilty as charged but guilty of some other (lesser) offence. However, the prosecution could be invited to have a separate information for the lesser offence, thus allowing the accused to plead guilty to that but not guilty to the original allegation. There is no special procedure for pleading autrefois acquit or autrefois convict (see 17.43) at summary trials, but the fact of a previous acquittal or conviction for the offence charged could be raised on an ordinary not guilty plea. Neither can one avoid pleading by claiming that one is unfit to plead, although it may be possible for the magistrates to make a hospital order under s 37(3) of the Mental Health Act 1983 without convicting the accused if there are medical reports showing him to be suffering from certain forms of mental disorder (see 10.73).

If the accused stays silent when the information is put to him, a not guilty plea must be entered on his behalf. Where a plea is ambiguous, the magistrates should try to resolve the ambiguity, but, if they cannot, again a not guilty plea should be entered. Ambiguous pleas at summary trials are normally referred to as 'equivocal pleas'. For the extended meaning given to the term 'equivocal plea', and for the consequences of the magistrates proceeding to sentence on a plea which remains equivocal, see 27.05.   **10.52**

Where the accused unequivocally pleads guilty, the procedure before sentence described in Chapter 22 may commence forthwith. Alternatively, the magistrates may prefer to adjourn for reports. Like a judge at the Crown Court, magistrates have a discretion to allow the accused to withdraw a guilty plea at any stage before sentence is passed (*S (an infant) v Recorder of Manchester* [1971] AC 481; *Bristol Justices ex parte Sawyers* [1988] Crim LR 754 and see 17.27 to 17.28). The procedure is set out in CrimPR, r 37.6, which lays down that the accused must lodge an application in writing with the court and the prosecutor, setting out the reasons why it would be unjust to allow his plea to stand, identifying any evidence and witnesses in support, and indicating whether he waives legal professional privilege.   **10.53**

Prosecution case

If the accused pleads not guilty, the prosecution have the right to an opening speech. Unless the case is particularly complicated, their representative tends to keep his remarks short since even lay magistrates are much more experienced at trying cases than jurors and do not need the kind of lengthy preliminary explanations which assist the latter. In, say, a simple road traffic matter, counsel or solicitor may dispense entirely with an opening.   **10.54**

After the opening (if any), the prosecution witnesses are called. The sequence of examination in chief, cross-examination, re-examination and questions from the bench is exactly the same as at a trial on indictment. The prosecution may also make use of s 9 of the Criminal Justice Act 1967 under which written statements may be read as evidence in criminal proceedings if (i) the statement contains a declaration that it is true to the best of the maker's knowledge and belief and he realizes the risk of prosecution for wilful misstatements, and (ii) a copy has been served on each of the other parties and none has objected within seven days of service to the statement being read. Should a prosecution witness, in giving evidence, depart significantly from earlier statement/s of which the prosecution are aware, the defence should be informed so that they can use the inconsistencies as a basis for cross-examination (see *Liverpool Crown Court ex parte Roberts* [1986] Crim LR 622 where the High Court quashed R's conviction for assaulting a   **10.55** police officer because his defence was that the officer had head-butted him, not vice versa, and the prosecution failed to tell the defence that the officer had earlier told his sergeant that 'he did not know what had happened but there must have been a clash of heads'). See also 9.31 and 9.54 on the prosecution duty of disclosure in summary trial.

10.56   Where the prosecution have notified the defence that they will be calling a witness, and the defence wish to have the opportunity of cross-examining that witness, the witness should be called by the prosecution even if they do not wish to examine him in chief. They can then tender the witness for cross-examination (*Wellingborough Justices ex parte Francois* (1994) JP 813). In any event, ultimately the justices have a power to call a witness not called by either party: *Haringey Justices ex parte DPP* [1996] QB 351.

10.57   A vexed question in respect of summary trials is how the magistrates should deal with objections to the admissibility of evidence. They are, of course, judges of both law and fact, so— at least in theory—they must rule on whether evidence should be allowed. But, in determining any objection to evidence, they will inevitably discover what the evidence is, and thus be somewhat influenced by it even if they rule it inadmissible. A more narrowly procedural problem is *when* the magistrates should decide if evidence is admissible and whether they are ever obliged to adopt the Crown Court procedure of holding a 'trial within a trial' (see 20.35 to 20.42). The general principle is that they have an unfettered discretion as to how they deal with objections to evidence. They can rule on the objection as a preliminary point; or they can deal with it immediately before the evidence would otherwise be given in the normal course of the trial; or they can receive the disputed evidence provisionally and then decide to ignore it once all the evidence in the case has been received (see *F v Chief Constable of Kent* [1982] Crim LR 682).

It followed from the decision in the last-mentioned case that the defence could not insist upon a trial within a trial even when they claimed that a confession was involuntary. If the accused wanted to testify that he was forced into confessing, he could only do so as part of the general defence case, and that exposed him to cross-examination on all matters relevant to guilt or innocence—i.e., he could not restrict his evidence to the admissibility or otherwise of his confession. The position has, however, been changed by s 76 of the Police and Criminal Evidence Act 1984 which now governs whether confessions are inadmissible as a matter of law. If the defence represent to the bench that a confession was obtained by oppression or in circumstances likely to render it unreliable, the general principle in *F v Chief Constable of Kent* does not apply and the magistrates are obliged forthwith to hold a 'trial within a trial' at which they rule on the confession's admissibility: *Liverpool Crown Court ex parte R* [1988] QB 1. However, where the court is asked to exclude a confession as a matter of discretion (e.g., because the police breached a provision in the Codes which govern their behaviour), the usual rules on objections to evidence in magistrates' courts apply—i.e., it is up to the justices when they make their decision on the objection. The objective is to secure a trial that is fair and just to both parties. The accused will therefore in some cases be given the opportunity to exclude the evidence before giving evidence on the main issues, so as to retain his right to remain silent on the main issues. This should certainly be the case where the confession is the main evidence against him, with the result that there may be no case to answer if it is excluded. In most cases, however, the whole of the prosecution case should be heard first, including the disputed evidence, so that regard can be had to 'all the circumstances' as s 78 requires. In making its decision, the court may take account of the extent of the issues raised by the accused's evidence in the trial within a trial: *Halawa v Federation Against Copyright Theft* [1995] 1 Cr App R 21.

Moreover, the *time* the ruling is made still does not overcome the basic problem that, having realized what the evidence is, the magistrates will not be able to put it out of their minds even if they do exclude it.

If either the prosecution or defence wish to call a witness, but have reason to think that he **10.58** might not attend court voluntarily, they should apply before trial to a magistrate or a magistrates' clerk for a summons requiring the witness to attend: MCA, s 97. If the summons is not obeyed and there appears to be no just excuse for the disobedience, the magistrates may issue a warrant for the witness's arrest, provided that they are satisfied by evidence on oath that the witness is likely to be able to give material evidence, that he has been served with the summons, and has been paid a reasonable sum to cover the costs of the court attendance. The magistrates may also adjourn the case until the witness is brought to court. In extreme cases, where a magistrate is satisfied by evidence on oath that a summons issued under s 97 is un-likely to be obeyed, he may before trial issue a warrant to arrest the witness. Section 97 may also be used for the issue of a summons where either the prosecution or the defence wants to obtain production of 'a document or thing likely to be material evidence' (see 9.57 to 9.62 for the implications in relation to 'third party disclosure').

The power under s 97 is conditional on the magistrate being satisfied that the witness can **10.59** give or produce material evidence. It cannot be used to conduct a 'fishing expedition', where the applicant just hopes something might turn up if the summons is granted, as opposed to showing that the person summoned actually has or can give material evidence: *Reading Justices ex parte Berkshire County Council* [1996] 1 Cr App R 239. Where the document is subject to legal professional privilege which has not been waived, a summons under s 97 should not be issued to compel its production: *Derby Magistrates' Court ex parte B* [1996] AC 487, HL.

Submission of no case

At the conclusion of the prosecution evidence, the defence may make a submission of no case **10.60** to answer. The submission should be upheld if *either* there is no evidence to prove an essential element of the offence charged *or* the prosecution evidence has been so discredited as a result of cross-examination *or* is so manifestly unreliable that no reasonable tribunal could safely convict on it. It is submitted that the magistrates may take into account on a submission of no case the fact that defence cross-examination has simply led them not to believe the prosecution witnesses, whereas a Crown Court judge at the equivalent stage of a trial on indictment should not be influenced by his personal view of a witness's credibility (see 20.48 to 20.55). Although this may seem anomalous, it is explained by magistrates being judges of both fact and law, whereas, at a trial on indictment, law is for the judge and facts for the jury. It would make little sense for the bench to sit through the defence evidence if they have already taken the view that the prosecution evidence will not allow them to convict. If a submission of no case is upheld, the accused is found not guilty and discharged. If the justices are provisionally minded to uphold the submission of no case to answer, they should call on the prosecution to address them, to avoid the possibility of injustice: *Barking and Dagenham Justices ex parte DPP* (1994) 159 JP 373.

Sometimes, the defence submission of no case to answer highlights a deficiency in the prosecution case which they are able to remedy. Should they be allowed to do so? In Hughes v DPP [2003] EWHC 2470 (Admin), the Divisional Court held that if the defence submission highlights a defect which has no bearing on the merits of the case, and the defect is one of omission, the prosecution can seek leave to recall the relevant witnesses to supplement its case. In such a case, the court ought to exercise its discretion to allow the prosecution to reopen its case. More specifically, the appellate courts have indicated a lack of sympathy for the defence in these circumstances where the defect in the prosecution case has not been identified as an issue prior to the submission itself. In *R(DPP) v Chorley Justices* [2006] EWHC 1795 (Admin), Thomas LJ stated:

> If a defendant refuses to identify what the issues are, one thing is clear: he can derive no advantage from that or seek, as appears to have happened in this case, to attempt an ambush at trial. The days of ambushing and taking last-minute technical points are gone. They are not consistent with the overriding objective of deciding cases justly, acquitting the innocent and convicting the guilty.

Defence case

10.61   Assuming there is a case to answer, the defence may but need not call evidence. Just as at a trial on indictment, the accused is a competent but not compellable witness in his own defence. If the prosecution know of a witness who can give material evidence and they do not themselves propose to call him, they are under a duty to make him available to the defence (see *Leyland Justices ex parte Hawthorn* [1979] QB 283 where failure by the prosecution to tell the defence of a witness who would have testified that H's car had stayed on the left-hand side of the road, rather than crossing the centre white line and colliding with the prosecution witness's car, led to H's conviction for careless driving being quashed and see 9.54 to 9.56 on disclosure in summary trials). After the defence evidence, defence counsel or solicitor has the right to a closing speech. The prosecution do not have a closing speech as such, although they may reply to any point of law raised by the defence in their closing.

10.62   As to closing speeches, the precise position is that the defence have the right to either an opening or a closing speech, and will almost always opt for the latter so as to have the advantage of the last word. Either party can apply to the magistrates to grant them a second speech. This is a matter solely within the court's discretion, but if one party obtains a second speech, the other must be given one as well. A second prosecution speech will be made before the defence closing speech. The above provisions are contained in CrimPR, r 37.1.

Verdict

10.63   A district judge sitting alone normally announces his decision immediately after the defence closing speech. Lay magistrates nearly always retire to consider their verdict. They need not be unanimous. In the event of an even-numbered court being equally divided, the chairman has no casting vote, and it will be necessary to adjourn the case for rehearing by a differently constituted bench: *Redbridge Justices ex parte Ram* (1991) 156 JP 203. One major difference between the powers of magistrates and of juries is that the former may not usually return a verdict of guilty of a lesser offence. They must either convict of the offence charged in the information or acquit. This applies even when the offence is triable either way and a jury, on an equivalently worded count in an indictment, could bring in an alternative verdict: *Lawrence v Same* [1968] 2 QB 93. Of course, as already mentioned, the prosecution may avoid the potential inconvenience of this rule by having two separate informations, one for the greater and one for the lesser offence. The magistrates may then choose on which, if either, charge to convict. Also the Road Traffic Offenders Act 1988, s 24, permits the bench, in respect of certain driving offences, to acquit of the offence charged and convict of another specified offence, e.g., where the defendant is charged with dangerous driving, the magistrates may acquit and convict him of careless driving. Further, s 12A(5) of the Theft Act 1968 constitutes another statutory exception to the general rule that magistrates do not have power to convict of a lesser offence. Thus where a defendant is charged with an aggravated offence of taking a vehicle without the owner's consent contrary to s 12A of the 1968 Act, he may be found guilty of the lesser offence of unauthorised taking of a vehicle contrary to s 12 of the Act. The specific authority for such a course of action, which is contained in s 12A(5) and is not confined to trial on indictment, overrides the general principle: *R (on the application of H) v Liverpool City Youth Court* [2001] Crim LR 487.

In *Malcolm v DPP* [2007] 1 WLR 1230, the Divisional Court considered whether a case could   **10.64** be re-opened, so as to allow further evidence to be called, after the magistrates had retired to consider their verdict. The defendant had been tried for driving with excess alcohol. Her advocate raised for the first time in her final speech that there had been no evidence of a warning (as is required by the Road Traffic Act 1988, s 7(7)) that failure to provide a specimen might render the accused liable to prosecution. She submitted therefore that there was no admissible evidence of alcohol on the accused's breath. The magistrates retired, and when they returned to court announced that the case would have to be dismissed for that reason. Before they formally dismissed the case, the prosecutor asked for leave to recall the officer who had conducted the breath test. The Divisional Court held that there were special circumstances which enabled the magistrates properly to re-open the case. The defence advocate had not properly laid the ground for a submission of no case. That should have been done either by calling evidence or by cross-examination. Stanley Burnton J said:

> Criminal trials are no longer to be treated as a game, in which each move is final and any omission by the prosecution leads to its failure. It is the duty of the defence to make its defence and the issues it raises clear to the prosecution and to the court at an early stage.

If, after convicting an accused, the magistrates have second thoughts about the correctness of their decision, they may direct that the case be reheard by different justices: MCA, s 142. The power is not available if the Crown Court or the High Court has determined an appeal in the case. The effect of a direction is that the conviction and any sentence subsequently imposed are nullified. The magistrates who rehear the case may, of course, convict the accused and pass whatever sentence they consider fit.

I   POWERS OF SENTENCING AFTER CONVICTION BY THE MAGISTRATES

The powers of the courts when sentencing offenders and the restrictions placed on the   **10.65** imposition of each form of sentence are dealt with in Chapters 24 and 25. This Section chiefly concerns certain additional restrictions which apply when magistrates are sentencing an offender for one or more *summary* offences. Some of the points made are equally relevant to summary sentencing for offences triable either way, but to obtain a full picture of the latter topic it will be necessary to read this Section in conjunction with 12.02 to 12.05, which deal in detail with the maximum custodial and financial penalties that magistrates may impose for such offences. In addition, the position as far as juveniles are concerned is somewhat different (see in particular 11.29 to 11.31).

10.66 Section 78 of the PCC(S)A 2000 provides that magistrates may not impose imprisonment for more than six months in respect of any one offence. This applies whether the offence is summary or triable either way. Thus, where a statute states that an offence created by it may be punished on summary conviction by imprisonment for a term exceeding six months, it must be understood as providing for a maximum summary penalty of six months. Subject to the above, the statute creating a summary offence sets out the term of imprisonment (if any) and/or fine which may be imposed as a maximum penalty for the offence. The fine will be expressed in terms of a level on a standard scale of fines. To take a random example, s 9(3) of the Criminal Attempts Act 1981 (as amended by the 1982 Act) provides that a person who commits the offence of interfering with a motor vehicle 'shall be liable on summary conviction to imprisonment for a term not exceeding three months or to a fine of an amount not exceeding level 4 on the standard scale or to both'. Level 4 on the standard scale is at present £2,500, so the maximum penalty for an offence under s 9 of the Criminal Attempts Act is three months' imprisonment and/or a £2,500 fine (see 25.54 to 25.56 for further detail).

10.67 A major change to the sentencing powers of magistrates is due when s 154 of the CJA 2003 comes into effect (no date for implementation had been given at the time of writing). It will increase the powers of magistrates to impose prison sentences of up to 12 months in respect of any one offence, unless a shorter term is prescribed by statute. At the same time, a number of statutory offences will have their maximum custodial terms increased to 51 weeks by Sch 26 to the 2003 Act. In addition, the maximum aggregate term which the magistrates can impose will be increased to 65 weeks. These provisions will apply also to the sentence of detention in a young offender institution, which will be abolished when s 61 of the Criminal Justice and Court Services Act 2000 is brought into force. They will not apply to the detention and training order (which is the standard custodial sentence for offenders under 18) where the maximum sentence which may be imposed by a youth court for a summary offence remains at six months, and 24 months for an offence triable either way.

10.68 When a court, be it the Crown Court or a magistrates' court, passes a sentence of imprisonment it may make the sentence take effect either after or at the same time as any other sentence of imprisonment which the offender may be serving. In the former case, the sentence is consecutive to the sentence already being served; in the latter case, it is concurrent with it. Similarly, where a court on one occasion sentences an offender to separate terms of imprisonment for two or more offences, the court can order that the terms run consecutively to or concurrently with each other. The magistrates' powers to order consecutive sentences are, however, limited in that if they sentence an offender for two or more summary offences, the aggregate sentence imposed must not exceed six months: MCA, s 133. If, therefore, magistrates convict an offender of three offences of interfering with a motor vehicle, they could sentence him to three terms of three months' imprisonment to run concurrently, or they could sentence him to three terms of two months to run consecutively, but they could not sentence him to three terms of three months to run consecutively. If an offender is convicted of one summary offence and one offence triable either way (e.g., interfering with a motor vehicle and theft of another vehicle) the magistrates are still restricted to an aggregate prison term not exceeding six months, but if they convict of two or more offences triable either way the aggregate term may exceed six months but must not exceed 12 months (see 12.02).

10.69 There are, of course, many methods of dealing with offenders apart from imprisoning them or fining them. For example, they can be absolutely or conditionally discharged, placed on probation, ordered to attend at an attendance centre, ordered to perform work for the community, or sent to a young offender institution. These sentencing powers and others are at the disposal of the Crown Court and magistrates' courts alike, although the availability of a sentence in any particular case will turn upon matters such as the age of the offender and whether the offence of which he has been convicted is punishable with imprisonment. Again like the Crown Court, magistrates can suspend sentences of imprisonment, but the term suspended must not exceed that which they could have imposed as an immediate sentence. Similarly, the term of any sentence of detention in a young offender institution must be within the maximum prison sentence that would be imposable were the offender aged 21.

Several of the sentences and orders mentioned above are available in the cases of some or all **10.70** young persons (under the age of 18). Occasionally a young person is tried and found guilty in an adult magistrates' court, not in the youth court. When this happens the adult court's sentencing powers are very restricted, and they usually have to remit the young person to the youth court to be sentenced (see 11.31 for details).

Having convicted an offender, the magistrates often feel that to sentence him properly they **10.71** must learn more about him. To that end, they can adjourn for inquiries to be made (e.g. through a probation officer preparing a pre-sentence report), but the adjournment must not be for more than four weeks if the offender is remanded on bail or for more than three weeks if he is remanded in custody: MCA, s 10(3).

Section 10(3) is supplemented by two further sections, namely MCA, s 30, and s 35 of the **10.72** Mental Health Act 1983. The former section provides that if magistrates trying an accused for an imprisonable offence are (a) satisfied that he 'did the act or made the omission charged' (i.e., committed the *actus reus* of the offence), and (b) are of the opinion that an inquiry should be made into his physical or mental condition to enable them to decide how to deal with him, then they must adjourn for medical reports to be prepared. If the accused is granted bail, attendance at a hospital for the preparation of the reports is made a condition of bail. The maximum period of the adjournment is again three or four weeks, depending on whether the remand is in custody or on bail. Section 35 of the Mental Health Act 1983 applies only if there is evidence from a suitably qualified doctor showing that the accused may be suffering from one or more of certain specified forms of mental disorder. The section enables the court to remand the accused to a hospital for the preparation of fuller reports on his mental condition. This is preferable to remanding him in custody, since incarceration—albeit in a prison hospital—is obviously undesirable for somebody who may be mentally disturbed. It also avoids the risk of absconding or non-cooperation in the preparation of reports which is inherent in a remand on bail.

Although remands under both s 30 of the MCA and s 35 of the Mental Health Act may, and **10.73** often will, take place after the magistrates have convicted the accused, a conviction is not a precondition of such remands. The magistrates may make use of the sections merely upon being satisfied that the accused committed the *actus reus* of the offence. This enables the court to avoid injustices which might otherwise result through an accused at a summary trial not being able to raise the issue of unfitness to plead (see 10.51). Should it appear that the accused might have mental problems such as to prevent him making a proper defence to the information, the magistrates can cause a not guilty plea to be entered on his behalf. The prosecution then call their evidence, and, if that satisfies the court that the accused committed the *actus reus*, the case may be adjourned under MCA, s 30 or Mental Health Act 1983, s 35, for the preparation of reports. Should those reports indicate that the accused is suffering from either mental illness or severe mental impairment, the magistrates may make a hospital order under s 37(3) of the Mental Health Act 1983 without completing the trial of the information, and without recording a conviction. The effect of the hospital order is that the accused is taken to hospital, and detained there for an initial period of six months, after which his discharge is dependent upon the improvement or otherwise in his mental condition. The procedure described above may be adopted even in cases where the offence charged is triable either way and the accused is too disturbed to give his consent personally to summary trial, provided he is legally represented and counsel or solicitor agrees on his behalf to the magistrates dealing with the case: *Lincoln (Kesteven) Magistrates' Court ex parte O'Connor* [1983] 1 WLR 335. For further details about remands under s 35 of the Mental Health Act 1983 and hospital orders, see 25.115 to 25.124.

10.74 It appears that the common law defence of insanity is available to a defendant in a summary trial where *mens rea* is in issue: *Horseferry Road Magistrates' Court ex parte K* [1996] 3 WLR 68.

J   ROLE OF THE CLERK

10.75 The court clerk plays a major role in the conduct of summary proceedings. He is not necessarily the magistrates' clerk himself, but may be a legal adviser qualified to act as a clerk in court (see 6.14). During the course of a hearing, the clerk's tasks include putting the information to the accused; taking a note of the evidence; helping an unrepresented accused in the presentation of his case, and advising the magistrates upon points of law or procedure as they arise. This last is probably his most important function, for, although the magistrates are the judges of both law and fact, lay magistrates do, as a matter of practice, accept their clerk's advice on matters of law. Because of the importance of his advice, it is desirable that when a point of law has to be decided during a hearing (e.g., as to the admissibility of evidence) the clerk should give his advice publicly so that the parties know what he has said. Where a clerk who was not present when legal submissions were made to the court is called by the justices to advise them, it is crucial that he hears those submissions himself, in open court, from the parties or their advocates (*Chichester Justices ex parte DPP* [1994] RTR 175). Similarly, if there is a point of law which has not been argued by the parties but which the clerk feels should be brought to the magistrates' attention, he should refer to the point in open court so that the parties have an opportunity of commenting upon the matter. Even if the justices have retired to consider their decision, if their clerk refers to additional cases not cited in argument, they should return to court and invite representations from the advocates on the new cases before finally making their decision (*W v W* (1993) *The Times*, 4 June 1993).

10.76 When the magistrates retire to consider their verdict, the clerk may retire with them, but only to advise them on the law and, if they are minded to convict, on their powers of sentencing. Generally speaking, he should not join the magistrates in their retirement unless asked to do so. However, in a complicated case, where the issues of fact and law are inextricably intertwined, it may be proper for him to stay with the magistrates for virtually the whole period of their retirement: *Consett Justices ex parte Postal Bingo Ltd* [1967] 2 QB 9. The essential point is that the clerk should neither interfere with the magistrates' decision on the facts, nor, through retiring with them when there is no good reason for doing so, put himself in a position where he might appear to be interfering with their decision. Thus, in *Stafford Justices ex parte Ross* [1962] 1 WLR 456 the High Court quashed R's conviction because, during the trial, the clerk had passed a note to the magistrates in which he suggested that R's defence was implausible. Similarly, in *Guildford Justices ex parte Harding* (1981) 145 JP 174 the conviction could not stand because, in a case where the law was absolutely straightforward, the clerk had retired with the magistrates to advise them on the standard of proof. The High Court appeared to regard this reason for wanting the clerk's advice as little better than a pretence.

Practice Direction (Criminal Proceedings: Consolidation) [2002] 1 WLR 2870, para V.55, summarizes the functions of the clerk.

KEY DOCUMENTS

Magistrates' Courts Act 1980, as amended.

Criminal Procedure Rules, Part 7, obtainable from: <http://www.justice.gov.uk/criminal/procrules_fin/index.htm>.

Magistrates' Court Case Progression Form for a Case to be tried in the Magistrates' Court, obtainable from: <http://www.hmcourts-service.gov.uk>.

11

TRIAL OF JUVENILES

11.01 A juvenile is normally tried by magistrates in a special form of magistrates' court, known as the 'youth court'. In the circumstances described below, it is either obligatory or possible for a juvenile to be tried on indictment (see 11.04 to 11.15) or in the adult magistrates' court (see 11.17 to 11.18). In all other cases, he must stay in the youth court, even if the offence charged is one which, if he were an adult, either could or would have to be tried on indictment.

11.02 By 'a juvenile' is meant a person who has not attained the age of 18. Juveniles are either children, who have not attained the age of 14, or young persons, who have attained the age of 14 but are not yet 18: Children and Young Persons Act 1969, s 70. For purposes of criminal procedure, children under the age of ten may be ignored as they have not yet reached the age of criminal responsibility. As far as method of trial is concerned, all persons aged 18 and over are treated in exactly the same way, and are referred to in this chapter simply as adults. However, if a person aged 18 to 20 inclusive is convicted of an offence, several methods of dealing with him are open to the courts which are not available in respect of offenders who have attained the age of 21.

11.03 Under the Criminal Justice Act 1991, what was the juvenile court was renamed the 'youth court' (s 70). In addition, the jurisdiction of the newly named youth courts was extended to 17-year-olds (s 68). Therefore, under the statutory provisions, adults are individuals aged 18 and over.

A   TRIAL OF JUVENILES ON INDICTMENT

11.04   Like adult accused, juveniles make their first court appearance before magistrates, even if they are ultimately tried on indictment. If a juvenile is charged by himself or with other juveniles, he will appear in the youth court (a special form of magistrates' court). If he is charged jointly with an adult, both he and the adult will come before the adult magistrates' court. The decision on whether a juvenile is tried summarily or on indictment is taken by the magistrates, applying the relevant statutory provisions. The juvenile never has the right to elect trial on indictment. Sometimes he must go to the Crown Court, and neither he nor the magistrates have a choice in the matter; sometimes the magistrates have a choice between summary trial and committal proceedings; usually, statute decrees that the trial must be summary. In no case, however, is the juvenile able to choose, although sometimes he or his legal representatives will be asked for their views on which court would be more appropriate.

11.05   Section 24(1) of the Magistrates' Courts Act 1980 provides that a juvenile *must* be tried summarily (i.e., in the youth court or in an adult magistrates' court) unless:

(a)   he is charged with an offence of homicide; *or*

(b)   he is charged jointly with an adult who is going to be tried on indictment, and the magistrates consider that it is in the interests of justice to commit them both for trial; *or*

(c)   the magistrates consider that he could properly be sentenced under the PCC(S)A 2000, s 91 if he were convicted on indictment, and he is charged with an offence carrying a maximum sentence of 14 years' imprisonment or more, or with a serious sexual offence listed in s 91(1) of the PCC(S)A 2000; *or*

(d)   he falls within the ambit of the dangerous offenders provisions of the CJA 2003 (see 24.34 to 24.42); or

(e)   he is charged with an offence under s 5 of the Firearms Act 1968, which makes him liable to a minimum term sentence under s 51A of that Act, and he was aged 16 or over at the time of the alleged commission of the offence.

In all the above cases, with the exception of (d), if the youth court decides that the juvenile must face trial in the Crown Court, then as matters stand at the time of writing, he will be sent by means of committal proceedings. However, in the case of the dangerous offender provisions ((d) above), the 'sending' to the Crown Court is under s 51A of the Crime and Disorder Act 1998 (CDA), and there are no committal proceedings (see 13.09 to 13.16). Once s 51A of the CDA is fully in force, then categories (a), (c), and (e) (homicide, s 91 cases, and relevant firearms cases) will also be sent direct to the Crown Court, rather than through committal proceedings.

11.06   Each of these circumstances for trial on indictment calls for further consideration.

(a)   **Offences of homicide.** These obviously include murder and manslaughter. Since these offences are triable only on indictment, the magistrates have no discretion as to the method of trial, but must send the juvenile to the Crown Court.

(b)   **Charged jointly with an adult.** If two or more accused are charged with having jointly committed an offence, it is, generally speaking, desirable to have them tried together (see 15.33 to 15.36). But, the question then arises of how there can be a joint trial if an adult and a juvenile are charged with an indictable offence and the adult either must be tried on indictment or rejects the offer of summary trial but the matter is one for which a juvenile would ordinarily have to be tried summarily. To deprive the adult of his funda-mental right to jury trial simply because he happens to be jointly charged with a juvenile would be unacceptable. So, Parliament has approached the problem from the opposite direction, and has given the magistrates a discretion to hold committal proceedings in respect of both accused and to send the juvenile for trial with the adult if that is in the inter-ests of justice (MCA, s 24(2)). Usually, 'jointly charged' in this context means charged with the same offence in the same information. Exceptionally, the driver and passenger of a motor vehicle taken without consent should be regarded as jointly charged, even though there is a different information in respect of each of them: *Ex parte Allgood* (1994) *The Times*, 25 November 1994. In exercising their discretion, the magistrates should balance the desirability of a joint trial against the undesirability of having youngsters put through the possibly traumatic experience of appearing in the Crown Court. The younger the juve-nile and the less serious the offence charged, the more likely it is that the magistrates will decide that the interests of justice do not require the juvenile to be committed for trial. If they do so decide, the adult will go to the Crown Court by himself, and the juvenile will be asked to plead to the charge in the magistrates' court. Should he plead not guilty, the adult court has a discretion (which it will almost certainly exercise) to remit him to the youth court to be tried: MCA, s 29. If he pleads guilty, the adult court should proceed to consider sentence, but their sentencing powers in respect of juveniles are limited (see 11.31), and, if those powers are not adequate to deal with the case, there will again have to be a remittal to the juvenile court. Where the juvenile is committed for trial with the adult, he may also be committed in respect of any other indictable offence which arose out of cir-cumstances the same as or connected with the circumstances of the joint charge: MCA s 24(2). Thus, if A (aged 18) and J (aged 16) are charged with burglary, and J is charged by himself with using a cheque book stolen in the burglary to obtain property by deception, the likely course of events is that both will appear together in the adult magistrates' court. As regards A, the magistrates will go through the normal procedure to determine the mode of trial. Possibly they will give him the option of summary trial, but, if he rejects it, they will have to consider whether committal proceedings are also appropriate in J's case. Since J is nearly an adult, the arguments for sending both accused to the Crown Court are strong. Assuming the prosecution can establish a prima facie case against them both in respect of the burglary, J could also be committed for trial on the deception charge, since that is linked to the joint charge. Should there not be a case to answer against A, the committal proceedings against J will be discontinued; he will be asked to plead to the two charges against him, and, if he pleads not guilty, the magistrates will be able to remit him to the youth court for trial.

(c) **Young persons at risk of a s 91 sentence.** When a juvenile is convicted in circumstances falling within the Powers of Criminal Courts (Sentencing) Act 2000, s 91 (see 24.69 to 24.72 for details), the Crown Court may sentence him to detention in accordance with the Home Secretary's directions for a term not exceeding the maximum prison term imposable in the case of an offender over 21. Sentences under s 91 are at present only possible if there has been a conviction on indictment (but see 11.08). Consequently, magistrates must be enabled to commit for trial where they think that the allegation is grave enough to warrant a sentence of detention, for otherwise the imposition of such a sentence will be precluded by the con-viction being in the wrong court. As already mentioned, s 24 of the MCA does give them that power. It should be noted, however, that s 91 detention (as opposed to detention in a young offender institution) is in practice reserved for a small minority of very serious cases. Thus, although burglary of a dwelling and handling carry 14 years' imprisonment, a youth court will almost automatically proceed with summary trial of such a charge unless alerted to the fact that there is something quite exceptional about the circumstances that might warrant a sentence of detention under s 91 were the young person to be found guilty on indictment.

(d)   The 'dangerous offender' provisions under the CJA 2003 apply to 'specified offences' (violent or sexual) which are set out in Sch 15. Where a juvenile is charged with a specified offence and it appears to the court that, if he were found guilty, the criteria for the imposition of a sentence of detention for life, detention for public protection, or an extended sentence would be met, the court shall send him forthwith to the Crown Court for trial for that offence. As to the criteria for the imposition of such a sentence, see 24.39 to 24.42.

(e)   A juvenile must be sent to the Crown Court for trial on any charge where, if convicted, he would be subject to the mandatory minimum sentence under the Firearms Act 1968, s 51 (see 24.46).

11.07   A good example of the way in which the powers under s 91 of the PCC(S)A should be exercised is *South Hackney Juvenile Court ex parte RB and CB* (1983) 77 Cr App R 294. RB (aged 15) and CB (aged 14) were charged, together with six other juveniles, with conspiracy to commit burglaries. They were also charged with having participated in a few specific burglaries, although the total number of burglaries committed by the gang as a whole was 15. In the course of those burglaries some £27,000 worth of property had been stolen. Moreover, the juveniles had planned the offences with care, found places to store the stolen property, and had arranged to sell it through a carefully organized distribution network. This set the case apart from the normal run of juvenile crime, and justified the juvenile court's decision to hold committal proceedings. The Divisional Court also held that the procedure adopted by the magistrates before embarking on committal proceedings—namely to hear representations from the prosecution and defence about which method of trial would be more appropriate, but not to consider evidence at that stage about the gravity of the allegations—was the correct one.

11.08   For some years, the power to commit for sentence under the PCC(S)A 2000, s 91, and its predecessors has been reserved for the situation where the young defendant is tried on indictment. However, when the CJA 2003, Sch 3, para 23 comes into force, the magistrates will be given a new power of committal for sentence by virtue of PCC(S)A 2000, s 3B. It will apply where a juvenile is charged with an offence to which the PCC(S)A, s 91, applies, and he indicates a guilty plea. The magistrates will then have the power to commit him to the Crown Court for sentence. The power will be available where the court is of the opinion that the offence (or the combination of the offence and one or more offences associated with it) is such that the Crown Court should have the power to deal with the juvenile under s 91. The Crown Court will then be able to sentence him under s 91, without a trial on indictment. The power will not apply where the juvenile pleads not guilty and is convicted after summary trial by the magistrates. In such circumstances, sentence must be passed by the youth court. At the time of writing, no date had been fixed for the introduction of s 3B of the PCC(S)A.

11.09   From time to time, the appellate courts have issued guidance on how the youth court ought to approach its task of deciding whether to send the young defendant for trial in the Crown Court. In *Fairhurst* (1987) Cr App R 19, the Court of Appeal said that it was not necessary that the crime 'should be one of exceptional gravity' before the magistrates should decline jurisdiction. The reasoning process which ought to govern the youth court's decision was spelt out in *Inner London Youth Court ex parte DPP* [1996] Crim LR 834, where the defendant, aged 15, was charged with causing grievous bodily harm. The prosecution case was that he had grabbed the victim, pushing her into a shop door and thrusting her head through the broken glass, whilst commenting upon how pleased he was with what he had done. The justices ruled that the case was suitable for summary trial. The prosecution, who had argued that the case should be tried on indictment in the Crown Court, appealed. The Divisional Court held that the application should be allowed, and remitted the matter for committal proceedings. Clearly the offence fell within the ambit of what is now s 91 of the Powers of Criminal Courts (Sentencing) Act 2000, since an offence under s 18 is punishable in the case of an adult with a maximum sentence of imprisonment of more than 14 years (the maximum available in the case of an adult is life imprisonment for a s 18 offence). Unless the accused was sent to the Crown Court for trial, the maximum sentence which could be imposed would be 24 months. The proper approach for the magistrates was to consider whether, if the defendant was convicted of the offence, it would be proper for the Crown Court to exercise its powers under s 91, and to sentence the defendant to a term of detention greater than the two years to which its powers would otherwise be limited. If the answer was yes, the magistrates must make it possible for such a sentence to be imposed, and they should have done so in this case.

In *R(D) v Sheffield Youth Court* (2003) 167 JP 159, Stanley Burnton J stated that the youth court, **11.10** in deciding whether the case was one where it ought to be possible to sentence the defendant in accordance with s 91, should consider the sentencing powers of the Crown Court, and the guidance that had been given as to how they should be exercised. If, on the basis of that guidance, there was no real possibility of such a sentence, it would not be appropriate to send the matter to the Crown Court. However, if the youth court considered that it ought to be possible to sentence him pursuant to s 91, then it had no discretion but should commit him to the Crown Court. In coming to its decision, it should take into account any undisputed facts in mitigation (e.g., the defendant's good character) and ignore any contentious mitigation. If the case was sent to the Crown Court and the defendant convicted, those disputed facts would be considered by that court.

Lord Woolf CJ put it rather differently in *R(W) v Southampton Youth Court* [2003] 1 Cr App R (S) **11.11** 455, saying:

> While the need to impose the appropriate sentence is important, so is the need to ensure that wherever possible the trial should take place in the appropriate setting. That is more satisfactorily achieved in a youth court than in a Crown Court. . . . [J]ustices should start off with a strong presumption against sending young offenders to the Crown Court unless they are satisfied that that is clearly required, notwithstanding the fact that the forum for trial will not be so appropriate as the youth court.

When the youth court makes its decision as to whether s 91 applies, it should be told of **11.12** any previous findings of guilt against the juvenile: *R (Tullet) v Medway Magistrates Court* (2003) 167 JP 541.

As with the decision about mode of trial for an adult, so the decision as to how a juvenile should **11.13** be tried is not irreversible. Having originally decided in favour of trial on indictment, the court may revert to summary trial at any stage of committal proceedings if it decides that the conditions described in sub-paragraphs 11.05 (b) and (c) above are not after all satisfied (see *Brent Juvenile Court ex parte S* (1991) *The Times*, 18 June 1991). Conversely, it may, up until the close of the prosecution evidence, switch from summary trial to committal proceedings (see MCA, s 25(5)–(7)). It has also been held that, where the court at a first hearing considers representations as to whether a juvenile's case should be committed for trial in view of the likelihood of a sentence of detention under s 91 and decides against that course, a differently constituted bench may not—at a subsequent hearing—reverse their colleagues' decision unless some fresh circumstance has arisen that was not before the court on the previous occasion: *Newham Juvenile Court ex parte F* [1986] 1 WLR 939. In *R (K) v Leeds Youth Court* (2001) 165 JP 694, the issue was whether a fresh circumstance had arisen so as to enable the magistrates to change their minds about accepting jurisdiction. K (aged 17) was charged with robbery. He entered a not guilty plea before the youth court, once it had accepted jurisdiction. The matter subsequently came back before a differently constituted bench of the youth court, and the prosecution submitted that the magistrates should commit to the Crown Court. After hearing a prosecution witness, the justices determined that the trial should be discontinued, so that the matter could be heard in the Crown Court, since their powers of sentencing would be inadequate if K were convicted. K applied for judicial review, arguing that the power to change the mode of trial should only be used where there had been a change of circumstances. The Divisional Court held that the youth court was entitled to keep the trial under review and change its decision if the original decision was no longer appropriate. Circumstances justifying such a decision were likely to vary, but included a change in circumstances, and instances where new material was adduced. There would also be cases, like this one, where as the evidence unfolded, the manner in which it was presented would justify such a decision. Once it became clear to the justices that the oral testimony had put a different perspective on the bare statement of the offences, they had been entitled to exercise their powers under s 25(6). The Divisional Court was saying, in effect, that the manner in which the evidence was presented was enough. Although such an interpretation does not exactly strain the statute, its subjective character might give rise to the suspicion that the real reason why the juvenile is sent to the Crown Court is because of a change of mind, and possibly a change of composition, on the part of the bench. In the light of *V v UK* (2000) 30 EHRR 121 (see 28.29), it is submitted that there ought to be a strong presumption in favour of trying juveniles in the youth court, and that the court's decision to change its mind and send a juvenile to the Crown Court should be firmly based upon fresh material.

11.14 Once the decision that a juvenile should be tried on indictment has been taken, the procedure generally follows the procedure in respect of adults. Just as in the case of an adult, the committal may be with or without consideration of the evidence (MCA, s 24(1)). At the trial on indictment, the juvenile has the same rights as an adult accused (e.g., to challenge jurors), and his defence is conducted in the same way as that of an adult. The court may also order that the media shall not reveal the name, address, school or any other identifying details of the juvenile charged or any juvenile who is a witness in the case: Children and Young Persons Act 1933, s 39. Sentencing of juveniles by the Crown Court is considered in 11.27 and 28.

11.15 In the wake of the European Court of Human Rights judgment in *V v UK*, the Lord Chief Justice issued a Practice Direction, (now para IV.39 of the *Practice Direction (Criminal Proceedings: Consolidation)* [2002] 1 WLR 2870) which emphasized that all possible steps should be taken to assist a young defendant to understand and participate in proceedings in the Crown Court (for details see the final points made at 28.29 to 28.33).

11.16 The PCC(S)A 2000, s 3C, deals with the committal of dangerous young offenders. Where a juvenile is convicted of an offence specified in the CJA 2003, s 224, the magistrates must consider whether the criteria for the imposition of a sentence under s 226(3) or s 228(2) of the CJA 2003 are met. If they are, then the magistrates must commit the juvenile to the Crown Court for sentence. The provisions relating to dangerous offenders, including the criteria, are dealt with in 24.36 to 24.42.

B   TRIAL OF JUVENILES IN AN ADULT MAGISTRATES' COURT

By a combination of s 46 of the Children and Young Persons Act 1933 and s 18 of the Children   **11.17** and Young Persons Act 1963, it is provided that a juvenile who is to be tried summarily shall be tried in a youth court unless:

(a) he is charged jointly with an adult; or
(b) he appears before the magistrates together with an adult and, although (a) above does not apply as the prosecution have chosen to charge them separately, the charge against him is that he aided and abetted commission of the offence alleged against the adult or vice versa; or
(c) he appears before the magistrates together with an adult, and the charge against him arises out of circumstances the same as or connected with the circumstances giving rise to the charge against the adult; or
(d) the adult magistrates' court began to hear the proceedings against him in the erroneous belief that he was an adult.

Where (a) above applies, the adult magistrates' court *must* try the juvenile unless the adult   **11.18** with whom he is jointly charged pleads guilty and he pleads not guilty, in which case the court may, and probably would, remit him to a youth court to be tried: Magistrates' Court Act 1980, s 29. According to *Ex parte Allgood* (1994) *The Times*, 25 November 1994, which was decided in the context of the trial of a juvenile on indictment (see 11.06), the driver and passenger of a motor vehicle taken without consent should be regarded as being jointly charged. Where (b) to (d) above apply the adult court merely has a discretion to hear the case if it so wishes.

Section 39 of the Children and Young Persons Act 1933 (orders restricting the reporting of   **11.19** the juvenile's name etc.—see 11.14) applies to trials of juveniles in an adult magistrates' court.

The position as far as the attendance of parents or guardians is concerned is governed by s 34A   **11.20** of the Children and Young Persons Act 1933: see 11.23.

C   TRIAL OF JUVENILES IN A YOUTH COURT

The great majority of charges against juveniles are tried in a special form of magistrates'   **11.21** court, known as a youth court. The basis upon which magistrates are authorized to hear cases in the youth court is set out in the CYPA 1933, s 45, which was amended by the Courts Act 2003. It lays down that the Lord Chancellor authorizes certain lay justices and district judges to sit in the youth court. It follows that, although the youth court is part of the magistrates' court, only some magistrates are able to sit on youth court cases, because such cases are frequently sensitive, and require special knowledge and understanding.

11.22   Youth courts differ from the ordinary adult courts in the ways described below:

(a)   The general public are excluded from youth courts. Only the parties and their legal representatives, officers of the court (e.g., court ushers), witnesses after they have given their evidence and others directly concerned in the case, probation officers and social workers, and members of the press are allowed in: Children and Young Persons Act 1933, s 47. In addition, the court may especially authorize other persons to be present (e.g., law students). By contrast, proceedings against juveniles in the adult magistrates' courts or Crown Court are normally in open court, although there is power to clear the court whenever a juvenile is called as a witness in relation to an offence against decency or morality: Children and Young Persons Act 1933, s 37.

(b)   The bench of magistrates hearing the case must consist of no more than three magistrates, and must include a man and a woman: Youth Courts (Constitution) Rules 1954, r 12. If, through unforeseen circumstances, the members of the youth court panel available for a sitting of a youth court are all male or all female, they can waive the above rule and form a single-sex court should they not consider it expedient to adjourn. A district judge (magistrates' court), however, may sit alone in the youth court.

(c)   All witnesses in the case, whether juveniles or adults, 'promise before Almighty God to tell the truth, the whole truth' etc. instead of swearing by Almighty God that they will do so. The different form of oath for youth courts was introduced by the Children and Young Persons Act 1963, s 28. It is also used by juveniles giving evidence in other courts. If the magistrates decide that the juvenile committed the offence charged, they do not 'convict' him, but 'record a finding of guilt'. When they deal with him for the offence, they do not 'sentence' him but 'make an order upon a finding of guilt': Children and Young Persons Act 1933, s 59. The same terminology should be employed for juveniles appearing in the adult magistrates' court.

(d)   Where the juvenile is not legally represented the court may permit his parent or guardian to assist him in conducting his defence (e.g., by cross-examining prosecution witnesses on his behalf).

(e)   The media may not report the name or any other identifying details of the juvenile charged or any other juvenile involved in the proceedings: Children and Young Persons Act 1933, s 49. The prohibition may be lifted if the court thinks that to be necessary in order (a) to avoid injustice to the juvenile or (b) to apprehend a juvenile who is unlawfully at large. This power of the court in respect of a juvenile who is unlawfully at large may be exercised only on application from the DPP, in a case where the juvenile is charged with a violent or sexual offence or an offence carrying a maximum sentence of 14 years in prison or more. Thus, in the adult magistrates' courts and in the Crown Court, the juvenile's name etc. may be published unless the court makes an order to the contrary; in the youth court, the position is the opposite. If the defendant turns 18 during the course of proceedings, the reporting restrictions under s 49 of the 1933 Act cease to apply: *T v DPP; North East Press Ltd* (2004) 168 JP 194.

(f)   In general, the atmosphere in a youth court is more relaxed and less formal than in an adult court. The juvenile charged does not go into a dock, but sits on a chair facing the magistrates, with his parents alongside or behind him. The magistrates are usually seated behind a slightly raised table. They address the juvenile by his first name, and, when making an order upon a finding of guilt, may talk to him in a semi-informal fashion.

D   ATTENDANCE OF PARENTS

A juvenile defendant will normally be accompanied by his parents. The youth court (like the **11.23** adult magistrates' court and the Crown Court) has the power to require the attendance of the juvenile's parents or guardians. It should require such attendance in the case of an accused aged 15 or under, unless satisfied that it would be unreasonable to do so. Where the accused is aged 16 or over, by contrast, the court *may* require a parent's attendance. It should be stressed that any element of choice is that of the court, not the parent, who is obliged to attend in the event that the court so orders.

E   SENTENCING POWERS OF THE COURTS DEALING WITH JUVENILES

Depending on matters such as his age, record, whether the offence of which he has been **11.24** found guilty is punishable with imprisonment and what the reports on him say, a juvenile is likely to be dealt with in one or more of the following ways: a sentence of detention under s 91 of the Powers of Criminal Courts (Sentencing) Act 2000 (PCC(S)A); a detention and training order; a youth community order; a reparation order; a fine; a supervision order; a hospital order under s 37 of the Mental Health Act 1983; a compensation order; a bind-over; a conditional discharge; or an absolute discharge. It is also possible to order the juvenile's parent or guardian to enter into a recognizance to take proper care of him or to ensure that he complies with the requirements of a community sentence. For driving offences the court may be able to disqualify the juvenile (which in effect postpones the date at which he can lawfully acquire a licence), or order that particulars of the offence be endorsed on any licence which he subsequently obtains.

Section 150 of the PCC(S)A 2000 places the court under a duty to bind over the parents of an **11.25** offender under the age of 16 if it is satisfied that it will help to prevent him from committing further offences. The court must state its reasons if it does not exercise the power. Where a juvenile offender is aged from 10 to 15 inclusive, and the court imposes a fine, it *must* order his parents to pay the fine (unless this would be unreasonable, or they cannot be found). In the case of juveniles aged 16 or 17, the parents *may* be ordered to pay (PCC(S)A, s 137). The court must take into account the means of the person whom it orders to pay (whether parent or child), just as it must do when it fines an adult offender. The same rules apply to compensation orders.

The nature of these various sentences, and the general restrictions on their imposition, are **11.26** described in Chapters 23 to 25. The following Sections deal with whether a sentence may be passed, in appropriate circumstances, by any of the courts having power to deal with juveniles, or by the Crown Court only, or by the Crown Court or a youth court.

The Crown Court

11.27 All the sentencing options available in the cases of juveniles are at the disposal of the Crown Court. However, s 8 of the PCC(S)A 2000 provides that, except in cases of homicide, the Crown Court must remit a juvenile convicted on indictment to the youth court to be sentenced, unless satisfied that it would be undesirable to do so. In *Lewis* (1984) 6 Cr App R (S) 44, Lord Lane CJ mentioned some of the reasons which will justify a Crown Court judge in not remitting for sentence. They include the following:

(a) that the judge, having presided over the trial of a not guilty plea by the juvenile, will be better informed about the case than the youth court could hope to be;

(b) that the juvenile and an adult have both been convicted on a joint charge, and sentencing the former in the youth court and the latter in the Crown Court would entail an unacceptable risk of disparity in sentencing; and

(c) that remitting would cause delay, unnecessary duplication of proceedings and unnecessary expense.

11.28 The third argument against remitting will apply in almost every case where a juvenile is convicted on indictment, so Lord Lane in effect seems to be saying that, notwithstanding the statutory provisions, juveniles should *not* normally be sent back to the youth court for sentence. His Lordship did, however, give one example of remittal being appropriate, namely where the Crown Court judge cannot sentence forthwith because no reports on the juvenile have been prepared but he realizes that he will not be available to pass sentence on the date to which the case will have to be adjourned.

The youth court

11.29 The youth court's powers are less extensive than those of the Crown Court in the following ways:

(a) It cannot pass a sentence of detention under s 91 of the PCC(S)A 2000. As explained in 11.06, such sentences are only appropriate in a minority of very serious cases.

(b) The maximum fine it may impose is £1,000 in the case of a young person and £250 in the case of a child (Magistrates' Courts Act 1980, s 24(3) and (4) and s 36). However, the court is unlikely in any event to want to fine a juvenile a large sum of money.

11.30 Prior to 1999, the youth court was restricted to a maximum custodial sentence of six months for a single offence or 12 months for two triable either-way offences. That meant that its custodial powers were less than those of the Crown Court on the committal of a juvenile offender for sentence (24 months). The position was changed with the introduction of the secure training order, replaced in due course by the detention and training order (see 24.75 to 24.77). The youth court, like the Crown Court, was given the power to pass a secure training order of 24 months in length, later to be replaced by the power to pass a detention and training order of 24 months, for an offence triable either way.

The adult magistrates' court

11.31 An adult magistrates' court's powers of dealing with a juvenile are very limited. It can fine him, or absolutely or conditionally discharge him, or make an order that his parents enter into a recognizance. It can also make any order which may be combined with a conditional discharge (e.g., disqualification from driving, an order that any subsequently obtained licence be endorsed, or an order ancillary to the sentence proper relating to a matter such as costs or the payment of compensation). If, in the court's opinion, the case cannot properly be dealt with by any of these methods, it must remit the juvenile to the youth court to be sentenced: Children and Young Persons Act 1969, s 7(8).

F   AGE LIMIT AND MODE OF TRIAL

The right of a person charged with an indictable offence to be tried on indictment depends **11.32** crucially upon whether he is under or over 18 (s 68 of the Criminal Justice Act 1991 made his 18th birthday the watershed). If he is under 18, s 24 of the Magistrates' Courts Act 1980 applies, and he will usually be tried in the youth court. Even if he is tried on indictment, it will be because the magistrates decided for one reason or another that summary trial was inappropriate, not because the juvenile elected to go to the Crown Court. On the other hand, if he is 18 or over, he will—depending on whether the offence charged is triable only on indictment or triable either way—either be obliged to stand his trial on indictment or will have the option of doing so. Unfortunately, the MCA does not make it clear whether the relevant consideration is the accused's age when he first appears in court charged with the offence, or his age at some subsequent stage in the procedure. However, case law on the subject, especially the House of Lords decision in *Islington North Juvenile Court ex parte Daley* [1983] 1 AC 347, does help to clarify the Act, although there are still some points of doubt. The position seems to be as follows:

(a)   If an accused is under 18 when he first appears in court charged with an indictable offence, but has attained that age by the time mode of trial is to be determined, he must be treated as an adult: *Ex parte Daley* (supra). In other words, he is entitled to refuse to plead in the youth court and can elect trial on indictment. Although the point was not directly in issue in *Ex parte Daley*, he could not be tried summarily for an offence triable only on indictment in the case of an adult, even if the offence is one which the youth court would have been entitled to deal with had he still been under 18 and he himself does not wish to go to the Crown Court (see *Rotherham Justices ex parte Brough* [1991] Crim LR 522, the facts of which are summarized at (f) below).

(b)   If the accused was under 18 when he admitted or denied the charge, his being 18 by the time the youth court is ready to hear the case does not give him a right to trial on indictment (see *Lewes Juvenile Court ex parte T* (1984) 149 JP 186, where T pleaded not guilty to a triable-either-way matter when 16—the 'watershed' age being 17 at that time; the case was immediately adjourned through lack of court time, and, although he reached 17 before the date fixed for the hearing, T had to be tried in the juvenile court).

(c)   Conversely, where the youth court has accepted summary jurisdiction before the accused turns 18, it cannot commit him to the Crown Court for trial after his 18th birthday. Again, the material date is that at which mode of trial is determined: *Nottingham Justices ex parte Taylor* [1992] QB 557.

(d)   The youth court does, however, have a discretion to transfer a case to the adult court where the defendant turns 18 during the course of proceedings, provided that the discretion is exercised (i) before the start of the trial or (ii) after conviction and before sentence (s 47(1) of the Crime and Disorder Act 1998). What distinguishes this option from the situation described in (c) is that the decision on transfer must take place either before the beginning or at the end of the trial process. It is also clear that it *is* a discretion, and that the youth court may well wish to retain the case, e.g., if the defendant is relatively immature.

(e)   If proceedings are begun against an accused when he is under 18, but he is 18 before they are completed, the youth court may deal with him as if he were still 17: Children and Young Persons Act 1963, s 29. The House of Lords in *Ex parte Daley* apparently ignored s 29. Clearly, in the light of the decision in *Daley*, the section cannot be used to deprive an accused of his right to trial on indictment if he is 18 before he is asked to plead. The section will apply, however, where an accused admits guilt or is found guilty in the youth court when 17, but reaches 18 during an adjournment prior to sentencing. The youth court retains the right to sentence him, and could even pass a sentence which is only available in the case of juveniles (see point (f) below). What is not clear is whether s 29 entitles a youth court to proceed with the trial of an 18-year-old if he was 17 when the proceedings commenced, and is going to be tried summarily because, although he was 18 when the information was put, he either elected for summary trial or had no right to trial on indictment as the offence was summary. Normally, of course, summary trial of an 18-year-old would take place in the adult magistrates' court, but it may be that the accused's age when the proceedings commenced allows the youth court to retain jurisdiction. In practice, the kinds of problems discussed in this Section can be avoided by ensuring that if an accused is approaching 18 the proceedings are expedited, and at least a plea is taken from him while he is under the crucial age.

(f)   It is implicit in the points discussed above that the age of the accused when he allegedly committed the offence is not the crucial factor. What if the prosecution manipulate the date of the accused's court appearance to ensure that the matter is dealt with by the court of their preference? In *Rotherham Justices ex parte Brough* [1991] Crim LR 522, B was aged 16 when he was involved in a 'glassing', and charged under s 18 of the Offences Against the Person Act 1861. The CPS ensured that process was issued on the day after his 17th birthday (which was the 'watershed' age at the time), so that, since he was an adult at the time when mode of trial was determined, the matter had to go to the Crown Court. B's solicitor applied to the justices for a stay on the grounds of abuse of process, claiming that the actions of the CPS were a deliberate manipulation of the situation to suit the purposes of the Crown. The bench concluded that the CPS had acted properly and without malice, and committed B to the Crown Court, on the s 18 charge. B applied to the Divisional Court for a quashing order, which was refused. Their lordships agreed that the conduct of the CPS was incorrect. They should have preferred the information and allowed matters to take their course. Their lordships concluded, however, that there was no misconduct on the Crown's side. The delay was just under a week. In any event, the youth court would probably have committed B to the Crown Court, so there was no prejudice. Notwithstanding this decision on the facts, however, the Divisional Court was firmly of the view that prosecutors should not manipulate the process in this way, but should allow the youth court to take the decision which the law entrusts to them.

G   AGE AND SENTENCE

The relevant date for sentence is the date of conviction, or in the case of a defendant who **11.33** pleads guilty, the date when a plea is entered: *Starkey* [1994] Crim LR 380 (see 24.67 for details). In *Aldis* [2002] 2 Cr App R (S) 400, the defendant turned 18 before conviction. It was held that the magistrates had the power, by virtue of the CYPA 1963, s 29, to treat him for pur- poses of sentence as under 18, provided that he was under 18 at the time when they deter- mined their jurisdiction to try him summarily. They were therefore able to sentence him to a detention and training order as if he were under 18. In *Bowker* [2007] EWCA Crim 1608, the Court of Appeal was dealing with a case where the offences took place two days before the appellant's 18th birthday, but he was sentenced some time after that. It was clear that the sen- tencing regime which is to be applied to an offender is that which flows from his age at the date of conviction. Nevertheless, the fact that he would have been subject to a more restrict- ed sentencing regime if sentenced when the offences were committed was a powerful factor for the court to bear in mind, even if it was not the sole or determining factor in relation to sentence.

KEY DOCUMENTS

Magistrates' Courts Act 1980, as amended.

Powers of Criminal Courts (Sentencing) Act 2000, as amended.

Practice Direction (*Criminal Proceedings: Consolidation*) [2002] 1 WLR 2870, para IV.39, available at: <http://www.hmcourts-service.gov.uk>.

Criminal Procedure Rules, Part 38, available at: <http://www.justice.gov.uk/criminal/ procrules_fin/index.htm>.

12

COMMITTAL FOR SENTENCE

Where a defendant is convicted or pleads guilty in the magistrates' court, the magistrates will **12.01** usually proceed to sentence, in accordance with the procedure detailed in Chapter 22. In doing so, however, they are limited by the restrictions on their powers of punishment. They should, of course, only have agreed to deal with an offence which is triable either way if they considered their powers of punishment adequate (see 8.16). However, in a case where the defendant indicates, at the plea before venue procedure, that he intends to plead guilty, then the magistrates will have proceeded to sentence without considering the adequacy of their powers of punishment.

A   MAGISTRATES' POWERS

The magistrates' sentencing powers in respect of an offence triable either way are set out in **12.02** ss 78 and 131 of the Powers of Criminal Courts (Sentencing) Act 2000 (PCC(S)A) and ss 32 and 133 of the Magistrates' Courts Act 1980 (MCA), and are as follows:

(a) If the offence is one of those listed in Sch 1 to the MCA, the magistrates may fine the offender up to £5,000 and/or pass a sentence of up to six months' imprisonment (s 32(1)). Offences listed in Sch 1 are those for which the offence-creating provision merely specifies a maximum penalty following conviction on indictment, they being made triable either way by MCA, s 17, and Sch 1 (see 8.06 to 8.08).

(b) If the offence is made triable either way by the statute creating it, the maximum sentence of imprisonment the magistrates can impose is six months or the maximum laid down in the statute, whichever is the *less* (s 78 of the PCC(S)A—see also 10.65 to 10.70). Conversely, the maximum fine is the *greater* of £5,000 or the sum prescribed in the statute. Thus, if a statute creating an either-way offence provides for a maximum penalty of 12 months' imprisonment and/or a fine of £1,000 on summary conviction, the actual maximum that may be imposed is six months and £5,000.

(c) Where the magistrates sentence an offender for two or more offences triable either way, they may pass sentences of imprisonment for each offence and make the sentences run consecutively to each other (and consecutively to sentences of imprisonment passed in respect of any summary offences of which they have also convicted the offender). The aggregate term of the sentence must not, however, exceed 12 months (s 133(2)). Thus, if magistrates convict an offender of two offences of theft and one of assaulting a police constable in the execution of his duty (i.e., of two offences triable either way and one summary offence), they may sentence him to six months' imprisonment for each offence to run concurrently; or they may sentence him to four months for each offence to run consecutively, but they may not sentence him to six months for each offence to run consecutively. If the offender was convicted of only one offence of theft and one of assaulting a police constable, the aggregate term would be restricted to six months (s 133(1) and see 10.68).

12.03 When s 154 of the CJA 2003 comes into effect (no date for implementation had been set at the time of writing), there will be a major change to the sentencing powers of magistrates. The maximum prison sentence which the magistrates can impose in respect of any one offence will be increased from six months to 12 months. The maximum aggregate term for two or more offences (whether triable either way or not) will be increased to 65 weeks (ss 154(3) and 155). The implementation of these proposals is tied to the introduction of 'custody plus' (see 24.78 to 24.80), which has considerable funding implications.

12.04 Other forms of sentence at the disposal of magistrates (e.g., community sentences) are mentioned at 10.69.

12.05 What if the accused pleads guilty, or the magistrates agree to summary trial, and on fuller consideration the magistrates believe that their powers of punishment are inadequate? There is an escape route, in the form of committal for sentence to the Crown Court.

B   COMMITTAL FOR SENTENCE UNDER THE POWERS OF CRIMINAL COURTS (SENTENCING) ACT 2000, s 3

12.06 The most important of the powers to commit for sentence which the magistrates possess is that contained in PCC(S)A, s 3, which reads in part as follows:

(1) Subject to subsection (4) below, this section applies where on the summary trial of an offence triable either way a person aged 18 or over is convicted of the offence.

(2) If the court is of opinion—
  (a) that the offence or the combination of the offence and one or more offences associated with it was so serious that greater punishment should be inflicted for the offence than the court has power to impose; or
  (b) in the case of a violent or sexual offence, that a custodial sentence for a term longer than the court has power to impose is necessary to protect the public from serious harm from him,

the court may commit the offender in custody or on bail to the Crown Court for sentence in accordance with s 5(1) below.

Section 5(1) essentially provides that, following a committal for sentence under s 3, the **12.07** Crown Court may deal with the offender as if he had just been convicted on indictment. From the wording of the statute, it is apparent that there are certain limitations to the power to commit under s 3. First, the accused must be aged 18 or more at the date of conviction. Although the statute is not explicit on the point, it is arguable that he should be aged 18 at the date when mode of trial was determined, by analogy with the cases where jurisdiction depends on age (see 11.32 and the cases cited there, especially *Islington North Juvenile Court ex parte Daley* [1983] 1 AC 347). Secondly, the offender must have been convicted of an offence triable either way. This excludes, in this context, an offence of criminal damage where the value involved is £5,000 or less (for the special procedure on such criminal damage charges, see 8.38 to 8.43). Thirdly, the magistrates must be of the opinion that their powers of punishment are inadequate for one of the two reasons set out in s 3. Either:

(a)   the offence is so serious that greater punishment should be imposed than they are empowered to inflict; or
(b)   in the case of a violent or sexual offence, the protection of the public demands a longer term of custody than they can impose.

The reasons reflect the criteria which the court eventually passing sentence must apply in determining the length of that sentence, and are explained in more detail in that context in Chapter 24.

The PCC(S)A, s 3, allows the magistrates to commit for sentence because of the limitations **12.08** imposed on their power to impose a fine, as well as those relating to custody: *North Essex Justices ex parte Lloyd* [2001] Crim LR 145.

In many cases, the magistrates will be considering sentence in a triable either-way case because **12.09** the defendant has indicated that he intends to plead guilty during the plea before venue procedure (see 8.16). In cases where the defendant indicates a plea of not guilty, however, the bench will have made a positive decision to accept jurisdiction after hearing representations from both prosecution and defence. As far as these latter cases are concerned, the seriousness of the offence, at least, ought to have been revealed at the time when mode of trial was determined. If the magistrates thought the offence was so serious that their powers of punishment were inadequate, they should have sent the matter to the Crown Court for trial. Exceptionally, however, there may be aspects of offence seriousness which emerge only after conviction, and which may lead the magistrates to commit to the Crown Court for sentence. These are:

(a)   where the defendant is revealed as having a record of previous convictions (the CJA 2003, s 143(2), states that, in determining offence seriousness, 'the court must treat each previous conviction as an aggravating factor if' it considers it reasonable to do so: see 23.52); or
(b)   where the defendant asks for further offences to be taken into consideration (for an explanation of this procedure see 22.60 to 22.65); or
(c)   where there are aggravating features about the offence charged, of which the magistrates were not aware when they accepted jurisdiction.

12.10 There has been some controversy about the extent to which the magistrates can, as it were, change their minds about the adequacy of their powers of punishment. That, after all, is what committal for sentence involves (other than in cases where a guilty plea was indicated). On a previous occasion the bench decided to accept jurisdiction. In order to do so, they must have concluded that their powers of punishment were adequate. By committing for sentence, they are now coming to a different conclusion. As far as categories (a) and (b) are concerned, such a change of mind seems quite legitimate. The magistrates are not supposed to know of any previous convictions, or offences which the defendant wants taken into consideration, when they decide on mode of trial. (The position will change once the new mode of trial procedure under the CJA 2003, Sch 3 comes into effect: see 8.48).

12.11 The difficulty arises over category (c). It has been argued that aggravating features about the offence charged can justify committal for sentence only where the magistrates were not aware of them when they accepted jurisdiction. If they were aware of them, so this line of argument runs, then either they should have refused jurisdiction, or the features are not such as to justify committal for sentence. After all, the offender gave up his right to jury trial in the knowledge that the magistrates had taken the view that their powers of punishment were adequate. For the magistrates to change their minds without new information would be inequitable. This was the conclusion of the Divisional Court in *Manchester Magistrates' Court ex parte Kaymanesh* [1994] Crim LR 401.

12.12 In *North Sefton Magistrates' Court ex parte Marsh* (1994) 159 JP 1, the Divisional Court came down firmly in favour of a broad interpretation of the statute, and stated that *Ex parte Kaymanesh* was wrongly decided. The magistrates had 'an open-textured decision' on whether to commit for sentence, which was apparently separate from their decision on mode of trial. However, the Divisional Court in *Ex parte Marsh* did stress that magistrates should think carefully when deciding to accept jurisdiction because normally an accused should be able to conclude that, once jurisdiction had been accepted, he would not on the same facts be committed for sentence.

12.13 The discretion of the magistrates in relation to committal is, however, subject to a general principle of 'legitimate expectation'. If the defendant has been led to believe, expressly or by implication, that he will be sentenced by the magistrates, then he should not subsequently be committed for sentence, whether by the same or a differently constituted bench: *Nottingham Magistrates' Court ex parte Davidson* [2000] 1 Cr App R (S) 167 and *Norwich Magistrates' Court ex parte Elliott* [2000] 1 Cr App R (S) 152. The burden is on the defendant who asserts that his expectations were aroused to establish that they were: *Sheffield Magistrates' Court ex parte Ojo* [2001] Crim LR 43. The defendant ought to have been warned of the court's power to commit, but the warning may have given the impression that the court is satisfied on the material that it has that the matter should remain in the magistrates' court unless new material emerges. If that is the case, and no such material emerges, then the defendant is entitled to expect that he will not be committed for sentence: *Wirral Magistrates' Court ex parte Jermyn* [2001] Crim LR 45.

12.14 Magistrates sometimes use the phrase 'all options open' when adjourning for a presentence report, in an effort to avoid arousing the expectations of the defendant. The question whether this includes the option to commit for sentence, or merely the option of a custodial sentence, arose in *Feltham Justices ex parte Rees* [2001] Crim LR 47. The Divisional Court held that it must be considered in context. The court echoed the observations in *ex parte Elliott* that if the justices had in mind that one of the options which they were considering was committal for sentence, they should specifically say so.

When s 41 and Sch 3, para 22 of the CJA 2003 come into force (no date had been set for **12.15** implementation at the time of writing), the position in relation to committal for sentence will be radically altered. The magistrates will no longer generally have the power to commit the defendant to the Crown Court. Once they have decided that the case is suitable for summary trial, and the defendant has, in turn, consented to summary trial, the option of committal to the Crown Court under s 3 of the PCC(S)A 2000 will no longer be available. The defendant may still, however, be committed for sentence under s 3A of the 2000 Act (which is inserted in the 2000 Act by the CJA 2003, Sch 3), where the criteria for an extended sentence or a sentence for public protection appear to be met (see 24.34 to 24.42 for an explanation of those sentences.) It follows that the power to commit for sentence will be confined to cases where:

(a)   a guilty plea has been indicated at plea before venue; or
(b)   the defendant is likely to be the subject of an extended sentence, or a sentence for public protection.

Committal for sentence after the plea before venue procedure

In *Warley Magistrates' Court ex parte DPP* [1998] 2 Cr App R 307, the Divisional Court set out **12.16** the following points of guidance for magistrates deciding whether to commit for sentence as a result of the plea before venue procedure:

(a)   In deciding whether their powers of punishment were adequate, they should take into account the discount granted on a plea of guilty.
(b)   Where it was obvious that the gravity of the offence required punishment which would exceed the magistrates' powers, they should commit to the Crown Court without seeking any pre-sentence report or hearing mitigation.
(c)   The defence should, however, be allowed to make a brief submission in opposition to this course of action, and the prosecution should be allowed to reply.
(d)   If there was any dispute as to the facts which triggered off the need for a *Newton* hearing, the magistrates should proceed to hold one if the decision whether to commit for sentence might depend on the outcome of the *Newton* hearing (see 22.11 to 22.30 for details of the *Newton* hearing procedure).
(e)   Similarly, a *Newton* hearing should be held if the magistrates considered that, whatever the outcome, their powers of sentencing would be adequate.
(f)   But if they considered that, whatever the outcome, the case would have to be committed for sentence, it was clearly preferable to leave the *Newton* hearing to the Crown Court (See *Gillan* [2007] EWHC 380, and 22.30 as to whether the Crown Court should conduct a *Newton* hearing when the magistrates have already done so).

Bail on committal for sentence

A committal for sentence under PCC(S)A, s 3, may be in custody or on bail. Traditionally, it **12.17** was rare for bail to be granted because by committing for sentence the magistrates have indicated that in their view, a relatively severe custodial sentence is called for.

12.18 In *Rafferty* [1998] 2 Cr App R (S) 449, the Court of Appeal dealt with the situation where the accused gives, as part of the plea before venue procedure (see 8.16), an indication that he will plead guilty, and is then committed to the Crown Court for sentence. Their lordships stated that it would not be usual, in most such cases, to alter the position as regards bail or custody. When a person who had been on bail pleaded guilty at the plea before venue, the usual practice would be to continue bail, even if it was anticipated that a custodial sentence would be imposed by the Crown Court, unless there were good reasons for remanding the accused in custody. By the same token, an accused who had been in custody could expect to remain there if the reasons for remanding in custody were unchanged. *Rafferty* does seem to reflect concern that, unless defendants could expect a reasonable chance of bail after an indication of a guilty plea, they would adopt a tactical not guilty plea in order to postpone the evil moment.

Powers of the Crown Court

12.19 When magistrates commit an offender for sentence under PCC(S)A, s 3 they should commit him to the most convenient location of the Crown Court, where the case is normally listed for hearing by a circuit judge or recorder. The offender is asked whether he admits that he was convicted by the magistrates and committed by them to the Crown Court for sentence. In the absence of an admission, the prosecution must call evidence to prove those facts (*Barker* [1951] 1 All ER 479), probably the evidence of a police officer who was present at the magistrates' court when the committal for sentence was made. Once the convictions and committal have been admitted or proved, the proceedings before sentence is passed are the same as those which follow a guilty plea on indictment (see Chapter 22).

12.20 When sentencing an offender who has been committed to it under s 3, the Crown Court can deal with him as if he had just been convicted of the offence(s) concerned on indictment: PCC(S)A, s 5. The maximum sentence upon a committal for sentence is consequently greater, and often much greater, than that which the magistrates have power to impose. For example, an offender convicted on indictment of theft may be sentenced to seven years' imprisonment and an unlimited fine. If he is convicted of two or more thefts, prison sentences for those offences may be made to run consecutively even if the aggregate term exceeds seven years. An offender who has been committed for sentence under s 3 in respect of offences of theft may be similarly sentenced. On the other hand, had he been sentenced by the magistrates, the maximum for one offence of theft would have been six months' imprisonment and a £5,000 fine, and the maximum prison term for several offences of theft would have been one year. Of course, the Crown Court would not in practice consider passing a sentence anywhere near the maximum it could pass for offences of theft which the magistrates considered suitable for summary trial. However, upon a committal for sentence the Crown Court may well inflict punishment considerably more severe than that which the magistrates could have inflicted.

C   OTHER POWERS TO COMMIT FOR SENTENCE

12.21 Section 3 of the PCC(S)A 2000 contains the most important but by no means the only power to commit for sentence. Some of the other powers to commit are necessary to deal with cases where, as a result of a summary conviction, the offender is liable to be dealt with by the Crown Court in respect of a matter such as breach of a community sentence or breach of a suspended sentence. Details will be found in Chapters 24 and 25, but it should be noted that magistrates can commit for sentence when:

(a) they have convicted an offender of an imprisonable offence (indictable or summary) committed during the operational period of a suspended sentence of imprisonment passed by the Crown Court (PCC(S)A, s 120); or

(b) they have convicted an offender of any offence committed during the period of an order for conditional discharge made by the Crown Court (PCC(S)A, s 13(5) and Sch 3).

Following a committal in the circumstances mentioned in (a) or (b) above the Crown Court can, respectively: bring the suspended sentence into force or sentence the offender for the offence for which he was conditionally discharged. The magistrates do not have jurisdiction to do either of those things.

The powers to commit for sentence mentioned so far are primary powers in the sense that **12.22** they may be exercised even though the magistrates have no other reason to commit. They are supplemented by a secondary power to commit for sentence contained in s 6 of the PCC(S)A 2000. This provides that, where magistrates have decided to commit for sentence under s 3 or any other of their primary powers, they may also commit the offender to be dealt with by the Crown Court for:

(a) any offence of which they (the magistrates) have convicted the offender;

(b) breach of a suspended sentence of imprisonment passed by their court or any other magistrates' court;

(c) breach of a community sentence or conditional discharge ordered by a magistrates' court, provided (if the order was not made by their court) they have been given permission to deal with the breach (see 25.29 to 25.36 for details).

When an offender has been committed under s 6, the Crown Court does *not* sentence him as **12.23** if he had just been convicted on indictment, but it deals with the matter which occasioned the committal in any way the magistrates could have done had they chosen not to commit. Thus, the purpose of s 6 is not to render the offender liable to a more severe punishment, but to enable the Crown Court to deal with all matters outstanding against him in cases where, were it not for the section, the sentencing function would have to be split between the magistrates and the Crown Court. Two examples will show the usefulness of the section. O is summarily convicted of stealing from a Ford Focus (an offence triable either way) and of interfering with a Renault Megane (a summary matter). Having heard about O's previous convictions, the magistrates decide to commit him under s 3 of the PCC(S)A in respect of the theft. They cannot commit under s 3 for interfering with the Megane, for the section only applies if there has been a conviction for an offence triable either way. Nor do any of the other primary powers of committal apply. However, it will be possible to have the Crown Court deal with both offences by committing the offence of interfering with a motor vehicle under s 6. As a second example of the operation of s 6, consider a case where O is convicted of the summary offence of assaulting a police officer in the execution of his duty. He committed the offence during the operational period of a suspended sentence of imprisonment passed by the Crown Court for an indictable offence of assault occasioning actual bodily harm. Magistrates have no power to bring into effect a suspended sentence passed by the Crown Court (see CJA 2003, Sch 12). They may, however, commit the offender under s 120 of the PCC(S)A 2000 with a view to the Crown Court doing what they cannot. Section 120 does not, however, entitle them to commit O to be sentenced for the offence which has put him in breach of the suspended sentence, and, since that offence is summary, s 3 is of no assistance. Again, the answer is to commit under s 6.

12.24 Section 4 of the PCC(S)A applies to the situation where the magistrates commit an accused for trial for some offences, but also have to deal with him for other related either-way offences to which he has indicated his intention to plead guilty at the plea before venue procedure (see 8.16). Offences are related to each other in this context if they can both be tried on the same indictment. The magistrates are given the power by s 4 to commit the accused to the Crown Court for sentence for the related offences, even if they do not meet the criteria laid down in s 3 (offence seriousness or public protection—see 12.06). Once the accused reaches the Crown Court, its powers to sentence him depend on whether:

(a)   it convicts him of one or more related offences; or

(b)   the magistrates' court in committing him for sentence under s 4 stated that it also had the power to do so under s 3.

If either of these conditions is fulfilled, the Crown Court can sentence the offender as if he had just been convicted on indictment. If they are not, the court's powers are limited to those of the magistrates.

12.25 In the great majority of cases, the offence which gives rise to the magistrates' primary power of committal (the 'relevant offence') will be indictable. If the primary committal is under s 3 of the MCA, that will inevitably be so. But, occasionally, the relevant offence is summary (e.g., when a summary conviction puts the offender in breach of a suspended sentence passed by the Crown Court in dealing with an appeal from the magistrates against conviction or sentence for a summary offence). In such cases, the power to commit under s 6 is more restricted than when the relevant offence is indictable. The magistrates are only able to commit in respect of (a) breach of a magistrates' court suspended sentence, and (b) any imprisonable or endorsable offences of which they have convicted the offender.

KEY DOCUMENTS

Powers of Criminal Courts (Sentencing) Act 2000, ss 3 to 6, as amended.

13

SENDING CASES TO THE CROWN COURT

A   INTRODUCTION

13.01   Trial on indictment always takes place in the Crown Court. However, before being sent to the Crown Court, the defendant will have been the subject of preliminary proceedings in the magistrates' court. Those proceedings are dealt with in this Chapter.

13.02   Historically, the decision to send the defendant to the Crown Court took the form of committal proceedings. In essence, this was a filter mechanism to ensure that there was sufficient evidence against the defendant to constitute a prima facie case that he had committed an indictable offence. The magistrates would consider the evidence, assuming that the decision had been taken in the first place that the matter should be tried in the Crown Court (in accordance with the mode of trial provisions dealt with in Chapter 8). They would then make a decision, after hearing representations from legal representatives if appropriate, whether there was sufficient evidence to send the case to the Crown Court. If there was, the case would be committed to the Crown Court for trial. If there was not, the defendant would be discharged.

13.03   Under the Magistrates' Courts Act, 1980, s 6, there were two methods of committal: 'with consideration of the evidence', and 'without consideration of the evidence'. At the time of writing, both are still in existence, but are due to be phased out (no date had been set at the time of writing for the implementation of these provisions) by provisions contained in the CJA 2003, Sch 3. Both forms of committal are described in 13.47 to 13.64.

13.04   Under the CJA 1987, s 4, new provisions were made for the transfer of serious fraud cases to the Crown Court. In the CJA 1991, s 53, rather similar provisions were brought in to transfer cases involving child witnesses to the Crown Court (see 13.29 to 13.43). Both of these forms of transfer are due to be replaced by equivalent provisions in the CJA 2003 (no date had been set for this change at the time of writing).

13.05   The recent historical trend has been away from a relatively detailed consideration of the evidence by the magistrates in the form of committal proceedings with witnesses (who might give evidence orally at the instance of the defence) to an increasingly paper exercise where the magistrates play a minimal role prior to dispatching the case to the Crown Court. A major step in this process took place with the enactment of the CDA 1998, s 51. This abolished committal proceedings in respect of indictable-only offences. It substituted an administrative exercise, with little judicial input, under which the case was sent to the Crown Court at an early stage—frequently after a single appearance by the defendant in the magistrates' court (see 13.09 to 13.28).

13.06   The latest step in this trend towards the abolition of committal proceedings is contained in the CJA 2003, Sch 3. It removes triable-either-way offences from the ambit of committal proceedings so that they will be governed by s 51 of the CDA 1998 (13.44 to 13.46).

13.07   The position in relation to the transfer of cases from magistrates' court to Crown Court, before the introduction of the CJA 2003, Sch 3, can therefore be summarized as follows:

(a) indictable-only offences are sent under the CDA 1998, s 51;
(b) serious fraud cases are sent under the CJA 1987, s 4;
(c) child witness cases are sent under the CJA, s 53;

(d) either-way offences are sent by committal proceedings, under the MCA 1980, s 6.

After the CJA 2003, Sch 3, comes into force, the position will be: **13.08**

(a) indictable offences (whether indictable-only or triable-either-way) sent to the Crown Court under CDA 1998, s 51 (adults) or s 51A (juveniles);
(b) serious fraud cases sent up under CDA 1998, s 51B;
(c) child witness cases sent up under CDA 1998, s 51C.

B   INDICTABLE-ONLY OFFENCES

A major new route to the Crown Court was opened up as a result of the the procedure set out **13.09** in s 51 of the Crime and Disorder Act 1998 (CDA). This lays down that offences which can be tried only on indictment, and those related to them, must be sent immediately to the Crown Court from a preliminary hearing in the magistrates' court.

Section 51 provides that the magistrates *must* send for trial in the Crown Court, without **13.10** holding committal proceedings:

(a) an adult defendant charged with an indictable-only offence, to be tried for that offence;
(b) an adult defendant sent for trial for an indictable-only offence, to be tried also for any related offence which is triable either way for which he appears at the same time;
(c) an adult defendant sent for trial for an indictable-only offence, to be tried also for any related summary offence for which he appears at the same time and which is imprisonable or carries disqualification from driving;
(d) an adult co-defendant appearing on the same occasion charged with a related offence which is triable either way.

In addition, the magistrates *may* send immediately to the Crown Court for trial: **13.11**

(a) an adult defendant already sent to the Crown Court for trial for an indictable-only offence, to be tried for a related offence which is triable either way (or summary and imprisonable and carrying disqualification) and which has been charged subsequently;
(b) an adult co-defendant charged with a related triable-either-way offence, who appears subsequently to a defendant sent to the Crown Court for an indictable-only offence;
(c) a juvenile jointly charged with an adult defendant with an indictable-only offence, where the magistrates consider that it is in the interests of justice for the juvenile to be tried jointly with the adult; and
(d) a juvenile sent to the Crown Court by virtue of (c), in respect of any related either-way or summary offence (provided it is imprisonable or carries disqualification).

For the purposes of these provisions, an offence triable either way is related to an indictable-only offence if they could be joined in the same indictment. A summary offence is related to an indictable-only offence if it arises out of circumstances which are the same as or connected with those giving rise to it.

Indictable-only offences and the transfer procedure

13.12   In cases where the notice of transfer procedure might otherwise be available to the prosecution, the provisions of s 51 of the CDA 1998 take precedence. In a child witness case, where s 53 of the CJA 1991 might have been considered as a route to the Crown Court, if the charge is indictable-only (e.g., rape), or is related to an indictable-only charge, the prosecution is not able to make use of the notice of transfer procedure, and must proceed according to s 51 of the CDA 1998 (see Sch 8, para 93 to the CDA 1998). Similarly, where a serious fraud is charged, the case will be governed by the indictable-only procedure, rather than the provisions of the CJA 1987 (see Sch 8, para 65 to the CDA 1998).

Procedure in the magistrates' court

13.13   The accused appears in the magistrates' court for a preliminary hearing. The court must send the case *forthwith* to the Crown Court (s 51(1)). The magistrates may however, adjourn (s 52(5)), for example where the situation is likely to change and it may not be necessary to send the case to the Crown Court, or where the defence needs to obtain information in order to mount a bail application.

13.14   Despite the historical link between the provision of advance information and the decision as to mode of trial, the CPS recommends that a standard package of advance information be served upon the defence for cases falling within the s 51 procedure, preferably prior to the preliminary hearing in the magistrates' court. This includes the charge sheet, any summary of the prosecution case which has been prepared, the key witness statements and a print-out of previous convictions.

13.15   The proceedings before the magistrates are subject to statutory provisions relating to reporting restrictions. Only details which are permitted by the CDA 1998, s 52A, can normally be published. Those permitted details include the identity of the court and the magistrates, the name, age, home address, and occupation of the defendant, the offence(s) with which he is charged, the names of the legal representatives, bail arrangements, and whether publicly funded representation has been granted. As far as any other details are concerned, they are subject to reporting restrictions, and may not be published unless the magistrates expressly lift the restrictions. The court may lift them if it is satisfied that it is in the interests of justice to do so, after hearing representations from the accused.

13.16   At the hearing, the magistrates' court states, in a notice, the offence(s) for which the accused is being sent for trial, and the location of the Crown Court at which he will be tried. Copies of the evidence on which the charges are based must then be served on the accused by the prosecutor. This must be done within 70 days of the first hearing in the Crown Court (50 days where the accused is in custody), subject to an application for extension: Crime and Disorder Act 1998 (Service of Prosecution Evidence) Regulations 2005 (SI 2005 No 902).

Summary-only offences sent under the CDA 1998, s 51

13.17   A summary-only offence may be sent to the Crown Court under the provisions of s 51 of the CDA 1998 if it is related to an indictable-only offence. When it is sent, it will be adjourned by the magistrates in accordance with s 51(10), i.e., no date will be fixed for it to be heard. If it is disposed of in the Crown Court in due course, in accordance with Sch 3, para 6 of the CDA 1998, then the magistrates do not need to deal with it. If it is not disposed of in the Crown Court, then it can, in effect, be remitted to the magistrates to deal with it. The procedure is similar to that under s 41 of the CJA 1988 (see 13.81).

Appearance in the Crown Court

After the preliminary hearing which sends the defendant to the Crown Court, the **13.18** magistrates' court will send a notice to the Crown Court. The magistrates' court or the Crown Court may decide that a preliminary hearing in the Crown Court is necessary after the case has been sent there. If this is necessary, then it should be held approximately 14 days after the accused is sent to the Crown Court. In any event, a plea and case management hearing should be held approximately 17 weeks after the case was sent up (14 weeks if the accused is in custody): *Practice Direction (Criminal Proceedings: Consolidation)* [2002] 1 WLR 2870, paras IV.41 and V.56, and see 16.05.

The bill of indictment must be served within 28 days of service of the prosecution case. It may **13.19** contain any count which is supported by the evidence contained in the papers served by the prosecution, either in addition to or in substitution for the charges upon which the defendant was sent to the Crown Court by the magistrates' court (Sch 8, para 5, CDA 1998). Any such counts must, however, be capable of being lawfully joined in the same indictment.

Discontinuance of the prosecution case

The prosecution has power to discontinue the case against the defendant not only in the **13.20** magistrates' court, but also, in the case of offences sent up to the Crown Court by s 51 of the CDA 1998, at any time before the indictment is preferred (Prosecution of Offences Act 1985, s 23A).

Applications for dismissal

The defence is able to challenge the prosecution case under the procedure set out in Sch 3 to **13.21** the CDA 1998. After the prosecution case has been served, but before arraignment, the defendant may apply to the Crown Court for the charges (or any of them) to be dismissed. The details of the procedure are covered in the Crime and Disorder Act 1998 (Dismissal of Charges Sent) Rules 1998 (SI 1998 No 3048). The application may be made orally (r 2) or in writing (r 3). Where the judge gives leave or so orders, then oral evidence may be given on the application. This may be done only, however, if the judge considers that it is in the interests of justice to do so (Sch 3, para 2(4)). The proceedings are covered by reporting restrictions (para 3).

Written notice of intention to make an oral application for dismissal is governed by r 13.2(2) **13.22** of the Criminal Procedure Rules 2005. Written applications for dismissal are dealt with in r 13.3. Applications for both must be made on the forms set out in the *Practice Direction (Criminal Proceedings: Consolidation)* [2002] 1 WLR 2870.

The position as far as evidence is concerned has been that oral evidence may be given on an **13.23** application for dismissal, but only if the judge decides, after an application, that the interests of justice require such evidence. However, the possibility of oral evidence at such a hearing will be removed when the CJA 2003, Sch 3, para 20(3)(b), comes into effect.

13.24 At the conclusion of the hearing, the judge must dismiss the charge, and quash any related count in the indictment if it appears to him that the evidence against the applicant would not be sufficient for a jury properly to convict him (Sch 3, para 2).

13.25 If a charge is dismissed by the judge as a result of an application, then further proceedings may only be brought by the prosecution in relation to that charge by way of a voluntary bill of indictment (see 13.75 to 13.77): CDA 1998, Sch 3, para 2(6).

13.26 The accused is not entitled to challenge by way of judicial review the decision of the judge in the Crown Court not to dismiss the charge: *R (Snelgrove) v Woolwich Crown Court* [2005] 1 WLR 3223. The reason is that the decision not to dismiss the charge is a matter relating to trial on indictment, and as a result it is excluded from the jurisdiction of the Divisional Court: Supreme Court Act 1981, s 29(3).

Effect of dismissal of charges

13.27 Where at least one indictable-only charge remains, then the Crown Court can proceed to deal with the indictment in the normal way. Where there are no indictable-only charges left as a result of a successful application for dismissal, however, then the remaining charges must be put on an indictment, which is read to the accused (Sch 3, paras 7 to 15). The Crown Court must then carry out, in respect of each triable-either-way offence, the plea before venue procedure and, if there is an indication of a not guilty plea or no indication, the mode of trial procedure (see 8.16). If, as a result, the case is to be tried summarily, it must be remitted to the magistrates' court. If not, the Crown Court will continue to deal with it. Where the defendant is under the age of 18, the Crown Court will remit the case to the youth court unless:

(a) the offence ought to be dealt with as a grave crime under the provisions of the PCC(S)A 2000, s 91; or

(b) there is an either-way offence in which the juvenile is charged jointly with an adult, and the Crown Court considers that it is in the interests of justice for them to be tried together.

13.28 In *Haye* [2003] Crim LR 287, the defendant was sent to the Crown Court by virtue of s 51 of the CDA 1998 on a charge of robbery. The prosecution dropped the indictable-only charge of robbery at the plea and directions hearing, and substituted a charge of theft (triable-either-way). The Crown Court should then have conducted a mode-of-trial hearing to determine where the theft charge should be dealt with. This was not done, and the defendant, after initially pleading not guilty, entered a guilty plea. He later appealed against conviction because the procedure set out in Sch 3 of the CDA 1998 had not been followed. The Court of Appeal upheld the appeal. The statutory procedure had not been followed. The defendant had the right to make representations and/or to exercise choice as to the mode of trial. Here there had been no conscious decision as to the appropriate mode of trial. The defendant had been deprived of an opportunity to persuade the judge that summary trial was more suitable. The proceedings leading to his conviction were a nullity. The Courts Act 2003, s 66 has given Crown Court judges the power to sit as district judges. As a result, if the *Haye* situation were be repeated today, the judge could utilize his powers as a district judge, determine mode of trial, commit the defendant for sentence, and could then (sitting once again as a Crown Court judge), pass sentence: *Ashton* [2007] 1 WLR 181. In *Ashton*, the Court of Appeal went on to indicate that 'if *Haye* were decided now the result would have been the other way'. Even if there had been a procedural failure such as occurred in *Haye*, the court must ask itself whether Parliament intended jurisdiction to be removed automatically in such an event. If it did not, then the court must look at whether the interests of justice meant that the error rendered the proceedings which followed invalid, having particular regard to whether the defendant or the prosecution suffered prejudice.

C NOTICES OF TRANSFER

The notice of transfer system was introduced for two very different situations: **13.29**

(a) in cases of serious and complex fraud; and
(b) in certain cases involving child witnesses.

Although the factual situations in (a) and (b) differ greatly, the procedural consequences are much the same. The notice of transfer system in serious fraud cases is dealt with first at 13.30 to 13.38, and those features which are peculiar to its use in child witness cases are discussed at 13.39 to 13.43.

Serious fraud cases

It was the report of the Roskill Committee in 1986 which led to the introduction of the **13.30** notice of transfer system in the Criminal Justice Act 1987 (CJA 1987). One of the primary difficulties highlighted by the report was the very considerable delay in the prosecution of major fraud, resulting from the hearing of oral evidence in the preliminary stages, when this was permitted for committals.

The CJA 1987 gave the Director of Public Prosecutions, the Director of the Serious Fraud **13.31** Office, the Commissioners of Inland Revenue, the Commissioners of Customs and Excise and the Secretary of State the status of 'designated authorities'. A notice of transfer may be given whenever a designated authority is of the opinion that the evidence against an accused charged with an indictable offence is:

(a) sufficient for him to be committed for trial; and
(b) 'reveals a fraud of such seriousness or complexity that it is appropriate that the management of the case should without delay be taken over by the Crown Court' (CJA 1987, s 4(1)(a) and (b)).

Notice of transfer may be given at any time between the accused being charged and the **13.32** commencement of committal proceedings. It must be given to the 'magistrates' court in whose jurisdiction the offence has been charged' (s 4(1)(a) and (c)).

13.33 The notice must specify the location of the Crown Court at which it is proposed that the trial should take place, and the charges to which it relates (s 5(1) and (2)).

13.34 Once served, the effect of a notice of transfer is that the functions of the magistrates' court cease, except in respect of bail, grant of legal representation and witness orders (s 4(1)).

13.35 The accused is provided with a measure of protection against being put on trial for offences in respect of which there is inadequate evidence. This is contained in s 6, which enables the accused to apply to the Crown Court for the dismissal of the transferred charges. The application for dismissal must be made within 28 days of the service of the notice of transfer, unless the Crown Court gives leave for late notice. The application itself may be presented and determined either orally or in writing, but an oral application must be preceded by written notice (Criminal Justice Act 1987 (Dismissal of Transferred Charges) Rules 1988 (SI 1988 No 1695), rr 2 and 3).

13.36 By s 6(3), oral evidence may be given at an application for dismissal only with the leave of the judge, such leave not to be given unless the interests of justice so require.

13.37 A judge determining an application for dismissal must dismiss any of the charges specified in the notice of transfer in respect of which 'it appears to him that the evidence against the applicant would not be sufficient for a jury properly to convict him' (s 6(1)). The corresponding counts in any indictment preferred against the accused must be quashed. The effect of a successful application for dismissal is basically the same as a refusal by examining justices to commit for trial, i.e., the accused is not acquitted but may be re-prosecuted for the same matters. It is provided that any further proceedings on the dismissed charges must be brought by way of a voluntary bill of indictment (s 6(5); see 13.75 to 13.77 for the voluntary bill procedure).

13.38 The CJA 2003, Sch 3 inserts a new s 51B in the CDA 1998, which is not in effect at the time of writing. It will not in any event have any major practical effect, since it replicates the CJA 1987, s 4 as set out above.

Child witnesses

13.39 The notice of transfer system was extended to cases of sexual offences and offences of violence involving child witnesses by s 53 of the Criminal Justice Act 1991. The intention was to protect the child witnesses in question from being compelled to give their evidence at committal with the trauma that almost inevitably involved. Further, the reform aimed to bring on the Crown Court trial more speedily by dispensing with committal proceedings altogether. This means both that the recollection of the child witness is likely to be more accurate, and that any therapy to help the child recover from the incident can begin as soon as possible.

13.40 In child witness cases, the Director of Public Prosecutions (rather than the list of 'designated authorities' in serious fraud cases) is authorized to serve a notice of transfer, in respect of proceedings for certain offences, and provided that certain conditions are fulfilled. The offences include any which involve an assault on, or injury or a threat of injury to, a person, offences of cruelty to persons under 16, sexual offences, and attempting or conspiring to commit, or aiding, abetting, counselling, procuring, or inciting any of those offences.

The conditions of which the DPP must be satisfied are that:

(a) the evidence of the offence would be sufficient for the accused to be committed for trial;
(b) a child who is alleged to be the victim or to have witnessed the commission of the offence, will be called as a witness at trial; and
(c) for the purpose of avoiding any prejudice to the welfare of the child, the case should be taken over and proceeded with without delay by the Crown Court.

According to s 53(6), the meaning of 'child' varies according to the offence with which the accused is charged. For an offence of violence or cruelty (or attempting or conspiring etc. to commit such an offence), it means a person aged under 14. For sexual offences, it means a person under 17. The relevant date for determining the child's age is not laid down in s 53, but the context suggests that it is the date of the notice of transfer. In each case, if a video recording was made of an interview about the offence by the child witness, when he was below the relevant age, then the age limit is increased by a year, to 15 or 18, as the case may be. The contents of a notice and, once served, its effect are much the same as in a serious fraud case (see 13.29 to 13.37). One notable difference is that, in an application for dismissal, the judge cannot give leave for oral evidence to be adduced from a child witness, as defined above. **13.41**

Special considerations arise where the defendant is a juvenile and the CPS is considering whether to make use of the notice of transfer procedure. In *T and C* [2001] Crim LR 398, the Court of Appeal stated that the prosecution should not consider using the notice of transfer procedure unless satisfied that a magistrates' court would be likely to find that it should be possible to sentence the defendant under PCC(S)A 2000, s 91 (see 11.04 to 11.15). The reason is that the interests of both the juvenile defendant and the young witness are served by a speedy trial. It follows that summary trial is desirable unless there is a need to ensure greater powers of punishment under s 91. **13.42**

The CJA 2003, Sch 3, inserts a new s 51C in the CDA 1998, which is not in effect at the time of writing. It will not in any event have any major practical effect, since it replicates the CJA 1991, s 53, as set out above. **13.43**

D EITHER-WAY OFFENCES

The CJA 2003, Sch 3, para 18, brings about a major change in the way in which triable-either-way cases reach the Crown Court. It was not in force at the time of writing, and no date had been announced for its implementation. Until that time, triable-either-way offences continue to be subject to committal proceedings (see 13.47 to 13.74). However, once the new system is in operation, the magistrates' court will follow the procedure set out in s 51 of the CDA 1998 for cases where an either-way case involving an adult defendant is allocated for trial on indictment. **13.44**

At the same time, s 50A(3) of the CDA 1998 sets out the order in which the magistrates will have to deal with the necessary procedures where an offence is triable-either-way. Where an adult is charged with an either-way offence, the court must take the following steps: **13.45**

(a) plea before venue;
(b) if the accused indicates a not guilty plea, deal with the mode of trial procedure;

(c) if the court declines jurisdiction, or the accused elects trial on indictment, send the case to the Crown Court by way of the CDA 1998, s 51.

13.46 The same set of provisions will insert into the CDA 1998 a new s 51A, which will replace the existing provisions for moving cases where defendants are under the age of 18 to the Crown Court for trial.

E   COMMITTAL PROCEEDINGS

13.47 Prior to 1967 the examining justices always considered the evidence put forward at committal proceedings so as to decide whether or not there was a prima facie case against the accused on which they should commit for trial. However, this led to waste of the court's time and unnecessary inconvenience for witnesses in cases where the defence conceded that there would have to be a committal. Accordingly, s 1 of the Criminal Justice Act 1967 introduced an alternative procedure by which the examining justices could, in certain circumstances, commit the accused for trial without considering the evidence against him. Section 1 of the 1967 Act was re-enacted in s 6(2) of the Magistrates' Courts Act 1980. Committals with consideration of the evidence are dealt with in s 6(1) of the Magistrates' Courts Act. Most committals then took place under s 6(2), i.e., without consideration of the evidence. Pressure continued during the 1980s and early 1990s for the role of committals to be reduced further. The Royal Commission on Criminal Justice, chaired by Lord Runciman, said in its report (Cm 2263, 1993) that more efficient ways should be found of weeding out the weak cases before they went to trial in the Crown Court. The Commission estimated that some 93 per cent of cases were committed to the Crown Court by the ritualistic formality of a 'paper committal' under MCA, s 6(2). The remaining 7 per cent went up to the Crown Court by way of s 6(1), but the Commission was even less impressed by the operation of this procedure, although for different reasons. The full committal was criticized for the amount of court time which it wasted (including the outdated requirement for the clerk to transcribe the depositions of witnesses), and for the pressure to which witnesses were subjected by being compelled to give their evidence twice over.

13.48 As a result of the complaints about the committal system, the government introduced, in the Criminal Justice and Public Order Act 1994, a system called 'transfer for trial', which was purely administrative rather than judicial. The transfer for trial system under the 1994 Act bore only a passing resemblance to the 'notice of transfer' system described in 13.29 to 13.43, despite the confusing similarity of terminology. In any event, it was widely perceived by practitioners as a bureaucratic nightmare, and was consigned to oblivion without ever being brought into force. In the Criminal Procedure and Investigations Act 1996, however, the committal system was subjected to radical reform. Crucially, the examining justices decided whether to commit to the Crown Court on the basis of a series of statements, and without any oral evidence.

13.49 There are still two types of committal procedure:

(a) committal where the evidence (consisting entirely of documents) is considered by the bench, and submissions are made by the parties as to whether the accused should be sent to the Crown Court for trial; and

(b) committal where the accused is committed without consideration of the evidence.

Committals as described in (a) are governed by s 6(1) of the MCA, and are held when the accused has no legal representative acting for him in the case, or his legal representative has requested the court to consider a submission of no case to answer (see 13.67 to 13.69 (MCA)).

The law on committal proceedings is contained chiefly in the Magistrates' Courts Act 1980 **13.50** and the CrimPR, Part 10. Before looking in detail at the two forms of committal proceedings, it will be convenient to consider topics relevant to both forms.

Presence of the accused and the public

Evidence tendered at committal proceedings must be given in the presence of the accused **13.51** unless the examining justices consider that his disorderly conduct makes that impracticable, or he cannot be present for health reasons but is legally represented and has consented to evidence being given in his absence: MCA, s 4(3) and (4). As with criminal proceedings in general, the public as well as the accused have a right to attend, although the justices do have a discretion to sit in camera if the ends of justice would not be served by an open court hearing: MCA, s 4(2). If proceedings are open to the public then they are also, of course, open to the press. However, special rules govern the extent to which the media may report committal proceedings. They are similar to those which are set out at 13.15 in relation to indictable-only cases sent straight to the Crown Court.

Number of accused

Committal proceedings may concern two or more accused persons. This is obviously **13.52** appropriate where they are charged jointly with committing a single offence. It is also appropriate where the accused persons are charged with separate offences which are linked together in some way so that it is in the interests of justice to have a single set of proceedings: *Camberwell Green Magistrates ex parte Christie* [1978] QB 602.

Abuse of process: discretion to halt proceedings

Examining justices have a discretion to discharge the accused without hearing the prosecution **13.53** evidence if there has been delay in bringing the proceedings of such magnitude as to render them an abuse of the court's process. The leading cases are *Derby Crown Court ex parte Brooks* (1984) 70 Cr App R 164, *Grays Justices ex parte Graham* [1982] QB 1239, *Bow Street Stipendiary Magistrate ex parte Director of Public Prosecutions* (1989) 91 Cr App R 283 and *Horseferry Road Magistrates' Court ex parte Bennett* [1993] 3 WLR 90. The principle emerging from those decisions is that justices are entitled to discharge the accused without considering the evidence on which committal is sought if *either* the prosecution have deliberately manipulated the normal criminal process so as to take unfair advantage of the accused (e.g., delayed commencing proceedings in the hope that a potential defence witness would die, emigrate or otherwise become unavailable), *or* there has been delay on the part of the prosecution which—although not deliberate—is none the less unjustifiable and is likely to prejudice the accused in the preparation and conduct of his defence (e.g., because potential witnesses will have forgotten the relevant events).

13.54   The doctrine of abuse of process is by now well established. It was applied in *Bow Street Stipendiary Magistrate ex parte Director of Public Prosecutions* (1989) 91 Cr App R 283. The Divisional Court made it clear that mere delay which gave rise to prejudice and unfairness might by itself amount to an abuse of process. It had to be shown that the delay had produced genuine prejudice and unfairness. In some cases, prejudice would be presumed from substantial delay which the Crown would have to rebut. The Director of Public Prosecutions had applied for judicial review of the magistrate's decision to refuse to commit police officers for trial. It was alleged that the officers concerned had conspired to pervert the course of justice. The prosecutions arose from the Wapping demonstrations on 24 January 1987. Notices of disciplinary proceedings were not served on the officers until 17 December 1987. At the committal on 3 May 1989, magistrate A declined jurisdiction on the ground that it would be an abuse of process to hear the charges. In addition, C, another police officer, applied for judicial review of the decision by magistrate B that his prosecution for assault was not an abuse of process. Again, the allegation arose from events on 24 January 1987. C was said to have assaulted W in the course of arrest. C was not served with a disciplinary notice until 16 February 1988 and the summons was not issued until January 1989. Magistrate B held that the delay was not an abuse of process and that C should be committed for trial. The Divisional Court refused the application of the Director of Public Prosecutions but granted C's, thus holding in effect that both prosecutions involved delays which were an abuse of process. It was perfectly proper, in the circumstances, to infer prejudice from the mere passage of time. With regard to the allegation of assault against C, such an inference was more easily drawn in the case of a single, brief, but confused event which must depend on the recollections of those involved.

13.55   The power of the justices is nevertheless strictly confined, and instances of the discretion not to proceed being exercised in favour of the accused are rare. Thus, in *Ex parte Brooks*, the decision of the Divisional Court was that examining justices had been right to consider the evidence and commit even though some five years had elapsed since the date of the offences. Similarly, in *Ex parte Graham*, the prosecution were not ready to start committal proceedings in respect of obtaining some £1,600-worth of goods by deception until December 1981, nearly two years after the offences. Had the matters been investigated with reasonable expedition, committal could have taken place in about six months. The officer in charge of the case admitted that the only reason for his not having acted more promptly was the size of his case load and the fact that he had more serious matters to investigate. Nevertheless, an application to the High Court for an order requiring the examining justices not to proceed was refused. The following passage from May LJ's judgment in *Ex parte Graham* shows the constraints which the higher courts have tended to put upon the discretion of examining justices:

> We are well aware that there is today a substantial amount of delay and inefficiency in criminal proceedings both before and at trial. This is to be deplored, and all concerned must do their utmost to bring criminal proceedings to trial and to verdict as swiftly and efficiently as possible. But we do not think that this court should create any artificial limitation period for criminal

proceedings where it cannot truly be said that the due process of the courts is being used improperly to harass a defendant.

In an appropriate case, however, the doctrine of abuse of process can certainly be invoked in **13.56** an accused's favour. Thus, in *Telford Justices ex parte Badhan* [1991] 2 QB 78, a complaint was made against the applicant in 1988 that he had committed an offence of rape in 1973 or 1974. He appeared before the examining justices in May 1989. It was submitted that the committal should not proceed, since it would be an abuse of process. The justices rejected the submission, and the applicant sought judicial review. In the Divisional Court, the prosecution argued that the doctrine of abuse of process had no application to committal proceedings, and that *Ex parte Brooks* and subsequent decisions were *per incuriam*. The Divisional Court allowed the application and granted prohibition. Examining justices had the power to decide that the initiation of the process of committal was an abuse of that process. If their decision was disputed, the complainant could seek judicial review. In the present case, it was for the accused to show on a balance of probabilities that he was prejudiced in his defence. Where the period of delay was long, it was legitimate for the court to infer prejudice. The period in question here was that between the date of the alleged offence and the opening of committal—some 15 or 16 years. The court could infer prejudice and conclude that a fair trial was impossible.

As to the procedure which the examining justices ought to adopt, it is submitted that they **13.57** should deal with the question prior to the committal proceedings proper. They should consider evidence on the course of proceedings thus far, particularly as to the extent of the delay, the reasons for it, and any prejudice which the defence may suffer as a result. They should hear from both the prosecution and the defence. Thus, in *Clerkenwell Stipendiary Magistrate ex parte Bell* [1991] Crim LR 468, the magistrate heard evidence from a police officer explaining that the delay of two and a half years between commission of the offence and committal proceedings was due to B's change of address. He declined to hear evidence from B, and then committed him for trial. The Divisional Court held that this was a breach of natural justice and quashed the committal. Conversely, in *Crawley Justices ex parte DPP* (1991) *The Times*, 5 April 1991, the Divisional Court quashed the decision of the justices to dismiss informations because of delay. The bench had not heard from the prosecution, nor enquired fully from the accused as to the facts.

For discussion of the linked question of whether magistrates have a discretion not to proceed **13.58** with a summary trial (as opposed to committal proceedings) on the grounds of delay, see 10.26 to 10.31. Reference should also be made to 20.14 to 20.20, which deals with the general principles, and with the judge's corresponding discretion at a trial on indictment.

Committals with consideration of the evidence

A committal under the MCA 1980, s 6(1) is held whenever: **13.59**

(a) the accused (or one of them) has no legal representative acting for him in the case; or
(b) the legal representative of the accused (or one of them) has requested the court to consider a submission of no case to answer (see 13.67 to 13.69).

13.60   The hallmark of a committal under s 6(1) is that the bench is charged with considering the evidence before deciding whether to send the accused to the Crown Court for trial. Proceedings begin when the accused is called into the dock and has the charges read out to him (but he does not plead since that will not be appropriate until arraignment in the Crown Court). If the prosecution wish to vary the charges (either by adding fresh ones or not proceeding on an original one), that can be explained to the bench. Any additional charge should have been put into writing and handed to the clerk so that he can read it to the accused.

13.61   The prosecution must be legally represented. The accused is entitled to be legally represented, or he may conduct his own defence.

13.62   The procedure is governed by CrimPR, r 10.3. The prosecutor is entitled to outline the case and explain any relevant points of law, before tendering the evidence (all of which is written). The evidence may be read through or, with the leave of the court, summarized. The magistrates' court may view any original exhibits and may retain them. No witnesses are called, and no depositions are taken during the course of the committal (such as used to be taken in s 6(1) committals before the changes introduced by the Criminal Procedure and Investigations Act 1996). No evidence can be tendered by the defence. The accused may then make a submission of no case to answer and, if he does so, or the court is minded not to commit for trial, the prosecutor is entitled to respond (see 13.67 to 13.69 for details about the submission of no case). The court then reaches its decision as to whether to commit the accused for trial in the Crown Court.

13.63   For evidence to be admissible at committal:

(a)   it must be tendered by the prosecutor (the defence is no longer able to adduce evidence at committal); and

(b)   it must fall within one of the categories of evidence defined in ss 5B, 5C, 5D, and 5E of the MCA.

In most cases, the evidence will be in the form of witness statements under MCA, s 5B. Any such statement may be admitted if it is adduced by the prosecutor and:

(a)   It is signed by the maker.

(b)   It contains a declaration by the maker that it is true to the best of his knowledge and belief, and that he made it knowing that if it were tendered in evidence he could be prosecuted for wilfully stating in it anything that he knew to be false or did not believe to be true.

(c)   The prosecution gives a copy of it to each of the other parties to the committal proceedings before tendering it to the court.

13.64   A statement under s 5B should give the maker's age if under 18. If the maker cannot read, it should be read through to him before he signs it, and should contain a declaration that it was so read. (Note that it is not necessary for any witness to write his statement personally, provided that he reads it through before signing it.) Where the statement refers to another document as an exhibit (e.g., a police officer's statement might refer to signed notes of an interview that he had with the accused at the police station), a copy of the exhibit should be given to each of the other parties. If a witness makes a statement to the police it is normally taken down on a standard form which incorporates the declaration that the statement is true etc. as required by s 5B.

Although the usual route for a statement to be admitted in committal proceedings is by **13.65** MCA, s 5B, there are other possibilities. Section 5C is an innovation introduced by the Criminal Procedure and Investigations Act 1996. It allows for evidence by way of deposition taken in advance of the committal where a prosecution witness is reluctant to provide a written statement. A further route is provided by s 5D, which allows in hearsay evidence.

Finally, documents which 'prove themselves' or are made admissible by other legislation, **13.66** such as certificates of conviction or DVLA certificates in road traffic proceedings, are made admissible in committal proceedings by s 5E.

After the prosecution have read or summarized their written statements, the defence have the **13.67** opportunity to submit that there is no case to answer: CrimPR, r 10.3(5). The question for the examining justices is whether the evidence discloses a prima facie case in respect of any indictable offence. If the answer is 'yes', the proceedings continue as described in the next Paragraph. If the answer is 'no', the accused is discharged—i.e., he is free to leave court unless he is being held in custody for some other matter (see 13.72 for details of the effect of discharge at committal proceedings). Unless it is obviously ill-founded, the prosecution will be invited to reply to the defence submission.

The test the justices should apply in deciding whether there is a case to answer has already **13.68** been described in general terms. It is likely that the bench will be concerned only with evidential sufficiency, and will leave questions of credibility to the Crown Court, where the jury will have a chance to assess the witnesses at first-hand. (For a discussion on submissions of no case to answer in the context of summary trial and trial on indictment, see 10.60 and 20.48 to 20.55 respectively.)

Finally, it should be noted that the question for the bench is not merely whether there is a **13.69** case to answer in respect of the charges preferred against the accused at the police station, as supplemented or amended during the course of the hearings. The question is whether *any* indictable offence has been disclosed. Thus, if the accused is charged with murder and the prosecution are seeking committal on that charge, the examining justices could decide that there is no evidence on which a reasonable jury might find that the accused acted with malice aforethought but there is ample evidence of unlawful killing. They would then refuse to commit for murder but allow the proceedings to continue on the basis of manslaughter. The fact that the accused has never been expressly charged with manslaughter is irrelevant. Of course, where two or more offences have been expressly charged (whether in the alternative or cumulatively), the justices can commit on one and refuse to commit on another.

If the submission of no case to answer is rejected (or the defence elect not to make a submission), **13.70** the charges on which the examining justices find there is a case must be read to the accused: MCR, r 7(7). Where the examining justices decide there is a case in respect of an offence with which the accused has not yet been charged, as when they refuse to commit on a charge of murder but consider that the evidence shows a prima facie case of manslaughter, the new charge must be put down in writing.

13.71 The examining justices will formally announce that they are committing the accused to the Crown Court to stand his trial on those charges for which there is sufficient evidence. A particular location of the Crown Court should be specified (see 14.11).

13.72 Discharge at committal proceedings is not equivalent to an acquittal, and the prosecution may therefore prefer fresh charges for the same offence or offences: *Manchester City Stipendiary Magistrate ex parte Snelson* [1977] 1 WLR 911. They may then seek to persuade either the examining justices who originally refused to commit for trial or a differently constituted bench that there is a case to answer. Should the prosecution act improperly or oppressively in making a second attempt to secure a committal for trial, the High Court has power to issue an order prohibiting the continuation of the second set of committal proceedings: *Horsham Justices ex parte Reeves* (1981) 75 Cr App R 236n.

Committals without consideration of the evidence

13.73 The Criminal Justice Act 1967 introduced a procedure by which the defence could agree to the examining justices committing the accused for trial without considering the evidence against him. The legislation is now contained in s 6(2) of the MCA 1980. Most committals take place under the provisions of this subsection.

13.74 The accused may be committed for trial without the examining justices considering the evidence against him if:

    (a)   the accused (or, if there is more than one accused, each of the accused) has a solicitor acting for him in the case, whether present in court or not, and

    (b)   there is no submission from counsel or solicitor for the accused (or any one of the accused) that there is no case to answer.

These conditions for a committal without consideration of the evidence should ensure that an accused is only so committed in cases where, were the examining justices to consider the evidence, they would conclude that there was a case to answer. It is the duty of the accused's legal representative to read through the statements and other documents, which should have been served beforehand, and only allow the committal to proceed under s 6(2) if the documents clearly disclose a prima facie case. However, it should be noted that, provided the accused has a solicitor acting for him in the case as a whole, no legal representative need be present in court for the committal itself—the accused himself may inform the examining justices that a committal without consideration of the evidence is acceptable. Committals without consideration of the evidence are a pure formality, and may take five minutes or less to accomplish.

F   VOLUNTARY BILLS OF INDICTMENT

13.75 In the great majority of cases, the accused is sent, transferred, or committed for trial by the magistrates in one of the ways described earlier in this Chapter. There is an alternative, however, namely a direction by a High Court judge for the preferment of a voluntary bill of indictment (see Administration of Justice (Miscellaneous Provisions) Act 1933, s 2 as amended). The terminology is explained in Chapter 15, but what it means essentially is that a High Court judge orders that the accused be tried on indictment.

In theory, the prosecution could always apply to a High Court judge for a voluntary bill. However, the *Consolidated Criminal Practice Direction* [2002] 1 WLR 2870, para IV.35.3 states that a voluntary bill should be granted 'only where the interests of justice, rather than considerations of administrative convenience require it'. **13.76**

The procedure for obtaining a High Court judge's consent to the preferment of a voluntary bill of indictment is set out in the Indictments Procedure Rules 1971. The application must be in writing, signed by the applicant or his solicitor. Unless there have already been unsuccessful committal proceedings, the application should state why it is being made. It should be accompanied by (i) the bill of indictment it is proposed to prefer, and (ii) proofs of evidence from the proposed prosecution witnesses and/or depositions taken and statements tendered at the committal proceedings (assuming there have been any). Save where the prosecutor is the Director of Public Prosecutions, there must also be an affidavit verifying that the statements contained in the application are true to the best of the applicant's knowledge and belief. However, a Crown Prosecutor applying for a voluntary bill on behalf of the DPP is, like the DPP himself, under no obligation to file an affidavit in support (*Liverpool Crown Court ex parte Bray* [1987] Crim LR 51). The actual decision on whether there should be a voluntary bill is taken by the judge in chambers. Normally neither the prosecution nor defence attend (i.e., the judge simply reads through the papers and notifies his decision to the parties in writing). The defence do not even have a right to make written representations to the judge, although there is a discretion to receive such representations (*Raymond* [1981] QB 910). Oral representations should be allowed only in quite extraordinary circumstances. **13.77**

G   LINKED SUMMARY AND INDICTABLE OFFENCES

An offence can be tried in the Crown Court if it is triable on indictment only, or triable either way (for an examination of how offences are classified see Paragraphs 8.01 to 8.08). This general rule is, however, subject to an exception, in that a limited category of summary offences can be sent to the Crown Court for trial if linked with an offence properly triable on indictment. This exception was introduced by s 40 of the Criminal Justice Act 1988. It is convenient to consider here, in addition, the procedure introduced by s 41 of the CJA 1988, by which a summary offence, linked to a triable-either-way offence can be sent up to the Crown Court for plea and sentence (see 13.81 to 13.83). **13.78**

Committal under the CJA 1988, s 40

Section 40 of the CJA 1988 provides that, if the accused has been sent or committed for trial in respect of an indictable offence and the evidence that was before the committing court **13.79** discloses also a summary offence, then the prosecution may include in the indictment a count for the latter. There are two further conditions that must be satisfied, namely that:

(i)   the summary charge is *either* founded on the same facts or evidence as the indictable charge *or* forms with it a series of offences of the same or a similar character; and

(ii) the summary charge is *either* for common assault or assault on a custody officer, taking a motor vehicle without the owner's consent, driving while disqualified or criminal damage falling within the special MCA, s 22 procedure, or it is punishable with imprisonment or disqualification and is specified by the Home Secretary in an order made by statutory instrument.

13.80   Points to notice about the s 40 procedure are that, although the evidence of the summary offence must be disclosed on the committal statements for the linked indictable matter, the initiative for putting it in the indictment must come from the prosecution—the magistrates are only required to commit for trial in respect of the indictable charge (contrast the procedure under s 41, see the next Section). Secondly, the legislation expressly includes within the s 40 procedure only certain specified summary offences. Thirdly, the summary offence must be linked with the indictable charge in one or other of the ways specified in s 40. The wording of that part of the section is taken from r 9 of the Indictment Rules, governing joinder of counts in one indictment (see 15.18 to 15.25). Fourthly, no method of challenging the joinder of a count for a summary offence is laid down by s 40. It is submitted, however, that the defence will be entitled to move to quash the count before arraignment if either the joinder is unlawful as falling outside the terms of s 40, or the committal statements do not disclose a case to answer for the offence. Lastly, assuming a count for a summary offence is validly included in an indictment by virtue of s 40, the method of trial will be exactly the same as for an indictable offence—i.e. the summary count will be put to the accused on arraignment together with the indictable count, and, if he pleads not guilty (either to both or even just to the former), a jury will be empanelled to hear the evidence and return a verdict. However, should he be convicted of the summary offence, the Crown Court's powers of sentence are limited to those the magistrates would have had (s 40(2)).

Committal under the CJA 1988, s 41

13.81   Section 41 supplements s 40 by providing that magistrates committing for trial for an either-way offence may also commit the accused for any summary offence punishable with imprisonment or disqualification that arises out of circumstances which are the same as or connected with the either-way matter. The summary offence need not actually be disclosed by the evidence tendered at the committal proceedings—it would seem to be sufficient for the prosecution representative simply to explain that, in the course of committing an either-way offence, the accused also allegedly committed a summary one. As regards the summary offence, the magistrates commit neither for trial nor for sentence. What they do is perhaps best described as 'committing for plea', although that term is not used in the section. Thus, the summary offence is not included in the indictment, and is only mentioned in the Crown Court if and when the accused pleads guilty to or is found guilty of the either-way charge(s). At that stage the summary allegation is put to him. If he pleads guilty, the Crown Court judge will sentence him for all matters, thus ensuring that the sentencing function for offences arising out of one incident is not split between the magistrates' court and the Crown Court. The sentence for the summary offence is, of course, limited to that which the magistrates could have imposed. Should the accused deny the offence, the case may be remitted to the magistrates for summary trial. Since the passage of the Courts Act 2003, Sch 3, para 303, the Crown Court may try him for the offence, its powers of sentencing again being limited to those of the magistrates.

The differences between the s 40 and s 41 procedures have already emerged in the course of the preceding Sections. However, a summary of them may illuminate the two sections. The differences are: **13.82**

(i) Section 40 applies only to those offences listed in the section plus any specified by the Home Secretary—s 41 applies to any summary offence punishable with imprisonment or disqualification.

(ii) The magistrates do not initiate the s 40 procedure, the onus being on the prosecution to include a count for a summary offence in the indictment if they consider that to be appropriate. Under s 41, it is the magistrates who must commit the summary offence to the Crown Court.

(iii) But, under s 41, the summary offence need not actually be disclosed by evidence at the committal proceedings, whereas under s 40 it must.

(iv) Under s 40, the summary offence must be founded on the same facts or form part of a series with the indictable charge; under s 41, it must arise out of the same or connected circumstances.

(v) Under s 41, the linked indictable charge must be triable either way (see *Miall* [1992] Crim LR 71), whereas under s 40 it does not matter whether it is triable either way or only on indictment.

Committal of a summary offence under s 41 does not preclude the prosecution from putting a count for it in the indictment under s 40 (see s 4(4)). If that is done, the s 41 committal is disregarded and the Crown Court proceeds only under s 40.

When the CJA 2003, Sch 3 (Part 2) comes into force (no date had been set at the time of writing), s 41 of the CJA 1988 will be repealed. This is because the amendments of the CDA 1998, s 51(3) will enable the magistrates, when sending an accused to the Crown Court for trial on indictment, to send him at the same time for trial in respect of any related offence. This power is subject to the proviso that, if the related offence is a summary one, it must be imprisonable or carry the power to disqualify from driving. Since a Crown Court judge had the powers of a District Judge (magistrates' court), by virtue of s 66 of the Courts Act 2003, he is empowered to try and (if appropriate) sentence the accused for the summary offence. **13.83**

KEY DOCUMENTS

Crime and Disorder Act 1998, ss 50 to 52 and Sch 3, as amended.

Criminal Justice Act 2003, Sch 3 (in so far as it is in force).

Criminal Procedure Rules 2005, Parts 10 and 13, obtainable from: <http://www.justice.gov.uk/criminal/procrules_fin/index.htm>.

PART 3

TRIAL ON INDICTMENT

14

THE CROWN COURT

14.01 The Courts Act 1971 created a new criminal court—the Crown Court—to replace the ancient courts of assize and quarter sessions which had formerly dealt with trials on indictment. The Courts Act has now been largely repealed and its provisions incorporated into the Supreme Court Act 1981 ('SCA').

14.02 The Crown Court is part of the Supreme Court: SCA, s 1. The main heads of its jurisdiction are as follows:

(i) It has exclusive jurisdiction over trials on indictment: SCA, s 46. In other words, all trials on indictment take place in the Crown Court.

(ii) It deals with offenders who have been committed for sentence by the magistrates' courts (see Chapter 12).

(iii) It hears appeals from the magistrates' courts against conviction and/or sentence (see Chapter 27).

(iv) It has a miscellaneous jurisdiction in respect of civil matters (e.g., hearing appeals against care orders made by youth courts or decisions of the licensing justices).

A   CROWN COURT JUDGES

14.03   High Court judges, circuit judges and recorders may all sit as judges of the Crown Court: SCA 1981, s 8(1).

High Court judges

14.04   At any one time there may be 20 or more High Court judges sitting in the Crown Court. They handle the most serious cases coming before the Court (see 14.10 for details of the way work is distributed amongst the various types of Crown Court judge). One would normally expect a High Court judge sitting in the Crown Court to come from the Queen's Bench Division and to have had some experience of criminal work as an advocate. In theory, however, there is nothing to stop a judge of, say, the Chancery Division being asked to sit.

Circuit judges

14.05   The office of circuit judge, like the Crown Court itself, was created by the Courts Act 1971. There are over 600 circuit judges, most of whom spend the bulk of their time sitting in the Crown Court. Circuit judges and recorders (see 14.07) handle most of the routine work of the Crown Court, and the circuit judge in particular may be regarded as the typical Crown Court judge, presiding over some 80 per cent of Crown Court trials. Circuit judges are appointed by the Queen on the recommendation of the Lord Chancellor. It is a full-time appointment which cannot be combined with practice as a barrister or solicitor. On appointment, a circuit judge must have had the right of audience in the Crown or county courts for ten years, or have been a recorder, or have held a full-time post such as a member of an administrative tribunal or a district judge (Courts and Legal Services Act 1990, s 71). Retirement is normally at the age of 72 although the Lord Chancellor may authorize continuance in office until the age of 75. Conversely, the Lord Chancellor could remove a circuit judge from office before normal retiring age on grounds of incapacity or misbehaviour.

14.06   Circuit judges may and, if possible, should sit in the county courts as well as the Crown Court. One of the suggestions made by Lord Beeching, on whose report the Courts Act was based, was that a reasonable 'mix' of civil work in the county courts and crime in the Crown Court would prevent circuit judges becoming jaded through lack of variety in their work. Accordingly, circuit judges are appointed to serve 'in the Crown Court and county courts': Courts Act 1971, s 16. Obviously, some circuit judges will be predominantly Crown Court judges and others predominantly county court judges, but the intention was that they should not be exclusively one or the other.

Recorders

14.07   Like circuit judges, recorders are appointed by the Queen on the recommendation of the Lord Chancellor. Unlike circuit judges, their appointment is a part-time one, and, when not sitting in the Crown Court, they may undertake private practice. The appointment is for a fixed term, during which the recorder agrees to make himself available to sit on a certain number of occasions. Barristers or solicitors of at least ten years' standing are eligible for appointment

(Courts Act 1971, s 21). There are about 1,400 recorders but only a minority of them will be sitting in the Crown Court at any one time. Recorders deal with some 15 per cent of trials in the Crown Court.

Deputy circuit judges

As a temporary measure, in order to assist the disposal of business in the Crown Court **14.08** (e.g., when there is a substantial backlog of cases waiting to be heard) the Lord Chancellor may appoint for a fixed period a deputy circuit judge: Courts Act 1971, s 24 as amended by SCA, s 146. For the period of his appointment a deputy circuit judge is in all ways equivalent to a circuit judge. Retired Lord Justices of Appeal, High Court judges and circuit judges are eligible for appointment as deputy circuit judges.

Mode of addressing Crown Court judges

High Court judges, all judges sitting at the Central Criminal Court (the Old Bailey) and any **14.09** circuit judge holding the office of honorary Recorder of the city in which he sits are addressed in court as 'My Lord' (or 'My Lady'). Except as stated above, circuit judges, recorders and deputy circuit judges are addressed as 'Your Honour'. The court list of cases for hearing in a particular court should refer to a circuit judge as 'His/Her Honour Judge...', and to a recorder as 'Mr/Mrs/Miss Recorder...' (see *Practice Direction (Criminal Proceedings: Consolidation)* [2002] 1 WLR 2870, para IV.30).

Distribution of work between High Court judges and circuit judges etc.

Practice directions given by the Lord Chief Justice govern the distribution of work between **14.10** the various types of Crown Court judge. The general principle is that the gravest offences either must or normally will be tried by a High Court judge; less serious cases are assigned to circuit judges or recorders. For details of the Practice Directions, see the next Section.

B ORGANIZATION OF THE CROWN COURT

The Crown Court is a single court but it sits in many different locations throughout the country. **14.11** Thus, strictly speaking, one should refer to the 'Crown Court sitting at Barchester' rather than the 'Barchester Crown Court'. One advantage of being a single court is that the Crown Court sitting anywhere in England or Wales may try any indictable offence over which the English courts have jurisdiction, irrespective of where it was allegedly committed (e.g., the Crown Court sitting at Plymouth can try an offence of, say, theft allegedly committed in Newcastle and vice versa). One of the few concessions to tradition made by the Courts Act 1971 was that when the Crown Court sat in the City of London (i.e. at the Old Bailey) it should continue to be known as the Central Criminal Court, not the Crown Court sitting in London. This nomenclature is preserved by s 8(3) of the SCA.

Locations of the Crown Court are classified as first, second, or third tier. The first tier locations **14.12** have facilities not only for Crown Court work but also for High Court civil work. They are attended by High Court judges as well as circuit judges and recorders. Second tier locations have no facilities for civil work but do have the services of at least one High Court judge on a regular basis; third tier locations have neither High Court work nor High Court judges. The various locations, of whatever tier, are grouped on a geographical basis into six circuits (Midland and Oxford, North-Eastern, Northern, South-Eastern, Wales and Chester, and Western). For each circuit there is appointed at least one High Court judge, known as the '*presiding judge*', who has special responsibility for the Crown Court locations within the circuit. In addition, each location has a '*resident judge*'. He is a senior circuit judge who, as the name implies, sits permanently at the location in question. Some of the presiding judge's duties in connection with the distribution of work (see below) may be devolved to the resident judge.

14.13   When a magistrates' court commits, sends or transfers an accused for trial it must specify the location of the Crown Court at which the trial is to take place. In selecting the appropriate location, the examining justices are to consider (Magistrates' Courts Act 1980, s 7 and Crime and Disorder Act 1998, s 51(10)):

(a)   the convenience of the defence, the prosecution and the witnesses;

(b)   the expediting of the trial; and

(c)   any direction given by the Lord Chief Justice under s 75 of the SCA.

The SCA, s 75 empowers the Lord Chief Justice, with the concurrence of the Lord Chancellor, to give directions concerning the distribution of business in the Crown Court. Directions are contained in *Practice Direction (Criminal Proceedings: Consolidation)* [2002] 1 WLR 2870, paras III.21 and IV.33. Their effect is as follows:

14.14   Offences are divided into four classes. Class 1 offences, consisting principally of murder, manslaughter and offences contrary to the Official Secrets Act 1911, *must* be tried by a High Court judge, save that murder trials may be released by or on the authority of the presiding judge to an approved circuit judge (i.e., one whom the Lord Chief Justice has approved for trying murder cases). Class 2 offences (principally, rape and other serious sexual offences) must be tried by a High Court judge unless a particular case is released by or on the authority of the presiding judge for trial by a circuit judge. As regards rape (and any serious sexual offence, whether a Class 2 offence or not), the circuit judge or recorder to whom it is released must be one approved by the Lord Chief Justice. Class 3 offences consist simply of those not in any of the other classes. They may be tried by a High Court judge, circuit judge or recorder in accordance with general or particular directions from the presiding judge. They should not be listed for trial by a High Court judge except with the consent of the judge concerned or the presiding judge. Thus, the presumption is that the great majority of Class 3 offences will be handled by a circuit judge or recorder.

14.15   It will be apparent that offences in Classes 1 and 2 either must or prima facie will be tried by a High Court judge; offences in Class 3 will prima facie be tried by a circuit judge or recorder. Accordingly, para 21.2 of the Directions states that, if the offence (or any one of the offences) for which an accused is being committed for trial is in Classes 1–2, the trial should take place at the most convenient location of the Crown Court at which a High Court judge or duly authorized circuit judge regularly sits. If all the offences are in Class 3, it should simply be the most convenient location. In deciding on the appropriate location the justices should have regard to the location/s which the presiding judge has specified as being those to which their division should normally send cases for trial. Thus, the decision on venue is, in practice, taken automatically, each magistrates' court knowing the location to which it is expected to send defendants.

However, the venue selected will not necessarily be that at which the case is tried, since s 76(1) **14.16** of the SCA provides that the Crown Court itself may give directions varying the place of a trial on indictment. In addition, either the prosecution or defence may apply to the Court for a change of venue. Such applications must be heard by a High Court judge in open court (s 76(4)). The application might be based on the matters specifically mentioned in s 7 of the Magistrates' Courts Act 1980, namely the convenience of the parties and witnesses. Occasionally, other reasons for a change are advanced (e.g., local hostility to the accused making it desirable to have the trial well away from where the offence was allegedly committed, or fear of an escape attempt necessitating a switch to a location which can be securely guarded). An application to vary the location to one where a higher proportion of black people live, in order to obtain a multiracial jury panel, is unlikely to be successful, following the Court of Appeal's judgment in *Ford* [1989] QB 868 (see 18.36 to 18.41).

C MAGISTRATES AS JUDGES OF THE CROWN COURT

The primary role of magistrates in the judicial system is, of course, to adjudicate in the magis- **14.17** trates' courts. They do, however, have a secondary role to play as judges of the Crown Court. When the Crown Court is dealing with an appeal from a magistrates' court it *must* consist of a 'professional' judge (i.e., a High Court judge, circuit judge, or recorder) sitting with not less than two and not more than four lay justices: SCA, s 74(1). In fact, para IV.33.4 of the *Consolidated Criminal Practice Direction* states that the professional judge should be an experienced circuit judge or recorder, not a High Court judge. Also, the hearing can continue if one or more of the justices initially comprising the court has withdrawn, or is absent for any reason (Criminal Procedure Rules 2005, r 63.8(2)). As well as being required to sit for appeals from the magistrates' court, lay justices *may* sit with a circuit judge or recorder for any Crown Court proceedings other than those listed for a not guilty plea. The idea is that working with a professional judge will broaden the magistrate's experience and assist him when he returns to his local bench.

Whenever magistrates sit in the Crown Court, whether their presence is obligatory or optional, **14.18** they should play a full part in all decisions of the court: *Orpin* [1975] QB 283. Indeed, in the event of disagreement, decisions are taken by a majority so that, at least in theory, the lay magistrates could overrule the professional judge: SCA, s 73(3). However, should the court be equally divided, the professional judge has a casting vote. Also, on any questions of law that arise, the magistrates must accept the judge's direction. Thus, if the defence contend during an appeal against conviction that a confession by the accused should not be admitted into evidence, the judge will tell his lay colleagues what the law on admissibility of confessions is, but any relevant findings of fact (e.g. as to whether a police officer used threats to obtain the confession) will be for the court as a whole, not just for the judge. At the sentencing stage, it is particularly important for the magistrates not only to contribute to the decision but to be *seen* to contribute.

14.19   As has been seen, a magistrate, sitting in the Crown Court upon the hearing of an appeal, plays a major role in the proceedings. If the appellant or offender were to find himself in the Crown Court before one of the magistrates who had previously decided against him, he might justifiably feel aggrieved. Rule 63.9 of the Criminal Procedure Rules provides, therefore, that a magistrate who was involved in the proceedings in the magistrates' court may not be a member of the court for the appeal.

14.20   Any Crown Court judge is able to exercise the powers of the District Judge (magistrates' court). Hence a judge sitting the Crown Court can deal with a summary offence which is linked to an indictable offence without having to send the matter back to the magistrates' court.

D   RIGHTS OF AUDIENCE IN THE CROWN COURT

14.21   Barristers, of course, have the right of audience in the Crown Court. In addition, the Courts and Legal Services Act 1990 enacted a statutory scheme for the definition and regulation of rights of audience before the courts. It preserved all existing rights of audience (see ss 31 and 32), and set up a framework for the granting of new rights (see s 27). Machinery was introduced for advocates who are not barristers to obtain rights of audience formerly held only by barristers. What has taken place, in particular, is the extension of rights of audience to certain solicitors, subject to training.

14.22   Even without the machinery introduced by the Courts and Legal Services Act 1990, however, the Bar's right of audience in the Crown Court has not been exclusive. The Lord Chancellor has issued directions entitling solicitors to 'appear in, conduct, defend and address the court' in appeals and committals for sentence where they, or a member of their firm, represented the accused in the magistrates' court.

14.23   The accused has the right to defend himself if he so wishes. As far as the prosecution in a trial on indictment is concerned, the position is governed by the Courts and Legal Services Act 1990, s 27(2)(c). This gives the Crown Court a discretion to allow a private individual to conduct a private prosecution before it. Glidewell LJ stated in *Southwark Crown Court ex parte Tawfick* (1994) *The Times*, 1 December 1994 that this was a discretion which would only be exercised occasionally, so almost invariably, the prosecution must be legally represented in the Crown Court even if it is a private prosecution.

E   THE LAYOUT OF THE CROWN COURT

14.24   This Chapter has described the legal structure of the Crown Court. It may be useful to conclude with a brief description of the physical appearance of a location of the Crown Court. Externally, the court buildings vary enormously, from modern glass and concrete structures to ornate Victoriana. Internally, the court rooms themselves also vary, but one may detect a basic pattern. At the front of the court is the raised bench where the judge sits in a throne-like chair beneath the Royal coat-of-arms. Below the judge is the clerk at his desk. Facing the judge, either at the rear or in the middle of the court, is the accused in the partitioned off area known as the dock. In front of the dock are the seats for counsel. To one side of the court is the jury box—twelve seats, usually in two tiered rows of six—and, on the other side, is the witness box from where the witnesses give their evidence. At the back of court, or in a gallery looking down from above, are seats for the public. Special areas in court may also be set aside for probation officers or social workers. A room leading off the court is reserved for the use of the jury, and it is to that room, at the end of the trial, that they retire to consider their verdict.

15

THE INDICTMENT

15.01 The indictment is the formal document containing a list of the charges against the accused, to which he pleads either guilty or not guilty at the beginning of his trial on indictment. A jury may try only one indictment at a time: *Crane v DPP* [1921] AC 299. The law on drafting indictments is contained principally in the Indictments Act 1915 (IA) and the CrimPR, Part 14.

15.02 On page 237 you will find the form of indictment which might be expected to follow from an imaginary incident involving three young men (David Wilson, John Burton, and Paul Green) who, after a football match, attacked two supporters of the opposition team (Barry and Charles Johnson). The police arrived to find Wilson and Burton kicking Barry Johnson as he lay on the ground. This caused sufficient severe bruising to require outpatient hospital treatment. Meanwhile Green was threatening Charles Johnson with a broken milk bottle, with which he had already inflicted a facial wound requiring stitches but not sufficiently serious to leave a subsequent scar.

15.03 The indictment illustrates certain fundamental points about indictments which will be discussed in detail later in the Chapter:

(a) The heading or commencement to the indictment is always in a standard form. At the top is the word 'INDICTMENT', followed by the place of trial and the name of the case. The prosecution is always formally in the name of the Queen. After the name of the case comes the standard phrase 'AB, CD etc. are charged as follows', known as the presentment.

(b) The offences alleged against the accused are set out in separate counts of the indictment. Each count must allege only one offence.

(c) Each count is divided into a Statement of Offence and Particulars of Offence. The Statement of Offence gives the name of the offence and, if it is statutory, the statute and section contravened: CrimPR, r 14.2(1)(a). If the offence is contrary to common law, that does not have to be expressly stated—e.g., had Barry Johnson died as a result of the kicks he received and had Wilson and Burton been charged with his unlawful killing, the Statement of Offence would simply have read 'manslaughter'.

(d) The Particulars of Offence give the names of the accused alleged to have committed the offence set out in the count, and 'such particulars of the conduct constituting the commission of the offence as to make clear what the prosecutor alleges against the defendant' (CrimPR, r 14.2(1)(b)).

(e) Although a count may allege only one offence, an indictment may contain two or more counts against an accused. Paul Green is charged with wounding Charles Johnson (the cut to the cheek) and with having an offensive weapon (the broken milk bottle). Had the injuries to Barry Johnson been more serious the prosecution might have included in the indictment a count for causing grievous bodily harm with intent against Wilson and Burton as well as the count for occasioning actual bodily harm. The jury could then convict on one count or the other depending on whether they thought the evidence established the more serious or the less serious offence. Green can, of course, be convicted on either or both of the counts against him.

(f) Two or more accused may be charged in a single count if the prosecution case is that they acted in concert to commit an offence. Wilson and Burton were both kicking Barry Johnson so it is proper to put them both in one count.

(g) Two or more accused may be charged in a single indictment even though they are not alleged to have committed any single offence together. Green was not involved in the attack

No 063210

INDICTMENT

The Crown Court at BARCHESTER
THE QUEEN v DAVID WILSON, JOHN BURTON and PAUL GREEN

DAVID WILSON, JOHN BURTON and PAUL GREEN are CHARGED AS FOLLOWS: —

Count 1   Statement of Offence
Assault occasioning actual bodily harm contrary to s 47 of the Offences Against the Person Act 1861.

Particulars of Offence
DAVID WILSON and JOHN BURTON, on the 1st day of January 2008, assaulted Barry Johnson thereby occasioning him actual bodily harm.

Count 2   Statement of Offence
Wounding contrary to s 20 of the Offences Against the Person Act 1861.

Particulars of Offence
PAUL GREEN, on the 1st day of January 2008, maliciously wounded Charles Johnson.

Count 3   Statement of Offence
Having an offensive weapon contrary to s 1(1) of the Prevention of Crime Act 1953.

Particulars of Offence
PAUL GREEN, on the 1st day of January 2008, without lawful authority or reasonable excuse had with him in a public place, namely Cathedral Row, Barchester, an offensive weapon, namely a broken milk bottle.

Date 1 March 2008

A. N. Other
Officer of the Crown Court

on Barry Johnson, but since his attack on Charles Johnson and the attack by the other two on Barry Johnson were all part of one incident they may all be joined in one indictment.

(h)   The indictment is signed by an officer of the Crown Court.

A   PREFERRING THE DRAFT INDICTMENT

An indictment must be signed by an officer of the Crown Court: Administration of Justice **15.04** (Miscellaneous Provisions) Act 1933, s 2(1). Technically, until the indictment is signed, it is merely a 'draft indictment'. The question arises as to the consequences if the draft indictment is not signed. In *Ashton* [2007] 1 WLR 181, the Court of Appeal set out the way in which procedural failures in relation to the indictment should be approached. Crucially, the court must concentrate upon the intention of Parliament, and ask whether it was intended that a procedural failure should render the proceedings invalid. Second, it must look at the interests of justice and consider whether the procedural failure caused any prejudice to any of the parties, such as to make it unjust to proceed. Their lordships concluded that there was no basis for deciding that Parliament had intended that proceedings would be automatically rendered invalid because an indictment had not been preferred or signed. As there was no prejudice or consequential injustice, the appeal was dismissed.

The approach in *Ashton* was followed by the Court of Appeal in *Clarke* [2008] UKHL 8, which was further appealed to the House of Lords. Lord Bingham, with the approval of the other members of the Judicial Committee, agreed with the Court of Appeal that the test was: what was Parliament's intention? He stated, however, that this could be broken down into two questions:

(a) What did Parliament intend to be the consequences of a failure to comply with the requirement in s 2(1) that a draft indictment should be signed? He said that the conclusion was 'inescapable' that Parliament's intention was that the draft indictment 'should not become an indictment unless and until it was duly signed by the proper officer'.

(b) What did Parliament intend to be the consequences of a trial proceeding on an unsigned draft indictment? Again, he believed that the answer was clear: 'Parliament intended that there could be no valid trial on indictment if there was no indictment'. The appeal therefore succeeded. As a result, the position is that trial upon an unsigned draft indictment is invalid.

15.05 In an attempt to reduce delays in the criminal process, CrimPR, r 14.1 provides that a bill of indictment must be preferred within 28 days of committal, the giving of a notice of transfer, consent to the preferment of a voluntary bill of indictment, or the serving of documents where a person is sent for trial under the CDA 1998, s 51. However, the rule does little in practice to expedite trials since it permits an officer of the Crown Court to extend the original 28-day period by 28 days, and further extensions can be granted by a Crown Court judge. Thus, the time-limit is an extremely flexible one, but even if the rule is not complied with (i.e., the bill of indictment is preferred outside the 28-day period with no extension of time having been obtained) it has been held that the accused may be validly tried and convicted on the indictment: *Sheerin* (1977) 64 Cr App R 68. In other words, the rule is directory not mandatory. It states what ought to be done, not what must be done. The distinction between an indictment and a bill of indictment is only relevant in the context of preferment of a bill of indictment, so further references will be simply to drafting an indictment.

15.06 Only in a minority of particularly important or complex cases are the papers sent to counsel for an indictment to be drafted. However, in *Newland* [1988] QB 402, the Court of Appeal expressed concern at the quality of some drafting, and stated that, before the indictment is put to the accused at the beginning of the trial, counsel for the prosecution should check that it complies with the Indictment Rules. In other words, it is counsel's responsibility to correct any errors in the Crown Court officer's drafting.

B   COUNTS WHICH MAY BE INCLUDED IN AN INDICTMENT

The first and most basic question for the person drafting the indictment is: What counts (i.e.,   **15.07**
charges) should be included in it? If there were committal proceedings, the drafter will have
been provided with copies of the documents from them. He will also know on what charges
the magistrates' court committed the accused and on what charges, if any, it refused to do so.
But, he is not bound by the magistrates' view as to the offences for which there is a case to
answer. Subject to the rules on joinder of counts (see below), he may include in the indictment counts for *any* indictable offence that he considers to be disclosed by the evidence
before the magistrates' court, whether or not the accused was committed for trial in respect of
that offence: Administration of Justice (Miscellaneous Provisions) Act 1933, s 2(2). Thus,
where the prosecution evidence is that the accused was found in possession of stolen goods
an hour after they were stolen and he has been sent for trial on a charge of theft, the indictment may include counts in the alternative for both theft and handling stolen goods to cover
the possibility of the accused saying that he did not steal the goods but merely received them.
Again, where the committal is for manslaughter, the indictment could contain a single count
for murder and no count for manslaughter if counsel or the Crown Court officer considers
that there is sufficient evidence of malice aforethought. That would be possible even if the
magistrates' court had been specifically asked to commit on a charge of murder, but had
refused and merely committed for manslaughter. The power to include a count for an
offence for which the magistrates' court expressly refused to commit should, however, be
very sparingly exercised: *Dawson* [1960] 1 WLR 163, quoted with approval in *Kempster* [1989]
1 WLR 1125. The count must in any event be based upon the evidence before the magistrates' court (see 15.51 to 15.54 for details). In addition, a charge upon which the accused
was not sent for trial can only form part of the indictment if it is 'in substitution for or in
addition to' a count upon which he *was* sent. Further, any such extra counts must be of a
kind that can 'lawfully' be joined in that indictment (proviso (i) to s 2(2) of the
Administration of Justice (Miscellaneous Provisions) Act 1933). Thus, in *Lombardi* [1989]
1 WLR 73, L faced two indictments. On the first he was convicted of three forgery offences.
On the second there were four bankruptcy offences (unrelated to the forgery counts), upon
which the magistrates had not committed him for trial, although there was ample evidence
to do so on the committal papers. The judge ruled the second indictment valid, whereupon
L pleaded guilty and then appealed. The Court of Appeal held that the second indictment
was invalid since the counts in it could not have been joined with the counts in the
first indictment without breaching the rules relating to joinder (now contained in CrimPR,
r 14.2(3) – see 15.21 to 15.25). Consequently, the counts in it were barred by s 2(2)(i) of the
1933 Act. (For the consequences where the indictment is invalid, see 15.56.)

C   CONTENTS OF THE COUNT

A count consists of a statement of offence, giving the short name of the offence and the statute   **15.08**
contravened if it is statutory, followed by particulars of the offence. IA, s 3 provides that the

indictment shall contain 'such particulars as may be necessary for giving reasonable information as to the nature of the charge'. CrimPR, r 14.2(1) is a little more specific, saying that where the offence is a statutory one, the particulars must identify 'any legislation that creates it'. It goes on to state that the count 'must contain such particulars of the conduct constituting the commission of the offence as to make clear what the prosecutor alleges against the defendant'.

15.09   The guidance on drafting particulars given by s 3 and CrimPR, Part 14 is so vague that the best advice to a person settling an indictment is to look up a precedent for any count he wishes to include. *Blackstone's Criminal Practice* contains specimen counts for the most common indictable offences, and the practitioner can usually follow the form of wording in there with safety. Specimen counts for some offences are set out at 15.60, but the following general comments may be helpful:

(a)   The particulars start with the forename and surname of the accused charged in the count. An error in giving the name will not be a good ground of appeal against conviction provided the accused could reasonably be identified from the name stated. Similarly, where any other person is referred to in the particulars, fore-name and surname should be stated but errors will not defeat a conviction.

(b)   The date of the alleged offence is then stated. Surprisingly, a conviction can be upheld even where the prosecution evidence shows that the offence was committed on a day other than that laid in the particulars, although if the change in date would prejudice the accused in his defence (e.g., he has an alibi for the date in the particulars) he should be granted an adjournment. If the exact date of the offence is unknown the particulars may allege that it was on a day unknown between the day before the earliest day on which it could have been committed and the day after the latest day on which it could have been committed. Thus, if property was stolen on 1 January 2008 and found in possession of the accused on 31 January, the count would allege that 'A.B., on a day unknown between the 31st day of December 2007 and the 1st day of February 2008 dishonestly received...'

(c)   The elements of the offence are alleged. It is not usually necessary to write out the elements in full. For example, in a count for theft, it is sufficient to allege that 'AB stole a wrist-watch belonging to CD'—one need not allege that 'AB dishonestly appropriated a wrist-watch belonging to CD with the intention of permanently depriving CD of the said wrist-watch.' However, in counts for certain offences such as handling stolen goods a fuller form of particulars is recommended.

(d)   Where property is mentioned in the particulars, the owner should be named in order to identify the property, but the value need not be given. If the owner is unknown the property can be referred to as 'belonging to a person or persons unknown'. If the property relevant to a count is cash, it may be described simply as money without specifying the individual coins and bank-notes (e.g., 'A.B., on..........stole a purse and £5.50 in money').

(e)   The place where the offence occurred need not be alleged, unless the definition of the offence requires that it be committed in or with reference to a limited range of places. Thus, a count for dangerous driving must specify the road where it occurred since the offence can only be committed on a road, and a count for burglary must specify the building burgled since the offence necessitates entering a building as a trespasser. Theft, on the other hand, can be committed anywhere so the count need not say from where the property was stolen.

D   THE RULE AGAINST DUPLICITY

An indictment may contain several counts, but each count must allege only one offence. If the **15.10** wording of a count in itself shows that it is alleging two or more offences, the count is said to be 'bad for duplicity', and the defence should bring a motion to quash, i.e., apply to the judge, before the indictment is put to the accused, to quash the count (see 15.1).

A count alleging that 'A.B., on . . . , murdered or unlawfully killed C.D.' is bad for duplicity or **15.11** duple, since both murder and manslaughter are particularized in one count. Similarly, a count alleging that 'Jane Smith, on 1st January 2006, stole a dress belonging to Spencer Ltd and on 2nd January 2006 stole a coat belonging to Marks Ltd' is duple because the different days and different victims named show that two quite separate thefts are being charged. On the other hand, a count for stealing a coat and dress from Spencer and Marks Ltd on 1st January is perfectly valid. The wording of the count is consistent with the accused having gone into one shop (Spencer and Marks Ltd) on one occasion and stolen two items. Of course, in strict logic it could be argued that there must have been two separate acts of appropriation, one in relation to the coat and the other in relation to the dress. Therefore, assuming the necessary *mens rea* was present, the accused committed two separate thefts which should be charged in separate counts. However, as Lord Diplock said in *DPP v Merriman* [1973] AC 584, 'the rule against duplicity has always been applied in a practical, rather than in a strictly analytical way', and if several items are stolen from one victim on one occasion it is standard practice to have just one count listing all the items. In other words, several criminal acts may be alleged in one count if they were so closely linked together as to form one activity or transaction. Whether there was one or more than one activity is a matter of degree, turning upon the facts of the individual case. In *Wilson* (1979) 69 Cr App R 83 the facts were that W went into a 'Boots' department store, and moved from department to department, taking items from each department. He left the store without paying, and went into 'Debenhams' where he behaved in similar fashion. The indictment against him contained two counts, one listing all the items stolen from 'Boots' and the other the items stolen from 'Debenhams'. The jury found W guilty, and he appealed on the basis that there should have been separate counts in relation to his conduct in each of the departments. The Court of Appeal upheld the convictions. W's acts in each store were not broken into separate activities by his leaving one department and entering another, and therefore two counts—one for each store—were sufficient. It is worth pointing out that *Wilson* and the other case law on duplicity must now be read in the light of CrimPR, r 14.2(2)—see 15.16. In sum, it seems that the acts in question must now 'amount to a course of conduct', whereas in *Wilson* the principle was put in the form that the acts must 'form one activity'. In practice, this may prove to be a distinction without a difference.

It is unusual for a count to name more than one victim of the offence alleged. Thus, in **15.12** *Mansfield* [1977] 1 WLR 1102, M's single act of setting fire to a hotel caused the deaths of seven victims, but the prosecution nonetheless elected to have seven separate counts for murder, each count naming one victim.

Where a count is not bad for duplicity, since its wording is consistent with the accused having **15.13** only committed one offence, but the prosecution evidence tends to show that his criminal conduct was broken into separate activities, the correct remedy is to apply to the judge to amend the indictment (see 15.47 to 15.50). The amendment would take the form of splitting the single count into several counts. Failure to amend would be a ground of appeal, but the Court of Appeal might well dismiss the appeal because there had been no miscarriage of justice.

'General deficiency' cases

15.14   The rule that separate activities should be charged in separate counts would be inconvenient if strictly applied in the not uncommon type of case where a person is suspected of having stolen cash or property from the same victim on a large number of separate occasions, but it is not possible to specify the precise dates when the thefts occurred or the precise amounts that were stolen (e.g., the prosecution case is that the manager of a shop has been taking small amounts from the till over a lengthy period, but their only evidence of that is that when the takings at the end of the period were compared with the amount of stock which had been sold there was found to be a significant shortfall). Such an allegation is usually referred to as 'theft of a general deficiency'. In such a case it is permissible to allege in the particulars of one count that the accused stole the *aggregate* amount on a day or days unknown during the whole period over which the appropriations must have occurred (see *Tomlin* (1954) 38 Cr App R 82 and *Lawson* (1952) 36 Cr App R 30).

Specimen or sample counts

15.15   Where a person is accused of a systematic course of criminal conduct, the prosecution may choose to proceed by way of specimen or sample counts. This might be the case, for example, where dishonesty over a period of time is alleged, or where a series of indecent assaults is alleged in a case of child abuse. In order to keep the indictment to a manageable length, a limited number of sample counts are included. In such a case, the prosecution should provide the defence with a list of all the offences of which those contained in the indictment are samples. Where the defendant pleads not guilty, the prosecution may decide to seek a trial by the procedure set out in the Domestic Violence, Crime and Victims Act 2004, s 17: see 19.12 for details.

Criminal Procedure Rules, r 14.2(2)

15.16   CrimPR, r 14.2(2) lays down that:

> More than one incident of an offence may be included in a count if those incidents taken together amount to a course of conduct having regard to the time place or purpose of commission.

In the *Consolidated Criminal Practice Direction*, guidance is given as to when it is appropriate to charge multiple offences within a count. The following examples are cited:

(a) the victim on each occasion was the same, or there was no identifiable victim (e.g., money laundering or drug importation);
(b) the incidents alleged involved a marked degree of repetition in the method or location;
(c) the incidents took place within a clearly defined period, e.g., no more than a year;
(d) the defence is such as to apply to every alleged incident.

(For consideration of the extent to which this formulation affects the rule against duplicity, see 15.11).

Counts for handling stolen goods

Section 22 of the Theft Act 1968 creates a single offence of handling stolen goods: *Griffiths v*   **15.17**
Freeman [1970] 1 WLR 659. It can be committed in some 18 different ways, by receiving the
goods, or by undertaking or assisting in their retention, removal, disposal, or realization by
or for the benefit of another person, or by arranging to do any of those things. Therefore, if
the particulars of a handling count merely allege that the accused *handled* certain stolen
goods namely... knowing or believing the same to be stolen, it is technically correct but it
hardly gives the defence a fair indication of how the prosecution intend to present their
case. The prosecution ought to 'nail their colours to the mast', and state in the count
whether they are alleging receiving or one or more of the other forms of handling. In a case
of genuine uncertainty, there should be two counts. The particulars of count one will allege
that the accused received the goods, and the particulars of count two that he undertook or
assisted in their retention, removal, disposal or realization by or for the benefit of another
person or arranged so to do. The jury can then choose whether to convict on count one (generally regarded as the most serious form of handling) or on count two (see *Nicklin* [1977]
1 WLR 403).

E   JOINDER OF COUNTS IN AN INDICTMENT

The circumstances in which several counts against one accused may be put in one indictment   **15.18**
are set out in CrimPR, r 14.2(3), which says:

> Charges for any offences may be joined in the same indictment if those charges are founded on
> the same facts, or form or are part of a series of offences of the same or a similar character.

The procedure which is described in the following paragraphs is illustrated in the flowchart
on page 244. The operation of the rule is illustrated by *Mansfield* [1977] 1 WLR 1102, where M
was charged in an indictment containing ten counts. Three counts were for arson, alleging
that on 12 December 1974 M had started a fire in the Worsley Hotel, Bayswater, and that on
19 December and 28 December 1974 he had started fires in the Piccadilly Hotel in the West
End of London. The three offences were a series of the same or a similar character, so counts
for them were rightly put in one indictment. The remaining counts were for murder, based on
the fact that seven people had died in the Worsley Hotel fire. Since these counts were founded on the same facts as the Worsley Hotel arson count, all ten counts could properly be joined
in one indictment.

Charges 'founded on the same facts'

The simplest application of the first limb of r 9 is to be found in cases such as *Mansfield* where   **15.19**
a single act by the accused (setting fire to a hotel) gives rise to several offences (arson and seven
murders). The rule will also apply where the accused allegedly committed several offences in
a continuous course of conduct. Thus, if X robs a bank; drives his 'get-away' car at high speeds
in a built up area to shake off pursuit, and then, when finally cornered, struggles with police
officers to avoid arrest, he could be charged in one indictment with robbery, dangerous

Figure 15.1 Indictments: Joinder

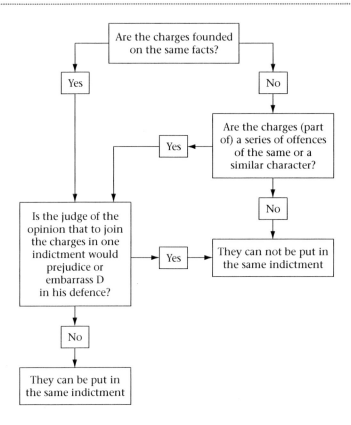

driving, and assault with intent to resist arrest. If he carried a shotgun and/or stole the get-away car, further counts could be added for theft and having a firearm to commit an indictable offence. But, substantial contemporaneity is not an essential prerequisite for the application of r 9. If two offences are separated in time, but the later one would not have happened without the prior occurrence of the first, then they may be said to be founded on the same facts: *Barrell and Wilson* (1979) 69 Cr App R 250. In that case, W was indicted for (i) assault and affray at a discotheque and (ii) attempting to pervert the course of justice. The prosecution case was that W, having been committed for trial for the offences of violence, tried to bribe witnesses not to testify against him. That obviously happened several weeks after the incident at the discotheque, but W would have had no cause to offer bribes unless he had faced prosecution for assault. Therefore, the Court of Appeal held that the time-lag did not prevent the charges being founded on the same facts. A simpler example of the same principle is where the accused allegedly used stolen cheques to purchase goods—he can be charged in one indictment with (i) theft or handling of the cheque book and (ii) obtaining property by deception in respect of each individual cheque tendered, regardless of how long elapsed between his getting the cheque book and his first dishonest use of it.

15.20   In *Barrell and Wilson*, the jury could—and indeed did—convict W on all the counts against him. A more difficult problem for the courts is whether two counts may be joined in one indictment if the prosecution cases on the counts are mutually destructive of each other—i.e., a verdict of guilty on count 1 would presuppose that the jury were not satisfied that the accused committed count 2 and vice versa. In *Bellman* [1989] AC 836, B had been convicted of obtaining money by deception. The indictment included a count both for that and conspiracy to import drugs. According to the prosecution, money had been paid to B by persons who expected him to use it to smuggle drugs into the country. Either B genuinely intended to carry out the plan to smuggle drugs (in which case he was guilty of conspiracy), or he did not (and was guilty of obtaining the money by deception). In the House of Lords [1989] AC 836, it was argued that it could never be right for mutually contradictory counts to be contained in one indictment. The House of Lords rejected that argument as without authority. Indeed it had long been the practice to include in one indictment counts for stealing and handling the same property, even though a conviction for theft would preclude a conviction for handling and vice versa (see 15.32).

Charges of 'the same or a similar character'

The meaning of this phrase was discussed by the House of Lords in *Ludlow v Metropolitan Police Commissioner* [1971] AC 29. Lord Pearson (their lordships all concurring) said that for two or more offences to form a series or part of a series of the same or a similar character there must be a nexus between them. The nexus must arise from a similarity both in law and in the facts constituting the offences. In *Ludlow*, L was charged in the first count with attempted theft and in the second count with robbery. The element of attempted or actual theft in both counts provided a sufficient similarity in law. The facts of the first count were that L was seen emerging from a window in the private part of a public house in Acton, the jury being asked to draw the inference that he had been disturbed when attempting theft. The facts of the second count were that 16 days later, at another public house in Acton, L paid for a drink and then snatched the money back, punching the barman. The House of Lords held that there was a sufficient similarity between the facts of the two offences to justify the joinder of the counts in one indictment. This might seem a surprising decision, since both offences happening to be committed in public houses appears purely coincidental, and otherwise the only similarity arises from the closeness in time and geographical location of the offences. The lesson to be drawn from *Ludlow* is that only a slight similarity on the facts is necessary to satisfy CrimPR, r 14.2(3)(b). Another point confirmed by *Ludlow* is that two offences are sufficient to constitute a series within the meaning of the rules. **15.21**

The time between the alleged offences may well be important in determining whether there is a sufficiently close nexus between them. After all, the second limb requires that the charges should be 'part of a series', and use of the word 'series' would seem to imply some limit as to time. **15.22**

In the case of *C* (1993) *The Times*, 4 February 1993, C was charged in the same indictment with the rape of his seven-year-old daughter in 1978, and an attempt to rape her in 1989. Notwithstanding the gap of 11 years, the Court of Appeal held that the counts were properly joined. The fact that the alleged victim was the same in each case, and that the offences were of a broadly similar character, meant that there was sufficient nexus. **15.23**

The requirements of CrimPR, r 14.2(3) are undemanding, but care must be taken not to forget those requirements completely. In *Harward* (1981) 73 Cr App R 168, the indictment against H contained a count for conspiring to use cheque cards to obtain money fraudulently from banks, and a count for handling stereo equipment which was found in H's possession shortly after it **15.24** had been stolen. H was acquitted on the conspiracy count, but convicted of handling. Quashing the conviction, the Court of Appeal held that joinder of the two counts in one indictment was not justified within the meaning of the rules, and was therefore unlawful. The offences were not founded on the same facts, and the only point of legal or factual similarity between them was that they both involved dishonesty. But the dishonesty alleged in the conspiracy count related to H's involvement in fraudulent practices, whereas that alleged in the handling count related to his state of mind when he received the relevant goods. There was not a sufficient nexus between the offences for them to form part of a series of the same or a similar character.

15.25   In *Williams* [1993] Crim LR 533, W was charged with (1) indecently assaulting a girl of 13 in a London hotel and (2) falsely imprisoning her five days later, by forcing her on to a seat in a train travelling from Stevenage to London. The Court of Appeal held that the two offences were not of a similar character, and had been wrongly joined in the same indictment.

Discretion to order separate trials

15.26   If the judge is of the opinion that the accused may be 'prejudiced or embarrassed in his defence' through a single trial of all the counts against him in an indictment, or if for any other reason he considers that separate trials of at least some of the counts is desirable, then he may make an order to that effect: IA, s 5(3). This is commonly referred to as severing the indictment. The power to sever given by s 5(3) is meant to deal with cases where the joinder of counts in one indictment is technically justified (i.e., there is no breach of CrimPR, r 14.2(3)), but, if the accused were to be tried by a single jury on all counts, there would be a risk of the jurors not considering some of the matters fairly. However, where the indictment is invalid because it contains counts which are neither founded on the same facts nor form part of a series of the same or similar character, the invalidity cannot be cured by a purported exercise of the power to sever: *Newland* [1988] QB 402. In *Newland*, N was indicted for possessing a controlled drug with intent to supply and totally unrelated offences of assault. Prosecuting counsel, realizing that the joinder was improper, applied successfully for severance and N thereupon pleaded guilty, but his convictions had to be quashed on appeal as they resulted from an invalid indictment. Watkins LJ stated that the prosecution could have partially rescued the situation by amending the indictment so as to delete either the drugs count or the assault counts—there could then have been a valid conviction on whatever part of the indictment remained (see 15.47 to 15.50 for amending the indictment). If they wished, the prosecution could then have brought fresh proceedings for the counts that had been deleted out, although that would have entailed either a second committal or a voluntary bill of indictment. But, what neither they nor the judge could do was to treat the indictment as if it had been properly drafted in the first place and then purport to exercise the statutory power to sever valid indictments.

15.27   Another way forward for the prosecution, when faced with an indictment which is invalid because of improper joinder, is to adopt the course approved in *Follett* [1989] QB 338. They may, in effect, ignore the invalid indictment and seek leave to prefer fresh, separate indictments out of time. They must then elect on which indictments they wish to proceed. They will obviously choose the replacement indictments. Then (and only then), the judge will be asked to quash the original, invalidly joined indictment.

15.28   The correct judicial approach to applications to sever under s 5(3) was explained by the House of Lords in *Ludlow v Metropolitan Police Commissioner* (see 15.21). The judge is under a duty to direct separate trials only if there is a special feature in the case which would make a joint trial of several counts prejudicial or embarrassing. Examples are cases where the evidence relevant to one count would be difficult to disentangle from the evidence relevant to the other counts, and cases where one of the counts is of a scandalous nature so that if the jury were satisfied that the accused had committed that offence they would be so prejudiced against him that they would convict on the other counts regardless of any lack of proof.

The argument for the appellant in *Ludlow* was that the offence of attempted theft was not **15.29** sufficiently similar to the offence of robbery for the jury to be entitled to consider the evidence on one count when deciding whether the accused committed the offence alleged in the other count (see works on evidence and especially *Blackstone's Criminal Practice 2008* F12 and the CJA 2003, s 103, for the current provisions on admissibility of the accused's propensity to commit similar offences). Therefore, it was argued, L was inevitably prejudiced and embarrassed in his defence on the attempted theft charge through the jury hearing irrelevant accusations about the robbery. The same applied in reverse on the robbery charge. The House of Lords rejected the argument. In a simple case, such as *Ludlow*, the jury were quite capable, given a suitable direction from the judge, of ignoring the evidence of the robbery when considering the attempted theft and vice versa. In more complicated cases, however, the difficulty of disentangling the evidence relevant on the various counts might necessitate an order for separate trials.

Alternative counts

Sometimes the evidence available to the prosecution clearly shows that the accused has **15.30** committed an indictable offence, but precisely what he has done is less obvious. In such cases, the indictment may include counts for *all* the offences that might be proved and the jury can then decide on which (if any) they should convict. The indictment will not expressly say that the counts are in the alternative, but counsel and/or the judge in his summing-up will explain to the jury that they are not being invited to find the accused guilty of everything alleged against him.

Alternative counts may be included in an indictment when the accused's conduct, depending **15.31** on his state of mind at the relevant time and/or the consequences of his acts, might make him guilty of one of a number of offences of differing degrees of gravity. Thus, if the accused injured a victim without breaking the skin, he might be indicted for (i) causing grievous bodily harm with intent contrary to s 18 of the Offences against the Person Act 1861; (ii) unlawfully and maliciously inflicting GBH contrary to s 20 of the same Act; and (iii) assault occasioning actual bodily harm contrary to s 47. If satisfied that the injuries amounted to really serious harm and that the accused intended to cause such harm, the jury would convict of (i); if satisfied as to the gravity of the injuries but not as to the accused's intentions, they would convict of (ii); if satisfied merely that the accused had occasioned some actual bodily harm by an assault, they would convict of (iii); and if in doubt as to all of the above, they would simply acquit. The judge would direct them to go through the counts in descending order of gravity.

Another common example of alternative counts is where the accused was allegedly found in **15.32** possession of stolen goods soon after they were stolen, and the prosecution ask the jury to convict him either of the theft or receiving. Here the alternatives are mutually exclusive as a matter of law, for s 22 of the Theft Act expressly provides that the act of handling must be otherwise than in the course of theft (contrast ss 18 and 20 of the Offences Against the Person

Act which are alternatives only in the sense that it would be oppressive to find the accused guilty of both when the lesser offence is virtually included in the greater). Despite the fact that theft and handling are thus true alternatives, it has never been doubted that it is appropriate to join them in one indictment on the basis that they are founded on the same facts within the first limb of r 9 of the Indictment Rules (see *Shelton* (1986) 83 Cr App R 379, where Lawton LJ said that the practice of charging theft and handling as alternatives should continue whenever there is a real possibility that the evidence might support one rather than the other). It is also common practice to have two separate handling counts as alternatives to each other, the particulars of one alleging that the accused 'received' stolen goods, and the particulars of the other alleging that he 'undertook their retention, removal, disposal or realization by or for the benefit of another person'. The jury can then convict either on the first limb of s 22 (which is generally considered the more serious) or on the less serious second limb.

F   JOINDER OF DEFENDANTS IN AN INDICTMENT

15.33   A count in an indictment may charge two or more defendants with committing a single offence. Further, two or more counts in an indictment may charge different defendants with separate offences even though there is no one count against them all collectively.

Joint counts

15.34   All parties to a single offence may—and normally will—be charged with it together in a single count. This applies not only to the principal offenders, but also to those who aid, abet, counsel or procure the commission of the offence, for s 8 of the Accessories and Abettors Act 1861 provides that all secondary parties are liable to be 'tried, indicted and punished as a principal offender'. Thus, if A provides information which assists B and C to enter a building as trespassers and steal property, whilst D keeps watch outside, the prosecution could have one count against them for burglary alleging that 'A, B, C and D, having entered a building known as . . . as trespassers, stole therein . . .'. In a sense, the count is inaccurate because A and D did not enter the building. However, should there be a not guilty plea, the prosecution can easily explain to the jury that A and D were not, so to speak, the actual burglars but may be held liable in law as burglars on the basis that they assisted B and C in their break-in. If found guilty, the actual sentence the judge passes (as opposed to the maximum which he could theoretically pass) will be related to whether they played a major or a minor role. Although it is convenient to word a count against an aider and abettor as if he were a principal offender, there is nothing to stop the prosecution specifically alleging that he was merely a secondary party. This might be preferable, for example, where the prosecution case is that a woman assisted a man to commit rape. Rather than confuse a jury with a count which apparently attributed the act of rape to a woman, the prosecution could make the statement of offence, 'Aiding and abetting rape contrary to s 1 of the Sexual Offences Act 1956', and the particulars of offence, 'Jane Smith aided and abetted Jack Brown to rape Jill Black'.

15.35   The jury are entitled to convict one or more but acquit other defendants named in a joint count. Furthermore, although the prosecution will not include defendants in a joint count unless their evidence suggests that there was a joint enterprise or cooperation between them, it has been held by the House of Lords in *DPP v Merriman* [1973] AC 584 that any or all of them may be convicted on the basis that they committed the offence independently of the others charged in the count.

The judge always has a discretion to order separate trials of defendants who are accused of **15.36** committing an offence jointly, but there are strong reasons for a single trial which usually outweigh any opposing arguments. In favour of a single trial are the saving of time and convenience to witnesses of only having the evidence given once; the desirability of the jury having a full picture of what occurred which is more likely to be given through a single trial, and the risk of differing verdicts being returned by different juries on virtually identical evidence should there be separate trials. These considerations led the Court of Appeal to state in *Moghal* (1977) 65 Cr App R 56 that separate trials of those joined in a single count should only be ordered in very exceptional cases. However, the decision is essentially one for the judge. The fact that a joint trial will result in the jury hearing evidence against A, which is inadmissible against B but highly prejudicial to him, does not oblige the judge to accede to an application by B for separate trials (see *Lake* (1977) 64 Cr App R 172, where the judge's refusal of a separate trial for L was upheld even though L's co-defendants had made confessions in L's absence which implicated not only themselves but L also). Similarly, the fact that A and B are going to put forward defences in which they put the entire blame for the offence on each other does not necessitate separate trials: *Grondkowski and Malinowski* [1946] KB 369. For an exceptional case, in which an appeal on these grounds succeeded, see *O'Boyle* (1990) 92 Cr App R 202. On the facts of that case, the Court of Appeal said that joint trial had prejudiced the appellant, whereas separate trials would have done little or no harm to his co-accused or the prosecution. Accordingly, the trial judge had erred in the exercise of his discretion.

Separate counts

An indictment may include separate counts each naming a different defendant, no defendant **15.37** being joined with any other defendant in a single count. The circumstances in which this may be done are not closely defined. It is a matter for the practice of the court, but there must be some linking factor between the offences to justify joining their alleged perpetrators in one indictment. The linking factor may be that the defendants were apparently acting in concert although committing separate offences, or that the offences all occurred in one incident (e.g., various assaults during a gang fight), or that they occurred successively (e.g., two witnesses at the same trial committing perjury one after the other). An example of correct joinder is *Assim* [1966] 2 QB 249. Two defendants were charged in a single indictment, one with unlawfully wounding X and the other with assaulting Y occasioning him actual bodily harm. Since their respective acts of violence had separate victims they could not be charged in a single count. The joinder of the separate counts in one indictment was, however, justified as the defendants were the doorman and receptionist at the same night-club, and X and Y were customers who were attempting to leave without paying their bills. The offences were linked by proximity in time and place, and by their apparent motive of discouraging bad payers.

The Theft Act 1968, s 27(1) provides for handlers of stolen property to be charged in one **15.38** indictment. All persons who at any time handle any portion of the goods stolen in one theft may be jointly indicted and jointly tried. So, if A, in the course of a burglary, steals a watch and a necklace which he sells to B and C respectively, and C sells on the necklace to D—all four can be indicted and tried together. The separate counts of handling against B, C, and D are properly put in one indictment because of s 27(1), and the burglary count against A is sufficiently linked with the handling counts to fall within the principle in *Assim*.

15.39   Where defendants are joined in one indictment but not charged in a joint count, the judge again has a discretion to order separate trials, even though the single indictment was justified. The arguments for and against splitting the indictment are similar to those rehearsed above in the context of defendants charged in a joint count, but the argument for a single trial is less strong where there is no joint count, as the evidence in the case of one defendant will not be so closely inter-twined with the evidence in the cases of the other defendants. An illustration of the circumstances in which a judge might think it fair to order separate trials is provided by *Johnson* [1995] 2 Cr App R 41. The indictment contained a count alleging that A assaulted B, and another count that C assaulted A. In other words, A was victim and defendant in the same trial. As the Court of Appeal pointed out, this had the effect that, if A gave evidence, counsel for the prosecution could ask him in cross-examination about C. It was inevitably prejudicial to C, especially when the issue was whether C was A's assailant. Their lordships said that separate trials would often (though not always) be preferable in such a situation. The avoidance of the unusual prejudice to C would normally outweigh the inconvenience of calling the same witnesses at two trials.

Overloading indictments

15.40   The preceding Paragraphs have shown that the rules governing joinder of counts and joinder of defendants are far from strict, and, if joinder is prima facie within the rules, the Court of Appeal are reluctant to quash a conviction on the ground that the judge, in the exercise of his discretion, refused to sever the indictment. However, their lordships have often warned of the danger of overloading indictments. For example, in *Thorne* (1978) 66 Cr App R 6, no fewer than 14 defendants were tried together on an indictment containing three counts for robbery and numerous related offences such as conspiracy to rob, handling the proceeds of the robberies and attempting to pervert the course of justice in respect of the robbery prosecutions. The trial, involving 27 counsel and 10 firms of solicitors, lasted 111 working days and included a 12-day summing-up from the judge. Although none of the appeals were allowed simply on the basis that the trial had been too long, the Court of Appeal stated that two or three shorter trials would have been far preferable. Such a huge trial placed an unfair burden on judge and jury.

15.41   If the accused's conduct on one occasion may possibly make him guilty of several offences, the prosecution should assess what the 'real' offence was and have a count for that, ignoring the other offences which as a matter of strict law are disclosed on the committal statements (see May LJ's comments in *Staton* [1983] Crim LR 190). Of course, where there is genuine uncertainty about what is the more appropriate charge the prosecution will need two or more counts in the alternative—the point being made in *Staton* and in *Thorne* is that the prosecution should not automatically include in an indictment as many counts and as many defendants as are technically justified by the rules. They should consider also whether joinder will make for a fairer and more efficient trial.

15.42   In *Laycock* (2003) *The Times*, 21 May 2003, the defendant had faced an indictment which contained a number of counts dealing with the possession of a firearm. One such count showed that he had been sentenced to a previous sentence of imprisonment, with the result that he was prohibited from possession of a firearm. The Court of Appeal criticized the inclusion of this count, as it caused prejudice to the defendant without adding to the judge's sentencing powers. Prosecutors were urged not to charge counts which would prejudice a defendant, unless there was a real purpose to be served.

The Code for Crown Prosecutors and the indictment

The Code for Crown Prosecutors (issued by the Director of Public Prosecutions—see **15.43** Paragraph 4.3) contains guidance as to the counts which ought to be included in an indictment (the Code refers to 'charges', which is the generic term, but 'counts' is the more appropriate term when dealing with an indictment). The Code exhorts Crown Prosecutors to 'select charges which (a) reflect the seriousness of the offending; (b) give the court adequate sentencing powers; and (c) enable the case to be presented in a clear and simple way'.

This means that Crown Prosecutors should not continue with more charges than are necessary **15.44** (para 7.1 of the Code). Further, Crown Prosecutors are told not to include more charges than are necessary just to encourage a defendant to plead guilty to a few. Nor should they include a more serious charge just to encourage the defendant to plead guilty to a lesser charge (para 7.2).

G   APPLICATIONS CONCERNING THE INDICTMENT

The following applications may be necessary: **15.45**

Application to sever the indictment

If the defence considers that two or more counts in the indictment against the accused should **15.46** be tried separately, or that he should not be tried with the other defendants named in the indictment, application must be made to the judge to sever the indictment. The application is usually made immediately after the pleas to the indictment have been taken. Such applications may be made to the trial judge in a pre-trial hearing, where there is provision for one.

Applications to amend the indictment

If the judge considers that the indictment is defective he must order it to be amended, unless **15.47** such amendment would cause injustice: IA, s 5(1). The amendment may be ordered before or at any stage during the trial, the defence, if necessary, being given an adjournment to consider the way their position has been affected: s 5(4). Subject always to not causing injustice, *any* defect in an indictment can be remedied by amendment, whether the defect be trivial (e.g., the misspelling of a name) or fundamental (e.g., omitting from the particulars an essential element of the offence charged in the count). Amendment is also appropriate where the evidence at the trial differs from the allegations in the particulars, although if such amendments are sought at a late stage, they may well be refused because of potential injustice. For example, in *Gregory* [1972] 1 WLR 991, the Court of Appeal quashed G's conviction on a count for handling a starter-motor because, after all the evidence had been given, the judge deleted from the particulars an allegation that the starter-motor belonged to 'W.A.W.' Much of the evidence had turned on whether a starter-motor, admittedly found in G's possession, was the one that had earlier been stolen from W.A.W. The defence contended that it was not, and that

G had legitimately bought the motor from a casual acquaintance whose name he did not know. By deleting the allegation as to ownership the judge altered the whole basis of the prosecution case, and, in effect, invited the jury to convict on the basis that even if G's story were correct, the circumstances of the purchase (at a quarter of the proper price) showed that the motor had been stolen from someone and that G knew it to be stolen. Had the amendment been made before the indictment was put to the accused, with the defence being offered an adjournment, it is unlikely that any appeal could have succeeded.

15.48 Amendment may also take the form of inserting new counts in the indictment either in substitution for or in addition to those originally drafted. This may be done after the accused has pleaded to the indictment: *Johal and Ram* [1973] QB 475. Indeed, in *Collison* (1980) 71 Cr App R 249, the Court of Appeal approved the addition of a count when, after the jury had retired to consider their verdict, a difficulty arose concerning whether they could properly return a verdict of guilty of a lesser offence (see 21.22 to 21.33). In *Johal* and *Collison* the fresh counts were needed to solve purely technical problems that had arisen on the indictments as originally drafted but they did not alter the nature of the prosecution case. If a count containing a genuinely fresh charge were to be added after the start of the evidence, it would almost certainly cause injustice.

15.49 The question may arise whether it is necessary for the amendment to be founded on the evidence disclosed at committal, where that is the route by which the defendant was sent to the Crown Court. In *Osieh* [1996] 1 WLR 1260, the Court of Appeal held that it was not necessary (although the amendment in the case in question *was* actually founded upon the committal evidence). However, the fact that an amendment raises for the first time something which is not foreshadowed in the committal evidence may be reason for refusing leave for an amendment, or allowing the defence an adjournment to cope with the change in direction (per Schiemann LJ in *Osieh*).

15.50 Where an amendment appears necessary counsel for the prosecution should apply for it. If he fails to do so, the judge may raise the matter on his own initiative, asking for the views of prosecution and defence.

Motion to quash the indictment

15.51 The defence may apply to the judge to quash the indictment. If the application (or motion) succeeds no further proceedings may take place on the indictment. It follows that the appropriate time for moving to quash is before the indictment is put, as success at that stage will mean that the accused does not even have to plead. The judge may, however, entertain an application at a later stage. A motion to quash may also be brought in respect of a single count in an indictment.

15.52 Motions to quash are not of great value to the defence for three reasons. First, even after a successful motion, the prosecution are entitled to commence fresh proceedings in respect of the same matters, hoping to avoid the mistake that led to the first indictment or count being quashed. Second, a suitable amendment to the indictment can often prevent the motion to quash from succeeding. Third, the grounds for a successful motion are very limited. Those grounds are that:

(a) the bill of indictment was preferred without authority, or

(b) the wording of the indictment or count reveals a fundamental defect, or

(c) the count is for an offence in respect of which the magistrates did not commit for trial, and no case to answer for that offence is revealed from the committal evidence (or the evidence upon which a notice of transfer or a voluntary bill of indictment is based, or the documents served when the accused is sent to the Crown Court: see Chapter 13).

As to (b) it must be stressed that the judge is only entitled to look at the wording of the indictment to see if there is something fundamentally wrong (e.g., a count fails to allege an essential element of the offence charged or is bad for duplicity). Except as described in (c), he may not be asked to consider any inadequacies in the prosecution evidence foreshadowed in the statements. In other words, a motion to quash is not a way of challenging the magistrates' court's decision to commit for trial on a certain charge. If the indictment or count is defectively worded the prosecution may prevent a successful motion to quash simply by applying to amend.

Perhaps the most valuable use of motions to quash is that mentioned in (c) above. If the **15.53** indictment contains a count alleging an offence for which the magistrates' court did not commit the accused for trial, the defence may invite the judge to read the evidence considered by the magistrates, and, if it does not disclose a case to answer, to quash the count. It is the one situation where, on a motion to quash, the judge considers the evidence: *Jones* (1974) 59 Cr App R 120. It is right that he should do so because either the magistrates' court held that there was not a case to answer for the offence charged in the count, or, at the very least, it was not invited to give a decision on the point.

In examining the evidence considered by the magistrates' court, the judge should ensure that **15.54** any offence in the indictment, other than one on which the defendant was sent for trial, is founded on the evidence. The evidence contained in the statements need not, however, be conclusive (*Biddis* [1993] Crim LR 392). In *Biddis*, a count of possessing a firearm was added to the charge of robbery on which the defendant had been committed. It was argued on appeal that the committal bundle did not include any evidence to show that the gun could be fired so that it could be a firearm within the meaning of the Firearms Act 1968, s 57(1). The Court of Appeal held that there was evidence that the gun had been loaded, and that this was, in the circumstances of the case, sufficient evidence from which the jury could reasonably have inferred that it was an effective weapon.

Staying the indictment

In addition to the powers referred to above, the court has power to stay (i.e., to postpone **15.55** proceedings) in relation to an indictment. This is part of its inherent power to regulate the efficient and fair disposal of criminal cases (*Connelly v DPP* [1964] AC 1254 at p. 1346). The court is also able to stay part of an indictment, so that, for example, proceedings continue against one defendant only or in respect of one count only (*Munro* [1993] Crim LR 393).

H   APPEALS BASED ON DEFECTIVE INDICTMENTS

An error in the indictment which is not corrected during the trial may provide the accused **15.56** with a good ground of appeal should he ultimately be convicted. Unfortunately the cases on the subject tend to turn upon technicalities as to the Court of Appeal's powers when determining an appeal. Since detailed consideration of appeals against conviction must wait until

Chapter 26, the propositions below are intended to summarize the position with regard to defective indictments without fully explaining the reasoning behind the decisions:

(a) A significant defect in the drafting of a count—e.g., omission from the Statement of Offence of the statute contravened, or a failure to allege the full particulars of the offence, or a discrepancy between the evidence at trial and the particulars—may amount to a ground for quashing a conviction. Where the mistake is very trivial (e.g., misspelling a name) it can be disregarded as being too minor to amount to a good ground of appeal. However, even a serious mistake will not automatically result in a successful appeal. The essential question is whether, in all the circumstances, the error in pleading prejudiced or embarrassed the accused. If it did not, the Court of Appeal will uphold the conviction on the basis that there has been no miscarriage of justice, i.e., it is safe. Lord Bridge in *Ayres* [1984] AC 447 stated the guiding principle thus:

> If the statement and particulars of offence can be seen fairly to relate to and be intended to charge a known and subsisting criminal offence but plead it in terms which are inaccurate, incomplete and otherwise imperfect, then the question whether a conviction on that indictment can properly be affirmed ... must depend on whether, in all the circumstances, it can be said with confidence that the particular error in the pleading cannot in any way have prejudiced or embarrassed the defendant.

There is a strong tendency for their lordships to hold that there has been no such prejudice. Thus, convictions have been upheld:

(i)   where the particulars of a count for possessing explosives contrary to s 4 of the Explosive Substances Act 1883 failed to allege that the accused knowingly had possession of the explosives, knowledge being an essential element of the offence (*McVitie* (1960) 44 Cr App R 201);

(ii) where the Statement of Offence in a count for having an offensive weapon in a public place omitted the statute contravened, namely s 1 of the Prevention of Crime Act 1953 (*Nelson* (1977) 65 Cr App R 119); and

(iii) where the Statement of Offence for an offence contrary to s 5 of the Perjury Act 1911 wrongly described the offence as 'perjury' when it should have been making a false declaration not on oath (*Power* (1977) 66 Cr App R 159);

(iv) where the particulars of a count of riot contrary to the Public Order Act 1986, s 1(1), charged that the defendant had 'used or threatened' unlawful violence, when the offence required that he should have 'used' unlawful violence (*Jefferson* [1994] 1 All ER 270).

In each of these cases, the court essentially reasoned that, while the indictment was defective, it described an offence known to law (albeit in terms which were inaccurate). Crucially, the accused had not, on the facts, been misled or prejudiced in the conduct of his defence by the error.

(b) Where, however, the defect consists not merely in the wording of a count but in a fundamental procedural error which renders the whole indictment a nullity, the conviction cannot stand. An example is where the committal proceedings that purported to justify the preferring of a bill of indictment were themselves invalid (*Phillips and Quayle* [1939] 1 KB 63). In such cases the Court of Appeal is obliged to quash the conviction but it may, in its discretion, order a *venire de novo* (i.e., sanction a fresh prosecution).

(c) Where counts are unlawfully joined in one indictment contrary to r 9 of the IR, the indictment is merely invalid, not a nullity. The prosecution can amend the indictment at trial by deleting one or more of the counts, so that what results is an indictment consisting of counts which are lawfully joined. If they fail to do so, the question arises as to the status of the subsequent proceedings. In *Lockley* [1997] Crim LR 455, the Court of Appeal held that technical points should not generally nullify the whole indictment, unless there was prejudice to the accused.

I   CONSPIRACY COUNTS

Counts for conspiracy have probably caused more drafting problems than counts for any other offence. Two particular points should be noted. **15.57**

First, where the conspiracy alleged is a complicated one the particulars need to be more detailed than is the case with other offences. If the judge considers that the particulars as originally drafted are too brief to give the defence a fair idea of how the prosecution put their case, he may order that further particulars be provided (see *Landy* (1981) 72 Cr App R 237). **15.58**

Second, the prosecution sometimes include in one indictment a count for (i) conspiracy to commit certain offences, and (ii) counts for actually committing those offences. The practice seems to have originated as a way of bringing before the jury evidence which was admissible on the conspiracy count but was, technically speaking, inadmissible on the substantive counts in the hope that, having heard the evidence, the jury would take it into consideration on all counts. However, in *Jones* (1974) 59 Cr App R 120 the Court of Appeal held that joinder of a conspiracy count with counts for the substantive offences can only be justified if *either* the evidence may turn out to be too weak for convictions on the latter but ample for conviction on the former, *or* a number of counts for minor substantive offences would not truly reflect the gravity of the accused's conduct. Moreover, the trial judge must require the prosecution to justify the joinder and, if they cannot, they must elect on which part of the indictment they wish to proceed. **15.59**

SPECIMEN COUNTS **15.60**

1   Murder

STATEMENT OF OFFENCE

Murder.

PARTICULARS OF OFFENCE

A, on the 1st day of January 2008, murdered B.

2   Manslaughter

STATEMENT OF OFFENCE

Manslaughter.

PARTICULARS OF OFFENCE

A, on the 1st day of January 2008, unlawfully killed B.

3   Grievous   STATEMENT OF OFFENCE
     bodily harm   Causing grievous bodily harm with intent, contrary to section
     with intent   18 of the Offences Against the Person Act 1861.
                              PARTICULARS OF OFFENCE
                    C, on the 1st day of January 2008, caused grievous bodily harm
                    to D with intent to do her grievous bodily harm.

4   Unlawful   STATEMENT OF OFFENCE
     wounding   Unlawful wounding, contrary to section 20 of the Offences
                    Against the Person Act 1861.
                              PARTICULARS OF OFFENCE
                    C, on the 1st day of January 2008, unlawfully and maliciously
                    wounded D.

5   Rape   STATEMENT OF OFFENCE
                    Rape, contrary to section 1(1) of the Sexual Offences Act 2003.
                              PARTICULARS OF OFFENCE
                    E, on the 1st day of January 2008, raped F.

6   Robbery   STATEMENT OF OFFENCE
                    Robbery, contrary to section 8(1) of the Theft Act 1968.
                              PARTICULARS OF OFFENCE
                    G, on the 1st day of January 2008, robbed H of a cloak, a necklace and
                    £100 in money.

7   Theft   STATEMENT OF OFFENCE
                    Theft, contrary to section 1(1) of the Theft Act 1968.
                              PARTICULARS OF OFFENCE
                    J, on the 1st day of January 2008, stole a pair of cuff links belonging to K.

8   Handling   STATEMENT OF OFFENCE
     stolen goods   Handling stolen goods, contrary to section 22(1) of the Theft Act 1968.
                              PARTICULARS OF OFFENCE
                    L, on a day unknown between the 31st day of December 2007 and the
                    1st day of February 2008, dishonestly received certain stolen goods,
                    namely a pair of cuff links belonging to K, knowing or believing the
                    same to be stolen goods.

     or

                              STATEMENT OF OFFENCE
                    Handling stolen goods, contrary to section 22(1) of the Theft Act
                    1968.

PARTICULARS OF OFFENCE

L, on a day unknown between the 31st day of December 2007 and the 1st day of February 2008, dishonestly undertook or assisted in the retention of certain stolen goods, namely a pair of cuff links belonging to K, by or for the benefit of J, knowing or believing the same to be stolen goods.

| 9 | Burglary | STATEMENT OF OFFENCE |

Burglary, contrary to section 9(1)(b) of the Theft Act 1968.

PARTICULARS OF OFFENCE

M and N, on the 1st day of January 2008, having entered as trespassers a building known as 1 Dickens Lane, Chertsey, Surrey, stole therein a cashbox and £100 in money.

| 10 | Obtaining by deception | STATEMENT OF OFFENCE |

Obtaining property by deception, contrary to section 15(1) of the Theft Act 1968.

PARTICULARS OF OFFENCE

O and P, on the 1st day of January 2006, dishonestly obtained from Q a gold watch with the intention of permanently depriving Q thereof by deception, namely by falsely representing to the said Q that they were employees of a watch repairer who had sent them to collect the said watch for repair.

| 11 | Going equipped | STATEMENT OF OFFENCE |

Going equipped for burglary, contrary to section 25(1) of the Theft Act 1968.

PARTICULARS OF OFFENCE

U, on the 1st day of January 2008, not being at his place of abode, had with him articles for use in the course of or in connection with burglary, namely a jemmy, a screwdriver and a torch.

| 12 | Criminal damage | STATEMENT OF OFFENCE |

Damaging property, contrary to section 1(1) of the Criminal Damage Act 1971.

PARTICULARS OF OFFENCE

V, on the 1st day of January 2008, without lawful excuse, damaged a dress belonging to W, intending to damage such property or being reckless as to whether such property would be damaged.

| 13 | Dangerous driving | STATEMENT OF OFFENCE |

Dangerous driving, contrary to section 2 of the Road Traffic Act 1988.

PARTICULARS OF OFFENCE

X, on the 1st day of January 2008, drove a mechanically propelled vehicle on a road, namely Willow Avenue, Banktown, Grahamshire, dangerously.

14   Possessing   STATEMENT OF OFFENCE
      drugs   Possessing a controlled drug, contrary to section 5(2) of the Misuse
                    of Drugs Act 1971.
                                    PARTICULARS OF OFFENCE
                    Y, on the 1st day of January 2008, had in his possession a controlled
                    drug of Class A, namely cocaine.

15   Perjury   STATEMENT OF OFFENCE
                    Perjury, contrary to section 1(1) of the Perjury Act 1911.
                                    PARTICULARS OF OFFENCE
                    A, on the 1st day of January 2008, having been lawfully sworn as
                    a witness in a judicial proceeding, namely the trial of a criminal
                    cause in the Crown Court entitled *The Queen v BC*, wilfully made
                    a statement material in that proceeding which he knew to be false,
                    namely that he saw BC speaking to DE on the 1st day of June
                    2005.

16   Conspiracy   STATEMENT OF OFFENCE
                    Conspiracy to murder, contrary to section 1(1) of the Criminal Law
                    Act 1977.
                                    PARTICULARS OF OFFENCE
                    FG and HJ, on divers days before the 1st day of January 2008, con-
                    spired together and with persons unknown to murder KL.

17   Attempt   STATEMENT OF OFFENCE
                    Attempted murder, contrary to section 1(1) of the Criminal
                    Attempts Act 1981.
                                    PARTICULARS OF OFFENCE
                    M, on the 5th day of November 2008, attempted to murder N.

KEY DOCUMENTS

Indictments Act 1915, as amended.
Indictment Rules 1971 (SI 1971 No 1573).
Code for Crown Prosecutors, available at: <http://www.cps.gov.uk>.

16

PRE-TRIAL PROCEEDINGS

In recent years, various reforms have aimed to increase the scope of pre-trial proceedings in **16.01** the Crown Court. The underlying aim is to enable the judge (preferably the one who will preside at trial but, if that is impossible, one of the other judges who are available at that Crown Court centre) to start the business of managing the trial before it begins. That means that the parties must supply information as to the issues and the way in which they intend to conduct their case; and that the judge must act upon that information by making any orders which seem necessary in order to assist the efficient conduct of the trial.

Perhaps the most important of the issues on which early information is necessary in the inter- **16.02** ests of efficiency is the intended plea of the defendant. If the defendant decides to plead guilty on the day of the trial, after a court and a judge have been allocated to the case, lawyers have prepared and witnesses have been summoned to attend court, then there is a substantial waste of resources. One aim of pre-trial management is therefore to ensure that the defendant's plea is taken at an early stage before the trial, and the main vehicle for this is provided by the appropriately named plea and case management hearing.

There are other points which need to be canvassed prior to the trial, however, such as the **16.03** points of law which are likely to arise, and any arguments as to the admissibility of evidence. It is important for the judge to know of these, since they will affect the course of the trial. Further, since points of law and admissibility are decided in the absence of the jury, as many of them as possible should be resolved in advance of the trial, so as to avoid extensive argument after the jury has been empanelled. If the judge ruling on these points is not the eventual trial judge, however, then much of the value of early resolution of the issues can be lost if the parties have an unfettered right to apply for the matter to be decided again (e.g., by the trial judge). As a result, it has been seen as desirable that the decisions taken prior to trial should be binding, at least to an extent, and this need has led to the statutory provisions on pre-trial rulings. In complex or lengthy matters, a more detailed framework of pre-trial proceedings has been thought necessary, and this is contained in the statutory regime which governs preparatory hearings.

16.04   This Chapter deals with the main forms of pre-trial proceedings as follows:

(a)   plea and case management hearings (16.05 to 16.07);
(b)   pre-trial rulings (16.08 to 16.11);
(c)   preparatory hearings (16.12 to 16.19).

Paragraph 16.20 summarizes the special measures which can be ordered preparatory to trial in order to protect vulnerable witnesses.

A   PLEA AND CASE MANAGEMENT HEARINGS

16.05   Before a trial on indictment can take place, both parties need to prepare, and the court needs to ensure that any necessary arrangements are made. In 1995, a new procedure was introduced to ensure that steps are taken to prepare cases committed to the Crown Court for trial. The procedure was known as the plea and directions hearing (PDH). It is now called a plea and case management hearing (PCMH). The *Practice Direction* (*Criminal Proceedings: Consolidation*) [2002] 1 WLR 2870 lays down that it should be held within 7 weeks after committal for trial, within 14 weeks after sending for trial (pursuant to s 51 of the Crime and Disorder Act 1998) where the defendant is in custody and within 17 weeks after sending for trial where the defendant is on bail (para V.56.5). They may be conducted by a judge other than the one who will preside at trial.

16.06   The arrangement is that each magistrates' court should commit the defendant to appear in the Crown Court on a specific date. The purpose of the PCMH is to ensure that any steps necessary for trial have been taken, and that the court is provided with sufficient information to fix a trial date. The advocate briefed in the case should appear in the PCMH wherever practicable. The defendant(s) should be present unless the court gives leave. Where a defendant intends to plead guilty, the court, prosecution and probation service must be notified as soon as possible.

16.07   At the PCMH, the defence must supply a full list of the prosecution witnesses whom they require to attend at trial. Both prosecution and defence should submit to the court and the other parties a summary of the issues on which the court's directions are sought, referring to any authorities which are relied on. For cases which are serious, lengthy or complex, a case summary should be prepared by the prosecution for use by the judge at the PCMH. At the PCMH, arraignment will normally take place (see 17.02 to 17.06 for details of the arraignment). If the defendant pleads guilty, the judge should proceed to sentencing whenever possible. Where the defendant pleads not guilty, or his pleas are not acceptable to the prosecution, the parties are expected to inform the court of the following matters (inter alia):

(a)   the estimated length of the prosecution and defence cases;
(b)   the witnesses the prosecution will call, and the order in which they will call them;

(c) any exhibits, CCTV evidence or electronic equipment required;

(d) any expert evidence to be called;

(e) any requirement for special measures or live TV links;

(f) any applications regarding hearsay or bad character evidence;

(g) whether a defence statement has been served;

(h) whether the defence alleges that the prosecution has failed to disclose any evidence.

Advocates fill in a detailed questionnaire and hand it to the judge at the PCMH. The intention is that, armed with this information, the judge will be able to fix a suitable date and make any other appropriate directions. Each of the parties, moreover, will be better fitted to prepare for trial with an indication of the likely issues at trial.

B PRE-TRIAL RULINGS

The plea and case management hearing described at 16.05 to 16.07 is now compulsory in all cases except serious fraud. It is meant to clarify the issues and enable the parties to focus upon them as they prepare for trial. One of the problems which has dogged such pre-trial proceedings over the years, however, has been the fact that whatever is decided may be overruled by the trial judge. This knowledge has undermined the effectiveness of such hearings, and frequently it has also meant that the advocates attending the PCMH have not been those who will represent the parties at trial, since, if the issues can be re-canvassed when the trial begins, there is little incentive for the trial advocates to disrupt their schedules by making themselves available for a preliminary procedural hearing of little importance. They have often succumbed to the temptation of sending someone much more junior along to 'hold the brief', secure in the knowledge that, if they do not like the outcome, they can always apply to the trial judge for a different ruling. **16.08**

Obviously, this attitude resulted in a diminution of value of the PCMH. Sections 39 to 43 of the Criminal Procedure and Investigations Act 1996 (CPIA) attempt to remedy the situation. The new statutory provisions apply to rulings made *before* the trial begins, i.e., before a jury is sworn or a guilty plea is accepted, or a preparatory hearing starts: s 39(3). It follows that the rulings in question may be made by someone other than the trial judge, who may not even be known at the time when they are made. Rulings may be made on any question as to the admissibility of evidence or any question of law relating to the case, either on application by a party to the case or on the judge's own motion. Once such a ruling is made, it has binding effect until the jury returns a verdict or the prosecutor decides not to proceed, unless a judge discharges or varies it. A judge may discharge or vary a ruling, either on the application of a party or on his own motion, where it appears in the interests of justice to do so. Where a party makes an application to vary an earlier ruling, he must show that there has been a material change of circumstances since the original ruling was made or (where there has been a previous application) since the last application was made (s 40). **16.09**

The result is that a pre-trial ruling acquires a status which means that it is not irreversible, but nor is it subject to automatic reconsideration at any time one of the parties so desires. It can be compared in this sense to a second decision to refuse bail, which can be challenged in the magistrates' court only if there are fresh circumstances. **16.10**

16.11 There are restrictions on the reporting of pre-trial rulings and the proceedings on applications relating to them. Reports may not be published or broadcast until the conclusion of the trial. There is no exemption in respect of formal details of the accused, in contrast to the restrictions on reporting of committals and preparatory hearings. However, a party may apply to the judge presiding at the pre-trial hearing for an order lifting reporting restrictions. If the accused (or one of them) objects, then the court may lift the restrictions only if it is satisfied that it is in the interests of justice to do so (ss 41 and 42 of the CPIA).

C   PREPARATORY HEARINGS

16.12 Sections 28 to 38 of the CPIA contain provisions for preparatory hearings in serious, long or complex cases. They originate from the procedure established for serious fraud cases, which came into force by virtue of the Criminal Justice Act 1987.

16.13 The decision to hold a preparatory hearing may be made by a Crown Court judge at any time before a jury is sworn, on the application of any of the parties, or by the court of its own motion. In practice, the decision is likely to be made at the PCMH (see 16.05 to 16.07). The preparatory hearing is in fact a stage of the trial itself, which may be used in order to settle various issues without requiring the jury to attend (s 30). In this respect, it differs from the pre-trial rulings described at 16.08 to 16.11. Since the trial begins with the preparatory hearing, the same judge must preside throughout, save for exceptional circumstances such as death or serious illness on his part (see *Southwark Crown Court ex parte Commissioners for Customs and Excise* [1993] 1 WLR 764, but contrast the position as far as the PCMH is concerned).

16.14 Among the powers available to the judge at a preparatory hearing is the power to order the prosecution to give the defence a case statement. This will differ from the bundle of evidence supplied at committal in that it should state the facts as the prosecution believe them to be, including, e.g., any inferences which they are asking the jury to draw from the evidence. Once the prosecution have supplied such a case statement, the judge may order the defence to supply a statement setting out in general terms the nature of the defence and the principal matters on which they take issue with the prosecution, any objections which they have to the prosecution case statement, and any points of law or admissibility which they wish to take and authorities on which they intend to rely (s 31). Although this is a form of defence disclosure, it is additional to, and may be more extensive than, the general duty of disclosure outlined in Chapter 9. Adverse comments and/or inferences are the sanctions which may flow from a failure to disclose, or a departure at trial from the case disclosed at a preparatory hearing. Although the sanctions are similar to those available for a breach of the general duty of disclosure, the preparatory hearing provisions apply to the prosecution as well, and there is a specific prohibition on any mention of the defence statement without the consent of the accused (s 34).

16.15 The judge may also make rulings as to any question of law relating to the case, including questions as to the admissibility of evidence (s 31(2)), but his powers in this respect may be circumscribed by the principle in *Gunawardena* [1990] 1 WLR 703. In that case, it was held that the power to make binding rulings in a preparatory hearing in a serious fraud case was limited by implication to the purposes for which preparatory hearings may be ordered. These purposes are set out in s 29(2), and may be summarized as:

(a) identifying material issues for the jury;
(b) assisting them to understand those issues;
(c) expediting proceedings before them;
(d) helping the judge to manage the trial; and
(e) considering questions as to the severance or joinder of charges.

An order or ruling is binding throughout the trial, but the judge may decide on application that the interests of justice require him to vary or discharge it. There is no restriction on applications for variation such as exists in the case of pre-trial rulings under s 40 (see 16.08 to 16.11). Perhaps such a restriction was not seen as necessary in view of the fact that the same judge will act throughout, and a party is likely to expect the application to meet the same fate unless there really is a change in circumstances. **16.16**

There are provisions for appealing from rulings made by the judge at a preparatory hearing to the Court of Appeal and, ultimately, the House of Lords (ss 35 and 36). Where leave to appeal has been granted, the preparatory hearing may continue, but the jury trial cannot begin until the appeal has been determined or abandoned. The provision of a system of interlocutory appeals is to ensure that issues of admissibility and law are definitively resolved *before* the jury begins to deliberate, so as to ensure that a complex and potentially lengthy trial does not prove to be abortive. **16.17**

Restrictions on reporting preparatory hearings are contained in s 37, although certain formal details (e.g., the names, ages, home addresses, and occupations of the accused and witnesses, and the offence(s) charged) may be published by virtue of s 37(9). The court has power to lift the restrictions (s 37(3)). **16.18**

The Criminal Justice Act 1987, enacted as a result of the 1986 report of the Roskill Committee, provides in ss 7 to 11 for special 'preparatory hearings' in cases of serious fraud. The provisions were the basis for those enacted on preparatory hearings in long or complex cases described in this Section. Further, efforts have been made to ensure that the preparatory hearings regime operating for fraud cases is consistent with that for long or complex cases (see CPIA, s 72 and Sch 3). **16.19**

D   SPECIAL MEASURES FOR CERTAIN WITNESSES

The Youth Justice and Criminal Evidence Act 1999 contains a series of special measures which the court can direct in respect of certain witnesses. Where appropriate, such measures would form the subject of pre-trial rulings as described in the preceding Sections in this Chapter. The measures are: **16.20**

(a) screening the witness from the accused (s 23);
(b) giving evidence by live television link (s 24);
(c) ordering the removal of wigs and gowns while the witness gives evidence (s 25);

(d) giving evidence in private (in a sexual case, or where there is a fear that the witness might be intimidated—s 26);

(e) video-recording of evidence-in-chief (s 27);

(f) video-recording of cross-examination or re-examination where the evidence-in-chief of the witness has been video recorded (s 28);

(g) examination through an intermediary in the case of a young or incapacitated witness (s 29); and

(h) provision of aids to communication for a young or incapacitated witness (s 30).

In deciding whether to make a direction incorporating any of these special measures, the court must determine whether it will improve the quality of the witness' evidence, which is stated in s 16(5) to refer to its completeness, coherence and accuracy. In order to qualify for special measures, a witness must be eligible on grounds of youth or incapacity (s 16), or be liable to suffer from fear or distress when giving evidence (s 17). The accused is specifically excluded from eligibility for special measures (s 16(1) and 17(1)). In *R (S) v Waltham Forest Youth Court* [2004] 2 Cr App R 335, the Divisional Court held that the fact that the special measures provisions were not available to defendants who might otherwise be thought to be vulnerable witnesses did not contravene Art 6 of the ECHR. It followed that a court or judge could not permit a defendant to give evidence by live link, since such permission would not be based upon the common law discretion to regulate the trial, but on specific statutory measures, from which Parliament had clearly intended to exclude defendants.

16.21 In *H (Special Measures)* (2003) *The Times*, 15 April 2003, the Court of Appeal went some way to alleviate the harshness of the exclusion of defendants from eligibility for special measures directions. Their Lordships suggested that the trial judge, in his discretion, might take the following steps to assist a defendant with learning difficulties:

(a) ask his legal representatives to provide a detailed defence statement which could be read to the jury if there was concern about his ability to recall events;

(b) if the defendant could recall matters only by reference to a past coherent account of events which he had given, the judge might allow him to refer to it;

(c) if the defendant could not read, it was open to the judge to decide that he could be asked leading questions in respect of the account in the defence statement.

E   EVIDENCE BY VIDEO RECORDING

16.22 When the CJA 2003, s 137 comes into effect the court will be able to permit a video recording of an interview with a witness (other than the defendant) to be admitted as the evidence-in-chief of the witness in a wide range of circumstances. The court will be able to authorize such a video recording to replace the witness' evidence-in-chief provided that:

(a) the person claims to be a witness to the offence, or part of it, or to events closely connected with it; and

(b) the video recording of the statement was made at a time when the events were fresh in the witness' memory; and

(c)   the offence is indictable-only, or is a triable-either-way offence prescribed by order of the Home Secretary.

If the recording satisfies (a) to (c), then the court may admit it provided that:

(i)   the witness's recollection of events is likely to be significantly better at the time the recording was made than by the time of the trial; and

(ii) it is in the interests of justice to admit it, having regard to whether it is an early and reliable account from the witness, whether the quality is adequate, and the witness's own views about using the recording.

Where a video recording is admitted under these provisions, it is to be treated as the final statement of any matters adequately dealt with in it (s 138).

F   LIVE LINKS

Section 51 of the CJA 2003 gives the court power to authorize witnesses, other than the defen- **16.23**
dant, to give evidence through a 'live link'. This will usually be a closed circuit television link, but is defined in such a way as to include any technology with a similar effect, such as video conferencing facilities or the internet. In December 2007, s 51 was brought into force, but only in relation to Crown Court proceedings for certain specified sexual offences.

The power to authorize the use of a live link is confined to serious sexual offences such as rape **16.24**
and sexual assault. Further, the court may only authorize the use of a live link if:

(a)   it is in the interests of the efficient or effective administration of justice for the witness to give evidence in this way (e.g., because he works in a different part of the country, and can give his evidence from his place of work via a live link); and

(b)   notification has been received that the necessary facilities are available in the area where the criminal proceedings are to take place. (It is up to the parties to ensure that there are facilities in the location from which the witness will give evidence).

Where a direction for a live link has been given, that means that the witness must give all his **16.25**
evidence in that way, so that cross-examination must also be conducted by live link. If it is in the interests of justice to do so, the court can rescind a direction for a live link.

KEY DOCUMENTS

Youth Justice and Criminal Evidence Act 1999, as amended.

Criminal Justice Act 2003, ss 51 and 137.

Practice Direction (Criminal Proceedings: Consolidation) [2002] 1 WLR 2870 and at: <http://www.hmcourts-service.gov.uk/cms/pds.htm> where relevant forms can also be found.

17

PLEAS

A trial on indictment begins with the arraignment, which consists of putting the counts in   **17.01**
the indictment to the accused so that he can plead guilty or not guilty. The clerk reads the
indictment, pausing after each count to ask those charged in it whether they plead guilty or
not guilty. A plea must be taken on each count, unless it is in the alternative to another count
to which the accused has already pleaded guilty. The consequences of the accused giving an
ambiguous answer when asked to plead, or saying absolutely nothing, or being incapable of
pleading rationally are discussed at 17.16, 17.34 to 17.35, and 17.36 to 17.41 respectively.

A   TIME-LIMITS

17.02   The trial should begin (i.e., the arraignment take place) not less than two and not more than eight weeks from the date of committal for trial: Supreme Court Act 1981, s 77 and r 39.1 of the Criminal Procedure Rules 2005. However, this is an indication of what ought to happen, rather than of what actually does happen, since a judge of the Crown Court may, and normally would, give permission for the trial to start after the eight-week period. Even if no permission is expressly given, a trial commencing outside that period would not be a nullity as s 77 is directory not mandatory (see *Urbanowski* [1976] 1 WLR 445 and *Governor of Spring Hill Prison ex parte Sohi* [1988] 1 WLR 596. Rule 12.2 of the Criminal Procedure Rules 2005 deals with the listing of the first Crown Court appearance of a defendant who has been *sent* for trial in accordance with s 51 of the Crime and Disorder Act 1998 (see 13.09 to 13.11). It is not required in every case, and is to be listed in accordance with any directions from the magistrates' court which sent the case up, or the Crown Court itself. The *Practice Direction (Criminal Proceedings: Consolidation)* [2002] 1 WLR 2870, V.56.4 makes it clear that such a hearing should only be ordered if it is necessary. If it is necessary, then it should be held about 14 days after the case has been sent to the Crown Court. In any event, a plea and case management hearing (PCMH) should be held within 14 weeks (where the defendant is in custody) or 17 weeks (where the defendant is on bail): see 16.05 for details of the PCMH.

17.03   More crucially, the date of arraignment may be affected by regulations pursuant to s 22 of the Prosecution of Offences Act 1985, which lay down that preliminary stages of criminal proceedings (including the committal to arraignment stage) should be completed within prescribed time-limits. The Act envisages two types of time-limit implemented by regulations:

(a)   Overall time-limits, which lay down the maximum period within which a particular stage (e.g., from committal to arraignment) must be completed. No overall time-limits have yet been prescribed.

(b)   Custody time-limits, which lay down the maximum period during which the accused may be kept in custody pending completion of a particular stage of proceedings. If a custody time-limit expires, it has important implications for the accused's right to bail. Custody time-limits are now in force throughout the country (see 7.23 to 7.25 for details).

17.04   The procedure on arraignment is that the accused is brought into the dock. If it is anticipated that he will plead not guilty to all counts in the indictment the men and women from whom the jury will be selected (the jury in waiting) may be permitted to sit at the back of court to hear him plead. If there is any chance of his pleading guilty to one count and not guilty to another, they should be kept out of court since, were they to know that he had admitted one charge, it might prejudice their trying him fairly on the others. They should also be kept out of court if some but not all the accused joined in the indictment are expected to plead guilty.

17.05   Although there is no rigid formula for what ought to be said, the clerk putting the indictment which appears on p. 237 might say—'David Wilson, John Burton and Paul Green, you are charged in an indictment containing three counts. The first count charges you David Wilson and you John Burton with assault occasioning actual bodily harm contrary to s 47 of the Offences

Against the Person Act 1861. The particulars of that offence are that, on the 1st day of January 2006 you assaulted Barry Johnson thereby occasioning him actual bodily harm. David Wilson, do you plead guilty or not guilty?...John Burton, do you plead guilty or not guilty?...The second count charges you, Paul Green, with wounding contrary to s 20 of the Offences Against the Person Act 1861. The particulars of the offence are that...' and so on through the indictment.

Where an indictment contains counts in the alternative which are of roughly equal gravity **17.06** (e.g., theft and handling the proceeds of the theft), and the accused wishes to plead guilty to one of the counts, it is advisable to tell the court of his intentions. The count to which he is pleading guilty can then be put to him first (irrespective of whether it is first on the indictment), and the other count need not be put. Counts are in the alternative if, given the nature of the prosecution evidence, a jury could properly convict on one count or the other but not on both counts. Paragraphs 17.22 to 17.26 deal with the procedure to be followed where alternative counts are not of equal gravity.

B PLEA OF 'NOT GUILTY'

A plea of not guilty puts the entire prosecution case in issue. Essentially, therefore, the **17.07** prosecution will have to prove to the requisite standard (i.e., beyond reasonable doubt) each essential element of the offence charged, as defined by the substantive law of crime. That is traditionally summarized by saying that they must establish (i) that the accused committed the *actus reus* of the crime (or aided, abetted, counselled or procured someone else in its commission), and (ii) that, at the relevant time, he had the appropriate *mens rea*. Moreover, the prosecution must be able to do this initially through evidence which they tender as part of their case. If they fail to adduce evidence on which a reasonable jury could find the accused guilty, the judge is obliged to direct the jury to acquit, and the trial never reaches the point of the defence being invited to present their case (see 20.48 to 20.54 for submissions of no case to answer). If there is a case to answer, then, of course, the prosecution must convince the jury on *all* the evidence (prosecution and defence) that the accused is guilty.

A further consequence of a not guilty plea is that, generally speaking, it requires the prosecu- **17.08** tion to negative any defences which are open to the accused (e.g., defences such as acting under duress, or non-insane automatism, or acting in reasonable self-defence if the charge is one of assault, or provocation if the charge is murder). It is, however, for the defence to raise the issue in the first place by showing (through cross-examination of prosecution witnesses and/or the testimony of defence witnesses) that the defence might be applicable. Once the possibility of the defence applying has been fairly raised, the prosecution must show beyond reasonable doubt that the accused is not entitled to rely on it. There are exceptions to this rule. For example, the accused must prove that he was insane or suffering from diminished responsibility at the time of the offence. It is also for him to prove that he comes within the terms of any exception, proviso, exemption or excuse provided by the statute creating the offence with which he is charged. Whenever the burden of proof is placed on the defence, they discharge it on a balance of probabilities. Details of these matters should be sought in works on evidence.

17.09   If the accused pleads not guilty to some or all of the counts on the indictment, the next step, in most cases, is to empanel a jury to decide whether he is guilty or not (see Chapter 18). However, sometimes the services of a jury are not required because the prosecution do not wish to proceed with the case save on those counts, if any, to which the accused pleaded guilty. There are then two options at the disposal of prosecuting counsel. One is to tell the judge that he proposes to offer no evidence, and the judge may then order that a verdict of not guilty be recorded in respect of each offence denied by the accused, that being equivalent to an acquittal by a jury: Criminal Law Act 1977, s 17. The second option is to ask that the counts to which the accused pleaded not guilty be left on the court file, marked not to be proceeded with without leave of the court or of the Court of Appeal. Offering no evidence is appropriate when the prosecution genuinely think, perhaps as a result of extra evidence discovered since the committal proceedings, that the accused ought not to be convicted. Leaving counts on the file most commonly happens when the accused pleads guilty to some but not all the counts against him. In such cases, the prosecution often elect not to proceed on the 'not guilty' counts simply because proving the case would be a waste of time and money in view of the guilty pleas which have also been entered. As they still believe the accused to be guilty as charged, the prosecution will be unwilling to offer no evidence and see him actually acquitted. Leaving the counts on the file is the obvious solution. It has the additional advantage that, should the Court of Appeal subsequently set aside the convictions on the other counts on the ground, for example, that the accused's pleas of guilty were involuntary (see 17.17 to 17.21), their lordships can give the prosecution leave to proceed with the counts left on the file. Given the possibility (however remote) of counts left on the file being re-activated, defendants occasionally object to that course being adopted, saying that the case should either go ahead or the judge should enter an acquittal. However, it would seem that, in the last resort, the decision is one for the trial judge, and there is no avenue by which an accused can appeal against an order that a count lie on the file: *Central Criminal Court ex parte Raymond* [1986] 1 WLR 710.

17.10   The plea of not guilty should be made by the accused personally, not by his advocate on his behalf. However, a deviation from the correct procedure for taking not guilty pleas will not necessarily give the accused a good ground of appeal against conviction should the jury find him guilty. In *Williams* [1978] QB 373 it was thought, through an administrative muddle, that W had pleaded not guilty. In fact, he had never been arraigned, although he undoubtedly intended to deny the charge. The trial proceeded exactly as if W had been arraigned and pleaded not guilty. W, who was the only person in court who knew that he had not pleaded, failed to raise any objection. The jury convicted, and the Court of Appeal dismissed the appeal, holding that the irregularity in the proceedings had not been sufficiently material to justify quashing the conviction.

17.11   To appreciate the significance of the rule that a not guilty plea puts the whole of the prosecution case in issue, consider a prosecution for assault occasioning actual bodily harm brought against two defendants, A1 and A2. The prosecution must establish (a) that the accused applied unlawful force to the victim, and (b) that this caused the victim some actual bodily harm. A1, when questioned by the police, admitted that he and A2 struck the victim, but claimed that they were acting in reasonable self-defence after the victim had threatened them with a knife. A2 said nothing to the police, but gives instructions to counsel for the defence that his co-accused's account of what happened is correct and a defence statement is submitted on his behalf to that effect. At the trial, both plead not guilty. The prosecution call the victim as a witness, but he has become confused about what occurred, and says that he can no longer be sure that A1 and A2 were involved in the attack on him. He does, however, confirm that he suffered injuries amounting to actual bodily harm, and he denies defence counsel's suggestion in cross-examination that he had been the aggressor. A police officer then gives evidence of A1's response to questioning. Assume that there is no other prosecution evidence, and that the judge decides that no inference under s 34 of the Criminal Justice and Public Order Act 1994 can be drawn from A2's silence in interview. The judge must direct the jury to acquit A2, since no evidence has been called to show that he used force against the victim. He made no admissions to the police, and what A1 said to the police on the subject cannot be used against A2 because of the rule against hearsay evidence. The fact that A2 would not in reality have disputed his involvement in the incident, and was planning to run a quite different type of defence does not release the prosecution from the obligation, imposed upon them by the not guilty plea, to establish a prima facie case against him in respect of every element of the offence. A2's defence statement cannot be used by the prosecution to establish a prima facie case (see 9.16 to 9.23). However, the case against A1 may proceed because the statement he made to the police *is* evidence against him that he struck the victim. Assuming A1 testifies in his own defence that the victim threatened him with a knife, the judge, when summing-up the case to the jury, must tell them only to convict if they are sure on all the evidence that A1 was not acting in reasonable self-defence. This is because of the rule that the prosecution must not only establish the elements of the offence but (subject to certain exceptions) must negative any defence fairly raised by the accused. It may well be that A1, in his testimony, will claim that A2 was also a party to the incident. If A2 were still a defendant, the jury could use A1's evidence as a basis for convicting A2 (what an accused testifies on oath is capable of being evidence against his co-accused whereas what he says to the police out of court is only capable of being evidence against himself).

C   PLEA OF 'GUILTY'

A plea of guilty must be entered by the accused personally. Counsel may not plead guilty on his behalf. If he purports to do so, the plea is a nullity, and will result in the Court of Appeal quashing the conviction entered upon the plea and ordering a retrial: *Ellis* (1973) 57 Cr App R 571. In *Williams* (see 17.10) the Court of Appeal stated that 'no qualification of or deviation from the rule that a plea of guilty must come from him who acknowledges guilt is permissible. A departure from the rule in a criminal trial would necessarily render the whole procedure void and ineffectual'. **17.12**

Following a plea of guilty there is no need to empanel a jury as the accused has convicted himself out of his own mouth. The court may proceed straight to sentence or, if it needs more information about the accused, it may adjourn for the preparation of reports. The procedure before sentence is passed is described in Chapter 22. If the accused pleads guilty on one count and not guilty on other counts, the judge will postpone sentencing him for the offence to which he has pleaded guilty until after the trial of the pleas of 'not guilty'. Should the jury convict him, the judge can sentence him at one time for all the offences. **17.13**

Pleas by co-accused

17.14 If two accused are charged in one indictment, and one pleads guilty and the other not guilty, the usual practice is for the judge to adjourn the case of the one who has pleaded guilty. He is remanded, either in custody or on bail, to come up for sentence at the conclusion of the trial of the accused pleading not guilty. The advantage of this course of action is that, during the trial before the jury, the judge learns from the evidence full details of the case against the accused who has denied the charge, and may also learn much that he would not otherwise have known about the case against the accused who has pleaded guilty. Should the former be convicted by the jury, the judge can sentence both accused at the same time, knowing from the evidence which, if either, of the two played the major role. Whether or not to adjourn is, however, a matter for the discretion of the judge. If he is satisfied that he has sufficient information about the accused who has pleaded guilty, he may sentence him forthwith without waiting for the other to be tried.

17.15 If the prosecution proposes to call the accused who has pleaded guilty to give evidence against his co-accused, there is a strong argument for sentencing the former before he gives his evidence. Not to do so leaves room for suspicion that, in testifying, he may have said what he thought the judge wanted him to say in order to receive a lighter sentence. However, in 1977 the Court of Appeal stated that, even where the accused is going to testify for the prosecution, the judge has a discretion either to sentence him forthwith or to postpone sentence until after the trial of the other accused. Subsequently, their lordships have, in a number of cases, strongly urged judges to adopt the latter course, pointing out that not to do so can lead to embarrassing disparities in sentence should the co-accused ultimately be convicted and receive a much heavier sentence than that earlier passed on his companion in crime (see especially *Weekes* (1980) 74 Cr App R 161). Even so, it is in the end a matter for the individual judge's discretion: *Palmer* (1994) 158 JP 138.

Ambiguous pleas

17.16 Instead of merely saying 'Guilty', an accused sometimes responds to the indictment in an ambiguous way. For example, he may answer to a count for handling by saying—'Guilty to receiving, but I wasn't sure if the goods were stolen'. The plea is ambiguous. He may mean—'I believed them to be stolen, although nobody told me in so many words that such was the case', or he may mean—'I was a bit suspicious about the goods, but didn't really think they were stolen'. In the former case, he should plead guilty, but not in the latter. The judge should try to elucidate the plea by explaining to the accused the elements of the offence charged. Then the indictment can be put to him again. If the plea remains ambiguous a not guilty plea must be entered on his behalf: Criminal Law Act 1967, s 6(1). If the judge proceeds to sentence upon a plea which remains ambiguous, the Court of Appeal will set aside the conviction and sentence and order that the accused be sent back to the Crown Court to plead again to the indictment. Similar principles apply whenever the accused says something when the indictment is put but will not give a direct answer to it (e.g., in a case where the motive for the offence alleged appears to be political he might say—'I do not recognize the authority of the court'). A plea of not guilty should be entered on his behalf, and the case proceeds as if he had actually pleaded not guilty.

Involuntary pleas

Not only must the plea of guilty come from the lips of the accused, but his mind must go **17.17** with his plea. In other words, where a guilty plea is extracted from the accused by pressure and the circumstances are such that he cannot genuinely choose between pleading guilty and pleading not guilty, then that plea is a nullity. If he appeals, the Court of Appeal will quash the conviction and order a retrial. The pressure necessary for a plea of guilty to be rendered a nullity may come either from the judge or from counsel. An example of the former is provided by *Barnes* (1970) 55 Cr App R 100. B pleaded not guilty, but half way through the prosecution case the judge, having sent the jury to their room, said in effect that B was plainly guilty and was wasting the court's time. Even so, B refused to change his plea to guilty, but, had he done so, the plea would have been a nullity. Allowing the appeal on other grounds, the Court of Appeal stated that the judge's conduct was 'wholly improper'.

A more subtle way in which the judge might pressurize the accused is illustrated by *Turner* **17.18** [1970] 2 QB 321. T pleaded not guilty to a charge of theft. After some of the prosecution witnesses had given their evidence, there was a lengthy adjournment during which T discussed the conduct of the case with his counsel and solicitor. At one stage counsel went to see the judge in his private room. On his return, counsel warned T that if he persisted in a not guilty plea and was found guilty there was a 'very real possibility' that he would receive a sentence of imprisonment, but that if he pleaded guilty he would be dealt with by a fine or other non-custodial sentence. Counsel was, in fact, expressing his personal opinion of the case, but inevitably it appeared to T that he was passing on what the judge had said. T changed his plea to guilty. The Court of Appeal (Lord Parker CJ presiding) quashed his conviction and ordered a retrial. Once T felt that the advice his counsel gave him as to sentence was 'an intimation emanating from the judge, it is really idle in the opinion of this court to think that he really had a free choice in the matter' of his plea.

Lord Parker's judgment in *Turner* clearly governs what the judge may say about sentence in open **17.19** court, in the hearing of the accused. It also governs what he may say privately to defence counsel on the matter, for one of the subsidiary points made in the case is that if there is a private discussion between the judge and counsel about sentence the latter should tell his client both that he has seen the judge and what the judge said (see 20.13 for further discussion).

The second source of pressure capable of rendering a plea of guilty a nullity is that which may **17.20** be exerted by the accused's own counsel. Advice by defence counsel along the lines that 'the prosecution case is so strong that your only possible course of action is to plead guilty whether you committed the offence charged or not' would cause any plea of guilty to be a nullity. The principles governing the advice that counsel should give the accused about his plea were dealt with comprehensively in *Goodyear* [2005] 3 All ER 117. It is counsel's duty to give the best advice he can, if need be in 'strong terms'. That advice may include his view on the strength of the prosecution case and the difficulties thrown up by the nature of the defence (e.g., he might warn the accused that a defence involving attacks on the characters of the prosecution witnesses would lead to his being cross-examined about his previous convictions if he chose to give evidence). The accused should also be told, if he does not know already, that a conviction upon a plea of guilty is likely to attract a more lenient sentence than a conviction following a not guilty plea. Counsel can also indicate his personal view of the sentence the judge is likely to pass. The mischief in *Turner* arose not from the nature of counsel's advice on sentence, but from the implication that the 'advice' was a repetition of what the judge had said. Finally, it must be emphasized to the accused that the choice of plea is one for him, not counsel, to make, and that he should only plead guilty if he is indeed guilty. The mere fact that the accused pleads guilty reluctantly after receiving strong advice from counsel does not make the plea a nullity. It is only a nullity if, when he makes it, the accused has lost the power to make a voluntary and deliberate choice: *Peace* [1976] Crim LR 119.

17.21 Inability to make a genuine choice may very occasionally arise from something for which only the accused himself is to blame. Even then the Court of Appeal has been willing to treat his plea as a nullity. The point is illustrated by *Swain* [1986] Crim LR 480, where S changed his plea to guilty half way through the prosecution case. He gave no coherent reason to counsel, merely saying—'Have you looked up at the sky lately? Have you seen the stars?' After he had been sentenced, it emerged through his mother that he had obtained drugs in prison, and had been under the influence of LSD at the relevant time. Psychiatric evidence was called before the Court of Appeal that LSD can put the user into a state akin to schizophrenia, where he drifts in and out of a delusional world and makes irrational decisions. That seemed to be the explanation for the change of plea, and the Court was therefore obliged to hold it a nullity and quash the conviction.

D PLEA OF 'GUILTY' TO A LESSER OFFENCE

17.22 Halfway between a plea of guilty and not guilty is the plea of guilty to a lesser offence. It is a corollary of the option given to juries in certain cases by s 6 of the Criminal Law Act 1967 to return a verdict of 'not guilty as charged but guilty of some other (lesser) offence' (see 21.22 to 21.33 for details). Familiar examples are that on a count for murder the jury can convict of manslaughter; on a count for burglary contrary to s 9(1)(b) of the Theft Act they can convict of theft, and on a count for wounding with intent contrary to the Offences Against the Person Act 1861, s 18 they can convict of unlawful wounding contrary to s 20. Whenever a count is put to the accused on which the jury could find him guilty of a lesser offence, he may offer a plea of not guilty as charged but guilty of the lesser offence: Criminal Law Act 1967, s 6(1)(b). If the plea is accepted, he stands acquitted of the offence charged, and the court proceeds to sentence him for the lesser matter: s 6(5).

17.23 The prosecution are not, of course, obliged to accept a proffered plea of guilty of a lesser offence. The Code for Crown Prosecutors (para 9.1) stipulates that the defendant's plea to a lesser charge should be accepted only if the court will be able to pass a sentence that matches the seriousness of the offence. Crown prosecutors are told that they must not accept a guilty plea just because it is convenient.

17.24 If the prosecutor is not prepared to accept the defendant's plea of guilty of a lesser offence, he can insist on the trial proceeding. The court then enters a straightforward not guilty plea on behalf of the accused and a jury is empanelled. The evidence is then called in the normal way. At the end of the case, the jury can either convict as charged, convict of the lesser offence, or even simply acquit. Even if the prosecution are willing to accept a plea of guilty to a lesser offence, the judge may indicate that it is not an appropriate course to adopt: *Soanes* [1948] 1 All ER 289. That case in fact suggests that the judge's consent to the plea is essential as a matter of law but, in the light of analogous later cases, the true position appears to be that the final decision is for the prosecution, although in practice they would rarely if ever act against the judge's expressed wishes (see 17.22 to 17.28). Strictly speaking, there should be something in the evidence on the committal statements or in the general circumstances of the case to suggest that the accused may not be guilty as charged—otherwise the trial ought to proceed. In practice, however, the savings in time and money to be derived from not having to hold a jury trial may make it fairly easy to persuade both prosecution and judge that a plea of guilty to a lesser offence is appropriate.

An odd consequence of rejecting a plea of guilty to a lesser offence is illustrated by *Hazeltine* **17.25** [1967] 2 QB 857. H pleaded not guilty to wounding with intent to cause grievous bodily harm but guilty of unlawful wounding. The plea was not accepted. The trial proceeded, and the jury simply acquitted H. They did not, as they were entitled to, find him not guilty as charged but guilty of unlawful wounding. The judge nevertheless proceeded to sentence H for that offence, relying on the fact that he had originally pleaded guilty to it. The Court of Appeal quashed the sentence. When the court entered on H's behalf a plea of not guilty to wounding with intent, his plea to unlawful wounding was by implication withdrawn and could not subsequently be reinstated by the judge. Nor could the prosecution prefer a fresh charge for unlawful wounding as the jury's acquittal for wounding with intent amounted impliedly to an acquittal for unlawful wounding also, and any proceedings would have been countered by the plea of autrefois acquit (see 17.43 to 17.45). However, the Court of Appeal did suggest a means by which a repetition of what happened in *Hazeltine* can be avoided. Upon realizing that the defence are putting forward a version of events which, if accepted, would result in a complete acquittal, prosecuting counsel should call evidence before the jury that the accused originally pleaded guilty to the lesser offence. In the absence of a convincing explanation of why, if he is completely innocent, he did not simply plead not guilty, the jury will almost certainly convict him at least of the lesser offence. But, should the prosecution not have called evidence of the original plea, the judge must not tell the jury about it in his summing-up. Nor can he direct the jury to convict of the lesser offence, as opposed to telling them that they have the option of doing so: *Lee* [1985] Crim LR 798; *Notman* [1994] Crim LR 518.

A variation on the theme of pleading guilty to a lesser offence in respect of a single count **17.26** arises when there are two counts on the indictment, one more serious than the other, and the prosecution case is such that they do not seek a conviction on both counts (i.e., the counts are in the alternative). An example is an indictment containing counts against the accused for robbery and for handling all or some of the proceeds of the robbery. If he pleads guilty to handling and not guilty to robbery, but the prosecution still want to try to prove the robbery against him, there is no need for the court to withdraw his plea of guilty to handling as that is a plea entered on a quite separate count. The trial proceeds on the robbery count, and if the accused is acquitted he can then be sentenced for handling. If he is convicted of robbery, he is sentenced for that, but not for handling. Although his plea of guilty to handling remains on the court file, he does not stand convicted of handling as, technically speaking, a guilty plea does not amount to a conviction until sentence has been passed (see *Cole* [1965] 2 QB 388).

E   CHANGE OF PLEA

17.27   The possibility of an accused changing his plea from not guilty to guilty has already been mentioned at 17.17 to 17.21 (see the discussion of *Barnes* and *Turner*). This may be done at any stage of the trial. The defence advocate asks for the indictment to be put again to his client, and, upon that being done, the accused pleads guilty. Like any other plea of guilty, it must come from the accused personally, not from his advocate on his behalf. In addition, the jury, empanelled as a result of the original not guilty plea, must return a formal verdict of guilty. If they fail to do so, the change of plea is ineffective, and the trial rendered a nullity: *Heyes* [1951] 1 KB 29. The judge in sentencing ought to give the accused some credit for having changed his plea, although it should not be as much as if he had admitted his guilt from the outset.

17.28   A change of plea from guilty to not guilty is also possible, but is subject to the judge giving his consent. The granting of consent is a matter of discretion, and is not automatically forthcoming even where the accused was unrepresented when he originally pleaded. Relevant considerations are whether he apparently understood the nature of the charge and/or genuinely intended to admit his guilt of it. If he seems merely to have changed his mind about plea out of tactical considerations (e.g., the judge's attitude when the prosecution summarized the facts makes him fear a heavier sentence than he first anticipated), the judge is fully entitled to hold him to his original admission (see, for example, *McNally* [1954] 1 WLR 933). Applications to withdraw a guilty plea may be made at any stage before sentence is passed: *S (an infant) v Recorder of Manchester* [1971] AC 481. They are often prompted by the accused using an adjournment between his plea an the date fixed for sentence to obtain legal advice for the first time, but, as already mentioned, his being unrepresented when he pleaded does not guarantee that the application will succeed. The procedure for a change from a plea of guilty is set out in CrimPR, r 39.3. The defence must apply as soon as practicable after becoming aware of the grounds for a change. The application should be served on the court and the prosecutor in writing, setting out:

(a)   the reasons why it would be unjust for the guilty plea to remain unchanged;
(b)   any evidence which the accused intends to call;
(c)   the identify of any proposed witness; and
(d)   whether legal professional privilege is waived, specifying any material name and date.

The final point is relevant where the accused is basing his change of plea upon legal advice received. Any such advice is privileged, and it will be his choice as to whether he reveals the advice in question, depending no doubt on whether such information assists his argument for a change of plea, without undermining his case generally.

F   PLEA BARGAINING

17.29   *Turner* [1970] 2 QB 321 was partly concerned with what Lord Parker described as the 'vexed question' of plea bargaining. The phrase is an imprecise one which may be used in at least four different senses. It can mean an agreement between the judge and the accused that if he pleads guilty to some or all of the offences charged against him the sentence will or will not take a certain form. A bargain in this sense can raise the issue of whether pressure has been applied to the defendant (see 17.17). Second, plea bargaining can mean an undertaking by the prosecution that if the accused will admit to certain charges they will refrain from putting more serious charges into the indictment or will ask the judge to impose a relatively light sentence. This form of bargaining is not possible under the English system as the indictment is drawn up quite independently of the defence, and, at the sentencing stage, the prosecution's function is merely to tell the judge the facts, not to suggest an appropriate sentence. Thirdly, plea bargaining may refer to the prosecution agreeing with the defence that if the accused pleads guilty to a lesser offence they will accept the plea (see 17.22 to 17.26), and, lastly, it may refer to the prosecution agreeing not to proceed on one or more counts in the indictment against the accused if he will plead guilty to the remainder.

Plea bargaining in the third and fourth senses described above is a frequent occurrence, **17.30** approved by the courts. It is not usually in the public interest to spend time and money proving the accused guilty precisely as charged if he is prepared to admit the bulk of the case against him, either by pleading guilty to a lesser offence or by pleading guilty to some but not all the counts. The bargain is usually struck by prosecuting and defence counsel outside court before the commencement of the trial. The question arises whether the judge must approve what is proposed. In *Coward* (1980) 70 Cr App R 70, Lawton LJ put the onus solely on prosecuting counsel, saying that it was for him to make up his mind what pleas to accept. No doubt, as a matter of courtesy, he will explain his decision to the judge and, should the latter not approve, he may say so in open court. In the light of the judge's comments counsel might well change his original decision. But, in the last resort, the judge cannot force the prosecution to proceed. In *Broad* (1979) 68 Cr App R 28, on the other hand, the prosecution had originally been prepared to offer no evidence against B if her co-accused pleaded guilty but, upon seeking the judge's views and discovering that he disapproved, decided to proceed. B was convicted. Dismissing her appeal, the Court of Appeal held that the judge was not a 'rubber stamp' to sanction whatever counsel thought appropriate. The Report of the Farquharson Committee (see 20.05 to 20.07 and the Trinity 1986 edition of *Counsel* magazine) suggested that if prosecuting counsel expressly asks for the judge's approval before agreeing to a defence proposal, he is bound by the judge's decision whatever it may be (*Broad* above). But, where counsel chooses to act without seeking prior approval, his only obligation is to explain to the judge the reasoning behind his decision. If the judge disapproves, counsel should reconsider his position and even consult the CPS about the matter. In the final analysis, however, counsel's views must prevail. The report of the Farquharson Committee was referred to with approval in *Grafton* [1993] QB 101, which focused on a disagreement between judge and prosecuting counsel about whether the prosecution could discontinue its case once the trial had commenced (see 20.86 to 20.88 for further discussion of this question).

Sometimes the defendant is willing to plead guilty on the basis of a particular version of the **17.31** facts. The defence and the prosecution may therefore try to reach agreement on the factual basis upon which a plea of guilty would be accepted, e.g., the prosecution might be prepared to accept that the defendant assaulted the victim recklessly (rather than intentionally). Such an agreement is likely to have an impact on the sentencing process. The issues arose in *Beswick* [1996] 1 Cr App R (S) 343, and are dealt with at 22.19.

17.32 In *Goodyear* [2005] 3 All ER 117, the Court of Appeal gave comprehensive guidance on judicial indications of sentence. It was made clear that it was for the defendant to seek such an indication (although the judge could remind the defence advocate that he was entitled to seek an indication). The judge could then decide whether to give one or not, or postpone doing so, and was not obliged to give reasons. Once an indication was given, it was binding both on the judge who gave it and also upon any other judge who became responsible for the case. However, if the defendant did not plead guilty after being given a reasonable opportunity to consider his position, the indication would cease to have effect, i.e., the judge would not be bound by the indication in the event of a not guilty plea, or even a guilty plea after a delay for some reason. As far as the defence advocate was concerned, he should not seek an indication without signed and written authority from his client. The defence advocate was personally responsible for ensuring that his client knows that:

(a) he should not plead guilty unless he is guilty;

(b) any sentence indication by the judge is subject to the possibility of a reference by the Attorney-General of an unduly lenient sentence to the Court of Appeal (see 26.80 to 26.87);

(c) any indication given by the judge reflects the situation at the time, and if a guilty plea is not tendered in the light of that indication, the indication ceases to have any effect;

(d) any indication given refers only to the matters about which it has been sought.

The judge should never be asked to indicate levels of sentence which he may have in mind depending on possible different pleas. As to the process, any sentence indication would normally be sought at the plea and case management hearing (PCMH: see 16.07). It should only be sought where the prosecution and the defence had agreed upon the factual basis of the plea. The hearing should normally take place in open court, with a full recording of the entire proceedings, and both sides represented, in the defendant's presence. An opening by the Crown, or a plea in mitigation by the defence was not envisaged. There would normally be reporting restrictions, which would be lifted if the defendant pleaded guilty. The procedure was not practicable for extension to the magistrates' court.

In *Kulah* [2007] EWCA Crim 1701, the Court of Appeal dealt with the situation where the judge is asked for an indication in respect of a case where the defendant may fall foul of the 'dangerous offender' provisions (see 24.34 to 24.42). The problem is that an indication might be given before the judge became aware that the defendant was likely to be shown to be a dangerous offender. Their lordships reminded judges that it was a matter of discretion whether to give an indication, and they had no obligation to do so. If any indication was given where the offence was one specified within Schedule 15 to the CJA 2003, and an assessment of future risk was still to be made, then the indication would be subject to that assessment. Any sentence mandated by the dangerous offender provisions (an indeterminate or extended sentence) would be imposed if the offender was assessed as dangerous. In that event, the indication would relate to the notional determinate term which would be used in calculating the minimum period which the offender would have to serve. If the offender was not assessed as dangerous, the indication would operate in the normal way.

In *Attorney-General's Reference (No 80 of 2005)* [2005] All ER (D) 214 (Nov), the Court of Appeal was at pains to emphasize that the purpose of the decision in *Goodyear* was not to encourage a return to the practice of counsel seeing the judge about sentence privately in his room. A hearing involving indication of sentence should normally occur in open court (one exception being where the defendant was unaware that he was terminally ill).

G   THE ACCUSED WHO WILL NOT OR CANNOT PLEAD

So far it has been assumed that when the accused is arraigned he says something rational in **17.33** answer to the charges. What he says may fall short of a proper plea of guilty or not guilty, but, at least, his response shows that he has heard and understood the clerk's words to him. However, the accused may be unwilling to reply when the indictment is put, or he may be incapable of replying in a sensible way. The first possibility raises the question of 'mute of malice', the second the question of unfitness to plead.

Muteness

If the accused remains silent, this may be by choice or because he is incapable of responding **17.34** to the arraignment. In the former case, he is said to be 'mute of malice'. A plea of not guilty is entered on behalf of an accused who is mute of malice, and the case then proceeds as if he had himself pleaded not guilty: Criminal Law Act 1967, s 6(1)(c).

If the accused is not mute of malice, he is said to be 'mute by visitation of God'. When the jury **17.35** return a verdict of mute by visitation of God, they are also asked to specify the cause of the muteness. If it arises from the accused being unable to speak, or deaf so that he cannot hear what the clerk says to him, the case is adjourned with a view to finding a way of communicating with him (e.g., through an expert in sign language). If the cause of the muteness seems to be that the accused suffers from mental problems, and so cannot reply when the indictment is put, the jury may be further asked to consider whether he is unfit to plead (see 17.36).

Unfitness to plead

An accused is unfit to plead or stand his trial if he cannot comprehend the course of the **17.36** proceedings so as to make a proper defence to the indictment. Whether he can understand so as to answer when arraigned is obviously one relevant factor. Other relevant factors are whether he is capable of challenging a juror to whom he might wish to object (see Chapter 18), whether he can instruct his legal representatives, and whether he would be able to follow the evidence. An accused is not unfit to plead merely because he is highly abnormal (*Berry* (1977) 66 Cr App R 157), or because he is likely to act against his own best interests (*Robertson* [1968] 1 WLR 1767), or even because he is suffering from amnesia so as not to be able to recall the alleged offence or the circumstances surrounding it: *Podola* [1960] 1 QB 325. Section 4(2) of the Criminal Procedure (Insanity) Act 1964 permits the court to postpone consideration of unfitness until any time up to the opening of the defence case. The court must be of the opinion that postponement is 'expedient' and 'in the interests of the accused'.

Where the accused may be unfit to plead, either the prosecution or the defence should, **17.37** before the arraignment, bring the matter to the judge's attention. Although one would normally expect the defence to do this, the prosecution might feel it their duty to take the initiative if, for instance, the accused is unrepresented but is clearly in no fit state to understand the proceedings. The decision whether the accused is unfit to plead was formerly decided by a jury, but the Domestic Violence, Crime and Victims Act 2004 changed the position, so that it is now decided by a judge. The burden and standard of proof depends upon who raised the issue. If it was the prosecution, they must prove unfitness beyond reasonable doubt; if it was the defence, they must do so on a balance of probabilities (see *Robertson* and *Podola* respectively).

17.38 Where the judge has determined that the accused is unfit to plead, s 4A of the Criminal Procedure (Insanity) Act 1964 applies. This provision lays down that it must then be determined by a jury whether the accused 'did the act or made the omission charged against him as the offence' (s 4A(2)). If they are satisfied that he did, they must find accordingly (s 4A(3)). If they are not satisfied, they must acquit.

17.39 Section 4(6) of the 1964 Act provides that the court may not determine the question of fitness to plead except on the evidence (written or oral) of two or more registered medical practitioners, at least one of whom must have been approved by the Secretary of State as having special experience in the diagnosis or treatment of mental disorder.

17.40 In *M* [2002] Crim LR 57, the Court of Appeal considered the above procedures in the light of the Human Rights Act 1998, and particularly in the context of Art 6 of the European Convention on Human Rights (see 28.19). The court held that the criminal charge provisions of Art 6 do not apply to proceedings under ss 4 and 4A of the 1964 Act, since those proceedings cannot result in a conviction. In any event, they concluded that the procedure under ss 4 and 4A of the 1964 Act constituted a fair procedure, providing an opportunity for investigation of the facts on behalf of a disabled person, so far as possible. It fairly balanced the public interest and the interest of the person alleged to have committed the act. Therefore, if Art 6 had applied to the procedure under the 1964 Act, it would not have been infringed. In addition, their lordships stated that the defence was able to make an application to stay proceedings for abuse of process when it appeared necessary, and this could be either before arraignment or before any question of disability fell to be determined. This decision was endorsed by the House of Lords in *M* [2003] 1 All ER 497. Any orders made following a finding that the accused did the act in question were said not to be punitive, but for his benefit, and that of the public.

17.41 Under s 5 of the 1964 Act (as amended in 1991), if the accused is found unfit to plead, and the jury determines that he did the act or made the omission as charged, then the court may make:

(a) an admission order to a hospital approved by the Secretary of State;
(b) a guardianship order under the Mental Health Act 1983;
(c) a supervision and treatment order; or
(d) an order for the accused's absolute discharge.

See 25.115 to 25.124 for further details.

H   DOUBLE JEOPARDY

17.42 It is a vital constitutional principle that no one should be prosecuted twice to acquittal or conviction for the same offence. The principle is often referred to as the 'rule against double jeopardy'. Where the accused contends that he has, on a previous occasion, been acquitted or convicted of an offence alleged in a count in the indictment, he can seek the protection of the rule against double jeopardy by raising a plea of 'autrefois acquit' or 'autrefois convict'. Those pleas are dealt with at 17.43 to 17.50. Paragraphs 17.51 to 17.53 deal with the question of issue estoppel, which has been distinguished from the situation where a plea of autrefois is available. Paragraphs 17.54 to 17.61 deal with two major inroads made on the rule against double jeopardy in recent legislation—the provision in the CPIA 1996 for retrial where there is a 'tainted acquittal', and the procedure under the CJA 2003 for retrial of serious offences where new evidence emerges.

Pleas of 'autrefois acquit' and 'autrefois convict'

If the accused contends that he has, on a previous occasion, been acquitted or convicted of **17.43** the offence in question, he can plead 'autrefois acquit' or 'autrefois convict', depending on the outcome of the previous trial. If one or other of the pleas is raised successfully it is a bar to all further proceedings on the count concerned. These pleas, together with the plea of pardon (see 17.62), are known as special pleas in bar. Despite the importance of the pleas being available to prevent harassment of the individual by repeated prosecutions for one crime, it is rare in practice for the defence to be forced to have recourse to them. This is because court records are available to establish clearly whether a person has previously been prosecuted for an offence, and if so, the result of that prosecution. If it ended in his being convicted or acquitted—as opposed, for example, to the jury being unable to agree on a verdict—he would not be prosecuted again for the same offence. However, although infrequently pleaded autrefois acquit and convict have led to a disproportionately large body of case law as the appellate courts have been called upon to define the precise limits of the pleas.

The plea is made in writing signed by the defence advocate on behalf of the accused. The form **17.44** of words suggested is—'John Smith says that the Queen ought not further to prosecute the indictment against him because he has been lawfully acquitted/convicted of the offence charged therein.' However, should the accused be unrepresented, he is allowed to make the plea orally. The correct time for doing so is before arraignment but the court has a discretion to entertain the plea at any stage during the trial. Assuming the prosecution do not accept the defence contention, they join issue through a written 'replication' signed by an appropriate officer of the Crown Court. It simply says— 'David Brown joins issue on behalf of the Queen.'

Until 1988, whether autrefois did or did not apply had to be decided by a jury sworn in for the **17.45** purpose. The Criminal Justice Act 1988 provided that— 'Where an accused pleads autrefois acquit or autrefois convict it shall be for the judge, *without the presence of a jury* to decide the issue.' Should the plea fail, the indictment is put in the normal way, the accused's right to plead not guilty being in no way affected: Criminal Law Act 1967, s 6(1)(a).

Applicability of the pleas

The following propositions are based mainly upon the speech of Lord Morris of Borth-y-Gest **17.46** in *Connelly v DPP* [1964] AC 1254 at pp. 1305–6. They must be read subject to the decision in *Beedie* [1997] 2 Cr App R 167 (see below), and to the provisions of the Criminal Procedure and Investigations Act 1996, and the CJA 2003 (see 17.54 to 17.61).

(a) A man cannot be tried for a crime in respect of which he has previously been acquitted or convicted. This is the straightforward application of autrefois acquit and convict. If the accused is charged with an offence which is identical in law and on the facts to one of which he has already been acquitted or convicted, then autrefois will bar any further proceedings on that charge.

(b)   A man cannot be tried for a crime in respect of which he could on some previous indict-ment have been convicted by way of a verdict of guilty of a lesser offence (see 21.22 to 21.33). This extension of (a) is necessary because, where jurors are entitled to convict of a lesser offence but choose simply to acquit, they decide by implication that the accused was not guilty both of the offence charged and the lesser matter. Accordingly, autrefois acquit bars proceedings for both offences. Thus, an acquittal on a count for murdering X entitles the accused to raise autrefois if he is subsequently indicted for the manslaughter of X.

(c)   A man cannot be tried for a crime proof of which would necessarily, as a matter of law, entail proof of another crime of which he has already been acquitted (per Lord Hodson in *Connelly* at p. 1332). Therefore, to reverse the example given in proposition (b) above, an accused who is charged with X's murder, having previously been acquitted of his manslaughter, is entitled to rely on autrefois acquit because, having regard to the legal definitions of murder and manslaughter, proof of the latter is a necessary step towards proving the former.

(d)   A man cannot be tried for a crime which is in effect the same or substantially the same as one of which he has previously been acquitted or convicted (or could have been convict-ed through a verdict of guilty of a lesser offence). Thus, in *King* [1897] 1 QB 214, K, who had previously been convicted of obtaining credit for goods by false pretences, was held to be entitled to rely on autrefois convict when subsequently indicted for larceny of the same goods. But, the cases are markedly inconsistent as to the degree of similarity necessary before it can be said that a later charge is 'substantially' the same as an earlier offence. *King* may, for example, be contrasted with *Kendrick and Smith* (1931) 23 Cr App R 1 where a con-viction for threatening to publish photographic negatives with intent to extort money did not bar a subsequent prosecution for sending letters demanding money with menaces, both prosecutions arising out of the same facts. Lord Devlin in *Connelly* suggested a means of avoiding elaborate attempts to reconcile the cases on this aspect of autrefois. He said that the pleas proper should be restricted to the circumstances set out in (a)–(c) above, but, in other analogous cases, the trial judge should use his discretionary power to halt the prosecution if letting it continue would be unfair or oppressive to the accused in the light of previous proceedings against him. So, in *Moxon-Tritsch* [1988] Crim LR 46, where M-T was privately prosecuted for causing the death of her passengers by reckless driving after the driving in question had earlier resulted in her being fined and disqualified for careless driving, the trial judge held that the proceedings were oppressive and the count should lie on the file marked not to be proceeded with.

(e)   A man may not be successively prosecuted for a number of offences arising out of the same criminal conduct where the later prosecutions are for aggravated forms of an offence of which he was earlier acquitted or convicted—e.g., if he has already been con-victed or acquitted of assault occasioning actual bodily harm he cannot, on the same facts, be indicted for unlawful wounding or causing grievous bodily harm (see *Elrington* (1861) 1 B & S 688). However, one important qualification to the principle should be noted, namely that a conviction for an offence of violence does not protect the offend-er from a prosecution for homicide should the victim later die of his injuries: *Thomas* (1949) 33 Cr App R 200.

(f)   A plea of autrefois may fail even though the prosecution allege the same facts and call the same evidence as they did at an earlier trial resulting in the accused's acquittal or conviction. The point is well illustrated by the facts of *Connelly*. C and three others took part in an office robbery, during the course of which a person was killed. They were charged with murder and convicted, but C's conviction was quashed because of errors in the conduct of the trial. He was therefore treated as if he had been acquitted of murder (see below). In line with the practice then prevailing, the murder indictment had not included any counts for other offences, so upon the murder conviction being quashed the prosecution sought to proceed against C on an indictment for robbery. Following an unsuccessful plea of autrefois acquit, they called the evidence which they had already used at the murder trial, and C was again convicted. The House of Lords held that the plea of autrefois had rightly been rejected. C could not bring himself within any of the four propositions (a) to (d) above. The crimes of murder and robbery were obviously not identical (proposition (a)), nor, in view of their totally different legal characteristics, could they be regarded as substantially the same (proposition (d)). On a count for murder, a jury are not entitled to bring in a verdict of guilty of robbery (proposition (b)), and, as a matter of *law*, the prosecution did not have to prove murder in order to prove robbery (proposition (c)).

(g)   The principles of autrefois acquit and convict apply equally in summary trials, although there is no special form of plea or procedure as there is at trials on indictment—the defence raise the issue on a simple not guilty plea.

In *Beedie* [1997] 2 Cr App R 167, however, the Court of Appeal was unable to accept that Lord **17.47** Morris's speech correctly represented the reasoning of the majority in the House of Lords. B was the landlord of a woman who died of carbon monoxide poisoning caused by the use of a defective gas fire at her bedsit. He was prosecuted under the Health and Safety at Work Act 1974 by the Health and Safety Executive, and was fined. He was subsequently prosecuted by the CPS for manslaughter on substantially the same facts. Rose LJ said that the principle of autrefois was confined to the situation where the second indictment charges the same offence as the first, and therefore did not operate to prevent B's prosecution for manslaughter. Judicial discretion should, however, be exercised to order a stay on the indictment in appropriate circumstances. Such a stay should have been ordered in circumstances such as those in *Beedie*. B's appeal succeeded, therefore. Although the trial judge had correctly analysed the case as falling outside the autrefois principle, he had failed properly to consider the discretion which he had to stay proceedings where the second offence arises out of substantially the same facts as the first. That discretion should be exercised in favour of the accused unless the prosecution discharges the onus of showing that there are special circumstances for not doing so. In this case, there were no special circumstances and the indictment should have been stayed.

What constitutes a conviction or an acquittal?

Many of the cases on autrefois are about what amounts to an acquittal or conviction for **17.48** purposes of the pleas. No distinction is drawn between acquittals or convictions on indictment and those following summary trial. However, for the pleas to apply, the court trying the case must have been acting within its jurisdiction (see *West* [1964] 1 QB 15 where a purported acquittal by magistrates on a charge which they were not entitled to try did not prevent their subsequently committing W for trial or his being convicted at quarter sessions). Discharge of the accused by the examining justices after committal proceedings is not an acquittal (*Manchester City Stipendiary Magistrate ex parte Snelson* [1977] 1 WLR 911), nor is the quashing of an indictment following a motion to quash. Where, however, the Court of Appeal quashes an accused's conviction, the successful appellant is treated as if he had been acquitted by the jury that tried him. Hence, he cannot be prosecuted again for the same offence unless the Court of Appeal has exercised its discretionary power to order a retrial (see s 7 of the Criminal Appeal Act 1968 as amended and 26.35 to 26.38).

17.49 In summary trial in the magistrates' court, there is an important distinction between the withdrawal of a charge by the prosecution and its dismissal by the justices. Where the summons is withdrawn without the justices considering the merits, there is no acquittal such as to found autrefois. On the other hand, if the accused pleads not guilty and the prosecution formally offer no evidence, so that the justices dismiss the summons, the accused is acquitted and there can be no further proceedings (see *Grays Justices ex parte Low* [1990] 1 QB 54 and 10.26 to 10.31). But no plea of autrefois can be founded on proceedings where the information is so faulty that the accused could never have been in jeopardy upon it (*DPP v Porthouse* (1988) 89 Cr App R 21).

17.50 To sustain a plea of autrefois convict, it is not enough that the court before which the defendant was first charged should have accepted his plea of guilty, or returned a verdict of guilty. It is necessary also that the court should have sentenced him, since the purpose of the doctrine is to avoid double punishment (*Richards v The Queen* [1993] AC 217). A finding of 'guilt' in disciplinary proceedings followed by the imposition of a penalty is not a conviction (*Hogan and Tompkins* [1960] 2 QB 513, where prison escapees, who had been punished for the escape by the visiting committee of magistrates under the Prison Rules, could not rely on autrefois convict at a subsequent trial for the offence of escaping by force). Similarly, if a court takes another offence into consideration when sentencing an offender for an offence of which he has been convicted, there is no conviction in respect of the offence taken into consideration: *Nicholson* (1947) 32 Cr App R 98 and see 22.60 to 22.65. Acquittals or convictions before foreign courts or by courts martial are in general sufficient grounds for autrefois (see, for example, *Aughet* (1919) 13 Cr App R 101). Where, however, an accused has been convicted and sentenced in his absence by a foreign court, but there is no realistic possibility of his ever returning to the country concerned to serve his sentence, autrefois convict will not apply if he is prosecuted for the same matter in England (*Thomas* [1985] QB 604).

Issue estoppel

17.51 Prior to 1976, it was from time to time suggested that, even if autrefois acquit did not apply, the prosecution could be estopped from re-opening a particular issue of fact which had clearly been decided in favour of the accused at an earlier trial ending in his acquittal. Opportunities to test the validity of this suggestion were rare, for nearly all criminal trials involve more than one issue, and if the jury simply find the accused not guilty it is impossible to know on what issue the prosecution failed to satisfy them. At last, however, a case arose in which the defence could plausibly point to an issue estoppel. The case was *DPP v Humphrys* [1977] AC 1. H was acquitted of driving while disqualified on a day in 1972. He admitted that he was disqualified on the relevant day, but gave evidence that he had not driven either on that day or at all in 1972. Thus, the only possible reason for the acquittal was that the jury were not satisfied that H had been driving on the relevant day. H was then prosecuted for perjury. To prove that his evidence at the driving while disqualified trial had been false, the prosecution again called the evidence they had used at that trial indicating that H had driven on the relevant day, and there was also evidence from other witnesses, not available for the first trial, that H had driven on other occasions in 1972. H was convicted and the House of Lords rejected his appeal. They held that the prosecution were entitled to re-open the issue of whether H drove on the relevant day, because the doctrine of issue estoppel has no place in criminal proceedings. Neither the prosecution nor the defence can rely on it. The decision in *Humphrys* might seem a dangerous one, allowing the prosecution in effect to challenge an acquittal by the device of prosecuting the acquitted person for perjury. However, the majority of the House of Lords emphasized that a trial judge has a discretion to prevent a prosecution continuing if it would be an abuse of the process of the court, and implied that the prosecution in *Humphrys* was only saved from being an abuse of process by the fact that the evidence of perjury related not just to H's evidence that he had not driven on the day of the driving while disqualified charge, but also to his evidence that he had not driven at all during 1972.

As stated above, the prosecution are no more able to rely on an issue estoppel than are the defence. This means that if the accused pleads not guilty to Offence A, having previously been convicted of Offence B, the prosecution must prove *all* the elements of Offence A even if they had to prove some of those elements to secure the conviction for Offence B. Lawson J's ruling at first instance in *Hogan* [1974] QB 398—that if, at a trial for murder, the prosecution can show that the accused has already been convicted on the same facts of causing grievous bodily harm with intent to the victim of the alleged murder, then the defence are estopped from denying all elements of the prosecution case apart from the causal link between the harm caused and the death of the victim—was held by the House of Lords in *Humphrys* to be incorrect. **17.52**

It appears that, notwithstanding the general rule outlined above, issue estoppel *does* have relevance in an application for habeas corpus (*Governor of Brixton Prison ex parte Osman* [1991] 1 WLR 281). **17.53**

Tainted acquittals

Sections 54 to 57 of the Criminal Procedure and Investigations Act 1996, which relate to 'tainted acquittals', constitute a major exception to the availability of autrefois acquit. They enable the prosecution of an accused for a second time for a crime of which he has already been acquitted at trial, if the following conditions are met: **17.54**

(a) a defendant has been acquitted of an offence (s 54(1)(a)); and

(b) a person has been convicted of an administration of justice offence involving interference with or intimidation of a juror or a witness or potential witness (s 54(1)(b)); and

(c) the court convicting of the administration of justice offence certifies that there is a real possibility that, but for the interference or intimidation, the acquitted person would not have been acquitted, and that it would not be contrary to the interests of justice to proceed against the acquitted person (s 54(2) and (5)).

An application may then be made to the High Court for an order quashing the acquittal. The High Court must make the order if the four conditions set out in s 55 are satisfied. These are that it appears to the High Court:

(i)   likely that, but for the interference or intimidation, the acquitted person would not have been acquitted;
(ii) that it is not contrary to the interests of justice to take proceedings against the acquitted person for the offence of which he was acquitted, e.g., because of the lapse of time;
(iii) that the acquitted person has been given a reasonable opportunity to make written representations to the High Court; and
(iv) that the conviction for the administration of justice offence will stand.

17.55   The provisions of ss 54 to 57 apply in relation to acquittals in respect of offences alleged to be committed on or after 15 April 1997. It should be emphasized that it is the *original* offence, i.e., the offence of which the defendant was acquitted, which must be alleged to have been committed on or after that date (s 54(7)).

New evidence retrials

17.56   This is the second major statutory exception to the rule against double jeopardy. It is contained in ss 75–97 of the CJA 2003.

Schedule 5 of the CJA 2003 list a series of 'qualifying offences' to which these provisions apply. They are all serious offences, which in the main carry a maximum sentence of life imprisonment. They include murder, manslaughter, rape and certain other serious sexual offences, supplying, importing or exporting class A drugs, arson endangering life, causing an explosion likely to endanger life or property, war crimes, and terrorism. The procedure for retrials after acquittal is set out in the flowchart on p. 287.

17.57   Section 76 allows a prosecutor to apply to the Court of Appeal for an order to quash the person's acquittal for a qualifying offence or a lesser qualifying offence of which he could have been convicted at that time. This takes into account an 'implied acquittal'. For example, where the person was acquitted of murder, this would also imply an acquittal for the offence of manslaughter. Section 76 encompasses the possibility of the acquitted person being retried for manslaughter, provided the other conditions are fulfilled. Acquittals after trial on indictment in England and Wales are covered by the Act, as are acquittals outside the United Kingdom (provided they would have amounted to or included the commission of a qualifying offence in the United Kingdom). However, an acquittal in Scotland of a qualifying offence is not covered by the Act, and cannot be quashed. Acquittals are susceptible to quashing whether the offence in question was committed before or after the relevant sections of the CJA 2003 came into effect on 4 April 2005.

17.58   The application to the Court of Appeal to quash the acquittal requires the personal written consent of the Director of Public Prosecutions who must be satisfied (s 76(4)) that:

(a) there is evidence which meets the requirements of s 78 (see 17.59);
(b) it is in the public interest for the application to proceed; and
(c) any trial is consistent with the country's obligations under the Treaty on European Union relating to the principle of *ne bis in idem* (which is the European equivalent of the prohibition of double jeopardy).

Figure 17.1 Retrials after Acquittal

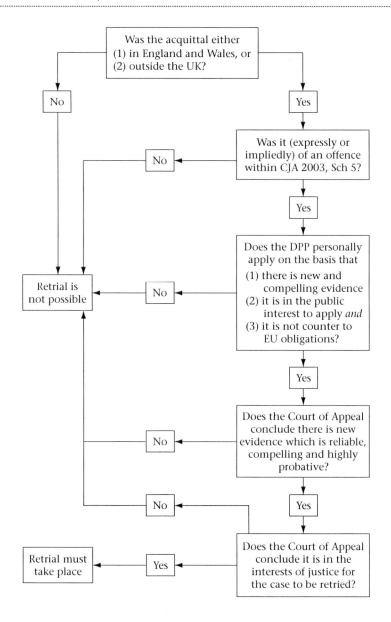

The latter point would be relevant where retrial is proposed for an offence already dealt with in another EU country.

The Court of Appeal must order a retrial if: **17.59**

(a) there is new and compelling evidence in the case; and
(b) it is in the interests of justice for an order to be made.

As to the evidence (s 78), it is 'new 'if it was not adduced at the original trial of the acquitted person. It is 'compelling' if the Court of Appeal considers it to be reliable and substantial and highly probative of the case against him. It is submitted that what is compelling will depend on the context of the previous trial. For example, if the identity of the offender was not in issue in the original trial, new evidence as to identification would not fit the evidence criterion so as to justify a retrial. Reporting restrictions may be imposed by the Court of Appeal in respect of matters surrounding the application for a retrial. The restrictions may last until the end of the retrial, or to the point at which it is clear that the acquitted person can no longer be retried (s 82). The restrictions may apply to any information in respect of the investigation and to the re-publication of matters previously published.

17.60 As to the interests of justice, the court will consider in particular whether a fair trial is unlikely (e.g., because of adverse publicity about the accused), the length of time since the alleged offence, and whether the police and prosecution have acted with due diligence and expedition with regard to the new evidence. These factors are set out in s 79, but they are not exhaustive, and the Court of Appeal can consider other relevant issues in determining whether a retrial would be in the interests of justice. An application to order or refuse a retrial can be the subject of an appeal to the House of Lords on a point of law (s 81).

17.61 The acquitted person must be served with a copy of the application within two days, and be charged with the offence in question. He is entitled to attend and be represented at the hearing at the Court of Appeal (s 80). If a retrial is ordered, it must be on an indictment preferred by the direction of the Court of Appeal (s 84). Arraignment must take place within two months of the date on which the Court of Appeal ordered a retrial, unless it specifies a longer period. The period can only be extended if the Court of Appeal is satisfied that the prosecutor has acted with due expedition since the order was made, and that there is still good and sufficient reason to hold the retrial despite any additional elapse of time. The retrial provisions were utilized in *Dunlop* [2006] EWCA Crim 1354. D had been tried for murder in 1989 and 1991. The jury failed to agree on both occasions, and an acquittal was then ordered. During the course of 1999, D confessed to the murder to a prison officer while in prison on an unrelated matter, and he made similar admissions to other people. He then pleaded guilty to perjury in 2000, and was sentenced to six years' imprisonment. In 2006, the Crown applied for an order under s 76 of the CJA quashing D's acquittal, and ordering a retrial. It was argued on D's behalf that an order would not be in the interests of justice because he had made his admissions, and pleaded guilty to perjury in the belief that he could not be tried again for murder. In addition, it was submitted that a fair trial would be impossible because of prejudicial publicity, and that there had been so great a delay as to make a retrial contrary to the interests of justice. The Court of Appeal quashed the acquittal and granted the application for retrial. It was not unjust that D should be retried. He had been aware of the possibility that the double jeopardy rule might be altered, and his motive for making some of his confessions was in order to obtain psychiatric help. As to prejudicial publicity, any recollection that jurors might have about it would pale into insignificance in comparison to the legitimate prejudicial effect of being told that he had on a number of occasions confessed to murder and pleaded guilty to perjury. The delay in the retrial was no longer than that which was common in relation to historic sexual offences. The only crumb of comfort for D was a suggestion from the court that the sentence which he had served for perjury might be taken into account when determining the minimum term to be served should he be convicted of murder.

I   OTHER POSSIBLE PLEAS

For the sake of completeness, three other pleas should be mentioned, although they are **17.62** hardly ever used in practice.

(a) **The plea of pardon.** Pardons are granted by the Crown, upon the advice of the Home Secretary, in the exercise of the royal prerogative of mercy (see 26.108 to 26.109 for further details). The effect of a pardon is that the recipient is freed from the consequences that would normally result from a crime which he allegedly committed. In previous centuries, pardons were occasionally granted prior to or during proceedings for the crime in question. The pardoned person would then plead the pardon either on being arraigned or (if it was granted after arraignment) at the first opportunity. The plea barred any further proceedings on the indictment. Thus, a properly pleaded pardon prevented an accused being convicted of his crime. In modern times, however, pardons are only granted *after* conviction and sentence. They are used in cases where the normal avenues of appeal have been exhausted or would probably prove unsuccessful, but there is good reason to doubt the correctness of the conviction. The pardon does not affect the fact of the conviction, but all adverse consequences flowing therefrom are removed (see *Foster* [1985] QB 115).

(b) **A plea to the jurisdiction,** which must be in writing, is to the effect that the court has no jurisdiction to try the offence. It would be appropriate in the unlikely event of the indictment alleging a summary offence (other than one falling within the Criminal Justice Act 1988, s 40). It could also be relied upon where the defence argue that the offence was committed outside the territorial jurisdiction of the English courts (see 5.30 to 5.31), although the point could equally well be taken on an ordinary not guilty plea. The Court of Appeal in *Cumberworth* (1989) 89 Cr App R 187 expressed the view that a point of territorial jurisdiction could have been raised by way of demurrer (see (c) below).

(c) **A demurrer,** which, like a plea to the jurisdiction, must be in writing, is an objection to the wording of an indictment. Any objection which could be taken on a demurrer can more conveniently be taken on a motion to quash. For that reason Lord Parker CJ expressed the wish that demurrer 'will be allowed to die naturally': *Deputy Chairman of Inner London Sessions ex parte Commissioner of Metropolitan Police* [1970] 2 QB 80. In *Cumberworth,* by contrast, the Court of Appeal suggested that a challenge to the jurisdiction, raised by the defence on a not guilty plea, could have been more sensibly dealt with by way of demurrer (although a plea to the jurisdiction would seem to be at least equally appropriate).

KEY DOCUMENTS

Criminal Procedure (Insanity) Act 1964, as amended.

Criminal Justice Act 2003, ss 75 to 97.

Practice Direction (Criminal Proceedings: Consolidation) [2002] 1 WLR 2870 available at: <http://www.hmcourts-service.gov.uk/cms/pds.htm>.

18

THE JURY

If the accused pleads not guilty, then, unless the prosecution chooses to offer no evidence, a **18.01** trial must be held. There are now limited exceptions to the general rule that trial on indictment must be by judge and jury (see Chapter 19). Subject to those exceptional situations, a jury must be empanelled (or, more colloquially, sworn in). The law concerning juries is contained chiefly in the Juries Act 1974, which is denoted in the remainder of this Chapter by the letters JA.

A ELIGIBILITY FOR JURY SERVICE

Jurors are drawn from a broad, though not complete, cross-section of the population. Subject **18.02** to the exceptions mentioned below, everyone aged 18 to 70, who is registered as a parliamentary or local government elector is eligible for jury service, provided he has been ordinarily resident in the United Kingdom for any period of at least five years since attaining the age of 13: JA, s 1. If it appears to a Crown Court officer that a person attending at the court for jury service may not have a sufficient understanding of English to be able to act effectively as a juror, he may bring that person before a judge of the court for a ruling that he be discharged from jury service: JA, s 10. As to the maximum age for jury service, that was raised from 65 to 70 by the Criminal Justice Act 1988.

18.03   Certain categories of people are excluded by Sch 1 to the JA from sitting as jurors. Those defined as 'mentally disordered' are ineligible—this includes anyone who suffers or has suffered from mental illness or mental handicap and is resident in a hospital or regularly attends for treatment by a doctor as a result. The following groups of people are disqualified for life:

(a)   those who are on bail in criminal proceedings;
(b)   those who have been sentenced to imprisonment for life or the equivalent for younger offenders;
(c)   those sentenced to imprisonment or detention for public protection;
(d)   those who have been given an extended sentence; and
(e)   those sentenced to imprisonment or detention for five years or more.

18.04   There are also certain categories who are disqualified for ten years:

(a)   those who have served any part of a sentence of imprisonment or detention;
(b)   those who have been subject to a community order, a community rehabilitation order, a community punishment order, a community rehabilitation and punishment order, a drug treatment and testing order, or a drug abstinence order.

18.05   Until 2004, a number of other groups were also ineligible (e.g., the judiciary, police officers, barristers and solicitors, the clergy). In an effort to make the scope of jury service more inclusive, however, the CJA 2003, s 321 did away with their exemption, together with the ability of other groups (e.g., those aged 65 to 70) to claim excusal from jury service as a right. As to the exclusion of some convicted criminals, it was formerly the case that suspended sentences of imprisonment, community service, and probation had no effect on eligibility for jury service. However, that was felt to be unsatisfactory in that too many 'villains' were sitting in the jury box with the result that some villains in the dock were being acquitted when they ought to have been convicted. Accordingly, the JA 1974 was amended by the Juries (Disqualification) Act 1984 and then further by the CJA 2003 so as to produce the present position. But, even now, an offender fined or given a conditional discharge remains entitled to serve on a jury. Since about half those convicted of indictable offences are so dealt with, it is perfectly possible for a person to be convicted by a jury one day and serve on a jury trying somebody else the next.

18.06   Notwithstanding the ineligible and excluded groups, the broad effect of s 1 and Sch 1 is that most adults are eligible for jury service. This may be contrasted with the pre-1974 position under which only householders were eligible. Juries were then criticized (or, depending on one's point of view, commended) for being 'middle-aged, middle-class and middle-income'. It would be difficult now to sustain such a criticism. Note, however, that a person's being eligible to sit on a jury does not inevitably mean that, if summoned for service, he will take his place in the jury box. The procedures for asking a juror to stand by and challenging jurors (see 18.23 to 18.41) are meant to prevent unsuitable, though eligible, jurors serving on the jury in a particular case.

A person who serves on a jury knowing that he is disqualified from jury service commits a **18.07** summary offence punishable with a fine of up to £5,000. Prosecutions for the offence are, however, very rare.

B   SUMMONING JURORS

The Lord Chancellor is responsible for summoning jurors to attend for jury service in the **18.08** Crown Court: JA, s 2. He acts, of course, through officers of the Crown Court. The summons, which must be in writing, may be sent by post. It requires the juror to attend on certain days at a stated location of the Crown Court. The location should, if possible, be within reasonable daily travelling distance of the juror's home, and the average period for which a juror is asked to attend is two weeks. At some courts, such as the Central Criminal Court, which regularly deal with long cases, the period may be greater. If a lengthy case is anticipated it is normal to ask jurors whether they have any objection to being involved. Jurors are, of course, entitled to payment in respect of *inter alia* travelling and subsistence expenses and loss of earnings, but the rates of payment laid down by the Lord Chancellor may not provide full compensation for the losses incurred. The summons should be accompanied by a notice explaining the restrictions on eligibility for jury service, the penalties for non-attendance when summoned and the possibility of being excused from jury service.

The names and addresses of the persons summoned for jury service are taken at random from **18.09** the names and addresses on the electoral roll. Save that the roll indicates those who are ineligible by reason of age, the summoning officer does not know and has no means of checking whether the persons he summons are entitled to sit on a jury. The courts rely on ineligible or disqualified 'jurors' reading the notice which accompanies the summons, and informing the court of their ineligibility.

There is a fundamental weakness in this exclusive reliance on the electoral register. Some people **18.10** (about 8 per cent of those eligible according to the Home Office's 1999 research) do not register. In respect of those who do register, the electoral register becomes increasingly inaccurate until it is updated. As a result, there is a significant minority of those who should be in the 'pool' for jury service who are ignored by the system. This becomes more serious when one considers that certain sections of the community are under-represented as a result, namely those aged 20–24, ethnic minorities, and those living in rented accommodation (see the Auld Report, p. 144).

The Lord Chancellor is also responsible, through the Crown Court officers, for drawing up **18.11** lists (or panels) of the names, addresses and dates for attendance of those who have been summoned for jury service at the various locations of the Crown Court: JA, s 5(1). The prosecution and defence are both entitled by s 5(2) to inspect the panel from which the jurors to try their case will be, or have been, drawn. By s 5(3), this may be done in advance of or during but not after the trial. The right to inspect the jury panel before trial enables the prosecution and defence, if they so wish, to make enquiries about the potential jurors with a view to objecting to one or more of them sitting on the jury. In practice, the defence do not have the resources to conduct such inquiries. The prosecution have relatively easy access, through the police computer system, to the criminal records of potential jurors, but their use of this information is restricted by the Attorney-General's Guidelines (see 18.27 to 18.29 and 18.42 to 18.43).

18.12 The usual pattern is to summon many more jurors for service than are likely to be required. Should a miscalculation occur, however, so that a full jury cannot be made up from those on the jury panel, the court may summon, without written notice, any person in, or in the vicinity of, the court to complete the jury: JA, s 6. The names of persons so summoned are added to the jury panel. There is only a very remote possibility of the court actually having to make use of s 6.

18.13 A person who is eligible and summoned for jury service is under a duty to attend as required, and, unless excused from doing so, commits an offence by not attending without reasonable cause: JA s 20. Sudden illness or bereavement would, no doubt, be a reasonable cause for not attending.

18.14 If the juror thinks there is a good reason why he should not be required to attend, he may apply to the appropriate officer for discretionary excusal.

18.15 Alternatively, application may be made for deferral of service. That would be appropriate where the dates for which the juror has been summoned clash with holidays or business commitments. If the application is granted, a later date is fixed for the service to be performed.

18.16 Excusal and deferral of jury service are dealt with in ss 8, 9, 9A, and 9B of the JA. Should the appropriate officer refuse an application under one or other of the sections, appeal may be made to a Crown Court judge.

18.17 Section 9B of the JA deals with the procedure where someone may be unable to act as a juror because of physical disability. It states that the judge 'shall affirm the summons unless he is of the opinion that the person will not, on account of his disability, be capable of acting effectively as a juror, in which case he shall discharge the summons'. In *Re Osman* [1996] 1 Cr App R 126, the Recorder of London held at first instance that a person summonsed to be a juror who was profoundly deaf should be excused from jury service pursuant to s 9B. In order to follow proceedings in court or in the jury room, the prospective juror needed the assistance of an interpreter in sign language. It was held to be an incurable irregularity in the proceedings for the interpreter to retire with the jury when they considered their verdict.

C   EMPANELLING A JURY

18.18 The next stage in the procedure is to select, from amongst the jury panel summoned to attend at a location of the Crown Court on a certain day, the twelve men and women who will form the jury to try a particular case. This is the empanelling or swearing-in of the jury.

18.19 Twenty or more members of the jury panel (known as the jury in waiting) are either in court when the accused pleads not guilty, or are brought into court by an usher immediately after the plea has been taken. The clerk of court calls the names of twelve of them, asking them to step into the jury box. He has the names of all the jurors in waiting, and must choose the ones he calls at random: JA, s 11—'the jury to try an issue before a court shall be selected by ballot in open court from the panel, or part of the panel, of jurors . . .'. (The importance of the random nature of the selection process was stressed in *Salt* [1996] Crim LR 517—a case where the son of one of the ushers at the Crown Court was called upon by his father to sit as a juror when the number available was insufficient!) The ballot is normally carried out by giving to the clerk some cards, each card having on it the name and address of a juror in waiting. He shuffles the cards, and calls the names on the top twelve.

In *Comerford* [1998] 1 Cr App R 235, the judge ordered that the names of the jurors should not **18.20** be read in open court, but that they should be called by numbers allocated to them. This unusual measure was meant to allay the jurors' fears of intimidation, in view of an earlier abortive trial. Although defence counsel objected to this course, the Court of Appeal held that it did not render the trial a nullity unless it made the proceedings unfair to the defendant or otherwise violated his rights. In the present case, there was no such violation, and the appeal was dismissed. It is submitted that there would be unfairness to the defendant if his right to challenge for cause was impeded by the adoption of this process. The defendant is entitled to as much information as the law and practical considerations allow in determining whether a potential juror may be prejudiced against him. The names of the potential jurors form part of that information. As defence counsel put it, 'a name may ring a bell where a face does not'. In *Comerford*, however, there was no denial of the defence's right to see in advance the names of those on the jury panel, and a challenge could have been formulated as a result of such an inspection, but was not.

Once twelve persons are in the jury box, the clerk says to the accused—'John Smith, the **18.21** names that you are about to hear called are the names of the jurors who are to try you. If therefore you wish to object to them or to any of them, you must do so as they come to the book to be sworn, and before they are sworn, and your objection shall be heard.' This is meant to inform the accused of his right to challenge jurors (see 18.23 to 18.34).

Next the clerk calls individually on each person in the jury box to take the juror's oath, which **18.22** is—'I swear by almighty God that I will faithfully try the defendant[s] and give a true verdict[s] according to the evidence'. The juror reads the words of the oath from a printed card while holding in his right hand the appropriate book (the Bible for Christians, Old Testament for Jews, Koran for Moslems, etc.). If he so wishes, he may affirm. It is possible for the parties to object to a juror before he takes the oath, either by asking him to stand by (prosecution only) or by challenging for cause. The procedure and grounds for doing so are explained in the following Paragraphs. If the objection succeeds, the juror is asked to leave the box and is replaced by another juror in waiting (who could himself be the subject of objection). However, as a result of the abolition of peremptory challenges (see 18.26) it is now far less likely than it used to be that a juror originally called into the box will be replaced. Once a full jury of twelve has taken the oath, the clerk formally asks them if they are all sworn and puts the accused in their charge. This is a traditional, although not strictly essential part of the procedure. The clerk says something to the effect that—'John Smith is charged in an indictment containing *X* counts. Count One is for theft contrary to section 1 of the Theft Act 1968, the particulars being that on the 1st of January 2006 he stole £10 belonging to Jane Brown. Count Two is for... [and so on through the indictment]. To this indictment he has pleaded not guilty. It is your charge, having heard the evidence, to say whether he be guilty or not.' If the accused has pleaded guilty to some counts on the indictment but not guilty to others, the jury are not told about the guilty pleas. Once the accused is in the jury's charge, prosecuting counsel begins his opening speech.

D   CHALLENGES TO JURORS

18.23   Two contrasting views may be held on the best way to select a jury. One is that the process should be left as much as possible to chance. According to this view, certain groups (e.g., children and the mentally sick) must inevitably be excluded from jury service, but these groups should be as narrowly defined as possible. Moreover, if a person has been chosen to serve on the jury for a particular case by whatever method of random selection the judicial system in question uses, then it should not be possible to object to his presence on the jury save on the ground that he comes within one of the excluded groups. Lawton LJ in *Mason* [1981] QB 881 suggested that this approach could lead to unfairness. For example, the jury to try an accused who, while out poaching, is alleged to have unlawfully wounded a gamekeeper might include a juror with several convictions for poaching, the convictions not having resulted in a sentence which would disqualify him from jury service. The counter argument is that the jury could just as well include a gamekeeper, and, anyway, the provisions for majority verdicts (see 18.50) prevent any one juror having a decisive influence on the case.

18.24   The second view on selecting a jury is that every effort should be made to choose jurors who have no discernible prejudices relevant to the case, whether it be a prejudice against the particular type of crime alleged, or for or against accused persons in general, or for or against the particular accused charged. This approach is adopted in some of the American states. It involves giving the parties the opportunity to examine a potential juror, call evidence about him and present argument about his suitability. The difficulty is that the process of selecting a jury can become almost as lengthy and expensive as the trial itself. It is probably no accident that the process has been developed in one of the wealthiest and most litigious societies in the world.

18.25   The approach of the English courts represents a compromise between the above views, although leaning strongly in favour of random selection. The groups not entitled to serve on juries are fairly small (see 18.02 to 18.07), the names of those to be summoned for jury service are chosen at random (see 18.08 to 18.17), and the selection from the jury panel of those who go into the jury box with a view to taking the oath and forming the jury is by ballot (see 18.18 to 18.22). However, the random nature of the choice is qualified by the possibility that either the prosecution or defence will prevent one or more of those originally picked from sitting on the jury. The prosecution can ask a juror to 'stand by'; both prosecution and defence can challenge a juror for cause. Until 1988 it was also possible for the defence to challenge jurors without giving a reason, but this right has now been lost (see the next Paragraph). The change reinforces the random nature of jury selection.

Abolition of peremptory challenges

18.26   For centuries, the defence had the right to prevent a certain number of jurors sitting on the jury without giving any reason whatsoever. All defence counsel had to do was say 'Challenge' immediately before a juror in waiting would otherwise have taken the oath, and that juror then had to leave the box to be replaced by another. Such challenges were known as challenges without cause or peremptory challenges. The number allowed per defendant was progressively reduced, from 25 to 12 in 1925; from 12 to 7 in 1948, and finally from 7 to 3 in 1977. None the less, protests still arose about alleged abuse of the right of peremptory challenge, it being said that defence counsel too often challenged for frivolous or down-right improper reasons. Finally, in the face of spirited resistance from the retentionists, it was decided to abolish peremptory challenges (CJA 1988, s 118).

Jurors asked to stand by

The prosecution never had a right of peremptory challenge as such. However, they did and do **18.27** have a right which is in effect just the same. It is the right to stand a juror by. If prosecuting counsel does not want someone on the jury, he says 'stand by' immediately before that person would otherwise take the oath. The 'juror' then leaves the box and is replaced by another juror in waiting. No reason need be given for the 'stand by'. It will only be necessary for him to give reasons in the unlikely event of the entire jury panel being exhausted without a full jury having been obtained. Since it is the practice of the courts to summon many more jurors for service than are ever likely to be needed at the same time, counsel would have to stand by an inordinately large number of potential jurors to be in danger of running through the whole panel. If, however, he were to do so, the first of those he stood by would be asked to return to the box, and would join the jury unless successfully challenged for cause (see 18.30 to 18.34).

The position of prosecuting counsel in standing jurors by was clarified in *Mason* [1981] **18.28** QB 881. The Court of Appeal (Lawton LJ giving judgment) held that the right to stand jurors by is not dependent upon counsel having a reason for so doing which would be capable of founding a successful challenge for cause. In theory, therefore, a juror can be stood by for any or no reason. But prosecuting counsel should use his power responsibly. The importance of the right of stand-by has since been vastly reduced by the *Attorney-General's Guidelines on Exercise by the Crown of its Right of Stand-by* (1989) 88 Cr App R 123 (see 18.43).

The defence have no right to stand jurors by: *Chandler* [1964] 2 QB 322. **18.29**

Challenges for cause

Both prosecution and defence are entitled to challenge as many individual jurors as they wish **18.30** for cause. A considerable volume of arcane eighteenth century law categorizes challenges for cause under a variety of headings such as *propter honoris respectum, propter defectum* and *propter affectum*. However, the upshot of the old cases is that a juror may be challenged *either* on the basis that he is ineligible for or disqualified from jury service, or on the basis that he is or may reasonably be suspected of being biased. As to bias, jurors have been successfully challenged when they were employed by or related to a party; when they had been entertained at the house of a party; when they had expressed a wish or opinion as to the outcome of the case; and when they had shown hostility to the accused (see *O'Coigley* (1798) 26 St Tr 1191 where the challenged juror, on looking at the defendants in the dock, said 'Damned rascals'). More recently, in *Kray* (1969) 53 Cr App R 412, the trial judge was prepared to exclude from the jury anyone who had read certain lurid and probably inaccurate newspaper accounts of the alleged gangland activities of the accused.

By contrast in *Pennington* [1985] Crim LR 394, the Court of Appeal implied that a juror who **18.31** had worked during the miners' strike of 1984–5 was fit to serve on a jury trying P, a leading striking miner, for an offence of criminal damage allegedly committed while on picket-line duty. The point was not, however, directly in issue as the defence did not discover the relevant facts until after the trial and so no challenge was actually made.

18.32 The procedure for making a challenge for cause is that the challenging party says 'challenge' immediately before the 'juror' takes the oath. The burden is then on him to satisfy the judge on a balance of probabilities that his objection is well founded. To discharge that burden he must normally call prima facie evidence of the juror's unsuitability—e.g., that he is disqualified on account of previous convictions, or ineligible by reason of his occupation, or biased one way or the other. Until that prima facie evidence has been led, no questions may be asked of the juror himself. In other words, the parties are not allowed to embark on a 'fishing expedition' asking each member of the jury panel about their attitudes, life-histories, etc. with a view to eliciting a possible ground for challenge. This restrictive rule has the advantage of shortening the process of jury selection. It has the disadvantage that, with jury panels at large Crown Court centres numbering several hundred, it is virtually impossible for the parties to check before trial whether the potential jurors for their case are suitable or not. Almost certainly a significant proportion of challengeable jurors go unchallenged simply because nobody has the necessary information at the relevant time. It is clear from *Morris* (1990) 93 Cr App R 102 that the right to challenge for cause is limited to the time when the jury is sworn, and cannot be exercised during the course of the trial. M was charged with stealing from a Marks and Spencer store. After the store detective had given evidence, one of the jurors said that she was a personnel assistant with a different branch of the company. The judge refused to discharge the juror, saying that the right way to deal with the matter was by a challenge for cause. The trial proceeded and M was convicted. The Court of Appeal allowed his appeal. By the time the facts about the juror had emerged, it was too late to challenge for cause, which could only be done when the jury was sworn.

18.33 Partly as a result of the procedural difficulties just described and partly because—if there was any doubt about a juror—it was far easier to use a peremptory challenge or stand him by, challenges for cause largely fell into disuse. The question for the future is whether, with the abolition of peremptory challenges, the defence in particular will resort again to challenges for cause. And should judges aid the process by allowing jurors in waiting to be questioned about their suitability *before* rather than after prima facie evidence of a ground for challenge has been led? The rule against putting preliminary questions to the whole jury in waiting is merely a judge-made one of practice and, even in the past, has been departed from in exceptional circumstances. Thus, in *Kray* (1969) 53 Cr App R 412 (see 18.30) the judge permitted each juror to be asked whether he had read the offending newspaper articles, even though there was no reason to suppose that any individual had done so.

18.34 A challenge to the whole jury panel may be made in addition to challenges to individual jurors. This is known as a challenge to the array, and is on the ground that the Crown Court officer appointed to summon the panel was biased or otherwise acted improperly. Although challenges to the array are preserved by s 12(6) of the JA, they are virtually unknown in modern times.

The judge's powers

18.35 The trial judge has a residual power to stand a juror by. The commonest example is where, on a juror beginning to take the oath, it becomes apparent that he would not be sufficiently literate to understand documentary evidence that will be advanced during the course of the trial. The judge can ask the juror to step down.

Whether it would ever be appropriate for a judge to intervene more generally so as to obtain **18.36** what he considers to be a properly balanced jury is an open question. It is a question which has arisen especially in the context of defendants from a racial minority who want to have representatives of their own race (or, at least, of the black community in general) on the jury. In *McCalla* [1986] Crim LR 335, the defence asked for at least two black jurors, but the judge said that granting their wish was beyond his powers since he could not properly interfere with the random selection of the jury from the jury panel, nor could he artificially enlarge the panel so as to incorporate more black people. Moreover, as a matter of principle, a defendant should not be allowed to stipulate the type of jury he wanted to try him.

The extent to which a judge may properly influence the composition of a jury is one that **18.37** has assumed greater importance with the abolition of peremptory challenges. In *Ford* [1989] QB 868, F appealed against his convictions for reckless driving and taking a motor vehicle without consent. It was argued on his behalf that the trial judge had wrongly refused an application for a racially balanced jury. The argument was rejected by the Court of Appeal. Any challenge to the array of jurors must be on the ground of bias or other irregularity on the part of the summoning officer. If there is a complaint of disproportion of persons of a certain ethnic group then it must be corrected by administrative (rather than judicial) intervention— unless due to bias or irregularity. As far as individual jurors are concerned, the mere fact that a juror is of a particular race or religion cannot found a challenge for cause on the ground of bias. Further, the judge may not discharge individual jurors selected in the ballot, in order to secure a jury of a particular racial mix.

The matter remained controversial, and the Royal Commission on Criminal Justice, appointed **18.38** in 1991 under the chairmanship of Lord Runciman, asked those submitting evidence whether the decision in *Ford* was satisfactory. If not, they asked, 'What procedure could be devised to permit judges in exceptional cases to exercise such a power (namely, to stand jurors by)?' The Commission for Racial Equality (CRE) responded, in its evidence, by voicing concern at the low proportion of jurors from ethnic minorities. It suggested that this might in part be due to such factors as a lower propensity to register on the electoral roll, and a lower rate of eligibility because of residence requirements. The CRE also pointed out that some accused are tried away from the area of the alleged offence, e.g., many accused from South London (with a relatively high ethnic minority population) are tried in Kingston-upon-Thames (which has a virtually all-white population). The CRE proposed to the Royal Commission that it should be possible for either the prosecution or the defence to apply to the judge before the trial for the selection of a jury containing up to three people from ethnic minority communities. If the judge granted the application, it would be for the jury bailiff to continue to draw names randomly selected from the available pool until three such people were drawn. The Royal Commission, in its Report (TSO 1993, p. 133) agreed with this proposal, provided that the prosecution or defence, as the case might be, could persuade the judge that such an approach was reasonable because of the unusual and special features of the case. The Royal Commission suggested that a black defendant charged with burglary would be unlikely to succeed in such an application. But black people accused of violence against a member of an extremist organization whom they alleged had been making racial taunts against them might well succeed.

18.39   When the Auld Report appeared in 2001, an alternative proposal was put forward (p. 159). In summary, it was proposed that the parties should be asked prior to trial whether race was likely to be an issue and, if so, whether steps should be taken to ensure ethnic minority representation on the jury. If so, a larger number of jurors would then be empanelled for that case. If those selected did not include a minimum of, say, three ethnic minority jurors, the remainder would be stood down until the minimum was reached. There has been no indication that either Lord Justice Auld's recommendation or that of the Royal Commission would find its way into the statute book.

18.40   In *Tarrant* [1998] Crim LR 342, the trial was held at Snaresbrook in the East End of London. The prosecution applied for the case to be moved from the area, because of fears that the jury might be intimidated. The judge refused to transfer the case, but ordered that a random panel of jurors be brought in from outside the area. The defendant was convicted, and appealed. The Court of Appeal emphasized that both the nomination of prospective jurors on to the panel, and the selection of jurors from the panel to try the case had to be random. Further, the process had to be carried out by the court administration, and not by the judge. Since the defendant had been deprived of a genuinely randomly selected jury, the conviction was quashed.

18.41   In *Smith* (2003) *The Times*, 3 March 2003, the Court of Appeal considered whether the HRA 1998 and Art 6 of the ECHR affected the standing of *Ford*. Their Lordships held that it remained good law, Pill LJ saying:

> We do not accept that it was unfair for the appellant to be tried by a randomly selected all-white jury or that the fair-minded and informed observer would regard it as unfair. We do not accept that, on the facts of this case, the trial could only be fair if members of the defendant's race were on the jury. It was not a case where consideration of the evidence required knowledge of the traditions or social circumstances of a particular racial group.

Jury vetting

18.42   A matter which has given rise to public controversy is whether the parties should be allowed to 'vet' the jury—i.e., make enquiries about the members of the jury panel with a view to exercising more effectively their rights of challenge and stand by. Jury vetting is not of itself illegal. On the contrary, it is facilitated by JA, s 5(2) which entitles the parties to inspect the jury panel prior to trial (see 18.11). By doing so, they can discover the names and addresses of the panellists, and there is then nothing in law to prevent them investigating the backgrounds, likely attitudes, etc. of those who have been summoned for service for the dates when their case is likely to be heard. In practice, the size of the jury panel makes it impossible for the defence to do any effective 'vetting'—the legal aid fund would certainly not pay for the army of private investigators that would be needed! The prosecution (through the police) have greater resources at their disposal, but, in general, the only check which they consider it right to make is into the panellists' criminal records. If it turns out that a juror in waiting has disqualifying convictions or (although not disqualified) is none the less unsuitable by reason of a previous offence, prosecuting counsel may challenge for cause. *Mason* [1981] QB 881 (see 18.28) expressly approved jury vetting in this limited sense although it must now be restricted further in practice by the *Attorney-General's Guidelines on Exercise by the Crown of its Right of Stand-by* (see 18.43). Shortly after the judgment in *Mason*, the Association of Chief Police Officers issued recommendations, indicating when the police would consider it appropriate to check the jury panellists for previous convictions. The recommendations are reported in (1989) 88 Cr App R 123 at p. 125. They identify three situations in which a check may be carried out. They are:

(a) it appears that an attempt is being made to introduce disqualified persons onto a jury, or that a particular juror may be disqualified; or
(b) it is believed that, in a previous related abortive trial, an attempt was made to interfere with jurors; or
(c) it is thought especially important, having regard to the nature of the particular case, to ensure that no disqualified person sits on the jury.

The police will not check jurors on behalf of the defence unless specifically requested to do so by the Director of Prosecutions. Nor will they carry out checks in addition to the check on convictions unless that is authorized under the Attorney-General's guidelines (see the next Paragraph below).

The Attorney-General's guidelines (1989) 88 Cr App R 123 state that, in two types of case, **18.43** enquiries about the jurors going beyond a mere check on convictions may be justified. The types of case are—(i) those in which national security is involved and part of the evidence is likely to be heard in camera, and (ii) terrorist cases. Extra checks are said to be needed because, in such cases, a person of extreme political views might allow those views to interfere with his objective assessment of the evidence. Further, as regards security cases, it is thought essential to exclude from the jury anybody who might be tempted to divulge evidence heard in camera. Therefore, in both categories of cases, the files of the police Special Branch may be consulted; in security cases, the aid of the security services themselves may additionally be sought. However, such checks require the personal authorization of the Attorney-General, and are consequently known as 'authorized checks'. The results of any authorized check are, at the discretion of the Director of Public Prosecutions, passed on to prosecuting counsel who may then—bearing in mind the risks against which the check was intended to guard—use the information to stand jurors by. Since the Attorney gives his authority only in a handful of cases, authorized checks are of little significance in the overall scheme of jury selection.

Jury protection

Where the judge is concerned about 'jury nobbling' (e.g., intimidation or bribery), he may **18.44** make a jury protection order. In essence, this will involve the police providing protection for the members of the jury during the course of the trial, so that their deliberations can be carried out without outside interference. Usually, such an order would be considered as a result of an application by the prosecution. Generally, the judge will be reluctant to accede to such an application without substantial grounds. There is the danger that a jury subjected to the intrusive attention which protection is likely to involve will assume that the defendant is to blame for the inconvenience, and must be the object of suspicion if he has associates suspected of jury nobbling. There is also the converse danger that the less robust among the jury may fear adverse consequences if they convict, and will decide to acquit. Nevertheless, the judge has a discretion as to whether to order jury protection. The prosecution will make its application in the absence of the jury, and wherever possible in the presence of the defence. Usually, reasons will be given by the prosecution, and evidence called, the witnesses being subject to cross-examination. Occasionally, a departure from this procedure may be sanctioned by the judge, e.g., to allow the prosecution to make its application in the absence of the defence or without calling evidence. But any departure from the usual procedure should not be sanctioned unless it is necessary and does not result in unfairness to the defendant. In any event, if the judge decides to authorize protection, there is no need for the jury to be told of the reasons, as to do so may merely compound the inevitable problems which the protection order involves. Some explanation, however, is usually necessary, and it is customary for a formula to be agreed between counsel and the judge, which will stress that the jurors should not be alarmed, and must in no way be prejudiced against the defendant by reason of the precautions taken. The phenomenon of jury protection, which is increasingly common, was analysed by the Court of Appeal in *Comerford* [1998] 1 Cr App R 235, from which the above points are taken.

Issues triable by one jury

18.45   A jury selected by the procedures described in the preceding Paragraphs will normally be kept together to try only one issue. The issue will nearly always be whether the accused is guilty or not guilty of the charges in the indictment preferred against him. Having brought in their verdict, the jury is disbanded and its constituent members are then available for selection for further juries. Section 11(4) of the JA does, however, provide that a jury may try more than one issue if the trial of the second (or last) issue begins within 24 hours of the time when the jury was constituted. This provision is useful in cases of muteness where the jury which found the accused mute of malice may go on to try the general issue of guilt or innocence (assuming, of course, that it took them less than a day to find that the accused was not mute by visitation of God). Outside of this unusual type of situation, juries are not in practice retained to try more than one issue even if that might be technically permissible under s 11(4). Thus, if a trial on indictment takes less than a day, the jurors will simply return to the pool of jurors in waiting rather than be asked to start a second trial.

E   THE COMPOSITION OF THE JURY AS A GROUND OF APPEAL

18.46   It is in the public interest that the verdicts of juries should be treated with respect, and should not be overturned on appeal unless there was some significant error during the trial which preceded the verdict (see Chapter 26 for the grounds on which the Court of Appeal upholds an appeal against conviction). If it were possible, as a matter of course, to challenge convictions by impugning the competence of individual jurors or the way they collectively came to their decision in the case, then public confidence in the jury system would be undermined, and members of the public would be reluctant to serve on juries for fear of being subsequently criticized before the Court of Appeal. So, Parliament and the Court of Appeal have combined to make it very difficult for an offender to challenge his conviction by attacking the jury.

18.47   First, the Court of Appeal has long had a settled principle that it will not investigate what occurred in the jury room, however strong the suspicion may be that there was some irregularity (see 21.10 to 21.17 for details). Secondly, if it is discovered by the defence after the trial that one of the jurors knew facts to the accused's detriment of which he ought to have been unaware and/or was heavily biased against the accused, that is not regarded as a good ground of appeal unless the defence can discharge the near impossible burden of showing that the juror concerned had made up his mind before the trial to convict the accused regardless of the evidence. Thus, in *Box and Box* [1964] 1 QB 430, the convictions were upheld despite the fact that the foreman of the jury knew that the appellants were ex-burglars, villains, and associates of prostitutes, and had said to an acquaintance that he 'did not need to hear the the the evidence' and 'would get them ten years'. Of course, it was quite wrong for the foreman to serve on the jury—he should have told the judge what he knew about the accused, and the judge would have released him. And, if the defence had known soon enough what the foreman knew, they would obviously have challenged him for cause, and the challenge would inevitably have succeeded. But, given that the relevant facts did not come to light until after verdict, the Court of Appeal decided that the conviction would have to be upheld, despite the doubts one may have as to whether the jury really decided the case fairly according to the evidence or were swayed by the foreman's anti-defence bias. Similarly, in *Pennington* (1985) 81 Cr App R 217 (see 18.31 for the facts) the alleged bias of the non-striking miner on the jury—even if it might have been a ground for a challenge for cause had it been discovered earlier—was unhesitatingly rejected as a reason for quashing P's conviction after the event. Finally, the Court of Appeal's approach in cases such as *Box and Box* has been statutorily confirmed by s 18 of the JA.

Section 18 provides that a conviction may not be quashed on any of the following grounds: **18.48**

(a) that the provisions of the JA about the summoning of jurors or their selection by ballot were not complied with;
(b) that a juror was not qualified to serve under s 1 of the JA;
(c) that a juror was misnamed or misdescribed (e.g., in the jury summons or on the panel);
(d) that a juror was unfit to serve.

Section 18 does not apply to breaches of the JA coming within (a) above if objection was made **18.49** at the time or as soon as practicable thereafter, and nothing was done to correct the irregularity. Nor does s 18 apply to cases where a person wrongfully served on a jury by impersonating somebody else who had been properly summoned for service. But, subject to those two provisos, the section will defeat appeals based on grounds such as a juror having been ineligible for or disqualified from or otherwise unfit for jury service, even though the relevant facts were not known until after the trial. In *Chapman and Lauday* (1976) 63 Cr App R 75, the appellants failed even though a juror was deaf, and had heard only half the evidence and none of the summing-up. Clearly, a juror who has not heard the proceedings is incapable of discharging his oath to give a true verdict according to the evidence, but the deaf juror was not challenged at the time (because nobody then knew of his disability), and there was no way in which the defence could disguise the fact that their ground of appeal was simply his unfitness to be a juror. In effect, the appellants had been tried by eleven, not twelve, jurors but s 18 still applied to save the conviction. Arguably, a juror is unfit within the meaning of s 18 not only when (as in *Chapman and Lauday*) he would be physically or mentally unsuited to serve on *any* jury, but also when his knowledge about or attitude to a particular accused makes him unsuitable to try that man, although he would be acceptable on other juries. Perhaps, though, such cases are best left to the common law principles explained in *Box and Box* (see above) and should not be brought within s 18.

18.50   In *Chapman and Lauday*, the Court of Appeal did suggest *obiter* an alternative approach which, in different circumstances, might ameliorate the apparently harsh effects of the section. That approach is to argue that the entire circumstances of the case—including but not limited to the alleged deficiency of the juror—give rise to lurking doubt that justice was not done, and that therefore the conviction is unsafe. For example, had the verdict in *Chapman and Lauday* been by the minimum permissible majority of 10–2 rather than being unanimous, their Lordships could not have been confident about the justice of a conviction which depended for its legality upon the vote of a juror who had not heard the evidence. They would therefore have quashed the conviction, notwithstanding s 18, on the ground of unsafeness.

F   DISCHARGE OF JURORS OR A JURY

18.51   Once a jury has been empanelled, the normal course of events is that those twelve men and women hear the entire case and return a verdict at the end of it. However, the judge may discharge up to three jurors and allow the trial to continue with the remainder. Alternatively, he may discharge the entire jury from giving a verdict, leaving open the possibility of a fresh jury being sworn in to try the accused at a later date. Discharge of jurors or the jury is frequently connected with allegations of misconduct by them during the course of the hearing. It is therefore convenient, first, to summarize the rules on the conduct of jurors.

Conduct of the jury during the trial

18.52   The trial judge has a discretion to allow the jury to separate from each other at any time prior to their retiring to consider their verdict: JA, s 13. This discretion is extended by the Criminal Justice and Public Order Act 1994, s 43, to cover the time after they have retired to consider their verdict. For obvious reasons it is normal to permit such separations both during lunch adjournments and overnight. But, when they first separate, the jury should be warned by the judge not to speak about the case to anyone who is not of their number (see *Prime* (1973) 57 Cr App R 632). It is especially important that they do not speak to the parties, witnesses, counsel, or anybody else actually involved in the trial. Neither, however, should they discuss the case with relatives, friends, etc. This is partly because they (and nobody else) are charged with the duty of ultimately returning a verdict, and partly because a person to whom they speak might have strong views on the issues raised by the trial and, whether by accident or design, colour the juror's attitude to the proceedings (see *Spencer*, described in 18.59, for an extreme example of this occurring). Breach of the above rules may lead to a juror or the entire jury being discharged (see 18.53 to 18.61).

Discharge of individual jurors

18.53   Section 16 of the JA provides that if, during the course of a trial, a juror dies or is discharged by the judge 'whether as being through illness incapable of continuing to act or for any other reason', the remainder of the jury may complete the hearing of the case and return a verdict provided their number is not reduced below nine. Section 16 does not itself define the reasons (other than incapacitating illness) which justify discharge. At common law, however, discharge is allowed only if there is an 'evident necessity' for it (see *Hamberry* [1977] QB 924).

What amounts to an evident necessity is essentially a matter for the judge's discretion, and it is not in practice particularly difficult to show it exists. Thus, in *Hamberry* a juror was discharged merely because the unexpectedly long duration of the trial meant that, had she remained on the jury, her holiday plans would have been interfered with. The Court of Appeal approved the trial judge's decision. Similarly, in *Richardson* [1979] 1 WLR 1316, their lordships had no difficulty in holding that it was right to discharge a juror whose husband had died during an overnight adjournment.

A suspicion of bias on the part of a juror may also necessitate his being discharged. The decided cases show two different strands of authority, revealing that different tests have been applied when considering questions of bias. The two competing tests have been identified as: **18.54**

(a)   whether there was a real danger of bias on the part of the juror concerned; and
(b)   whether a reasonable person might reasonably suspect bias on the juror's part.

In *Porter v Magill* [2002] AC 357, the House of Lords considered the claims of the two competing tests in relation to the courts generally, and approved the following formulation: would a fair-minded and informed observer conclude that there was a real possibility, or real danger (the two being the same) that the tribunal was biased? This test has been adopted by the Court of Appeal in a series of criminal cases (see, for example, *Mason* [2002] 2 Cr App R 628). It also appears to be in accordance with the approach of the European Court of Human Rights in Strasbourg: *Sander v United Kingdom* [2000] Crim LR 767. **18.55**

In *Sander v UK*, the European Court of Human Rights emphasized that any allegation of bias must be looked at from an objective, as well as a subjective point of view. In other words, a finding that the jury were not in fact biased did not end the matter. There was a further question which had to be posed: were there 'sufficient guarantees to exclude any objectively justified or legitimate doubts as to the impartiality' of the jury. **18.56**

In *Sawyer* (1980) 71 Cr App R 283 three jurors had been seen talking to prosecution witnesses in the court restaurant but, when asked by the judge what the conversation had been about, they assured him that it was on neutral matters unconnected with the trial. The judge decided that there was no real danger of prejudice and refused to discharge the jurors, which decision was approved by the Court of Appeal. Similar principles apply if it is discovered during the course of the trial that a juror knows the accused and/or knows that he is of bad character; or knows a witness in the case; or has expressed an opinion about the case suggesting that he might have made his mind up in advance. If there is a real risk of prejudice, the judge must certainly discharge the juror, and he may have to consider discharging the whole jury (see *Hood* [1968] 1 WLR 773). **18.57**

Discharge of a juror does not require the consent of the parties. The former rule that consent was needed in murder cases has been abolished by the Criminal Justice Act 1988. Normally, the judge would ask for representations before making any decision but even that is not essential. Indeed, the judge can exercise the power of discharge otherwise than in open court and without telling the parties what he has done (see *Richardson* (above) where the juror was told over the telephone that she was discharged, and the judge failed even to announce his decision in open court so that, on the trial resuming, counsel did not immediately realize that a juror was missing—nonetheless the conviction was upheld). **18.58**

Discharge of the whole jury

18.59   The judge has a discretion to discharge the whole jury from giving a verdict. If he does so, the accused does not stand acquitted of the offence charged but can be retried by a different jury on the same indictment. The main situations for discharge of a jury are as follows:

(a)   **Where they cannot agree upon their verdict**. This is discussed in Chapter 20.

(b)   **Where inadmissible 'evidence' prejudicial to the accused has inadvertently been given**. Thus, if a witness tells the jury that the accused has previous convictions and it is not one of the exceptional cases where evidence of character is allowed, then there is a good chance that the judge will accede to a defence application to discharge the jury. But, it remains a matter for discretion, and the judge will consider especially how explicit the reference to bad character was; how far the defence were to blame for what happened through asking ill-advised questions in cross-examination; and what impact the inadmissible information is likely to have on the jury. In *Weaver* [1968] 1 QB 353, cross-examination by defence counsel of a police officer led to answers which, in effect, revealed to the jury that the accused had previous convictions. The judge refused to discharge the jury and W was convicted. The Court of Appeal dismissed the appeal. The factors weighing against discharge were (a) that defence counsel was himself responsible for inviting the answers which he then complained of; and (b) the judge's summing-up had minimized the degree of prejudice. Contrast the case of *Boyes* [1991] Crim LR 717, in which, as the judge concluded his summing-up on charges of rape and indecent assault, the complainant's mother shouted from the public gallery, 'When is it going to come out about the other five girls he has attacked?' The judge told the jury not to pay any attention to the outburst. The jury convicted. The Court of Appeal allowed the appeal. One of the bases for their decision was the judge's failure to enquire of the jury whether they had heard the outburst. If they had, one could hardly think of more damaging and prejudicial evidence being taken to the jury room. The judge should have considered a fresh trial.

In *McCann* [1991] Crim LR 136, M and others were tried for conspiracy to murder Mr King, then Secretary of State for Northern Ireland, and others. They elected not to give evidence. During the closing stages of the trial, the Home Secretary announced in the House of Commons the Government's intention of changing the law on the right to silence. That night, interviews with Mr King and Lord Denning were televized, expressing in strong terms their view that in terrorist cases a failure to answer questions or give evidence was tantamount to guilt. The trial judge refused to dismiss the jury, and the defendants were convicted. The Court of Appeal allowed the appeal. There was a real risk that the jury had been influenced by the statements. The only way in which justice could be done and be obviously seen to be done was by discharging the jury and ordering a retrial.

The problems outlined in relation to the revelation of matters prejudicial to the accused may also arise where it is discovered that one of the jurors has personal knowledge of the accused, or of one of the witnesses in the case. The judge would then need to decide, on the basis of the 'real danger' test outlined in *Porter v Magill* [2002] 2 AC 357 (see 18.55), whether the individual juror, or the whole jury, should be discharged. If there is a real danger of bias on the part of the individual juror, then the suspicion must also be addressed that he will have contaminated the other members of the jury by communicating his prejudice to them. If that is the case, then the whole jury should be discharged.

(c) **Where one or more jurors have been guilty of misconduct and/or might be prejudiced against the accused, and the matter cannot be satisfactorily dealt with by
discharge of the individual jurors concerned.** The test for whether the jury
should be discharged in such cases is the one stated in *Porter v Magill* (see 18.55).
Again, this is essentially a matter for the judge's discretion. Therefore, the Court of
Appeal will overturn a conviction only if the appellant can show that the judge's refusal
to discharge was totally unreasonable and/or arrived at by applying incorrect principles.
In *Spencer* [1987] AC 128, however, the House of Lords did quash S's conviction on the
basis of non-discharge. The facts were that S was charged with ill-treating patients during
the course of his employment as a nurse at Rampton special security mental hospital.
During the trial a juror (Mr Peet) evinced signs of obvious hostility towards the accused
(e.g., by showing impatience at having to listen to the cross-examination of the patients
called as prosecution witnesses). On the penultimate day of the trial an usher discovered
that Mr Peet's wife worked at another mental hospital and may well have heard gossip
about what allegedly went on at Rampton, which she in turn could have passed on to her
husband. The usher told the judge, and the judge discharged Mr Peet. However, the judge
allowed him to continue his usual practice of driving three of the remaining jurors home
from the Crown Court to the nearby town where they all lived. A warning was given that
they should not discuss the case as Mr Peet was no longer a member of the jury. The next
morning defence counsel asked for the whole jury to be discharged on the basis that, in
the car rides home, Mr Peet would almost certainly have infected the other three jurors
with his anti-defence bias. The judge refused the application, apparently holding that
the defence had to show a 'very high risk' that Mr Peet had improperly influenced other
jury-members. Both the Court of Appeal and the House of Lords affirmed that that was
the wrong test—the defence merely had to show a real danger of prejudice. However, the
Court of Appeal dismissed the appeal as, in their view, there was no such danger on the
facts of the case. The House of Lords reversed that decision (i.e., quashed the conviction)
but only because they had before them an affidavit from Mr Peet in which he admitted
that he had disobeyed the judge's warning and had discussed the case with the other
three jurors during the car journey home on the evening after he had been discharged.
There was a real risk that—piqued by being off the jury and desperate to ensure a conviction—Mr Peet would then have imparted information derived from his wife of which
neither he nor any juror should have been aware. However, the implication of the House
of Lords judgments is that, on the facts known to him at the time, the trial judge was justified in refusing the application for discharge.

One difficult set of cases deals with approaches made to the jury by outsiders in an attempt to   **18.60**
influence their decision. In *Thorpe* [1996] Crim LR 273, the Court of Appeal said that a distinction should be drawn between a case where the approach is immediately reported to the
judge, and a case where the matter comes to light only after the verdict has been delivered.
If the juror who has been approached reports it immediately to the judge, that will be an
indication that his integrity remains intact, and the approach has not influenced him.

The CJA 2003 did away with the exemption of various groups from jury service, including the   **18.61**
judiciary, barristers, solicitors and police officers (see 18.05). As a result, a number of people
familiar with the criminal justice system, and potentially identified with either the prosecution or the defence, have become eligible to serve as jurors. Their position was considered in

three cases heard together under the name of *Abdroikof* [2007] UKHL 37.

(a)   In one of the cases, the foreman of the jury was a lawyer employed by the local CPS. Lord Bingham, speaking for the majority who upheld the appeal, stated:

> Justice is not seen to be done if one discharging the very important neutral role of juror is a full-time, salaried, long-serving employee of the prosecutor.

The problem arose because the juror's employer was the prosecutor, and it may be that such a person could serve on the jury where another agency prosecuted. In addition, Baroness Hale indicated that the position might be different if the employee was not a lawyer.

(b)   In the second case, there was a crucial dispute between the appellant and a police sergeant on the evidence. Their lordships made it clear that they did not regard the mere presence of a police officer as a member of the jury as, in itself, rendering a verdict unsafe. However, one of the jurors was a serving police officer who shared the same local service background as the sergeant giving evidence in the case, and the defendant disputed that evidence. The appeal was upheld on the grounds that this 'would be judged by a fair-minded and informed observer to be a real and possible source of unfairness, beyond the reach of standard judicial warnings and directions'. Lord Bingham referred with apparent approval to Metropolitan Police Notice 20-2004, which advised staff that they should not attend the court where their Operational Command Unit committed its cases.

(c)   With respect to the third case, the presence of a police officer was held not to be objectionable. This case did not hinge upon a contest between police evidence and that adduced by the defence.

18.62   Where a judge does decide to discharge the jury—whether for one of the reasons summarized above or for a totally inadequate reason—and the accused is subsequently convicted at a retrial, no appeal can be brought on the basis that the first trial should have been allowed to continue: *Gorman* [1987] 1 WLR 545.

KEY DOCUMENTS

Juries Act 1974, as amended.

19

JUDGE-ONLY TRIALS

Historically, trial on indictment in England and Wales has always been in front of a judge and **19.01** jury. The principle, which for some has acquired virtually constitutional status, is that someone accused of a serious crime has the right to be tried by a jury of his peers, who are the sole determiners of guilt. Central to the argument in favour of jury involvement in trial on indictment is the concept that ordinary citizens ought to participate in the criminal justice system in this central role, as a crucial part of the democratic process. As Lord Devlin put it, the jury is 'the lamp that shows that freedom lives'.

Nevertheless, the jury has its critics, some of whom regard it as an unwieldy and inaccurate **19.02** tool for doing justice. Others regard it as all very well in its place, but inappropriate for certain complex or sensitive matters. The CJA 2003, ss 43 to 50, introduced for the first time in England and Wales the concept of trial on indictment without a jury. These provisions dealt in part with serious or complex fraud (19.04 to 19.05) and in part with allegations of jury tampering (19.06 to 19.11). The provisions relating to jury tampering came into force during 2006. Those dealing with serious or complex fraud are not yet in force.

There is another procedure, introduced by the Domestic Violence, Crime and Victims Act **19.03** 2004 (DVCVA), which may be regarded as sanctioning a particular form of judge-only trial in the Crown Court. Although it is rather different in scope, it is also dealt with in this Chapter. It was brought into effect in 2007 and is dealt with in 19.12.

A SERIOUS OR COMPLEX FRAUD

Once s 43 of the CJA 2003 comes into force, the prosecution will be able to apply for a trial in **19.04** the Crown Court to take place without a jury (i.e., in front of a judge sitting alone) in the case of serious or complex fraud (s 43). The application would have to be determined at a preparatory hearing (see 16.12 to 16.19). The court must be satisfied that the length and/or complexity of the trial is likely to make it so burdensome that the interests of justice require serious consideration to be given to conducting the trial without a jury. In considering the matter, the judge must consider whether anything can reasonably be done to make the trial less complex and lengthy. However, in doing so, the court is not to regard as reasonable any measures which would significantly disadvantage the prosecution. If it is satisfied that the interests of justice require serious consideration of a trial without a jury, then it has a discretion to order that it should proceed without a jury. However, such an order requires the approval of the Lord Chief Justice or a judge nominated by him.

19.05   Section 43 proved particularly controversial during the debates on the CJA 2003 in Parliament. As a result, a deal was struck in order to ensure the passage of the legislation, by which it may only be brought into effect by affirmative resolution of each House of Parliament. Since then, the Government have made various efforts to bring s 43 into effect, but these have not proved successful by the time of writing.

B   JURY TAMPERING

19.06   The second set of provisions under the CJA 2003 covers the situation where there is perceived to be a danger of jury tampering. The prosecution is then able to apply for the trial to be conducted without a jury. Further, where the jury has been discharged in the course of a trial because of jury tampering, the prosecution is able to apply for it to continue without a jury. 'Jury tampering' includes threatened or actual harm to, or intimidation or bribery of, a jury or any of its members, or their family or friends or property. For the prosecution's application to be granted in respect of a trial which has yet to take place, the court must be satisfied that two conditions are fulfilled:

(a)   there is evidence of a real and present danger that jury tampering will take place; and

(b)   there is so substantial a risk of jury tampering that it is necessary in the interests of justice for the trial to be conducted without a jury, notwithstanding any steps (e.g., police protection) which might reasonably be taken to prevent the risk.

19.07   Where the trial is already under way and the judge is minded to discharge the jury in accordance with his common law powers (see 18.51 to 18.61) because jury tampering appears to have occurred, he must hear representations from the defence and the prosecution as to how he should proceed. If he then decides to discharge the jury, he may order that the trial shall continue without a jury if he is satisfied that this would be fair to the defendant. Alternatively, he may terminate the trial, and has the option of ordering that the retrial is to take place without a jury (s 45). Again, he must be satisfied that the danger of jury tampering is such as to make trial without jury necessary in the interests of justice, notwithstanding any steps that could be taken to prevent jury tampering.

19.08   There is a right of appeal to the Court of Appeal by both the defence and the prosecution against any decision made by the court at a preparatory hearing on any application for a trial without a jury (s 47). There will also be a right of appeal against any order to continue a trial in the absence of a jury, or for a retrial to be conducted in the absence of a jury (s 47).

19.09   Where a court orders a trial to be conducted or continued without a jury, the trial will proceed in the usual way, except that functions which a jury would have performed will be performed by the judge alone. If the defendant is convicted, then the judge will have to give reasons for the conviction (s 48(5)).

Figure 19.1 Judge only Trials

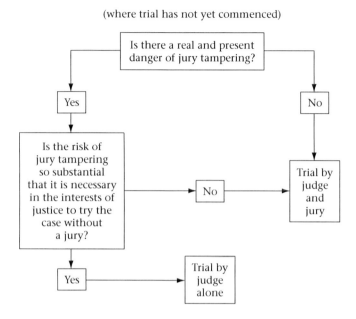

(where trial has not yet commenced)

The question: 'when is there evidence of a real and present danger of jury tampering?' is **19.10** answered, in part, in s 44(6) which gives 'examples' of such a danger as follows:

(a) the case is a retrial, and the jury in the previous hearing was discharged because of jury tampering;
(b) jury tampering has taken place in previous criminal proceedings involving the defendant (or any of them);
(c) there has been intimidation of a likely witness in the trial.

As these are examples, they are not exhaustive, nor do they constitute any sort of definition.

By contrast with the fraud provisions dealt with in 19.04 and 19.05, there are no special **19.11** conditions for the commencement of the provisions relating to jury tampering. They were brought into effect on 24 July 2006. The procedure involved is set out in the flowchart on this page.

C SAMPLE COUNTS

A further avenue by which the prosecution can seek trial on indictment without a jury is **19.12** opened up by s 17 of the DVCVA 2004. It was brought into effect for cases sent or committed to the Crown Court on or after 8 January 2007. In essence, the procedure allows the jury to try sample counts, with the remaining counts in the indictment capable of being tried by a judge sitting alone. The application by the prosecution may be acceded to by the judge if the following conditions are fulfilled:

(a) that the number of counts in the indictment is such that a trial of them all by jury would be impracticable;

(b) that each count to be tried by the jury can be regarded as a sample of counts which could for their part be tried by a judge alone; and

(c) that it is in the interests of justice to grant the order sought.

The judge should have regard to any steps which might be taken to facilitate a jury trial, but not if that might result in the defendant receiving a lesser sentence. If the judge accedes to the application, the sample counts are tried by the jury. If the jury finds the defendant guilty of one or more of the sample counts, the judge then tries the remaining counts in the light of the jury's verdict, and passes sentence in accordance with the overall culpability of the defendant.

KEY DOCUMENTS

Criminal Justice Act 2003, ss 43 to 50.
Domestic Violence, Crime and Victims Act 2004, s 17.

20

THE COURSE OF THE TRIAL

A   COUNSEL AND THE JUDGE

20.01   The judge at a trial on indictment must be a professional judge (i.e., a High Court judge; circuit judge or deputy circuit judge; or recorder). The distribution of work between these various types of judge is described at 14.14. The prosecution *must* be legally represented; the accused usually chooses to be so, and will probably be able to obtain representation from the Criminal Defence Service. Although some solicitors now have rights of audience in the Crown Court, legal representation for trial on indictment still usually involves instructing solicitors who in turn brief counsel (see 14.21 to 14.23). The following Paragraphs deal with some aspects of the role of prosecuting and defence counsel, and their relationship with the judge. The discussion is based upon decided cases and also upon the Code of Conduct for the Bar. The Code does not have the force of law, but is of great persuasive value, and a barrister who conforms with its spirit cannot be guilty of a breach of professional discipline.

20.02   The criminal justice system in this country is essentially adversarial. It is the duty of the prosecution to present the case for the Crown; and the role of counsel for the defence is to represent the accused. It follows that the judge's interventions must be limited to providing a framework in which counsel carry out their duties efficiently and fairly. In *Whybrow* (1994) *The Times*, 14 February 1994, the appellants complained that the judge had prevented them from giving their evidence in chief properly, and had intervened with such frequency and hostility as to deny them a fair trial. The Court of Appeal quashed their convictions, and ordered a retrial. Their lordships stressed that there were occasions when the judge could, and indeed should intervene. For example, if a witness gave an ambiguous answer, the judge should have it clarified 'as briefly as possible'. If he did not hear an answer, he could have it repeated so that he could note it accurately. He should 'intervene to curb prolixity and repetition and to exclude irrelevance, discursiveness and oppression of witnesses'. In this case, however, the Court of Appeal took the view that the judge's interventions went 'far beyond the bounds of legitimate judicial conduct'. One of the cases on which their lordships relied was *Hulusi* (1973) 58 Cr App R 378, in which it was said (per Lawton LJ at p. 385):

> It is a fundamental principle of an English trial that, if an accused gives evidence, he must be allowed to do so without being badgered and interrupted. Judges should remember that most people go into the witness-box, whether they be witnesses for the Crown or the defence, in a state of nervousness. They are anxious to do their best. They expect to receive a courteous hearing, and when they find, almost as soon as they get into the witness-box and are starting to tell their story, that the judge of all people is intervening in a hostile way, then, human nature being what it is, they are liable to become confused and not to do as well as they would have done had they not been badgered and interrupted.

The role of prosecuting counsel

20.03   Counsel for the prosecution is not in court to win the case at all costs. Of course, he should present the prosecution evidence as persuasively as possible, and cross-examine the defence witnesses with all proper vigour and guile. Nevertheless, as Avory J put it in *Banks* [1916] 2 KB 621, prosecuting counsel 'ought not to struggle for the verdict against the prisoner, but they ought to bear themselves rather in the character of ministers of justice assisting in the administration of justice'. One aspect of this role is that, should the defence suggest a plea of guilty to a lesser offence or guilty on some but not all the counts in the indictment (see Chapter 15), prosecuting counsel does not consider only whether the evidence he has available might secure a conviction on all counts as charged, but whether the proposed pleas represent a fair way of dealing with the case. If they do, and subject to any comments by the judge, he should accept the pleas, even though that means giving up the chance of 'extra' convictions.

In *Gomez* [1999] All ER (D) 674, the Court of Appeal endorsed the description of prosecuting counsel as a minister of justice, stating that it was incumbent on him not to be betrayed by personal feelings, not to excite emotions or to inflame the minds of the jury and not to make comments which could reasonably be construed as racist and bigoted. He was to be clinical and dispassionate. **20.04**

In 1986, the Chairman of the Bar set up a committee to consider the role of prosecuting counsel in the light of the imminent introduction of the Crown Prosecution Service. The committee was chaired by Farquharson J and also included distinguished members of the Bar. Its report was published in the Trinity 1986 edition of *Counsel* magazine. Appropriate points have been incorporated in the Written Standards contained in the Bar's Code of Conduct. **20.05**

The Report began by reiterating the special duty of prosecuting counsel to be fair, etc. and to conduct himself as a 'minister of justice'. This duty does entail counsel having 'greater independence from those instructing him than enjoyed by other counsel', although on the whole differences of opinion between him and the CPS should be resolved by sensible give-and-take on both sides, not by counsel insisting upon his rights. Most *tactical* decisions concerning the conduct of a trial (e.g., whether or not to call a certain witness, or what submissions to make as to the relevant law) arise at court when counsel is probably attended only by an unqualified clerk, and in such circumstances the only practical course is for counsel to take the decision himself. If the CPS do not approve, they have the sanction available to all disappointed solicitors of not briefing that counsel again. There are also what may be described as *policy* decisions, in particular as to whether to accept proffered pleas of guilty to part of the indictment or to a lesser offence and whether to offer no evidence at all. Is counsel then entitled to act contrary to his instructions?—i.e., accept the plea even though the CPS want him to continue or vice versa. The Committee state, first, that counsel should strive to prevent such a situation arising by advising promptly before trial on the point in question. If the CPS do not like the advice, they can take a second opinion and, if need be, brief other counsel. Where, however, the question arises too close to trial for that to be a realistic option and discussions between CPS lawyers and counsel have failed to resolve the disagreement, then—as a last resort—counsel must do what he conscientiously believes to be right, even if that means acting contrary to instructions. After trial, the Attorney-General might require him to submit a written report as to why he acted as he did. **20.06**

Thus, in respect of trials on indictment, counsel is the person ultimately in charge of the case for the prosecution and cannot be forced to act contrary to his views of what ought to be done. **20.07**

The role of defence counsel

20.08 Counsel for the defence is not placed under the same constraints as prosecuting counsel. He is under no duty to regard himself as a minister of justice, or to be fair to the prosecution, or to tell them that his client or one of his witnesses has previous convictions. Subject to what is said below, he may use all means at his disposal to secure an acquittal. Nevertheless, he has 'an over-riding duty to the court to ensure in the public interest that the proper and efficient adminis-tration of justice is achieved: he must assist the court in the administration of justice and must not deceive or knowingly or recklessly mislead the court' (para 202 of the Code of Conduct). If a procedural irregularity, such as a juror leaving the jury room after they have retired to con-sider their verdict, comes to defence counsel's knowledge before the verdict is announced, he should inform the court as soon as he can. He should not keep silent so as to be able to raise the irregularity on appeal should there be a conviction (*Smith* [1994] Crim LR 458).

20.09 The greater latitude afforded to defence counsel should not be exaggerated. Like all counsel, he owes a duty not just to his client but to the court. It follows that he must not deliberately mis-lead the court, or behave unethically in any other way. While he may point out the difficulties in the defence the accused wants to put forward, he must not suggest or invent a more plausi-ble defence. Although he need not reveal that the accused or his witness has convictions, he must not positively assert that they are of good character if he knows that to be false.

20.10 Perhaps the clearest statement of defence counsel's role is to be found in some principles outlined by the Chairman of the Bar (see 62 Cr App R 193). The statement followed criticism by Melford Stevenson J in the case of *McFadden and Cunningham* (1976) 62 Cr App R 187, of the way in which defence counsel had presented their case and cross-examined police wit-nesses. The Chairman of the Bar said that defence counsel's duty is to present to the court, 'fearlessly and without regard to his personal interests', the defence of the accused. His personal opinion of the truth or falsity of the defence, or of the character of the accused, or of the nature of the charge should all be left out of account—'that is a cardinal rule of the Bar, and it would be a grave matter in any free society were it not'. Of course, if the accused tells counsel that he is guilty, it would not be right for counsel to call evidence suggesting the opposite, as he would be deliberately misleading the court. If the accused insists on pleading not guilty despite his admission to counsel, guidance is provided by the Bar's Code of Conduct, Written Standards, paras 13.1 to 13.6. Where counsel does continue to act, he should confine himself to cross-examining the prosecution witnesses with a view to showing that their evidence does not establish guilt beyond a reasonable doubt. Provided, however, that the accused has not actually said he is guilty, counsel may, and indeed is under a duty, to put forward the defence as persuasively as possible, even though his personal opinion is that it is a tissue of lies.

20.11 However, the relationship between the duty of the advocate to the court and to his client must be interpreted in the light of changes in practice and procedure made by relevant legis-lation. For example, the duty laid upon the defence to make disclosure of the case which it will present at trial (see 9.16 to 9.30) has implications for the conduct of defence advocates. It may not be wise or proper to seek to gain advantage by omitting an issue relating to the charge from a defence statement, or concealing it during the plea and directions hearing, and then raising it for the first time in a submission of 'no case to answer', for example. In *Gleeson* [2003] Crim LR 579, Auld LJ said:

For defence advocates to seek to take advantage of such errors by deliberately delaying identification of an issue of fact or law in the case until the last possible moment is, in our view, no longer acceptable, given the legislative and procedural changes to our criminal justice process in recent years. Indeed, we consider it to be contrary to the requirement on an accused in [the CPIA 1996] s.5(6) . . . to indicate 'the matters on which he takes issue with the prosecution' and to their professional duty to the court – and not in the legitimate interests of the defendant.

Further examples of the difference between the prosecution and defence approach to a case will be found in the remainder of this Chapter. For a critical analysis of the difference, see Blake and Ashworth, 'Some Ethical Issues in Prosecuting and Defending' [1998] Crim LR 16.   **20.12**

Counsel seeing the judge in private

In appropriate circumstances, counsel should be permitted to see the judge in his private room in order to discuss with him matters relevant to the case in the absence of the parties and the public. As Lord Parker CJ put in in *Turner* [1970] 2 QB 321 (see also 17.18), 'there must be freedom of access between counsel and judge'. But his Lordship went on to say: **20.13**

> It is of course imperative that, as far as possible, justice must be administered in open court. Counsel should, therefore, only ask to see the judge when it is felt to be really necessary, and the judge must be careful only to treat such communications as private where, in fairness to the accused person, this is necessary.

Since *Turner* the Court of Appeal have stressed in cases such as *Coward* (1980) 70 Cr App R 70 and *Llewellyn* (1977) 67 Cr App R 149, that private access to the judge should be kept to an absolute minimum. One clear example of private access being appropriate is where defence counsel, who is to mitigate on behalf of an offender prior to sentencing, receives instructions that his client believes himself to be healthy but is in fact suffering from an incurable disease. Clearly the judge should be told of the offender's ill health, so as to avoid, if at all possible, passing a sentence which would result in his dying in prison. Equally clearly, to mention the fact in open court with the offender listening could have disastrous consequences. One of the problems which arises where a confidential meeting is held between counsel and the judge, however, is that what is said may be misunderstood by the defendant and lead to later allegations that pressure was put on him to plead guilty. This is the problem which arose in *Turner* [1970] 2 QB 321, and which is described in 17.18. More recently, detailed guidance has been provided in *Goodyear* [2005] 3 All ER 117 for cases where the judge is asked to provide an advance indication of sentence: see 17.32.

B   ABUSE OF PROCESS

Once an indictment against the accused has been signed there is very little the defence can do to prevent the prosecution going ahead. They can move to quash the indictment, or raise a special plea in bar (autrefois acquit, autrefois convict, or pardon), or plead that the Crown Court has no jurisdiction to try the case, but all these remedies are of limited scope and rarely assist in practice. If, however, defence counsel thinks that the prosecution is grossly unfair he has one further remedy at his disposal. He can ask the judge to intervene and stay the   **20.14** prosecution, i.e., order that it shall not proceed without leave of the court or of the Court of Appeal. It is now beyond doubt that the Crown Court has inherent power to prevent its process from abuse (for the position in the magistrates' court see 10.26 to 10.31 and 13.53 to 13.58). In *Connelly v DPP* [1964] AC 1254, for example, Lord Devlin stated at p. 1355 that, where particular criminal proceedings constitute an abuse of process, the court is empowered to refuse to allow the indictment to proceed to trial.

In *Beckford* [1996] 1 Cr App R 94, Neill LJ analysed the authorities and concluded that there were two main bases upon which the power to stay proceedings on the ground of abuse of process was exercised:

(a)   where the accused could not receive a fair trial; and
(b)   where it would be unfair for the accused to be tried.

Whilst this analysis provides a general test, it is also worth considering the various categories of cases in which the courts have made use of their power to stay on grounds of abuse. These include lengthy delay (coupled with prejudice to the defendant), failing to secure (or destroying) evidence, going back on a promise made to the defendant, and abuse of executive power (this list is by no means exhaustive). In the representations made by the defence and prosecution as to whether a stay should be granted, it is customary nowadays for the parties to deal in argument with the right to a fair trial under Art 6 of the ECHR, and the overriding objective under the CrimPR to deal with cases 'justly'.

20.15   Several cases have considered the issue of whether undue delay can constitute an abuse of process. There is, of course, no general time-limit upon the issue of proceedings for indictable offences (compare the six-month time-limit in respect of summary offences discussed in 10.18). Nevertheless, in *Bell v DPP of Jamaica* [1985] AC 397, the Privy Council accepted that courts have an inherent jurisdiction to prevent a trial which would be oppressive because of unreasonable delay. Generally, a stay on the basis of delay will only be granted if there has been prejudice to the defendant as a result. In terms of the analysis of Neill LJ in *Beckford* (see 20.14), the argument is whether the case falls within category (a): Could the accused receive a fair trial? In *Central Criminal Court ex parte Randle* [1991] Crim LR 551, for example, the applicants were charged with offences arising out of the escape from custody of George Blake while he was serving a 42-year sentence for spying. They appeared before the Central Criminal Court in 1990, some 23 years after the alleged offences. They applied for proceedings to be stayed on the grounds of unreasonable delay. The judge refused, and they sought judicial review of that decision. Whilst the Divisional Court refused their application, it was accepted that delay could by itself, in appropriate circumstances, be such as to render criminal proceedings an abuse of process. In this case, however, the applicants had published a book in 1989, which had provided much of the material upon which the prosecution relied. In the light of its contents, the plea of failing memory could not be advanced, and the Divisional Court would not interfere with the judge's discretion. The trial therefore had to proceed, although the accused were in due course found not guilty by the jury.

20.16   In *Attorney-General's Reference (No 2 of 2001)* [2004] 2 WLR 1, the House of Lords considered the principle that the right to a fair trial under Art 6 of the ECHR includes the right to have a trial within a reasonable time. In cases where the reasonable time requirement in Art 6(1) had been breached, should the proceedings be stayed? Their Lordships held that they should only be stayed if a fair hearing was no longer possible, or if for any compelling reason it was unfair to try the defendant. A crucial reason for so holding was that it would be anomalous if breach of the reasonable time requirement were to have an effect which was more far-reaching than other breaches of the defendant's rights under Art 6(1). The House of Lords also held that a stay of proceedings would never be an appropriate remedy if a lesser remedy would rescue the defendant's rights under the ECHR. It follows that a stay of proceedings will be the appropriate remedy where there has been prejudice caused to the defendant which can only be remedied by a stay of the proceedings. If there is no such prejudice, a stay will not be justified. In appropriate circumstances, the prejudice to the defendant may be overcome, for example, by a warning from the judge in summing up about the difficulties faced by the defence due to elapse of time since the events in question. *In Bell v DPP* the Privy Council laid down guidelines for determining whether the delay would deprive the accused of a fair trial. The relevant factors were said to be:

(a)   length of delay;
(b)   the prosecution's reasons to justify the delay;
(c)   the accused's efforts to assert his rights; and
(d)   the prejudice caused to the accused.

Clearly in *ex parte Randle*, the lack of prejudice to the defendants was held to be fatal to their argument, despite a delay of 23 years. In *Buzalek* [1991] Crim LR 115, the appellants were convicted of fraudulent trading, the case having been tried some six and a half years after they had been suspended from their jobs. The alleged fraud was of a mammoth nature, requiring the inspection of a great number of documents, many of which had to be translated from German. The trial judge had held that there was no reason why they should not receive a fair trial. The Court of Appeal dismissed the appeal. The case turned largely on documents, and it was possible for the memories of witnesses to be refreshed by referring to them. The passage of time would be much more prejudicial where a case turned, for example, on what witnesses saw in an affray, an assault or a road accident.

In *Dobson* [2001] All ER (D) 109, the Court of Appeal considered the position where police **20.17** had failed to obtain CCTV footage relating to the defendant's defence of alibi. Their lordships said that, in determining whether there was an abuse of process, it was appropriate to consider:

(a)   what was the duty of the police;
(b)   whether they had failed in it by not obtaining or retaining the appropriate video footage;
(c)   whether there was serious prejudice which rendered a fair trial impossible; and
(d)   whether the police failure was a result of bad faith or serious fault independently from the serious prejudice so that a trial would not be fair.

In the instant case, the police should have looked at the CCTV footage, and had failed in their duty to do so. However, the prejudice was not serious because it was uncertain that the footage would have assisted the defence, the defendant was in a position to understand the relevance of the footage and could have requested it and/or sought other evidence to support his alibi. There was no question of malice or intentional omission as opposed to oversight on behalf of the police. The judge was therefore right to conclude that a fair trial was possible and the conviction was upheld. Similar points were made by Brooke LJ in *R (Ebrahim) v Feltham*

Magistrates' Court [2001] 2 Cr App R 23. He also emphasized that most challenges to the prosecution case could be dealt with fairly within the trial process itself.

20.18 A further category of cases where abuse of process may apply is the situation where police or prosecutor gives an undertaking that a person will not be prosecuted. In *Jones v Whalley* [2007] 1 AC 63, the defendant was cautioned by the police for an offence, and the caution specifically stated that he would not have to go to face proceedings in a criminal court in connection with the matter. He was then the subject of a private prosecution for the offence. The House of Lords held that this was an abuse of process. Although he might receive a fair trial (evidence of his admission to the police and the caution could be excluded) it was not fair that he should be tried at all in view of the assurance which he had been given.

20.19 Another area of case law on the subject deals with the abuse of executive power or, to put it another way, cases where proceeding against the defendant would bring justice into disrepute. In *Mullen* [2000] QB 520, the police and security services brought about the accused's unlawful deportation from Zimbabwe, avoiding extradition proceedings. The Court of Appeal reasoned that it was an abuse of power to try him, even though he had received a fair trial, with the result that his conviction was unsafe and his appeal succeeded. Cases of entrapment also fall within this category. Although entrapment is not a defence in English law, where the defendant is able to show entrapment, the proceedings may be stayed as an abuse of process: *Looseley* [2001] 1 WLR 2060. The reason is that it is an affront to public conscience for the police to conduct themselves in such a way as to create crime. However, the police will not be regarded as instigating the crime if the defendant merely took advantage of an opportunity to commit a crime with the police officer, rather than someone else.

20.20 In the Crown Court, the procedure for an abuse of process application is set out in the *Consolidated Criminal Practice Direction* [2002] 1 WLR 2870, para IV.36. Written notice must be given to the court and the parties at least 14 days before trial, setting out the grounds on which the application is made. Skeleton arguments must be served by both sides prior to the hearing. The court may decide on the application prior to the commencement of the trial, and this will frequently be what the defence seeks. However, the court may well wish to deal with the matter at the conclusion of evidence, when the impact of the allegedly unfair features in the case faced by the defendant will be clearer.

C   THE PROSECUTION OPENING

20.21 After the accused has been put in the charge of the jury, prosecuting counsel opens his case. The prosecution opening gives the members of the jury an overall view of the case. Counsel will remind them of the charges against the accused, which the clerk has just read out to them, explaining any relevant points of law which may not be familiar to lay persons. Probably he will tell them that the prosecution has to prove its case so that they are sure of the accused's guilt, and, if they are not so convinced, they must acquit. Whenever counsel refer to the law it is usual to warn the jury that what they (counsel) say about the law is merely intended as a guide, and is subject to whatever the judge may rule—the jury take the law from the judge not from counsel.

After his explanation of the charges, counsel summarizes the evidence he intends to call. In **20.22** his brief, counsel has copies of the statements of prosecution witnesses. Basing himself on these he tells the jury the main facts which (he hopes) his various witnesses will prove, and indicates how the pieces of testimony fit together so as to show, beyond reasonable doubt, that the accused committed the offence charged. Having had a general picture of the case, the jury will be able to appreciate the significance of each witness's evidence as it is given. Three detailed points relevant to the opening are that:

(a) If counsel is told by the defence that they intend to object to certain pieces of prosecution evidence, that evidence should not be included in the prosecution's opening to the jury.

(b) It is sometimes advisable to 'open the case low'—i.e., slightly to underplay what a witness is expected to say. If counsel puts great weight on what a witness is going to prove, and then, in the event, the evidence is not quite as strong as the jury were led to expect, they may think that the whole prosecution case has been undermined.

(c) As part of his duty not to 'struggle after the verdict' counsel should avoid unnecessarily emotive language. Indeed, in cases where the facts alleged are likely to cause especial sympathy for the victim or repugnance towards the criminal, it is desirable for the opening to warn the jury against such natural feelings. They should return a verdict upon the evidence, not upon feelings of sympathy or horror.

D   THE PROSECUTION CASE

Next, the prosecution call witnesses to give oral evidence and tender in evidence written **20.23** statements which are read to the jury. At this point the subjects of evidence and procedure become intertwined. This book does not attempt to deal with evidence *per se*, so reference should be made to works on the subject for information on topics such as the competence and compellability of witnesses, oaths and affirmations and unsworn evidence, the course of a witness' examination, the admissibility of similar fact evidence and character evidence, the extent to which an accused may be cross-examined about his previous convictions, the rule against hearsay, exceptions to it such as confessions, and the various exclusionary rules of evidence. However, some matters which are, in a sense, part of the law of evidence, also have important procedural aspects, and these will be considered in the succeeding Sections. (For a summary of the order in which events take place at trial, see Appendix 3.)

The witnesses the prosecution should call

The persons who made written statements or depositions which were tendered by the pros- **20.24** ecution at committal or sent to the Crown Court under s 51 of the CDA 1998 are known collectively as 'witnesses whose names appear on the back of the indictment'. The term derives from the old practice of literally writing the names on the reverse of the indictment. The defence naturally assume that the prosecution will call at the trial on indictment all the witnesses whose names are on the back of the indictment (or that they will read out a statement or deposition made by the witness if that is permissible by virtue of one of the provisions described in 20.34). However, it does not follow that because a witness is on the back of the

indictment, and thus prima facie favourable to the prosecution, that the defence will necessarily be pleased if he is not called. It may be that part of the witness' anticipated evidence
will support the accused's case, or that the defence hope through skilled cross-examination
so to undermine the witness' testimony that doubt will be cast on the entire prosecution
case. In such a case, the defence would feel aggrieved if the prosecution did not call the witness. Therefore, the rule is that prosecuting counsel must call a witness whose name is on the
back of the indictment unless *either* it will be possible to read out his statement or deposition,
or the witness has failed to come to court despite the prosecution having taken all reasonable
steps to secure his attendance (see 20.27 to 20.31), *or* the witness does not appear to be a credible witness worthy of belief. In the latter case the prosecution remain under a duty to secure
the witness' attendance at court so that the defence can call him if they so wish.

20.25 In the normal course of events the prosecution would not, at committal proceedings, make
use of evidence from a person considered to be unworthy of belief. Thus, almost by definition,
a witness on the back of the indictment is a witness the prosecution regard as credible.
However, it can happen that the prosecution view of a witness changes between committal
proceedings and trial on indictment, and it is in that situation that prosecuting counsel might
decline to call the witness. In *Oliva* [1965] 1 WLR 1028, for example, the witness (W) had been
the victim of an offence of causing grievous bodily harm. He made a statement to the police
naming O as the culprit, and in evidence on the first day of committal proceedings testified
for the prosecution to that effect. Following an overnight adjournment, he reversed his evidence and exonerated O, but O was nevertheless committed for trial on the basis of other evidence. Since W had been called by the prosecution at committal proceedings, he was a
witness whose name appeared on the back of the indictment, but the Court of Appeal held
that prosecuting counsel rightly refused to call him at the trial as his sudden change of evidence at committal proceedings showed he was not worthy of belief. Had prosecuting counsel been forced to call W the jury would have been confused by a prosecution witness who
flatly contradicted the prosecution case, and counsel would have found it difficult to
challenge W's evidence because of the rule that one cannot cross-examine one's own witness.
As it was, defence counsel was given a not unfair choice between managing without W's evidence all together and calling W himself, in which event prosecuting counsel would be able
to cross-examine.

20.26 Sometimes, when the prosecution do not need a person's evidence (e.g., because several
witnesses have already given the relevant evidence which he could give) but they consider
him a credible witness, they 'tender him for cross-examination'. This means that they call
him, establish his name and address, and then allow the defence to question him as they see
fit. Where the judge considers that the prosecution are wrong not to call a witness, he may
himself call the person concerned.

Securing the attendance of witnesses

20.27 It is the prosecution's duty to take all reasonable steps to secure the attendance at court of the
witnesses whose names appear on the back of the indictment unless, in the case of any particular witness, they will be able to read his deposition or written statement to the jury under
the rules described in 20.34. The defence must arrange for the attendance of the witnesses

they wish to call. If a witness is not at court on the day of the trial the judge has a discretion either to adjourn the case or allow it to continue, notwithstanding that the jury will possibly be deprived of useful evidence. The exercise of the judge's discretion will turn upon matters such as the importance of the evidence the witness is likely to give; the reason for his absence (sickness, disappearance, absence abroad, possible intimidation etc.), and the likelihood of his attending on the next occasion were the case to be adjourned for a short time. Where the prosecution wish the case to proceed even though one of their witnesses is absent, the judge should especially consider the extent to which the absent witness might in part support the defence case: *Cavanagh and Shaw* [1972] 1 WLR 676.

The parties may need assistance in securing the attendance of the witnesses whom they wish **20.28** to call at trial. As far as the prosecution is concerned, they may wish to call a particular witness, or to have his evidence read. If the defence wishes to have that witness attend, however, it is entitled to object to that course of action. The position now is that all evidence tendered at committal 'may without further proof be read as evidence on the trial of the accused... unless a party to the proceedings objects'. Since only the prosecution can tender evidence at committal, the objection will in practice come from the accused (or one of them). If there is no objection from the defence, the prosecution can decide to call the witness in question, or read his statement. If the defence wishes to object, then it must give written notification to the prosecutor and the Crown Court within 14 days of committal (CrimPR, r 10.4). The defence objection will not necessarily conclude the matter, as it may be overruled by the trial judge (see 20.34).

In addition, a party wishing to secure the attendance of a witness at trial may apply to the **20.29** Crown Court for a witness summons under s 2 of the Criminal Procedure (Attendance of Witnesses) Act 1965. The Crown Court must be satisfied that the witness is likely to give material evidence, or produce a document or exhibit which is likely to be material evidence; and that he will not do so voluntarily. The application must be made as soon as reasonably practicable after the committal. A witness summons is useful where the prosecution or defence wish to call a witness who was not involved at the committal proceedings. If a witness who is subject to a witness summons fails to attend before the Crown Court when required, the judge can order that a notice be served on him telling him to attend at a time specified in the notice. Alternatively, if a notice has already been served or if there are reasonable grounds for believing that the witness has failed to attend without just excuse, the judge can issue a warrant to arrest him and bring him before the court: s 4(2). He can then be remanded in custody or on bail until he gives his evidence. Failure to obey, without just excuse, a witness order or summons is a contempt of court punishable with up to three months imprisonment: s 3.

The test for a 'just excuse' as laid down by the Court of Appeal in *Abdulaziz* [1989] Crim LR **20.30** 717 is remarkably strict: only sheer impossibility of attendance seems to constitute a good enough reason.

While the 1965 Act is a useful aid in securing the attendance of reluctant witnesses, it is worth **20.31** bearing in mind that no legislation can force a witness to give the evidence desired by the party calling him. A reluctant witness may be a difficult witness, who does more harm than good to his side's case.

Additional evidence

20.32   A witness may be called for the prosecution at a trial on indictment even though they did not tender his statement or deposition at committal proceedings. The obvious reason for not making use of a witness' evidence at committal proceedings but calling him at the trial is that the prosecution only became aware that the witness could give relevant evidence during the period between committal and the trial's commencement. However, even where the prosecution, at the time of the committal proceedings, know of the evidence the witness is able to give and intend to call him at the Crown Court, they are under no duty to tender his statement before the examining justices: *Epping and Harlow Justices ex parte Massaro* [1973] QB 433. In fact, there is little or nothing to be gained by not revealing the evidence at committal proceedings, since the prosecution at the trial on indictment are not allowed to take the defence by surprise with evidence of which they have given no prior warning. The rule is that a notice of intention to call an additional witness, together with a written account of the evidence it is proposed he should give, should be served by the prosecution on both the defence and the court. Usually they serve a copy of a statement signed by the witness and complying with the requirements of the Criminal Justice Act 1967, s 9 (see 20.34). The advantage of so doing is that, if the defence do not object, the original statement can be tendered in evidence, thus avoiding the need to call the witness.

20.33   Where no notice is served, the defence should be granted an adjournment so that they can deal properly with the additional evidence.

Depositions and written statements as evidence

20.34   As a general rule a witness, whether for the prosecution or the defence, should give his evidence orally in court. The jury can then see him, hear him and decide how trustworthy he is, and the party against whom he is called can challenge his evidence by cross-examination. In certain exceptional cases, however, a deposition or written statement may be read to the jury as evidence, and there is thus no need to call the maker as a witness. Although these exceptional cases might be regarded as part of the law of evidence—it is appropriate to describe them here because of their relevance to the question of which witnesses the parties should arrange to have at court.

    (a)   The Criminal Procedure and Investigations Act 1996, Sch 2, provides for the statements tendered at committal by the prosecution to be read in evidence at the subsequent Crown Court trial. Identical provisions apply to a deposition taken under s 97A of the Magistrates' Courts Act 1980, and tendered in evidence at committal. The defence must give written notification to the prosecutor and the Crown Court within 14 days of committal, stating that there is objection to the statement or objection being read at trial. That does not, however, conclude the matter. The objection of the defence can be overruled by the trial judge. According to para 1(4) of Sch 2 to the CPIA, 'the court of trial may order that the objection shall have no effect if the court considers it to be in the interests of justice so to order'. It is submitted that the Crown Court ought to be extremely wary about overruling the objections of the defence, and thus denying the accused the right to see those who are giving evidence against him, let alone the right to cross-examine them. Any suspicion that objections were overruled for reasons which were less than compelling would be contrary to well-established principle, and would be likely to lead to the prospect of a challenge based upon Art 6(3)(d) of the European Convention on Human Rights (see Chapter 28).

(b) A deposition taken out of court under the Children and Young Persons Act 1933, s 42, from a child or young person who was the victim of one of a list of sexual or violent offences is admissible in evidence at the trial on indictment if the court is satisfied, upon medical evidence, that the attendance of the child or young person before the court would involve serious danger to his life or health (s 43 of the 1933 Act). The deposition is only admissible against the accused if he was given notice of the intention to take it and an opportunity to cross-examine the child or young person.

(c) The Criminal Justice Act 1967, s 9 provides for the admissibility of written statements in criminal proceedings other than committal proceedings. To be admissible under s 9 the statement must be signed and contain a declaration that it is true to the best of the maker's knowledge and belief etc. The party proposing to tender the statement in evidence must serve a copy of it on each of the other parties. If one of those parties, during the period of seven days from the date of the service of the copy on him, serves notice on the party wishing to use the statement that he objects to it going into evidence, the statement cannot be tendered. Thus, s 9 statements are only admissible if all the parties agree. Even where a statement is admissible under s 9 the court may require that the maker attend to give oral evidence. This would be appropriate where the defence dispute the contents of a s 9 statement but, through inadvertence, failed to serve notice objecting to it being tendered. Section 9 applies both to summary trials and to trials on indictment. At the latter, it is chiefly used where the prosecution wish to adduce evidence additional to that which they used at committal proceedings (see 20.32 to 20.33).

(d) Sections 114 to 120 of the CJA 2003 make provision for the introduction of hearsay evidence. The process for the introduction of such evidence is described in Part 34 of the CrimPR, Part 34 (see Chapter 2). The evidential points at issue are dealt with in detail in *Blackstone's Criminal Practice 2008*, F16.

Defence objections to proposed prosecution evidence

Having read the committal statements, the defence may consider that some of the proposed **20.35** prosecution evidence is inadmissible. It is a fundamental principle of trials on indictment that questions of law, including the admissibility of evidence, are decided by the judge not the jury. Therefore, the defence will have to ask the judge to exclude the evidence to which they object. Should the objection be upheld, it would obviously be prejudicial for the jury to hear reference to the inadmissible material. The procedure described below is designed to prevent that occurring.

Before the start of the trial, defence counsel should warn his opponent that he intends to **20.36** object to certain evidence. In his opening speech counsel therefore refrains from mentioning that evidence. He then calls his remaining evidence in the normal way up to the point when the disputed material would otherwise be introduced. Then one or other counsel (probably defence) invites the judge to ask the jury to leave court, perhaps saying that a point of law has arisen which only concerns the lawyers. Once the jury have retired to their room, defence counsel makes his objection to the evidence; prosecuting counsel replies, and the judge makes his ruling. If the evidence is inadmissible, the jury hear nothing about it; if it is admissible, it is called immediately upon their returning to court; in either event, they are told nothing of what occurred in their absence. The above procedure is all that is needed where the admissibility of the evidence can be decided solely by reference to the relevant law and the evidence itself as foreshadowed in the committal statements. Sometimes, however, admissibility depends upon the circumstances in which the evidence was obtained, and those circumstances may themselves be in dispute. It is then for the judge to decide (i) the factual question of how the prosecution got the evidence, and (ii) the legal question of whether, in the light of his findings of fact, the evidence is admissible. In such cases, there has to be a *trial on the 'voir dire'*. By far the commonest example of this occurring is where the defence represent that a confession should be excluded under s 76 and/or s 78 of the Police and Criminal Evidence Act 1984. It will therefore be convenient to describe 'voir dires' through the illustration of challenges to confessions, although such challenges are not the only possible reason for adopting the procedure.

20.37   Up to the jury leaving court, the procedure is as for any other dispute on evidence—i.e., prosecuting counsel does not refer to the confession in his opening speech; the case proceeds as normal until the police officer to whom the confession was made is about to testify about it, and the jury are then sent out. Next, the officer gives evidence before the judge as to the making of the confession. He will probably say that he and a fellow officer interviewed the accused at the police station; that a contemporaneous note was taken of what was said, and that, at the end, the accused read through and signed the note. The signed note, containing damaging admissions, is then produced before the judge. Defence counsel may then cross-examine the officer. Typically it will be suggested that threats were made in order to induce the confession; or bail was promised; or the accused was held for an unacceptably long period without access to a solicitor or proper rest, refreshment, etc. The second officer who was present at the interview (and any other prosecution witnesses who can give relevant evidence) may then be called and cross-examined. After that, the accused himself is at liberty to testify and may also call witnesses (e.g., a doctor who examined him immediately after his release from the police station and saw bruises consistent with his claim that he was beaten up by the police). All these witnesses give their testimony on a special form of oath, known as the 'voir dire', the wording of which is— 'I swear by almighty God that I will true answer make to all such questions as the court shall demand of me'. The questions they are asked on the voir dire, whether in chief or cross-examination, must relate only to the admissibility or otherwise of the confession. At common law the accused could not even be asked if the confession was true (see *Wong Kam-Ming v R* [1980] AC 247). The same rule applies under s 76 of PACE, since—unless the prosecution prove that the confession was not obtained in contravention of the section—it must be excluded 'notwithstanding that it may be true' (see s 76(2)(b)). Once the evidence on the voir dire has been given, the judge listens to counsel's submissions and announces his decision, both as to the facts and their legal consequences. If the confession is held inadmissible, the jury, of course, hear nothing of it. If it is admissible, the self-same evidence and cross-examination as was advanced on the voir dire may be advanced again before the jury as part of the general prosecution and defence cases. At this stage, however, the evidence goes merely to the weight that the jury should attach to the confession, not to the question of admissibility. Should the accused choose to testify before the jury, he cannot be asked about anything he said on the voir dire, save that if he gives evidence as to how he came to confess which is inconsistent with the explanation he gave at the voir dire stage, he can be cross examined about the discrepancy (see *Wong Kam-Ming v R* above). For obvious reasons, the above procedure is colloquially known as a 'trial within a trial'.

20.38   As already stated, trials within a trial are not by law restricted to confession cases. However, they should only be held if the decision on admissibility of evidence genuinely cannot be reached without making prior determinations of fact. Outside of inadmissible confessions, it will nearly always be possible for the judge to make his ruling simply on the basis of the committal statements without hearing evidence. Thus in *Flemming* (1987) 86 Cr App R 32 the Court of Appeal upheld the judge's decision to admit identification evidence despite a defence contention that its quality was so poor that its prejudicial effect would exceed its probative value, but criticized him for holding a full trial within a trial. The relevant considerations (i.e., the circumstances of the identification and alleged breach of the rules on holding identification parades) emerged perfectly well from the committal statements. On the other hand, the trial within a trial procedure has been commended by the Court of Appeal to judges deciding upon the admissibility of a computer printout (*Minors* [1989] 1 WLR 441).

The voir dire procedure is intended for the benefit of the defence. It follows that they should **20.39** not be forced to adopt it against their will. The disadvantage that some defence advocates perceive in having a trial within a trial is that the prosecution witnesses dealing with the obtaining of the allegedly inadmissible evidence are alerted to the defence line of attack. Should the judge rule that the evidence is admissible, the witnesses will be able to counter the defence cross-examination before the jury more effectively than if they had not had, so to speak, a 'dry run' on the voir dire. Lord Bridge, giving the judgment of the Privy Council in *Ajodha v The State* [1982] AC 204, said *obiter* that, at the 'vast majority' of trials where the admissibility of a confession is to be challenged, the procedure already described will be adopted. But, as an alternative, it is open to defence counsel merely to impugn the confession before the jury during the ordinary course of cross-examination of prosecution witnesses and calling of defence evidence. At the end of the evidence, he may then ask the judge to rule the confession inadmissible as a matter of law. If the judge agrees, he will tell the jury in his summing-up to ignore the confession completely or, if there is no case to answer without it, direct them to acquit the accused. In *Airey* [1985] Crim LR 305, the Court of Appeal quashed A's conviction because the judge had not allowed the defence to follow such a course. In *Sat-Bhambra* (1988) 88 Cr App R 55, however, the Court of Appeal held that the defence could not seek a retrospective ruling on the admissibility of a confession on the basis of s 76 of PACE because of the wording of that section. It refers to a decision about evidence which has not yet been put before the court, using the formulae 'proposes to be given in evidence' and 'shall not allow the confession to be given'. The same logic would seem to apply to an objection based on s 78 of PACE, which also applies where 'the prosecution proposes to rely on evidence'. There remains a common law discretion for the judge to exclude evidence (preserved by s 82(3) of PACE), which can be exercised after a confession has been admitted in evidence (see for details, *Blackstone's Criminal Practice 2008*, F17.22 and F17.48).

In any event, it is clear that the Court still regards a hearing on the voir dire as the normal and **20.40** preferred way of dealing with objections to confessions, and their Lordships have held that— where the alternative procedure is adopted—the defence cannot ask the judge to consider the confession's admissibility at the end of the prosecution evidence but must wait until the end of *all* the evidence: *Jackson* [1985] Crim LR 444. This means that defence counsel is forced to take the vital decision on whether to call his client without knowing whether the jury will be told to ignore the confession completely or merely told to give it such weight as they think proper. It should also be noted that the judge is given a discretion by s 76(3) of PACE to raise the issue of a confession's admissibility on his own initiative, in which event a trial within a trial would presumably be held whether defence counsel wanted it or not.

20.41   According to *Hendry* (1988) 88 Cr App R 187 the judge has the power to ask the jury to retire during submissions on the admissibility of evidence, even if that is against the wishes of the defence.

20.42   A further variation on the standard procedure for objecting to evidence is that the judge can be asked to deal with the question as a preliminary issue immediately after the jury has been empanelled. This is an appropriate course to adopt when the prosecution case depends very largely on the challenged evidence, and counsel could not sensibly open his case to the jury without referring to it (see *Hammond* [1941] 3 All ER 318). If the judge rules the evidence inadmissible, counsel will probably offer no evidence; if it is admissible, counsel's potential problem with his opening speech is overcome.

Limits set on defence cross-examination

20.43   In general, defence counsel may ask a prosecution witness any question in cross-examination provided it is relevant, and provided the answer will not involve inadmissible material such as hearsay or non-expert opinion. A question is relevant if it concerns an issue in the case, i.e., it relates directly to whether the accused committed the offence, or it relates to a fact which increases or decreases the likelihood of his having done so. A question is also relevant if it concerns the credit of the witness, i.e., it relates to a fact from which the jury may conclude that he is not the sort of person who can be trusted to speak the truth. Thus, counsel is free, to a large extent, to cross-examine on whatever he thinks will assist his client's case. This freedom is limited by the Bar's Code of Conduct, with which barristers have a duty to comply. The following extracts from the Written Standards contained in the Code are particularly relevant:

(a)   Counsel must at all times promote and protect fearlessly and by all proper and lawful means his lay client's best interests (para 5.1);

(b)   he must not make statements or ask questions which are merely scandalous, or intended or calculated only to vilify, insult or annoy the witness or some other person (para 5.10(e));

(c)   he must not in a speech impugn a witness whom he has had an opportunity to cross-examine, unless in cross-examination he gave the witness an opportunity to answer the allegation (para 5.10(g));

(d)   he must not suggest that a victim, witness or other person is guilty of crime, fraud or misconduct, or attribute to another person the crime with which his client is charged, unless such allegations go to a matter in issue (including credibility of the witness) material to his client's case, and appear to him to be supported by reasonable grounds (para 5.10(h)).

The above rules also apply where appropriate to prosecution cross-examination of defence witnesses.

Formal admissions

20.44   Reading a witness' deposition or written statement (see 20.34) is a convenient method of proving facts which are not in dispute. Another way of proving an undisputed fact is for the party against whom evidence of the fact would otherwise be led, to admit formally that it is true. The formal admission is conclusive evidence of the fact admitted, so no evidence on the matter need be adduced. The Criminal Justice Act 1967, s 10 which applies both to summary trials and to trials on indictment, governs the making of formal admissions.

Section 10 provides that any fact of which oral evidence may be given in criminal proceedings **20.45** may be formally admitted, for purposes of those proceedings, by either the prosecution or defence. The admission may be made at or before trial. Unless made in court (e.g., at the trial or at a pre-trial review), it must be in writing and signed. An admission by the defence must be made by the accused personally or by counsel or solicitor on his behalf. If the admission is made by the accused personally before trial, it must be approved by counsel or solicitor on his behalf either at the time it is made or subsequently. The admission only binds the party making it in the criminal proceedings for purposes of which it was made and in any subsequent criminal proceedings, such as a retrial or appeal, arising out of the original proceedings. Thus, if the defence at a trial on indictment for dangerous driving formally admit that on 1 January 2008 the accused was driving car number ABC 123 in Acacia Avenue, they cannot deny that fact either at the trial or on an appeal to the Court of Appeal against conviction, but if the accused is subsequently prosecuted for driving while disqualified on the same occasion or issued in civil proceedings based on the alleged dangerous driving, he is free to deny that he was driving the car. The formal admission in the dangerous driving proceedings might be used as evidence against him in the other proceedings, but it would not be conclusive evidence. Even in the proceedings for purposes of which it was made a formal admission can be withdrawn with leave of the court: s 10(4).

Where an admission is made by counsel in argument in court but in the absence of the jury, **20.46** it may be treated as an admission in terms of s 10 of the Criminal Justice Act 1967, even though it was not intended as such (*Lewis* [1989] Crim LR 61). Counsel therefore needs to be careful not to make unguarded statements during the course of an argument before the judge.

A formal admission by the defence under s 10 must not be confused with a confession by the **20.47** accused in which he informally admits to the police or some other person that he committed the crime (or admits a fact which makes it more likely he committed the crime). Provided it was not obtained by oppression or as a result of words or conduct likely to render it unreliable, a confession is admissible evidence to prove the facts stated in it. Often it is very powerful evidence, but it is not conclusive evidence of the facts admitted as a formal admission is. The defence may, and often do, agree that the accused made a confession, but deny the truth of the facts confessed; if they have made a formal admission they cannot deny the fact admitted, unless the court gives leave for the admission to be withdrawn. Also, whereas a formal admission made out of court must be in writing and approved by counsel or solicitor, neither of these two conditions apply to confessions—indeed, it is hard to imagine defence counsel ever approving a confession if he could block its admissibility by withholding approval.

E SUBMISSION OF NO CASE TO ANSWER

After the prosecution evidence, oral and written, has been adduced, prosecuting counsel **20.48** closes his case by saying 'that is the case for the prosecution', or words to that effect. Defence counsel may then, if he so wishes, submit that there is no case to answer (see 10.60 and 13.67 to 13.69 for the equivalent submissions in summary trials and committal proceedings, respectively). If the accused is unrepresented, or even if he is but counsel apparently is not going to make a submission when one is called for, the judge can raise the matter on his own initiative. The submission may be made on all or any of the counts, or on behalf of all or any of the accused joined in the indictment. If a submission on a count succeeds the judge directs the jury to acquit on that count the accused on whose behalf the submission was made.

20.49   There is no case to answer if the prosecution have failed to adduce evidence on which a jury, properly directed by the judge in his summing-up, could properly convict: *Galbraith* [1981] 1 WLR 1039. If there is literally no evidence relating to an essential element of the offence (e.g., because a prosecution witness has failed to give the evidence expected of him), a submission of no case must clearly succeed. A submission should also succeed if the prosecution rely on circumstantial evidence to establish an element of the offence, but the inferences they ask the jury to draw from the evidence cannot reasonably be drawn. Thus, on a charge of handling stolen goods, the judge could rule no case to answer if the only evidence of guilty knowledge is that the accused bought the goods at an under-value, but the difference between the price he paid and the true value was too small to put the accused on suspicion that the goods might be stolen.

20.50   Difficult problems arise where there is some evidence that the accused committed the offence but, for one reason or another, it seems unconvincing. The basic principle is that the jury should decide whether witnesses are telling the truth or not, and the judge should not usurp their function by directing them to acquit merely because he thinks the prosecution witnesses are lying. As it was put in *Galbraith* [1981] 1 WLR 1039 (at p. 1042):

> How then should the judge approach a submission of 'no case?' (1) If there is no evidence that the crime alleged has been committed by the defendant, there is no difficulty. The judge will of course stop the case. (2) The difficulty arises where there is some evidence but it is of a tenuous character, for example because of inherent weakness or vagueness or because it is inconsistent with other evidence. (a) Where the judge comes to the conclusion that the prosecution evidence, taken at its highest, is such that a jury properly directed could not properly convict upon it, it is his duty, upon a submission being made, to stop the case. (b) Where however the prosecution evidence is such that its strength or weakness depends on the view to be taken of a witness's reliability, or other matters which are generally speaking within the province of the jury and where on one possible view of the facts there *is* evidence upon which a jury could properly come to the conclusion that the defendant is guilty, then the judge should allow the matter to be tried by the jury.

There is some room for interpretation of the judge's role as set out in *Galbraith*, however. In two more recent cases, the Court of Appeal has indicated that a judge must ensure that the case should not go to the jury if it would be unsafe to convict. In *Brown* [1998] Crim LR 196 Rose LJ said:

> It seems to us that, throughout a trial, the judge has a responsibility not to allow a jury to consider evidence on which they could not safely convict . . . . If, at the conclusion of all the evidence, a trial judge is of the view that no reasonable jury, properly directed, could safely convict, he should, generally speaking, whether a submission of no case has been made at the conclusion of the prosecution case or not, raise that view for discussion with counsel, in the absence of the jury. If, having heard submissions, he remains of that view, then he should, in our judgment, withdraw the case from the jury . . .

20.51   In *Shire* [2001] EWCA Crim 2800, the accused was charged with causing death by dangerous driving. The Court of Appeal considered the evidence of a group of his friends who appeared, according to impartial observers to be 'in high spirits' at the time of the accident, and may have been trying to get the accused's bus to stop so they could board it. There were inconsistencies in their statements, which were at odds in important respects with those of the impartial observers. Nevertheless, it could be said 'on one possible view of the facts' (to quote *Galbraith*) that a jury could have concluded that the accused was guilty. The Court of Appeal, however, did not seem to think that the jury could have done so 'properly', and stated that:

> The inherent risk of unreliability of the evidence given by that group was such that when considered in the light of the discrepancies in the evidence, it would be necessary, before leaving it to the jury, to have some evidence independent of that evidence which could justify the jury concluding that it could be reliable evidence.

To put it another way, as Turner J did at first instance in *Shippey* [1988] Crim LR 767, the obligation to 'take the prosecution case at its highest' does not require a trial judge to 'take out the plums, leaving the duff behind'.

The procedure for a submission of no case is that the jury are asked to leave court. This is so **20.52** that counsel and the judge can comment freely upon the quality and significance of the evidence without the risk of the jury being influenced by what is said. Once the jury have gone, defence counsel makes his submission, and prosecuting counsel is given an opportunity to reply. The judge then announces his decision, and the jury are brought back into court. If the judge has decided that there is no case to answer on all counts, he explains briefly to the jury the decision he has reached. He then asks them to appoint a foreman to speak for them, and the clerk of court takes from the foreman on each count a verdict of not guilty upon the judge's direction. If the decision was that there is no case to answer on one or more counts, but there is a case to answer on other counts, the judge tells the jury that at the end of the trial he will be directing them to return a verdict of not guilty on the counts in respect of which there is no case, and so, for the remainder of the trial, they should ignore those counts. However, on the remaining counts, the case will proceed as normal. If the submission failed on all counts, the jury are told nothing of what went on in their absence.

The judge's power to direct an acquittal after a submission of no case to answer is an impor- **20.53** tant one, although the number of cases in which it is used appears to be decreasing. According to the CPS Report for 2006/7, 4.5 per cent of all acquittals in the Crown Court were directed by the judge at the close of the prosecution case.

In one important type of case the correct approach to submissions of no case has been **20.54** explained by the Court of Appeal with some precision. Where the main issue in the case is one of mistaken identity (i.e., the case against the accused depends substantially on the correctness of one or more identifications of him which the defence allege to be mistaken), the judge should assess the quality of the identifying evidence. If it is poor, and if there is no other evidence to support the correctness of the identification, the judge should withdraw the case from the jury: *Turnbull* [1977] QB 224. Identification evidence is poor if the witnesses only saw whoever committed the offence for a short space of time, or saw him in circumstances of fear or confusion, or if the lighting conditions were bad, or if a long time elapsed between seeing the culprit and picking out the accused at an identification parade. The detailed guidance given to judges on how they should decide submissions of no case in identification cases is necessary because judicial experience has shown mistaken identifications by honest witnesses to be a prime factor in wrongful convictions.

For similar reasons, special guidance was laid down in *MacKenzie* (1992) 96 Cr App R 98, for a trial judge who is considering a submission of no case to answer in certain cases depending on a confession by the accused. The judge should withdraw the case from the jury if all the following conditions apply:

(a) the prosecution case depended wholly upon confessions;

(b) the defendant suffered from a significant degree of mental handicap; and

(c) the confessions were unconvincing to a point where a jury properly directed could not properly convict upon them.

Confessions might be unconvincing, for example, because they lacked the incriminating details to be expected of a guilty and willing confessor, because they were inconsistent with other evidence, or because they were otherwise inherently improbable.

20.55 There is a different procedure which must be followed where the defendant is charged in the same trial with murder or manslaughter and an offence under the Domestic Violence, Crime and Violence Act 2004, s 5, in respect of the same death. That provision deals with the offence of causing or allowing the death of a child or a vulnerable adult. In such a case, the question whether there is a case to answer on the murder or manslaughter charge must not be considered before the close of all the evidence.

F   THE DEFENCE CASE

20.56 Assuming there is a prosecution case to answer, the next stage of the trial is for the defence to present their case. Since it is for the prosecution to prove each element of the offence charged beyond reasonable doubt, the defence are under no obligation to adduce any evidence whatsoever. Defence counsel can, without calling evidence of his own, submit to the jury in a closing speech that the accused should be acquitted as the prosecution evidence fails to establish their case to the requisite standard of proof. Such a strategy may be right when the prosecution's case is weak, but in general there are obvious dangers in the jury only hearing evidence favouring the prosecution. It is therefore unusual for the defence not to call evidence.

Defence opening speech

20.57 If defence counsel is calling evidence as to the facts of the case other than or in addition to the evidence of the accused, he has the right to make an opening speech to the jury. In that speech he may both outline his own case and criticise the evidence which has been called by the prosecution. Where the only defence evidence is from the accused, or from the accused and witnesses who speak only as to his good character, defence counsel does not have an opening speech: Criminal Evidence Act 1898, s 2.

Defence evidence

20.58 The accused is a competent but not compellable witness for the defence (Criminal Evidence Act 1898, s 1)—i.e., he is entitled but cannot be forced to give evidence, e.g., by a co-defendant. Irrespective of whether he goes into the witness-box, other persons may be called for the defence, and may testify about the factual issues in dispute or the character of the accused or both. The defence may also take advantage of the various statutory provisions permitting the reading of depositions and written statements (see 20.34). Where defence witnesses are to be called in addition to the accused, the latter should normally be called first. This is partly because the accused is the person best able to tell the jury what the defence case is, and partly because he is allowed to be in court throughout the trial and so, if permitted to testify after his witnesses, would be able to tailor his evidence to fit in with what he has heard them say. Witnesses other than the accused, whether called for the prosecution or defence, are kept out of court until after they have testified. The judge does, however, have a discretion to let a defence witness be called before the accused: Police and Criminal Evidence Act 1984, s 79. It might be appropriate to exercise that discretion if, for example, the witness has a pressing engagement elsewhere and his evidence is unlikely to be challenged by the prosecution.

Details about the accused as a witness must be sought in the books on evidence. Very briefly, **20.59** the position is that he is treated like any other witness except that:

(a) He can be asked questions which tend to incriminate him as to the offence charged, and to that extent cannot, as witnesses normally can, claim a privilege against self-incrimination: Criminal Evidence Act 1898, s 1(e). It would obviously be absurd if the accused could give evidence exonerating himself and then avoid any questions in cross-examination which might tend to show him guilty.
(b) The rules relating to the admission of evidence of bad character are different for the defendant from those in respect of other witnesses: see CJA 2003, ss 98 to 108, which are dealt with in detail in *Blackstone's Criminal Practice 2008*, F12 and F14.

Nothing should be said or done to suggest to the jury that the accused, as a witness, is inferi- **20.60** or to the other witnesses in the case. This is illustrated in a symbolic way by the fact that in the absence of compelling reasons to the contrary (e.g., the risk of violence or attempted escape), the accused should testify from the witness box not the dock (Criminal Evidence Act 1898, s 1(g) and see *Farnham Justices ex parte Gibson* [1991] Crim LR 642). However, being treated essentially like the other witnesses is often a dubious advantage for the accused, as he is exposed to cross-examination by prosecuting counsel. This is particularly damaging where he is of bad character, and evidence as to his previous convictions is admissible (see 20.59(b)). Until fairly recently the accused could avoid the risks inherent in cross-examination, but still tell the jury his side of the story, by making an unsworn statement while standing in the dock. He was not then subject to questioning either by his own counsel, or prosecuting counsel or anybody else. However, the right to make an unsworn statement was abolished by s 72 of the Criminal Justice Act 1982. Thus the accused now faces a stark choice. He can say nothing, which may well lead to the jury drawing an unfavourable inference as to his guilt (Criminal Justice and Public Order Act 1994, s 35; see *Blackstone's Criminal Practice 2008*, F19.20); or he may give evidence on oath which, of course, will be subject to cross-examination. The decision must be his. As the Bar's Code of Conduct puts it (Written Standards, para 11.4):

> A barrister acting for a defendant should advise his client as to whether or not to give evidence in his own defence but the decision must be taken by the client himself.

Should the decision be against going into the box, defence counsel should always record the decision and ensure that the defendant signs the record, indicating (a) that he has decided of his own accord not to give evidence and (b) that he has so decided bearing in mind the advice (regardless of what it was) given by counsel (*Bevan* (1994) 98 Cr App R 354). The usual way in which this is done is for the record to be endorsed in a note on counsel's brief.

Disclosure and alibi evidence

20.61   As part of their duty of disclosure (see 9.16 to 9.29), the defence should have served the prosecution and the court, prior to trial, with a statement setting out the terms of the defence, the matters on which they take issue with the prosecution case and the reasons why (Criminal Procedure and Investigations Act 1996, s 5(6)). In addition, they should have given certain particulars if the defence involves an alibi, e.g., the name, address, date of birth and other information to aid tracing, of any witness who is able to give evidence in support of alibi (s 5(7)).

20.62   The general consequences which flow from the service (or non-service) of a defence statement are dealt with at 9.41 to 9.53. These consequences apply equally to a defence statement which raises alibi. The peculiar feature of alibi as a defence, however, is that it requires the accused to provide details of prospective witnesses in the defence statement. The definition of 'alibi' contained in s 5(8) is therefore important; 'alibi' means evidence 'tending to show that by reason of the presence of the (accused) at a particular place . . . at a particular time he was not . . . at the place where the offence is alleged to have been committed' at the relevant time. Evidence which merely indicates that the accused was not present as the place where the offence was committed is not 'evidence in support of an alibi'. To be caught by the definition in s 5(8), the evidence must be evidence that the accused was at some other place (*Johnson* [1995] 2 Cr App R 41). When the defence duty to notify *all* witnesses comes into force, (CJA 2003, s 33 (2)) the distinction between alibi evidence and other evidence for the defence will become less important.

20.63   Although defence counsel has general authority to make tactical decisions about the way a case should be run and need not obtain his client's express approval at every point, any decision not to call alibi evidence is so fundamental that it should not be taken unless there has been prior consultation at which the accused agrees (preferably in writing) that the alibi should not after all be advanced. Thus, in *Irwin* [1987] 1 WLR 902 counsel's conduct in taking a spot decision while the appellant was in the witness box not to call his wife and daughter in support of his alibi amounted to a material irregularity in the course of the trial that necessitated the quashing of the conviction. Although *Irwin* was said in *Ensor* [1989] 1 WLR 497 to be 'regarded as being confined to its own facts', it is submitted that it remains good authority in relation to a decision by counsel, without consultation, not to call an alibi witness (see further 26.31).

Expert evidence

20.64   The requirement to reveal to the prosecution, in advance of trial, any expert evidence which the defence propose to adduce is set out in Part 24 of the CrimPR, Part 24.

20.65   In brief, the rules state that, unless he has already done so, a party to a trial on indictment who proposes to adduce expert evidence shall, as soon as possible after committal, provide the other parties with a written statement setting out his expert's finding or opinion. If the expert bases his view upon some experiment, observation, calculation or other procedure that he has carried out, the other parties are also entitled, on request, to a record of or opportunity to examine the experiment, etc. Exemption from the requirements of the rules may be sought on the ground that compliance might lead to intimidation of the expert or other interference with the course of justice. Assuming no exemption has been granted, non-compliance will mean that the expert evidence can only be adduced with leave of the court. The sanction is therefore different in kind from that imposed in other cases of incomplete defence disclosure (see 9.16 to 9.29). It applies to the prosecution also, although it is to be expected that any expert evidence for the prosecution will in any event be served when the case is committed or sent to the Crown Court for trial, or thereafter by way of a notice of additional evidence.

Part 33 of the CrimPR lays down that the duty of an expert to the court overrides any duty to **20.66** the person who instructs him. It also gives the court power to order that experts instructed by different parties should meet prior to the trial and determine which matters they are agreed upon, and which matters are in dispute between them.

More than one accused in the indictment

If two or more accused are charged in one indictment and are separately represented their **20.67** cases are presented in the order in which their names appear on the indictment. Thus, if Robert Smith precedes John Brown on the indictment, counsel for Smith makes his opening speech (if he has the right to one), then calls Smith and his other witnesses. Counsel for Brown may question each witness after his evidence in chief and before cross-examination by the prosecution. Then Brown's counsel opens his case, and so forth. There is little authority on who should be named first on an indictment. It may seem strange that the order of the defence cases depends on how prosecuting counsel or an officer of the Crown Court chooses to draft the indictment.

Where two or more accused are jointly represented they are treated as, in effect, presenting a **20.68** joint defence. Counsel has one opening speech on behalf of both accused, and may then call them in turn to give evidence.

The unrepresented accused

Although an accused at the Crown Court is encouraged to obtain legal representation, he is **20.69** entitled to conduct his own defence throughout, or, indeed, to start with the benefit of legal representation and dismiss his counsel at any stage of the trial (subject to the limitation dealt with below). The judge should assist an unrepresented accused in matters such as the cross-examination of the prosecution witnesses, the giving of his own evidence, and the examination in chief of any witnesses he may choose to call. Often a judge has to explain to the accused that when he cross-examines a witness he must ask questions rather than make a speech of his own disagreeing with what the witness has said. It is particularly important that at the close of the prosecution case the accused should be told that he may give evidence himself and/or call other witnesses. The judge's failure to ask the accused if he wishes to call evidence in his defence may lead to any conviction being quashed: *Carter* (1960) 44 Cr App R 225.

20.70 The Youth Justice and Criminal Evidence Act 1999 restricts the right of the unrepresented defendant to cross-examine certain witnesses. The 1999 Act lays down that:

(a) A defendant charged with rape or other specified sexual offences who chooses to conduct his own defence may not himself cross-examine the alleged victim of the offence. This prohibition also extends to any other offence with which the defendant is charged in the proceedings.

(b) A defendant who is charged with an offence of violence, a specified sexual offence, kidnapping, false imprisonment or abduction may not cross-examine a child who is an alleged victim or witness to the commission of the offence.

(c) The court is given power to prohibit unrepresented defendants from cross-examining witnesses in cases not covered by the specific prohibitions laid down in (a) and (b) if it is satisfied that the circumstances of the witness and the case merit it and that a prohibition would not be contrary to the interests of justice.

(d) Where the accused is barred from cross-examining a witness, a representative can be appointed by him to carry out that cross-examination.

(e) If he does not appoint a legal representative to carry out the cross-examination, the court has to consider whether it is necessary, in the interests of justice, for the witness's evidence to be tested. If it decides that it is, it will appoint a legal representative to cross-examine the witness. That representative will not, however, be instructed by the defendant, and will not be responsible to him.

Presence of the accused

20.71 The accused must be present at the start of a trial on indictment in order to plead. If he is not, the judge will adjourn and, unless there is some good reason for the absence such as sickness, issue a bench warrant for the accused's arrest under s 7 of the Bail Act 1976.

20.72 Having attended for the arraignment, the general rule is that the accused should be present throughout the trial. It is obviously fair that he should hear what the prosecution and their witnesses have to say against him so as to be in a position to answer their allegations. Should he, at any stage of the trial, fail or be unable to appear in court the judge will normally have to adjourn the case and, depending on the circumstances, issue a warrant for arrest. If his absence looks like being prolonged (e.g., he has contracted an illness which will last several days) the judge will consider discharging the jury from giving a verdict. The case will then re-commence before a different jury once the accused is able to attend. The principle that the accused should be present during his trial demands that he should be able to understand proceedings. It follows that the failure to ensure that an interpreter translates the evidence constitutes a substantial miscarriage of justice: *Kunnath v The State* [1993] 1 WLR 1315.

20.73 There are, however, two main situations in which the judge has a discretion to allow the trial to proceed in the accused's absence. The first is when he shouts, misbehaves, or otherwise makes such a nuisance of himself that it is impracticable to continue with him present (per Lord Reading CJ in *Lee Kung* [1916] 1 KB 337). The second is if he voluntarily absents himself. In *Hayward* [2001] 3 WLR 125, the Court of Appeal considered the principles which the trial judge ought to apply when dealing with an absent defendant, and summarized them as follows:

(a) A defendant has, in general, a right to be present at his trial and a right to be legally represented.

(b) Those rights can be waived, separately or together, wholly or in part, by the defendant himself:

  (i) They may be wholly waived if, knowing or having the means of knowledge as to when and where his trial is to take place, he deliberately and voluntarily absents himself and/or withdraws instructions from those representing him.

  (ii) They may be waived in part if, being present and represented at the outset, the defendant, during the course of the trial, behaves in such a way as to obstruct the proper course of the proceedings and/or withdraws his instructions from those representing him.

(c) The trial judge has a discretion as to whether a trial should take place or continue in the absence of a defendant and/or his legal representatives.

(d) That discretion must be exercised with great care and it is only in rare and exceptional cases that it should be exercised in favour of a trial taking place or continuing, particularly if the defendant is unrepresented.

(e) In exercising that discretion, fairness to the defence is of prime importance but fairness to the prosecution must also be taken into account. The judge must have regard to all the circumstances of the case including, in particular:

  (i) the nature and circumstances of the behaviour in absenting himself from the trial or disrupting it, as the case may be and, in particular, whether his behaviour was deliberate, voluntary and such as plainly waived his right to appear;

  (ii) whether an adjournment might result in the defendant being caught or attending voluntarily and/or not disrupting the proceedings;

  (iii) the likely length of such an adjournment;

  (iv) whether the defendant, though absent, is, or wishes to be, legally represented at the trial or has, by his conduct, waived his right to representation;

  (v) whether an absent defendant's legal representatives are able to receive instructions from him during the trial and the extent to which they are able to present his defence;

  (vi) the extent of the disadvantage to the defendant in not being able to give his account of events, having regard to the nature of the evidence against him;

  (vii) the risk of the jury reaching an improper conclusion about the absence of the defendant;

  (viii) the seriousness of the offence, which affects defendant, victim and public;

  (ix) the general public interest and the particular interest of victims and witnesses that a trial should take place within a reasonable time of the events to which it relates;

  (x) the effect of delay on the memories of witnesses;

  (xi) where there is more than one defendant and not all have absconded, the undesirability of separate trials, and the prospects of a fair trial for the defendants who are present.

(f) If the judge decides that a trial should take place or continue in the absence of an unrepresented defendant, he must ensure that the trial is as fair as the circumstances permit. He must, in particular, take reasonable steps, both during the giving of evidence and in the summing up, to expose weaknesses in the prosecution case and to make such points on behalf of the defendant as the evidence permits. In summing up he must warn the jury that absence is not an admission of guilt and adds nothing to the prosecution case.

The overall effect is to underline the need for caution before proceeding with the trial when the defendant is absent. In view of the need to ensure compliance with Art 6 of the European Convention on Human Rights, that caution is entirely proper. It is also right that the focus in determining whether to proceed should be upon the defendant's right to attend the trial and be represented at it. The notion of participation in the criminal proceedings is crucial not only from the perspective of the defendant, but also in ensuring the legitimacy of the system. It is submitted that the court ought to be particularly cautious in concluding that the defendant has waived his rights. There is considerable merit in the suggestion made by counsel for the appellant in *Hayward* that such waiver should be established to the criminal standard. Although that point was not expressly adopted by their lordships, it is submitted that it is in accordance with the spirit of the guidelines set out in the case.

G   COUNSELS' CLOSING SPEECHES

20.74   After the close of the defence case (or the last of the defence cases where there are more than one accused separately represented) prosecuting counsel may sum up his case to the jury. In doing so he should continue to regard himself as a 'minister of justice', not an advocate striving at all costs for a conviction. In his speech he can for example remind the jury of the most cogent parts of the prosecution evidence, and comment upon any implausibilities in the defence case. The only situation where the prosecution does not have the right to a closing speech is where an accused is unrepresented and did not call evidence as to the facts other than his own. It does not follow, however, that whenever counsel has the right to a speech he should necessarily make one. If the defence are represented but choose not to call evidence, prosecuting counsel is still entitled to a closing speech but may well consider that he need not make one: *Bryant* [1979] QB 108. In that case it was further said by Watkin J that 'the majority of speeches by prosecuting and defence counsel should bear the becoming hallmark of brevity'—advice which perhaps is not followed on all occasions.

20.75   The last word, in a criminal trial, leaving aside the judge's summing-up, belongs to the defence. After the prosecution closing speech, defence counsel sums up his case to the jury. He has a broad discretion to say anything he considers desirable on the whole case, but he should not allege as fact matters of which no evidence has been given. As it was put in *Bateson* (1991) *The Times*, 10 April 1991, he should not 'conjure explanations out of the air', but he is entitled to suggest, for example, that there might be an innocent explanation for his client's lies, if there was evidence in the case on which to base such an explanation. The rule applies equally to prosecuting counsel, but defence counsel may be more tempted to transgress it. If there are two or more accused separately represented the speeches on their behalves are given in the order in which their names appear on the indictment. An unrepresented accused can, of course, make both a closing and, if he is entitled to one, an opening speech on his own behalf.

H   JURY STOPPING THE CASE

20.76   Paragraphs 20.48 to 20.55 dealt with the judge's duty to *direct* the jury to acquit if the evidence called by the prosecution is so weak that no jury could properly convict on it. As explained in that Section, the Court of Appeal's judgment in *Galbraith* [1981] 1 WLR 1039 has narrowed the circumstances in which it is right to direct an acquittal. However, it does not follow that, because a submission of no case has failed, the trial will inevitably run its full course. At any stage after the close of the prosecution case, the jury may say that they do not wish the proceedings to continue, whereupon they acquit the accused. Since few juries will be aware that they possess this power, it is open to the judge to 'remind' them of it, although he should not in so many words invite them to acquit (see *Kemp* [1995] 1 Cr App R 151 and *Falconer-Atlee* (1973) 58 Cr App R 348). The judge might remind the jury of their power to acquit forthwith if the prosecution case is a little too strong for him to direct an acquittal, but nonetheless their evidence looks feeble in the light of defence cross-examination. In *Speechley* (2004) *The Times*, 1 December 2004, the Court of Appeal held that it was not open to the jury to return a verdict until the judge had invited them to do so. It was the judge's duty to decide when the jury was to be permitted to reach a decision. It should be stressed that the jury may not, of course, *convict* without first listening to the entire case.

I   THE JUDGE'S SUMMING-UP

The final and very significant stage of a trial on indictment is the judge's summing-up. In it **20.77** he directs the jury on the law and assists them in their task of deciding the facts. While it is impossible to know the reasons for a jury returning a certain verdict, a reasonable assumption is that the judge's apparent view of the case sways them considerably. Having heard persuasive and eloquent speeches from the various counsel in the case which usually arrive at directly opposite conclusions, the jurors turn with relief to the judge who can put the arguments in perspective, identify the 'red herrings' and clarify the issues. Counsel, of course, are not always as convinced of the impartiality and wisdom of the judge as the jurors may be.

In preparing the summing-up, the judge will have been able to draw upon the specimen **20.78** directions of the Judicial Studies Board (see Key Documents at the end of this Chapter), suitably adapted. The following matters are usually dealt with in a summing-up:

(a) The judge explains to the jury his and their respective roles—i.e., the judge decides on the law, and they must accept whatever he says about the law; the jury decide what facts have been proved, in which task they may be helped but are in no way bound by what he says. As was said in *Wootton* [1990] Crim LR 201, this explanation of functions is no mere formality. Its omission may by itself ground a successful appeal.

(b) The jury are told that it is for the prosecution to prove the guilt of the accused, that the accused does not have to prove anything, and that, unless they are satisfied beyond reasonable doubt on all the evidence that the accused committed the offence charged, they must acquit him. An acceptable alternative is to direct the jury that in order to find the defendant guilty they must be 'sure' or 'satisfied so that they feel sure'. An amalgam of the two alternatives, along the lines of 'You must be satisfied beyond reasonable doubt so that you feel sure of the defendant's guilt' has also been suggested (see *Ferguson v The Queen* [1979] 1 WLR 94).

(c) The judge defines the offence charged, explaining the matters which the prosecution have to prove in order to establish guilt. If possible he keeps his statement of the law simple and basic. For example, if Smith is charged with stealing Jones' umbrella and the defence is mistaken identity, the judge might say something like—'Members of the jury, you all know what is meant by stealing—it is taking somebody else's property dishonestly, knowing it does not belong to you, and intending that they shall not get it back again. Now, Mr Jones has told you that at 1 p.m. he left his umbrella in the cloak-room, and that at 2 p.m. when he returned to collect it it had gone, and he did not see it again until he was shown it at the police station. That evidence was not disputed by the defence, so you may not have much difficulty in deciding—it's a matter entirely for you, ladies and gentlemen—that somebody stole the umbrella. The question is, was it this defendant? . . . ' If the defence raised by Smith was mistake (he took the umbrella think-ing it was his own) or an unauthorized loan (he took the umbrella for use in a heavy shower intending to return it), the judge would have to emphasize, in the one case, that the appropriation must be dishonest and, in the other, that there must be an intention permanently to deprive.

(d) Depending on the evidence called in the particular case, it may be necessary to explain some evidential points to the jury. For example, the basic direction on the burden and standard of proof is inadequate where, on an assault charge, the accused raises the defence of acting in reasonable self-defence, for the jury might be left with the impression that the accused has to show that he was so acting. The judge should therefore tell the jury expressly that it is for the prosecution to prove beyond reasonable doubt that the accused was not acting in reasonable self-defence. Similar principles apply where the defence raised is one of alibi. Conversely, if the burden of establishing a defence is, by way of exception to the general rule, upon the accused (e.g., where a defence of dimin-ished responsibility is raised upon a charge of murder) the judge explains both that and the standard of proof required of the defence (i.e., upon a balance of probabilities). Where the defence is mistaken identity the judge should mention the special need for caution before convicting on the basis of the evidence from the identifying witnesses (see *Turnbull* [1977] QB 224 for full details of what the judge should say in mistaken identity cases). If the accused's character, good or bad, has been put into evidence, the judge should explain the bearing it has upon the case. Depending on the evidence in the par-ticular case many other points may have to be considered in the summing-up.

(e) If two or more accused are joined in one indictment, the judge must direct the jury to con-sider the case of each accused separately. In particular, if evidence has been given against A which, although inadmissible against B, is prejudicial to his defence (e.g., A has made a confession in B's absence which implicates both himself and B), the jury must be told to ignore that evidence when reaching their verdict on B. Similarly, if an accused is charged in one indictment with two or more offences, the jury are warned to give separate con-sideration to each count. The fact that they have decided to convict or acquit the accused on count one is normally irrelevant to their decision on count two, and vice versa.

(f) The last part of the summing-up deals with the evidence in the case. Using the note of evidence which he takes during the trial, the judge reminds the jury of the evidence they have heard and comments upon it. Judges vary in the way they discharge this part of their duty. Some merely read out the significant parts of each witness' evidence, concen-trating upon the evidence in chief, others seek to define the issues in the case, and relate the evidence to those issues. Some keep their own view of the case discreetly hidden, others, whether directly or indirectly, let the jury know their opinion of the facts. In *Charles* (1979) 68 Cr App R 334, Lawton LJ commented upon the desirable method of summing-up in a long case. In a trial which lasted for a total of 35 days and involved complex allegations of fraudulent business dealings, the summing-up took three days. After an introductory survey of the law and issues relevant to the case, the judge adopted the technique of reading out from his notes what each witness had said. The Court of Appeal criticized his approach because, in long fraud cases especially, it is important for the judge to 'analyse the issues and relate the evidence to the issues' (p. 341). Merely reading a note of the evidence is unsatisfactory, not least because 'it must bore the jury to sleep' (p. 339). In general, judges 'should not indulge in long-winded summings-up which are more likely to confuse than help the jury' (p. 341). Whatever method of summing-up the judge uses, it is essential that he put the defence before the jury in a form which they can appreciate. He is entitled to express his opinion on that defence (or, indeed, on any of the facts of the case), provided that he leaves the issues of fact to the jury to determine. As it was trenchantly put by Lord Lane CJ in *Marr* (1989) 90 Cr App R 154, however distasteful the crime, however repulsive the accused, however laughable the defence, he was entitled to have his case presented fairly by both counsel and judge. That especially applied when the cards seemed stacked against him. In preparing the summing-up, the judge will have been able to draw upon the specimen directions from the Judicial Studies Board, which set out formulae for many of the points of law, procedure, and evidence which are likely to arise in a jury trial (see Key Documents at the end of this Chapter for the address of the website). Of course, the specimen directions then have to be tailored by the judge to meet the facts of the particular case where his view of the law is that the defence's own version of events itself shows the accused to be guilty as charged, he should still leave the ultimate issue of guilt or innocence with the jury, albeit with the comment that the evidence all points in one direction (see *DPP v Stonehouse* [1978] AC 55 and *Thompson* [1984] 1 WLR 962).

(g) Occasionally, the question arises whether the judge is confined, when summarizing the case against the defendant, to the same basis as that on which the prosecution has put its case. In *Falconer-Atlee* (1973) 58 Cr App R 348, the judge left it open to the jury to convict on a basis which had never been put forward by the prosecution. This was one of the reasons given by the Court of Appeal for quashing the conviction. But in *Japes* [1994] Crim LR 605, the Court of Appeal said that a judge was not bound by the way in which the Crown opened its case. As the evidence developed, it might become apparent that the offence may have been committed on a somewhat different factual basis, e.g., the appropriation necessary for theft may have taken place at a later stage than the prosecution originally thought. If so, the judge was not debarred from putting that basis before the jury to consider, so long as the defendant was not disadvantaged or prejudiced by this course of action.

(h) At the very end of the summing-up, the judge advises the jury to appoint one of themselves to be their foreman. The foreman will act as their spokesman and, in due course, announce their verdict. Finally, the judge tells them to retire, consider their verdict and seek to reach a unanimous decision. Where the prosecution have put their case on more than one basis it may be necessary to tell the jury that, in order to convict, they must be unanimous not only as to the accused being guilty but also as to the *basis* on which he is guilty: *Brown* (1984) 79 Cr App R 115. In that case, the prosecution alleged the obtaining of property by the use of two deceptions, and the Court of Appeal held that the jury should have been directed that—if not unanimous that B used both deceptions—they should at least all agree as to which one he used. If six thought he used deception *a* and the remainder thought he used deception *b*, he should not be convicted. See generally J.C. Smith, 'Satisfying the jury' [1988] Crim LR 335 and *Mitchell* [1994] Crim LR 66.

20.79   Before he starts summing-up, the judge may ask counsel to assist him on the law and facts with which he is to deal, but he should never seek counsel's help after the jury have retired, and only in exceptional circumstances should he discuss the law with counsel after finishing his summing-up but before the jury's retirement: *Cocks* (1976) 63 Cr App R 79. Asking counsel to interrupt the summing-up in order to correct any errors as they are made is also unwise as it may disrupt the jury's train of thought and appear to undermine the judge's authority (*Charles* (1979) 68 Cr App R 334 where counsel intervened 33 times in the course of a three-day summing-up). If, having listened to the summing-up, prosecuting counsel appreciates that there has been some misdirection of law or fact, he should raise the matter with the judge before the jury retire so that the error can be corrected. Failure to do so may expose counsel to criticism if the defence subsequently appeal (for an example, see *Donoghue* [1988] Crim LR 60). Although the point is not free from doubt, it seems that defence counsel is under no duty to mention any error he may notice. If he thinks it in the best interests of his client, he may say nothing in the hope that, should the accused be found guilty, he will be able to appeal successfully against conviction (see the comments of Robert Goff LJ in *Edwards* (1983) 77 Cr App R 5). He obviously takes a risk in doing so, even though the dismissal of an appeal based on these circumstances is not inevitable (*Holden* [1991] Crim LR 478). The position appears to be different where a procedural irregularity is in issue (see 20.08 and *Smith* [1994] Crim LR 458).

20.80   What if the judge does realize that his summing-up is in error (whether as a result of counsel's intervention or of his own accord)? He should expressly refer to the error, tell the jury to disregard it, and then give the correct direction (*Cole* [1994] Crim LR 300).

20.81   Counsel should take a note of the summing-up. This will assist him when advising on the merits of an appeal and drafting the initial Grounds of Appeal, at which stage a transcript of the shorthand writer's note of the summing-up is unlikely to be available (see 26.46).

J   EVIDENCE GIVEN OUT OF THE NORMAL ORDER

20.82   The prosecution may not in general call evidence after they have closed their case, or even cross-examine the accused about matters which they could have proved as part of their case had they so chosen.

20.83   The rule is illustrated by *Day* [1940] 1 All ER 402. D's conviction for forging a cheque was quashed because, after the defence had closed their case, the judge allowed the prosecution to call a handwriting expert to compare the writing on the cheque with a sample of D's writing.

20.84   The exceptions to the general rule are as follows:

(a)   If, in the course of the defence case, a matter arises *ex improviso*, which no human ingenuity can foresee, the prosecution may adduce evidence to rebut the defence evidence on the matter. In *Blick* (1966) 50 Cr App R 280, for example, B who, according to the police, was arrested following a chase and charged with robbery, testified that at the time of the chase he was in a public lavatory. The prosecution were correctly allowed to reopen their case and call evidence that at the relevant time the lavatory was closed for repairs. No human ingenuity could have foreseen that access to a public lavatory would be relevant to the case against B. *Blick* may be compared with *Day* where the prosecution should have anticipated that a handwriting expert would be needed to help establish that the writing on the cheque was D's.

(b) The judge has a discretion to allow the prosecution to call a witness who was not available to them before they closed their case, even though his evidence does not go to rebut a matter raised *ex improviso* by the defence. Cases where it is proper to exercise the discretion are rare. Leave to call the witness should be refused if the only reason for the prosecution not calling him before they closed their case was that they wished to 'keep him up their sleeve' or had not been sufficiently diligent in preparing the case. In *Doran* (1972) 56 Cr App R 429 prosecuting counsel was informed, after he had closed his case, that two members of the public sitting in the gallery, had realized that they could give relevant evidence. He was allowed to call them, and the Court of Appeal confirmed the conviction because, although the case did not fall within the principle of (a) above, the prosecution could not have found out about the witnesses before closing their case.

(c) Where the prosecution inadvertently omit to lead evidence of a purely formal nature the judge may allow them to reopen their case and repair the omission. Evidence that a steamroller is made mainly of iron or steel comes within the category of evidence of a purely formal nature (*McKenna* (1957) 40 Cr App R 65, where M was charged with exporting manufactured goods 'wholly or mainly of iron or steel'). The principle has been extended somewhat to cover cases where the prosecution by mistake fail to call evidence identifying the accused as the person who committed the *actus reus* of the offence (see, for example, *Francis* [1990] 1 WLR 1264). Even in a case where identity is not in dispute, this could hardly be said to be evidence of a purely formal nature, but it seems that the court has a discretion to let prosecuting counsel reopen his case.

(d) The rule of evidence that a party cross-examining the other side's witness about matters going only to the witness' credibility, not the issues in the case, cannot adduce his own evidence to rebut the answer he receives in cross-examination does not apply if the witness is asked about his previous convictions, previous inconsistent statement or bias. Therefore, if prosecuting counsel asks a defence witness about, for example, his previous convictions and the witness denies having any, the prosecution can adduce evidence to prove the convictions even though their case will obviously have been closed before the defence witness was called to testify.

Where there are proper grounds for allowing the prosecution to reopen their case, their evidence may be called during or at the close of the defence case, or even after counsel's closing speeches: *Flynn* (1958) 42 Cr App R 15. The judge also has a broad discretion to allow the defence to reopen their case. In *Sanderson* [1953] 1 WLR 392, where a defence witness did not arrive until the summing-up was virtually completed, the judge rightly allowed the witness to testify at the end of the summing-up, and then delivered a supplementary summing-up dealing with his evidence.   **20.85**

K   POWER OF JUDGE TO CALL WITNESSES

20.86   The judge has a right to call a witness if, in his opinion, it is necessary for him to do so in the interests of justice.

20.87   The judge asks the witness questions, and then allows either or both counsel to cross-examine. However, the judge's power to call a witness should be exercised sparingly. In any event, the judge must not call any further prosecution witnesses in a case where the Crown has decided not to continue the prosecution. To do so would be, in effect, to take the prosecution over (*Grafton* [1993] QB 101). If the witness is likely to favour the prosecution and they have already closed their case, the judge should only call him if the circumstances are such that he could accede to a prosecution application to reopen their case were one to be made. One situation where a judge might call a witness is where the witness is named on the back of the indictment but the prosecution decline to call him (see *Oliva* [1965] 1 WLR 1028 and 20.25).

20.88   The judge has a discretion to recall for further questioning witnesses who have been called by the prosecution or defence, provided this does not allow the prosecution improperly to reopen their case. The power to recall witnesses includes power to recall the accused himself if he has testified. Where assertions are made by counsel or witnesses in the course of the defence case which should have been put to a prosecution witness in the course of cross-examination, the witness can be recalled to deal with the assertions.

L   HEARING IN OPEN COURT AND PUBLICITY

20.89   It is not only the parties who have an interest in criminal proceedings—the public also are concerned that, as far as is possible, the innocent shall be acquitted, the guilty convicted and offenders properly sentenced. Therefore, it is a fundamental principle of common law that justice shall be administered in open court. The principle was re-stated by Lord Diplock in *AG v Leveller Magazine* [1980] AC 440 at p. 450A–D:

> As a general rule the English system of administering justice does require that it be done in public. If the way that the courts behave cannot be hidden from the public ear and eye this provides a safeguard against judicial arbitrariness or idiosyncrasy and maintains the public confidence in the administration of justice. The application of the principle of open justice has two aspects: as respects proceedings in the court itself it requires that they should be held in open court to which the press and public are admitted and that, in criminal cases at any rate, all evidence communicated to the court is communicated publicly. As respects the publication to a wider public of fair and accurate reports of proceedings that have taken place in court the principle requires that nothing should be done to discourage this.

Thus, according to Lord Diplock, the principle of open justice has two main aspects, although the first really sub-divides into two. First, hearings should be in open court, not in camera; second, evidence communicated to the court should be communicated openly; and, third, the press should be free to report all that is openly done and communicated in open court. At common law, each aspect of the principle may be departed from if, and only if, insisting on the principle in its entirely would frustrate the ends of justice in the particular case before the court. Moreover, such departure as is allowed must be no more than is strictly necessary to overcome the perceived threat to justice.

The overwhelming trend of appellate decisions is to limit approval for derogations from the principle of open justice to very exceptional cases. Thus, sitting in camera is not justified by possible danger to an offender through mitigation (including the fact that he was a 'super-grass') being presented in open court and thereafter reported: *Reigate Justices ex parte Argus Newspapers* (1983) 5 Cr App R (S) 181. Nor is it justified by a drink-driver's 'overwhelming fear' of having embarrassing details about her personal life and medical problems aired publicly (*Malvern Justices ex parte Evans* [1988] QB 540), or by the supposed undesirability of the general public being entertained with salacious items of evidence (per Viscount Haldane LC in *Scott v Scott* [1913] AC 417), or even by considerations of national safety (per Lord Scarman in *AG v Leveller Magazine* above). In fact, almost the only clear example given in the decided cases of closed hearings being appropriate is where feelings about a case are running so high that there would be a risk of 'tumult or disorder' should the public be admitted (per Lord Loreburn in *Scott v Scott* above). There are also dicta suggesting that excluding the public is justifiable if, given the nature of the anticipated evidence and/or the occupation of the witnesses, there is no realistic prospect of their being willing to testify unless guaranteed confidentiality (see Viscount Haldane in *Scott v Scott* and Lord Scarman in *AG v Leveller Magazine*). **20.90**

Sometimes the adverse consequences of an open hearing can be largely avoided by allowing a certain piece of evidence to be communicated to the court privately. By far the commonest example is where a witness is allowed to write down his name and/or address instead of giving it orally. Thus, in *AG v Leveller Magazine* the House of Lords was unanimous in its approval of the examining justices' decision to proceed in open court but with the intelligence officer mentioned above referred to simply as 'Colonel B'. Blackmail victims are also commonly protected by pseudonyms. However, the courts are far less willing to afford the same protection to the accused himself. In *Evesham Justices ex parte McDonagh* [1988] QB 553 the High Court held that magistrates trying an information for using a car without a valid MOT test certificate should have insisted on the accused giving his address orally. His reason for wanting to write it down—namely, that he feared harassment from his ex-wife should she find out where he was living—was insufficient. According to Watkins LJ, the accused's 'comfort and feelings' cannot outweigh the public interest in knowing precisely who has been charged with or found guilty of an offence. **20.91**

The strictness of the common law principle of open justice is modified by miscellaneous statutory provisions which permit restrictions either on public access to the court or on the reporting of what takes place in open court. The chief provisions are as follows: **20.92**

(a) *Official Secrets Act 1920, s 8.* Where the publication of any part of proceedings for an offence under the Official Secrets Acts would be 'prejudicial to the national safety', the court may, on the prosecution's application, order that the public shall be excluded from the hearing. Sentence, however, must be passed in open court.

(b) *Children and Young Persons Act 1933, ss 36, 37, and 39.* Save when their presence is required as witnesses or defendants, children under 14 are not permitted in court during criminal proceedings (s 36). Where a juvenile is called as a witness in proceedings for an offence of indecency the court may direct that the public, but not the press, shall be excluded while the juvenile testifies (s 37). In proceedings of any description the court may direct that the media shall not publish identifying details of any juvenile involved, irrespective of whether he is the accused, a witness or concerned in some other way (s 39). There are also special statutory rules governing access to and reporting of youth court hearings (see Chapter 11).

(c) *Contempt of Court Act 1981, s 4.* At common law, any media reporting that creates a substantial risk of prejudice to the course of justice amounts to contempt of court, and is punishable even if the offender had no intention of causing such prejudice. This 'strict liability' rule is preserved by s 2 of the Contempt of Court Act 1981. The Act also preserves the major common law exception to liability, namely that fair and accurate reporting of legal proceedings held in public is not contempt, provided the report is published contemporaneously and in good faith (see s 4(1)). Far from discouraging such reporting, the courts have recognized its vital role in the administration of justice (e.g., Lord Diplock's judgment in *AG v Leveller Magazine*). However, s 4(2) creates an exception to the exception in that it empowers a court to order that publication of reports of all or part of its proceedings shall be postponed. An order may be made only if 'it appears to be necessary for avoiding a substantial risk of prejudice to the administration of justice' in the proceedings before the court or in any other 'pending or imminent proceedings'. Both in scope and duration an order must not exceed that which is strictly necessary to remove the threatened prejudice (see *Horsham Justices ex parte Farquharson* [1982] QB 762). Any publication in breach of a s 4(2) order is automatically to be regarded as having been made in bad faith, and therefore those responsible cannot claim the protection of s 4(1) even if there was no actual damage to the interests of justice (per the majority in *ex parte Farquharson*, Lord Denning dissenting on the point). At Crown Court level, orders under s 4(2) are especially appropriate where the accused is to be tried within a short space of time on two separate indictments. To avoid prejudicing the jurors for the second trial, the judge at the first trial might postpone reporting until after the second's conclusion. Similarly, where the jury are excluded from a trial within a trial, the judge may postpone reporting until he has decided whether the disputed evidence is admissible (see *AG v Leveller Magazine* at p. 450). Before postponing publication in this way, however, the judge should be satisfied that postponement 'appears to be necessary for avoiding' the risk of prejudice, as s 4(2) requires (*The Telegraph* [1994] Crim LR 114).

(d) *Contempt of Court Act 1981, s 11.* Where a court validly exercises its common law power to order that a name or other piece of evidence be communicated to it privately (see above), it may further impose a permanent ban on publication of that material. This is to cover against the possibility of the media discovering and reporting what the court had wanted withheld from the public.

(e) *Sexual Offences (Amendment) Act 1992.* This section, as amended, essentially prevents the media naming or giving the address of the complainant in a case of rape or one of the serious sexual offences covered by the 1992 Act, or publishing anything else likely to enable the public to identify her. The protection given by the section operates from the moment of the complaint being made, and lasts for the complainant's lifetime. The Crown Court has a discretion both before and at trial to order that the section shall not apply (e.g., because the accused needs publicity in order for witnesses to come forward). A parallel provision which used to protect the accused's identity unless and until he was convicted, was repealed by the Criminal Justice Act 1988.

(f) Part 16 of the Criminal Procedure Rules 2005 gives the court powers to make reporting directions under the Youth Justice and Criminal Evidence Act 1999, s 46. If such a direction is made, no matter relating to the witness which is likely to lead to identify him may be included in any publication during his lifetime.

The above discussion of open justice has covered both Crown Court and magistrates' courts' **20.93** proceedings, since the same basic principles apply in both courts. However, special statutory rules apply both to access to youth court proceedings and reporting of committal proceedings. They are dealt with in Chapters 11 and 13 respectively.

KEY DOCUMENTS

Code of Conduct of the Bar of England and Wales.

Criminal Procedure Rules 2005, available at <http://www.justice.gov.uk/criminal/procrules_fin/index.htm>.

Consolidated Criminal Practice Direction, available at <http://www.hmcourts-service.gov.uk/cms/pds.htm>.

21

THE VERDICT

A RETIREMENT OF THE JURY

When the judge has finished his summing-up, a court usher takes an oath to keep the jury in **21.01** some 'private and convenient place', to prevent anybody speaking to them without leave of the court, and not to speak to them himself 'except it be to ask them if they are agreed upon their verdict'. Having so sworn, the usher, who is referred to as the jury bailiff, leads the jury to their room and stations himself outside. During the period of their retirement the jury are kept together so that through discussion and argument they can arrive at a unanimous verdict (or, at least, at a verdict upon which ten of them are agreed: see 21.34 to 21.37). As far as possible, they are kept apart from everybody else, because no outside influences should affect a jury's verdict. They and they alone must reach a decision on the guilt or innocence of the accused, and they should reach that decision solely on the basis of the evidence and speeches they have heard in court combined with their own experience of life and good sense. Three interconnected rules are designed to ensure that nothing untoward occurs while the jury are considering their verdict.

21.02 First, the jury must stay in the custody of the jury bailiff. This means that the jury bailiff must be in a position to prevent anybody speaking to the jury or any individual member of it. He should not himself go into the jury room or speak to the jurors unless the judge orders him to do so (e.g., to pass on a message from the judge or ask a question). Convictions have been quashed where either the whole jury or a juror left the jury bailiff's custody. In *Neal* [1949] 2 KB 590, the jury, with the judge's permission but after having retired to consider their verdict, left the court building to go to a restaurant for lunch. The jury bailiff did not go with them. Having lunched, they returned to court and convicted N. The conviction was quashed because they had been out of the bailiff's custody for a substantial period, during which time numerous persons could have spoken to them about the case. Similarly, in *Ketteridge* [1915] 1 KB 467, K's conviction was quashed because a member of the jury, instead of retiring with his colleagues to the jury room, by mistake left the court building and was absent for fifteen minutes before rejoining the other jurors. Just as in *Neal* there was ample opportunity for non-jury members to speak to the juror.

21.03 Second, the jury must not leave their room without the judge's permission. The commonest reason for the jury leaving their room is the judge asking them to return to court for further directions about the case or for the answer to a question they have asked. Also, in cases of 'evident necessity', the judge may let them leave not just their room but the entire court buildings: *Neal* (above). Although the Court of Criminal Appeal in *Neal* did not find it necessary to decide whether the judge could properly have allowed the jury to go to a restaurant in the custody of the jury bailiff, the obtaining of refreshments away from the court building could hardly now amount to an 'evident necessity' as the jury may have sandwiches brought to them (they may be allowed reasonable refreshment at their own expense—Juries Act 1974, s 15). Where the jury are far from agreement and it is getting late, the judge may decide that there is an evident necessity for them to be taken to an hotel for the night, so that they can return to their room the next morning refreshed by a good sleep. This is only appropriate in very long or complex cases where it is reasonable for the jury to take a day or more to consider their verdict. Normally, if a jury have been given several hours to deliberate and are still nowhere near a verdict, the judge discharges them (see 21.38 to 21.41). If the jury are kept at an hotel for the night or allowed to leave their room for any reason, they must still remain in the custody of the jury bailiff.

21.04 The third rule, which is really a corollary of the second, is that the jury must not separate, save with the permission of the judge. Until 1994, the jury had to be kept together after they had retired to consider their verdict, even if this meant that they had to stay overnight in a hotel. The position now is that the judge has a discretion to permit the jury to separate at any time during the trial, even if it is after they have retired to consider their verdict (Criminal Justice and Public Order Act 1994, s 43). It is still possible that the judge will decide against allowing the jury to separate, thus necessitating an overnight stay in a hotel, but at least there is a judicial discretion. In *Oliver* [1996] 2 Cr App R 514, the Court of Appeal said that, if the judge permitted the jury to separate during consideration of their evidence, then he should tell them:

(a)   to decide the case on the evidence and the arguments seen and heard in court, and not on anything seen or heard outside the court;

(b)   that the evidence had been completed and it would be wrong for any juror to seek or receive further evidence or information of any sort about the case;

(c)   not to talk to anyone about the case save to the other members of the jury and then only when they were deliberating in the jury room;

(d)   not to allow anyone to talk to them about the case unless that person was a juror and he or she was in the jury room deliberating about the case; and

(e)   on leaving the court, to set the case on one side until they retired to the jury room to continue the process of deliberating about their verdict.

An infringement of the rules described above, however trivial, is an irregularity in the course **21.05** of the trial but it will not lead to a conviction being quashed by the Court of Appeal unless it 'goes to the root of the case'. Thus, in *Alexander* [1974] 1 WLR 422 a conviction was upheld where, after the jury had left court in the charge of the jury bailiff, one of them returned to collect an exhibit (the judge had told them that they might see any exhibit they wanted). Technically the juror had both separated himself from his colleagues and left the custody of the jury bailiff, but since the separation was for a matter of seconds only and since he had been observed by defence counsel throughout those few seconds, the irregularity did not go to the root of the case. In *Goodson* [1975] 1 WLR 549, on the other hand, the jury bailiff allowed a juror to leave the jury room to use a telephone. By chance, prosecuting counsel discovered what was happening, and took steps to prevent the juror rejoining his colleagues. The judge discharged him from the jury, and the remaining eleven convicted. The Court of Appeal held that the irregularity was such that the conviction had to be quashed. The bailiff's error, for which the court had to take ultimate responsibility, had deprived G 'of the voice of one juror in the jury room' (per James LJ at p. 552).

In a more recent case, however, the fact that a juror had communicated with the outside **21.06** world by telephone was viewed as irregular, but not sufficiently material to ground a successful appeal. In *Farooq* (1994) *The Times*, 12 May 1994, a juror made two telephone calls to ask about a sick child. The Court of Appeal saw no valid reason to disbelieve the juror, and was satisfied that no miscarriage of justice had occurred. It did, however, criticize the procedure which the judge had adopted to deal with the matter. When told about the telephone calls, he had asked the chief clerk to make enquiries. The clerk then told counsel informally what the juror said about the telephone calls. The judge was then told that all counsel had said they were satisfied, and the jury continued with their deliberations. The Court of Appeal said that the court should have been reconvened, the relevant facts stated in open court, and counsel given the opportunity to ask for further clarification. The same reasoning applied to a juror's use of the internet in *Karakaya* (2005) *The Times*, 25 February 2005. The Court of Appeal made it clear that a juror should not conduct private research for material which might have a bearing on the trial. If such material were obtained, two fundamental linked rules were violated: the first was that of open justice, and the second was that prosecution and defence were entitled to a fair opportunity to address all material considered by the jury when reaching their verdict.

Questions from the jury

Even though they have retired to consider their verdict, the jury may ask the judge for further **21.07** explanation of matters of law arising in the case. They may also ask him to remind them of any part of the evidence. If they ask for information about a point on which no evidence has, in fact, been given the judge must tell them there is no evidence on the matter and that they must decide the case on the evidence they have heard. No evidence should be adduced before the jury once they have begun to consider their verdict (*Owen* [1952] 2 QB 362). This was thought to be an absolute rule, but in *Hallam* [2007] EWCA Crim 1495, the Court of Appeal quashed a conviction in circumstances where the defence sought to have a (lately discovered) photograph put before the jury after it had retired to consider its verdict. The Court stated that what had previously been regarded as the very firm rule that evidence could not be admitted after the retirement of the jury was not absolute—in each case, the question was: what did justice require? In *Stewart* (1989) 89 Cr App R 273, the Court of Appeal held that the trial judge had erred in letting the jury have a pair of scales after they had retired. The case was one in which the weight of a quantity of drugs was highly relevant. The Court of Appeal was clearly concerned that the jury had, in effect, been permitted to carry out experiments without judge, counsel, or accused being present. In *Maggs* (1990) 91 Cr App R 243, on the other hand, it was stated that the supply of a tape measure or a magnifying glass would not normally raise the prospect of such experiments, and would be unobjectionable. In any event, the jury are normally entitled to take the exhibits in the case with them when they retire, including a tape of an interview which has been played to them during the trial (*Emmerson* (1990) 92 Cr App R 284). Where the tape has not been played during the trial, but the jury have been given a transcript, then if they ask after retirement to hear the tape, they are entitled to hear it. The tape is the exhibit, and the transcript is merely a convenient method of presenting it. Although it is a matter for the judge's discretion, the best course in these circumstances is to bring the jury back into court to hear the tape. Problems might arise if they are allowed free access to the tape, including the risk that they might hear matters left on it which they should not hear, e.g., evidence which is inadmissible (*Riaz* (1991) 94 Cr App R 339). In *Rawlings* [1995] 1 WLR 178, the Court of Appeal said that the jury would usually, though not always, be allowed to see an exhibit on request. This general rule would apply to a request from the jury to see a replay of a video. It appears that the judge may, if asked by the jury to remind them of a witness' evidence-in-chief, use his discretion as to whether to remind them also of the cross-examination and re-examination (*Morgan* [1996] Crim LR 600).

21.08   Where the jury have a question or communication for the judge, they should write it down and give it to the jury bailiff, who passes it on to the judge. The judge then asks for counsel and the accused to return to court; the note is read out, and counsel may be invited to comment on the appropriate method of dealing with it. Next, the jury are brought back. The judge confirms with them the question they wish to raise, and the answer is given. Where the jury's note reveals something that should really be kept confidential (e.g., their provisional voting figures), the judge should summarize its contents omitting what ought not to be disclosed (see *Gorman* [1987] 1 WLR 545). Numerous cases over the years have dealt with the proper way of answering jury questions. Although they may differ on points of detail, their guiding principle is that both the question and the answer should be given publicly in open court at the time the matter is raised by the jury, and certainly before they return their verdict. Any suggestion that the judge has indulged in secret communications with the jury is likely to lead to a successful appeal, even if what he actually told them was unexceptionable. Indeed, this is one area of procedure where the *appearance* of justice is as important as its reality. Whether departure from the proper practice will necessitate the quashing of the accused's conviction does, however, depend upon the facts of the individual case, in particular the extent of the departure and the strength of the prosecution evidence.

It does seem that there is a distinction to be drawn between matters affecting the trial, and **21.09** what has been termed 'domestic management'. As far as the first category is concerned, the judge should, other than in the most exceptional cases, inform counsel of the fact and general nature of the communication. In cases where the communication relates to 'domestic management', the same principle applies, but the integrity of the trial process is not harmed, and any appeal is unlikely to succeed. Although this distinction was set out by the Court of Appeal in *Conroy* [1997] 2 Cr App R 285, it is not always easy to say which category a communication falls into. Overall, it would seem that the safest course for the judge is to disclose all communications from the jury to counsel (with the exception of confidential matters such as provisional voting figures).

The privacy of the jury room

The extreme reluctance of the Court of Appeal to quash a conviction because of any **21.10** inadequacy, or apparent bias, or misconduct by a juror has already been noted (see 18.46 to 18.50). This reluctance is complemented by a refusal to enquire, for purposes of an appeal, into what took place during the jury's deliberations. The general public interest requires that jurors should feel free, in the privacy of their room, to express whatever view they wish about the case, without the fear that a wrong word could be seized upon by the defence, following a conviction, and made the subject of an appeal. While the broad principle is understandable it may sometimes work apparent injustice in the case of an individual appellant. In *Thompson* [1962] 1 All ER 65 the Court of Criminal Appeal refused to hear evidence that the jury, in a case where T's character had not been revealed in evidence, were going to acquit until the foreman read to them a list of T's previous convictions which, in some unexplained way, had come into his possession.

The approach of the Court of Appeal will be different, however, where bias can be established **21.11** without calling evidence of the juror's conduct during the course of deliberations. In *Box* [1964] 1 QB 430, the complaint was that a juror was biased because of his prior knowledge of the accused's character. Because the evidence backing that complaint came from remarks made out of court to non-jurors, the appeal was not invalid *ab initio*, although it did not succeed (see also 18.47).

The confidentiality of jury deliberations is reinforced by s 8 of the Contempt of Court Act 1981, **21.12** which makes it an offence to obtain or disclose information about such deliberations. The main purpose of s 8 was apparently to prevent newspapers interviewing jurors after a particularly newsworthy trial, and publishing an account of why the jurors reached the verdict they did.

A particularly blatant example was provided by the publication in 1992 of an article in the **21.13** *Mail on Sunday* which referred to accounts by three jurors of their deliberations in the Blue Arrow fraud trial. The jurors described how they reached their decisions, commented on the evidence in issue at the trial, and gave an opinion of one of the other jurors. Fines of £30,000, £20,000 and £10,000 were imposed on the publisher, editor, and journalist respectively (*Attorney-General v Associated Newspapers Ltd* [1994] 2 AC 238). The prohibition does not only apply to the media, however. In *Mickleburgh* [1995] 1 Cr App R 297, the Court of Appeal made it clear that it applies to court officials, ushers, and jury bailiffs as much as to anyone else. In *Attorney-General v Scotcher* [2005] 1 WLR 1867, a member of the jury which convicted the defendants by a majority wrote to their mother at the end of the trial. He informed her of discussions which had taken place in the jury room, and which he felt would show the verdict was unsafe. The mother referred the matter to a solicitor, who informed the Court of Appeal. The Attorney-General prosecuted the juror under s 8(1) of the Contempt of Court Act 1981. He was found guilty, and in due course appealed to the House of Lords, which dismissed his appeal. He had been in contempt of court in writing to a third party. He would not have contravened the statute if he had communicated with the officers of the Crown Court or the Court of Appeal.

21.14   Whilst there are clear reasons of public policy for preserving the privacy of the jury room from intrusion, the Contempt of Court Act 1981, s 8, does have the unfortunate effect of making unlawful an important and potentially useful field of research into the way jurors approach their task, and the factors which influence them. The Royal Commission on Criminal Justice therefore recommended in its report (TSO, 1993, p. 2) that the Act ought to be amended to allow research into the deliberations of juries, 'so that informed debate can take place rather than argument based only on surmise and anecdote'.

21.15   The prohibition does not, in any event, extend to events happening outside the jury room, e.g., in the hotel at which the jury is accommodated overnight: *Young* [1995] QB 324. In this case, the jurors stayed overnight in an hotel, after they had retired to consider their verdict in a murder trial. Several of them got together and sought the views of the deceased as to the defendant's guilt, using a ouija board to summon up his spirit! The Court of Appeal took the view that this incident was not 'in the course of' the jury's deliberations, but during an overnight break from those deliberations. Their Lordships held, therefore, that they were entitled to enquire into the incident. Having done so, they allowed the appeal and ordered a retrial.

21.16   The issues surrounding the confidentiality of jury deliberations were considered in detail in *Connor* [2004] 1 All ER 925. The House of Lords considered two conjoined cases. In each of them, a letter had been written to the trial court by one of the jurors. In the case of the appellant Mirza, the letter alleged that other jurors had been racially prejudiced against the defendant. In the case of the appellants Connor and Rollock, the juror in question complained that the other members of the jury had been anxious to reach a verdict as quickly as possible, and had not considered the case against each defendant separately because it would take too long to do so. The Court of Appeal dismissed each of the defendants' appeals against conviction, applying the common-law rule that, after the verdict had been returned, evidence as to what had been said by the jurors in private was inadmissible, and stating that this was reinforced by s 8 of the Contempt of Court Act 1981. The defendants in both cases appealed, and the Court of Appeal certified two questions of public importance as follows:

> Should the common law prohibition of evidence of the jury's deliberations prevail even if the Court of Appeal is presented with a statement from the juror which, if admitted, would provide prima facie evidence of jury partiality in breach of Article 6 [of the ECHR]?
> Does s 8 of the Contempt of Court Act 1981, when interpreted in the light of s 3 of the HRA 1998 and Article 6 ... prohibit the admission into evidence of a statement from a juror which if admitted, would provide prima facie evidence of partiality in breach of Article 6? If so, is s 8 compatible with Article 6 to the extent that it prohibits the admission into evidence of such a statement?

Four of their Lordships answered the first question in the affirmative and the second in the negative, holding that the common-law principle prohibiting evidence of jury deliberations from within the jury was in accordance with Art 6. They endorsed the rule relating to confidentiality, and stated that it underpinned the independence and impartiality of the jury as a whole. Consequently, confidentiality was not just compatible with Art 6, but helped to guarantee a fair trial by helping the jury to operate as a collective body impartially, and independently of outside influences. In the cases which were before them, their Lordships concluded that the evidence as to deliberations of the jury could not be admitted, and dismissed the appeals. The basis for the decision was the common-law rule as to confidentiality rather than s 8 of the Contempt of Court Act 1981. In a powerful dissent, Lord Steyn concluded that there were substantial grounds, in the case of the appellant Mirza, for finding 'that the jury reached their verdict on perverse grounds which included a pronounced racial element'. He poured scorn on the argument of counsel for the prosecution that, if the foreman of the jury took a coin out of his pocket in the jury room, the evidence about the tossing of a coin in the jury room to obtain a verdict was inadmissible. He called this argument 'absurd' and stated that it did not reflect well on our jurisprudence. He suggested that the European Court of Human Rights would uphold the guarantee of a fair trial above the sanctity of privacy in the jury room, and quoted from their decision in *Remli v France* (1996) 22 EHRR 253:

> ... the Court considers that Article 6(1) of the Convention imposes an obligation on every national court to check whether, as constituted, it is 'an impartial tribunal' within the meaning of that provision where, as in the instant case, this is disputed on a ground which is not manifestly devoid of merit.

As far as the statutory provisions were concerned, all the Law Lords were agreed that they did **21.17** not affect the duty of the trial court and the Court of Appeal to investigate any irregularity in the conduct of the jury within the limits of the common law, so as to ensure that the accused received a fair trial. The court could not be said to be in contempt of itself if it did so (contrary to what had been suggested in *Young*). Their Lordships went on to advise that certain measures should be taken to strengthen the jury system. Jurors should be told to inform the court clerk or the judge in writing (either individually or collectively) if anything improper came to their notice. They should be reminded that what was said during their deliberations was confidential to them and could not be repeated or discussed outside the jury room. Their duty of confidentiality continued after the verdict. The adequacy of the existing jury video should be reviewed in order to ensure that it dealt with the rights and duties of jurors in these matters. The Judicial Studies Board (which trains judges, and issues advice to them) should consider the implications of the opinions delivered in the instant cases and whether trial judges should receive additional guidance as a result.

B RETURNING THE VERDICT

At the end of his summing-up the judge directs the jury to try to reach a unanimous verdict. **21.18** If they succeed in doing so, they come into court, and the clerk asks the foreman if they have reached a verdict on which they are all agreed. He answers 'yes', after which their verdict on each count is announced. The jury must return a verdict on each count, and in respect of each accused joined in a count, unless they are discharged from giving a verdict on a certain count (see 21.21). They can, of course, find an accused guilty on some counts and not guilty on others, or they can find one accused guilty and his co-accused not guilty. They can also find the accused guilty of, for example, stealing a part but not all of the goods named in a count for theft: *Furlong* [1950] 1 All ER 636. In asking for the verdicts, the clerk says something like— 'On count one, which charges the defendant with theft, do you find the defendant guilty or not guilty? . . . On count two, which charges the defendant with going equipped to steal, do you find him guilty or not guilty?' . . . and so on, through the indictment. If there are more than one accused joined in the indictment the clerk obviously has to name the accused in respect of whom he requests a verdict, rather than just referring to the defendant. Where, after a submission of no case to answer, the judge ruled that there was no case on count one, but that the trial should proceed on count two, the clerk says—'On count one, charging the defendant with . . . do you, upon His Honour's direction, find the defendant not guilty?' The foreman obediently replies 'not guilty', and the verdict on count two is taken in the normal way. Unless one of them protests at the time, it is conclusively presumed that the jurors are in agreement with the verdicts returned on their behalf: *Roads* [1967] 2 QB 108.

21.19   In *Austin* [2003] Crim LR 426, the Court of Appeal stated that, where a verdict was given in the sight and hearing of the whole jury without any dissent from any of its members, there was a presumption (which could be rebutted) that they had all assented to it.

21.20   The circumstances in which a jury may return a majority verdict and the procedure for doing so are described in 21.34 to 21.37. In *C* [2007] Crim LR 984, after the jury had been deliberating for some time on an indictment alleging a number of sexual offences, they sent a note to the judge saying that they were split on five of the counts (8 to 4 and 9 to 3 in favour of a guilty verdict), and were set to give unanimous verdicts of not guilty on the remaining counts. The judge called the jury into court with a view to taking the unanimous verdicts and giving the majority direction in respect of the remainder. However, when the jury came into court, the foreman gave answers indicating unanimous verdicts of guilty in relation to the five counts. One juror reported to the jury bailiff that the guilty verdicts had not been unanimous. The judge did not inform counsel of the contents of the note, and the jury was allowed to disperse. A member of the jury then sent a letter to the Crown Court stating that the foreman had stated wrongly that the guilty verdicts were unanimous. In the subsequent appeal, it was held that the trial judge had had jurisdiction to investigate whether the foreman had given a true verdict. That jurisdiction was also available to the Court of Appeal, which decided that the convictions were unsafe and must be quashed.

C   VERDICTS ON COUNTS IN THE ALTERNATIVE

21.21   The prosecution case on two counts is sometimes such that the accused may be found guilty on one count or the other but not on both (e.g., if the evidence is that the accused was found in possession of stolen goods shortly after they were stolen and he failed to give an explanation of how he came by the goods, then the jury can convict him of either theft or handling—see 15.30 to 15.32 on alternative counts). If, on an indictment containing alternative counts, the jury convict on, say, count one and are discharged from giving a verdict on count two, the Court of Appeal have power to quash the conviction on count one and substitute a conviction on count two provided it appears to them that the jury must have been satisfied of facts which proved the accused guilty on that count: Criminal Appeal Act 1968, s 3. If, on the other hand, the jury convict on count one and actually acquit on count two, the Court of Appeal cannot overturn the latter verdict: *Melvin and Eden* [1953] 1 QB 481. Therefore, if the count one conviction has to be quashed, the accused will stand acquitted on both counts, even though the Court of Appeal consider that he richly deserved to be convicted on the second count. To avoid such a miscarriage of justice, the foreman of the jury should be asked, in a case where there are counts in the alternative, whether the jury find the accused guilty on either count. If the answer is 'yes', he is further asked to name the count on which they wish to convict, and the verdict is taken on that count. The judge then discharges them from giving a verdict on the other count. If the answer is 'no', the clerk confirms that the jury acquit the accused on both counts.

D   VERDICTS OF GUILTY OF AN ALTERNATIVE OFFENCE

Normally, when the jury are considering their verdict on a count, they have a simple choice **21.22** between acquitting and convicting the accused. Sometimes, however, a third option is open to them. They can find the accused not guilty as charged in the count, but guilty of some other (lesser) indictable offence. The circumstances in which they may do this are set out in the Criminal Law Act 1967, s 6(2)–(4) and s 4(2). (For discussion of the related topic of a plea of guilty to a lesser offence, see 17.22 to 17.26.)

The general provision

If the allegations in a count for an offence other than treason or murder 'amount to or include **21.23** (expressly or by implication) an allegation of another [indictable] offence', the jury may find the accused not guilty of the offence charged but guilty of the other offence: Criminal Law Act 1967, s 6(3).

A count *expressly* includes an allegation of another offence if, having struck out from the part- **21.24** iculars those allegations which have not or might not have been established by the evidence led before the jury, there remain valid particulars for the other offence. This is illustrated by the facts of the leading case of *Lillis* [1972] 2 QB 236. L was charged with burglary contrary to s 9(1)(b) of the Theft Act 1968 in that he had entered a building as a trespasser on a certain date and had stolen therein a lawnmower. The prosecution evidence in fact showed that he had had permission both to enter the building and to borrow the lawnmower, but he had failed to return it when he ought. The judge ruled that there was no case to answer in respect of burglary, but that the jury could convict of theft on the basis that L had appropriated the mower dishonestly by keeping it. The jury did so convict, and L argued on appeal that a count which essentially alleged that he had stolen property inside a building on a certain day should not expose him to the risk of conviction for subsequently stealing the property outside the building. The argument was rejected. The Court of Appeal held that, omitting everything in the count the prosecution could not prove (namely the entry as a trespasser and the place where the offence occurred), there was still a valid count for theft, i.e., 'L, on … stole a lawnmower'. Admittedly, the date alleged for the theft was incorrect, but a variation between the date laid in the indictment and the evidence as to when the offence occurred will only be a good ground of appeal if the variation prejudiced or embarrassed the accused in the presentation of his defence (see 15.56). On the facts of *Lillis*, there was no such prejudice.

21.25 The test to apply when deciding whether a count *by implication* includes an allegation of another offence was elaborated by the House of Lords decision in *Wilson* [1984] AC 242. Three main propositions emerge from the leading judgment of Lord Roskill;

(a) If committing the offence alleged in a count would inevitably have involved the accused committing another offence, the jury may convict of that other offence. In other words, a verdict of guilty of an alternative offence may lawfully be returned when committing the alternative is a *necessary step* towards committing the offence charged. Thus, on a count for robbery, the jury may acquit of robbery but convict of theft. The count will merely state, for example, that 'AB, on . . . robbed CD of a wallet and £20 in cash'. Clearly, there is no express allegation of theft. But, s 8 of the Theft Act 1968 provides that a person is guilty of robbery 'if he *steals*, and in order to do so he uses force on any person or puts or seeks to put any person in fear of being then and there subjected to force'. In view of that statutory definition, it is literally impossible for a person to commit robbery without committing theft. Therefore, if the jury are not satisfied that AB used or threatened force, but they are satisfied that he stole the wallet and money, they should convict him of theft. By a similar reasoning process, it has been held that on a count for either rape or unlawful sexual intercourse with a girl under 16 the accused may be convicted of indecent assault (see *Hodgson* [1973] 1 QB 565 and *McCormack* [1969] 2 QB 442).

(b) In *Wilson* the question for the House of Lords was whether the appellants had lawfully been convicted of assault occasioning actual bodily harm on counts which charged them with (respectively) maliciously inflicting grievous bodily harm contrary to s 20 of the Offences Against the Person Act 1861 and burglary by entering a building as a trespasser and inflicting grievous bodily harm on a person therein contrary to s 9(1)(b) of the Theft Act 1968. In other words, does an allegation of inflicting grievous bodily harm impliedly include an allegation of assault occasioning actual bodily harm? The House assumed in favour of the appellants that it is possible to inflict harm without assaulting the victim (e.g., by deliberately causing panic in a crowded building so that people hurt themselves in a rush for the exits). Nonetheless, it is obvious that in the vast majority of cases harm will be inflicted through an assault. Their Lordships upheld the convictions. It is difficult to extract any clear *ratio* from Lord Roskill's judgment. However, the thrust of it seems to be that a count for Offence A impliedly contains an allegation of Offence B not only when commission of B is in law a necessary step towards committing A but also when a person committing the one offence will, *in the normal course of events*, commit the other also.

Application of *Wilson* led the Court of Appeal to hold that, on a count for burglary contrary to s 9(1)(b) of the Theft Act, there may be a verdict of guilty of s 9(1)(a) burglary (see *Whiting* [1987] Crim LR 473, reversing the earlier decision in *Hollis* [1971] Crim LR 525). Croom-Johnson LJ conceded that the s 9(1)(b) offence of entering a building as a trespasser and then stealing does not require the offender to have formed a theftous intent at the moment of entering, whereas s 9(1)(a) (entering as a trespasser with intent to steal) clearly does. However, the alternative verdict was available since, 'in the vast majority of cases', a trespasser who steals will have had the intent to steal before he entered and thus be guilty under both limbs of s 9(1). The impact of *Wilson* has been greatest, however, in the field of offences against the person. The *Wilson* case itself restored a conviction for assault occasioning actual bodily harm contrary to s 47 of the Offences Against the Person Act 1861, where the count in the indictment alleged inflicting grievous bodily harm contrary to s 20. In *Savage* [1992] 1 AC 699, the House of Lords held that a verdict of guilty of assault contrary to s 47 is a permissible alternative verdict on a count alleging unlawful wounding contrary to s 20. In *Mandair* [1995] 1 AC 208, the House of Lords held that 'causing' grievous bodily harm contrary to s 18 was wide enough to include any action that could amount to inflicting grievous bodily harm under s 20.

(c) In determining the questions posed by (a) and (b) above, the courts are not entitled to take into account the manner in which, according to the prosecution witnesses, the offence alleged was actually committed. Whether an alternative verdict is open to the jury is a question of law decided solely by reference to the wording of the count and the legal definitions of the offence charged and the proposed alternative. For example, if the accused is charged only with burglary in that he entered a building as a trespasser with intent to steal, he could not be convicted of criminal damage even if the prosecution case had always been that he broke a window to effect the entry. Criminal damage is not a necessary step towards burglary; nor is it even an offence which will in the normal course of events be committed by a burglar. Therefore if the accused admits that he broke the window but says that his purpose was merely to find shelter for the night, the prosecution will not be entitled to invite the jury to convict of criminal damage in the event of their believing the accused's story. Of course, if the indictment included counts for both burglary and criminal damage, the jury could convict on one or other or both. Thus, if there is any doubt as to the availability of an alternative verdict, the prosecution should have separate counts for the various alternatives (see also below).

The sensible course for the prosecution to follow in cases of doubt is to have several counts **21.26** (e.g., one for causing grievous bodily harm with intent; one for inflicting grievous bodily harm; and a third for assault occasioning actual bodily harm). If the jury convict on the most serious count, they will be discharged from giving a verdict on the other counts; if they acquit on the major count, it is still open to them to convict on one or other of the less serious ones (see *Mandair* [1995] 1 AC 208 and *Lahaye* [2006] Crim LR 241).

Reference has just been made to 'the major count' and the 'less serious counts', and it is **21.27** natural to think of s 6(3) of the Criminal Law Act 1967 in terms of a greater offence charged in the count and a lesser offence of which the jury may convict as an alternative. However, as was pointed out by Lord Roskill in *Wilson*, those expressions are not used in the subsection. It is therefore possible that the alternative offence will be of equivalent gravity to—or even more serious than—the count offence.

Specific provisions

The Criminal Law Act 1967, s 6(3), which makes general provision for verdicts of guilty of a **21.28** lesser offence, is supplemented by three further subsections of the 1967 Act and s 24 of the Road Traffic Offenders Act 1988, which all deal with the verdicts which may be returned in particular types of case. If the jury find the accused not guilty of the offence charged in the count then:

(a) On a count for murder they may convict of any one of the following—manslaughter, causing grievous bodily harm with intent, infanticide, child destruction, or attempt to commit any of the aforementioned: Criminal Law Act 1967, s 6(2).

(b) On a count for a completed offence the jury may convict of an attempt to commit that offence or of an attempt to commit another offence of which the accused could be convicted on the count: Criminal Law Act 1967, s 6(4). Thus, if the accused is charged with robbery, the jury could convict him of attempted robbery or attempted theft. In the converse case of the accused merely being charged with the attempt but the evidence showing that the completed offence was committed, the jury may convict of the attempt or the judge may, in his discretion, discharge them from giving a verdict so that a fresh indictment may be preferred alleging the completed offence.

(c) On a count for an arrestable offence, if the jury are satisfied that the offence charged (or another of which they could convict on the count) was committed by someone other than the accused, they may convict the accused of assisting whoever the offender was by impeding his apprehension or prosecution: Criminal Law Act 1967, s 4(2). Thus, on a count for murder, the accused could be convicted of assisting an offender who had committed either the murder or manslaughter or any other of the offences listed in (a) above.

(d) On a count for dangerous driving or causing death by dangerous driving the jury may convict the accused of careless driving (Road Traffic Offenders Act 1988, s 24). This is an unusual provision in that it allows a jury to convict of a summary offence (other than one specified in s 40 of the Criminal Justice Act 1988: see 13.79 to 13.80).

Judge's discretion

21.29   Even when the jury could as a matter of law return a verdict of guilty of a lesser offence, the judge has a discretion not to mention that option to them in his summing-up. The existence of the discretion was emphasized by Lord Roskill in *Wilson* [1984] AC 242 to counter the argument that extending the availability of alternative verdicts by abandoning the *Springfield* test (see 21.25) was unfair to the defence. His Lordship said—'a judge must always ensure, before deciding to leave the possibility of another offence to the jury, that that course will involve no risk of injustice to the defendant'. If the alternative offence has not been the subject of argument and submission in counsel's speeches, it is certainly wrong to introduce it for the first time in the summing-up: *Hazell* [1985] Crim LR 513. Counsel should at least be warned beforehand of what the judge has in mind, and given the opportunity to make a supplementary closing speech. In *Harris* (1993) *The Times*, 22 March 1993, the introduction by the prosecution of an alternative offence after the defence case and before closing speeches was held to be prejudicial. Steyn LJ said that such a course of action was only appropriate if it caused no risk to the defendant, and he was allowed a full opportunity to deal with the altered basis of the case against him.

21.30   In appropriate cases, there is, of course, nothing to stop counsel dealing with the issue in their respective closing speeches. However, the implication of *Fairbanks* [1986] 1 WLR 1202 is that the judge still has a discretion to tell the jury that they should ignore the alternative mentioned by counsel and either convict as charged or acquit. Mustill LJ summarized the principles involved by saying (at pp. 1205H–1206E) that 'the judge is obliged to leave the lesser alternative only if this is necessary in the interests of justice'. Where the case has been presented to the court in such a way that the lesser verdict simply does not arise (e.g., the defence have agreed that somebody committed the offence charged in the count but deny that it was the accused), mentioning the possibility in the summing-up would merely confuse the jury and so be contrary to the interests of justice. Similarly, if the alternative is very trivial by comparison with the actual charge, it is best not to distract the jury 'by forcing them to consider something which is remote from the real point of the case'. Where, however, the issue of a lesser offence clearly arises on the case as presented to the jury and where directing them on that issue would not be distracting or confusing, the judge should leave the alternative to them, even if one or other counsel objects. The interests of justice 'include the interests of the public as well as those of the defendant, and if the evidence is such that he ought at least to be convicted of the lesser offence, it would be wrong for him to be acquitted altogether merely because the jury cannot be sure that he was guilty of the greater'.

In *Fairbanks* it was the defence rather than the prosecution who wanted the alternative left. **21.31** F was indicted for causing death by reckless driving (the equivalent offence today would be causing death by dangerous driving). The essence of the prosecution case was that he had been responsible for a fatal accident by driving at recklessly high speeds along narrow country lanes. The defence more or less conceded that he had driven too fast but challenged, with some success, the actual speeds alleged by the prosecution. In his closing speech counsel argued that the jury might be sure that F was careless but not that he was reckless. Counsel for the prosecution, on the other hand, maintained a 'neck or nothing' approach— the jury should either convict as charged or acquit. Tactically, counsel did not wish them to have the easy option of conviction merely of careless driving. After argument, the judge took the prosecution's line, telling the jury that they should put careless driving 'out of their minds altogether' and consider only whether F's conduct was reckless. The jury convicted as charged, but only after a five-hour retirement in which questions they asked indicated that a conviction for careless driving (as suggested by defence counsel) might have been attractive to them. The Court of Appeal, applying the principles summarized above, held that failure to leave the alternative in the summing-up was a material irregularity and they therefore substituted a conviction for the lesser offence.

The decision in *Fairbanks* was approved by the House of Lords in *Maxwell* [1990] 1 WLR 401. **21.32** M was charged with robbery. He admitted that he would have pleaded guilty to burglary, but denied that he had intended any violence to the victims. The prosecution declined to apply to amend the indictment to include a count of burglary. A verdict of guilty of burglary was not, in law, open to the jury on the robbery count. About an hour after the jury had retired, they returned with the question: 'We would like to know if there is a lesser charge that we can bring against M... other than robbery?' The judge took the question as being directed to whether the jury were entitled to bring in a verdict of burglary. He directed that they could not. The jury could, of course, have been directed that they were entitled to bring in a verdict of guilty to the even lesser charge of theft. The judge did not deal with that possibility. After retiring for a further three and a half hours, the jury found M guilty of robbery. M appealed and his appeal was dismissed by the Court of Appeal. On appeal to the House of Lords, it was held that (a) the prosecution were entitled, on the evidence, to take the view that the jury should not be distracted by an inappropriate alternative count of burglary; (b) the judge had been entitled to accept that view; (c) the judge had been entitled to decline to leave the alternative of theft to the jury since it was relatively trifling, and the essential issue was: Did M intend violence to be used?

In *Coutts* [2006] 1 WLR 2154, the House of Lords considered an appeal by C against his conviction for murder . His defence at trial had been that he and the victim were engaged in consensual sex involving asphyxiation, and that her resultant death was an accident. The judge, in accordance with the views urged on him by both prosecution and defence, did not direct the jury on manslaughter. C appealed on the basis that the judge should have given the jury directions on manslaughter. The House of Lords allowed the appeal. Lord Bingham stated that the trial judge should leave to the jury:

> subject to any appropriate caution or warning, but irrespective of the wishes of trial counsel, any obvious alternative offence which there is evidence to support....I would.....confine the rule to alternative verdicts obviously raised by the evidence. By that I refer to alternatives which should suggest themselves to the mind of any ordinarily knowledgeable and alert criminal judge, excluding alternatives which ingenious counsel may identify through diligent research after the trial.

Decision on the offence charged

21.33   The power to bring in an alternative verdict under both CLA, s 6(2) (counts for murder) and s 6(3) (the general provision) only arises if the accused is found not guilty of the offence charged. In *Collison* (1980) 71 Cr App R 249 the jury sent a note to the judge saying that they were agreed that C was guilty of the alternative of unlawful wounding but could not agree that he should be acquitted of wounding with intent as alleged in the indictment. The ironic possibility therefore arose that the jury might have to be discharged from giving any verdict whatsoever as an acquittal for the greater offence appeared to be a precondition of a conviction for the lesser. The judge rescued the situation by allowing an amendment to the indictment so as to add a separate count for the lesser offence. The jury then convicted on the new count and were discharged from giving a verdict on the original one. The Court of Appeal approved the course of action adopted. A similar issue arose in *Khela* [2006] Crim LR 526 in two conjoined appeals. In the first, the appellant had been charged with causing death by careless driving while unfit through drink or drugs. The trial judge stayed that charge because the relevant evidence (the car) had been destroyed by the police. He then invited the jury to bring in a verdict on the alternative charge of driving while unfit through drink or drugs. This is an alternative verdict under the Road Traffic Offenders Act 1988, s 24, provided that the defendant is found not guilty of the charge of causing death by careless driving while unfit through drink or drugs. However, the jury did not find the defendant not guilty of that charge but just proceeded immediately to consider the lesser alternative, and found him guilty of that. In the second appeal, the appellant was tried for racially aggravated assault. The jury was directed in the judge's summing up on the basis of the alternative offence of assault without the racial aggravation. This is an alternative offence in accordance with s 31 of the Crime and Disorder Act 1998, if the defendant is found not guilty of the racially aggravated form of assault. In due course, the jury indicated in a note that they had reached a unanimous verdict on the alternative offence, but told the judge in answer to a question that there was no realistic likelihood of their reaching a majority verdict on the racially aggravated assault. The judge then discharged them from reaching a verdict on the count in the indictment, and the jury delivered a unanimous verdict of guilty in relation to the non-racially aggravated charge. Both appeals were allowed. In each case, the jury only had jurisdiction to convict of the alternative offence if they had found the defendant not guilty of the primary offence. In neither case had they delivered such a verdict, with the result that there was no jurisdiction to convict of the alternative offence.

E   MAJORITY VERDICTS

Until 1967 the verdict of a jury had to be unanimous. This may have helped prevent mistaken convictions, but it had the disadvantage that one obstinate or unreasonable juror could prevent his colleagues reaching a verdict when, in truth, the evidence one way or the other was absolutely clear. There was also the possibility that a juror could be threatened or bribed into refusing to agree to a conviction. The Criminal Justice Act 1967, therefore, departed from centuries of tradition by introducing majority verdicts. The present legislation is contained in the Juries Act 1974, s 17. **21.34**

Section 17 provides for verdicts by a majority of 11 to 1 or 10 to 2, or, if the jury is reduced below twelve, by a majority of 10 to 1 or 9 to 1. A majority of 9 to 2 is not acceptable. If the jury is reduced to nine they must be unanimous. A jury can both acquit and convict by a majority, although if they convict the foreman must state in open court what the majority was: s 17(3). The chief restriction upon majority verdicts is that before one may be accepted by the court the jury must have had two hours, or such longer period as the judge 'thinks reasonable having regard to the nature and complexity of the case', in which to try to reach a unanimous verdict: s 17(4). It is for this reason that the judge, at the end of his summing-up, directs the jury that they must try to reach a verdict on which they are all agreed. He is entitled also, if he so wishes, to indicate that the possibility of their returning a verdict which is not the verdict of them all may arise at some future stage, in which event he will give them further directions. He should not, however, indicate precisely how long must elapse before he can give such directions: *Thomas* [1983] Crim LR 745. In *Guthrie* (1994) *The Times*, 23 February 1994, the Court of Appeal confirmed that it was desirable not to mention the time at which a majority direction could be given, but said that on the facts of the case, mentioning the time did not amount to pressure on the jury. The two-hour minimum period laid down in s 17 has, in effect, been extended slightly by *Practice Direction (Crime: Majority Verdict)* [1970] 1 WLR 916, which states that at least two hours and ten minutes must elapse between the jury leaving their box and their returning with a majority verdict. The extra ten minutes is meant to allow them time for going to their room, settling down in their room, returning to court with any questions and any other matters which reduce the period they actually spend deliberating their verdict.

The procedure for the taking of majority verdicts is set out in the *Practice Direction (Criminal Proceedings: Consolidation)* [2002] 1 WLR 2870, para IV.46. Should the jury come into court, apparently with a verdict, before the two hours and ten minutes or such longer period as the judge considers reasonable has elapsed, the clerk asks the foreman if they have reached a verdict on which they are all agreed (see 21.18). If they have, the verdict is taken in the usual way; if not, the judge sends them out again with a further direction to arrive if possible at **21.35** a unanimous verdict. If the jury return to court or are sent for by the judge after the two hours and ten minutes or longer period, they are again asked if they have agreed unanimously. At this stage, however, should the foreman answer 'no', the judge gives them the majority verdict direction—i.e., he tells them they should retire once more and endeavour to reach a unanimous verdict, but if they cannot he will accept a majority verdict. He then informs them what the permissible majorities are. When the jury finally return to court after the majority verdict direction, the clerk asks—'Have at least ten [or, if the jury has only 10 members, nine] of you agreed upon your verdict?' If they have, the verdict is taken, the clerk stressing that the foreman should only answer 'Guilty' or 'Not Guilty'. This is to avoid the foreman saying 'Not Guilty by a majority', as the whole aim of the rather elaborate procedure prescribed by the Practice Direction is to prevent the public knowing, if it be the case, that the accused, although acquitted, was only acquitted by a majority. Accordingly, if the verdict is not guilty, nothing further is said. If, however, the jury convict they are asked if their decision was by a majority, and, if so, the foreman states the majority. Although a literal reading of s 17(3) of the Juries Act might lead to an opposite conclusion, it is not necessary for the foreman to state expressly both how many jurors agreed and how many disagreed—it is sufficient if he says ten or eleven, as the case may be, agreed, leaving the size of the minority to be calculated by the most elementary arithmetic: *Pigg* [1983] 1 WLR 6. On an appeal against conviction the Court of Appeal may, in a border-line case, be swayed in their decision by the fact that the verdict was only by a 10 to 2 majority.

21.36   Although the Court of Appeal have stressed the importance of the procedure in the practice direction being followed, the direction does not have the force of law and failure to comply with it will not in itself lead to a conviction being quashed (*Gilbert* (1978) 66 Cr App R 237; *Trickett* [1991] Crim LR 59). The position is different where s 17 itself is contravened through a majority verdict being returned within the two hour period or the foreman failing to say by what majority the jury decided to convict. The verdict then is not 'a proper or lawful one', so an appeal must succeed: *Barry* [1975] 1 WLR 1190. *Barry* can be contrasted with *Shields* [1997] Crim LR 758, where, although the judge gave a majority direction after an hour and 47 minutes, this was remedied by telling the jury (once the mistake was discovered) that it was too early for a majority verdict, and they must reach a unanimous verdict. The jury did not in fact return a verdict until three hours and 47 minutes after their original retirement, and the conviction by a majority of 10 to 2 was upheld by the Court of Appeal.

21.37   The readiness of the judge to accept a majority verdict varies depending upon the gravity and complexity of the case and the views of the individual judge on the desirability of unanimity. In *Mansfield* [1977] 1 WLR 1102, for example, Cobb J twice had the jury back into court to stress the 'utter desirability' of a unanimous verdict, and delayed for over six hours before giving a majority verdict direction. Melford Stevenson J, on the other hand, in *Gilbert* (above) told the jury that he would accept a majority verdict after only the bare statutory minimum period had elapsed. In both *Mansfield* and *Gilbert* the accused was charged with murder, although the former was admittedly the more serious case in that there were seven counts of murder and three of arson. The evidence in *Mansfield* was also more complicated than that in *Gilbert*. Even so, the reluctance in the one case and the readiness in the other to accept a majority verdict seemed to spring essentially from the attitude of the judges concerned to such verdicts. Some indication of the Court of Appeal's view on how long the jury should have to reach a unanimous verdict is derived from *Rose* [1982] 1 WLR 614. In the circumstances of that case—a complicated murder trial lasting 15 days—two hours and forty minutes after retirement was 'a little soon' for the majority verdict direction. However, in a case which is not especially serious or complicated one would expect the direction to be given soon after the two hours and ten minutes have elapsed.

F   DISCHARGING THE JURY FROM GIVING A VERDICT

Where a jury cannot agree upon their verdict, the judge discharges them from giving one. The **21.38** procedure is that, after giving them the majority verdict direction, the judge allows them whatever time he thinks reasonable for further deliberations. If they still do not return with a verdict, he has them brought back into court and finds out from the foreman whether there is any real possibility of their arriving at a decision. Should the answer be that they are so badly split that, even given more time, they would not reach a verdict, the judge discharges them. Discharge of the jury from giving a verdict is not equivalent to an acquittal. Therefore, the accused may be tried again by a fresh jury on the same indictment, and a plea of autrefois acquit will fail. In theory, there could be an infinite number of trials for the same offence, with the jury failing to agree and being discharged on each occasion. In practice, if two juries have disagreed, the prosecution offer no evidence at the start of what would otherwise be the third trial, and the judge enters a verdict of not guilty. In *Henworth* [2001] Crim LR 505, it was stressed that this was a convention, rather a proposition of law. In some cases, a further trial might be proper, e.g., if a jury had been tampered with, or some cogent piece of evidence for the Crown had since been discovered. Whether it was an abuse of process for the prosecution to seek a further trial must depend on the facts, including:

(a) the overall period of the delay and the reasons for it;
(b) the results of the previous trials;
(c) the seriousness of the offence; and (possibly)
(d) the extent to which the case against the defendant had changed since previous trials.

However anxious the judge is for the jury to agree he must not pressurise them into doing so. **21.39** Subject to being discharged from giving a verdict, the jury must be allowed as much time as they need to deliberate freely and reach a proper verdict. If the judge does exert undue pressure, any conviction will be quashed. An example is provided by *McKenna* [1960] 1 QB 411. At 2.40 p.m., after the jury had been considering their verdict for two and a quarter hours, the judge told them that he was leaving court within ten minutes, and if they had not by then agreed they would have to be 'kept all night'. The reason for this ultimatum was that the judge was anxious to catch a train. After six minutes the jury returned with a verdict of guilty. Describing the judge's words as a threat, and pointing out that the jury might have thought that they would be locked in their room until the next morning, the Court of Criminal Appeal quashed the conviction. As Cassels J said at p. 422—'It is a cardinal principle of our criminal law that in considering their verdict . . . a jury shall deliberate in complete freedom, uninfluenced by any promise, unintimidated by any threat'. The attitude of the Court of Appeal in *McKenna* is a far cry from that which prevailed a century or so earlier. Until 1860, the jury bailiff swore to keep the jury without food, water, or light, which must have given them a powerful incentive to agree upon a verdict quickly!

21.40   The Court of Appeal has also disapproved of less blatant forms of pressure, e.g., telling the jury during the majority direction that if they failed to agree, another trial might have to take place (*Boyes* [1991] Crim LR 717).

Failure by the jury to agree is regrettable for all concerned. To encourage awkward jurors to listen to their colleagues' arguments while not putting undue pressure on them to change their minds, judges over the years have used a form of direction first sanctioned by Lord Goddard CJ in *Walhein* (1952) 36 Cr App R 167. The so-called '*Walhein*' direction had two elements. First, the jurors were told that, in order to return a collective verdict, there necessarily had to be some give and take between them and a willingness on the part of the minority to subordinate their views to the majority, while always bearing in mind that each of them had to stay true to his juror's oath to return what he regarded as 'a true verdict according to the evidence'. Secondly, the judge could point out the inconvenience and expense caused by one or more jurors being unwilling to listen to the arguments of the rest. Quite often juries which had appeared hopelessly deadlocked returned a verdict shortly after receiving such a direction, the clinching factor probably being the reference to public expense. The introduction of majority verdicts greatly reduced the need for *Walhein* directions because one or two obstinate or unreasonable jurors could be outvoted by the others.

21.41   Because of uncertainties over the propriety of *Walhein* directions, the issue was considered by a five-judge Court of Appeal in *Watson* [1988] QB 690, judgment given by the Lord Chief Justice. The main points are that:

(i)   The original *Walhein* direction was capable of putting improper pressure on juries to agree, chiefly because of the reference to the adverse consequences of disagreements.

(ii)   But, there is no reason why juries should not be directed as follows:

Each of you has taken an oath to return to true verdict according to the evidence. No one must be false to that oath, but you have a duty not only as individuals but collectively. That is the strength of the jury system. Each of you takes into the jury box with you your individual experience and wisdom. Your task is to pool that experience and wisdom. You do that by giving your views and listening to the views of others. There must necessarily be discussion, argument and give and take within the scope of your oath. That is the way in which agreement is reached. If, unhappily, [10 of] you cannot reach agreement you must say so.

(iii)   There will usually be no need to give such a direction. Whether to do so or not is a matter for the judge's discretion. Similarly, the stage at which it is given (whether before or after the majority verdict direction) is a matter for discretion.

As to (iii), giving the *Watson* direction before the majority verdict direction might be appropriate where the jury take the initiative by sending the judge a note to the effect that they are split in such a way that even decision by a majority will be impossible unless some of them are prepared to change their minds. More usually, the judge will consider giving the *Watson* direction after the jury has had a reasonable time to consider the majority direction. It is in any event clear from *Buono* (1992) 95 Cr App R 338, that a *Watson* direction should never be given at the same time as a majority direction. Finally, it should be stressed that a *Watson* direction is unusual, even within the strict limits laid down by the Court of Appeal. In the great majority of cases, the trial judge will, when it becomes plain that the jury cannot agree even on a majority basis, discharge them.

G ACCEPTING THE VERDICT

In general, the judge has no power to reject the jury's verdict however much he may disagree **21.42** with it: *Lester* (1940) 27 Cr App R 8—for exceptions, see below. Nor should he ask the jury any questions about the verdict (e.g., the reason why they convicted of manslaughter and not murder—*Larkin* [1943] KB 174). Once the jury have completed giving their verdict they are discharged. If the accused has been acquitted on all counts, he is discharged as well. If he has been convicted on any count, the judge either proceeds to sentence him forthwith, or adjourns so that reports on him can be prepared. He may be released on bail or kept in custody for the period of the adjournment. The procedure before sentence is passed is dealt with in Chapter 22. Should the jury realize before they have dispersed that they have inadvertently announced the wrong verdict, the judge has a discretion to let them correct their error (see 21.19).

In the following cases the judge is not obliged to accept the first verdict returned by the jury: **21.43**

(a) If their verdict is one which, on the indictment, they have no power to return the judge will ask them to reconsider it. An example is if the jury purport to convict of an offence not charged in the indictment which does not fall within the provisions of the Criminal Law Act 1967 on alternative verdicts.

(b) If a verdict on a count is ambiguous the judge should not accept it in the form it is given, but should ask questions to resolve the ambiguity and, if need be, further direct the jury on the law. Usually the verdict is an unambiguous guilty, not guilty or guilty of another offence, but occasionally something more is said which raises a doubt as to what the jury's decision really is. In *Hawkes* (1931) 22 Cr App R 172 the foreman said 'Guilty' when asked the jury's verdict on a count for driving while unfit through drink, but a moment later he added 'We find the defendant guilty of being under the influence of drink'. This remark introduced an element of ambiguity into the original verdict, since it might have meant that the jury, although satisfied that H had consumed alcohol, were not satisfied that it had impaired his ability to drive. The judge failed to take steps to clear up the ambiguity, so the conviction had to be quashed.

(c) If a verdict appears, having regard to the evidence adduced at the trial, to be inconsistent with another verdict returned by the jury in the same case the judge may ask them to reconsider the verdicts. He should only do this if the verdicts genuinely cannot be reconciled. If there is a possible, though unlikely, view of the evidence on which they can be supported, the judge should accept them. In *Burrows* [1970] Crim LR 419, where the jury were trying three accused on a joint count for theft of a purse and one of the three on a second count, in the alternative, for handling the purse, the judge thought that acquittals of all three on the theft count were inconsistent with a conviction on the handling count. He asked the jury how they could convict the handler when they had found that the purse was not stolen by acquitting all the alleged thieves. The Court of Appeal held that the verdicts were not inconsistent. The jury might have been satisfied that one of the three accused had stolen the purse, but were unable to say which it was.

If the judge, in a proper case, declines to accept the jury's first verdict, and, as a result of his **21.44** further directions, they alter their verdict, the second verdict is the operative one. If, despite the judge's efforts, the jury insist upon their **first** verdict it seems that it would have to be accepted although any conviction would have to be quashed on appeal.

KEY DOCUMENTS

Code of Conduct of the Bar of England and Wales available on the website of the Bar
   Standards Board: <http://www.barstandardsboard.org.uk/standardsandguidance/codeof
   conduct/>.
Criminal Procedure Rules 2005, available at <http://www.hmcourts-service.gov.uk/cms/
   pds.htm>.
Specimen Directions available on the website of the Judicial Studies Board: <http://www.jsboard.
   co.uk/>. then click on Specimen Direction from the list of JSB publications.

PART 4

SENTENCING

22

PROCEDURE BEFORE SENTENCING

22.01 This chapter, and the three which follow, summarize the sentencing process, placing emphasis upon its procedural aspects. For more detail, reference should be made to *Blackstone's Criminal Practice 2008*, Part E.

22.02 Once the accused has pleaded guilty or been found guilty by the jury or magistrates, the court's task is to sentence him. Before it does so, the procedures described in this Chapter must be gone through. The court may either embark on them immediately after conviction, or it may adjourn (e.g., to obtain reports on the offender, or to await the outcome of a co-accused's trial so that, in the event of his being convicted as well, they can both be sentenced together). During the period of any adjournment the offender may be remanded in custody or on bail at the court's discretion. The description that follows is mainly of procedure preparatory to sentencing in the Crown Court. Although the same basic principles apply in the magistrates' courts, what happens there tends to be less elaborate and less formal than the Crown Court equivalent. Paragraphs 22.75 to 22.76 deal with the differences.

22.03 In the magistrates' courts the decision on what sentence to impose, like the decision as to verdict, may be taken by a majority of the magistrates. In the Crown Court, the responsibility for sentencing rests solely upon the judge and any magistrates with whom he may be sitting. The only way a jury may try to influence sentence is by adding a rider to their verdict recommending leniency. They very rarely do so. Since counsel in their speeches and the judge in his summing-up do not refer to the possibility of recommending leniency, the jurors probably do not even know that they could make such a recommendation. Moreover, in *Sahota* [1980] Crim LR 678, where the jury asked if they could recommend leniency and the judge answered 'yes', the Court of Appeal stated that he should have told them that matters of sentencing were not for their consideration.

22.04 If the jury indicate on their own initiative a view of the facts which is relevant to sentence, the judge is not bound by that view when he decides upon sentence. In *Mills* [2003] Crim LR 896, the defendant was convicted of being knowingly concerned in fraudulently evading the prohibition on the importation of cocaine and other drugs. The judge stated he would sentence on the basis that the defendant knew he was importing drugs with a high value, and sentenced him to 16 years' imprisonment. The jury submitted a note signed by 11 of them stating that their verdict of guilty was based on a view that the accused genuinely believed that the goods he was importing were not drugs but were prohibited. The sentencing judge concluded that he was not bound by the note, and refused to vary the sentence. The Court of Appeal agreed that he was not bound by the jury's finding, and dismissed the appeal.

22.05 The procedure before sentencing is divided into the presentation of the facts of the offence by the prosecution; the reading of any reports on the offender; and mitigation by the defence.

A   THE FACTS OF THE OFFENCE

22.06 Where the offender has pleaded not guilty and has been convicted by the jury, the Crown Court judge, having heard the evidence, knows full well the facts of the offence, and does not need to be reminded of them. If the offender pleads guilty, on the other hand, it is prosecuting counsel's duty to summarize the facts of the offence. He does this partly to assist the judge, partly to establish the prosecution version of how the offence was committed, and partly so that the public may know what occurred and form their own views on the justice of the sentence passed. The Attorney-General has issued guidance (*Guidelines on Acceptance of Pleas and the Prosecutor's Role in the Sentencing Exercise*) which lays down that the prosecution must set out in advance, and in writing:

- the aggravating and mitigating features of the offence which will form the opening of its case;
- any statutory provisions or guidelines on sentencing applicable to the offence or the offender;
- evidence of impact on the victim and community;
- any ancillary orders which the prosecution intends to apply for.

The intention is that this statement will be notified in advance to the court and the defence. The guidelines apply to all cases before the Crown Court, and cases in the magistrates' court where the issues are complex or there is scope for misunderstanding.

22.07 In summarizing the facts, counsel makes use of copies, given to him in his brief, of the statements made by the prosecution witnesses for purposes of the committal proceedings. He explains how the offence was committed, mentioning facts especially relevant to its gravity—e.g., if it was an offence of theft, he tells the judge the value of the property stolen and the amount which has been recovered; if it was an offence of violence, he recites the injuries suffered by the victim. He goes on to describe the arrest of the offender, and his reaction when asked about the offence. If the offender was immediately cooperative, admitting his guilt to the police, it is a point in his favour which may result in the sentence being lighter than it would otherwise have been. Therefore, prosecuting counsel should acknowledge, if it be the case, that the offender did frankly confess to the crime. If there was a formal interview with the offender at the police station, counsel could either read out the record of it in full, or, more usually, summarize its contents and leave the defence to refer to it in more detail if they so wish.

At the sentencing stage, the prosecution take a neutral attitude towards the case. They do not suggest any particular sentence, nor do they advocate a severe sentence. Prosecuting counsel is still to regard himself as a minister of justice (see 20.06), conceding to the defence those points which can fairly be made on the offender's behalf. This general statement is subject to some qualifications. For example: **22.08**

(a) Prosecuting counsel should apply for compensation, confiscation or forfeiture, backing up the application with evidence and argument if necessary (see 25.96 to 25.110 for details).

(b) Counsel should assist the judge by drawing attention to any limits on the court's sentencing powers, so that no unlawful sentence is passed. This duty applies also to defence counsel (*Komsta* (1990) 12 Cr App R (S) 63). Prosecuting counsel should also draw the judge's attention to guidelines cases (*Panayioutou* (1989) 11 Cr App R (S) 535; see 23.23 to 23.27 for the role of guideline cases).

Rather more controversial is the question of the extent to which the prosecution should make reference to the impact of the offence on the victim. In *Attorney-General's Reference (No 2 of 1995)* [1996] 1 Cr App R (S) 274, the Court of Appeal said it was appropriate that a judge should receive factual information as to the impact of offending on the victim. Any such information should, however, be put in proper form, e.g., a witness statement, served on the defence in advance and forming part of the judge's papers (see *Hobstaff* (1993) 14 Cr App R (S) 632, where the point was also made that the prosecution should avoid colourful and emotive language in dealing with the impact on the victim). In *H* (1999) *The Times*, 18 March 1999, the Court of Appeal emphasized that where the prosecution does provide a statement from the victim, then the sentencer should approach it with some care. Since it was generally inappropriate for the defence to investigate such a statement, it would necessarily reflect one side of the case only. **22.09**

In *Perks* [2001] 1 Cr App R (8) 66, the following guidelines were laid down for courts when taking into account what have become known as 'victim impact statements': **22.10**

(a) a sentencer should not make assumptions unsupported by the evidence about the effect of an offence on the victim;

(b) if the offence had a particularly distressing or disturbing effect upon the victim, the court should be so informed and account should be taken of this fact in passing sentence;

(c) evidence of an offence on the victim should be in the proper form as a witness statement or expert report, and be properly served on the defence prior to sentence;

(d) evidence of the victim should be approached with care, particularly if it dealt with matters which the defence could not be expected to investigate; and

(e)   opinions of the victim's close relatives on the appropriate level of sentence should not be taken into account.

22.11   In any event, the prosecution should not accept the defence version of the offence if it does not accord with the account given by the prosecution witnesses. Hence, there is the possibility of a dispute arising about the facts of the offence, even after the offender has quite properly entered a plea of guilty. If the dispute is on a minor point, it can be glossed over because the sentence the judge passes will be the same irrespective of which of the opposing contentions he believes. But, where there is a 'substantial conflict between the two sides' involving a 'sharp divergence on questions of fact', the judge, having heard submissions from counsel, must *either*:

(a)   obtain the answer to the problem from a jury; or
(b)   accept the defence account 'as far as that is possible', *or*
(c)   give both parties the opportunity to call evidence about the disputed matters,

and then decide himself what happened 'acting so to speak as his own jury on the issue which is the root of the problem'.

What he must *not* do is to come down in favour of the prosecution version of events without hearing evidence. The benefit of any reasonable doubt should be given to the offender. The above statement of the law is based on Lord Lane CJ's judgment in the leading case of *Newton* (1982) 77 Cr App R 13, the facts of which illustrate the importance which can attach to disputes about the facts after a guilty plea. N pleaded guilty to buggery of his wife. Buggery of a female was at that time an offence punishable with life imprisonment, regardless of whether the 'victim' consented. The wife, in a complaint she made to the police, said that she had not consented, but N claimed that she had. On his own admission, he was guilty as charged, but the appropriate sentence would be significantly more severe if he acted against his wife's will. Without hearing evidence from N or from the wife, the judge announced that he was sentencing on the basis that she had not consented, and he imprisoned N for seven years. The Court of Appeal (in reducing the term of imprisonment so as to allow for N's immediate release) said that the judge should not have decided such an important issue against the defence without hearing evidence. (The substantive law has been amended. Buggery of a man or woman now constitutes rape where the victim did not consent and the accused knew of that lack of consent or was reckless as to whether there was consent or not. If N was to be dealt with today, the indictment would no doubt include a count of rape, and the procedural problem would be resolved in that way.)

22.12   Uncertainty about the facts of the offence can also occur where the offender pleaded not guilty and was found guilty by the jury. For example, in *Stosiek* (1982) 4 Cr App R (S) 205, S, who had punched a plain-clothes police officer and broken his nose, was found guilty of assault occasioning actual bodily harm. Prior to the assault, the officer had touched S lightly on the arm, shown him his warrant card, and said 'I want a word with you'. The evidence was consistent either with S having realized that a policeman was trying to arrest him and committing the assault to resist arrest, or with his not noticing the warrant-card and over-reacting to what he took to be a minor assault on him by a member of the public. On either hypothesis, the jury would have to convict, but on the first-mentioned hypothesis a sentence of imprisonment was almost inevitable, whereas on the second (given that S was of previous good character) non-custodial sanctions were appropriate. The Court of Appeal held that in such cases it is for the judge to assess the evidence led before the jury, and decide on the basis thereof what the facts of the offence were. He is not obliged to accept the least serious construction of the evidence consistent with the jury's verdict (*Solomon* [1984] Crim LR 433), but he should be 'extremely astute' to give the benefit of any doubt to the offender (*Stosiek*). In passing sentence, the judge must always respect the jury's verdict, so that if the offender was found guilty merely of a lesser offence the sentence must be appropriate to that lesser offence, even if the judge thinks that the evidence showed beyond doubt that the offender was guilty as charged: *Hazelwood* [1984] Crim LR 375.

A judge must not, under guise of hearing evidence about the facts of what occurred, in effect **22.13** find the accused guilty of an offence more serious than that to which he has pleaded guilty. (*Courtie* [1984] AC 463).

The decision in *Nottingham Crown Court ex parte Director of Public Prosecutions* [1995] Crim LR **22.14** 902 would appear to run counter to the well-established principle outlined in the preceding paragraph. In that case, the prosecution charged assault by beating contrary to s 39 of the Criminal Justice Act 1988 (which requires no proof of injury), rather than assault contrary to s 47 of the Offences Against the Person Act 1861 (which does). The Divisional Court held that the sentencer should have taken into account, in passing sentence, injuries caused to the victim. It is submitted that the decision is best viewed as confined to the offence of assault by beating, and should not be extended to other offences.

A judge must also not use an inquiry into the facts of the offence as a means of deciding that **22.15** the offender has committed similar offences on other occasions. This principle is important to bear in mind should the prosecution, in their summary of the facts following a guilty plea, suggest that the counts on the indictment merely represent a sample of a continuing course of conduct by the offender. If this is accepted by the defence, the judge may pass sentence on that basis. There is also the possibility that the prosecution may make formal application under s 25 of the Domestic Violence, Crime and Victims Act 2004 for some of the counts to be treated as a sample, with the remainder being tried by the judge alone (see 15.15 for detail of this procedure). However, if neither of these events occur, then the judge must ignore the allegations about a continuing course of conduct, and sentence on the basis of the offences to which the defendant has pleaded guilty. Thus, in *Huchison* [1972] 1 All ER 936, the Court of Appeal halved a four-year sentence passed on H for incest with his daughter. The indictment contained one count to which H pleaded guilty. The prosecution alleged that there had been regular intercourse over a long period, whereas the defence said it had only happened the once. Having heard evidence from both the daughter and H, the judge believed the daughter, and sentenced on the basis that the count represented but a small part of a continuing course of conduct. Their Lordships held that the judge had adopted the wrong procedure. Instead of hearing evidence himself, he should have sentenced H strictly for the one offence to which he had pleaded guilty, leaving the prosecution to commence further proceedings for the other alleged acts of incest if they so wished. In *Canavan* [1998] 1 Cr App R 79, the Court of Appeal said that the court below could not base its decision as to sentence on the commission of offences not forming part of the offence for which the offender was to be sentenced. This seems to resolve the matter authoritatively.

Since the Court of Appeal's decision in *Newton* (supra) there has been a plethora of decisions **22.16** refining and expanding upon Lord Lane CJ's basic dictum that, if the prosecution and defence disagree about the facts of the offence, the judge must either proceed on the basis most favourable to the defence or himself hear evidence on the disputed issues. Among the points dealt with in the post-*Newton* cases are those set out in the following Paragraphs.

22.17   The Court of Appeal has stated that counsel are under a duty to make it clear when a *Newton* hearing is appropriate. In *Gardener* (1994) 15 Cr App R (S) 667, the court said that where there is a dispute about relevant facts which might affect sentence, defence counsel should make that clear to the prosecution. The court should be informed at the outset of the hearing, if not by the prosecution then by the defence. If for any reason this did not happen, defence counsel should ensure during mitigation that the judge was aware, not merely that there was a dispute, but that the defence wished to have it resolved in a *Newton* hearing. The Court of Appeal would not normally consider an argument that the sentencer had failed to order a hearing unless the possibility of such a hearing was raised unequivocally and expressly in the Crown Court (see also *Attorney-General's References (Nos 3 and 4 of 1996)* [1996] Crim LR 607). In *Tolera* [1998] Crim LR 425, the Court of Appeal said that the initiative rested with the defence to make it clear that it was asking the court to pass sentence on any basis other than that disclosed by the prosecution case. The mere fact that the defendant put forward an alternative version to the probation service, which was reflected in the pre-sentence report, was not sufficient to alert the judge to the need for a *Newton* hearing. If the defendant wanted that account to be used as the basis of sentence, he should expressly draw the relevant paragraphs of the report to the attention of the court, and ask that he be sentenced on that basis.

22.18   Some difficulty arises where the defendant changes his plea to guilty after some evidence has been given by prosecution witnesses. In *Mottram* (1981) 3 Cr App R (S) 123, it was held that the judge should then hear evidence from the defendant (and, presumably from any witnesses the defence wished to call), before deciding on the version of the facts which will form the basis for sentence. The totality of the evidence received on the point relevant to sentence can then be treated as a *Newton* hearing (see also *Archer* [1994] Crim LR 80).

22.19   Sometimes an agreement is reached between prosecution and defence as to the basis on which a plea of guilty will be given and accepted, e.g., the accused agrees to plead guilty to assault occasioning actual bodily harm, but only on the basis of recklessness, and the prosecution are willing to accept this. In *Beswick* [1996] 1 Cr App R (S) 343, the Court of Appeal set out principles to guide the court in such cases. It stressed that the court should sentence an offender on a basis which was true, and that the prosecution should not lend itself to any agreement with the defence based upon an unreal set of facts. If that had happened, then the judge was entitled to call for a *Newton* hearing to determine the true factual basis for sentence. The judge's decision to do so did not of itself entitle the defendant to change his plea from guilty to not guilty. Once the judge had decided to hold a *Newton* hearing, then the prosecution should no longer regard themselves as bound by the original agreement which they had made with the defence, which was conditional on the sentencer's approval. They should therefore assist the court in the conduct of the *Newton* hearing by presenting evidence and testing any evidence called by the defence.

22.20   In *Underwood* [2005] 1 Cr App R 178, the Court of Appeal stressed that, where the Crown agreed the defendant's account of facts, which were originally disputed, the agreement should be set out in writing and signed by both advocates. It should then be made available to the judge before he was invited to approve acceptance of the plea. Crucially, the Crown's acceptance of the proposed basis of the plea of guilty must be conditional upon the judge's acceptance of it. Where, on the other hand, the defendant's version was rejected by the Crown, the precise facts in dispute should be identified in a document for the attention of the court. In any event, it was for the judge to determine whether there should be a *Newton* hearing to ascertain the truth about those facts.

In *Oudkerk* [1994] Crim LR 700, it was held that where the imposition of a longer than normal **22.21** sentence is contemplated, the sentencing court must resolve by a *Newton* hearing any important issue relevant to the application of that provision (see 24.34 to 24.42 for longer than normal sentences).

If the court decides to have a '*Newton* hearing', the same rules apply regarding burden and **22.22** standard of proof as apply at the trial of a not guilty plea. In other words, the court may sentence on the prosecution version of what occurred only if satisfied beyond reasonable doubt that the defence version is wrong (see dicta in *Ahmed* (1984) 6 Cr App R (S) 391 and *Stosiek* (above)). In *Ahmed*, the Court of Appeal also intimated that they will not interfere with the Crown Court's decision as to the facts established at a *Newton* hearing unless the appellant can show that it was totally unreasonable or arrived at by applying incorrect principles (e.g., not giving him the benefit of any doubt). *Gandy* (1989) 11 Cr App R (S) 564 makes it clear that, where there is a *Newton* hearing:

(i)   the rules of evidence should be strictly followed; and
(ii) the judge should direct himself appropriately as the trier of fact, e.g., in accordance with the guidance in *Turnbull* [1977] QB 224 on identification evidence.

Where the differences between the prosecution and defence as to what occurred are too **22.23** slight to affect sentence, the Crown Court may sentence on the basis of the facts alleged by the prosecution without hearing evidence. (In such a case, the judge will frequently indicate that he is accepting the defence version purely for the purpose of sentence. Since it will not make any difference to the outcome, there is no point giving the offender a sense of grievance by openly disbelieving what is put forward on his behalf.) Thus, in *Bent* (1986) 8 Cr App R (S) 19, the Court of Appeal dismissed B's appeal against a sentence of six months' youth custody for assaulting a store detective who tried to arrest him for shoplifting since, although the judge in passing sentence clearly accepted the prosecution case that B had used a stick in attacking the detective (whereas defence counsel had said in mitigation that his client merely *threatened* to use a stick), the gravamen of the charge was that the appellant had resisted arrest. As there was no suggestion even from the prosecution that the store detective had suffered actual harm through the assault, the question of whether the stick had lightly come into contact with his face or had merely been waved threateningly was peripheral to sentence.

Sometimes it is possible to avoid a *Newton* hearing by inviting the prosecution to add a sub- **22.24** sidiary count to the indictment which will enable a jury, in effect, to decide how the offence alleged in the primary count was committed. Thus, if the accused pleads guilty to robbery but denies the prosecution allegation that he used a firearm to commit the offence, the correct procedure is to have a second count for carrying a firearm with intent to commit an indictable offence. The accused will presumably deny that charge, and, if the jury acquit him, the sentence for robbery will have to be passed on the basis that it was committed unarmed.

22.25   The principles explained in *Newton* do not apply when the facts advanced by the defence in mitigation are peculiarly within the knowledge of the accused himself, so that the prosecution cannot realistically be expected either to accept or to challenge what is put forward on his behalf, for example, where the accused pleads guilty to importing cocaine but says that he thought the drug was cannabis, or where he claims to have committed an offence as a result of threats that fell short of actual duress. In such cases, which have been usefully described as 'reverse *Newton*' situations, the onus would seem to be on the defence to establish the mitigation. Whether they do so simply by counsel making assertions of fact in his speech in mitigation (see 22.53 to 22.59) or by calling evidence, is a matter for their judgment. In *Guppy* (1994) 16 Cr App R (S) 25, the Court of Appeal held that where the defendant raised extraneous matters of mitigation, a burden of proof rested upon the defence, i.e., on the balance of probabilities to the civil standard. The court did state, however, that in the general run of cases the sentencer would readily accept the accuracy of defence counsel's statements. In *Tolera* [1998] Crim LR 425, however, the defendant pleaded guilty to the possession of heroin with intent to supply, and claimed that he had been threatened with violence if he did not assist in the drug dealing. The Court of Appeal held that there was an onus on the prosecution to rebut an explanation of this kind, and reduced the sentence from five to four years because they had not done so. In *Underwood* [2005] 1 Cr App R 178, the Court of Appeal stated that neither the prosecution nor the judge is bound to agree facts merely because the prosecution was unable to disprove the defendant's account. In these cases where an issue raised by the defence is outside the knowledge of the prosecution, both prosecution and defence should call any relevant evidence. Where the issue arises from facts which are within the exclusive knowledge of the defendant, he should be called as a witness and, if he is not, the judge may draw such inferences as he sees fit, subject to any explanation put forward.

22.26   The judge is entitled to decide that the defence version is not capable of belief and thus does not warrant the holding of a *Newton* hearing (see, for example, *Kerr* (1980) 2 Cr App R (S) 54, *Gandhi* (1986) 8 Cr App R (S) 391). The judge's view that the defence version is manifestly absurd must, however, be in accordance with the facts. In *Costley* (1989) 11 Cr App R (S) 357, C pleaded guilty to inflicting grievous bodily harm. The prosecution alleged that C hit V about the head and body with a piece of wood, causing a fractured rib, a broken arm and extensive bruises. C claimed he struck V with his fists only, after V had made a homosexual approach and dripped blood on him, claiming that he was suffering from AIDS and would pass the condition on to C. The judge sentenced C solely on the basis of the prosecution opening and the defence speech in mitigation. He said:

> I find as a fact that the attack was totally unprovoked by anything [V] said or did . . . I reject your explanation for the use of violence as being wholly incredible.

The Court of Appeal held that it was not open to the judge to come to these conclusions, and upheld the appeal against sentence. In a case where the judge is faced with a substantial conflict on issues such as this, a *Newton* hearing should be held. In *Tolera* [1998] Crim LR 425, the Court of Appeal stressed that, while the judge was not bound to hold a *Newton* hearing where the defence version was manifestly implausible, he should indicate his view to the defendant. The defendant would then have the opportunity to convince the judge of the truth of his story.

When one accused pleads guilty and a co-accused pleads not guilty, two principles for determining the factual basis of sentence come into conflict. Should the judge hold a *Newton* hearing (which would normally be done in respect of a guilty plea)? Or should he rely on the evidence heard in the trial (as would be the usual procedure for the accused who pleaded not guilty)? In *Smith* (1988) 87 Cr App R 393, S pleaded guilty to conspiracy to obtain property by deception, the prosecution case being that he had supplied stolen credit cards to his co-accused (cashiers at a petrol filling-station), who used them to create receipts for non-existent transactions. Two of his co-accused pleaded not guilty, and ran the defence that they acted under duress from S. They were convicted. When the judge came to sentence both S and the co-accused, he said that he was taking the preliminary view that S was the ringleader, but offered S an opportunity to testify that he was not. The invitation was declined, and S was sentenced to 21 months' imprisonment, while his co-accused were given community service. The Court of Appeal held that the judge was entitled, in sentencing S, to take into account evidence at the trial of his co-accused. There was no need to recall the witnesses for cross-examination on S's behalf, notwithstanding the fact that his counsel had had no opportunity to cross-examine them during the trial. As the judge had given S a chance to give evidence himself, he had handled the procedure impeccably, and the appeal was dismissed. The approach in *Smith*, while understandable as a pragmatic solution to a difficult problem, may lead to a sense of unfairness being felt by an offender who is sentenced on a view of the facts which he disputes and which his counsel has not been able to test in the usual way by cross-examination of the witnesses who support the prosecution case. It is worth noting that the Court of Appeal in *Smith* did stress that the sentencing judge should bear in mind that evidence at the trial had not been tested by cross-examination on behalf of the offender who had pleaded guilty (see also *Winter* [1997] Crim LR 66 and *Taylor* [2007] Crim LR 491). **22.27**

A further anomaly appears when one compares the approach outlined in *Smith* with that adopted in a case such as *Gandy* (see 22.26). In *Gandy*, G pleaded guilty to violent disorder. His co-accused were then tried. Once their trial was completed, the judge held a *Newton* hearing to determine whether G had thrown a glass, causing the loss of V's eye. The Court of Appeal held that the judge should, in the *Newton* hearing, have followed the rules which would govern the use of evidence in a jury trial. Clearly, there is no equivalent protection for the accused where the *Smith* procedure is concerned. The resultant distinction seems arbitrary and exacerbates the sense of unfairness already referred to. **22.28**

In *Underwood* [2005] 1 Cr App R 178, the Court of Appeal considered the application of the principle that credit should be given for a guilty plea (see 23.39 to 23.46) to a case where a *Newton* hearing had been necessary. Clearly, if the issues on the hearing were resolved in the defendant's favour, the credit due to him should not be reduced. On the other hand, if he was disbelieved or obliged the prosecution to call a witness causing unnecessary distress, and conveyed to the judge a lack of remorse for his offence, the judge might reduce the discount, particularly if the plea was tendered at a very late stage. In an exceptional case, the entitlement to credit might be completely dissipated by the *Newton* hearing, but if that was the case, the judge should explain his reasons. **22.29**

In appropriate cases, the Court of Appeal can itself hold a *Newton* hearing: *Guppy* (1995) 16 Cr App R (S) 25. As to the situation where the magistrates court has held a *Newton* hearing and the defendant requests a further such hearing upon committal to the Crown Court, see 22.76. **22.30**

B ANTECEDENTS

22.31 Immediately following the committal of the case to the Crown Court, the police should prepare a document containing what are known as the Crown Court antecedents. These should be provided to the CPS, the defence, and the Crown Court within 21 days of committal or transfer, and checked and updated seven days before the hearing: *Practice Direction (Criminal Proceedings: Consolidation)* [2002] 1 WLR 2870, para III.27.6 and 7.

22.32 The antecedents should contain details of the offender's age, education, past and present employment, his domestic circumstances and income, the date of his arrest, whether he has been remanded in custody or on bail, and the date of his last release from prison or other custodial institution. There should also be a summary of his previous convictions and findings of guilt. This may include findings of guilt made when the offender was under 14, despite the Children and Young Persons Act 1963, s 16(2), which provides that in proceedings against a person who has attained the age of 21 findings of guilt when under 14 shall be disregarded for the purposes of evidence relating to previous convictions. Attached to the antecedents is a form giving full details of the offender's criminal record, save that, unlike the summary, it omits mention of s 16(2) findings of guilt. As regards each conviction or finding of guilt on it, the form states the name of the convicting court, the offence dealt with, the sentence passed, and the date of release if the sentence was a custodial one. Convictions which are spent (see 22.39 to 22.43) are included in both the summary of convictions and the previous convictions form, but they should be marked as such on the latter. The defence are entitled before or at any stage during the trial to be supplied with details of the accused's previous convictions. The judge also knows about them, in contrast to magistrates trying a case summarily who, if possible, are kept in ignorance of the accused's criminal record until after conviction. In the Crown Court, the police are expected to provide brief details of the circumstances of the last three similar convictions, and also of any other convictions likely to be of interest to the court. This information is provided separately, and attached to the antecedents. Formal cautions (see 5.06 to 5.11) may be cited in court, although they should appear on a separate sheet from previous convictions.

22.33 In the great majority of cases where the contents of the antecedents are not challenged, prosecuting counsel will summarize the information which they contain. The judge has the full list and may not want to hear the details of all of them, and so may say, for example, 'last three only', or 'starting from 2001'. Counsel will then read out the last three convictions, or those dating from 2001, as the case may be.

22.34 *Practice Direction (Criminal Proceedings: Consolidation)* [2002] 1 WLR 2870, para 27 deals with the contents of the antecedents.

22.35 After these matters have been dealt with, the prosecution case is closed.

Challenges to the antecedents

22.36 Where the defence challenge the prosecution version of the antecedents, it would be usual for the prosecution to call the police officer in the case. If the prosecution assertions remain in dispute, the onus remains upon them to satisfy the judge of the truth of the assertion by calling evidence of a type which would be admissible during the trial of a not guilty plea—not, for example, inadmissible hearsay or opinion. If the prosecution fail so to satisfy the judge, he should ignore the challenged assertion in passing sentence, and state that he is ignoring it: *Campbell* (1911) 6 Cr App R 131.

The prosecution should, in any event, be restrained from making generalized allegations, **22.37** prejudicial to the offender, which are incapable of strict proof or disproof. In *Van Pelz* (1942) 29 Cr App R 10, where VP had been convicted of an offence of larceny, the Court of Criminal Appeal criticized the prosecution for allowing the officer giving the antecedents to say that VP had led a loose and immoral life, was very well known as a prostitute, had associated constantly with thieves, and was regarded as a very dangerous woman indeed. Even where a prejudicial allegation is specific, it should be made by an officer with first-hand knowledge of the matter, not by an officer relying upon what others have told him. In *Wilkins* (1978) 66 Cr App R 49, the Court of Appeal reduced W's sentence for living on the earnings of prostitution from three years to two years because the officer giving the antecedents evidence testified that some 82 women, who had worked for an escort agency run by W, had stated that they used the agency as a medium for prostitution. The evidence at W's trial, while satisfying the jury that he had lived on the earnings of prostitution, had not suggested that he was involved in the organization of prostitution on such a substantial scale. Clearly, the officer in making his allegations was not speaking of matters within his first-hand knowledge—he was repeating what the prostitutes had said.

If the defence challenge the correctness of the prosecution evidence about any of the previous **22.38** convictions, the principles described above apply, so the prosecution must provide strict proof of the conviction. They can do this by (a) producing a certificate of conviction, signed by the clerk of the convicting court, and (b) adducing evidence that the offender who is to be sentenced is the person named in the certificate: Police and Criminal Evidence Act 1984, s 73. The evidence of identity could come from someone who was present in court on the occasion of the previous conviction. Alternatively, s 39 of the Criminal Justice Act 1948 enables the prosecution to produce further certificates, establishing that the fingerprints of the person named in the certificate of conviction are identical to the fingerprints of the offender.

Spent convictions

The Rehabilitation of Offenders Act 1974 is meant to enable offenders to 'live down' their **22.39** past. Broadly speaking, the scheme of the Act is that after the elapsing from the date of conviction of a certain period of time (known as the 'rehabilitation period'), the offender becomes a rehabilitated person and his conviction is spent. A rehabilitated person is treated 'for all purposes in law as a person who has not committed . . . or been convicted of or sentenced for the offence or offences' of which he was convicted (s 4(1) of the Act). This means, for example, that when a rehabilitated person applies for a job he does not, generally speaking, have to disclose his spent convictions, and any questions on the job application form about the applicant's criminal record are deemed not to relate to such convictions. Similarly, in most civil proceedings questions about spent convictions and evidence of the offences to which they related are inadmissible.

Section 4(1) is subject to the remainder of the Act, which contains provisions restricting the **22.40** circumstances in which the subsection is to apply. Thus, a person wishing to follow certain professions or occupations designated by the Home Secretary may be asked about spent convictions by a person assessing his suitability for the profession or occupation. Not surprisingly, any would-be barristers, solicitors or judges must declare their spent convictions. More to the point as far as criminal procedure is concerned, s 7(2) provides that s 4(1) is not to apply at all to criminal proceedings—i.e., there is no statutory restriction on the evidence which may be given of, and questions which may be asked about, spent convictions that does not apply equally to convictions which are not spent. However, the *Practice Direction (Criminal Proceedings: Consolidation)* [2002] 1 WLR 2870, para I.6 states that both courts and counsel should give effect to the general intention of Parliament expressed in the debates leading up to the passing of the Act, and should not refer to a spent conviction when that can reasonably be avoided. Indeed, counsel must always obtain the judge's authority before mentioning a spent conviction, that authority only being given where the interests of justice so require. At the sentencing stage of proceedings, the record supplied to the court of the offender's convictions should mark those which are spent. In passing sentence, the judge may disclose the existence of a spent conviction only if that is necessary to explain the sentence he is passing (e.g., because it would seem unreasonably severe were it not revealed that in the relatively recent past the offender had committed an offence similar to that for which he is now being sentenced).

22.41 The period after which a conviction becomes spent (the rehabilitation period) depends upon the sentence passed for the offence. The periods for the most common sentences are as follows:

(a) If the offender was sentenced to imprisonment for life or for a term exceeding 30 months (or to equivalent sentences of detention in a young offender institution or detention under PCC(S)A 2000, s 91) then the conviction never becomes spent.

(b) If the sentence was one of more than six but not more than 30 months' imprisonment, detention in a young offender institution or youth custody, the period is ten years for an adult, five years for a juvenile.

(c) If the sentence is one of imprisonment, detention in a young offender institution or youth custody for six months or less, the period is seven years for an adult, three and a half years for a juvenile.

(d) Where the offender was given a detention and training order and was aged 15 or over at the date of conviction, the period is five years if the order exceeded six months, and three and a half years if it did not.

(e) Where the offender received a detention and training order and was aged under 15 at the date of conviction, the period is one year after the order expired.

(f) For most community sentences, the period is five years for an adult, two and a half years for a juvenile.

(g) For bindovers and conditional discharges, the period is one year or the date on which the order ceases, whichever is the longer.

(h) For supervision orders the period ends on the date when the order ceases or after one year, whichever is the longer.

(i) For attendance centre orders and secure training orders, the period ends one year after the order expires.

(j) For disqualification from driving, the period is that for which the offender remains disqualified.

(k) If discharged absolutely the period ends after six months.

Where a custodial sentence is suspended, the period is the same as if it had been immediate.

Where more than one sentence is imposed for a conviction (e.g., for a drink/driving offence **22.42** the offender is sentenced to six months' imprisonment suspended for two years; is fined £100, and disqualified from driving for three years), the rehabilitation period is the longest of the relevant periods (i.e., in the example given above, seven years for the suspended prison sentence, not five years for the fine or three years for the disqualification).

A convicted person can be rehabilitated only if not reconvicted during the rehabilitation **22.43** period (s 6(4)). If an offender is reconvicted of anything other than a summary offence, the rehabilitation period for the first offence continues to run until the expiry of the rehabilitation period for the second offence. This is very important in practice, since it means that persistent offenders are unlikely to have any spent convictions. The rehabilitation periods for their early convictions are extended by their later convictions. This subsequent-offence rule does not, however, apply to orders of disqualification (s 6(5)).

Suspended sentence etc.

If the offence of which the offender has been convicted was committed during the operational **22.44** period of a suspended sentence, the Crown Court or, in certain circumstances, a magistrates' court can bring the suspended sentence into effect (see 24.61 to 24.63). Also, if the offence was committed during the currency of a conditional discharge the court may sentence the offender for the original offence (see 25.71). When it becomes apparent during the evidence of previous convictions that the offender is in breach of a suspended sentence or conditional discharge, he should be asked whether he admits the breach. If he does, the court may deal with him for that matter when it sentences him for the present offence. If he does not, strict proof must be provided of the previous conviction and sentence (see 22.36 to 22.38). Upon such proof, the court may deal with the breach.

C   REPORTS ON THE OFFENDER

After the prosecution opening, the judge reads any reports which have been prepared on the **22.45** offender. The defence are given copies of the reports. Counsel may refer to their contents in mitigation, but it is not normal practice to read them out in full. Where medical or psychiatric reports are concerned, it is obviously necessary to use them with discretion.

Pre-sentence reports are prepared by probation officers if the offender is an adult. In the cases **22.46** of offenders under 18 the report is prepared by a probation officer, a social worker, or a member of a youth offending team. Typically, the report should address the offender's explanation for the offence, acceptance of responsibility, feelings of remorse, motivations, character, criminal history, relationships, personal problems such as alcohol or drug misuse, difficulties with finance, housing or employment, and any medical or psychiatric information available.

It is customary for reports to make proposals, particularly as to any community sentence **22.47** which might be suitable. If the pre-sentence report proposes a community punishment order (see Chapter 25 for details), then it must state whether it is available. By the CJA 2003, s 156, the court must obtain a pre-sentence report when it is considering passing a custodial sentence or community sentence. Where the offender is aged 18 or over, however, the court need not have a pre-sentence report if it is of the opinion that it is unnecessary to have one. Where the offender is aged 17 or under, the court must obtain a pre-sentence report, unless there is a pre-existing report and the court has considered its content.

22.48   Even if there is no statutory requirement to have a report, the court may well regard it as good sentencing practice to have one, particularly if it is firmly requested by the defence. Nevertheless, even where the obtaining of a pre-sentence report is 'mandatory', the court's failure to obtain one will not of itself invalidate the sentence. If the case is appealed, however, the appellate court must obtain and consider a pre-sentence report unless that is thought to be unnecessary. Should the court want a report but one is not available when an offender initially appears to be sentenced, there will have to be an adjournment. To avoid such unnecessary delays, the probation service often prepare reports in advance of conviction. They are generally reluctant to prepare pre-trial reports on defendants who plead not guilty, because the accused obviously cannot be asked about his or her attitude to the offence. Practice as to pre-trial reports in the adult magistrates' courts and youth courts varies too much for any helpful generalizations to be made. A copy of the report must be given to counsel or solicitor for the offender, or, if he is unrepresented, to the offender himself. If the offender is a juvenile and unrepresented, the report may be given to his parent or guardian: PCC(S)A 2000, s 156. The prosecution are also given a copy of the pre-sentence report. The defence may ask for the probation officer who prepared the report to give evidence, so that for instance they can challenge unfavourable comment about the offender contained in the report. In *S* [2006] Crim LR 459, however, the Court of Appeal stated that it would only be in very rare cases that the judge would be obliged to permit the author of a pre-sentence report to be cross-examined in relation to an assessment of seriousness (that is, in respect of whether an offender was to be categorized as dangerous—see 24.39 to 24.42).

22.49   Medical and psychiatric reports may also be required. As already explained at 10.72, a magistrates' court has power to remand a person (in custody or on bail) for the preparation of medical reports. Following conviction on indictment or prior to sentencing on a committal for sentence, the Crown Court also may adjourn with a view to the preparation of medical reports. Again, the offender may be remanded in custody or on bail as the court sees fit. A further option—namely to remand an accused person/offender to hospital for the preparation of reports on his mental condition—has been given to the courts by s 35 of the Mental Health Act 1983 (see 25.124).

22.50   Medical and psychiatric reports are essential if the court is to make an order under s 37 of the Mental Health Act 1983 (detention in a mental hospital), or under PCC(S)A 2000, s 42 (community rehabilitation) with a requirement that the probationer receive treatment for a mental condition). In addition the court must order a medical report to be prepared on any offender who appears to be mentally disordered before a custodial sentence (other than for murder) is passed (Criminal Justice Act 1991, s 4(1)). The court need not obtain one if it thinks it unnecessary (s 4(2)). Failure to comply does not render the sentence invalid, but places a duty to obtain one on the appellate court where the matter is appealed (s 4(4)). Where the offender is legally represented, a copy of the report must be given to his counsel or solicitor, but if he is unrepresented he is not entitled to look at the report himself although the gist of it should be disclosed to him: Mental Health Act 1983, s 54(3). The practitioner who prepared the report may be required to attend to give oral evidence, and evidence may be called on behalf of the offender to rebut that contained in the report. In practice, it is often difficult to obtain psychiatric reports through the court, and it may be necessary for defence solicitors to take the initiative and ask a consultant who has been treating their client for a mental condition to prepare a report on him. It appears to be open to the defence to choose whether to put that report in front of the sentencer. The psychiatrist, on the other hand, if he discovers that his evidence is not to be put before the judge, is free to make it available through other channels, e.g., via the prosecution (*Crozier* [1991] Crim LR 138).

In the case of a juvenile, there may be reports from social workers involved with the juvenile **22.51** and his family. Where the juvenile, prior to being dealt with for the offence, is remanded in the care of a local authority, detailed reports may be prepared on him covering matters such as his intelligence, behaviour in care, reaction to persons in authority and relationships with his peers. There may also be a report from his school.

The mere act of adjourning for a pre-sentence report can raise in the offender's mind an **22.52** expectation that, should the report be favourable in the sense of recommending a non-custodial disposition, the court will follow the recommendation. If, notwithstanding a favourable report, he is then given a custodial sentence, he will have an understandable sense of grievance, and the Court of Appeal will feel obliged to quash the custodial sentence, even if it was perfectly justifiable in the light of the gravity of the offence and the offender's record (see *Gillam* (1980) 2 Cr App R (S) 267). To avoid such an outcome, a court adjourning for reports but wishing to leave all options open should tell the offender that there is no implied promise of a lenient sentence, and, whatever the reports say, the eventual outcome may well be imprisonment or detention. Provided the above was made clear at the time of the adjournment, there can be no objection to the court rejecting a non-custodial recommendation in a report: *Horton and Alexander* (1985) 7 Cr App R (S) 299. Moreover, the mere fact that the judge, on adjourning for reports, remains silent as to the prospect of a custodial sentence, should not be taken as an indication that a non-custodial sentence will eventually be passed (*Renan* [1994] Crim LR 379).

D   MITIGATION

Once the reports have been read and, if necessary, the makers of the reports called to give **22.53** evidence, defence counsel presents the mitigation on behalf of the offender. Much of it may be foreshadowed in the reports, and counsel can refer the judge to passages in them which are of especial assistance to his argument. Usually, counsel deals with the immediate circumstances of the offence, stressing any factor which may lessen its gravity. If it is an offence of dishonesty, he may be able to say that it was committed on the impulse of the moment, when temptation was suddenly and unexpectedly placed in the offender's way. If it is an offence of violence, he could point to extreme provocation which led the offender to lose his temper. Counsel must be careful, however, not to put forward in mitigation anything which in fact amounts to a defence to the charge—e.g., he should not assert that an assault was committed in self-defence. Where there is nothing that can sensibly be said with a view to making the offence appear less serious, it is best to turn rapidly to the circumstances of the offender. If the offence was committed when the offender was going through a period of difficulty, financial or otherwise, that may provide some explanation for what occurred. Looking to the future, there may have been a change in the offender's circumstances which offers hope for him staying out of trouble—he may have found a good job, or been reconciled with his wife, or accepted treatment for a drink problem which contributed to his offending. Finally, a co-operative attitude with the police when arrested, and a plea of guilty in court are both good points in mitigation.

22.54 In addition to his speech in mitigation counsel may call character witnesses on behalf of the offender to say (e.g.) that the offence was completely out of character and that they are convinced nothing like it will ever happen again. Such character witnesses can be called at the beginning or end of mitigation, or in the middle. If the offender has no previous convictions it is, of course, a very strong argument in mitigation whether or not any character witnesses are called. (For further details see 23.49 to 23.53.)

22.55 The Criminal Procedure and Investigations Act 1996, s 58 gives a court power to impose reporting restrictions on false or irrelevant assertions made during a speech in mitigation, where they are derogatory to a person's character. No such order can be made if the assertion has been made at an earlier stage of proceedings, e.g., at trial. Orders may be revoked at any time by the court, and if not revoked expire after a year. It is an offence to publish or broadcast in breach of such an order.

22.56 The offender may decline legal representation and put forward his mitigation in person if he so wishes. Generally speaking, however, it is of assistance to the court to have counsel or solicitor emphasize those matters which genuinely argue for a light sentence—an offender in person, through ignorance, may concentrate upon points which if anything exacerbate the offence and ignore some which are good mitigation. Legal representation for the offender is especially important where he is in danger of a first sentence of imprisonment. Except as a last resort when it is really unavoidable, the courts should try to avoid sending to prison an offender who has not previously been there, if only because having experienced prison he may become hardened to it, and not deterred by the risk of it as he was before serving his sentence. So that all possible alternatives to imprisonment can be explored, it is desirable to have a lawyer mitigate for the offender. As Lord Bridge of Harwich put it in *Re McC (A Minor)*, [1985] AC 528:

> No one should be liable to a first sentence of imprisonment . . . unless he has had the opportunity of having his case in mitigation presented to the court in the best possible light. For an inarticulate defendant, such presentation may be crucial to his liberty.

22.57 Therefore, the PCC(S)A 2000, s 83 provides that a court shall not pass a sentence of imprisonment on an offender who is not legally represented, and who has not previously been so sentenced unless he has been informed of his right to apply for representation by the Criminal Defence Service and has had the opportunity to do so but has failed to make any application. Broadly speaking, the effect of s 83 is that a court considering a first sentence of imprisonment must tell an unrepresented offender that he can apply for free legal representation, and grant, say, a week's adjournment to allow him to make the application. If he makes the application and is represented at the resumed hearing, the object of the section has been achieved. If he fails to make any application and is still unrepresented, the court has done all it reasonably could to persuade him to be represented, and is at liberty to pass whatever sentence it thinks fit.

Legal representation is also important whenever a court is considering depriving a young **22.58** offender of his liberty. Therefore, identical provisions apply to the passing of a sentence of a detention and training order or detention under s 91 of the PCC(S)A 2000. In the above cases, no distinction is drawn between an offender who has, and an offender who has not, previously been dealt with by means of the sentence or order in question.

A sentence of imprisonment which is suspended (see 24.48 to 24.63) is nonetheless a prison **22.59** sentence, and so s 83 of the PCC(S)A 2000 will apply when a court is considering suspended imprisonment just as it applies when it is considering immediate imprisonment. But the statute provides that, for purposes of deciding whether or not an offender has previously been sentenced to imprisonment, a suspended sentence which has not been brought into force shall be disregarded. Thus, before passing even a suspended sentence on an unrepresented offender whose only previous prison sentence is an unactivated suspended one, the court is obliged by s 83 to adjourn to let him apply for free legal representation.

E   TAKING OTHER OFFENCES INTO CONSIDERATION

A suspect who is questioned by the police about an offence and admits that he committed it **22.60** may be further questioned about other crimes, as yet unsolved, which bear some similarity to the crime to which he has confessed. If the suspect is responsible for some or all of these other crimes, he might nevertheless be unwilling to acknowledge responsibility should each crime appear as a separate count on an indictment against him. A system has therefore developed which allows an offender to admit to other offences without actually being convicted of them. It is known as taking other offences into consideration when passing sentence. The procedure can be used in both the magistrates' courts and Crown Court.

The police prepare a list of the other offences which they believe or suspect the offender has also **22.61** committed. The offender studies the list, and, if he so wishes, indicates that he did commit at least some of the offences. He then signs the list, those offences which he denies having been deleted. At the trial, the offender pleads guilty to the counts in the indictment. During his summary of the facts, prosecuting counsel tells the judge that he understands that the offender wishes to have other offences taken into consideration. The judge, who is given the list of offences which the offender has signed, asks him whether he admits committing each of the offences and whether he wants them taken into consideration when sentence is passed. Upon the offender answering 'yes' the judge will nearly always comply with his request. Prosecuting counsel will not give full details of the way the other offences were committed, but he may tell the judge for instance the total value of the property stolen in the other offences and the amount recovered.

In passing sentence, the maximum sentence the court may impose is the maximum for the **22.62** offences of which the offender has been convicted. This, in practice, is not a significant limitation on the court's powers, since maximum penalties are usually far in excess of that which the court would want to impose even for a serious instance of the offence in question. To take a typical example, an offender might plead guilty to an indictment containing two counts of theft from cars and a burglary from a dwelling-house. He might also ask for three further counts of thefts from cars to be taken into consideration. Theft carries a maximum penalty of

7 years' imprisonment and burglary from a dwelling-house 14 years. He would therefore face a total of 28 years' imprisonment for the counts on the indictment. Even with the additional offences taken into consideration, it is most unlikely that he would face a sentence of more than a fraction of the maximum.

22.63 The judge should not automatically take other offences into consideration merely because the prosecution and defence wish him to do so. Where the other offences are of a different type from those charged in the indictment, it may not be right to agree to the request to take them into consideration. Certainly, an offence which is punishable with endorsement of the driving licence and discretionary or obligatory disqualification from driving should not be taken into consideration when none of the offences on the indictment are so punishable: *Collins* [1947] KB 560. The reason is that, since the court's powers of sentencing are limited to those it possesses in respect of the counts in the indictment, an offender who was allowed to 't.i.c.' an endorsable offence when none of the offences on the indictment carried endorsement, would unfairly escape endorsement of his licence and possible disqualification. It is also wrong for magistrates to take into consideration offences which they have no jurisdiction to try—i.e., they should not 't.i.c.' offences triable only on indictment.

22.64 Where an offence is taken into consideration, the offender is not convicted of it and accordingly could not successfully raise the plea of autrefois convict if subsequently prosecuted for the offence: *Nicholson* [1947] 2 All ER 535. In practice, the police would never consider instituting proceedings for an offence which was taken into consideration. The 't.i.c.' system helps them to reduce the list of unsolved crimes by encouraging offenders who have little option but to admit to one offence to admit, at the same time, to other offences which, in the absence of such admission, it would be difficult or impossible to prove against them. The obvious question is— why should an offender admit to and ask to have taken into consideration other offences when, if the police had had sufficient evidence against him, they would have arrested him for those other offences? The answer is that, although the judge may increase his sentence somewhat because of the 't.i.c.' offences, the increase is unlikely to be significant, and the offender has the advantage of having his 'slate wiped clean'. When he has served his sentence, he can lead an honest life without worrying about the police uncovering evidence which would enable them to prosecute him for one of his past crimes.

22.65 The above discussion of taking offences into consideration has proceeded on the assumption that the offender is pleading guilty to the counts in the indictment or the informations preferred against him. However, there is nothing to stop the police asking an accused who is pleading not guilty whether, in the event of a conviction, he would like to have other offences considered, or there may be an opportunity between conviction and sentence to raise the matter with him. In general, though, the 't.i.c.' system is geared to the offender who is pleading guilty.

F   VARIATION OF SENTENCE

22.66 The sentence imposed or other order made by the Crown Court when dealing with an offender may be varied or rescinded within a period of 28 days beginning with the date of sentence: PCC(S)A 2000, s 155. The obvious use of s 155 is to correct some technical error in the original sentence, or to alter it substantially to the offender's advantage if the judge after sentencing thinks he might have been too severe. The section may, however, be used to add to a sentence (e.g., *Reilly* [1982] QB 1208 in which the Court of Appeal held that the Crown Court judge had power to add to his original sentence of three years' imprisonment a criminal bankruptcy order in the sum of £178,000). Only in the most exceptional circumstances, however, would it be right to increase the length of a custodial sentence or to replace an original non-custodial sentence with a custodial one. Thus, in *Grice* (1978) 66 Cr App R 167, where the judge had passed a suspended sentence for an offence of unlawful sexual intercourse, the Court of Appeal reversed his subsequent decision to make the sentence immediate. The reason for the variation was that the judge had suspended the sentence in return for G promising that he would not go near his adopted daughter, with whom he had committed the offence. G's breaking his promise within the 28-day period for variation was not a sufficient reason for 'unsuspending' his sentence. There is one group of cases where the power to increase sentence is likely to be held to be properly exercised. That is where the trial judge has failed to implement the 'dangerous offender' provisions, for example by failing to impose an extended sentence or a sentence of imprisonment for public protection (see 24.34 to 24.42). In such a case, the increase upon variation will be seen as the court seeking to comply with its statutory obligations: *Reynolds* [2007] Crim LR 493.

22.67 Once the period specified in s 155 has elapsed the Crown Court has no power to vary or rescind its sentence. Thus, an order made outside the relevant period that the offender should forfeit money which he had been carrying in order to facilitate the commission of drugs offences, was quashed by the House of Lords because the addition of a forfeiture order amounted to a variation of sentence, and so had to be made within the statutory time limits (*Menocal* [1980] AC 598). In *Reynolds* [2007] Crim LR 493, it was held that the Crown Court had power, after rescinding its original order in whole or in part, to adjourn the final sentence until a later date. In effect, this will result in an extension of the period for variation beyond 28 days. (In so deciding, the Court of Appeal refused to follow *Stilwell* (1991) 94 Cr App R 65).

22.68 A magistrates' court can also vary or rescind a sentence or other order made when dealing with an offender: Magistrates' Courts Act 1980, s 142(1). Similar provisions apply when a magistrates' court has convicted an accused, and the magistrates who made up the court have doubts about the correctness of their decision (see 10.64).

G DEFERRING SENTENCE

22.69 Counsel mitigating for an offender often makes optimistic or even extravagant claims on his behalf. If given a chance by the court (i.e., not sent to prison) his client will cease to commit crime; settle down in society; hold a steady job; marry his girl-friend, and make full reparation to the victims of his past offences. The court, having perhaps heard such claims on many previous occasions and not always found them borne out by subsequent events, may not be convinced by counsel's argument, but nevertheless may feel that the offender deserves a chance to prove himself. Time will show whether he can live up to the promises made on his behalf. To give him that time, the court may defer sentencing him.

22.70 Sections 1 to 1D of the PCC(S)A 2000 empower both the Crown Court and magistrates' courts to defer passing sentence on an offender for up to *six months* so that, when the court does come to determine what the sentence shall be, it may have regard to (a) the offender's conduct after conviction and (b) any change in his circumstances. Conduct after conviction is expressly stated to include making reparation for the offence where that is appropriate. Deferment under s 1 is always conditional upon the offender consenting to it and, subject to an exception explained below, is not allowed more than once per case. Moreover, it is desirable that sentence should actually be passed on the date specified by the court when it deferred sentencing. However, the court does not lose jurisdiction to sentence if it cannot deal with the offender on that date (e.g., because the judge reserved the case to himself and then is unavailable on the relevant day, or because the offender fails to appear, or because necessary reports have not been prepared)—see *Anderson* (1983) 78 Cr App R 251.

22.71 The approach to and procedure for deferring sentence was summarized by Lord Lane CJ in his judgment in *George* [1984] 1 WLR 1082. It is the responsibility of the deferring court to make it clear to the offender why sentence is being deferred, and what conduct is expected of him during the deferment. Obviously, he will be expected not to commit further offences, but he might also be told that he should stay in and/or make genuine efforts to find employment, or that he should accept help and advice from a probation officer, or that he should save money with a view to making reparation for the offence, or that he should cut down on his consumption of alcohol. It is not appropriate, however, to tell the offender that he must go to hospital to receive treatment for a mental condition, for such restrictions on an offender's freedom of action should be imposed by virtue of a hospital order or probation order with a requirement for treatment, not as a side wind of a deferment of sentence: *Skelton* [1983] Crim LR 686. In general, the courts should not defer sentence when the desired improvements in the offender's conduct are sufficiently precise to be included in requirements attached to a community sentence (see 25.16 to 25.17). The court should make a note of the reasons for deferment and give a copy to the offender and to his probation officer or other person appointed to supervise him (PCC(S)A 2000, s 1(5)). When the offender appears to be sentenced, the sentencing court may then easily ascertain, with the help of up-to-date reports, whether he has 'substantially conformed or attempted to conform with the proper expectations of the deferring court'. If he has, an immediate custodial sentence should not be imposed; if he has not, the sentencing court should state precisely in what respects there has been failure (see Lord Lane CJ's judgment in *George* at p. 1085). Commission of further offences during the deferment period is likely to result in a custodial sentence both for the subsequent offence and the deferred-sentence offence. But, merely staying out of trouble will not necessarily guarantee the offender a non-custodial sentence. Thus, in *Smith* (1977) 64 Cr App R 116 the Court of Appeal upheld a sentence of 18 months' immediate imprisonment for several burglaries, the facts being that S (with a bad record for dishonesty) had had sentence deferred to see if he would (a) work regularly and (b) cut down on his drinking. He had done neither, and his not having committed further offences was not sufficient to save him from prison. Conversely, if the offender has both 'gone straight' and done at least most of what the deferring court required of him, an immediate custodial sentence will be wrong in principle (see *Smith* (1979) 1 Cr App R (S) 339 for an example). *Aquilina* (1990) 11 Cr App R (S) 431 deals with the situation where it is alleged that the offender has committed offences during the period of deferment, but the allegations remain unresolved. It was held that they should not influence sentence in any way unless and until he has been convicted of the later alleged offences.

One of the reasons for asking courts to make a note of why they defer sentence is that the **22.72** sentencing court may well not comprise the same judge or magistrates who deferred sentence. Wherever possible, though, the deferring judge or magistrates should make themselves available to pass sentence (*Gurney* [1974] Crim LR 472), and counsel who represented the offender at deferment should also do his utmost to be there for sentencing (*Ryan* [1976] Crim LR 508).

When sentence is deferred, the offender is not bailed, but is simply told that he must come to **22.73** court on the appropriate day. If he fails to do so, a summons or warrant for his arrest may be issued. Conviction for a further offence during the deferment period entitles the deferring court to sentence the offender immediately upon securing his attendance before it. Alternatively, the court convicting of the subsequent offence may also sentence for the deferred-sentence offence, save that a magistrates' court may not deal with a matter in respect of which the Crown Court deferred sentence. Also, the Crown Court, when dealing with a matter in respect of which magistrates deferred, is limited to the sentencing powers which a magistrates' court dealing with the offender would have.

It was stated above that sentence may only be deferred once. There is one exception to this **22.74** rule, which arises as follows. The exercise by magistrates of their power to defer sentence does not preclude them, when the offender appears to be sentenced, from committing him to the Crown Court to be dealt with. The Crown Court may then, if it chooses, also defer sentence.

H   SENTENCING IN MAGISTRATES' COURTS

The pre-sentencing procedure described in this Chapter is essentially applicable in both the **22.75** Crown Court and magistrates' courts. Thus, Crown Court judges and justices alike must be told the facts of the offence and be informed about the offender's antecedents, after which they read reports and listen to mitigation. Similarly, specific procedures such as taking other offences into consideration and deferring sentence are the same in both the higher and lower tribunals. However, in the magistrates' courts, the whole sequence of events is swifter and less formalized than in the Crown Court. In particular, the antecedents are given simply by the prosecutor handing to the court a list of previous convictions. Furthermore, where the court is merely dealing with a road traffic matter, the practice is not to obtain a full list of previous convictions but to sentence on the basis of the endorsements shown on the motorist's licence. If there is no licence, a print out of the offender's driving record is obtained from the Drivers and Vehicles Licensing Centre in Swansea.

The justices are required to hold a *Newton* hearing in the same circumstances as a Crown **22.76** Court judge. What if an offender is committed to the Crown Court for sentence (see Chapter 12) and there is a dispute about the facts of the case upon which he has been committed? Which court ought to hold the *Newton* hearing: the Crown Court or the magistrates court? In *Munroe v Crown Prosecution Service* [1988] Crim LR 823, the Divisional Court held that:

(a)   Where the matter arises before the magistrates, they should conduct the *Newton* hearing, and, if they decide to commit, ensure that the Crown Court is informed of their findings of fact. The Crown Court should sentence on that basis.

(b)   If the issue arises for the first time in the Crown Court, then it should conduct the *Newton* hearing.

(c)   Where there was doubt whether the issue had been raised before the magistrates, then the Crown Court could either resolve the matter itself, or remit it to the magistrates, at its discretion.

What was said in *Munroe* should now be read subject to *Warley Magistrates' Court ex parte DPP* [1998] 2 Cr App R 307 (see 12.16). If it appears to the magistrates that they will be committing the case to the Crown Court for sentence in any event, then they should not conduct the *Newton* hearing, but should leave it for the Crown Court to do so. If the outcome of the *Newton* hearing is crucial to their decision whether to commit for sentence, however, then the magistrates must conduct it. It may therefore still happen that the magistrates conduct a *Newton* hearing where the matter ends up in the Crown Court. In *Gillan* [2007] EWHC 380, it was held that, where the magistrates have held a *Newton* hearing and found against the defendant, the Crown Court has power to hold a second *Newton* hearing, but is not obliged to do so.

23

DETERMINING THE SENTENCE

Chapter 22 dealt with the procedure which the court follows prior to passing sentence. The **23.01** sentencer should therefore have the information upon which to decide sentence. That decision involves a choice between a series of options. In any particular case, the range of options will be in part determined by the circumstances of the offence (e.g., whether it is imprisonable and the maximum punishment which the law lays down) and of the offender (e.g., his age). Usually, however, the sentencer has a fairly wide range of possibilities for disposing of the case. The various options for sentence are considered in detail in Chapters 24 and 25. Without any attempt to be exhaustive, such options include (in roughly increasing order of gravity):

(a) an absolute or conditional discharge,
(b) a fine,
(c) a community sentence,
(d) a suspended sentence,
(e) an immediate custodial sentence.

As already mentioned, the nature of the offence and the characteristics of the offender impose **23.02** certain limitations upon the freedom which the sentencer has to choose between the available options. In addition, a legislative framework is laid down in the Criminal Justice Act 2003 (CJA) which imposes criteria for determining whether the sentencer may pass a custodial sentence, for example. This legislative framework is detailed in 23.07 to 23.13.

23.03   Within that framework, the decisions of the courts provide further guidance in determining the sentence which a court is likely to impose (as distinct from the question of the sentence which it is empowered to impose). Certain points need to be borne in mind in considering the guidance available from the courts, however.

23.04   On passing sentence, judges need to keep the reasons short and simple so that the offender can readily understand what is being said to him. The principles governing the sentencing process therefore have to be deduced from sources other than the words of the sentencing judges themselves.

23.05   In addition, it should be emphasized that precedent plays a relatively small part in sentencing. This is for three reasons. First, the truism that every case turns upon its own facts is never truer than in the context of sentencing. No two offenders and no two offences are ever precisely the same, whatever the similarities between them. Therefore, if told about a Court of Appeal decision in a comparable case, a judge can always find a reason for distinguishing it if he so chooses. Second, the Court of Appeal does not attempt to prescribe the one right sentence for a particular case. Instead, their lordships allow Crown Court judges a broad discretion, and, in general, only interfere to reduce a sentence if it is outside the range of sentences appropriate to the gravity of the offence when taken in conjunction with any mitigating factors. Third, until the passing of ss 35 and 36 of the Criminal Justice Act 1988 (see 26.80 to 26.87) there was no procedure that was apt to allow the Court of Appeal to pronounce a sentence too light. It remains the case that, if the defence appeal, the Court of Appeal has no power to increase sentence, although their lordships do on occasion state that, if they had been sitting in the Crown Court, they would have imposed a harsher penalty.

23.06   Despite these limitations, and the growth in importance of the statutory dimension, reports of Court of Appeal decisions provide a useful guide to the way in which judges arrive, or should arrive, at their sentencing decisions. A number of sources are available to assist the court, and counsel appearing before it. There is a series of reports consisting entirely of sentencing appeals: *Criminal Appeal Reports (Sentencing)* cited as Cr App R (S). The *Criminal Law Review* publishes reports of sentencing decisions on a monthly basis. *Blackstone's Criminal Practice 2008* contains a substantial section on sentencing (Part E), and deals with the guideline cases, which encapsulate the Court of Appeal's views on sentencing for particular offences, under the offences in question (Parts B and C). A great number of decisions of the Court of Appeal are collected together and organized according to subject-matter in the encyclopaedia, *Current Sentencing Practice*. Even more important in providing a framework for the sentencer are the guidelines issued by the Sentencing Guidelines Council, which are described in greater detail in 23.17 to 23.27 and 23.41 to 23.46.

A   THRESHOLDS AND PURPOSES

23.07   The CJA 2003 lays down the criteria which the sentencer must consider in deciding:

(a)   whether to impose a community sentence; and

(b)   whether to impose a custodial sentence.

These provisions are perhaps best seen as thresholds. In other words, the sentencer must **23.08** consider whether the offender has crossed the threshold for a community sentence, or, as the case may be, a custodial sentence.

Under s 148 of the CJA 2003, a court shall not pass a community sentence 'unless it is of **23.09** the opinion that the offence, or the combination of the offence and one or more offences associated with it, was serious enough to warrant such a sentence'.

The position as far as custodial sentences is concerned is slightly more complex, in that **23.10** the court must find one of three alternative justifications for such a sentence. By s 152 of the CJA 2003 such a sentence may be imposed if either:

(a)   the offence (in combination if necessary with one or more offences associated with it) was so serious that only a custodial sentence is justified; or
(b)   the offender fails to express his willingness to comply with a requirement which the court proposes to include in a community order, where the requirement requires an expression of such willingness; or
(c)   he fails to comply with an order for pre-sentence drug testing.

The concept of seriousness is examined in rather more detail below (see 23.14 to 23.21), **23.11** together with the related concept of offence combination (23.28 to 23.33). The overall effect of these provisions is to create a hierarchy of sentencing bands. In the bottom band are the discharges (whether absolute or conditional). In the next band comes the fine. No specific conditions have to be met for the imposition of these relatively less severe penalties, although there are, of course, considerations which the court must bear in mind in deciding, for example, the size of the fine (see Chapter 25). The next band upward is occupied by community sentences. Before imposing such a sentence, the court must have formed the view that the offence is sufficiently serious to warrant it. In the top band come the various forms of custodial sentence. Again, the court must decide whether the offender has passed over the custodial threshold, applying this time the alternative criteria set out above.

Section 142 of the CJA 2003 sets out in legislation for the first time the purposes of sentencing. **23.12** Those aged under 18 at the time of conviction are excluded from its ambit, as are those convicted of murder, those subject to mandatory minimum sentences (see 24.43 to 24.47), those who come within the provisions for dangerous offenders (see 24.34 to 24.42), and those where the sentencer makes a disposal of the offender which is directed towards his treatment for a mental disorder (e.g., a hospital order). For the remainder of offenders, the 'purposes of sentencing' specified in s 142(1) apply. They are listed as follows:

(a)   the punishment of offenders;
(b)   the reduction of crime (including its reduction by deterrence);
(c)   the reform and rehabilitation of offenders;
(d)   the protection of the public; and
(e)   the making of reparation by offenders to persons affected by their offences.

Whilst it is helpful to have these purposes set out, what is notably absent is any sort of priority as between them. Some of the purposes may conflict, e.g., punishment and reparation, or deterrence and rehabilitation, and no guidance is given to the sentencer (or the advocate) on how such conflict might be resolved.

23.13   The CJA 2003 has made a noteworthy change to the way in which the thresholds described in this section will operate. The change is contained in s 151(2). The subsection states that 'the court may make a community order in respect of the current offence instead of imposing a fine if it considers that, having regard to all the circumstances including [where relevant, the offender's previous convictions], it would be in the interests of justice to do so'. This provision serves to emphasize that a community sentence may be imposed on an offender with limited financial means, rather than a fine, provided that the offence is of sufficient seriousness to justify a community penalty. Conversely, a substantial fine can properly be imposed for a case which is above the community sentence threshold. The change appears to be a reflection of the current approach of the courts, and is not likely to result in any major change in practice.

B   OFFENCE SERIOUSNESS

23.14   It is the seriousness of the offence which is the sole criterion in determining whether a community sentence or a custodial sentence may be passed. Offence seriousness is, again, the crucial factor in determining the length of a custodial sentence. It also looms large in fixing the amount of a fine.

23.15   The question of whether an offence is a serious one is clearly, then, a vital one for the sentencer. There are really two issues at stake:

(a)   What is the test to apply in determining whether an offence is serious?
(b)   What *material* ought the court to take into account in deciding whether an offence is serious?

23.16   As far as (a) is concerned, some statutory assistance is provided by s 143(1) of the CJA 2003, which states:

> In considering the seriousness of any offence, the court must consider the offender's culpability in committing the offence and any harm which the offence may have caused, was intended to cause or might foreseeably have caused.

It follows that the distinct but related concepts of harm and culpability have been selected as determinative of the seriousness of the offence. As a result, they are central to the way in which the sentencer must deal with the offence.

23.17   The Sentencing Guidelines Council chose 'seriousness' as one of the first topics on which it issued guidelines in December 2004. (The Council's website can be accessed at <http://www.sentencing-guidelines.gov.uk>, and more information about the way in which the guidelines system operates is set out in 23.23 to 23.26). Following the scheme of the statute, the Guidelines on Seriousness deal with two main parameters: the culpability of the offender and the harm caused or risked by the offence.

23.18   The Guidelines (in para 1.7) identify four levels of criminal culpability for sentencing purposes:

(a)   The offender has the *intention* to cause harm, with the highest culpability where the offence is planned. The worse the harm intended, the greater the seriousness.

(b) The offender is *reckless* as to whether harm is caused, i.e., he appreciates at least some harm would be caused but proceeds giving no thought to the consequences despite a risk which would be obvious to most people.

(c) The offender has *knowledge* of the specific risks entailed by his actions but does not intend to cause the harm that results.

(d) The offender is guilty of *negligence*.

This analysis is, of course, quite separate from the requirement for a particular mental state as the *mens rea* for an offence, e.g., intention or recklessness. In dealing with the sentencing aspect, the focus is upon intention to cause harm, recklessness as to whether harm is caused etc. The Guidelines (para 1.22) set out a list of some 21 'factors indicating higher culpability' which includes some statutory factors (e.g., offence committed on bail, racial or religious aggravation) and others based upon common law (e.g., planning, professional offending, abuse of a position of trust). It is also emphasized (para 1.17) that culpability will be greater if an offender:

(a) deliberately causes more harm than is necessary for the commission of the offence; or

(b) targets a vulnerable victim (because of their old age, youth, disability or by virtue of the job they do).

The Guidelines also distinguish between different types of harm. In some cases, what will be crucial will be the impact upon an individual victim. Such harm may take the form of physical injury, sexual violation, financial loss, damage to health, or psychological distress. Other offences may cause harm to the community at large, as well as or instead of an individual victim, e.g., economic loss, harm to public health, or interference with the administration of justice. The Guidelines (para 1.23) set out factors indicating a more than usually serious degree of harm, such as multiple victims, an offence committed against those providing a service to the public, high value in property offences. **23.19**

The Guidelines (para 1.25) make brief reference to mitigating factors, stating that the following factors indicate significantly lower culpability: **23.20**

(a) a greater degree of provocation than normally expected;

(b) mental illness or disability;

(c) youth or age, where it affects the responsibility of the individual defendant;

(d) the fact that the offender played only a minor role in the offence.

In addition, mention is made of the statutory provisions in relation to mitigation, and the separate set of Guidelines issued on reduction for a guilty plea (see 23.41 to 23.46).

The guidelines on seriousness also deal with the issue of prevalence and its relationship to offence seriousness (para 1.39). What is said, in effect, is that the sentences laid down as general guidance by the Court of Appeal already take into account the need to deter offences which are prevalent nationally. It is therefore 'wrong to further penalise individual offenders by increasing sentence length for committing an individual offence of that type'. If a sentencer is minded to increase a sentence on the basis that a particular crime is prevalent in the locality, he must have supporting evidence from an external source (e.g., the local Criminal Justice Board) to show that the crime is in fact more prevalent than it is nationally (see *Oosthuizen* [2005] Crim LR 979 for an application of this principle). **23.21**

23.22 When we come to the material which the court should consider in deciding whether an offence is serious then the statute is directly helpful in the following respects:

(i) In certain circumstances, the court must obtain and consider a pre-sentence report (CJA 2003, s 156 and see 22.47).

(ii) The court must take into account any matters that, in its opinion, 'are relevant in mitigation of sentence' (CJA 2003, s 166(1)).

(iii) By virtue of CJA 2003, s 143(1), the court may have regard to previous convictions and the failure to respond to previous sentences in considering the seriousness of the current offence. This provision is considered further at 23.49 to 23.53.

(iv) CJA 2003, s 143(3), states that the court must treat the fact that an offence was committed on bail as an aggravating factor—hence increasing its seriousness. The reason would seem to be that an offender committing an offence while on bail is in breach of the trust reposed in him by the court.

C   GUIDELINES

23.23 During the 1980s, the Court of Appeal developed the practice of issuing sentencing guidelines when dealing with an appeal (or linked appeals) against sentence. It would consider the existing practice in sentencing for the offence in question, identify mitigating and aggravating features, and set out a starting point for judges passing sentence at first instance. It would then deal with the appeal before it in accordance with the guidelines suggested. By and large, these judgments concentrated upon relatively serious cases emanating from the Crown Court, e.g. *Billam* (1986) 8 Cr App R (S) on rape, *Aramah* (1982) 4 Cr App R(S) on drugs offences and *Barrick* (1985) 7 Cr App R (S) on theft in breach of trust. In addition, the Magistrates' Association developed, with the approval of the senior judges, their own *Sentencing Guidelines*.

23.24 The CDA 1998, ss 80–81 charged the Court of Appeal with the responsibility for producing guidelines for criminal offences, and established the Sentencing Advisory Panel to act as an independent body to assist it in this function. The machinery for setting guidelines was amended by the CJA 2003. Section 167 establishes the Sentencing Guidelines Council, chaired by the Lord Chief Justice, with seven judicial and four non-judicial members. The judicial members must include a circuit judge, a district judge (magistrates' court), and a lay justice, as well as the senior judges. They are appointed by the Lord Chancellor. The non-judicial members, who are appointed by the Home Secretary, must have experience in policing, criminal prosecution, criminal defence, and the promotion of the welfare of victims of crime. The Sentencing Panel remains in being, constituted as before, but with the role of advising and assisting the Guidelines Council, rather than the Court of Appeal. It is chaired by Professor Andrew Ashworth QC, a distinguished academic, and consists of a mixture of sentencers, members with experience of other criminal justice agencies such as the police, prosecution, prisons and probation service, and others who have no prior connection with criminal justice. The Panel consults widely in the process of determining the advice which it will give to the Council. Its advice is generally followed when the Council draws up *its* draft guidelines, which in turn form the subject of consultation.

By s 170, the Council is to issue guidelines on both sentencing and 'allocation', or mode of **23.25** trial (the current version is in the *Practice Direction (Criminal Proceedings: Consolidation)* [2002] 1 WLR 2870, para 51). Section 172 of the CJA 2003 requires that 'every court must . . . in sentencing an offender, have regard to any guidelines which are relevant in the offender's case.' The Act makes it clear that the sentencing guideline cases dealt with by the Court of Appeal before the Council came into being retain their authority (Sch 38, para 2). In future, however, it is not expected that the Court of Appeal will continue to issue guideline judgments, although it will amplify and explain the Council's guidelines.

It follows that the Guidelines form the most important source material for those who wish to **23.26** ascertain the likely sentence which a court will impose in respect of a particular offence. To a lesser extent, Draft Guidelines may be regarded by the court as persuasive, even though it is under no obligation to follow them. The Guidelines, together with consultation material, are available on the website of the Sentencing Guidelines Council (for the address, see Key Documents at the end of this Chapter).

At the time of writing, the Sentencing Guidelines Council had produced eleven sets of guide- **23.27** lines. Some of them deal with general principles, while others focus upon specific offences. They are entitled:

(a) *Overarching Principles: Seriousness* (see 23.14 to 23.20).

(b) *New Sentences: Criminal Justice Act 2003* (see Chapters 24 and 25).

(c) *Reduction in Sentence for a Guilty Plea* (see 23.39 to 23.46).

(d) *Breach of a Protective Order*. This deals with sentencing for breach of restraining orders and non-molestation orders.

(e) *Overarching Principles: Domestic Violence*. This sets out the approach to sentencing for the variety of offences which can form part of this increasingly important area of practice. Domestic violence is defined to include 'any incident of threatening behaviour, violence or abuse [psychological, physical, sexual, financial or emotional] between adults who are or have been intimate partners or family members, regardless of gender or sexuality'.

(f) *Failure to Surrender to Bail*. This sets out starting points and sentencing ranges for this common offence against the Bail Act.

(g) *Manslaughter by Reason of Provocation*. This lays down starting points of 12, eight, and three years, based on low, substantial, and high provocation. The starting points are then subject to variation in accordance with aggravating and mitigating factors.

(h) *Robbery*. These Guidelines deal with street robbery and robberies of small businesses, rather than major robberies of banks. Starting points of 12 months, four years, and eight years are set out, depending on the degree of force used and any injury, and subject to various aggravating and mitigating factors.

(i) *Sexual Offences*. The very wide range of offences in the Sexual Offences Act 2003 is covered in a substantial and comprehensive document.

(j) *Assault and other offences against the person*—again, a detailed and comprehensive document.

(k) *Assaults on children and cruelty to a child*.

In addition to these Guidelines, there was in preparation at the time of writing an important set of Draft Guidelines, namely the *Revised Magistrates' Court Guidelines*. These were expected to be implemented in August 2008.

All these Draft Guidelines can be accessed on the Sentencing Guidelines website, and all are of some persuasive force until the definitive version is approved and issued, whereupon they will have the statutory effect described in 23.25.

D   COMBINATION OF OFFENCES

23.28 How should the courts deal with cases where the offender has to be sentenced for two or more offences? The court may consider 'the offence, or the combination of the offence and one or more other offences associated with it' when determining whether the case crosses over the seriousness threshold so as to justify custody (CJA 2003, s 152(1)) or a community sentence (s 148).

23.29 As a result, the sentencer can lump together a series of minor offences and decide that they merit custody (or a community sentence) once viewed together. In order to do so, however, the offences must be 'associated'. Section 161 of the PCC(S)A 2000 lays down that offences are associated if:

    (i)   the offender is convicted of the offences in the same proceedings (a plea of guilty being equivalent to a conviction);

    (ii)   the offender is sentenced for the offences at the same time; or

    (iii)   the offender is convicted of one offence and asks for the other or others to be taken into consideration.

23.30 If the court has decided on a custodial sentence, can it aggregate a number of offences for the purpose of deciding on the proper length of the sentence? This time, the answer is contained in CJA 2003, s 152(2), which states that the court may have regard to 'the combination of the offence and one or more offences associated with it' in determining the duration of the sentence. Again, the meaning of 'associated' offences is to be found in s 161of the PCC(S)A 2000.

23.31 There are some offences which do not fall within the scope of 'associated offences', however, e.g., an earlier offence for which a suspended sentence was imposed, of which the offender is now in breach: *Crawford* (1993) 98 Cr App R 297. Similarly, where an offender has been convicted of a number of charges described as 'sample counts', offences not on the indictment or formally taken into consideration are not associated offences: *Canavan* [1998] 1 Cr App R (S) 79.

23.32 The way in which the principle operates is illustrated by *Clugston* (1992) 13 Cr App R (S) 165. The approach in this case is consistent with the current statutory rules, although it predates them. C obtained £5,000 by deception in 100 transactions worth £50 each. The court aggregated the offences and imposed a sentence of three years' imprisonment, which was upheld on appeal. The severity of the sentence could be justified only by the process of aggregating the various offences.

23.33 Where an offender is being sentenced for several offences, there is a danger that the total sentence might be disproportionate to the overall seriousness of what the offender has done. In order to avoid such a result, the 'totality principle' has evolved. This requires a court to consider the overall sentence in relation to the totality of the offending, and in relation to sentence levels for other crimes. Hence it would be wrong just to perform the arithmetic and pass a sentence for a number of offences of theft which exceeded that for a single offence of, say, rape. This sentencing principle now finds statutory expression in the CJA 2003, s 166(3)(b), which states that 'nothing shall prevent a court…in the case of an offender who is convicted of one or more other offences, from mitigating his sentence by applying any rule of law as to the totality of sentences'.

E   MITIGATING AND AGGRAVATING FACTORS

Some of the potential effect of mitigation both in relation to the offence, and personal to the   **23.34** offender has already been indicated in this Chapter. The paragraphs which follow deal first with the statutory considerations which affect the court's consideration of mitigation (and its converse, aggravation), and then discuss some of the factors taken into account.

The statutory framework

The CJA 2003 makes specific mention of mitigating factors, usually in conjunction with   **23.35** aggravating factors, as follows:

(a) Before imposing a discretionary custodial sentence, the 'court must take into account all such information as is available to it about the circumstances of the offence or (as the case may be) of the offence and the offence or offences associated with it, including any aggravating or mitigating factors' (s 156(1)).
(b) There is a similar requirement in relation to any decision to impose a community sentence.
(c) The same obligations attach to the consideration of the *length* of any custodial sentence.
(d) The above points need to be considered alongside s 166(1), which makes provision for the sentencer to take account of any matters which 'in the opinion of the court are relevant in mitigation of sentence'.

It seems that there is a distinction between the provisions summarized in (a), (b) and (c), on   **23.36** the one hand, and the way in which (d) is meant to operate. In considering the matters under (a), (b), and (c), the court is looking at the factors which affect the seriousness of the offence. It is under an obligation to consider those factors. The scope of its duty includes both mitigation (e.g., provocation, acting on impulse rather than with premeditation, peripheral role in the enterprise), and aggravation (e.g., abuse of trust, gratuitous violence, the high value of unrecovered property stolen).

Section 166(1), however, is rather different (see (d) above). It encompasses matters other than   **23.37** the seriousness of the offence which the court might wish to take into account in deciding whether to impose a custodial sentence, and its length, or, for that matter, a community sentence. It permits consideration of *mitigating* factors only. It gives the court a *discretion* to consider such factors if it wishes to take them into account. Notwithstanding this discretionary form, it is submitted that the courts will continue to take into account the variety of factors relating to the offender's personal circumstances which they have considered in the past. Further, failure to do so will no doubt provide good grounds of appeal in appropriate cases. The following paragraphs deal with four of the grounds most commonly relied on by the defence as good mitigation.

23.38   One general point which should be borne in mind is that, even if the offence is such that it passes the custody threshold, personal mitigation such as that set out below may pull the offender back from the threshold, so that he receives a non-custodial sentence: *Cox* [1993] 1 WLR 188. This principle receives statutory confirmation in the CJA 2003, s 166(2).

Plea of guilty

23.39   A judge must not increase the sentence he passes because the accused pleaded not guilty, even if he considers that the accused, in giving evidence in his own defence, committed perjury (*Quinn* (1932) 23 Cr App R 196). Nor must he increase sentence because the nature of the defence involved grave allegations against the police officers in the case (*Skone* (1967) 51 Cr App R 165), or because, by pleading not guilty, the accused forced the prosecution to call witnesses who might well have found giving evidence particularly distressing or even harmful (e.g., child witnesses to a sexual offence). The principle is, however, slightly unreal because it is a well established common law principle (now set out in statute) that a guilty plea attracts a somewhat lighter sentence than a conviction following a not guilty plea (*Cain* [1976] QB 496), and, if the accused does not know this before he decides on his plea, he should be told it by advocate. In other words, a guilty plea is an excellent reason for reducing sentence, but a not guilty plea is no justification for increasing sentence.

23.40   The common law principle that a discount should be given for a guilty plea is given statutory backing by the CJA 2003, s 144. This section deals with the determination of sentence where the offender has pleaded guilty. It states that the court must take into account—

(a)   the stage in the proceedings for the offence at which the offender indicated his intention to plead guilty, and

(b)   the circumstances in which this indication was given.

23.41   In 2004, the Sentencing Guidelines Council produced guidelines on *Reduction in Sentence for a Guilty Plea*, and they were amended after consultation in 2007. The purposes of the reduction are set out in para 2.2. A guilty plea avoids the need for trial, enabling other cases to be disposed of more expeditiously. It shortens the gap between charge and sentence. It saves considerable cost. Finally, in the case of an early plea, it saves the victim and witnesses from concern about having to give evidence. The statement constitutes a frank summary of what are (in the main and with the important exception in relation to sparing victims and witnesses) advantages to the criminal justice system. There is a clear recognition that an incentive is desirable in order to deal with cases more efficiently and cheaply. This is rather different from the historical justification put forward for the reduction: that the plea reflected remorse on the part of the offender which ought to be rewarded with some credit. In fact, the guidelines go on to spell out that 'the sentencer should address separately the issue of remorse, together with any other mitigating features, *before* calculating the reduction for the guilty plea' (para 2.4).

23.42   The guidelines make it clear (para 2.3) that the reduction principle can result in a sentence which is different in *type*, e.g., where the sentencer is in doubt as to whether a custodial sentence is appropriate, in appropriate circumstances a fine or discharge can be imposed rather than a community sentence, or a community sentence rather than a custodial one, as a result of the offender's plea of guilty.

More usually, however, the reduction will be a proportion of the total sentence imposed, **23.43** depending on the stage of the proceedings at which the guilty plea was entered. Generally, it will operate as follows:

(a) a maximum of one-third where the guilty plea was entered at the first reasonable opportunity in relation to the offence for which the sentence is being imposed (para 4.2). The first reasonable opportunity may be the first time that a defendant appears before the court and has the opportunity to plead guilty, although the court may consider that an indication of willingness to plead guilty could have been given earlier, perhaps in interview. In any event, the court will need to be satisfied that the defendant and any legal adviser had sufficient information about the allegations (annex 1);
(b) in the region of 30 per cent where an offence triable either way is committed to the Crown Court for trial and the defendant pleads guilty at the first opportunity in that court (annex 1, para 3(c));
(c) a maximum of one-quarter where a trial date has been set (para 4.2);
(d) a maximum of one-tenth for a guilty plea entered at the door of the court, or after the trial has begun (para 4.2).
(e) in murder cases, the process of determining the level of reduction is different (paras 6.1 to 6.6). In brief, any reduction should not exceed one sixth, and will never exceed five years.

Where a court has decided to sentence on the basis of dangerousness (see 24.34 to 24.42) for **23.44** the protection of the public, the minimum custodial term (but *not* the protection of the public element of the sentence) should be reduced to reflect the plea.

One of the issues which led to the consultation about the revision of these guidelines was the **23.45** extent to which credit should be withheld or reduced because the offender was caught 'redhanded'. The version of the guidelines issued in 2004 stated that the normal sliding scale should apply. That position is modified in the 2007 version, which states:

> Where the prosecution case is overwhelming, it may not be appropriate to give the full reduction that would otherwise be given. Whilst there is a presumption in favour of the full reduction being given where a plea has been indicated at the first reasonable opportunity, the fact that the prosecution case is overwhelming without relying on admissions from the defendant may be a reason justifying departure from the guideline....Where a court is satisfied that a lower reduction should be given for this reason, a recommended reduction of 20% is likely to be appropriate where the guilty plea was indicated at the first reasonable opportunity (paras 5.3 and 5.4).

In a case where the offender enters a guilty plea in the magistrates' court, with the result that **23.46** the bench decides to deal with the matter themselves, rather than commit to the Crown Court, they may impose the maximum sentence available, e.g., a sentence of six months' imprisonment for a single either-way offence, where the offence would have attracted a sentence in the region of nine months if it had been committed to the Crown Court (para 5.5).

Similarly, a detention and training order of 24 months might be imposed on an offender aged under 18 if the offence was one which, but for the plea, would have attracted a sentence of long-term detention in excess of 24 months under the PCC(S)A 2000, s 91.

Co-operation with the police

23.47   Co-operation with the police, in the sense of not resisting arrest and confessing frankly to the offence at the police station, is good mitigation, although it may not add much to the effect of an early guilty plea. Co-operation in the sense of giving 'Queen's evidence' (evidence for the prosecution against one's accomplices) may lead to a substantial reduction in sentence. Even greater reductions are available for the handful of offenders who give information and/or evidence which leads to the conviction of large numbers of their criminal associates: *Lowe* (1977) 66 Cr App R 122. In *King* (1985) 7 Cr App R (S) 227, the Court of Appeal indicated that an offender who has given really substantial help to the police in relation to serious crime, including naming names and either confronting the persons named or giving evidence against them, is entitled to as much as a half to two-thirds off the normal 'tariff' sentence. Other cases have shown that a proportionate reduction should also be made in more trivial cases where neither the crimes for which the offender is sentenced nor those about which he gives evidence or information are in the first rank of gravity (see *Thomas* (1985) 7 Cr App R (S) 95). In *Wood* [1997] 1 Cr App R (S) 347, the amount of discount was said to depend on the quality, quantity, accuracy, and timeliness of the information.

23.48   Credit for giving Queen's evidence was given statutory form in SOCPA 2005. It provides (s 73) for the court to give a reduction to reflect assistance given or offered to the authorities, and to this extent reflects the common law. It lays down that the statutory scheme is conditional upon a guilty plea, and a written agreement with a designated prosecutor (the CPS and the usual public prosecuting authorities are designated). The statute says that the judge must state in open court that a lesser sentence has been given because of the assistance, unless it is not in the public interest to do so. The discount can later be reviewed if the assistance is not forthcoming, or if further assistance is given (resulting presumably in an upward or downward movement in sentence accordingly). Even if the offender is not given a discount at the time of sentence and later gives assistance, his (non-discounted) sentence can be reviewed. The provisions were subject to analysis by the Court of Appeal in *P* [2007] EWCA Crim 2290. Their lordships made it clear that the provisions relating to review of sentences could apply even if the crime was committed and sentence passed before the provisions came into operation. The discount for assistance should be assessed first, and the notional sentence calculated should then be further discounted for the guilty plea. Where an agreement was reached under s 73, sentences should usually be concurrent. This was likely to be of importance, as the offender would be disclosing criminal activities of his own which would probably not have come to light without an agreement being reached. In deciding on the sentence to be imposed, the normal level of reduction for substantial assistance in relation to serious crimes should continue to be between one half and two thirds of the total sentence which would otherwise be passed. Only in the most exceptional case would the appropriate level of reduction exceed three quarters of the total sentence which would otherwise be passed.

Good and bad character

Traditionally, the courts have regarded the previous good character of the offender as **23.49** excellent mitigation. The long-standing sentencing policy of the courts, underpinned by the decisions of the Court of Appeal, is to treat first offenders with leniency.

A variation on the argument that the offender has no previous convictions whatsoever is that **23.50** he has no previous for the kind of offence of which he has been convicted. For example, counsel in mitigation might say that, although his client has a record for petty dishonesty, he has no history of violence so that *vis-à-vis* the assault for which he is to be sentenced he should be treated as a person of good character. Yet another argument is that there has been a substantial gap between the present offence and the last one, indicating that the offender has made a genuine effort to 'go straight'. Thus, in *Canfield* (1982) 4 Cr App R (S) 94, a nine-month prison sentence for a clumsy attempted burglary from a social club was replaced with community service. C (aged 32) had had an appalling record for burglary during the period 1967 to 1976 but, after his release from prison in 1977, he had changed his way of life, found a job and married. Apart from some road traffic matters (which had led to loss of his job), this was the first time he had been in trouble since 1977. The five years of good behaviour saved him from going to prison again.

The common law principles set out above have been characterized as 'progressive loss of **23.51** mitigation'. The offender may be thought of as starting with substantial credit for good character. That credit is progressively diminished by each offence of which he or she is convicted. If there is a break in offending, some credit accumulates again, only to be diminished with a subsequent offence.

The principles are reinforced by the CJA 2003, s 143(2), which states: **23.52**

> In considering the seriousness of an offence ('the current offence') committed by an offender who has one or more previous convictions, the court must treat each previous conviction as an aggravating factor if (in the case of that conviction) the court considers that it can reasonably be so treated, having regard, in particular, to—
> (a) the nature of the offence to which the conviction relates and its relevance to the current offence, and
> (b) the time that has elapsed since the conviction.

In *Howells* [1998] Crim LR 836, Lord Bingham CJ said that leniency would ordinarily be **23.53** extended to offenders of previous good character, the more so if there was evidence of positive good character (such as a solid employment record or faithful discharge of family duties) as opposed to a mere absence of previous convictions. Such 'positive good character' was given weight, for example, in *Clark* (1999) *The Times*, 27 January 1999. The Court of Appeal were dealing with an offender who had brought up her four nephews and nieces in difficult circumstances when their mother died, and who was involved in a number of local community and charitable activities. Although she had pleaded guilty to two offences of false accounting and one of obtaining property by deception, amounting to fraud of £18,000 in total, her sentence of six months' imprisonment was reduced to seven days.

Youth

23.54   The youth of the offender can be a most important mitigating factor. If a young offender is given a custodial sentence, its length is likely to be shorter than the corresponding sentence of imprisonment which an offender over 21 would receive. For example, in *Storey* [1984] Crim LR 438, sentences of five years' detention passed on three 16-year-olds who had burnt down part of their school, causing £370,000-worth of damage, were reduced to three years. The Court of Appeal's reason was that, although severe sentences were called for because of the exceptional nature of the case, the term chosen should not be so long that 'to young men like this [the end would] seem completely out of sight'. More generally, youth is accepted as an important mitigating factor in the various sets of guidelines issued by the Sentencing Guidelines Council. For example, the *Guidelines on Sexual Offences* state that 'youth and immaturity must always be potential mitigating factors' unless the offence is 'particularly serious'.

23.55   There is also some authority for the view that youth can be crucial, not just in reducing sentence length, but in determining the type of sentence (see, for example, *Seymour* (1983) 5 Cr App R (S) 85, where the Court of Appeal urged the use of community sentences rather than custody in dealing with certain categories of burglary committed by young offenders).

Racial or religious aggravation

23.56   The Court of Appeal has made it clear for a number of years that racial motivation for an offence is 'gravely aggravating' (*Attorney-General's References (Nos. 29, 30 and 31 of 1994)* (1994) 16 Cr App R (S) 698. This principle was given statutory backing by the CJA 2003, s 145 which states that, if an offence is racially aggravated, the court must treat it as a factor which increases the seriousness of the offence.

23.57   Section 145 applies to sentencing generally, except where the court is imposing a sentence for one of the racially or religiously aggravated offences set out in the CDA 1998, ss 29 to 32 (certain aggravated assaults, aggravated criminal damage, certain aggravated public order offences, and aggravated harassment). As far as those offences are concerned, they carry higher maximum penalties than their non-aggravated equivalents, and would be expected to attract enhanced sentences in any event.

Aggravation related to disability or sexual orientation

23.58   By s 146 of the CJA 2003, sentencers are compelled by statute to take two further factors into account—aggravation related to disability or sexual orientation.

KEY DOCUMENTS

Powers of Criminal Courts (Sentencing) Act 2000, as amended.
Criminal Justice Act 2003, as amended.

The guidelines produced by the Sentencing Guidelines Council are available on: <http://www.sentencing-guidelines.gov.uk>. On the homepage, go to Guidelines, then Council Guidelines, then Final

The guidelines produced by the Magistrates' Association can be found on the Judicial Studies Board website: <http://www.jsboard.co.uk/>, then go to Adult Court Benchbook under JSB Publications

24

CUSTODIAL SENTENCES

24.01 This Chapter and the one following describe the sentencing options open to the courts. The general nature of a particular sentence, the age group for which it is intended and any restrictions on its imposition are explained. The special limitations on the powers of the magistrates' courts, and on the powers of an adult magistrates' court when dealing with a juvenile have already been explained (see 10.65 to 10.73, 11.29 to 11.31 and 12.02 to 12.05). This Chapter concentrates upon those sentences which can be described as 'custodial'.

24.02 It covers imprisonment (in the case of an adult), whether immediate or suspended and its equivalent, in the case of those under 21.

A PRISONS

24.03 Prisons are classified into various types. There are open and closed prisons, and there are also local and training ones. *Closed prisons*, as the name implies, have a boundary wall or fence, and strict perimeter security. The movement of prisoners about the institution is more or less strictly controlled, and they are locked up at nights. Probably, the accommodation will consist of the traditional cell. *Open prisons* have a far more relaxed regime, depending for security on regular roll-calls rather than perimeter security and other physical controls. Only about a tenth of male prisoners (a third of females) are detained in open prisons. *Local prisons* house prisoners on remand awaiting trial or sentence; offenders who have been given a short or shortish prison term; and long-term prisoners who are awaiting allocation to a suitable training prison. Local prisons are always closed, are nearly always located near large centres of population, and, since they tend to date from the Victorian era, are often notoriously inadequate for modern needs. *Training prisons* may be either open or closed, although the majority are the latter. They are meant to provide better standards of accommodation, better work facilities and better recreational opportunities than the local prisons. *Young offender institutions* are for sentenced prisoners under the age of 21.

24.04 The closed training prisons subdivide into a minority of maximum-security dispersal prisons at which the most dangerous prisoners are detained, plus category B and C prisons which cater for lower-risk inmates. Where an offender serves his sentence will depend mainly on the length of the term and the security classification he is given. As already mentioned, a prisoner given a short term (say, less than six months) will probably serve the whole of it in a local prison. Category A prisoners are the most dangerous, and they are held at the dispersal prisons. Some Category B prisoners (the next security classification down) also go to dispersal prisons, although the actual regime they are subjected to there will not be as tight as that enforced in respect of Category A prisoners. The remainder are sent to the Category B non-dispersal training prisons. Category C prisoners (those who cannot be trusted in open conditions but who are reckoned incapable of making a determined escape attempt) go either to Category B or Category C training prisons. Category D prisoners are eligible for detention in open conditions, but whether they are so detained will depend amongst other things, on the availability of places in open prison. A prisoner who is initially classified as being in one of the higher-risk categories may be put into a lower group as his sentence progresses, and, often, a long-term prisoner is allowed to spend the last few months of his sentence in open conditions so as to prepare him for release. Conversely, a Category D prisoner who absconds would be reclassified in the B or C groups.

The annual reports of Her Majesty's Chief Inspector of Prisons are an interesting and often **24.05** alarming guide to conditions in prisons. Over the years the reports have stressed three interlocking problems. One is the lack of space in prisons. Over a third of prisoners share (sometimes with two or three others) cells originally designed for one. Secondly, most prisons were built in the last century, and are becoming dilapidated.

Lastly, although the Prison Rules state that a prisoner serving a sentence may be required to **24.06** work for a certain number of hours a week, it is often difficult to provide work, and such work as there is may be boring and repetitive. The result of prisoners not being able to work is that they are locked up in their cells not only at night, but also for much of the day. The problem is especially acute in the local prisons, where the need to employ prison officers on tasks such as escorting remand prisoners to court often means that there are no officers available to supervise working parties.

B   MINIMUM AGE FOR IMPRISONMENT

The minimum age for a sentence of imprisonment is 21: Powers of Criminal Courts **24.07** (Sentencing) Act 2000 (PCC(S)A), s 89. The relevant consideration is the offender's age when sentence is passed, not his age when the offence was committed or even his age when he was found or pleaded guilty if that and the passing of sentence occur on different days. It should be noted, however, that s 89 merely prohibits *sentences* of imprisonment in the cases of under-21s—it does not say that a young offender can never in any circumstances be detained in prison. In fact, a minority of 17–20-year-olds sentenced to detention in a young offender institution serve all or part of the term imposed in prison, but that does not alter the fact that the sentence was one of detention rather than imprisonment. There will be a change when the Criminal Justice and Court Services Act 2000, s 61, comes into effect. It will abolish sentences of detention in a young offender institution and custody for life. Offenders aged 18 to 20 will then be sentenced to imprisonment. No date has been set for its implementation.

C   REQUIREMENTS FOR CUSTODIAL SENTENCES

When it is considering the imposition of a custodial sentence, the court has to abide by **24.08** certain statutory requirements. In particular:

(a)   A court shall not pass a first sentence of imprisonment upon an offender who is not legally represented, without giving him a chance to be legally represented (PCC(S)A 2000, s 83: see 22.53 to 22.59 for details).

(b) Before passing a custodial sentence, the court must be satisfied that it is justified on the basis of the criteria set out in the CJA 2003, s 152. These criteria are discussed at 23.07 and 23.14 to 23.21 (which deals with offence seriousness).

(c) In order to determine whether those criteria are satisfied, the court is obliged in certain circumstances to 'obtain and consider a pre-sentence report' (CJA 2003, s 156). These reports are discussed at 24.09 to 24.10.

(d) In addition to its consideration of the pre-sentence report, the court must take into account all such information about the circumstances of the offence (including any aggravating or mitigating factors) as is available to it (CJA 2003, s 156(1) discussed in 23.34 to 23.58).

(e) Any court passing a custodial sentence must state its reasons (CJA 2003 s 174: see 24.11).

Pre-sentence reports

24.09 As mentioned at 22.45 to 22.52, reports on an offender frequently play a major role in the court's decision on sentence. When the court is deciding whether one of the grounds specified in s 152 of the CJA 2003 is made out, so as to justify a custodial sentence, then it must obtain and consider a pre-sentence report. It has a similar obligation when deciding upon the length of a discretionary custodial sentence (s 153(2)). The court has power, however, to dispense with a pre-sentence report, which varies according to the age of the offender:

(a) In the case of an offender aged 18 or over, the obligation to obtain a pre-sentence report when considering a custodial sentence does not apply if the court is of the opinion that a report is not necessary.

(b) Where the offender is under 18, the court may not decide that a pre-sentence report is unnecessary unless there exists a previous pre-sentence report which the court has regard to (CJA 2003, s 156(5)).

24.10 In any event, s 156(6) of the CJA 2003 states that no sentence shall be invalidated by failure to comply with s 156(1). In the event of an appeal against a custodial sentence passed in the absence of a pre-sentence report, however, the Court of Appeal shall obtain and consider one unless the court below was justified in dispensing with one, or there is no longer any need to obtain one.

Giving reasons for custody

24.11 When passing a custodial sentence, any court has a duty (see CJA 2003, s 174,) to state in open court that such a sentence is justified under s 152(2) (offence seriousness) and why it has come to that view. Further, it must set out any reduction given for a guilty plea, and mention any aggravating or mitigating features of particular importance. In addition, it must explain to the offender 'in ordinary language and in general terms, its reasons for deciding on the sentence passed'. The court must also state, where there are relevant guidelines and it has chosen not to follow them, what its reasons are for that course of action. Further, in the magistrates' court, the reason must be recorded in the warrant of commitment and the court register. It would seem that failure to comply with these procedural requirements will not of itself invalidate any custodial sentence passed (see, by analogy, *McQueen* (1989) 11 Cr App R (S) 196).

Explaining what the sentence will mean in practice

The *Practice Direction (Criminal Proceedings: Consolidation)* [2002] 1 WLR 2870, para I.7 imposes **24.12** a requirement on sentencers in the Crown Court to explain the practical effect of any custodial sentence which is imposed. Sentencers must give the explanation in terms of their own choosing, whilst ensuring that it is clear and accurate (see also CJA 2003 s 174). The *Practice Direction* (which is to be found in *Blackstone's Criminal Practice 2008*, Appendix 7) sets out short statements which the sentencer can adapt.

D   MAXIMUM TERMS OF IMPRISONMENT

Common law offences are prima facie punishable with imprisonment for life. In other **24.13** words, the court may, at its discretion, pass a fixed term of any length or make the sentence extend to the term of the offender's life. In fact, there are very few remaining common law offences, and for most that do remain statute has altered the common law position as regards penalty. Thus, the maximum sentence for the common law offence of common assault is now a mere six months and for conspiracy to defraud it is 10 years (see CJA 1988, s 39 and CJA 1987, s 12 respectively). By contrast the penalty for murder is a mandatory life sentence (see 24.27 to 24.33). Manslaughter provides the best example of a common law offence for which the penalty is simply a discretionary life sentence.

The table below indicates the maximum terms of imprisonment imposable for some common statutory offences:

Offence	Penalty
Child destruction, abortion, rape, causing grievous bodily harm with intent, possessing a firearm with intent to endanger life or carrying one with intent to commit an indictable offence, criminal damage committed with an intent to endanger life or by the use of fire, aggravated burglary, robbery, importing or supplying controlled drugs in Class A.	Imprisonment for life
Burglary of a dwelling, handling stolen goods, blackmail, obtaining or communicating etc. information useful to an enemy contrary to s 1 of the Official Secrets Act 1911, supplying controlled drugs in Class B or C, causing death by dangerous driving, sexual activity with a child.	14 years
Obtaining property by deception, burglary (other than of a dwelling), non-aggravated criminal damage, sexual assault, and forgery and counterfeiting offences where the offender's intention in making, using etc. the forgery/counterfeit was to pass it off as genuine to the prejudice of another.	10 years
Theft, perjury, bigamy, and having possession of a Class A controlled drug.	7 years

Continued

Offence	Penalty
Unlawful wounding, inflicting grievous bodily harm, assault occasioning actual bodily harm, obtaining services by deception, evading liability by deception and having possession of a Class B controlled drug.	5 years
Going equipped for burglary, theft, or cheat.	3 years
Dangerous driving, forgery and counterfeiting offences where there was no intention to pass off the article concerned as genuine, making off without payment, having an offensive weapon, and having possession of a Class C controlled drug.	2 years
Assaulting a police constable in the execution of his duty, drink/driving offences, driving while disqualified, taking a motor vehicle without the owner's consent, and using threatening behaviour with intent to put a person in fear of violence, etc.	6 months
Interfering with a motor vehicle, criminal damage dealt with as a summary offence under the special procedure in s 22 of the MCA, and drink/being in charge of a motor vehicle offences.	3 months
Obstructing a police constable in the execution of his duty.	1 month

24.14 If a statute creates an indictable offence, provides that it is to be punishable with imprisonment, but fails to state what the maximum term shall be, the offence is punishable with up to two years' imprisonment upon conviction on indictment: PCC(S)A 2000, s 77. For attempts contrary to s 1 of the Criminal Attempts Act 1981 and conspiracy contrary to s 1 of the Criminal Law Act 1977, the maximum is the same as for the offence to which the attempt or conspiracy related. A magistrates' court cannot impose more than six months' imprisonment for one offence (PCC(S)A 2000, s 78 and see 10.65 to 10.68).

24.15 When the CJA 2003, s 154, comes into effect (this is not in force at the time of writing), the sentencing powers of magistrates will be increased.

24.16 As will be seen from the above, the maximum terms roughly, but only roughly, reflect the relative gravity of the various offences. There are apparent anomalies, such as handling stolen goods being punishable with a sentence twice as long as perjury. For many indictable offences, including burglary, handling, theft and criminal damage, the maxima are much higher than the terms which would actually be imposed save in the gravest of cases, but fixing the maximum term high allows for suitable punishment for the man who steals the Crown jewels or damages the National Gallery's most valuable painting. It should not be thought that the penalty which could theoretically be imposed plays a major part in determining the penalty which is actually imposed on a particular offender for a particular crime— i.e., a judge does not pass a sentence of three and a half years' imprisonment for an offence of theft which he regards as being of average gravity on the basis that the maximum for theft is seven years. Subject, of course, to not exceeding the lawful maximum, the sentence will reflect the character of the offender and the gravity of his conduct, not the label (robbery, burglary, theft, handling or whatever) which is attached to that conduct.

E   CONCURRENT AND CONSECUTIVE SENTENCES

When a court deals with an offender for two or more offences by means of sentences of **24.17** imprisonment it may either order that the terms of imprisonment shall run at the same time as each other, or it may order that they shall run one after the other. In the former case, the sentences of imprisonment are *concurrent;* in the latter case, they are *consecutive.* Similarly, if a court passes a sentence of imprisonment on an offender who is already serving a term of imprisonment it may order that the term it imposes shall run concurrently with or consecutively to the other term. The judge or presiding magistrate should expressly state whether prison sentences are concurrent or consecutive. If nothing is said, they are presumed to be concurrent. Where consecutive sentences are imposed for two or more offences the aggregate sentence may exceed that which could have been imposed for any one of them (see *Blake* [1962] 2 QB 377 where for five offences under the Official Secrets Act 1911, B was sentenced to a total of 42 years' imprisonment, even though 14 years is the maximum for one such offence). A magistrates' court's power to impose consecutive sentences is limited by s 133 of the Magistrates' Courts Act 1980 (see 10.65 to 10.68).

Consecutive sentences are wrong in principle if they are imposed for offences which, **24.18** although distinct in law, arose out of a single act so that—looking at what the offender did in a common-sense way—he really only committed one crime. *Hussain* [1962] Crim LR 712 illustrates the appellate court's attitude to consecutive and concurrent sentences. H, who tried unsuccessfully to smuggle Indian hemp through customs at Heathrow airport, was given three years for possessing a dangerous drug and two years to run consecutively for unloading prohibited goods from an aircraft. The Court of Criminal Appeal held that, since both offences consisted of precisely the same act (i.e., leaving the plane at Heathrow with Indian hemp in his possession), it was wrong to impose consecutive sentences. H's pleasure at a successful appeal was short-lived, because the sentence was varied to one of five years' imprisonment for each offence to run concurrently.

Where an offender is convicted of several similar offences committed at different times, he **24.19** could be sentenced to consecutive terms of imprisonment. The danger with such an approach is that the individual sentences may, in themselves, be short and well justified by the criminal conduct in respect of which they are passed, but taken in the aggregate they can amount to an unreasonably severe punishment. To avoid this danger, a judge sentencing an offender for, say, five offences of burglary from dwelling-houses committed over a six-month period should first decide whether the offences together justify a custodial sentence (see 23.28 to 23.33). He should then look at the totality of the offences during the period, and decide upon the appropriate sentence for that criminal conduct overall (using the criteria discussed at 24.21 to 24.26). He might, as a result of this process, decide that three years' imprisonment is right. He will then pass a sentence of three years' imprisonment for the most serious of the burglaries and make the sentences for the other burglaries run concurrently with each other and with the three-year sentence.

Generally, the principle is that sentences should be concurrent if offences arise out of the **24.20** same incident. In *Noble* [2003] 1 Cr App R (S) 312, for example, it was held that concurrent sentences should be imposed where multiple deaths arose from a single incident of dangerous driving.

In *Cosco* [2005] 2 Cr App R (S) 405, C exposed himself indecently on three occasions during a single afternoon. This was held to be a single course of conduct, for which concurrent sentences were appropriate. However, there are certain situations where consecutive sentences are applied, as a matter of policy. For example, there is authority for saying that a custodial sentence for failure to surrender to bail should be consecutive to any sentence for the offence in respect of which bail was granted: *White* [2003] 2 Cr App R (S) 133, and this approach now has the support of the Sentencing Guidelines Council (see their Guidelines on *Failure to Surrender to Bail*).

F   LENGTH OF CUSTODIAL SENTENCE

24.21   Once the sentencer has made the decision that an offender's conduct passes the custody 'threshold' (see 23.07 and 23.14 to 23.21), so that a custodial sentence is justified, that does not mean that a custodial sentence is inevitable. The Guideline issued by the Sentencing Guidelines Council on Seriousness states (para 1.32) that custody can still be avoided, e.g., in the light of personal mitigation or because a suitable community sentence is available. If the sentencer has come to the conclusion that custody is inevitable after this further stage in the decision-making process, the important question remains: what should the length of the sentence be? That issue is addressed in CJA 2003, s 153, which reads:

> (1) This section applies where a court passes a custodial sentence other than one fixed by law or falling to be imposed under ss. 225 or 226.
> (2) Subject to s. 51A of the Firearms Act 1968, ss. 110(2) and 111(2) of the [PCC(S)A 2000] and ss. 227(2) and 228(2) of this Act, the custodial sentence must be for the shortest term (not exceeding the permitted maximum) that in the opinion of the court is commensurate with the seriousness of the offence, or the combination of the offence and one or more offences associated with it.

24.22   As can be seen, the fundamental principle is that the custodial sentence should be the shortest one compatible with the seriousness of the offence. However, the terms of s 153 exclude the following from the ambit of this principle:

(a) sentences fixed by law, i.e., murder (see 24.27 to 24.33);
(b) sentences to be imposed under ss 225 and 226 (imprisonment or detention for life or for public protection for serious offences: see 24.34 to 24.38);
(c) mandatory minimum sentences for firearms, Class A drug and burglary offences (see 24.43 to 24.47);
(d) sentences to be imposed under ss 227 and 228 (extended sentences: see 24.37 to 24.38).

24.23   Any sentence imposed must be within the permitted maximum. This means, of course, that the sentence must be within the maximum applicable to the offence in question (see 24.13 to 24.16), as well as those which relate to the offender's age (see 24.64) and the powers of the court (see 10.65 to 10.67 for the limits on the magistrates' powers).

24.24   Looking first at the criterion embodied in s 153(1) it gives primacy to the principle of proportionality—the sentence should primarily be determined by (or proportionate to) the seriousness of the offence. Clearly in considering the seriousness of the offence as the determinant of length, the court must take into account any aggravating or mitigating circumstances which have bearing upon the seriousness of the offence itself. It should also have regard to mitigating factors which relate to the offender himself, even if they are totally irrelevant to the seriousness of the offence(s) for which he is being sentenced, e.g., the fact that he has pleaded guilty. (See s 166(1) and 23.34 to 23.55 for a fuller exposition of the main factors which provide good mitigation.)

'Clang of the prison gates'

In interpreting the criterion of 'offence seriousness', in particular, the approach of the Court **24.25** of Appeal to the length of custodial sentences in such cases as *Bibi* [1980] 1 WLR 1193 has been reinforced by the new statutory framework in CJA 1991. That case articulated the important principle that, where loss of liberty is inevitable, the sentence should be kept as short as possible. As Lord Lane CJ put it in *Bibi*:

> It is no secret that our prisons are at the moment dangerously overcrowded. So much so that sentencing courts must be particularly careful to examine each case to ensure, if an immediate custodial sentence is necessary, that the sentence is as short as possible consistent only with the duty to protect the interests of the public and to punish and deter the criminal. Many offenders can be dealt with equally justly and effectively by a sentence of six or nine months imprisonment as by one of 18 months or three years.

The Lord Chief Justice emphasized that this applied not only to first offenders (who are **24.26** often given disproportionately short sentences on the basis that merely hearing the prison gates 'clang shut' behind them will be a severe punishment), but also to those with criminal records and even to those with past experience of custodial penalties. Similar sentiments were expressed by Lord Phillips CJ in *Seed and Stark* [2007] EWCA Crim 254, in the context of the increasing problem of prison overcrowding at that date.

G MURDER

An offender aged 21 or over who has been convicted of murder *must* be sentenced to life **24.27** imprisonment (Murder (Abolition of Death Penalty) Act 1965, s 1(1)). As is well known, the term 'life imprisonment' does not normally mean that the offender will stay in prison for the whole of his natural life. At a certain point, the offender's release on licence is likely to come up for consideration, just as it does in the case of a determinate sentence. With a life sentence, that consideration comes up on the expiry of the 'minimum term'. The CJA 2003, ss 269 to 277 and Sch 21 lays down a detailed statutory scheme for setting minimum terms in all murder cases, whether the offender is adult or juvenile. It follows that the length of a minimum term has a different impact from the length of a sentence. The minimum term of a life sentence must be served in full before release on licence can be ordered, whereas an offender serving a long determinate sentence would normally be released at some point after half of that sentence. A minimum term of 15 years can therefore be compared to a determinate sentence of 30 years (for detailed exposition of the provisions, and the concepts involved, see *Blackstone's Guide to the Criminal Justice Act 2003*, Chapter 11.8). After release, the ex-prisoner is on licence for the rest of his life. In that sense, a life sentence is just that.

24.28 The CJA 2003 lays down a starting point of 15 years as the minimum term for murder for offenders aged 18 and over. For those aged under 18, it is 12 years. In these cases, the sentence is one of custody for life, or detention at Her Majesty's pleasure, respectively.

24.29 Where the murder falls within certain categories, however, the Act lays down a minimum term starting point of 30 years. These include:

(a)   murder of a police or prison officer in the course of duty;

(b)   murder involving a firearm or explosive;

(c)   murder done for gain (e.g., in the course of robbery or burglary);

(d)   murder intended to obstruct the course of justice;

(e)   murder involving sexual or sadistic conduct;

(f)   murder of two or more persons;

(g)   murder racially or religiously aggravated, or aggravated by sexual orientation.

If the murder falls within the following categories, and is committed by a person aged 21 or over, it attracts a minimum starting point of 'a whole life order':

(a)   the murder of two or more persons, where each murder involved a substantial degree of premeditation or planning, or the abduction of the victim, or sexual or sadistic conduct;

(b)   the murder of a person under 21 involving abduction or sexual or sadistic motivation;

(c)   political, religious, or ideological murder;

(d)   murder by a person with a previous conviction for murder.

In relation to these latter categories, there are starting points of 15 years for offenders aged 18 to 20; and 12 years for those aged under 18. The Act also lists aggravating and mitigating factors, which operate to modify the starting point in relation to offenders of all ages. In addition, the starting points are subject to appropriate reduction for a plea of guilty.

24.30 The new scheme marks a controversial departure from established practice, in that it aims to set legislative standards for sentencing, rather than entrusting that task to the newly formed Sentencing Guidelines Council. It sharply increases (sometimes doubling) the starting points which had been laid down by the Lord Chief Justice after widespread consultation. One feature of the scheme which has attracted particular criticism is the sharp difference between the starting points for those over and those under 18 years of age. In *Attorney-General's References (Nos 143 and 144 of 2006)* [2007] Crim LR 735, the Court of Appeal considered the correct approach where there were two co-defendants who had committed a murder jointly, and where one was 17 years and nine months old, and the other 18 years and seven months old. In such a case, said their lordships, the sentencer should move from each starting point to a position where any disparity between the sentences was no more than a fair reflection of the age difference between the two offenders. The result was that the offenders in question ended up with life sentences with minimum terms of 20 and 21 years respectively.

24.31 The procedure is that the court must select the minimum term appropriate to the seriousness of the offence or the combination of the offence and other offences associated with it, making allowance for any period spent in custody on remand. The court must select a minimum term unless the offender was aged 21 or over when he committed the offence and it considers that, 'because of the seriousness of the offence . . . no order should be made' (s 269(4)). This is to allow for the setting of a 'whole life term' in cases such as those indicated above. Section

269(5) states that when considering the seriousness of a murder case, the court must have regard to

(a) the general principles set out in Sch 21; and
(b) any guidelines relevant to the case which are not incompatible with the provisions of that schedule.

The general principles, including the starting points set out in the schedule, are not mandatory—the court must 'have regard' to them. But the court must state in open court and in ordinary language the reasons for its sentence, stating which starting point has been chosen and why, with reasons for any departure from it. The Home Secretary has power to amend the terms of Sch 21 by order, after consultation with the Sentencing Guidelines Council.

There can be no appeal against a mandatory life sentence. However, an offender can appeal against the minimum term set by the court in a murder case, or a decision to set a 'whole life term' (CJA 2003, s 271, inserting a new s 9(1A) in the Criminal Appeal Act 1968). The Attorney-General is also able to refer a minimum term in a murder case to the Court of Appeal as an unduly lenient sentence under ss 35 and 36 of the CJA 1988 (see 26.80 to 26.87). If the reference is successful, the Court of Appeal is precluded by s 36(3A) of the CJA 1988 from giving the offender the customary discount for the 'double jeopardy' of being sentenced twice (see 26.87). This exception to the usual principle was introduced by s 272 of the CJA 2003. **24.32**

Sections 269 to 277 and Schs 21 and 22 of the 2003 Act came into force on 18 December 2003. They apply to all cases in which a court passes a mandatory life sentence for murder on or after that date. The fact that the relevant date is the date of sentence, rather than the date of commission of the offence may well trigger off a challenge under Art 7 of the ECHR (see Chapter 28). That states: **24.33**

> 'Nor shall a heavier penalty be imposed than the one that was applicable at the time the criminal offence was committed'.

H   DANGEROUS OFFENDERS

The CJA 2003, ss 224 to 236 and Sch 15, introduced a new framework for sentencing 'dangerous offenders'. It is aimed at offenders who have been assessed as dangerous, and who have committed one of the specified violent or sexual offences, where the court is of the opinion that 'there is a significant risk to members of the public of serious harm occasioned by the commission by him of further specified offences'. Central to the understanding of these provisions are the definitions upon which they are based: **24.34**

(a) 'Specified offences' are those which are listed in Sch 15 of the CJA 2003. All of them carry a maximum penalty of two years' imprisonment or more.
(b) Violent offences are those which are listed in Part 1 of Sch 15, so that they are all included within the category of 'specified offences'. There are some 65 of them.
(c) Sexual offences are those which are listed in Part 2 of Sch 15. There are 88 of them, and they are again all included within the category of 'specified offences'.

Figure 24.1 Dangerous Offenders—Assessing Dangerousness

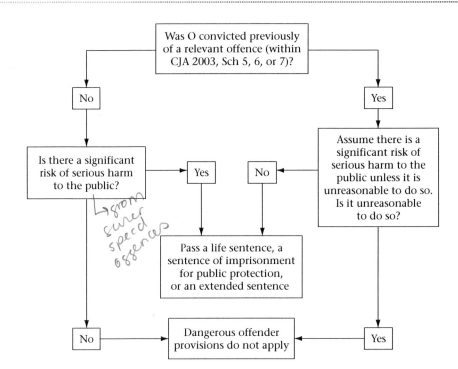

(d) Serious offences are those violent or sexual offences contained within Sch 15 for which the maximum penalty is either life imprisonment, or 10 years or more.

The issues involved are set out in the flowcharts on pages 420 and 422.

Life sentence or imprisonment for public protection

24.35   Section 225(1) of the CJA 2003 applies to offences committed on or after 4 April 2005 and where:

(a)   the offender is aged 18 or over; and

(b)   he is convicted of one of the serious offences set out in Sch 15 (that is, one of those offences carrying a maximum penalty of ten years or more); and

(c)   the court is of the opinion that there is a significant risk to members of the public of serious harm occasioned by the commission by him of further specified offences (that is, any of the offences set out in Sch 15, whether designated 'serious' or not).

Where these conditions are fulfilled, the court must impose a life sentence if:

(i)   the offence carries life as its maximum penalty, and

(ii)   the court considers that the seriousness of the offence, or of the offence and one or more offences associated with it, is such as to justify the imposition of a life sentence.

If the conditions set out above as (a), (b), and (c) are fulfilled, but either (i) or (ii) is not fulfilled, then the court must impose a sentence of public protection.

Figure 24.2 Dangerous Offenders—Adults

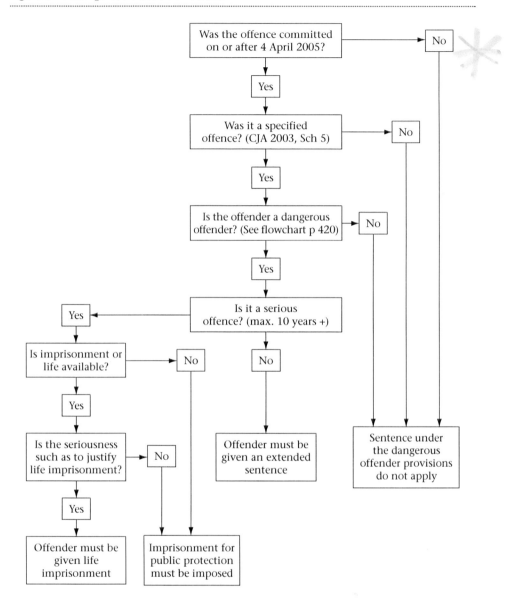

Detention of young offenders for life, or for public protection

Section 226 of the CJA 2003 contains provisions equivalent to those in s 225, but aimed at young   **24.36**
offenders. It applies to offences committed on or after 4 April 2005 where:

(a) the offender is under 18; and
(b) he is convicted of a serious offence in Sch 15 (that is, such an offence carrying a maximum
     penalty of ten years or more); and
(c) the court is of the opinion that there is a significant risk to members of the public of seri-
     ous harm occasioned by the commission by him of further specified offences (that is,
     offences within Sch 15, whether designated 'serious' or not).

Figure 24.3 Dangerous Offenders—Youths

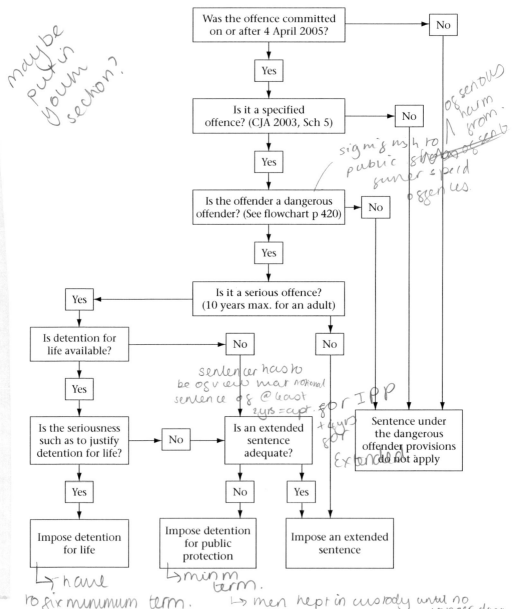

[handwritten notes: "maybe put in youth section?"]

[handwritten notes: "sig mis mght to public sthere of gunier s peed o gger us."]

[handwritten notes: "of serious harm from. orom of serb"]

[handwritten notes around flowchart: "sentencer has to be of view that notional sentence of @ least 2yrs = apt. for IPP + 4yrs for Extended"]

[handwritten notes: "have no six minimum term."]

[handwritten notes: "min m term."]

[handwritten notes: "men hept in custody until no longer dang"]

In such a case, if the offence for which the young offender has been convicted carries detention for life under s 91 of the PCC(S)A 2000 as its maximum penalty, and the court considers that the seriousness of the offence, together with associated offences, is such as to justify detention for life, the court must impose detention for life (s 226(2)). If the circumstances do not fall within s 226(2) the court must either impose a sentence of detention for public protection, or an extended sentence. If it is of the opinion that an extended sentence would not be adequate for public protection, it must impose a sentence of detention for public protection.

[handwritten notes: "can be serve more man 5 yar max."]

Extended sentences

Section 227 of the CJA 2003 deals with extended sentences and their imposition upon **24.37** dangerous offenders in certain circumstances. It applies to offences committed on or after 4 April 2005 where:

(a) the offender is aged 18 or over; and

(b) he is convicted of an offence in Sch 15 other than a serious offence (i.e., his conviction is for an offence which carries a maximum penalty of between two and ten years); and

(c) the court is of the opinion that there is a significant risk to members of the public of serious harm occasioned by the commission by him of further specified offences.

In such a case, the court is obliged to pass an extended prison sentence. This is will be for a term of imprisonment (not exceeding the maximum for the offence) which is equal to the sum of:

(a) the appropriate custodial term; and

(b) a further term (the extension period) on licence, of such length as the court considers necessary to protect members of the public from serious harm occasioned by the commission by him of further specified offences (s 227(2)).

Section 227(3) lays down that the custodial term of the extended sentence is the commensurate sentence appropriate to the offence, or 12 months, whichever is the longer. The extension period may be up to five years for a specified violent offence, and up to eight years for a specified sexual offence.

Equivalent and broadly similar provisions applicable to those aged under 18 are set out in s 228.   **24.38**

The assessment of dangerousness

Crucial to the operation of the provisions relating to dangerous offenders is the question: how **24.39** does the court determine whether the offender poses 'a significant risk to the public of serious harm occasioned by the commission by him of further specified offences'?('dangerousness'). That enquiry into dangerousness is central to the application of those sections of the CJA 2003 which are dealt with at 24.34 to 24.38 above. The issues involved in the enquiry are set out in the flowchart on page 420.

If, at the time that the specified offence was committed, the offender had not previously **24.40** been convicted of any specified offence, or was aged under 18, the court, in deciding on dangerousness:

(a) must take into account all such information as is available to it about the nature and circumstances of the offences; and

(b) may take into account any information which is before it about any pattern of behaviour of which the offence forms part; and

(c) may take into account any information about the offender which is before it.

The basis of the enquiry is altered if the offender was aged 18 or over at the time that the spec- **24.41** ified offence was committed, and had previously been convicted of a specified offence. In such a case, the court must assume that the offender 'poses a significant risk to the public...', unless it considers that it would be unreasonable to do so after taking into account:

(a) all the information available to it about the nature and circumstances of each of the offences; and

(b) where appropriate, any information about any pattern of behaviour of which any of the offences forms part; and

(c) any information about the offender which is before it. (CJA 2003, s 229(3)).

24.42 In *Lang* [2006] 1 WLR 2509, the Court of Appeal set out the following factors to be considered in assessing dangerousness for the purposes of imposing discretionary life sentences, imprisonment or detention for public protection, and extended sentences:

(a) The risk identified must be significant. Rose LJ stated that for a risk to be significant, it must be more than a possibility. It must be 'noteworthy, of considerable amount or importance'.

(b) Pre-sentence reports would be required to show the nature and circumstances of the current offence, the history and pattern of offending, relevant social and economic factors such as drug or alcohol abuse, and the attitudes of the offender.

(c) Significant risk must not be assumed because the foreseen specified offence was serious.

(d) If the foreseen specified offence was not serious, there would be few cases where risk of serious harm would be regarded as significant.

(e) Where the court had to presume a significant risk unless it would be unreasonable to do so (by virtue of s 229(3) CJA 2003, see 24.41), it had been accorded a discretion to conclude that there was no significant risk, i.e., the presumption was rebuttable.

(f) In any event, there was no such presumption where the offender was under 18 or had not committed a specified offence prior to that being sentenced. In such a case, the court's discretion was unfettered.

(g) With particularly young offenders, indeterminate sentences may be inappropriate for serious offences even where there was a risk of harm from further offences (see *Hollie D* [2006] Crim LR 73).

(h) The Act was intended to protect the public from serious harm and not to provide for the imposition of indeterminate sentences for minor offences.

(i) Sentencers should give their reasons for their conclusions, particularly as to whether there was a significant risk of further offences and/or serious harm, and for making (or not making) the statutory assumption in s 229(3). In *Johnson* [2007] Crim LR 177, the Court of Appeal stressed that the sentence of imprisonment for public protection was concerned with future risk rather than punishment for past offending.

I   MANDATORY MINIMUM SENTENCES

24.43 The PCC(S)A 2000 sets out mandatory minimum sentences for certain specified offences. This was something of an innovation in this jurisdiction, although their introduction had become increasingly widespread in the United States. The new sentences attracted fierce controversy, since their inevitable effect is to fetter the judge who is passing sentence, and eliminate the possibility of taking the circumstances of the offence or the offender into account, other than within the constraints of the statutory minimum. Nevertheless, such sentences are now part of the sentencing landscape, and there is no suggestion of any domestic initiative to remove them, although the impact of the European Convention on Human Rights (ECHR) in this field has not yet been fully determined.

Section 110 of the PCC(S)A 2000 applies to any person aged 18 or over who is convicted of **24.44** a Class A drug trafficking offence, and who has previously been convicted on two separate occasions of such offences. Such an offender must receive a minimum of seven years' imprisonment. There is a discretion available to the court, however. The court need not impose the minimum term if it is of the opinion that there are specific circumstances which (a) relate to any of the offences or to the offender; and (b) would make the prescribed minimum sentence unjust in all the circumstances.

Section 111 deals with repeat offences of burglary. It lays down a minimum sentence of three **24.45** years' imprisonment for the third conviction of burglary of a dwelling. The court is given the same discretion as applies to s 110.

The CJA 2003, s 287 brought into force a mandatory minimum sentence for certain serious **24.46** firearms offences. It lays down a minimum custodial sentence of five years in the case of an offender aged 18 or over, and a minimum sentence of three years for an offender aged 16 or over at the time of the commission of the offence. The offences in question are possessing or distributing certain prohibited weapons or ammunition, and possessing or distributing a firearm disguised as another object. The prescribed sentence must be imposed unless there are 'exceptional circumstances relating to the offence or to the offender which justify its not doing so'. The formula is broadly similar to those for Class A drug trafficking and domestic burglary described above. Crucially, however, the minimum sentence for firearms offences applies even to a first offence, while the other two apply only to repeat offenders. The Violent Crime Reduction Act 2006, ss 28 and 29 lay down a minimum sentence of five years for the offence of using another person to look after, hide or transport certain prohibited firearms, so as to make the firearm available to the offender for an unlawful purpose. The minimum sentence applies where the offender is aged 18 or over at the time of conviction.

A concession to the rigidity of the minimum sentence imposed by ss 110 and 111 is laid **24.47** down in s 152(3) of the CJA 2003, s 144, which allows the court to give a discount for a guilty plea by reducing the actual sentence passed to 80 per cent of the statutory minimum. Even this falls somewhat short of the recognized reduction of up to one-third for an early guilty plea (see 23.43). It does not appear, however, that the minimum sentence which must be imposed in the case of certain firearms offences is subject to any discount for a guilty plea.

J SUSPENDED SENTENCES

The court has the power to suspend certain sentences of imprisonment. This power is now set **24.48** out in CJA 2003, s 189, which came into effect on 4 April 2005 (in a modified version) and applies to offences committed on or after that date. For the position in relation to offences committed before that date, reference should be made to previous editions of this book. The power to suspend a sentence applies not only to sentences of imprisonment for those aged 21 and over, but also to those aged 18 and over who are sentenced to detention in a young offender institution.

24.49 The provisions in CJA 2003, ss 143, 152, 153, 156, and 174, relating to the passing of a cus-todial sentence (in relation to justifying its imposition, determining its length, pre-sentence reports, stating reasons etc.: see 24.08 to 24.12) apply equally to the passing of a suspended sentence (see s 189(6)). The court must, in particular, be clear that it would have passed a sen-tence of immediate imprisonment if it did not have the power to suspend.

Passing a suspended sentence

24.50 Where the Crown Court passes a sentence of imprisonment of at least 14 days but not more than 12 months, it may suspend it. In the case of the magistrates' court, the minimum period of 14 days also applies, but the maximum is 6 months. As already indicated, the power applies not only to sentences of imprisonment of the appropriate length (as it did previously) but also to sentences of detention in a young offender institution. The period of suspension (called 'the operational period') may be between six months and two years. At the same time as sus-pending the sentence, the court may order the offender to comply with one or more require-ments (see 24.51) for the duration of a period of supervision. The period of supervision must also be between six months and two years, but it must not end after the operational period.

24.51 During the 'supervision period', one or more requirements can be imposed. These are listed in s 190 of the CJA 2003 as follows:

(a)   an unpaid work requirement;
(b)   an activity requirement;
(c)   a programme requirement;
(d)   a prohibited activity requirement;
(e)   a curfew requirement;
(f)   an exclusion requirement;
(g)   a residence requirement;
(h)   a mental health requirement;
(i)   a drug rehabilitation requirement;
(j)   an alcohol treatment requirement;
(k)   a supervision requirement;
(l)   in a case where the offender is aged under 25, an attendance centre requirement.

same as
community order

24.52 Where a court imposes two or more sentences on the same occasion to be served consecu-tively, the power to suspend sentence cannot be exercised unless the *aggregate* of the terms does not exceed 12 months (6 months in the case of the magistrates): CJA 2003, s 189(2).

24.53 The operational period of a suspended sentence is the period during which commission of an offence carries with it the risk of the sentence being activated. The period runs from the date of the sentence, and is fixed by the court when it passes the sentence, within the statutory limits of not less than six months and not more than two years.

24.54 But it is not only the commission of an offence during the operational period which puts the offender at risk of the implementation of the suspended sentence. If he fails to carry out the requirement(s) imposed by the court when it made the suspended sentence order, then he will also be in breach of that order, and the suspended sentence is likely to be implemented.

24.55 For the court to make the initial decision to pass a suspended sentence order, the offence must have passed the custody threshold. In the Guideline issued by the Sentencing Guidelines

Council on *New Sentences: Criminal Justice Act 2003* (para 2.2.11), sentencers are told that the relevant steps in the decision-making process are:

(a)   Has the custody threshold been passed?
(b)   If so, is it unavoidable that a custodial sentence be imposed?
(c)   If so, can that sentence be suspended? (Sentencers should be clear that they would have imposed a custodial sentence if the power to suspend had not been available.)

The court must also decide upon the requirements which it will set to be complied with dur-   **24.56**
ing the supervision period. In the Guideline referred to above (para 2.2.14), the Sentencing Guidelines Council states that:

> Because of the very clear deterrent threat involved in a suspended sentence, requirements imposed as part of that sentence should generally be less onerous than those imposed as part of a community sentence. A court wishing to impose onerous or intensive requirements on an offender should reconsider its decision to suspend sentence and consider whether a community sentence might be more appropriate.

It has in the past been common practice for the courts to add a fine to the suspended sentence.   **24.57**
This is still permitted, as would be a compensation, restitution or similar order. However, the court may not impose a community sentence at the same time as it imposes a suspended sentence (s 189(5)), as this would create a confusing situation in the light of the imposition of requirements as an integral part of the suspended sentence itself. There is also precedent for saying that a suspended sentence should not be imposed at the same time as an immediate prison sentence, or upon an offender already serving a prison sentence (see *Sapiano* (1968) 52 Cr App R 674 and *Butters* (1971) 55 Cr App R 515 respectively). There is no reason, however, why a suspended sentence should not be imposed on the same occasion as a discharge is imposed for another offence.

When it imposes a suspended sentence, the court may order that it is subject to periodic   **24.58**
review at review hearings, and specify when those hearings are to take place. At such a hearing, the court may amend any community requirement of the suspended sentence order. However, it cannot add a requirement of a different kind or amend a drug rehabilitation requirement, or an alcohol or mental health treatment order unless the offender consents. The court may extend the supervision period as a result of the review, provided that the period remains within the statutory limits (s 192).

Breach of a suspended sentence

As has been indicated, the suspended sentence may be brought into operation if: **24.59**

(a)   the offender is convicted of a further offence (the offence in question need not itself be imprisonable);
(b)   the offender is in breach of any of the community requirements of the suspended sentence.

The procedure for dealing with either event is set out in Sch 12; para 8 of which describes the powers of the court. If it is proved to the satisfaction of the court that the offender is in breach of any of the community requirements or has been convicted of an offence committed during the operational period, it must:

(a)   order that the suspended sentence is to take effect with the original term and custodial period unaltered;

(b) order that it is to take effect with a lesser term (but not less than 28 weeks) or a shorter custodial period (but not less than 14 days); or

(c) amend the order by imposing more onerous community requirements or extending the supervision period or the operational period (but not to more than two years, nor so that the supervision period ends later than the operational period): see Sch 12, para 8(2).

24.60   In considering these options, the presumption is that the suspended prison sentence will be activated, either with its original term or a lesser term, unless the court considers that this would be unjust (Sch 12, para 8(3)). In deciding whether it would be unjust, the court should consider both the extent to which the offender has complied with the requirements, and the facts of the new offence (para 2.2.15 of the Guideline on *New Sentences: Criminal Justice Act 2003*). If the offender is near the end of the operational period and has complied with its requirements, and then commits a new offence, it may be more appropriate to amend the order than to activate it (para 2.2.19). If the new offence is less serious than the one for which the suspended sentence was passed, it may justify activating the sentence with a reduced term, or amending the terms of the order (para 2.2.20). It is expected that the activated suspended sentence will be consecutive to the sentence imposed for the new offence (2.2.21).

Powers to deal with breach of a suspended sentence

24.61   The Crown Court, when sentencing an offender who turns out to be in breach of a suspended sentence, has power to deal with the breach irrespective of whether the sentence was passed by the Crown Court or by a magistrates' court: CJA 2003, Sch 12, para 11(1). A magistrates' court has power to deal with a breach only if the suspended sentence was passed by itself or another magistrates' court. Should a summary conviction put an offender in breach of a Crown Court suspended sentence, para 11(2) places two options at the disposal of the magistrates. They may either commit the offender to the Crown Court to be dealt with for the breach, or they can decline to commit but give notice of the conviction to the Crown Court. In the latter event, the Crown Court may (but need not) issue a summons or warrant for arrest to secure the offender's attendance before it, with a view to activating the suspended sentence if it sees fit: para 12.

24.62   A committal to the Crown Court to be dealt with for breach of a suspended sentence may be in custody or on bail. At the same time as they commit for the breach, the magistrates commit the offender to be sentenced for the offence of which they have just convicted him, so that one court can deal with both matters.

24.63   If the magistrates choose merely to notify the Crown Court of the breach, they sentence the offender for the subsequent offence. By not committing him, they obviously indicate their view that the subsequent offence does not require activation of the suspended sentence, but the decision is one for the Crown Court not them. Therefore, they should not deal with the subsequent offence in a way which would make it impossible for the Crown Court to bring the suspended sentence into effect. Since a conviction which results in the offender being discharged conditionally or absolutely is deemed not to be a conviction, magistrates should not use this method when sentencing an offender in breach of a Crown Court suspended sentence: *Tarry* [1970] 2 QB 561. It is also undesirable for the magistrates to impose a community sentence for the subsequent offence, since that will render the task of the Crown Court in dealing with the suspended sentence much more difficult (*Stewart* (1984) 6 Cr App R (S) 166). If they think that a discharge, or a community sentence is appropriate they should commit the offender to the Crown Court under Sch 12, para11(1) (for breach of the suspended sentence) and under PCC(S)A 2000, s6 for the subsequent offence, and hope that the Crown Court judge will share their view of the case.

K   CUSTODY FOR OFFENDERS UNDER 21

In youth section?

At present, a sentence of imprisonment cannot be passed upon an offender who is under 21. **24.64** There are four custodial sentences which can be imposed on an offender under the age of 21, depending on his age. They are:

(a)   detention in a young offender institution;
(b)   detention under s 91 of the PCC(S)A 2000;
(c)   custody for life;
(d)   a detention and training order.

The position will change when the Criminal Justice and Court Services Act 2000, s 61, comes into force. It will abolish the sentences of detention in a young offender institution and custody for life. Young offenders who would have received such sentences will instead be sentenced to imprisonment, which will be available as a sentence for those aged 18 and over.

It will be convenient to refer to the totality of offenders under 21 by the phrase 'young **24.65** offenders', although that term is not used in legislation.

As was described at 24.08 to 24.12, there is now a statutory scheme which lays down the cri- **24.66** teria and procedure for custodial sentences generally. It applies to young offenders just as it does to adults.

In sentencing young offenders, it is necessary to know the relevant date for determining age, **24.67** so that the sentences available can be ascertained, as well as the length of any custodial sentence. In *Starkey* [1994] Crim LR 380, the offender turned 18 between being committed for sentence by the magistrates and his appearance for sentence in the Crown Court. He was 18 when the court sentenced him to one year and six weeks, and the question arose whether this sentence was lawful, the statutory maximum at that time for a juvenile of 17 being 12 months. It was held by the Court of Appeal that the relevant date was the date of conviction, when he was 17, with the result that the sentence had to be reduced to 12 months.

Sentence of detention in a young offender institution

Detention in a young offender institution is restricted to offenders aged 18, 19, and 20. As far **24.68** as juveniles are concerned, it has been replaced by the detention and training order (see 24.75 to 24.77). The term of a sentence of detention in a young offender institution may never exceed the maximum term of imprisonment that could be imposed for the offence if the offender were 21 or over. The minimum term is 21 days.

Sentences of detention under s 91 of the Powers of Criminal Courts (Sentencing) Act 2000

Where the offence is such that it merits a longer custodial sentence than that described in the **24.69** preceding Section, the court may consider a sentence under s 91. Such sentences, although not as uncommon as they used to be, remain very few in proportion to the number of juveniles sentenced for offences that theoretically could have been dealt with in that way. The qualifying conditions for a s 91 sentence are that the offender must be a person aged from 10 to 17 inclusive who is *convicted on indictment* of:

(a) an offence punishable in the case of an adult with at least 14 years' imprisonment; or

(b) an offence under ss 3, 13, 25 or 26 of the Sexual Offences Act 2003 (sexual assault and sexual offences involving children); or

(c) possessing or distributing certain prohibited weapons or ammunition contrary to s 5(1) or 5(1A) of the Firearms Act 1968 (where the offence was committed when the offender was aged 16 or over).

The court must be of the opinion that none of the other methods of dealing with the juvenile (including a detention and training order) is appropriate. The term of the sentence may be anything up to the maximum prison sentence imposable for the offence. While serving the sentence, the offender is held in accordance with the Home Secretary's directions. That will probably mean that he is kept in a young offender institution, but, depending on his age and needs, the Home Secretary might direct that he go to a mental hospital or even allow him to live in a community home. A s 91 detainee may be released at any stage of his sentence by the Home Secretary acting on a recommendation from the Parole Board. He then remains on licence for the remainder of the term passed by the court. Both the provisions about service of s 91 sentences and the release provisions mean that the sentence is much more flexible than a sentence of detention in a young offender institution. The appellate courts have issued guidance as to the cases where a sentence under s 91 should be imposed (see 11.06 to 11.15).

24.70   Note that time spent in custody (or local authority secure accommodation) on remand counts towards a sentence imposed under s 91, just as it does for other custodial sentences.

24.71   The crucial limitation on the implementation of s 91 is the fact that the subsection requires the offender to have been convicted on indictment. As explained in 11.01, youth courts tend almost automatically to proceed to the summary trial of a juvenile without considering whether he should be committed for trial so as to leave open the option of a more severe sentence than they can impose. In fixing the term of a sentence under s 91, the court must abide by the provisions of the CJA 2003, s 153 (see 24.21 to 24.23). Offence seriousness will therefore determine the length of sentence. Moreover the judge should realize that a term of, say, five years will seem like an eternity to a youngster. Therefore, it may well be proper to make the term much less than would have been appropriate in the case of an older offender convicted of a similar crime (see *Storey* [1984] Crim LR 438).

24.72   An offender convicted of murder, who was under 18 when he committed the offence, must be sentenced to be detained during Her Majesty's pleasure: PCC(S)A 2000, s 90. To all intents and purposes, the effect of the sentence is precisely the same as a sentence of detention for life under s 91. One oddity of the sentence of detention during Her Majesty's pleasure is that the relevant consideration is the offender's age when he committed the offence, not his age at the date of sentence. The reason for the apparent anomaly is that, in the days of capital punishment, the rule was that only those over 18 when they killed were liable to be hanged, and detention during Her Majesty's pleasure was made the alternative for younger murderers.

Custody for life

This is the equivalent for 18 to 20-year-olds of life imprisonment for older offenders. Section **24.73**
94 of the PCC(S)A 2000 provides that an offender who has attained the age of 18 but is not yet
21 may be sentenced to custody for life if the offence of which he has been convicted carries
life imprisonment. For murder, there is a *mandatory* sentence of custody for life if the offender
is under 21, unless he was under 18 when he committed the offence, in which case the sentence is detention during Her Majesty's pleasure (s 94). When s 61 of the Criminal Justice and
Court Services Act 2000 is brought into effect, the sentence of custody for life will be abolished
Those convicted of murder who are aged 18 and over will then be subject to the mandatory
penalty of life imprisonment.

An offender sentenced to custody for life must be detained in a young offender institution **24.74**
unless the Home Secretary directs otherwise.

Detention and training order

The detention and training order is now the standard form of custodial sentence for young **24.75**
offenders aged under 18. Its availability extends down to those as young as 10. It is a custodial sentence for the purposes of ss 152 to 156 of the CJA 2003 and the court must be satisfied
that the custody threshold has been reached before imposing such an order (see 24.08 to
24.12). In addition, in the case of an offender under the age of 15 at the time of conviction,
the court may not make a detention and training order unless it is satisfied that he is 'a persistent offender'. Further, where the offender is under the age of 12 at the time of conviction,
the court may only pass such an order if satisfied that 'only a custodial sentence would be adequate to protect the public from further offending from him'. (The power to pass a detention
and training order in respect of an offender aged 10 or 11 will in any event be dependent upon
a further order from the Secretary of State.)

As far as the length of the order is concerned, that is governed by s 101, which states that it **24.76**
shall be for 4, 6, 8, 10, 12, 18, or 24 months. It appears that any of the periods specified in s
101 can be imposed by the youth court (as well as the Crown Court), up to a maximum of 24
months: *Medway Crown Court ex parte A* (1999) *The Times*, 30 June 1999. That case concerned
a secure training order, but the Divisional Court made it clear that the same reasoning would
apply to a detention and training order.

Half of whatever period imposed is to be spent in custody, in detention and training. When **24.77**
that portion is complete, a period of supervision under the auspices of a probation officer,
social worker or member of a youth sentencing team commences, and continues until the
end of the sentence.

L 'CUSTODY PLUS'

A new scheme, which was entitled 'custody plus' in the Halliday Report (*Making* **24.78**
Punishments Work; Report of a Review of the Sentencing Framework in England and Wales, July
2001, Home Office) takes statutory form in the CJA 2003, ss 181 and 182. It had not been

introduced at the time of writing. When it is, it will replace all sentences of imprisonment under 12 months in length (with the exception of intermittent custody—see 24.81 to 24.82). It will consist of a total sentence term of between 28 and 51 weeks. That term will consist of two parts. The first part will be the custodial period, of between two and 13 weeks, in respect of any one offence. This is expected to fulfil the punitive part of the sentence. During the second part of the sentence, the offender will be released on licence under supervision in the community. This part must be at least 26 weeks in length, and aims to fulfil the reparative and crime reduction purposes of the sentence.

24.79 If the court imposes two or more consecutive terms of custody plus, the aggregate length of the sentence must not exceed 65 weeks, and the aggregate length of the custodial periods must not exceed 26 weeks.

24.80 The court will have the power to attach one or more of the following list of requirements to the sentence, in order to fulfil the aim of rehabilitating the offender:

(a) an unpaid work requirement;

(b) an activity requirement;

(c) a programme requirement;

(d) a prohibited activity requirement;

(e) a curfew requirement;

(f) an exclusion requirement;

(g) a supervision requirement; and

(h) in a case where the offender is aged under 25, an attendance centre requirement.

M   INTERMITTENT CUSTODY

24.81 The CJA 2003, ss 183 to 185, introduced a scheme of intermittent custody on a pilot basis for certain trial courts, starting in January 2004. The aim is to avoid some of the most destructive consequences of imprisonment such as the loss of home, employment, and family, by allowing the court to limit custody to the weekends, for example.

24.82 Where a court passes a sentence of imprisonment of between 28 and 51 weeks, it may impose an 'intermittent custody order'. The order will specify the total number of days the offender must spend in custody, and provide for his release on temporary periods of licence, subject to specified conditions, until the total number of days have been served. The total number of custodial days must be between 14 and 90 for any one offence. The offender must consent to serving the custodial part of his sentence intermittently. If two or more consecutive terms of intermittent custody are imposed, the aggregate length of the terms must not exceed 65 weeks, and the aggregate number of custodial days must not exceed 180. The court may attach requirements to the licence period of an intermittent custody order, which mirror those for custody plus (see 24.80).

N   RELEASE ON LICENCE

24.83 As is well known, the stated length of the sentence which an offender receives is almost invariably longer than the term which he actually has to serve. The usual position is that part of the term of imprisonment or detention is actually served in custody, with the prisoner then being released to serve the remainder of his term on licence.

The term served and the period on licence will vary according to the nature of the sentence **24.84** imposed. The main rules are set out in ss 244 to 264 CJA 2003, and may be briefly summarized as follows:

(a) Sentences of imprisonment of less than 12 months—the intention is that this length of sentence will in due course be governed by the new 'custody plus' scheme, where the court will lay down a custodial period of between 2 and 13 weeks (see 24.78). The offender will then be released on licence for the remainder of the term—up to a total of 51 weeks.

(b) Those sentenced to terms of imprisonment of less than 12 months prior to the implementation of 'custody plus' will be subject to the old rules set out in the PCC(S)A 2000, and will serve half their sentence in custody.

(c) Sentences of imprisonment for 12 months or more (other than life imprisonment, imprisonment for public protection, or extended sentences)—the offender will be released on licence after serving one-half of the sentence.

(d) Intermittent custody orders—release on licence takes place after each intermittent custody period.

(e) Persons serving consecutive or concurrent sentences—the period is that required for the longest sentence (for concurrent terms) or the aggregate of the custodial terms (for consecutive terms).

(f) Extended sentences for offences specified in Sch 15 of the CJA 2003 (see 24.34 to 24.42)—there is no automatic release until the end of the sentence. However, the Parole Board may direct release on licence at any time after the half-way point of the custodial period and prior to the expiry of the full term. There is then an extended licence period.

(g) Life imprisonment or imprisonment for public protection—the offender must serve the minimum term set by the court under the PCC(S)A 2000, s 82A. After that, he is dependent for release on the decision of the Parole Board. Again, there is an extended licence period, which in the case of life imprisonment carries on for life.

Once released on licence, the offender will be subject to conditions which, depending on the **24.85** circumstances, will be determined by the sentencing court or the Secretary of State. Breach of those conditions (including commission of a further offence) is likely to result in the offender being recalled to prison by the Secretary of State, subject to the authority of the Parole Board (CJA 2003, ss 252 and 254).

O CREDITING PERIODS OF REMAND

If the court makes a direction under the CJA 2003, s 240(3), time spent on remand in custody **24.86** is to count as time served by the prisoner as part of his sentence of imprisonment, provided that the remand was in connection with the same offence, or a related offence. The court has a discretion not to give such a direction if it is in the interests of justice not to do so. In any event, the credit for remand is not automatic, as it used to be in the past, so it is incumbent on the offender's representative to be aware of the amount of time spent on remand in custody, and to seek a direction under s 240(3). If time is credited, it will count towards the time served as part of the sentence so as to calculate whether the offender is eligible for release under licence (see 24.83 to 24.85). Time spent on remand is defined in s 242 in such a way that it does not include time spent in police detention, which is presumably seen as something incidental to the investigative process, rather than imposed by the courts. Hence, time spent in police detention will not count towards the sentence ultimately imposed. Another anomaly is that there is no entitlement to credit for time spent in custody on remand in respect of a detention and training order. When imposing such an order, the sentencer is supposed instead to take into account the length of time spent in custody on remand in determining the length of the order (the statute lays down that the order must be for two, four, six, eight, ten, 12, 18, or 24 months—see 24.76).

KEY DOCUMENTS

Powers of Criminal Courts (Sentencing) Act, 2000, as amended.
Criminal Justice Act 2003, as amended.
Guidelines on New Sentences: Criminal Justice Act 2003, produced by the Sentencing Guidelines
    Council and available at <http://www.sentencing-guidelines.gov.uk>.

25

SENTENCES OTHER THAN CUSTODY

25.01   Chapter 24 dealt with the range of custodial penalties at the court's disposal. The great majority of offenders, however, are dealt with by some means other than custody, and this Chapter is concerned with the non-custodial options.

25.02   This Chapter begins with some general points about community sentences (25.03 to 25.11), and then goes on to deal with the various community sentences in more detail, followed by financial penalties and the range of other orders which the court may make (without attempting to be exhaustive).

A COMMUNITY SENTENCES

25.03   The CJA 2003 laid down a new framework for the range of community sentences. There is now a single community sentence, which includes one or more from a list of 'requirements' at the option of the sentencing court. This unified community sentence, however, applies only in respect of offences committed on or after 4 April 2005. Further, it is limited at the time of writing to those aged 18 or over. For those aged under 18 (and for all offenders in respect of offences committed before 4 April 2005) there are various *different* community sentences.

They are dealt with from 25.12 to 25.50, and are expected to remain in force until April 2009 when the provisions for their repeal, contained in the CJA 2003, are brought into effect.

25.04 As far as the unified community sentence available in respect of offenders over 18 for offences committed on or after 4 April 2005, the requirements which a court may impose are listed in CJA 2003, s 177, and consist of the following:

(a) an unpaid work requirement. It consists of an order that the offender should perform not less than 40 and not more than 300 hours' unpaid work, which should be completed within 12 months (s 199);

(b) an activity requirement—this is a requirement that the offender must present himself to a specified person at a specified place (e.g., a community rehabilitation centre) for a stated number of days, and/or that he take part in specified activities, in each case for a stated number of days not exceeding 60 (s 201);

(c) a programme requirement—this will stipulate that the offender must take part in an accredited programme at a specified venue, for a stated number of days (e.g., an anger management course) (s 202);

(d) a prohibited activity requirement (e.g., not to attend football matches for a specified period) (s 203);

(e) a curfew requirement, i.e., that the offender stay at a particular place for certain periods of time, each being not less than 2 nor more than 12 hours in any given day (s 204)—it will normally be linked to an electronic monitoring requirement and must not last for more than six months;

(f) an exclusion requirement, which prohibits the offender from entering a particular place or area during any specified period (e.g., to stay away from a particular public house or the street where the victim lives)—it may not last longer than two years (s 205); it will also normally be linked to an electronic monitoring requirement (s 177(3));

(g) a residence requirement, that the offender will reside at a specified place for a stated period of time (s 206);

(h) a mental health treatment requirement, i.e., to undergo treatment by a doctor or psychologist (s 207)—an approved doctor must be satisfied that such a requirement is appropriate, and the offender must have given his consent;

(i) a drug rehabilitation requirement—this includes drug treatment and testing; it involves the offender agreeing to a course of treatment under the direction of a specified and suitably qualified person (ss 209–211);

(j) an alcohol treatment requirement, again subject to the offender's consent (s 212);

(k) a supervision requirement; the offender must, for the duration of the community sentence, attend appointments with the responsible officer (s 213);

(l) an attendance centre requirement—this option is only available to the court where the offender is aged under 25; where ordered, the offender must attend the centre specified for a certain number of hours between 12 and 36 (s 214).

25.05 Generally, these requirements reflect the various community orders in existence prior to the CJA 2003. Compliance with any of them can be enforced by means of electronic monitoring, which does not constitute a sentence in its own right, but can be ordered in conjunction with any of the other requirements. Where it imposes a curfew or exclusion requirement, the court must also impose an electronic monitoring requirement, unless it considers that it would be inappropriate to do so, and it may do so in the case of any of the other requirements.

Justifying community sentences

25.06   There is a threshold requirement for the imposition of a community sentence, in the same way as there is for a custodial sentence. A community sentence can only be justified on the basis of offence seriousness (CJA 2003, s 148). The court must consider the seriousness of 'the offence, or the combination of the offence and one or more offences associated with it', which is the same formulation as is contained in s 152 in relation to custody: see 23.14 to 23.21.

Objectives for community sentences

25.07   Once the court has decided that the offence (together with any associated offences) passes the community sentence threshold then CJA 2003, s 148, comes into play. It requires that the court must, in choosing the appropriate community order(s) achieve two objectives. First, the restrictions on liberty imposed by the order(s) must be 'commensurate with the seriousness of the offence'. Second, the sentence must be 'the most suitable for the offender'.

Pre-sentence reports

25.08   According to CJA 2003, s 156, a pre-sentence report is mandatory whenever a court is considering the imposition of a community sentence.

However the sentencing court may dispense with a pre-sentence report if it regards it as 'unnecessary', and the offender is aged 18 or over. For offenders under the age of 18, on the other hand, the court is required to obtain a pre-sentence report unless there is one already in existence, and it has sight of it. If there is more than one report, it should consider the most recent one.

25.09   In any event, the court is required, prior to deciding whether a community sentence is justified, and which one to impose, to 'take into account all such information about the circumstances of the offence (including any aggravating or mitigating factors) as is available to it' (this provision again mirrors that relating to custodial sentences). In carrying out this duty, the court would no doubt frequently obtain a pre-sentence report, even if it is not statutorily obliged to do so.

Consent to certain community sentences

25.10   The position now, by virtue of the CJA 2003, s 153(2), is that the consent of the offender is needed for the imposition of:

(a) mental health requirement;
(b) a drug rehabilitation requirement; or
(c) an alcohol treatment requirement.

25.11   Where the offender refuses to consent, the court may impose a custodial sentence. Its decision to do so need not be justified on the usual basis of offence seriousness, since the imposition of a custodial sentence in these circumstances constitutes an exception to the usual need to find justification on this ground (CJA 2003, s 152(3)).

B COMMUNITY REHABILITATION ORDERS

A community rehabilitation order may be imposed on an offender:　　　　　　　　**25.12**

(a)　aged 18 or over who has been convicted of an offence committed before 4 April 2005; or

(b)　aged 16 or 17 convicted of an offence either before or after that date.

Before it passes such a sentence, however, the court must be satisfied that the offence is suffi-　　**25.13**
ciently serious to pass the threshold set out in s 35(1) of the PCC(S)A 2000. This is in similar
terms to CJA 2003, s 148, so that the court:

> shall not pass a community sentence on an offender unless it is of the opinion that the offence,
> or the combination of the offence and one or more offences associated with it, was serious
> enough to warrant such a sentence.

The court may place such an offender on a community rehabilitation order for a period of　　**25.14**
between six months and three years. The effect is that the offender must accept the supervision of, and keep in touch with, his probation officer.

The purposes of a community rehabilitation order are (according to the PCC(S)A 2000, s 41):　　**25.15**

(a)　the rehabilitation of the offender, or

(b)　protecting the public from him or preventing the commission by him of further
　　offences.

Inherent in the order is a requirement that the offender submit to being supervised by a　　**25.16**
probation officer, whom he must visit at times fixed by the officer. The officer assigned
to look after him will be one of those appointed for or attached to the petty sessional area in
which he resides, and the magistrates' court for that area—which has certain responsibilities
in connection with the enforcement of the order—is known as the 'supervising court'.

There are standard conditions inserted in community rehabilitation order. They require that　　**25.17**
the offender:

(a)　be of good behaviour and lead an industrious life;

(b)　inform the probation officer immediately of any change of address or employment;

(c)　comply with the probation officer's instructions about reporting to the officer and
　　receiving visits from the officer at home.

In addition, the court may impose additional requirements, e.g., as to residence and
activities.

C COMMUNITY PUNISHMENT ORDERS

A community punishment order may be imposed on an offender:　　　　　　　　**25.18**

(a)　aged 18 or over who has been convicted of an offence committed before 4 April 2005; or

(b)　aged 16 or 17 convicted of an offence either before or after that date.

Before passing such an order, the court must be satisfied that the offence passes the threshold set out in s 35(1) of the PCC(S)A 2000 (see 25.13 above).

25.19 In the case of such an offender, the court may make a community punishment order, i.e., an order that he perform, without pay, work of value to the community. The order fixes the number of hours to be worked within a minimum of 40 and a maximum of 240 hours.

25.20 For a court to have power to make a community punishment order, certain additional conditions must be satisfied:

(a) the offender must have been convicted of an imprisonable offence;

(b) he must have attained the age of 16;

(c) the court must be satisfied, in the light of a probation officer's or social worker's report, that the offender is a suitable person for a community punishment order;

(d) the court must be satisfied that arrangements can be made for him to perform the work ordered in the petty sessions area in which he resides;

(e) the court must obtain and consider a pre-sentence report before imposing such an order, subject to the qualifications set out in 25.08.

Subject to not going outside the statutory limits of 40–240 hours, the court has total discretion in fixing the hours of service to be performed. The work is performed under the instructions of a probation officer for the area in which the offender resides. Normally, it should be completed within 12 months at times which do not clash with the offender's school or working hours.

25.21 A court dealing with an offender for two or more offences may make a community punishment order in respect of each offence. It may further order that the hours specified in each order be worked concurrently with or consecutively to each other, but in the latter case the aggregate number of hours must not exceed 240 (s 46(8)).

25.22 The attraction of a community punishment order as a 'last resort' alternative to custody is that it genuinely punishes the offender in that he loses his leisure time doing work for which he is not paid. On the other hand, if he cooperates in doing the work, the contact with those running the scheme can be genuinely constructive and rewarding. Certainly, the sentence is said to be successful in the sense that most offenders do the work they are ordered to do and do not have to come back before the court to be fined or even sentenced for the original offence.

D   COMMUNITY PUNISHMENT AND REHABILITATION ORDERS

25.23 In effect, this order is a mixture of the community rehabilitation and community punishment orders. It may be imposed on an offender:

(a) aged 18 or over who has been convicted of an offence committed before 4 April 2005; or

(b) aged 16 or 17 and convicted of an offence either before or after that date.

25.24 The community rehabilitation element in the combination must be for a minimum of 12 months (whereas the usual minimum is 6 months). The maximum is three years. As far as the community punishment element is concerned, that must be for between 40 and 100 hours (compare the usual maximum of 240 hours). Other points worth bearing in mind about such orders are:

(a) The court must obtain and consider a pre-sentence report before imposing such an order (PCC(S)A 2000, s 36(4)) subject to the qualifications set out at 25.08.
(b) The offender must be over the age of 16.
(c) The offence must be punishable with imprisonment.
(d) The court must be satisfied, before making the order, that it is desirable in the interests of securing the offender's rehabilitation, or protecting the public from harm from him or preventing the commission by him of further offences (as for a community rehabilitation order: see 25.15).
(e) The court can insert any of the additional requirements which it could have inserted into a community rehabilitation order, provided that they do not prevent the fulfilment of the community punishment element of the order.
(f) The community punishment element must be completed within 12 months of the making of the order.

A community rehabilitation order and a community punishment order cannot be imposed on the same occasion, even for separate offences, except in the form of a community punishment and rehabilitation order (s 35(2) of the PCC(S)A 2000).

E   CURFEW ORDERS

A curfew order may be imposed on an offender: **25.25**

(a) aged 18 or over who has been convicted of an offence committed before 4 April 2005; or
(b) aged 16 or 17 and convicted of an offence either before or after that date.

It requires the offender to remain at a particular place (e.g., at home) for between 2 and 12 hours on any days, over a period which must not exceed six months from the date when the order is made. In the White Paper *Crime, Justice and Protecting the Public* (Cm 965) (London: HMSO, 1990), the government stated that:

> Curfews could be helpful in reducing some forms of crime, thefts of and from cars, pub brawls and other types of disorder. A curfew order could be used to keep people away from particular places, such as shopping centres or pubs, or to keep them at home in the evenings or at weekends.

As the White Paper pointed out, the imposition of a curfew order would not prevent **25.26** the offender from working, attending a training course or a probation centre, or receiving treatment for, say, drug abuse.

Provided that it is within the limits indicated above, the curfew order may specify different **25.27** places or periods of curfew in respect of different days. The order must name the person who is to be responsible for monitoring the offender's whereabouts during curfew periods. A pre-sentence report must be obtained and considered before a curfew order is imposed (subject to the qualifications set out at 25.08). The court must have information about the place to which the offender is to be restricted, including information about the attitude of any persons likely to be affected by his enforced presence there (s 12(6)).

25.28 A curfew order may include requirements for electronic monitoring, so as to keep a check upon the offender's whereabouts during the curfew (s 13). Such a requirement can only be imposed where an electronic monitoring scheme is in operation in the area in question.

F   BREACH, REVOCATION, AND AMENDMENT OF COMMUNITY SENTENCES

25.29 There are two different schemes for the enforcement of community sentences, depending on whether the sentence in question was imposed

(a) under the CJA 2003; or

(b) under the provisions which pre-dated the 2003 Act.

25.30 Sentences under the CJA 2003 are those imposed on offenders aged 18 or over, in respect of offences committed on or after 4 April 2005. The procedure where there is a breach of such a sentence (i.e., a failure to comply with its terms rather than the commission of a further offence) is set out in CJA 2003, Sch 8, and can be summarized as follows:

(a) If the responsible officer decides that an offender has failed without reasonable excuse to comply with any of the requirements of the community order, he must warn the offender that another failure in the next 12 months will mean that he is brought back to court.

(b) If there is a further such failure within the next 12 months, the officer lays an information before the court.

(c) If the court in question is the magistrates' court and it decides that the offender has failed to comply with any of the requirements of the community order without reasonable excuse, then it must deal with him in one of the following ways:

(i) by amending the terms of the community order so as to impose more onerous conditions;

(ii) where the order was made by a magistrates' court, by revoking the order and dealing with him in any way in which the court could have dealt with him if he had just been convicted;

(iii) where the community order was made by a magistrates' court in respect of an offence not punishable with imprisonment, and the offender is aged 18 or over, and has wilfully and persistently failed to comply with the order, it may revoke it and impose a custodial term of up to 51 weeks;

(iv) where the order was made by the Crown Court, the magistrates may commit the offender to the Crown Court.

(d) Where the Crown Court decides that a community order has been breached without reasonable excuse, it must deal with the offender in one of the following ways:

(i) by amending the terms of the order so as to impose more onerous requirements;

(ii) by revoking the order and dealing with him in any way in which he could have been dealt with for that offence by the court which made the order;

(iii) where the offence in respect of which the order was made was not imprisonable, and the offender has wilfully and persistently failed to comply with the order's terms, it may revoke the order and impose a custodial term of up to 51 weeks.

(e) Whichever court deals with the offender, it must take into account the extent to which he has complied with the requirements of the community order. For example, if he has performed 50 hours of an unpaid work requirement, then the new sentence must give him credit for that.

The position in relation to breach of those community sentences which predate the CJA 2003   **25.31**
is somewhat different.

The breach of community rehabilitation orders, community punishment orders, curfew orders, exclusion orders, drug treatment and testing orders, and community rehabilitation and punishment orders is dealt with in Sch 3 to the PCC(S)A 2000 (for the position in relation to supervision and attendance centre orders, see 25.38 to 25.41 and 25.42 to 25.48).

If there has been a breach of one of these orders (i.e., a failure to comply with the terms of the   **25.32**
order rather than the commission of a further offence) the offender is brought before the magistrates' court for the area. The question which the court must then consider is: has he failed without reasonable excuse to comply with the requirements of the order? If he has, then the magistrates can adopt one of the following courses of action:

(a) Impose a fine up to a maximum of £1,000.
(b) Impose a community punishment order up to a maximum of 60 hours.
(c) If the offender is in breach of a community rehabilitation order, make an attendance centre order.
(d) If the original order was imposed by the Crown Court, commit him to the Crown Court in custody or on bail.
(e) If the original order was imposed by a magistrates' court, revoke the order and deal with him in respect of the original offence, in any way in which they could deal with him if he had just been convicted by them.

If the decision which the magistrates make is (a), (b) or (c), then the order may continue in   **25.33**
force. If the course decided upon is (d), then the fate of the original order awaits the Crown Court's disposition. If the option which the magistrates choose is (e), then the order ceases to have effect, and the court re-sentences. In doing so, it must take into effect the extent that the offender has complied with the original order.

Assume, on the other hand, that the magistrates decide upon option (d). In that case, the   **25.34**
matter will in due course come before the Crown Court. The Crown Court can for its part decide on any of the options (a) to (c). Alternatively, it, too, may revoke the order and deal with the offender in any manner in which the Crown Court could deal with him if he had just been convicted by it of the offence.

Whether the community sentence was imposed under the CJA 2003, or the earlier legislation,   **25.35**
revocation is to be distinguished from breach. A community order may be revoked because it has been breached (as in (e) above). More generally, however, the court may revoke the order if it is in the interests of justice to do so. This may be either a simple revocation (e.g., because of the offender's good progress) or revocation coupled with re-sentencing for the original offence. The commission of a further offence would be likely, but not certain, to trigger off revocation and re-sentencing in this way.

If they do revoke and re-sentence, the court must again give credit to the offender for the extent   **25.36**
to which he has complied with the original order. If that order was made by the Crown Court, the magistrates should commit any offender who falls to be re-sentenced to the Crown Court.

25.37 Any of the community sentences can be amended. This might be done to take account of a change in the offender's circumstances, e.g., his area of residence, the success of treatment, ill-health.

G   SUPERVISION ORDERS

25.38 The Crown Court or a youth court, when dealing with a young person aged under 18 for an offence, may make a supervision order (PCC(S)A 2000, s 63). There is power to make a supervision order even if the offence concerned is non-imprisonable. Subject to earlier discharge, the order lasts for three years or such shorter period as the court may specify (s 63(7)). The supervisor is designated in the order, and is usually the local authority in whose area the offender resides, although it may be a probation officer (s 63). It is the duty of the supervisor to 'advise, assist and befriend' the supervisee (s 64). Where the local authority is the supervisor it discharges that duty through social workers. The order may contain appropriate provisions to help the supervisor carry out his functions. In addition, the court may include in a supervision order one or more of a wide range of requirements.

25.39 Supervision orders are clearly comparable to community rehabilitation orders, although they are applicable to a younger age group (the supervision order being available for an offender under 18, the community rehabilitation order if he is over 16).

25.40 The sanctions for breach of a supervision order are:

(a) payment of a fine not exceeding £1,000;

(b) a curfew order;

(c) an attendance centre order;

(d) if the supervision order was made by a relevant court, it may discharge the order and deal with the offender, for the offence in respect of which the order was made, in any manner in which he could have been dealt with for that offence by the court which made the order if the order had not been made;

(e) if the supervision order was made by the Crown Court, the relevant court may commit the offender in custody or release him on bail to appear before the Crown Court.

25.41 It is primarily the supervisor's responsibility to apply to the court for the discharge or variation of an order or its replacement by a care order, although the supervisee also has the right to apply. Enforcement of a supervision order by bringing any breach of requirement to the court's attention is entirely a matter for the supervisor. The court to which application must be made is a youth court in the case of a supervisee who is under 18 and an adult magistrates' court in other cases.

H   ATTENDANCE CENTRE ORDERS

25.42 Attendance centre orders can be imposed:

(a) on an offender aged under 18 irrespective of the date when the offence was committed;

(b) on an offender aged 18 to 20 inclusive in respect of an offence committed before 4 April 2005.

Magistrates' courts have been able to make attendance centre orders since 1948. The present **25.43** legislation on the subject is contained in ss 60 and 62 of the PCC(S)A 2000. Section 62(2) defines an attendance centre as a place where offenders under 21 'may be required to attend and be given under supervision appropriate occupation or instruction'. Most centres open on Saturday afternoons, and are run by police officers in their spare time at premises such as schools or youth clubs. Typically, an offender might be required to attend at a centre for six two-hour sessions, during which he will be kept under firm discipline and will engage in activities such as physical training and handicrafts. The aim is not only to punish an offender by depriving him of his leisure time, but also to encourage him to use his leisure more con- structively once it is restored to him. Most attendance centres are for boys under 17, but in recent years efforts have been made to provide more centres for males aged 17 to 20 and girls.

A court dealing with an offender under the age of 21 for an imprisonable offence may make **25.44** an attendance centre order provided that the court has been notified that there is a suitable centre available for him to attend. This constitutes a significant restriction on the making of attendance centre orders because the centre to be attended, which must be specified in the order, should be reasonably accessible to the offender, and there may not be a centre for persons of his or her age and sex near where he or she lives.

Attendance centre orders are equally at the disposal of the Crown Court, youth court and **25.45** adult magistrates' court, save that the last-mentioned may not make an order in respect of a juvenile.

The number of hours for which the offender must attend is fixed in the order. It must be at **25.46** least 12, save that in the case of a child under 14 the court may order less if 12 hours' attendance would be excessive (s 60(3)). It must not be more than 12 unless, in all the circumstances, the court thinks that 12 hours is inadequate, in which case the maximum is 24 hours. Failure to attend in accordance with an order may result in its being revoked and the offender being dealt with for the offence in respect of which it was made in any way the court which made it could have dealt with him (Sch 5). The same applies if the offender attends the centre but misbehaves. In dealing with the offender for the original offence, the court must take into account the extent to which he has complied with the attendance centre order.

As an alternative to discharging the attendance centre order, the court can decide that the **25.47** order should continue, but impose a fine not exceeding £1,000.

Attendance centre orders may be made not only when sentencing for an offence but also **25.48** when dealing with a young person for default in paying a fine or breach of requirements in a supervision order (see PCC(S)A 2000, s 60(1)(b) and Sch 7, para 4).

I DRUG TREATMENT AND TESTING ORDERS

A court dealing with an offender aged 16 or over can impose a drug treatment and testing **25.49** order (PCC(S)A 2000, ss 52 to 55). Before making a drug treatment and testing order, the court must be satisfied that the offender is dependent on, or has a propensity to misuse drugs, and that the dependency requires and may be susceptible to treatment. As is implied by the name, the order has elements of treatment (to eliminate the dependency or propensity) and testing (to ascertain whether the offender has any drugs in his body). There is provision for review of the offender's progress at monthly intervals, and the order as a whole must last for a period of between six months and three years. It is a community sentence, and is subject to the general provisions relating to such sentences, e.g., as to the threshold for imposition, penalties for breach (see 25.06 and 25.21 to 25.37).

J   ACTION PLAN ORDER

25.50 This is a community sentence, and is subject to the general provisions for such sentences set out at 25.03 to 25.11. It is available in the case of an offender under the age of 18 at the time of conviction by the youth court or the Crown Court. It requires him to comply for a period of three months with an action plan which lays down certain requirements about his actions and whereabouts. For the period of the order, the offender is put under the supervision of a probation officer. The order is dealt within ss 69 to 71, PCC(S)A 2000. The court is able to include a drug treatment and testing requirement into an action plan order, in certain pilot areas.

K   REPARATION ORDER

25.51 A reparation order requires an offender aged under 18 to make reparation to the victim or someone 'otherwise affected' by the offence. It is not a community sentence, and is not subject to the general provisions relating to such sentences, e.g., as to threshold. The reparations in question consist of a certain amount of work up to a maximum of 24 hours (for details, see PCC(S)A 2000, ss 73 and 74).

L   ORDERS AFFECTING PARENTS

25.52 The Crown Court and the youth court have the power to impose a parenting order upon the parent or guardian of a juvenile offender where he has been convicted of any offence. The order may be for a period up to 12 months, and may impose certain requirements upon the parent in question during that period, e.g., to ensure that the child is accompanied to and from school each day, and is kept within the home from a certain hour each evening. In any event, the order must include a requirement that the parent attends specified counselling or guidance sessions. This order was introduced by ss 8 to 10 of the Crime and Disorder Act 1998.

Further, a court dealing with a young person for an offence may order his parent or guardian to enter into a recognizance to take proper care of him and exercise proper control over him (PCC(S)A 2000, s 150). Such a binding-over order may be made by the Crown Court, adult magistrates' court, or youth court. The court is under a duty to make such an order in the case of the parents of a young offender who is under 16, if it is satisfied that it is desirable in order to prevent further offences by the young offender. If the court is not so satisfied, it should state its reasons in open court. The offence concerned need not be imprisonable. Further, whenever the court has passed a community order in respect of an offender under the age of 16, it may include in the recognizance a provision that the offender's parent or guardian must ensure that the offender complies with the requirements of the sentence. The effect of an order is that the parent or guardian has to undertake to take care of and exercise control over the juvenile, upon pain of forfeiting a certain sum of money should he fail to do so. The sum to be forfeited and the period for which the undertaking is to last are fixed by the court within maxima of £1,000 and three years respectively. Of course, no money is handed to the court when the undertaking is entered into—the liability to pay only arises should the undertaking be breached.

M FINES

The fine is by far the commonest penalty imposed for summary offences. In addition, it is also **25.53** the most frequent penalty for offences which are triable either way. The Sections which follow deal first with the maximum fines which can be imposed by the different courts in respect of different offences and offenders (25.55 to 25.57); then with the way in which the court should decide how much to fine an individual offender (25.58 to 25.60); then the practicalities of recovering fines are described, including imprisonment in default (25.61 to 25.66); and finally, the question of combining a fine with another form of penalty is considered (25.67).

From the point of view of the offender, fines are not the only financial orders which may be **25.54** imposed. An order to pay compensation to the victim, or an order for restitution, confiscation or forfeiture will have similar effects (see 25.96 to 25.111).

Maximum fines

There is no statutory limit on the size of the fine which the Crown Court may impose on an **25.55** offender who has been convicted on indictment or committed for sentence under s 3 of the PCC(S)A 2000. Following summary conviction for an offence triable either way, the magistrates may, generally speaking, impose a fine of up to £5,000 (see 12.02 to 12.05 for further details). For summary offences, the maximum fines imposable are fixed by reference to a *standard scale of fines*. The vast majority of summary offences have been classified as either a level 1 offence, or a level 2 offence, and so on up to level 5. For each level, the standard scale specifies the maximum fine which the magistrates may order the offender to pay.

The relevant maxima are set out below. **25.56**

Level on the scale	Amount of fine
1	£200
2	£500
3	£1,000
4	£2,500
5	£5,000

At present the highest sum on the standard scale corresponds with the 'prescribed sum' (i.e., the maximum fine, again variable by the Home Secretary, which can be imposed by the magistrates following conviction for an either-way offence listed in Sch 1 to the Magistrates' Courts Act 1980). There is no reason why the prescribed sum should always be the same as the sum at level 5 on the standard scale. However, if Parliament wishes a maximum fine imposable on summary conviction (either for a summary offence or for an either-way offence not listed in Sch 1) to be the same as whatever the prescribed sum shall from time to time be, it simply provides that the fine shall not exceed the '*statutory maximum*'.

25.57 Where an offender under the age of 18 is fined in the magistrates' or youth court, the maximum is £1,000. The limit for those under 14 is £250. There is no statutory limit on the fine which the Crown Court may impose upon a juvenile.

Determining the size of a fine

25.58 The court needs to take a series of steps in deciding the size of the fine to impose. The first step is to determine what fine would reflect the seriousness of the offence (PCC(S)A 2000, s 128), including any aggravating or mitigating factors which relate to the offence itself. Secondly, any mitigation personal to the offender should be taken into account (s 158). Then the court should turn to the financial circumstances of the offender, and make any appropriate adjustments (s 128(3)). This must be done whether it increases or reduces the amount of the fine (s 128(4)).

25.59 In the Magistrates' Association's *Sentencing Guidelines* (2005), guideline fines are set out in relation to some of the common offences which are likely to be dealt with by way of fine. The decision-making sequence suggested in the *Sentencing Guidelines* is as follows. Magistrates are advised to consider first the seriousness of the offence, then to look at aggravating and mitigating factors, and mitigation appropriate to the offender. They are told to consider their sentence at that stage, and compare it with the suggested guidelines. They should reconsider their reasons carefully if they have chosen a sentence at a different level. A discount should be considered for a timely guilty plea. They should then decide their sentence. The Guidelines set out indicative fines, based upon weekly income net of tax and national insurance, and taking into account other relevant outgoings. There are three levels of guideline fine, A, B, and C, which represent one half of weekly income, weekly income, and one and a half times weekly income respectively. For example, the guideline fine for evasion of payment of a TV licence is level A, for careless driving it is level B, and for failing to stop and report an accident it is level C.

25.60 Although the *Sentencing Guidelines* apply to the magistrates' court, the essentials of the decision-making process are the same in the Crown Court.

Time to pay

25.61 A court imposing a fine is usually under a duty to give the offender time to pay. Even when it is not under a duty to do so, the court always has a discretion to allow time. The only occasions on which a court may refuse an offender time to pay are when:

(a) the offence is imprisonable, and he appears to have the money to pay forthwith; or

(b) he is of no fixed abode or is likely to leave the United Kingdom; or

(c) he is already serving a custodial sentence, or is given a custodial sentence by the court at the same time as it imposes the fine (Magistrates' Courts Act 1980, s 82).

The court may order the offender to be searched, so that money found on him can be used to pay the fine (PCC(S)A 2000, s 80(1)). When a court grants time to pay it either fixes a period within which the entire sum must be paid, or it orders that the sum be paid by fixed instalments. In *Olliver* (1989) 11 Cr App R (S) 10 the Court of Appeal said that a period of two years would seldom be too long, and three years might be acceptable in an appropriate case. The Magistrates' Association *Sentencing Guidelines* (2005) state, however, that 'The fine is payable in full on the day and the defendant should always be asked for immediate payment. If periodic payments are allowed, the fine should normally be payable within a maximum of 12 months.'

If the court refuses time to pay, and the offender does not produce the money forthwith, he may **25.62** be committed to prison until either he does pay or he has served the term in default (subject to the points made in 25.64). Part-payment results in a proportionate reduction of the term (see 25.65 to 25.66). If time to pay is granted, enforcement is the responsibility of a magistrates' court. Where the fine was imposed by the Crown Court, the enforcing magistrates' court is either named in the fine order or is the court which committed the offender for trial or sentence; where the fine was imposed by a magistrates' court, that court is the enforcing court; in either case, the initial enforcing court can transfer its responsibilities to the court for the area in which the offender resides. If the offender realizes that he will have difficulty in paying, he may apply to the enforcing court for more time to pay. Should he fail to pay (either within the time originally ordered or within any extension of time he may have obtained), the enforcing court summons him to appear before a *means inquiry* and orders him, for purposes of that inquiry, to provide a statement of his means. Following the inquiry, the magistrates may, if changes in circumstances since the fine was imposed make it just to do so, remit part or all of the fine. If the fine was imposed by the Crown Court, they need that court's consent. Where, on the other hand, the magistrates consider that the defaulter is to blame for his failure to pay by reason of 'wilful refusal or culpable neglect' and that other methods of enforcement would not work, they may issue a warrant committing him to prison for, in the case of a Crown Court fine, the term in default fixed by the Crown Court judge, or, in the case of a magistrates' court fine, a term not exceeding the maximum allowed by Sch 4 to the Magistrates' Courts Act 1980 for the size of the fine in question. If part-payment has already been made, the term fixed by the Crown Court judge or maximum term allowed by Sch 4 is reduced proportionately. As an alternative to sending the defaulter to prison forthwith, the magistrates may suspend issue of the warrant upon condition that he comply with stated terms as to payment. If he subsequently fails to comply, the warrant may be issued and the defaulter consequently committed to prison without a further court hearing.

The law on enforcement of fines is contained in the Magistrates' Courts Act 1980, ss 75 to 91 **25.63** and the Powers of Criminal Courts Act 1973, s 32.

Before committing the defaulter to prison, the magistrates must consider alternative means **25.64** of payment. These can be summarized as follows:

(a) imposing a money payment supervision order;

(b) in respect of those under 25, imposing an attendance centre order;

(c)   requesting the Department of Work and Pensions to make payments direct from the offender's benefit;

(d)   making an attachment of earnings order, requiring the offender's employer to pay sums from wages direct to the court;

(e)   issuing a distress warrant authorizing bailiffs to seize the offender's belongings;

(f)   issuing a warrant of overnight detention.

Imprisonment in default

25.65   At the same time as it imposes a fine, the Crown Court must fix a term of imprisonment to be served in default of payment. The maximum terms which may be fixed in default are prescribed by a table contained in PCC(S)A 2000, s 139(4). At the bottom end of the scale, the term in default for a fine of £200 or less must not exceed seven days; at the very top of the scale, the term for a fine exceeding £1 million (!) must not exceed ten years. Needless to say, fines of the latter amount are very rare indeed. In *Szrajber* [1994] Crim LR 543, it was made clear that the default term in relation to each band of fines was a *maximum*. In fixing the period to be served in default, the court had a discretion and would normally decide on a term between the maximum for the band applicable and the maximum of the band below, in line with the circumstances of the case.

25.66   When a magistrates' court fines an offender, it has no power to fix a term in default unless the circumstances are such that it need not grant time to pay (Magistrates' Courts Act 1980, s 82(2)). As explained above, it is only in exceptional cases that time to pay can be refused. If, however, the court *could* order immediate payment, it may fix a default term whether or not it in fact grants time. A table in Sch 4 to the Magistrates' Courts Act 1980 prescribes the maximum terms that may be fixed.

Combining a fine with another penalty

25.67   It is possible for the courts to combine a financial penalty with any of the community sentences. In addition, the courts continue to be able to combine a fine or compensation order with a custodial sentence, whether immediate or suspended, provided that the custodial sentence is justified by the seriousness of the offence, and proper regard is had to the offender's means of fixing the fine. A hospital order cannot be combined with a fine (Mental Health Act 1983, s 37(8)). A fine cannot be imposed at the same time as a discharge when sentencing for a single offence: *McClelland* [1951] 1 All ER 557.

N   CONDITIONAL AND ABSOLUTE DISCHARGES

25.68   When a court dealing with an offender for an offence considers that it is inexpedient to inflict punishment it may make an order discharging him either absolutely or on condition that, during a period specified in the order, he commits no offence. The specified period runs from the date of the order, and must not exceed three years. The law relating to discharges is contained in ss 12 to 15 of the PCC(S)A 2000.

A court may discharge an offender whatever his age and whatever offence he has been **25.69** convicted of (provided, of course, the sentence is not fixed by law). A discharge for an offence may be combined with an ancillary order, but not with any other sentence, although if an offender is dealt with for more than one offence he may be discharged for one and otherwise dealt with for the remainder. It is, in fact, quite common for an offender to be given a substantial sentence for the most serious offence of which he has been convicted, and to be conditionally discharged for other less serious ones.

An absolute discharge has no adverse effects at all on the offender—it is a complete 'let-off'. **25.70** Thus, it is appropriate in those cases where the offender is technically guilty of an offence, but no blame whatsoever attaches to him. If an offender is conditionally discharged, and does not commit an offence during the period of the discharge, he is never sentenced for the offence for which he was discharged (the 'original offence'). Where an offence is committed while subject to a conditional discharge, the offender may be sentenced for the original offence as well as for the subsequent offence (in which case the discharge ceases to have effect), or the courts may choose not to sentence him for the original offence (in which case he will still be subject to the discharge). When making a conditional discharge, the court should explain its effect to the offender.

A conditional discharge has something in common with a suspended sentence in that, if the **25.71** offender does not commit an offence during the period of the discharge, no actual penalty is inflicted on him, just as an offender who avoids committing an imprisonable offence during the operational period of a suspended sentence never serves the term of imprisonment. However, the two ways of dealing with offenders are markedly different in other respects. In particular, a court dealing with an offender for breach of a suspended sentence cannot itself choose how to sentence him for the offence for which he was given the sentence—essentially, the court either does or does not activate the sentence of imprisonment which the court on the previous occasion saw fit to suspend. On the other hand, conviction for an offence committed during a conditional discharge entitles the appropriate court to sentence the offender for the original offence as if he had just been convicted of it, and so the court has a full range of sentencing options at its disposal. Also, breach of a suspended sentence normally results in the term of imprisonment being brought into effect, whereas it is commonplace for the courts to overlook a breach of conditional discharge in the sense that the offender is merely sentenced for the subsequent offence with the conditional discharge being allowed to continue in force.

O BINDING OVER

Two other methods of dealing with offenders—namely binding over to keep the peace and **25.72** binding over to come up for judgment—may conveniently be described at this point.

First, if there is material before a court leading it to fear that, unless steps are taken to prevent **25.73** it, there might be a breach of the peace, it may order a person to be bound over to keep the peace and be of good behaviour. The person concerned must then enter into an undertaking (or recognizance) that he will keep the peace for a certain period upon pain of forfeiting a certain sum of money if he fails to do so. Both the period and the sum are fixed by the court when it orders the bind-over. If the person refuses to enter into the undertaking, he can be sent to prison for contempt of court. If he enters into the undertaking and breaks it, e.g., by committing an offence such as common assault during the relevant period, the court which bound him over can order him to forfeit part or all of the sum specified. Binding over is essentially a measure of preventive justice, designed to avoid future breaches of the peace. It is not appropriate where an offender has been convicted of an offence such as theft, repetition of which is most unlikely to involve violence or public disturbance. It is appropriate—and common—in cases of petty violence, especially in disputes between neighbours where Smith alleges that he was assaulted by Jones and Jones alleges that he was assaulted by Smith, and the magistrates metaphorically knock their heads together by ordering that they both be bound over to keep the peace for a year. A bind-over may be ordered in addition to another penalty for an offence, or instead of any other penalty, or even where the person concerned has not been convicted of an offence. Thus, in the example of Smith and Jones, the magistrates could acquit either or both of them and still order them both to be bound over. Another common occurrence is for an accused charged with a minor public order offence (e.g., threatening behaviour likely to cause alarm, harassment or distress) to plead not guilty but agree to be bound over on the prosecution undertaking to offer no evidence against him. Again, the bind-over will specify a sum of money to be forfeited in the event of breach. Even where a person appears before a court solely in the capacity of a witness (e.g., a hunt saboteur allegedly assaulted by a member of the hunt), a bind-over is possible. The power of magistrates to bind a person over to keep the peace is contained in the Magistrates' Courts Act 1980, s 115 and the Justices of the Peace Act 1361. The power of the Crown Court to do so is confirmed by the Justices of the Peace Act 1968, s 1(7).

25.74   Secondly, provided he consents, the Crown Court (but not a magistrates' court) has power at common law to bind an offender over to come up for judgment—i.e., he is released without being sentenced but enters into an undertaking that he will appear before the court to be sentenced on a certain day or on a day to be notified to him, upon pain of forfeiting a specified sum of money if he fails to do so. If the court merely wishes to adjourn before sentencing an offender, it is much more convenient to remand him on bail rather than binding him over. Similarly, if the court wants to defer sentence there is power to do so under s 1 of the PCC(S)A 2000 (see 22.69 to 22.74). The real value of a bind-over to come up for judgment lies in the conditions which may be attached to it, and often the hope is that, if the offender abides by these conditions there will be no need to sentence him at all.

25.75   In *Hashman v UK* [2000] Crim LR 185, the European Court of Human Rights dealt with a complaint by two applicants who disturbed a fox hunt by blowing a horn and shouting at the hounds. They were bound over to keep the peace and be of good behaviour. On appeal to the Crown Court, it was decided that there had been no breach of the peace, but they were nevertheless bound over to be of good behaviour for a year. The European Court found that there had been a violation of Art 10 of the ECHR, which guarantees freedom of expression. The non-violent protest conducted by the applicants was an exercise of their right to freedom of expression. It would be legitimate to restrict this right if Art 10(2) applied, but that paragraph requires any interference with freedom of expression to be 'prescribed by law'. The law that is relied upon must be 'certain' in the sense that it must be 'formulated with sufficient precision to enable the citizen to regulate his conduct'. The phrase 'to be of good behaviour' (which English law defines as 'behaviour which is wrong rather than right in the judgment of the majority of contemporary fellow citizens') was too imprecise, and did not give the applicants sufficiently clear guidance on how they should behave in future. It appears, therefore, that the bindover 'to be of good behaviour' is contary to the Convention, unless the good behaviour in question is defined with some particularity. The decision does not, however, affect the power to bind over to keep the peace.

P ENDORSEMENT AND DISQUALIFICATION FROM DRIVING

Most road traffic offences are endorsable, i.e., in the absence of special reasons for not doing **25.76** so, the court must order that particulars of a conviction for the offence be endorsed on the offender's driving licence. Unless the offender is disqualified from driving on the occasion when endorsement is ordered, the number of penalty points appropriate to the offence are also endorsed on the licence. Drink/driving offences and causing death by dangerous driving carry obligatory disqualification from driving for a period of at least a year (two years in the latter case) unless there are special reasons for not disqualifying (or for disqualifying for less than a year). Other endorsable offences carry disqualification at the discretion of the court. If the offender has been convicted of an endorsable offence, and the penalty points for that offence added to any other points endorsed on the licence total 12 or more, then—provided the offences concerned were all committed within a three year period—he must be disqualified for at least six months unless, having regard to all the circumstances, the court thinks fit not to disqualify him (or to disqualify him for less than six months).

The law on endorsement and disqualification is detailed and in parts complex, so within the **25.77** scope of this book it is only possible to summarize the relevant provisions. Of greatest importance are ss 34 and 35 of the Road Traffic Offenders Act 1988 and Sch 2 to that Act. Further details can be found in Sections C7 and C8 of *Blackstone's Criminal Practice 2008*. The Road Safety Act 2006 introduced 'driving records' maintained by the Secretary of State. The driving record will be endorsed with particulars of any offences committed by the person whose record it is. The new system is due to be implemented in two stages. Initially, the driving records will be created only in respect of foreign and unlicensed drivers. The second stage will involve driving records for all drivers, including those from Great Britain. Neither set of provisions had been brought into effect by the time of writing.

Endorsement of an offender's driving licence

Offences carrying endorsement are listed in Sch 2 to the Road Traffic Offenders Act 1988. **25.78** There are over 30 of them, but by no means all offences connected with motor vehicles are endorsable. For example, failing to stop one's vehicle when required by a police constable to do so, not having an MOT test certificate and most offences connected with the condition of one's vehicle are non-endorsable. Each endorsable offence carries a certain number of penalty points, the number being prescribed by Sch 2 to the Road Traffic Offenders Act

1988. Below is a table setting out the commonest endorsable offences and their penalty points:

Offence	Statute creating the offence	Penalty points
Driving when unfit through drink or drugs	RTA 1988, s 4(1)	3–11
Driving with excess alcohol in the breath, blood or urine	RTA 1988, s 5(1)(a)	3–11
Being in charge of motor vehicle when unfit or with excess alcohol	RTA 1988, s 4(2) and 5(1)(b)	10
Causing death by dangerous driving	RTA 1988, s 1	3–11
Dangerous driving	RTA 1988, s 2	3–11
Careless driving	RTA 1988, s 3	3–9
Failing to stop after accident or give particulars or report an accident	RTA 1988, s 170	5–10
Speeding	Road Traffic Regulation Act 1984, s 89	3–6
Disobeying traffic lights	RTA 1988, s 36	3
Driving while disqualified	RTA 1988, s 103(1)(b)	6
Using uninsured motor vehicle	RTA 1988, s 143	6–8

Unless there are special reasons for not doing so, a court dealing with an offender for an endorsable offence *must* order that particulars of the conviction (i.e., the date of the conviction, the convicting court, the offence committed and the penalty imposed) be endorsed on the offender's licence (Road Traffic Offenders Act 1988, s 44). Since any special reasons for not endorsing must be connected with the circumstances of the offence not the offender, and since such reasons are very narrowly defined, a conviction for an endorsable offence almost always results in endorsement. If the offender is disqualified on the occasion of an endorsement, particulars of the disqualification are also endorsed but there are no penalty points—the disqualification is considered a sufficient penalty without putting the offender on the path to a further disqualification under the 'totting-up' provisions (see 25.88 to 25.92). If the offender is not disqualified, the appropriate number of penalty points is endorsed. Where Sch 2 to the Road Traffic Offenders Act 1988 prescribes a range of penalty points (e.g., for careless driving and using a motor vehicle without insurance), the court fixes the number to be endorsed within the prescribed range. Where an offender is convicted of two or more endorsable offences committed on the same occasion, points are usually endorsed only in respect of the offence carrying the highest number (or, if they all carry the same number, in respect of one of the offences). Thus, an offender who on one occasion commits offences of taking a motor vehicle (8 points), dangerous driving (3–11 points) and using a motor vehicle without insurance (6–8 points) will normally acquire only 11 penalty points, not 17–27 points. However, the court may, under s 28(5) of the Road Traffic Offenders

Act 1988, order endorsement with penalty points for more than one offence committed on the same occasion.

An offender charged with an endorsable offence must deliver or post his licence to the court **25.79** prior to the hearing, or have it with him at the hearing (Road Traffic Offenders Act 1988, s 27). If he is convicted, the licence is shown to the court, and any endorsements on it are taken into account when passing sentence. Failure to produce one's licence is a summary offence, but it is a defence to establish that one has applied for a new licence and not received it. After the elapse of a prescribed period a person who has had his licence endorsed can apply for the issue of a new licence free of the endorsement (Road Traffic Offenders Act 1988, s 45(5)). The period is 11 years if the endorsement was for a drink/driving offence involving obligatory disqualification (see the next Section), and four years in other cases. The period runs from the date of commission of the offence if the offender was not disqualified, and from the date of the conviction if he was.

Obligatory disqualification

The following offences are the main ones to carry obligatory disqualification: **25.80**

(a) causing death by dangerous driving, contrary to RTA 1988, s 1;
(b) dangerous driving, contrary to RTA 1988, s 2;
(c) causing death by careless driving while under the influence of drink or drugs, contrary to RTA 1988, s 3A;
(d) driving or attempting to drive when unfit through drink or drugs, contrary to RTA 1988, s 4(1);
(e) driving or attempting to drive with excess alcohol in breath, blood or urine, contrary to RTA 1988, s 5(1)(a); and
(f) failing to provide a specimen required to ascertain one's ability to drive or the proportion of alcohol in one's system at the time of driving or attempting to drive, contrary to RTA 1988, s 7(6).

A court dealing with an offender for an offence carrying obligatory disqualification *must* **25.81** disqualify him for at least 12 months (2 years in the case of causing death by dangerous driving, or by careless driving when under the influence of drink or drugs) unless there are special reasons (Road Traffic Offenders Act 1988, s 36). If an offender is convicted of a drink/ driving offence carrying obligatory disqualification and it was committed within 10 years of a previous conviction for such an offence, the minimum period of disqualification is increased to three years. Where a court has power to disqualify, there is no statutory limit on the period for which it may order disqualification, and therefore it is always open to the court to disqualify for more than the obligatory minimum. It might well do so, for example, in a case where the proportion of alcohol in a drunken driver's breath was more than twice the legal maximum.

Any special reasons put forward for not disqualifying (or for disqualifying for less than the nor- **25.82** mal minimum) must relate to the circumstances of the offence itself, not the circumstances of the offender, and the courts are usually very reluctant to find that special reasons have been established. Thus, in *Jackson* [1970] 1 QB 647, the Court of Appeal held that a medical condition of which the offender was unaware and which caused him to retain alcohol for an unusually long time, was not a sufficient reason for shorter or non-disqualification. Exceptional hardship which the offender will suffer through disqualification (e.g., losing his employment) is incapable of being a special reason (contrast the position where a conviction for an offence carrying discretionary disqualification makes the offender liable to a 'totting-up' disqualification). Reasons which might justify non-disqualification are that the offender's non-alcoholic drink was 'laced' without his knowledge thus putting his alcohol level just above the legal limit.

25.83   *Chatters and Burke* [1986] 1 WLR 1321 lists the following factors which the court ought to consider in deciding whether there are special reasons:

    (a)   how far the vehicle was driven,
    (b)   in what manner it was driven,
    (c)   what was the state of the vehicle,
    (d)   whether it was the driver's intention to drive any further,
    (e)   the prevailing conditions with regard to the road and traffic on it,
    (f)   whether there was any possibility of danger by contact with other road users,
    (g)   what was the reason for the vehicle being driven at all.

25.84   Offences involving obligatory disqualification carry only three penalty points, whereas there are other less serious offences carrying anything up to 10 points (see the table at 25.78). This apparent anomaly is explained by the fact that when an offender is disqualified no points are endorsed on the licence, whatever the nature of the offence of which he has been convicted. If an offender is not disqualified for an offence involving obligatory disqualification, it means that there must have been something quite exceptional about the circumstances rendering the offence much less serious than an offence of that type is normally considered to be. Therefore, it is understandable that the penalty points are kept low.

Discretionary disqualification

25.85   A court dealing with an offender for an offence carrying discretionary disqualification may, but need not, disqualify him: Road Traffic Offenders Act 1988, s 34(2). There is no limit on the period of disqualification which may be imposed, but the trend is against overlong disqualifications because they merely invite further offending in the shape of driving while disqualified. Indeed, it is unusual for an offender to be disqualified at all for an offence merely carrying discretionary disqualification unless the offence makes him liable to a 'totting-up' disqualification (see 25.88 to 25.92). Offences such as careless driving, speeding, going through a red traffic light, failing to stop after an accident, and even not having insurance are mostly dealt with by means of a fine and endorsement, without disqualification. A bad case of careless driving would probably attract disqualification. Speeds of 100 mph plus on the motorway also tend to result in disqualification, although the period may be as short as a fortnight.

25.86   A disqualification commences immediately upon its being ordered. It follows that a court has no power to make a disqualification consecutive to another disqualification which it imposes on the same occasion, or which another court has imposed on a previous occasion.

25.87   Section 42 of the Road Traffic Offenders Act 1988 allows an offender who has been disqualified by a court for more than two years to apply to the court which disqualified him for early removal of the disqualification—the period the offender must wait before being able to apply varies depending upon the length of the disqualification.

Disqualification under the penalty points procedure

Section 35 of the Road Traffic Offenders Act 1988 deals with what are colloquially known as 'totting-up' disqualifications. **25.88**

Essentially, the section provides that where an offender is being dealt with for an endorsable offence (the 'present offence'), and the penalty points to be taken into consideration under the section (the 'relevant points') total 12 or more, then the offender *must* be disqualified for at least six months unless there are special grounds for not doing so. The relevant points are those which will be endorsed for the present offence if the offender is not disqualified, and those already endorsed on the licence in respect of offences committed in the three years preceding commission of the present offence. **25.89**

An offender who has acquired 12 or more relevant points need not be disqualified, or may be disqualified for less than the full six months, if the court is satisfied that 'there are grounds for mitigating the normal consequences of the conviction. Whereas special reasons for not disqualifying for an offence involving obligatory disqualification must be connected with the offence itself (see 25.82 to 25.83), there is no such restriction on the grounds which are capable of justifying non-disqualification of a 'totter'—subject to s 35(4) (see below), the court may have regard to 'all the circumstances', including those personal to the offender. Thus, it is much easier to avoid a six-month 'totting-up' disqualification than it is to avoid the obligatory 12 months for an offence such as driving with excess alcohol in the blood. However, s 35(4)(b) provides that the court may only take into account 'exceptional hardship'. Parliament was apparently concerned that offenders were avoiding disqualification by advancing the flimsiest suggestion of hardship, but there is no attempt in the Act to define 'exceptional hardship'. Loss of one's job, either because it involves driving or because it is virtually impossible to reach the place of work by public transport, is likely to constitute exceptional hardship (see *Owen v Jones* (1989) 9 Cr App R (S) 34). Less extreme consequences of disqualification (e.g., inconvenience in getting to work by public transport) might be 'hardship' but fall short of being 'exceptional hardship', and so would not be grounds for non-disqualification. Section 35(4) also provides (in subsection (a)) that the triviality of the present offence is not a ground for non-disqualification, while the House of Lords has indicated that the triviality of the previous offences for which penalty points were endorsed is of, at most, marginal significance (see *Woodage v Lambie* [1971] 1 WLR 754). Lastly, s 35(4)(c) applies to a 'totter' who has, in the three years preceding his present court appearance, been excused a 'totting-up' disqualification because there were special grounds. He is not allowed, on the present occasion, to rely on any circumstances which the court took into account on the previous occasion. Thus, for example, somebody who earns his living by driving cannot repeatedly avoid disqualification by arguing that loss of his licence would involve loss of his job. **25.90**

Where a court decides that s 35 obliges it to disqualify for, say, six months that is, of course, a minimum period, and the actual disqualification will be for whatever period the court considers appropriate having regard to the gravity of the offence, the offender's previous record and any other relevant circumstances. If an offender is convicted on one occasion of two or more endorsable offences which each render him liable to a s 35 disqualification, the length of the disqualification should reflect the fact that there were several offences. **25.91**

25.92 The following additional points about 'totting-up' disqualifications should be noted:

(a) If, within the three years preceding the commission of the present offence (or most recent endorsed offence if that was committed after the present offence), the offender has been disqualified once for a period of 56 days or more, then the normal minimum period for a 'totting-up' disqualification is increased from six months to one year. If there are two or more such disqualifications then it is increased to two years.

(b) It is for the offender to establish, on a balance of probabilities, that there are grounds for mitigating the normal consequences of acquiring 12 penalty points. This will normally involve him going into the witness box to give evidence, contrary to the general practice which is that, at the sentencing stage of proceedings, the offender stays silent in the dock while his advocate mitigates on his behalf. Similarly, an offender convicted of an offence involving obligatory disqualification who wishes to argue special reasons for not disqualifying must testify about the special reasons.

Probationary period disqualification

25.93 There is a probationary period of two years, which begins when a new driver qualifies. If he acquires six or more penalty points in that period, he will have his licence revoked and be required to present himself for re-testing.

Disqualification, endorsement, and other penalties

25.94 A disqualification is valid even if no other penalty is imposed for the offence (*Bignell* (1968) 52 Cr App R 10), but orders for endorsement and disqualification are almost invariably combined with some other sentence or order in lieu of sentence. Minor endorsable offences are normally dealt with by a fine or conditional discharge plus endorsement. Disqualification is unlikely except where the 'totting-up' provisions apply. More serious endorsable offences (e.g., taking a motor vehicle without consent, causing death by dangerous driving, possibly drink/driving offences) could well involve a custodial or community sentence plus endorsement and disqualification.

Disqualification under s 147 of the Powers of Criminal Courts (Sentencing) Act 2000

25.95 Where an offender is convicted on indictment of an offence carrying two years or more imprisonment, or is committed for sentence under PCC(S)A 2000, s 3, to be sentenced for such an offence, the Crown Court may disqualify him for such period as it thinks fit if satisfied that a motor vehicle was used in committing the offence: PCC(S)A 2000, s 147. This applies even if the offence is not endorsable, and even if the offender disqualified did not himself use the vehicle (i.e., it was used by an accomplice).

Q   FORFEITURE (OR DEPRIVATION) ORDERS

25.96 A court (Crown Court or magistrates' court) dealing with an offender for an offence of any description may order the forfeiture of any property which was in his possession or under his control at the time of his apprehension, provided the court is satisfied that the property has been used to commit or facilitate the commission of an offence or was intended by him to be used for that purpose (PCC(S)A 2000, s 143).

Forfeiture orders are used as ancillaries to a primary sentence such as imprisonment, fine   **25.97**
or community service. But, unlike other ancillary orders, they are regarded by the courts as essentially punitive—not compensatory—in purpose. Thus, the Court of Appeal held in *Lidster* [1976] Crim LR 80 that it was wrong in principle to deal with one offence by a combination of conditional discharge plus forfeiture order, since the former order implies that the court considers it 'inexpedient to inflict punishment' and so is inconsistent with the simultaneous imposition of a punitive ancillary order. The actual effect of the decision in *Lidster* has been reversed by statute. However, the case still illustrates the general attitude of the courts to such orders. An order may be made irrespective of the offence of which the offender has been convicted. Property in his possession at the time of the issue of a summons may be forfeited.

Provided the offender *intended* the relevant property to be used to commit/facilitate the   **25.98**
commission of an offence, a forfeiture order may be made even though neither he—nor, indeed, anybody else—actually did use the property for that purpose. 'Facilitating the commission of an offence' includes taking steps after its commission to avoid arrest or detection, or to dispose of any property to which it related. In decided cases, forfeiture orders have been made to deprive a handler of the car he had used to transport stolen goods at the request of the thieves; to deprive burglars of a motor-caravan in which they had driven to the scene of the crime and had intended to make their 'getaway' afterwards, and to deprive a petrol thief of a specially adapted pump by which he had siphoned off petrol from the tanks of numerous cars. The court should, however, have regard to the value of the property that it is considering forfeiting and to the likely financial effect on the offender of the making of the order, taken in conjunction with any other penalty (financial or otherwise) which may be imposed (see s 143(5) of the PCC(S)A 2000). In other words, the forfeiture order must be treated as part of the global penalty for the offence, and must not be allowed to make that penalty out of proportion to the gravity of what the offender did (see *Scully* (1985) 7 Cr App R (S) 119).

The effect of a s 143 order is to deprive the offender of his rights, if any, in the property   **25.99**
concerned. The property is taken into the possession of the police. If a person other than the offender claims to be entitled to the property, he has six months in which to apply to a magistrates' court for an order that it be returned to him. To succeed, he must not only satisfy the magistrates of his right to the property, but must also show that he either did not consent to the offender having the property or did not know the purpose for which it was to be used.

In addition to the general power of the PCC(S)A 2000, s 143, certain statutes contain their   **25.100**
own specific forfeiture provisions, e.g., the Misuse of Drugs Act 1971, the Firearms Act 1968, and the Prevention of Crime Act 1953 (in relation to offensive weapons). See also 25.111, which deals with confiscation orders.

R   COMPENSATION ORDERS

25.101 The power to order an offender to pay compensation to the victim of his offence is now contained in the PCC(S)A 2000, s 130. The propositions below summarize the position the law has now reached:

(i)   A court dealing with an offender for an offence (whether summary or indictable, imprisonable or non-imprisonable) may make an order requiring him to pay compensation for any 'personal injury, loss or damage resulting from that offence' or any other offence taken into consideration (s 130(1)(a)). Where the offence results in a death (other than death in a road traffic accident), the court may further order that the offender make payments for funeral expenses and/or bereavement (s 130(1)(b)).

(ii) A compensation order may be made instead of or in addition to dealing with the offender in any other way for the offence (s 130(1)). Thus, an order may be combined with non-punitive sentences, such as a discharge. It may even be employed as a sentence in its own right—i.e., as the only order made by a court when dealing with an offender.

(iii) If a court, having power to make a compensation order, chooses not to do so, it must give its reasons (s 130(3)). The requirement for reasons for not making an order reflects the Government's apparent anxiety, expressed in numerous speeches by Home Office ministers, that the courts should use their powers to order compensation to the full.

(iv) Where, as a result of an offence under the Theft Act 1968 or the Fraud Act 2006, the owner of property is temporarily deprived thereof but it is subsequently restored to him, any damage to the property occurring while it was out of his possession is conclusively presumed to have resulted from the offence, regardless of how it actually occurred (s 130(5)).

(v)   As regards loss arising from road traffic accidents, the general policy is that the victim should recover from the offender's insurers rather than direct from the offender himself. Thus, s 130(6) provides that compensation may not be ordered in respect of injury, loss or damage 'due to an accident arising out of the presence of a motor vehicle on a road', unless *either* the loss is attributed to the offender by virtue of s 130(5) (damage caused while stolen property was out of the owner's possession conclusively presumed to have been caused by the thief), *or* the offender was uninsured and the victim cannot claim under the Motor Insurers' Bureau Scheme.

(vi) In deciding the amount of compensation that is appropriate, the court shall have regard to any evidence and to any 'representations' made by or on behalf of the accused or the prosecution (s 130(4)).

(vii) The imposition of a compensation order is given statutory priority over a fine (s 130(12)). In effect, this means that a fine should be reduced or, if necessary, dispensed with altogether to enable compensation to be paid.

(viii) Where a juvenile is convicted of an offence and the court orders compensation, it should normally order the juvenile's parent or guardian to pay the compensation order (s 137).

In the magistrates' court, the maximum compensation order which can be imposed in respect of any offence is £5,000 (s 131). There is no statutory limit on the compensation which the Crown Court can order.

Numerous Court of Appeal decisions have outlined the correct judicial approach to the mak- **25.102**
ing of compensation orders. They are not intended as punitive orders *per se*, nor even as a
means of depriving the offender of the proceeds of his crime. They are, rather, meant to provide
the victim with a 'convenient and rapid means of avoiding the expense of resorting to civil
litigation when the criminal clearly has means which would enable the compensation to be
paid' (see *Inwood* (1975) 60 Cr App R 70). In other words, the victim obtains quickly and without expense through the criminal courts a remedy which he could otherwise have obtained
through civil proceedings. However, it is undesirable that the criminal courts should become
embroiled in complicated questions of civil law. Therefore, compensation orders are appropriate only where there is no real doubt about the offender's liability to compensate (see *Vivian*
[1979] 1 WLR 291).

Where the offender is convicted on a specimen count or counts, it is unlawful to base the **25.103**
value of the compensation order on losses alleged to result from offences which were neither
charged nor taken into consideration (*Crutchley* (1994) 15 Cr App R (S) 627).

One area of difficulty for the courts is the amount to order as compensation for personal **25.104**
injury, since assessing the 'value' of a cut eye or a broken jaw or whatever other injury was suffered by the victim, is notoriously difficult. The sentencer may, however, properly obtain
guidance on appropriate compensation from the amounts paid by the Criminal Injuries
Compensation Board in comparable cases (see dicta in *Broughton* (1986) 8 Cr App R (S) 380).

The Magistrates' Association *Sentencing Guidelines* (2005) set out guidance from which the fol- **25.105**
lowing, for examples are taken:

Type of injury		Guideline
Graze	Some pain for a few days and depending on size	up to £75
Bruise	Depending on size	up to £100
Black eye		£125
Cut (no permanent scarring)	Depending on size and whether stitched	£100–500
Sprain	Depending on loss of mobility	£100–1,000
Loss of tooth	Depending on position of tooth and cosmetic effect	£500–1,500

These figures are not to be regarded as a fixed tariff, but only as a guide. They reflect the element
which relates to general damages (pain, suffering, loss of facility) and should be added to
special damages for financial loss sustained (e.g., loss of earnings, dental expenses etc.).

Even where the offender's liability to make compensation is admitted or incontrovertibly **25.106**
established, the court should only make such order as is reasonably within his ability to pay.
An order which is beyond his means is likely to be quashed or reduced on appeal. Because of
the tendency of offenders to make extravagant claims as to their ability to compensate in the
hope of thereby avoiding or reducing a custodial sentence, counsel and solicitors for the
defence are under a duty to investigate any proposals for compensation, and should put them
before the court only if satisfied that the information provided by the offender as to his means
is correct (see *Huish* (1985) 7 Cr App R (S) 272). If an offender misleads the court into believing he can pay compensation, his subsequent appeal against the compensation order will not

succeed: *Dando* [1996] 1 Cr App R (S) 155. He must pay the compensation, or serve the term in default which will be imposed.

25.107   Of course, compensation is not usually ordered to be paid forthwith but may be made payable by instalments. The factors to be considered in relation to length of payment are similar to those in the case of a fine. An order for compensation should normally be payable within 12 months, but this can be exceeded up to a 3-year limit where the circumstances justify it (see *Olliver* (1989) 11 Cr App R (S) 10 and 25.61 for the analogous position relating to a fine). Any other financial orders the court may make will obviously affect the ability to make compensation. However, it is specifically provided by s 130(12) that, if a sentencer is considering both compensation and a fine, but the offender would not have the means to pay both, priority should be given to the compensation.

25.108   As to the procedure for obtaining a compensation order, it is not necessary for the victim to attend court and make an application in person. Usually, he will indicate on his statement to the police the extent of his loss and his desire for compensation. In addition, the CPS file may include a form specifying the amount claimed and the name and address of the claimant, which form can be handed in to the court. Receipts, etc. confirming the claim are also of value. Armed with this material, the prosecutor will ask for compensation in the appropriate sum at the end of his summary of the facts (assuming it is a guilty plea). If the plea is not guilty, evidence relevant to compensation will no doubt emerge during the course of the trial. If the criminal court refuses to make a compensation order (or makes an order for less than the full amount of the loss), the victim's civil rights are not, of course, affected, and he may commence proceedings in the county court or High Court for the amount by which his true loss exceeds the amount of the compensation order.

S   RESTITUTION ORDERS

25.109   Section 148 of the PCC(S)A 2000 provides that, where goods have been stolen and an offender is convicted of an offence with reference to the theft (or has such an offence taken into consideration), the court may order anyone having possession or control of the goods to restore them to any person entitled to recover them from him. 'Stolen goods' include goods obtained by deception or through blackmail, and 'an offence with reference to theft' includes handling stolen goods and, possibly, conspiracy to steal or assisting a thief. Persons other than the offender may be ordered to restore goods under s 148, but the court would only make an order against a third party in the clearest of cases. The obvious application of s 148 is where a convicted thief or handler was caught in possession of the stolen goods. If there is no doubt as to the true owner, the court can, at the conclusion of the trial, order that the goods be restored to him.

25.110   There is also power under s 148 to order that goods in the offender's possession which directly or indirectly represent the stolen goods be transferred to the person entitled to the stolen goods (e.g., if O steals A's television set and exchanges it for a DVD player, O could be ordered to transfer the DVD player to A). Lastly, the court may order that, out of money taken from the offender's possession on his arrest, the person entitled to the stolen goods shall be paid a sum not exceeding their value. In view of the wide powers the courts now have to order compensation under the PCC(S)A 2000, s 130, orders for payment of money under s 148 seem to be of limited value.

T CONFISCATION ORDERS

The Crown Court has important powers to confiscate the assets of those convicted of criminal **25.111** offences, by virtue of the Proceeds of Crime Act 2002 ('PCA 2002'). The details are beyond the scope of this work, and reference should be made to *Blackstone's Criminal Practice 2008*, Section E21. The PCA 2002 replaces the previous powers contained in the Drug Trafficking Act 1994 and the Proceeds of Crime Act 1995. The procedure is set out in detail in the Criminal Procedure Rules 2005, Parts 56 to 62. In outline, the scheme provides as follows.

(1) The court determines whether the offender convicted of an offence has a 'criminal lifestyle' (defined in s 75 and Sch 2). If he does have a criminal lifestyle, the court must decide whether he has benefited from his 'general criminal conduct'. If he does not, it must decide whether he has benefited from his 'particular criminal conduct' (defined in s 76).

(2) If he does have a criminal lifestyle, then the court is obliged to make certain assumptions to determine whether he has benefited from his general criminal conduct, and to what extent.

(3) The prosecutor must provide the court with a statement of information where it wishes to seek confiscation under the PCA 2002, or where the court so orders. The court may then order the offender to indicate the extent to which he accepts the allegations in it, and any matters upon which he proposes to rely. In the event of a failure to respond without reasonable excuse, the court may draw any appropriate inference.

(4) If the court decides that the offender has benefited from his criminal conduct, it must decide the 'recoverable amount', and make a confiscation order requiring him to repay that amount. The recoverable amount is either the amount of the offender's benefit from the conduct concerned, or such lesser 'available amount' as the court believes is just (ss 7 and 9).

(5) The confiscation order is normally made before sentencing the offender for the offence. It should be taken into account in fixing any fine, forfeiture, or deprivation of property, but should be left out of account in determining the sentence. The court may postpone confiscation proceedings for up to two years from the date of conviction (s 14).

(6) The power to make a confiscation order is confined to the Crown Court, but the magistrates may commit an offender to the Crown Court for that purpose.

U RECOMMENDATIONS FOR DEPORTATION

Where a non-British citizen, who has attained the age of 17, is convicted of an imprisonable **25.112** offence, the court dealing with him for the offence may recommend that he be deported.

25.113 Recommendations for deportation are dealt with in s 3 of the Immigration Act 1971, as amended by the British Nationality Act 1981. Such recommendations may be made by both the Crown Court and magistrates' courts. The recommendation is made to the Home Secretary, who, in deciding whether to act upon it, may take into account matters which could not properly be considered by the court (e.g., the possibility of the offender being persecuted if returned to his own country). A recommendation for deportation may be made in addition to any other penalty (custodial or otherwise) imposed for the offence. Even if no custodial sentence is passed the offender may be detained pending the Home Secretary's decision. The court may not recommend deportation unless the offender has been given notice in writing explaining that British citizens are not liable to deportation, and describing the persons who fall within that category. The notice must be given at least seven days before the recommendation is made. Failure to give such notice did not, however, necessarily render a recommendation for deportation invalid, it was held in *Abdi* [2007] EWCA Crim 1913. The reasoning in the Court of Appeal was that the purpose of the notice provision was to preclude the risk of deporting a British citizen, and the offender in question was not a British citizen.

25.114 A full enquiry into the circumstances of the case should be made before deportation is recommended, and reasons for a recommendation should be given. If considering making a recommendation, it is advisable for a judge to ask counsel for the offender to address him on the matter. The court must consider whether the offender's continued presence in the United Kingdom would be to the country's detriment (*Caird* (1970) 54 Cr App R 499), but the fact that he has a criminal record is not in itself a sufficient reason for deporting him. The question is whether, in the light of the present offence and his previous record, he is likely to re-offend. If he is, that would be a good ground for recommending his deportation. If, on the other hand, he is likely to be completely rehabilitated after serving whatever sentence is imposed, he should be allowed to stay in the country. In *Carmona* [2006] Crim LR 657, the Court of Appeal considered the procedure for recommending deportation in the light of the Human Rights Act 1998. Their lordships took the view that, as the recommendation did not equate to a final decision to deport, but was merely a stage in reaching such a decision, the rights of the offender were not engaged by the process of making a recommendation. It would be for the Home Secretary and, if appropriate, the Asylum and Immigration Tribunal, to consider those matters in due course.

V   HOSPITAL ORDERS

25.115 Upon receiving appropriate medical evidence, a court dealing with an offender for an imprisonable offence may order that he be admitted to and detained in a hospital where he will receive treatment for a mental disorder. Such an order is known as a 'hospital order'. When the Crown Court makes a hospital order it may add to it a 'restriction order', the effect of which is that the offender may only be discharged from hospital upon the direction of either the Home Secretary or a Mental Health Review Tribunal (Mental Health Act 1983, ss 37 to 43).

25.116 Hospital orders and imprisonment have this in common—they are the only two forms of sentence which entail the compulsory detention of offenders who have attained the age of

21. In other respects they are totally dissimilar. A hospital order is intended to assist and cure the offender, not to punish or deter him, and once he is in hospital he is subject to essentially the same regime as applies to non-offender compulsory patients. For these reasons it is better to think of a hospital order as being in lieu of sentence, rather than as a sentence in the strict sense of the word. The law on the subject is now contained in the Mental Health Act 1983 which consolidated earlier legislation.

Irrespective of the age of the offender, both the Crown Court and magistrates' courts have power to make a hospital order. The preconditions for the making of an order, set out in s 37(1) and (2) of the Mental Health Act 1983, are that: **25.117**

(a) The court must be dealing with the offender for an imprisonable offence.
(b) The court must be satisfied that:
   (i) the offender is suffering from mental illness, psychopathic disorder, mental impairment or severe mental impairment; and
   (ii) the mental illness etc. is of a nature which makes it appropriate for the offender to be detained in hospital for medical treatment; and
   (iii) in the case of psychopathic disorder or mental impairment, the treatment is likely to alleviate or prevent a deterioration in his condition; or
   (iv) in the case of an offender who has attained the age of 16 years, the mental disorder is of a nature or degree which warrants his reception into guardianship under the Act.
(c) The court must be satisfied that arrangements have been made for the offender's admission within 28 days to the hospital which it is proposed to name in the order.
(d) Having regard to matters such as the nature of the offence and the antecedents of the offender, the court must be of the opinion that a hospital order is the most suitable method of dealing with the case.

As to the matters mentioned in (b) above, the court must have evidence (written or oral) from two registered medical practitioners, one of whom must be a specialist in the diagnosis or treatment of mental illness. The significance of (d) above is that if the court considers that, notwithstanding his mental problems, the offender ought to be punished for what he has done, it may choose a custodial sentence in preference to a hospital order (see *Gunnell* (1966) 50 Cr App R 242).

Broadly speaking, the effect of a hospital order is to authorize the offender's conveyance to hospital and his detention there for an initial period of six months. Even during the six months, the doctor in charge of the offender's treatment may discharge him from hospital. Conversely, after the six months, the doctor may authorize detention for a further six months, and thereafter he may authorize further detention at yearly intervals. If the offender is dissatisfied with the doctor's decision to authorize further detention, he may apply to a Mental Health Review Tribunal (MHRT), which may direct that he be discharged. A Mental Health Review Tribunal consists of a legally qualified chairman, a psychiatrist, and a layman who, in deciding whether or not to direct discharge, consider whether the offender is still suffering from mental disorder; whether, if he is, his health or safety or the protection of others require that he should continue to receive treatment, and whether he would be able to look after himself properly out of hospital. Precisely the same considerations govern the discharge of non-offender patients. **25.118**

25.119 The system of discharge described above is satisfactory in the cases of mentally disordered offenders who present little or no danger to the public. However, where the offender has committed or might in the future commit serious offences, especially offences of violence, it is thought unwise to leave the date of his discharge from hospital in the hands initially of the doctor in charge of his treatment. Accordingly, s 41 of the Mental Health Act 1983 provides that when the Crown Court makes a hospital order it may add to it a *'restriction order'* if it considers that such an order is necessary to protect the public from serious harm. (See *Birch* (1989) 11 Cr App R (S) 202 for the way in which the court should approach such cases.) A restriction order may be for a fixed term or without a time limit. Its effect is that, for its duration, the offender can be discharged from hospital only on the direction of the Home Secretary or an MHRT. The offender may make yearly applications to the MHRT for discharge, and, if no application is made for three years, the Home Secretary is under a duty to refer the case to them for consideration.

25.120 It has been held to be contrary to Art 5 of the European Convention on Human Rights (see Chapter 28) to continue a restriction order if the patient's mental condition does not justify it. Danger to the public alone cannot be sufficient grounds for continuing detention under a restriction order: *X v UK* (1981) 4 EHRR 188.

25.121 A magistrates' court has no power to make a restriction order. However, where magistrates have convicted an offender aged 14 or over of an imprisonable offence and they consider that a hospital order with restriction order is called for, they may commit the offender to the Crown Court: Mental Health Act 1983, s 43. The Crown Court may then make a hospital order (with or without a restriction order), or deal with the offender in any way the magistrates could have dealt with him. While awaiting sentence at the Crown Court, the offender is either kept in custody or detained in a suitable hospital: s 44.

25.122 As an alternative to making a hospital order, the Crown Court or a magistrates' court may, in appropriate cases, make a guardianship order. The effect of such an order is that the offender is placed under the guardianship of a local social services authority or a person approved by the authority. The guardian may *inter alia* require the offender to reside at a certain address, and require him to attend places for treatment, training or education.

25.123 There are various other ways in which the process of criminal justice can result in a person being detained in a mental hospital:

(a) Upon a finding of not guilty by reason of insanity or unfitness to plead, the court may order that the accused be admitted to a hospital specified by the Home Secretary: Criminal Procedure (Insanity) Act 1964, s 5 (see 17.36 to 17.41).

(b) Magistrates may make a hospital order under s 37(3) of the Mental Health Act 1983 without convicting the accused (see 10.73).

(c) The Home Secretary may, upon receiving appropriate medical evidence, order that a person serving a prison sentence be transferred from prison to a mental hospital: Mental Health Act 1983, s 47.

25.124 Finally, it is necessary to summarize three powers given to the courts by ss 35, 36 and 38 of the Mental Health Act 1983, the broad aim of which is to facilitate the making of hospital orders. Section 35 provides that, where medical evidence suggests that an accused may be suffering from one of the forms of mental disorder which would justify the making of a hospital order, the court may remand him *to a hospital* for full reports on his condition. Magistrates may exercise this power in respect of somebody they have convicted of an imprisonable offence, or in respect of somebody charged with such an offence who either consents to the remand or who has been shown to the magistrates' satisfaction to have committed the *actus reus* of the offence. The Crown Court may exercise the power in respect of somebody who is awaiting trial on indictment, who is being tried on indictment or who has been convicted on indictment but not yet sentenced. A remand under s 35 must not be for more than 28 days. Although there may be further remands after the initial one, the total period must not exceed 12 weeks. The advantage of s 35 remands is that the court does not take the chance of allowing the accused to remain at liberty, but it avoids sending a disturbed person to prison or remand centre. Section 35 is complemented by s 36, which allows the Crown Court (but not magistrates) to remand an accused to hospital for treatment for mental illness or severe mental impairment. The power may be used only in respect of persons committed for trial in custody or remanded in custody during the course of the Crown Court proceedings. In effect, it is a means of transferring an accused from prison to hospital. The maximum period for s 36 remands is the same as for s 35 ones. Section 38, unlike ss 35 and 36, only applies after conviction. If there is medical evidence showing that the offender is suffering from a mental disorder which would permit the making of a hospital order, the court (magistrates' or Crown) may make an interim hospital order with a view to seeing whether a full hospital order will ultimately be appropriate. An interim order may authorise the offender's detention in hospital for a period of up to 12 weeks, and may be renewed for periods not exceeding 28 days at a time up to a total period of 12 months.

W DRINKING BANNING ORDERS

The Violent Crime Reduction Act 2006, Chapter 1 (not yet in force) gives a court the power **25.125** to impose a drinking banning order on conviction. The court must be satisfied that the offender has been engaged in criminal or disorderly conduct while under the influence of alcohol. A further condition is that it must have concluded that such an order is necessary to protect others from further conduct of that kind while under the influence of alcohol. The order can impose any prohibitions necessary to achieve that aim, for a period of between two months and two years.

X ANTI-SOCIAL BEHAVIOUR ORDERS

The Anti-Social Behaviour Order (ASBO) was introduced by the CDA 1998. A court may make **25.126** an ASBO if it considers it necessary to protect people from further anti-social acts by an offender aged 10 or over (CDA 1998, s 1). Anti-social acts are defined as those which cause, or are likely to cause, harassment, alarm, or distress on the part of those not of the same household as the offender. Application may be made by the police, a registered social landlord, a housing action trust, or a local authority. An application for an ASBO is made to the magistrates' court which serves the area concerned. The procedure is civil, rather than criminal in nature. The behaviour upon which the application is based need not amount to a criminal offence. Nevertheless, the court ought to apply the criminal standard of proof where the allegations being made would have serious consequences for the defendant: *R (McCann) v Crown Court at Manchester* [2003] 1 AC 787.

25.127 The order may prohibit the offender from doing anything which is described in it. It has effect for the period (not less than two years) specified in the order. If the person subject to the order contravenes it he is liable on conviction to imprisonment for up to five years (six months if dealt with by the magistrates). If an ASBO is imposed by the magistrates, it can be appealed to the Crown Court (CDA 1998, s 4) or by way of judicial review (but only if the process before the magistrates amounted to an excess of jurisdiction).

25.128 The preceding paragraphs deal with the situation where there has been an application for an ASBO by one of the relevant authorities. In addition, an ASBO may be imposed after conviction in criminal proceedings (CDA 1998, s 1C). The proceedings in question are, again, civil in nature, with the result that hearsay evidence is admissible on the basis of the civil rules although the court must consider carefully the weight of such evidence: *R(W) v Acton Youth Court* [2005] EWHC Admin 954. It is immaterial that the evidence would not have been admissible in the proceedings in which the offender has just been convicted. However, the court must satisfy itself to the criminal standard that he has acted in the anti-social manner alleged: *W and F* [2007] 1 WLR 339.

25.129 If a person, without reasonable excuse, breaches his ASBO, he commits an offence, and is liable to five years upon conviction in the Crown Court (six months or a fine of £5,000 in the magistrates' court). Often this penalty will be in excess of the maximum for any criminal offence otherwise constituted by the breach (and the breach may not amount to a criminal offence in any event).The appellate courts have stressed that the use of an ASBO to punish is unlawful, and that an ASBO should not be used merely to increase the sentence of imprisonment which an offender might otherwise receive (*Boness* [2005] EWCA Crim 2395).

25.130 The Crime and Disorder Act 1998, ss 1AA and 1AB, enables the court to make a new order where an ASBO has already been granted against a juvenile defendant. The individual support order may be made where an ASBO has already been made against a defendant aged 10 to 17. If made, it requires the defendant to comply for up to six months with its requirements, which may include participating in specified activities, presenting himself to a specified person, or complying with educational requirements.

Y   REGISTRATION UNDER THE SEX OFFENCES ACT 2003

25.131 Certain categories of sex offenders are required to notify the police of their name and home address within three days of conviction, and any subsequent changes of name or address within 14 days. Unreasonable failure to comply with the registration requirements is itself an offence.

The offences which trigger off liability to register are listed in Sch 3 of the 2003 Act. They **25.132** include rape, indecent assault, buggery, unlawful sexual intercourse, and offences relating to indecent photographs of children. Conviction of a listed offence automatically entails the liability to register, and there is no separate decision required on the part of the sentencer. The duty to register is imposed not just on those convicted, but also on those who are cautioned for one of the offences in question. Once the offender becomes liable to register, he will continue on the register for a period varying from the period of a conditional discharge to life, depending on the sentence imposed.

Z   DISQUALIFICATION FROM WORKING WITH CHILDREN

If an offender has been convicted of an offence committed against a child, he can (and in some **25.133** cases must) be disqualified by the court from working with children in future. The position is that:

(a) where the offender is aged 18 or over and has received a qualifying sentence (custodial of over 12 months, or a hospital or guardianship order), a disqualification order must be made, unless the offender can prove to the civil standard that he is unlikely to commit a further offence against a child;

(b) where the offender is aged under 18 and a qualifying sentence has been passed, the court has power to make a disqualifying order;

(c) whatever the age of the offender, and irrespective of the sentence passed, if he has been convicted of an offence committed against a child, the court has power to make a disqualifying order.

KEY DOCUMENTS

Powers of Criminal Courts (Sentencing) Act 2000, as amended.
Criminal Justice Act 2003, as amended.

PART 5

APPEALS AND ANCILLARY MATTERS

26

APPEALS FROM THE CROWN COURT

26.01 Appeals against conviction on indictment, against sentence following conviction on indictment, and against sentence passed following committal to the Crown Court for sentence, are all heard in the Criminal Division of the Court of Appeal. Decisions of the Crown Court in matters not relating to trial on indictment (e.g., in disposing of appeals from magistrates' courts) may be challenged by appealing by way of case stated to a Divisional Court of the Queen's Bench Division, or by applying for judicial review. Since appeals by case stated and applications for judicial review are chiefly used to correct errors made by magistrates, they are described in Chapter 27. The structure of the criminal appeal system is summarized in Figure 26.1.

Figure 26.1 Structure of the criminal appeal system

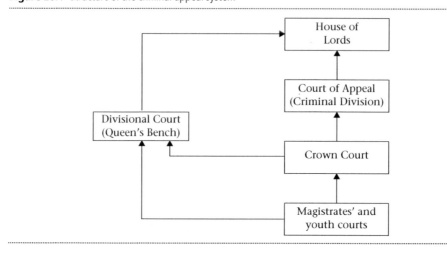

A   THE CRIMINAL DIVISION OF THE COURT OF APPEAL

Prior to 1907, a person convicted on indictment had no general right of appeal, but the trial **26.02** judge might in his discretion reserve a point of law for consideration by the Court of Crown Cases Reserved. The Criminal Appeal Act of 1907 created the Court of Criminal Appeal, which replaced the Court of Crown Cases Reserved. It had a much wider jurisdiction than the latter court, being able to hear appeals against conviction based on grounds of fact or mixed law and fact, and appeals against sentence where the appellant argued that his sentence, although lawful, was too severe. The Court of Criminal Appeal was in its turn abolished by the Criminal Appeal Act 1966, which transferred its jurisdiction to the Criminal Division of the Court of Appeal. The present legislation on the membership of the Criminal Division and its composition for particular types of hearing is contained in the Supreme Court Act 1981. The jurisdiction, powers and procedure of the Division are principally governed by the Criminal Appeal Act 1968 (CAA) and the CrimPR, Parts 65–69.

The Court of Appeal consists of up to 37 Lords Justices of Appeal and certain *ex officio* judges, **26.03** in particular the Lord Chief Justice: Supreme Court Act 1981, s 2(2). Any member of the Court of Appeal is equally entitled to sit in the Criminal and Civil Divisions of the Court, but in practice the Lords Justices who exercise the jurisdiction of the Criminal Division are likely to have had experience as advocates or judges in the Crown Court. The Lord Chief Justice is president of the Criminal Division: Supreme Court Act 1981, s 3(2). He may request any High Court or circuit judge to act as a judge of the Division: s 9(1). A request under s 9(1) is more in the nature of a command, because it is the judge's duty to comply with it: s 9(3).

Any number of courts of the Criminal Division may sit simultaneously: Supreme Court Act **26.04** 1981, s 3(5). When determining an appeal against conviction a court must consist of at least three judges: s 55(2). The same applies when there is an application for leave to appeal from the Court of Appeal to the House of Lords and when a person is appealing against a finding that he was unfit to plead or a verdict of not guilty by reason of insanity. Appeals against sentence may be determined by a two judge court. There is nothing to stop a court comprising more than three judges, provided the number is uneven. In fact, five judge courts are a rarity, confined to cases of exceptional importance or difficulty, e.g., *Turnbull* [1977] QB 224 where the Court of Appeal gave guidance to Crown Court judges on how they should deal with identification evidence.

Many applications incidental to the conduct of an appeal are decided not by a court but by a **26.05** single judge. The judge does not usually hear argument from the parties, but merely reads through the papers in the case. Matters commonly dealt with by a single judge are applications for leave to appeal, for bail pending determination of the appeal, or for an order that a witness attend court with a view to giving evidence at the hearing of the appeal. If the single judge decides against the appellant, he may renew the application before a court, which need only consist of two judges.

The decision of a court of the Criminal Division may be taken by a majority of its members. If **26.06** a two judge court is divided on what its decision should be, the matter should be re-argued before a three judge court: Supreme Court Act 1981, s 55(5). Even where the judges are not unanimous, the usual rule is that only one judgment is pronounced: s 59. However, the judge presiding in the court (i.e., the Lord Chief Justice if he is sitting, otherwise the most senior Lord Justice) may allow separate judgments if he considers that the question raised is one of law and that more than one judgment would be convenient. If there is only one judgment, the presiding judge either pronounces it himself or asks one of the other members of the court to undertake the task. A single judgment in a case makes for certainty in the law, and certainty in the criminal law is even more important than it is in the civil law.

26.07 In order to carry out its work, the Criminal Division needs administrative support. This is provided by the Registrar of Criminal Appeals and his staff. The Registrar is a barrister or solicitor of at least ten years' standing, appointed by the Lord Chancellor: Supreme Court Act 1981, s 89(1). Notices of appeal and notices of application for leave to appeal (see 26.48 to 26.50) are sent to the Registrar by the Crown Court officer on whom they were initially served. The Registrar's responsibilities then include obtaining any necessary transcript of the note taken by the shorthand writer of the Crown Court proceedings, obtaining from the Crown Court any exhibits or information it has relevant to the appeal, instructing counsel to represent an appellant who does not have a solicitor, and giving notice of the time fixed for the hearing of the appeal.

26.08 As already mentioned, Queen's Bench Division judges may be, and often are, asked to sit in the Criminal Division. The single judge who decides incidental applications is also usually a QBD judge. Queen's Bench Division judges also sit as Crown Court judges and circuit judges may also be asked to sit in the Court of Appeal (though not as a single judge). Therefore, the possibility arises of a judge hearing an appeal against his own decision. To avoid this happening, s 56(2) of the Supreme Court Act 1981 provides that a judge must not sit in the Criminal Division for the hearing of, or make any incidental decision connected with, an appeal against conviction or sentence if he was the judge in the lower court.

B   THE RIGHT OF APPEAL AGAINST CONVICTION

26.09 Subject to obtaining leave to appeal when that is necessary, a person convicted on indictment may appeal to the Court of Appeal against his conviction: CAA, s 1(1). Leave to appeal is granted by the court itself, usually acting through a single judge.

Appeals based on trial judge's certificate

26.10 No leave to appeal against conviction is required if the trial judge from the Crown Court has granted a certificate that the case is fit for appeal: CAA, s 1(2)(a). In all other cases, leave must be obtained.

26.11 A certificate of fitness for appeal may mention a ground of fact, mixed law and fact or pure law. It is very rare for the trial judge to grant a certificate. It will not be granted merely because the judge is uneasy about the verdict. There must be a particular and cogent ground of appeal with a substantial chance of success (*Parkin* (1928) 20 Cr App R 173, and *Practice Direction* (*Criminal Proceedings: Consolidation*) [2002] 1 WLR 2870, para IV.50.4).

Appeals with leave

The power to grant leave to appeal is one of the powers of the Court of Appeal which may be— **26.12** and most frequently is—exercised not by a court, but by a single judge. The procedure is described in more detail at 26.54 to 26.56, but, in essence, it involves the papers in the case being handed to the single judge for his consideration. The papers will include the appellant's 'Notice of Application for Leave to Appeal' and 'Grounds of Appeal', often together with an Advice on Appeal. They may also include a transcript of the trial judge's summing-up and possibly, depending on the nature of the points raised in the Grounds of Appeal, a transcript of part of the evidence. The judge reads through the papers privately. He could, but hardly ever does, call on counsel for the appellant to present argument. Having read the papers, he decides whether to grant leave or not. If leave is refused, the appellant has the right to have the application decided by a court of the Criminal Division. The risk, from his point of view, in exercising that right is that if the court, like the single judge, refuses leave, it may well order that time he has spent in custody since the commencement of the appeal shall not count as part of any custodial sentence imposed upon him (see CAA, s 29 and 26.58 to 26.62 on directions for loss of time). Most appellants who are refused leave to appeal by a single judge do not renew the application before the court.

In granting or refusing leave to appeal the single judge acts as a kind of filter, ensuring that **26.13** cases do not go before a court for a full hearing unless there is an arguable point.

Appeal against conviction following guilty plea

In entitling persons convicted on indictment to appeal against conviction, s 1 of the CAA **26.14** does not distinguish between those who pleaded guilty and those who denied the charge. On the face of it, the former have as much right to appeal as the latter. But, for obvious reasons, the Court of Appeal is most reluctant to grant leave to appeal against conviction if the appellant admitted his guilt in the Crown Court. The classic passage on the matter comes from Avory J in *Forde* [1923] 2 KB 400, although it has since been stressed that it should not be construed as a comprehensive statement of all the situations in which an appeal may be heard despite there having been a guilty plea. Avory J said:

> A plea of guilty having been recorded, this court can only entertain an appeal against conviction if it appears (1) that the appellant did not appreciate the nature of the charge or did not intend to admit he was guilty of it, or (2) that upon the admitted facts he could not in law have been convicted of the offence charged.

The first of the two situations mentioned by his lordship covers *inter alia* cases where a purported plea of guilty is said to have been a nullity because of pressure brought to bear on the accused by the judge and/or counsel (see *Turner* [1970] 2 QB 321 and 17.17 to 17.21). The second situation does not often arise in practice, since it presupposes that both the prosecution and the defence at the Crown Court were mistaken about the essential elements which the prosecution had to prove to establish the offence charged—if the defence had not been mistaken as well as the prosecution, they ought not to have allowed the case to proceed on a guilty plea.

In addition to cases which can clearly be brought within the terms of Avory J's proposition, **26.15** appeals are heard where a plea of guilty is induced by the trial judge's wrong ruling in law.

Thus, in *Clarke* [1972] 1 All ER 219, C successfully appealed against a conviction for shoplifting, the facts being that she abandoned her original plea of not guilty after the judge decided that her defence (that she put the goods into her bag in a moment of absent-mindedness and then forgot to pay) amounted to a plea of not guilty by reason of insanity. Not surprisingly, C preferred to plead guilty rather than be found not guilty and made the subject of a hospital order. In the circumstances, her change of plea did not preclude her appealing. Finally, there will be occasional cases which are not covered by any of the headings described above, but where the interests of justice demand that the appeal be allowed to proceed. An excellent example is *Lee* [1984] 1 WLR 578. Although fit to plead, L was of very low intelligence. He was charged with numerous offences of arson and manslaughter. The case against him consisted entirely of confessions which he had made to the police, but, notwithstanding the confessions, he instructed his legal representatives until shortly before the trial that he intended to plead not guilty. He then changed his mind and pleaded guilty to all counts. He subsequently attributed this *volte-face* to his having been told that a place had been found for him at a special mental hospital, so that if he pleaded guilty he would leave prison (where he had been for several months on remand) and be sent to hospital under a hospital order. That was in fact what happened. There was no question of L being pressured by counsel or judge into pleading guilty—on the contrary counsel told the judge privately that he was most unhappy about what L was doing, not least because a public inquiry into the cause of one fire which L now admitted to starting had concluded that it began by accident. Subsequent investigations by the *Sunday Times* cast more doubt on the correctness of L's convictions, and suggested that for at least some of the offences he had convincing alibis. Thus encouraged, L applied for leave to appeal out of time. The defence attributed his confessions to his low intelligence, a desire for 'notoriety and publicity' and the remorseless nature of the police interrogation. In the highly unusual circumstances of the case, L was given leave to appeal. As Ackner LJ said:

> The fact that the appellant was fit to plead; knew what he was doing; intended to make the pleas he did; pleaded guilty without equivocation after receiving expert advice, although factors highly relevant to [whether the appeal should ultimately succeed] cannot of themselves deprive the court of the jurisdiction to hear [the appeal].

26.16 In *Chalkley* [1998] 2 Cr App R 79, the Court of Appeal distinguished:

(a) cases where an incorrect ruling of law on admitted facts left a defendant with no legal escape from a verdict guilty on those facts; and

(b) cases where an accused was influenced to change his plea to guilty because he recognized that as a result of a ruling to admit strong evidence against him, his case was hopeless.

It was held that a conviction under category (a) was unsafe, whereas a conviction under category (b) was not.

26.17 In *Togher* [2001] 3 All ER 463, the Court of Appeal stated that the approach to an appeal against conviction of a plea of guilty following a judge's ruling depended on a choice between:

(a) a 'narrow' approach, that an appeal could be entertained only where the ruling left no legal basis for a plea of not guilty; and

(b) a 'wide' approach, that a plea of guilty following a material irregularity could also found an appeal.

The Court of Appeal adopted the wide approach in preference to the narrower approach adopted in *Chalkley* [1998] 2 Cr App R 79. In particular, the word 'unsafe' should be applied in a way compatible with the European Convention on Human Rights. Fairness of trial and safety of conviction went together. If a defendant were denied a fair trial it was almost inevitable that the conviction would be unsafe. Also, if he pleaded guilty in ignorance of matters which might amount to abuse of process and justify a stay of the prosecution, such conviction might properly be set aside.

C APPEAL AGAINST SENTENCE

Appellants to the Court of Appeal against sentence fall into two categories—those who were **26.18** sentenced for an offence following conviction on indictment, and those who were sentenced for an offence following summary conviction and committal to the Crown Court for sentence. Leave to appeal is always required, unless the judge who passed sentence grants a certificate that the case is fit for appeal.

Sentence following conviction on indictment

A person convicted on indictment may appeal to the Court of Appeal against any sentence **26.19** passed on him by the Crown Court for the offence: CAA, s 9. For purposes of the CAA, 'sentence' has a wide meaning. It includes 'any order made by a court when dealing with an offender': CAA, s 50. Thus, an offender may appeal not only against an order which is obviously a punishment (e.g., imprisonment, detention in a young offender institution, or a fine) but also against non-punitive orders such as a conditional discharge or even an absolute discharge. Section 50 specifically provides that hospital orders and recommendations for deportation are 'sentences'. Even orders which are normally regarded as ancillary to the sentence proper (e.g., costs for the prosecution or compensation for the victim) are orders made 'when dealing with an offender', and so fall within the s 50 definition.

Sentence following summary conviction

Section 10 of the Criminal Appeal Act 1968 provides that a person sentenced by the Crown **26.20** Court for an offence following summary conviction and committal for sentence (see Chapter 12) may appeal against his sentence.

Section 10 also gives a right of appeal to an offender who, following a summary conviction **26.21** which puts him in breach of probation or a conditional discharge, is dealt with by the Crown Court for the original offence.

Leave to appeal against sentence

Unless the Crown Court judge certifies that the case is fit for appeal, an appeal against sentence **26.22** lies only with leave: CAA, s 11(1). This applies whether the appeal is brought under s 9 or s 10 of the CAA, and whether it is on a point of law or otherwise. The Court of Appeal has, however, discouraged Crown Court judges from exercising the power (see, for example, *Grant*

(1990) 12 Cr App R (S) 441). Indeed it is hard to see why a judge should readily declare that a sentence he has just passed is appealable—if he thought the sentence was too severe, he presumably would not have passed it. As a result, virtually all offenders seeking a reduction in their sentence require leave. The procedure for obtaining leave is the same as for obtaining leave to appeal against conviction (see 26.12 to 26.13).

D   DETERMINATION OF APPEALS AGAINST CONVICTION

26.23   Section 2(1) of the CAA 1968 provides the statutory framework for the determination of appeals against conviction. It states that the Court of Appeal 'shall allow an appeal against conviction if they think that the conviction is unsafe; and ... shall dismiss an appeal in any other case'. This new simplified test was introduced by the Criminal Appeal Act 1995. Before that, the Court of Appeal had to consider whether the conviction was unsafe or unsatisfactory, whether the judge had made a wrong decision on a question of law, or whether there had been a material irregularity in the course of the trial. If they decided that one of these conditions was met, the Court of Appeal had then to proceed to determine whether a miscarriage of justice had actually occurred. The test is now greatly simplified, but the historical position should be borne in mind in studying cases decided before s 2 of the CAA 1968 was amended by the 1995 Act.

26.24   In any event, it is clear that the intention of Parliament was that there should be no change in effect despite the simplified wording. In moving the Second Reading of the Criminal Appeal Bill, the then Home Secretary said: 'In substance it restates the existing practice of the Court of Appeal.' It was made clear that this statement followed upon consultation with the Lord Chief Justice (*Hansard*, vol. 256, para 24, 6 March 1995; and see also Standing Committee B, 21 March 1995, col. 26). The fact that there is no difference in practice between the old and the new tests is illustrated by the case of *Mullen* [1999] Crim LR 561, where an appeal was based upon the circumstances in which the appellant was brought to trial. The English prosecuting authorities, in collusion with Zimbabwean authorities, had procured his deportation from Zimbabwe to England in circumstances which were illegal and amounted to an abuse of process. The Court of Appeal described the conduct of the British authorities as so unworthy or shameful that it was an affront to the public conscience to allow the prosecution to succeed. Nevertheless, the conduct of the trial itself was not challenged. The real question was whether it was fair to try the accused in view of the way in which he had been brought before the court. In applying the statutory test relating to appeals, did this mean that the conviction was unsafe? The Court of Appeal had recourse to *Hansard*, from which it was apparent that the new form of s 2 of the CAA was intended to restate the existing practice of the Court of Appeal. That practice allowed abuse of process to be a ground for quashing a conviction. Furthermore, for a conviction to be safe, it must be lawful. If the trial should never have taken place, then the conviction could not be regarded as safe.

26.25   Another illustration of the way in which the test (safety of the conviction) is applied is provided by the case of *Smith* (1999) *The Times*, 31 May 1999. Here the ground of appeal was the wrongful rejection of a submission of no case to answer. After the submission had been rejected, the defendant gave evidence and in cross-examination admitted his guilt! Before the unified test for appeals was introduced, the authorities favoured the view that in such a case the appeal should succeed since the accused had been deprived, by the wrong ruling, of the absolute certainty of an acquittal upon the judge's direction (*Cockley* (1984) 79 Cr App R 181). Since the accused had admitted his guilt in court, however, how accurate was it to say, under the new test, that the conviction was 'unsafe'? In *Smith*, the Court of Appeal had no hesitation in doing so. Even in an extreme case, such as this one, the wrongful rejection of a submission of no case to answer meant that the appeal must succeed. Again, it would appear that the change in wording in s 2 of the CAA had had no practical effect.

It is becoming increasingly clear that the new test is meant to reflect the practice adopted by   **26.26** the Court of Appeal in interpreting the old one. The restrictive reading of the word 'unsafe' anticipated by some commentators has not generally found favour in practice, despite dicta to the contrary, e.g., in *Chalkley* [1998] 3 WLR 146.

In *Condron v UK* [2000] Crim LR 679, the European Court of Human Rights emphasized the need for the Court of Appeal to focus upon the fairness of the trial, rather than the safety of the conviction, in deciding whether to uphold an appeal from the Crown Court. In para 65 of their judgment, the Court said:

> The question whether or not the rights of the defence guaranteed to an accused under Art 6 of the Convention were secured in any given case cannot be assimilated to a finding that his conviction was safe in the absence of any enquiry into the issue of fairness.

In *Togher* [2001] 3 All ER 463, the Court of Appeal considered the relationship between the   **26.27** requirement for a fair trial and the safety of any conviction which resulted. Lord Woolf CJ said that if the accused had been denied a fair trial, it was almost inevitable that his conviction would be regarded as unsafe, now that the Convention had been incorporated into domestic law.

In their grounds of appeal, many appellants refer first to specific legal or procedural errors   **26.28** which arose at their trial, and then supplement these specific grounds with a general claim that the conviction was therefore unsafe. There is a school of thought that all misdirections in the summing-up should be classified as factors rendering the conviction unsafe rather than as wrong decisions of law or material irregularities. But, nothing in s 2(1) of the CAA expressly limits appeals based on the unsafe nature of the conviction to cases where the appellant can point to some specific mistake in the conduct of his trial. As a matter of pure statutory construction, he may legitimately argue that the evidence against him (although just sufficient to establish a prima facie case) was so weak that the jury's verdict should not stand. However, in practice it is very difficult to raise a doubt in their lordships' minds about the safety of a conviction merely by attacking the quality of the evidence given at trial. They take the view that the jury saw and heard the witnesses (unlike themselves who rarely have more than a transcript of the summing-up). What seems a thin case on paper may have been totally convincing 'in the flesh'. Therefore, 'if all the material was before the jury and the summing-up was impeccable . . . the court shall not lightly interfere' (per Lord Widgery CJ in *Cooper* [1969] 1 QB 267). In other words, assuming the trial to have been legally error-free, the appellant will only succeed if he can point to something exceptional in the overall circumstances which absolutely drives the court to the conclusion that an injustice may have been done. In *Cooper* itself the special factors which led to C's conviction for assault being quashed were that the case against him rested on a somewhat dubious identification by the victim, and there was evidence that X (who closely resembled C and had a record for violence) had privately confessed to the crime. C had been able to call the third person to whom X had made his confession, but for obvious reasons he was unable to call X himself. Similarly, in *Pattinson* (1974) 58 Cr App R 417, P's appeal against a conviction for robbery succeeded because the prosecution's only evidence was a confession which P had allegedly made at the police station, and the circumstances of that confession were too bizarre for the police to be believed (after he had been charged—and so could not be further questioned—P, according to the police, had talked to himself when he thought he was not being overheard and had obligingly admitted his involvement in the robbery).

Errors in the trial as grounds of appeal

26.29   As indicated in the previous Section, the Court of Appeal will be most reluctant to uphold a conviction where the trial was legally error-free. Such errors therefore form the grounds on which most appeals are argued. Among the commonest grounds of appeal put forward are errors in the judge's summing-up, e.g., wrongly defining the elements of the offence, failing to leave to the jury a defence for which a foundation has been laid by the evidence, failing to give an adequate direction on the burden and/or standard of proof. Other grounds frequently relied on amount to procedural errors in the course of the trial, e.g., allowing the prosecution to amend the indictment when that involved the risk of injustice, allowing evidence to be admitted when it should have been excluded, failing to deal properly with a note from the jury, failing to comply with the statutory limitations on majority verdicts. All of these are common examples from an endless list of potential errors in a trial. In the end, however, the crucial question (however many errors there were) is: was the conviction safe?

26.30   Sometimes an appellant relies on alleged errors by counsel defending him at the Crown Court as a basis for appeal. Traditionally the Court of Appeal has been very reluctant to accept such arguments. In *Clinton* [1993] 1 WLR 1181, their lordships said it was rare for a verdict to be quashed because of defence counsel's conduct of the trial. The correct approach was whether the conviction was unsafe or unsatisfactory under all the circumstances. In *Clinton*, C had been charged with kidnapping and indecent assault. The complainant described her attacker in terms sharply at variance with the appearance of C (including a history of tattoos and scars). C did not give or call evidence at the trial. He was convicted, the case being almost entirely based on the complainant's evidence. The Court of Appeal, in allowing the appeal, said that C should have been strongly advised to give evidence to underline the discrepancies. His counsel had not in fact tried to wean him from his reluctance to testify, and that was a grave error. Exceptionally, where a tactical decision (such as not calling the defendant) was taken without proper instructions or against the promptings of good sense, the Court of Appeal could set aside the verdict.

26.31   Prior to *Clinton*, there was a line of cases, culminating in *Ensor* [1989] 1 WLR 497, in which the Court of Appeal concentrated its attention on the extent of counsel's alleged ineptitude. In *Ensor* E was charged with two counts of rape. He told his counsel that he wanted them severed, and it was common ground at appeal that an application to sever, if made, should have succeeded. For tactical reasons, E's counsel decided not to apply to sever. He did not inform E of his decision. E was convicted on both counts, and appealed on the basis of his counsel's conduct. The Court of Appeal stated that a conviction could not be set aside on the ground that counsel's action was mistaken or unwise, even if it was also contrary to the accused's wishes. There was an exception in the case of 'flagrantly incompetent advocacy'. Here counsel's actions, even if erroneous, were not incompetent, let alone flagrantly so. In another decision, the Court of Appeal held that failure by counsel to discuss with his client whether or not to call alibi witnesses could afford a ground of appeal (see *Irwin* [1987] 2 All ER 1085, which, however, was said in *Ensor* ought to be regarded as confined to its own facts).

Clinton, it is submitted, puts the consideration of alleged errors by counsel in a proper per- **26.32** spective. It must surely be better to concentrate on the extent to which the trial was affected, rather than the standard of advocacy. The proper question is, therefore, that posed by the statute: was the conviction unsafe?

In *Ullah* [2000] Crim LR 108, the Court of Appeal emphasized that in a case of this kind, the **26.33** crucial question was whether the conviction was safe, but ineptitude on the part of counsel was a necessary prerequisite. In considering whether counsel had been incompetent, their Lordships suggest that the test might be whether his conduct was based on such fundamentally flawed reasons that it might properly be regarded as *Wednesbury* unreasonable (applying the criteria in *Associated Picture Houses Ltd v Wednesbury Corporation* [1948] 1 KB 223).

In *Nangle* [2001] Crim LR 506, the Court of Appeal stated that 'flagrant incompetence' might **26.34** not now be the appropriate measure to apply in deciding whether to quash a conviction. In the light of the Human Rights Act 1998 and Art 6 of the European Convention on Human Rights, what was required was that the hearing of the charges against the defendant should be fair. If the conduct of his legal advisers was such that this objective had not been met, then the Court of Appeal might be compelled to intervene. The issue had been considered by the European Court of Human Rights in *Daud v Portugal* [1999] EHRLR 634, where the defence lawyer had only three days to prepare for a complex fraud trial which resulted in a nine-year prison sentence. It was held that the defendant's right under Art 6(3)(c) had been violated, since he had not had the benefit of a practical and effective defence. The time given was too short for a serious and complex case. As is stated in Professor Ashworth's commentary on *Nangle*, this suggests that a test less demanding than 'flagrant incompetence' may now be appropriate. In any event, it seems increasingly clear that the focus is upon the impact of the lawyer's errors, rather than their extent.

The effect of a successful appeal

If the Court of Appeal finds that the conviction is unsafe it must allow the appeal and quash **26.35** the appellant's conviction (CAA, s 2(2)). Unless the Court also orders that the appellant be re-tried, the effect of quashing a conviction is that the Crown Court is directed to record an acquittal instead of a conviction, and the appellant is treated just as if the jury had found him not guilty: s 2(3). Consequently, any attempt by the prosecution to re-prosecute him for the same offence would be barred by the plea of autrefois acquit.

Section 7 of the CAA deals with ordering retrials. Until it was amended by the Criminal Justice **26.36** Act 1988, s 7 applied only when the Court allowed an appeal on the basis of fresh evidence which it had heard. Such cases, as explained at 26.68, account for only a tiny fraction of the Court's workload. Therefore, retrials on the direction of the Court of Appeal were very rare. That position has been transformed by the amendments, passed in 1988, the effect of which is that, whenever they allow an appeal, their lordships have a discretion to order a retrial should they consider that the interests of justice so require. The Court of Appeal has indicated that the period which elapsed since the original trial, whether or not the appellant had been in custody for that period, and the apparent strength of the case against him were factors they would take into account in deciding where the interests of justice lay (see *Saunders* (1973) 58 Cr App R 248 and *Flower* (1965) 50 Cr App R 22).

26.37   One issue which must sometimes be considered in deciding whether a retrial should be held is the publicity surrounding the original trial and the appeal, in view of the potential impact on any future jury. In *Taylor* (1994) 98 Cr App R 361, the Court of Appeal, having upheld an appeal against conviction for murder in part because of the sensational and inaccurate publicity surrounding the trial, went on to say:

> Moreover, by reason of the view we take of the way in which this case was reported, we do not think that a fair trial could now take place. Hence we do not order a retrial.

In *Stone* [2001] Crim LR 465, the Court of Appeal considered whether exceptional publicity surrounding both the original trial for murder and the successful appeal of the appellant precluded a retrial. Although the publicity was sensational and possibly inaccurate in parts, the court was not satisfied on the balance of probabilities that it was such as to make a retrial oppressive or unfair or make a verdict in the retrial unsafe. A retrial was ordered.

26.38   Section 8, as amended, deals with the procedure when a retrial is ordered. A fresh indictment is preferred. Normally that will be for the self-same offence as was alleged in the original indictment, but the Court may order that the appellant be retried for an offence of which he could have been convicted at the first trial by way of alternative verdict, or an offence alleged in an alternative count in respect of which the jury were discharged from giving a verdict because they convicted on the other count (see s 7(2)(b) and (c)). The new indictment should be preferred promptly since an arraignment more than two months after the order for retrial will require leave from the Court: s 8(1A). Pending a retrial, the appellant is remanded in custody or on bail at the discretion of the Court of Appeal. Should he again be convicted, the sentence passed must not be more severe than that imposed after the first trial, although it may, of course, be more lenient (see Sch 2 to the CAA).

A writ of *venire de novo*

26.39   In the vast majority of cases coming before it, the Court of Appeal will rely on the powers given it by s 2 of the CAA in order to quash or, as the case may be, uphold a conviction. However, the Court also has a power, independent of statute and inherited from the old Court of Crown Cases Reserved, to quash a conviction and issue a writ of *venire de novo*. The effect of issuing the writ is virtually the same as ordering a retrial.

26.40   The somewhat arcane law on the subject is summarized in the propositions below which are based on dicta from Lord Diplock's judgment in *Rose* [1982] AC 822) and Watkins LJ's in *Newland* [1988] QB 402.

(i) The power to issue a writ of *venire de novo* arises only when a procedural irregularity occurred before or at the outset of the Crown Court proceedings which was of such a fundamental nature as to render the appellant's so-called 'trial' a total mistrial, with the consequence that he was never at any stage of the hearing before the jury in danger of a valid conviction. Examples are where the committal proceedings purporting to justify the preferment of a bill of indictment were invalid, or where a jury were asked to try two separate indictments simultaneously. *Venire de novo* is not, however, appropriate when the appellant complains of an irregularity occurring during a validly commenced trial, even if it is the type of error that seems to go to the root of the jury's power to return a verdict (e.g., the jury returned a majority verdict when the provisions of s 17 of the Juries Act were not complied with). In such cases, the appellant must simply rely on the grounds of appeal specified in s 2(1) of the CAA (see especially *Rose* [1982] AC 822 at pp. 831–3).

(ii) If the Court does have power to issue *venire de novo*, it may, at its discretion, simply quash the conviction and do no more—i.e., it is not obliged to order that the successful appellant be retried.

(iii) As issue of *venire de novo* presupposes that the appellant's trial was a total nullity, whereas the ground for allowing an appeal set out in s 2(1) of the CAA presupposes the opposite, there will never be circumstances in which the Court can choose to quash a conviction either by virtue of its inherent common law power or by virtue of its statutory powers (see especially *Rose* at p. 833; *Newland* at p. 408).

(iv) Now that the Court of Appeal has a discretion to order a retrial whenever it allows an appeal under s 2(1) and not just in fresh evidence cases, much of the point of distinguishing between *venire de novo* situations and 'ordinary' appeals has been lost.

Partially successful appeals

If an appellant was convicted at the Crown Court on two or more counts, and appeals against 26.41 all those convictions, the Court of Appeal may, of course, allow the appeal on some but not all the counts. Further, where the indictment against the appellant was such that the jury could have convicted him on it of an offence other than the one of which they did convict him, the Court may substitute for the jury's verdict a verdict of guilty of that other offence: CAA, s 3. The Court of Appeal must take the view that the jury must have been satisfied of the facts proving the appellant guilty of the other offence. Section 3 may apply in two situations. First, if the jury, on a count in the indictment, convicted the appellant as charged, but could have returned a verdict of not guilty as charged but guilty of a lesser offence, the Court of Appeal can substitute for their verdict a conviction for the lesser offence. Secondly, if the jury convicted of one of two counts on the indictment in the alternative, and were discharged from giving a verdict on the other count, the Court of Appeal can reverse the verdicts (i.e., quash the conviction and enter a verdict of guilty of the offence in respect of which the jury were discharged from giving a verdict) (see 21.21). In *Worton* (1990) 154 JP 201, for example, W was one of several charged with violent disorder under s 2 of the Public Order Act 1986. The trial judge failed to direct the jury correctly as to the effect on the case against W of his co-accused being acquitted (i.e., it might reduce the number participating to under three and therefore make the only possible verdict affray rather than violent disorder). The Court of Appeal quashed the conviction, then substituted a conviction for affray. Even if the appellant pleaded guilty in the Crown Court, a verdict of guilty of an alternative offence can now be substituted by the Court of Appeal, by virtue of s 3A of the CAA, as inserted by the CJA 2003, s 316.

Single right of appeal

26.42 Once an appeal has been dealt with, the appellant is debarred from bringing a second appeal in the matter (*Pinfold* [1988] QB 462). This is the case even if the point to be raised at the second appeal is entirely different from that which was dealt with at the first. In *Pinfold*, P's original appeal was on the basis of a misdirection in the summing-up. His proposed second appeal would have relied on fresh evidence. It was held that the court had no jurisdiction to determine a second appeal in the light of the dismissal of the earlier one.

26.43 The rule restricting the appellant to a single appeal can create a strange anomaly where there are several grounds of appeal, and the Court of Appeal indicates that it will allow the appeal on one ground, without hearing argument on the others, in order to save time. It may then be open to the Crown to appeal to the House of Lords against the Court of Appeal's decision to allow the appeal (see 26.105 to 26.107). If the Crown is successful in the House of Lords, the appellant will be unable to revive those grounds which were never considered by the Court of Appeal. The problem can be avoided if the Crown indicates to the Court of Appeal, immediately an appeal is allowed on one of several grounds, that it is likely to take the matter to the House of Lords. The Court of Appeal can then decide whether to consider the other grounds of appeal (see *Berry* [1994] Crim LR 276, where this procedure was commended as a way out of the dilemma). Another possibility is for the House of Lords to exercise the powers of the Court of Appeal in relation to any grounds not disposed of by the latter court (*Mandair* [1995] 1 AC 208). The rule in *Pinfold* does not apply where the case has been referred to the Court of Appeal by the Criminal Cases Review Commission under the powers given to it by s 13 of the CAA 1995: *Thomas* [2002] Crim LR 912.

E   DETERMINATION OF APPEALS AGAINST SENTENCE

26.44 On an appeal against sentence, the Court of Appeal may quash any sentence or order which is the subject of the appeal, and replace it with the sentence or order it considers appropriate provided:

(a)   the sentence it passes or order it makes is one which the Crown Court could have passed or made, and

(b)   taking the case as a whole, the appellant is not more severely dealt with on appeal than he was by the Crown Court: CAA, s 11(3).

Unlike the old Court of Criminal Appeal, the Court of Appeal does not have the power to increase sentence in cases where the appeal is brought by the sentenced offender. Where, however, the Court allows an appeal in respect of one count but confirms the conviction in respect of another count, it may increase the sentence for the count on which the appellant still stands convicted, provided it does not make the sentence more severe than the total sentence passed by the Crown Court on both counts: s 4. If the Court of Appeal substitutes for the jury's verdict a verdict of guilty of a lesser offence (see 26.41) it may pass a sentence for the lesser offence which again must not be more severe than the Crown Court sentence: s 3(2). Despite the prohibition on increasing sentence, an appellant serving a custodial sentence may find that his sentence has in effect been increased through the court directing that the time he has spent in custody pending determination of his appeal shall not count as part of his sentence. Section 11 (no increase in sentence) should therefore be considered in conjunction with s 29 (directions for loss of time: see 26.58 to 26.62). It should also be borne in mind that the Attorney-General may refer a sentence to the Court of Appeal if he considers it too lenient, and their Lordships may then deal with the offender more severely than the Crown Court judge did (see 26.80 to 26.87). Attorney-General's sentencing references are, however, quite distinct from appeals by the offender, where the basic rule is still that the Court cannot increase sentence. In *Reynolds* [2007] Crim LR 493, the Court of Appeal considered the position where the sentencing judge had failed to pass the sentence which the law required upon a dangerous offender e.g. an extended sentence or imprisonment for public protection (see 24.34 to 24.42). Their lordships held that they could not effectively increase the sentence by imposing the sentence which the law required. The restrictions laid down in s 11 prevailed, but the 'unlawful' sentence imposed by the court below must still be served.

Apart from ruling out any increase in the appellant's sentence, s 11(3) of the CAA places no **26.45** restriction on the Court of Appeal's approach to determining appeals. There is no statutory bar on the Court habitually substituting its own view of what the sentence should have been for the sentence actually passed, even if the reduction in sentence is very slight. However, their Lordships have always recognized that views on sentencing legitimately vary from judge to judge—some are bound to be on the severe side, others on the lenient side, and the individual sentencer is entitled to a measure of discretion in performing his task.

Thus, there is no one right sentence for a particular case but rather an acceptable range within which the sentence actually imposed should fall. Provided the appellant's sentence was within the acceptable range, it is unlikely to be reduced on appeal, even if it was at the top end of the range and greater than the individual members of the Court of Appeal would have imposed had they been the judges at first instance. As Lord Hewart CJ expressed it in *Gumbs* (1926) 19 Cr App R 74:

> This court never interferes with the discretion of the court below merely on the ground that this court might have passed a somewhat different sentence; for this court to revise a sentence there must be some error in principle.

The principal situations in which an appeal is likely to succeed are as follows:

(a) **Sentence wrong in law.** If the Crown Court judge's sentence was one which he was not in law entitled to pass, the Court of Appeal will replace it with a lawful sentence (subject to the decision in *Reynolds* dealt with in 26.44).

(b) **Sentence wrong in principle or manifestly excessive.** This is by far the commonest basis for a successful appeal. As explained above, the appellant must do more than show that his sentence was 'on the severe side'. He must show that it was outside the commonly accepted range of penalties for his type of case. 'Wrong in principle' is a phrase particularly apt to cover cases where the judge chose completely the wrong type of sentence—e.g., passed a custodial sentence when the offence did not pass the 'custody threshold' as laid down in the Criminal Justice Act 1991, s 1(2). 'Manifestly excessive' applies when the right form of sentence is chosen, but it is simply much too severe, or the sentence is clearly disproportionate to the offence.

(c) **Wrong approach to sentencing.** If it is apparent from the judge's remarks when he passed sentence that he dealt with the offender more severely than he would otherwise have done on account of a factor which he ought to have left out of consideration, the sentence will probably be reduced. Examples are when the judge says that he is increasing sentence because the offender pleaded not guilty and/or ran a defence in which imputations were cast on the conduct or veracity of the prosecution witnesses (*Skone* (1967) 51 Cr App R 165).

(d) **Wrong procedure prior to sentence.** Several cases were described in Chapter 22 where faulty procedures were adopted in the Crown Court between conviction and sentence to the potential detriment of the offender (e.g., *Newton* (1982) 77 Cr App R 13 where the judge accepted the prosecution version of the facts of the offence without hearing evidence, and *Wilkins* (1978) 66 Cr App R 49 where antecedents evidence prejudicial to the offender was tendered by an officer without first-hand knowledge of the matters about which he testified). The Court of Appeal will usually mark their disapproval of such irregularities by reducing the sentence. However, they sometimes say that the sentence itself was the correct one despite the procedural lapse, and therefore uphold it.

(e) **Disparity.** A marked difference in the treatment handed out to co-offenders, when that cannot be justified either by their differing degrees of involvement in the offence or the differing amounts of mitigation at their disposal, is sometimes put forward by the one more severely dealt with as a ground for reducing his sentence. The Court of Appeal's attitude to such arguments has been very inconsistent. One approach is to allow the appeal if the disparity is so marked that (even though the sentence received by the appellant was not wrong in principle or manifestly excessive) he would be left with a burning and understandable sense of grievance as he contemplated the more lenient penalty with which his equally culpable co-offender escaped (see *Dickinson* [1977] Crim LR 303). The alternative approach is to say that 'two wrongs do not make a right'. The fact that O1 was given too lenient a sentence is no justification for reducing the sentence of his accomplice, O2, assuming that O2's sentence would not otherwise be open to criticism. As it was put in *Stroud* (1977) 65 Cr App R 150: 'The appellant's proposition is that where you have one wrong sentence and one right sentence, this Court should produce two wrong sentences. That is a submission which this Court cannot accept.' According to *Stroud*, disparity should never be regarded as a good ground for appealing a sentence. However, there have certainly been cases since *Stroud* where it has seemed to be the major if not the only argument relied on by a successful appellant (see, for example, *Wood* (1983) 5 Cr App R (S) 381). Perhaps the true position is that disparity of sentence between co-offenders is a factor which the Court of Appeal ought to take into consideration when the more heavily sentenced offender appeals, but if the sentence was well within the accepted norms the appeal will probably fail. If, however, the sentence (even viewed in isolation) was on the severe side, the added consideration of disparity and the appearance of unfairness in the original treatment of the appellant will tip the scales in favour of reducing the sentence. It may also be easier to succeed on the ground of disparity when the co-offenders were sentenced by the same judge on the same occasion.

F   PROCEDURE FOR APPEALING

In outline, the standard procedure for appealing against conviction or sentence is as follows: **26.46**

(a)   Within 28 days of conviction or sentence, depending on which the appeal is against, the appellant serves on the Crown Court a notice of application for leave to appeal. The notice must be accompanied by grounds of appeal. If counsel has advised the appeal, he settles and signs the grounds. Otherwise, the appellant does the drafting himself. It is regarded as good practice, where counsel advises on appeal, that the advice should be sent to the solicitor within 14 days of conviction and that the solicitor should ensure that the lay client receives it within a further 7 days. If the appellant was publicly funded for the proceedings in the Crown Court, that funding covers advice on the merits of an appeal and, if so advised, the serving of notice and drafting of grounds of appeal. Having received the notice and grounds, the Crown Court forwards them to the Registrar of Criminal Appeals.

(b)   Where the appeal is against conviction, the drafting of grounds of appeal nearly always falls into two stages. The grounds submitted with the notice of application for leave to appeal (the 'initial grounds') are based on counsel's longhand note of what happened at the Crown Court. Inevitably, the note will be incomplete and partially inaccurate. However, a shorthand writer takes a full note of Crown Court proceedings, and counsel asks the registrar to obtain a transcript of as much of the note as he (counsel) considers is needed for the proper presentation of the appeal. Unless the registrar thinks that counsel is making unjustified demands, he does as requested, and delivers a copy of the transcript to counsel. A transcript of the judge's summing-up is hardly ever refused. A transcript of at least part of the evidence may also be necessary, depending on the nature of the initial grounds. Having read the transcript, counsel may advise that the appeal be abandoned. This, of course, does not prevent the appellant continuing the appeal without legal assistance, but if he does so he runs the risk of a direction for loss of time (see 26.58 to 26.62). On the other hand, if counsel continues to think that the appellant has a reasonably arguable case, he *perfects* his initial grounds of appeal—i.e., he amends them in the light of and with cross-references to the transcript. For what the perfected grounds should contain, see 26.51 to 26.52.

(c)   The papers in the case are put before a single judge. The papers will include the perfected grounds of appeal, the transcript and any other relevant documents (e.g., documentary exhibits adduced in evidence at the Crown Court, or a statement from a witness who has just come forward and whom the appellant wishes to call at the hearing of the appeal). In the light of these documents, the single judge decides whether to grant leave to appeal. If he does so, he might also *inter alia* grant the appellant an order for legal representation at the hearing, grant him bail pending determination of the appeal, or order that a potential witness attend for examination.

(d)   The appellant is notified of the single judge's decision. If it is unfavourable, he has 14 days in which to notify the registrar that he wishes to renew the application before a court of the Criminal Division (see 26.54 to 26.56). Assuming leave to appeal is granted (whether by the single judge or a court on a renewed application), the registrar and his staff check that the papers are all in order, prepare a summary of the case and fix a hearing date. The summary is read by the judges who are to hear the appeal, and is available to counsel in the case. It is a purely factual document, which does not contain any views on the merits of the case.

(e) At the hearing, counsel for the appellant presents argument. If the appeal is against conviction, the Crown will almost certainly be represented, and may be called upon in reply to the appellant's case. Occasionally witnesses are called by the appellant (e.g., an alibi witness whose identity could not have been known at the time of the trial on indictment), but usually the appeal will involve only consideration of the transcript and of counsel's arguments. At an appeal against sentence only, the Crown is unlikely to be represented, as it is not the prosecution's task, either at the Crown Court or on appeal, to argue for a high sentence.

There are two main variations on the above standard procedure. First, of course, the appellant may have received a certificate from the trial judge (see 26.10 to 26.11). In that event, he gives notice of appeal (not notice of application for leave to appeal), and the registrar simply lists the case for full hearing by a court. The second possibility is that the registrar, looking at the grounds of appeal served on behalf of an appellant who does need leave, sees that the appeal prima facie has a good chance of success. The registrar might then bypass the single judge procedure through listing the application for leave to appeal for hearing by a court. The court can then grant leave to appeal and proceed forthwith to determine the appeal.

26.47 In the Paragraphs which follow, some of the matters touched upon in the above outline of appeal procedure are explained in more detail. The reader may also wish to refer to a booklet issued by the registrar which has the approval of the Lord Chief Justice and which is entitled 'A Guide to Proceedings in the Court of Appeal Criminal Division'.

Notice of application for leave to appeal

26.48 The appellant's notice of application for leave to appeal must be given on a standard form provided by the CrimPR, r 68.3.

26.49 The notice should be served within 28 days of conviction or sentence (whichever is appealed against): CAA, s 18. Notice and grounds are sent to the location of the Crown Court where the appellant's case was heard. An officer of the Crown Court will then forward the document to the Court of Appeal. The Court has a discretion to give the appellant leave to apply for leave to appeal out of time, but there must be good reasons for the failure to serve the notice within the statutory period.

26.50 The fairly strict enforcement of the 28-day limit for giving notice ought not to lead to injustice. If the appellant is legally represented at the Crown Court, counsel or a representative of the solicitors will normally see him after the verdict and sentence, and advise informally on whether there are grounds for appeal. Most defendants at the Crown Court are publicly funded, and those funds cover a written advice from counsel on the merits of an appeal and, if so advised, the drafting of grounds of appeal. Having received the grounds from counsel the solicitors obtain a notice form from the Criminal Appeal Office or the Crown Court, complete it on behalf of the appellant, and serve it, together with the grounds, on the Crown Court. If the appellant is unrepresented, or his representatives advise against an appeal, he may complete the forms himself. If he is in custody, the forms are available at the prison etc. where he is detained.

Grounds of appeal

In preparing his grounds of appeal, which should accompany the notice, the appellant must **26.51** again make use of a standard form from the Criminal Appeal Office. If counsel settles and signs the grounds they are typed on a separate sheet, which is served together with the notice and grounds forms. As already explained, the grounds as initially settled may not be fit to go before the single judge. Once perfected, they should enable the single judge or court to identify the particular matters put forward by the appellant for their consideration (see para 2.2 of the registrar's Guide). It is not enough to state in general terms that 'the conviction is unsafe or unsatisfactory' or 'the sentence was too severe in all the circumstances of the case' without giving reasons for those assertions. No particular formality is required in the phrasing of the grounds, provided the point or points the appellant wishes to raise are made clear. A convenient method of drafting is to deal with the errors of which complaint is made in chronological order—e.g., ground one might deal with the trial judge failing to sever the indictment, ground two with his failing to uphold a submission of no case to answer, ground three with his wrongly allowing the appellant to be cross-examined about his previous convictions, and ground four with various misdirections in the summing-up. The grounds should refer by page number and letter to relevant passages in the transcript, and should cite authorities on which counsel intends to rely (para 4.4 of the Guide). Where the appellant wishes to call a witness at the hearing of the appeal, the reasons for doing so should be fully developed. If counsel settles grounds, he should only include those which are reasonable, have some real prospect of success and are such that he is prepared to argue them before the court (see para 2.4 of the registrar's Guide). If no such grounds exist, the appellant must be left to pursue his appeal in person if he so wishes. An example of grounds of appeal appears on page 507.

Sometimes counsel later supplements his grounds with a skeleton argument which their **26.52** Lordships can read prior to the hearing of the appeal. In complicated cases, this may save some time which would otherwise be wasted in orally laying the groundwork of the appellant's argument. The *Practice Direction* (*Criminal Proceedings: Consolidation*) [2002] 1 WLR 2870 lays down the requirements for skeleton arguments in appeals against conviction. The advocate for the appellant must lodge a skeleton argument with the registrar, and serve it on the prosecuting authority, within 14 days of receipt by the advocate of leave to appeal against conviction (unless a longer period is directed). The prosecutor should lodge a skeleton argument within 14 days of receipt of the appellant's skeleton (unless directed otherwise).

Transcripts

A shorthand writer takes a note of any proceedings in the Crown Court upon which an **26.53** appeal may lie to the Court of Appeal. The registrar and any 'interested party' has a right to be supplied with a transcript of the note, but only upon payment of a fixed charge: r 68.13 of the CrimPR, r 68.13. The cost of a transcript would inhibit most appellants from obtaining one, but the registrar has a discretion to order a transcript and supply a copy free of charge to any publicly funded appellant. Virtually all appellants are publicly funded, so, essentially, the supplying of transcripts depends on the registrar's discretion. In his initial grounds of appeal, counsel specifies those parts of the transcript which he needs providing names of witnesses, dates and times where necessary (para 3.2 of the Guide). If it is an appeal against conviction, he will almost certainly ask for and be given a transcript of the summing-up. It is also reasonable to have a transcript of any evidence said to be inadmissible. However, counsel should not request a transcript of *all* the evidence unless that really is essential to the determination of the appeal, since obtaining it will be both time-consuming and expensive (see *Flemming* (1987) 86 Cr App R 32 at p. 39, where Woolf LJ criticized counsel for ordering six bundles of transcript and then only referring to two at the hearing of the appeal). For an appeal against sentence, a transcript of the antecedents evidence, counsel's mitigation and any remarks the judge made when passing sentence may be of value. If the appellant pleaded guilty, the prosecution's summary of the facts could also be included. The registrar may decline to order some or all of the transcript which counsel requests. If dissatisfied with the registrar's decision, counsel may have the question referred to a single judge.

Applications to a single judge: Criminal Appeal Act 1968, s 31

26.54 The following ancillary powers of the Court of Appeal may be, and most frequently are, exercised by a single judge (i.e., a Lord Justice of Appeal or a High Court judge whom the Lord Chief Justice has asked to assist in the work of the Criminal Division):

(a) granting leave to appeal;
(b) granting leave to commence an appeal or to apply for leave to appeal out of time;
(c) allowing an appellant to be present at proceedings connected with his appeal when he is in custody and has no right to attend;
(d) ordering a witness, whose evidence the appellant wishes to adduce before the court, to attend for examination;
(e) granting bail to the appellant;
(f) granting an order for legal representation; and
(g) making a direction for loss of time.

Most of these powers have already been referred to; those which have not are described in the succeeding Sections. By far the most significant of the single judge's powers is that of granting leave to appeal. As already explained, he normally considers the application privately, without counsel attending. His decision is based upon a reading of the papers in the case, in particular the transcript and counsel's grounds of appeal.

26.55 Notification of the single judge's decision is given to the appellant. If the application is refused (whether it be an application for leave to appeal or an application for any other of the single judge's powers to be exercised in his favour), the appellant has a right to renew the application before a court: CAA, s 31(3). He must, however, serve the appropriate notice on the registrar within 14 days of being told of the single judge's adverse decision: CrimPR, r 68.6. Although there is power to extend the period for giving notice, this is only done if the appellant had good reason for not acting within time. To assist the appellant in deciding whether to renew the application, brief written reasons why he rejected it may be given by the single judge. On a renewed application for leave to appeal, the court will announce its decision in open court and give reasons.

26.56 Although the standard procedure is to make an ancillary application first to the single judge and then, perhaps, to a court if the single judge proves adverse, there is nothing to stop the application being made direct to a court. For the purposes both of applications initially made to a court and of applications renewed before a court after being turned down by the single judge, the court need only consist of two judges. The one exception to this is that a two-judge court cannot refuse (although it can grant) an application for leave to appeal against conviction made to it without prior unsuccessful application to a single judge.

Applications to the Registrar

The Registrar of the Court of Appeal is given certain powers by s 31A(2) of the CAA 1968: **26.57**

(a) to extend the time within which notice of appeal or application for leave to appeal may be given;
(b) to order a witness to attend for examination; and
(c) to vary an appellant's conditions of bail.

As far as (c) is concerned, the registrar may vary conditions only if the respondent does not object. In relation to any of the powers, if the registrar refuses an application by the appellant, the appellant is entitled to have it determined by the single judge.

Directions concerning loss of time: Criminal Appeal Act 1968, s 29

Unless a direction to the contrary is given, the time that the appellant spends in custody **26.58** between commencing his appeal and its being determined counts as part of any custodial sentence which he is serving, whether the sentence was imposed in the Crown Court proceedings which are the subject of the appeal or on some previous occasion. A direction to the contrary (i.e., a direction for loss of time) may be given by the single judge on refusing an application for leave to appeal, or by the court on an unsuccessful renewal of an application for leave to appeal, or by the court when dismissing an appeal on a ground of pure law. Directions for loss of time are a means of penalizing an appellant for commencing a meritless appeal which wastes the time of the court. It should be stressed that the Court of Appeal has no power to increase an appellant's sentence, in the strict sense.

In the *Practice Direction (Criminal Proceedings: Consolidation)* [2002] 1 WLR 2870, para II.16.1, an **26.59** indication is given as to the way in which the power to direct a loss of time will be exercised. It is stressed, not only that there should be grounds for appeal, but that they 'should be substantial and particularised and not a mere formula'. The direction goes on to state:

> Where an application devoid of merit has been refused by the single judge and a direction for loss of time has been made, the Full Court, on renewal of the application, may direct that additional time shall be lost . . .

A direction for loss of time may relate to part only of the time the appellant has been in cus- **26.60** tody since commencing his appeal. Thus, in a case where grounds have not been settled by counsel, the single judge could order that the appellant lose, say, a month's time, and, if he were unwise enough to renew the application, the court could order that he lose a further two months.

Whether the Court of Appeal should have power to make directions for loss of time is an **26.61** arguable point. Certainly, the knowledge that his custodial sentence might, in effect, be increased if he is thought to be wasting the court's time, will discourage a frivolous appeal.

Time-wasting applications for leave to appeal need to be discouraged because they delay the consideration of applications which have merit. The counter-argument is that fear of a direction for loss of time might discourage not only the worthless but some worthwhile appeals. It may also seem unfair that those who have not received custodial sentences may appeal with impunity, whereas those who are serving custodial sentences and, prima facie, have more urgent reasons for appealing, are liable to possible sanctions if they do so.

26.62 In practice, directions for loss of time have thus far been very rare, although the Court of Appeal does from time to time warn that it has the power and will make use of it. In *Hart* [2006] EWCA Crim 3239, the Court stated that the number of applications totally without merit was so substantial that it would have to consider exercise of the power with greater frequency than in the past. Two of the four unrelated applications which it heard in that case were made the subject of directions for loss of time. In each case, the direction was that 28 days of the period spent in custody should not count towards sentence.

Bail pending hearing of the appeal: Criminal Appeal Act 1968, s 19

26.63 The Court of Appeal's power to grant bail to an appellant, pending determination of his appeal, is exercisable by a single judge. The procedure is to indicate on the notice of application for leave to appeal form that the appellant is also applying for bail. In addition, a form giving details of the application must be served on the registrar. Bail is rarely granted as, in the event of the appeal failing, the appellant will suffer the trauma of being returned to prison. The question is—'Are there exceptional circumstances which would drive the court to the conclusion that justice can only be done by the granting of bail?': *Watton* (1979) 68 Cr App R 293. The fact that the single judge has granted leave to appeal against conviction does not in itself justify bail, but the appellant might be bailed where either the appeal seems likely to succeed, or he is serving a short custodial sentence which, in the absence of bail, is likely to be completed before the appeal is heard. The seriousness of the offence and the likelihood or otherwise of a retrial being ordered will no doubt also enter into consideration in deciding on bail.

26.64 If, and only if, he has certified that the case is fit for appeal, the appropriate Crown Court judge may bail an appellant pending determination of the appeal. If the appeal is against conviction or against sentence following conviction on indictment, the appropriate judge is the judge at the trial on indictment; if the appeal is against sentence following a committal for sentence, the appropriate judge is the judge who passed sentence. The power to grant bail must be exercised within 28 days of conviction or sentence depending on what the appeal is against, and the power is lost if the appellant chooses to apply for bail to the Court of Appeal itself. The Court of Appeal can always revoke bail granted by the Crown Court judge or vary the conditions on which he granted it. If bail is granted before the 'appellant' has served a notice of appeal or a notice of application for leave to appeal, the serving of notice is made a condition of bail.

26.65 The Court of Appeal has indicated that the power should be used sparingly. In *Grant* (1990) 12 Cr App R (S) 441, their lordships stated that, if the sentencer is persuaded that he has made the wrong decision, he should use his own powers to vary sentence within 28 days (Supreme Court Act 1981, s 47(2)—see 22.66 to 22.68), or allow the case to take the normal route

through the appeal system. The powers to certify as fit for appeal and to grant bail
reserved for cases where there is a 'particular and cogent ground of appeal'.

Presence at the appeal: Criminal Appeal Act 1968, s 22

An appellant need not be present at the hearing of his appeal but, subject to what is mentioned **26.66**
below, he is entitled to attend if he so wishes. This applies both to the actual determination of
the appeal and to ancillary applications. However, by way of exception to the general rule, an
appellant who is in custody requires leave from a single judge if he is to attend either ancillary
applications or, if the appeal is on a ground of law alone, the hearing proper.

Evidence called before the Court of Appeal: Criminal Appeal Act 1968, s 23

The Court of Appeal has a discretionary power to receive evidence under s 23 of the Criminal **26.67**
Appeals Act 1968. This power is unfettered, but the factors which the Court ought to take into
account are those listed in s 23(2), which states that their lordships should, in considering
whether to receive any evidence, have regard in particular to whether:

(a) it appears credible;
(b) it appears that it may afford any ground for allowing the appeal;
(c) it would have been admissible at trial; and
(d) there is a reasonable explanation for the failure to adduce the evidence at trial.

It is clear that points (a) to (d) are not conditions which must be satisfied before the evidence
can be heard. They are factors for the Court of Appeal to take into account in exercising its
discretion.

To decide whether proposed evidence is likely to be credible (see point (a) above) the judges **26.68**
in the Court of Appeal consider the testimony it is anticipated the witness will give in the context of the case as a whole: *Parks* [1961] 1 WLR 1484. Relevant factors are whether the witness'
proof of evidence is intrinsically credible, and whether it fits in with at least some of the other
evidence in the case. As to factor (d) any explanation for not adducing the evidence at the
Crown Court is closely examined by the court. The general principle is that all the relevant
evidence should be put before the jury so that they can make a once and for all decision on
the issues of fact. As Edmund Davies LJ expressed it in *Stafford and Luvaglio* (1969) 53 Cr App
R 1 at p. 3:

> public mischief would ensue and legal process could become indefinitely prolonged were it the
> case that evidence produced at any time will generally be admitted when verdicts are being
> reviewed.

In a sample of 102 appeals which were successful in 1992, only four were allowed on the
grounds of fresh evidence (Research Study No 17 for the Royal Commission on Criminal
Justice by Kate Malleson (London: HMSO, 1993)). The reason often given is that explained
above—the jury, not the Court of Appeal, are the tribunal of fact, and all the relevant evidence should be put before them. Where, however, the evidence the appellant wishes to
adduce appears exceptionally cogent the court will, in the interests of justice to the individual, hear it.

ɔ.69   Having heard evidence, the members of the court ask themselves whether in the light of that evidence and all the circumstances of the case the conviction is unsafe. In *Pendleton* [2002] Crim LR 398, the House of Lords considered the approach which the Court of Appeal ought to adopt in determining the safety of the conviction where they had decided to admit fresh evidence. Lord Bingham said it was important that 'the Court of Appeal bears very clearly in mind that the question for its consideration is whether the conviction is safe and not whether the accused is guilty'. He stated:

> ... it will usually be wise for the Court of Appeal, in a case of any difficulty, to test their own provisional view by asking whether the evidence, if given at the trial, might reasonably have affected the decision of the trial jury to convict. If it might, the conviction must be thought to be unsafe.

Should they allow the appeal, their lordships will have to consider whether or not to order a retrial. If the fresh evidence points strongly to the appellant's innocence, they are unlikely to order a retrial (for other factors, see 26.36 and 26.37).

26.70   What if the fresh evidence which the appellant wants considered promotes a line of defence not raised at trial? That was the position in *Ahluwahlia* [1992] 4 All ER 889. A killed her husband 'after enduring many years of violence and humiliation' from him, by throwing petrol into his bedroom and setting it alight. She was tried for murder. Her case was that she did not intend to kill him or cause him really serious harm. Provocation was her secondary line of defence. The jury rejected both lines of defence and convicted her of murder. She appealed on three grounds. The first two related to the trial judge's directions on provocation and were dismissed. The third ground was that she relied on evidence of diminished responsibility, which had not been raised as a defence at trial. A number of psychiatric reports were put before the Court of Appeal, expressing the opinion that A's responsibility was diminished at the time that she killed her husband. Their lordships decided to admit the reports as fresh evidence. They concluded that there may well have been an arguable defence which was not put forward at trial, for reasons which were unexplained. They upheld the appeal on the basis that the verdict was 'unsafe and unsatisfactory', and ordered a retrial.

26.71   An appellant who wishes to adduce evidence before the court should indicate on his notice of application for leave to appeal form that he is also asking for leave to call a witness. The court will be aware of the nature of the proposed evidence because the appellant's solicitors should have sent to the registrar either an affidavit sworn by the witness or a statement by him complying with s 9 of the Criminal Justice Act 1967 (see 20.34). If a witness is unwilling to cooperate, a single judge can order him to attend court prior to the hearing of the appeal so that an officer appointed by the Court of Appeal can take a deposition from him: CrimPR, r 68.15 and 68.16.

26.72   Where the court does decide to receive the evidence, and the witness would have been compellable at the trial on indictment, he may be called by the court, rather than by one of the parties, examined in chief by a member of the court, and then tendered to both parties for cross-examination. If the court does not call the witness but gives leave for one of the parties to call him, the normal procedure for examining witnesses applies—the party calling him examines him in chief, the other party cross-examines and the court may ask any questions it thinks fit. Normally it will be the appellant who wishes the court to receive evidence, but the prosecution may seek to call a witness to rebut the evidence the court has heard on behalf of the appellant.

When determining appeals against sentence, the Court of Appeal often has the benefit of pre- **26.73**
sentence, medical, psychiatric and other reports. Up-to-date reports of the progress the appellant is making in the prison or young offender institution are also of value. When an appeal
against conviction involves an allegation of an irregularity in the course of the trial, such as
the judge constantly interrupting the defence or bringing improper pressure to bear on the
accused to persuade him to plead guilty, the court may accept informal 'evidence' of what
occurred in the shape of statements by counsel or a note from the judge.

Publicly funded representation and costs

A person wishing to appeal to the Court of Appeal (Criminal Division) may be granted an **26.74**
order for legal representation for that purpose. The order may only be made by the Criminal
Division itself, not by the Crown Court: Criminal Defence Service (General) (No 2)
Regulations 2001 (SI 2001 No 1437), reg 10. The Division may exercise its powers through a
single judge or through the registrar. For the initial stages of the appeal procedure, an appellant who had a representation order for the Crown Court proceedings will not need to have
any further order made in his favour, since the Crown Court order will cover advice on the
merits of an appeal and—if so advised—the service of notice and drafting of grounds of
appeal. Assuming the single judge grants leave to appeal, he will almost certainly make an
order to cover representation at the hearing. Unless a lot of preparatory work still needs to be
done, the order will be 'for counsel only', rather than for 'counsel and solicitor'. In the former
case, counsel is assigned by the registrar. Save that the registrar then provides him with a brief
and the papers, he does not act as counsel's solicitor. Where leave to appeal is refused, the
Crown Court order will pay for advice on whether it is worth renewing the application before
a court, but will not pay for representation at the renewed hearing (see *Gibson* [1983] 1 WLR
1038 and *Kearney* [1983] 1 WLR 1046). If the appellant was not publicly funded in the Crown
Court, he may apply to the registrar for the grant of an order which will at least cover initial
advice on and preparation for appeal.

A successful appellant against conviction may be awarded his costs out of central (i.e., govern- **26.75**
ment) funds: Prosecution of Offences Act 1985, s 16(4). This is known as a 'defendant's costs
order' (see Chapter 29 for general consideration of costs). If the appeal fails, the appellant may
be ordered to pay to the prosecution (or any other person named by the Court of Appeal, such
as the provider of the transcript of the Crown Court proceedings) whatever costs the Court
considers 'just and reasonable': POA 1985, s 18(2).

G OTHER WAYS IN WHICH MATTERS COME BEFORE
THE COURT OF APPEAL

The main function of the Court of Appeal (Criminal Division) is to quash convictions or **26.76**
reduce sentences upon an appeal brought by the defendant in Crown Court proceedings.
Originally that was virtually its only function, and the prosecution had no right of redress if
it considered that the accused had been wrongly acquitted or sentenced too leniently.
However, since 1972, there has been a procedure by which the prosecution can test the

correctness of a ruling on law given by the Crown Court judge during the course of the trial which culminated in an acquittal, although the accused himself remains acquitted come what may. In addition, the Court of Appeal was given the power by the CJA 1988 actually to increase an offender's sentence. Both of these procedures require the reference to be made by the Attorney-General. Further, as a result of ss 55 to 74 of the CJA 2003, the prosecution is now entitled to appeal against certain rulings made by the judge in the course of the trial.

26.77   Paragraphs 26.78 to 26.87 deal with the Attorney-General's references on points of law and sentencing. Paragraphs 26.88 to 26.96 deal with prosecution appeals against rulings by the judge in the course of the trial. Paragraphs 26.97 to 26.99 deal with appeals against a verdict of 'not guilty by reason of insanity'.

Reference by the Attorney-General: Criminal Justice Act 1972, s 36

26.78   Until 1972, no procedure existed for testing the correctness of a decision or statement of law made by a judge during the course of a trial on indictment which ended in the acquittal of the accused. This was because the prosecution could not, and still cannot, appeal against an acquittal on indictment. The absence of any method of appeal left open the possibility that a ruling by a Crown Court judge which was unduly favourable to the accused might be reported, and become accepted as representing the law, when it was, in fact, mistaken. To avoid this happening, s 36 of the Criminal Justice Act 1972 provides that where a person has been tried on indictment and acquitted (whether on the whole indictment or some counts only), the Attorney-General may refer to the Court of Appeal for their opinion any point of law which arose in the case. Before giving their opinion on the point referred, the Court must hear argument by or on behalf of the Attorney-General. The person acquitted also has the right to have counsel present argument on his behalf. However, despite his right to be represented at the hearing, the person acquitted is not put in peril by the proceedings. Whatever the opinion expressed by the Court of Appeal—even if they decide that the trial judge was wrong and the facts of the case were such that the accused clearly ought to have been convicted—the acquittal is unaffected: s 36(7). By making a reference, the Attorney-General may obtain a ruling which will assist the prosecution in future cases against other suspects, but he cannot set aside the acquittal of the particular accused whose case gave rise to the reference.

26.79   In *Attorney-General's Reference (No 1 of 1975)* [1975] QB 733, Lord Widgery CJ stated that references by the Attorney-General should not be confined to cases where 'very heavy questions of law arise', but should also be made when 'short but important points require a quick ruling of [the Court of Appeal] before a potentially false decision of law has too wide a circulation in the courts'. The usefulness of Attorney-General's references is illustrated by *Attorney-General's References (Nos 1 and 2 of 1979)* [1979] 3 All ER 143, where 'burglars' surprised when committing the offence, had been acquitted following rulings that, although there was evidence of entering a building with intent to steal anything of value which might be found therein, s 9(1)(a) of the Theft Act 1968 required an intent to steal a specific item within the building entered, and the prosecution were unable to prove such an intent. The rulings could be interpreted as a 'burglar's charter', but the Attorney-General was able to refer the point of law to the Court of Appeal which quickly clarified the position—on a charge of burglary with intent to steal, the accused is guilty even if he intended to steal only if he found something in the building worth stealing. Had the Attorney-General not made the reference, the mistaken view of the law expressed by the Crown Court judges might have taken hold, with amending legislation the only way of remedying the situation.

Sentencing references: Criminal Justice Act 1988, ss 35 and 36

These are dealt with in ss 35–36 of the Criminal Justice Act 1988. Where an offender has been **26.80** sentenced in the Crown Court for either (i) an offence triable only on indictment, or (ii) an offence triable either way which is amongst those specified in an order made by the Home Secretary by statutory instrument, and the Attorney-General considers that the offender was dealt with unduly leniently, he may refer the sentence to the Court of Appeal for them to review: s 36(1). On such a review, their Lordships may quash the sentence and replace it with the sentence they consider appropriate. The substituted sentence may be *more severe* than that imposed at first instance, although it must, of course, be one that the Crown Court could lawfully have passed. The bringing of the reference is subject to the Court of Appeal granting leave.

In 1994, the power to refer indictable-only offences was supplemented by the Criminal **26.81** Justice Act 1988 (Reviews of Sentencing) Order 1994 (SI 1994 No 119) which extended that power to the following triable-either-way offences: indecent assault on a woman or a man, threats to kill, cruelty to a person under 16, attempt, or incitement to commit any of these offences. It was further extended in 2000 to cover serious fraud cases (i.e., those tried under the notice of transfer provisions in the Criminal Justice Act 1987) and certain smuggling and drug offences. Another extension took place in 2003, to bring any case in which sentence is passed on a person for a racially or religiously aggravated assault, criminal damage, public order, or harassment offence within the ambit of these provisions. (The triable-either-way offences which can be the subject of a reference are set out in the Criminal Justice Act 1988 (Reviews of Sentencing) Order: SI 2006, No 1116). Where an offender has been sentenced in the same proceedings for one offence in respect of which a reference is permissible and for a second in respect of which a reference could not otherwise be made, the Attorney-General may refer the sentencing for both matters to the Court of Appeal, which may consequently increase the sentence for both.

In *Attorney-General's Reference (No 14 of 2003), The Times* 18 April 2003, the Court of Appeal **26.82** emphasized the safeguards which applied before any increase of sentence could be ordered. First, the Attorney-General must consider the case, and decide whether he himself considers the sentence to be unduly lenient. Second, he must exercise his discretion as to whether to refer the case to the Court of Appeal. Third, the Court of Appeal must consider whether to grant leave for the reference and, in cases where leave was granted, whether the sentence was unduly lenient. Where these safeguards had not been complied with (as was the case here, since the Attorney-General had exercised his discretion on an erroneous factual basis) the application would be defective, and leave to refer the sentence would be refused.

In *Attorney-General's Reference (No 4 of 1989)* [1990] 1 WLR 41 at pp. 45–6, the Court of Appeal **26.83** set out their approach in these terms:

> The first thing to be observed is that it is implicit in the section that this court may only increase sentences which it concludes were *unduly* lenient. It cannot, we are confident, have been the intention of Parliament to subject defendants to the risk of having their sentences

increased—with all the anxiety that this naturally gives rise to—merely because in the opinion of this court the sentence was less than this court would have imposed. A sentence is unduly lenient, we would hold, where it falls outside the range of sentences which the judge, applying his mind to all the relevant factors, could reasonably consider appropriate. In that connection regard must of course be had to reported cases, and in particular to the guidance given by this court from time to time in the so-called guideline cases. However it must always be remembered that sentencing is an art rather than a science; that the trial judge is particularly well placed to assess the weight to be given to various competing considerations; and that leniency is not in itself a vice. That mercy should season justice is a proposition as soundly based in law as it is in literature.

The second thing to be observed about the section is that, even where it considers that the sentence was unduly lenient, this court has a discretion as to whether to exercise its powers. Without attempting an exhaustive definition of the circumstances in which this court might refuse to increase an unduly lenient sentence, we mention one obvious instance; where in the light of events since the trial it appears either that the sentence can be justified or that to increase it would be unfair to the offender or detrimental to others for whose well-being the court ought to be concerned.

Finally, we point to the fact that, where this court grants leave for a reference, its powers are not confined to increasing the sentence.

26.84 In the case under consideration, their lordships quashed a suspended sentence, and replaced it with a three-year probation order. Hence, a sentence referred on the basis that it was too lenient can be replaced (albeit exceptionally) with one which is more lenient.

26.85 More generally, the Court of Appeal has said that it will not intervene unless there was some error of principle in the Crown Court sentence, so that public confidence would be damaged if the sentence were not altered (*Attorney-General's Reference (No 5 of 1989)* (1990) 90 Cr App R 358).

26.86 The Court of Appeal has also made it plain that, in suitable circumstances, the increased sentence which it has to pass will be mitigated by the fact that the offender has had to face the prospect of being sentenced twice over. Thus, in *Attorney-General's Reference (No 1 of 1991)* [1991] Crim LR 725, the trial judge had imposed a sentence of five years. In the view of the Court of Appeal, a minimum of eight years would have been appropriate. As the offender had the added anxiety of waiting for the outcome of the reference, some allowance would be made, and a sentence of seven years substituted.

26.87 Section 271 of the CJA 2003 provides that an offender can appeal against the minimum term set by the court in a murder case, or against a decision by that court to set a 'whole life' term (see 24.27 to 24.33). Consequently, the Attorney-General may also refer a minimum term in a murder case to the Court of Appeal on the basis that it is unduly lenient. Section 272 provides that, if the Court of Appeal decides that the minimum term was unduly lenient, it 'shall not ... make any allowance for the fact that the person to whom it relates is being sentenced for the second time'. This makes the customary adjustment for 'double sentencing jeopardy' unlawful in murder cases.

Prosecution appeals against rulings of the trial judge

26.88 The CJA 2003 brought about a major change in the shape of the Crown Court trial by establishing the right of the prosecution to appeal against certain rulings made by the trial judge.

The new powers, contained in ss 57 to 74 of the CJA, introduce two types of appeal which the prosecution can institute:

(a) 'terminating' rulings under ss 57 to 61; and
(b) evidentiary rulings, which are dealt with in ss 62 to 66.

The prosecution is prohibited from appealing against rulings on the discharge of the jury, and   **26.89**
from challenging under these provisions the rulings which it may appeal under other legislation, e.g., from preparatory hearings on points of law. Further, it was held in *Thompson* [2007] Crim LR 387 that the procedure does not apply to a ruling that a count be dismissed in accordance with para 2 of Sch 3 to the CDA 1998 (see 13.21 to 13.26). In any event, the prosecution has to obtain leave to appeal, either from the trial judge, or from the Court of Appeal.

Figure 26.2 Prosecution Appeals: Terminating Ruling

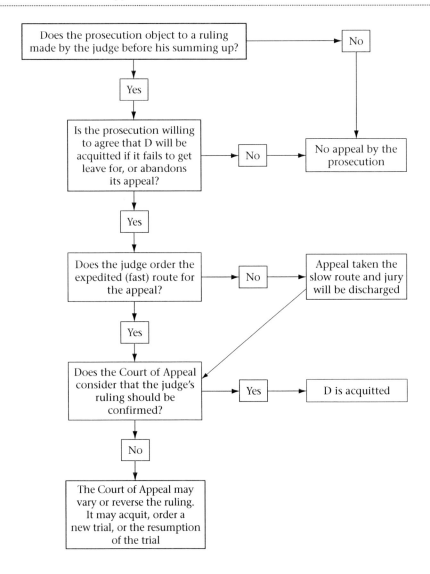

26.90 'Terminating' rulings are dealt with in ss 57 to 74. The procedure followed is set out in the flowchart on page 501. Although the term 'terminating ruling' itself is not used, it is an apt description, for reasons which will become apparent. This category of prosecution appeals came into force on 4 April 2005. It gives the prosecution a general right of appeal against a ruling made at any time up to the start of the judge's summing up to the jury. The procedure is that, following the ruling, the prosecution must either inform the court that it intends to appeal, or request an adjournment to consider whether to appeal. Under this section, the appeal by the prosecution is against one ruling only. However, where that ruling is that there is no case to answer, the prosecutor may put forward other rulings relating to the same offence, for the Court of Appeal to consider at the same time. The prosecution must pay a price for exercising its right to appeal, however. It must agree (s 58(9)) that if it fails to obtain leave to appeal, or abandons the appeal, an acquittal must inevitably follow. In consequence, the right is only likely to be exercised in cases where the ruling is 'terminating' in the sense that it is so fatal to the prosecution case that, in the absence of a right of appeal, the prosecution would offer no evidence (or no further evidence if it has already opened its case).

26.91 Two alternative appeal routes are laid down—an expedited (fast) route and a non-expedited (slow) route (s 59). It is for the judge to determine which route the appeal must follow. In the case of an expedited appeal, the trial may be adjourned. Where the appeal follows the non-expedited route, the judge may either adjourn the proceedings or discharge the jury. Either the judge or the Court of Appeal may reverse a decision to expedite an appeal. The effect is to transfer the case to the slower route. If this happens, the jury may be discharged. Section 60 enables the judge to direct that the proceedings may continue in relation to any offence to which the appeal does not apply.

26.92 The powers of the Court of Appeal in determining a prosecution appeal are set out in s 61. It may confirm, reverse, or vary a ruling appealed against. When it confirms the ruling, it must order the defendant's acquittal. Where it varies or reverses a ruling, it must either order a resumption of the Crown Court proceedings or a fresh trial, or the acquittal of the defendant for the offences under appeal. It must only order resumption of Crown Court proceedings or a fresh trial where it considers it necessary in the interests of justice to do so.

26.93 Sections 62 to 66 of the CJA 2003 deal with evidentiary rulings. These provisions were not in force at the time of writing, and no date had been set for their introduction. Under s 62, the prosecution is given an additional right to appeal against one or more evidentiary rulings made by a judge in relation to a trial on indictment before the opening of the case for the defence. The ruling must relate to a qualifying offence. The qualifying offences are set out in Sch 4. They include a series of serious violent, sexual, and drug trafficking offences, most of which carry a maximum sentence of life imprisonment.

26.94 Where it is appealing against evidentiary rulings, the prosecution must inform the court, before the opening of the case for the defence, that it intends to appeal. It must give details of the ruling or rulings to which the appeal relates. Again, leave to appeal is required. Unlike an appeal against a terminating ruling, the prosecution does not have to agree that if the appeal fails an acquittal must follow. But a specific condition must be met in the case of the appeal against evidentiary rulings: that the ruling or rulings in question significantly weaken the prosecution case in relation to the offence or offences which are the subject of the appeal. Again, the judge must decide whether the appeal is to take an expedited or a non-expedited route. The proceedings in relation to any offence to which the appeal does not apply may continue while the appeal proceeds.

When determining a prosecution appeal against an evidentiary ruling, the Court of Appeal **26.95** may confirm, reverse, or vary the ruling in question. Once it has decided, it must order a resumption of the trial, a fresh trial, or the acquittal of the defendant(s) for the offence(s) under appeal. It may only order an acquittal if the prosecution has indicated that it does not intend to continue with prosecuting that offence.

The conditions which must be satisfied before the Court of Appeal can overturn a ruling by **26.96** the trial judge are the same in the case of both terminating appeals and appeals against evidentiary rulings. Section 67 states that the Court of Appeal may not reverse a ruling unless it is satisfied that :

(a)   the ruling was wrong in law; or
(b)   the ruling involved an error of law or principle; or
(c)   the ruling was a ruling that it was not reasonable for the judge to have made.

Both prosecution and defence are given a right of appeal to the House of Lords from a decision by the Court of Appeal on a prosecution appeal under these provisions (s 68(1)).

Appeal against verdict of 'Not guilty by reason of insanity': Criminal Appeal Act 1968, ss 12–14

A person who is found not guilty by reason of insanity may appeal to the Court of Appeal **26.97** against the verdict. The provisions as to leave to appeal and determination of the appeal parallel those which apply to appeals against conviction. If the appeal is allowed on a ground relating to the finding that the appellant was insane, the Court of Appeal may substitute a verdict of guilty of the offence charged (or guilty of a lesser offence) for the verdict of the jury. The appellant may then be sentenced for the offence. If the appeal is allowed on other grounds (i.e., even in the absence of a finding of insanity, a conviction could not have been sustained), the Court of Appeal replaces the jury's verdict with a straightforward acquittal. It may, however, order that the appellant be admitted to a mental hospital specified by the Home Secretary.

A person who has been found unfit to plead may appeal against the finding: s 15. If the issue **26.98** of fitness to plead was determined after arraignment, and the Court of Appeal thinks that before it was determined the appellant should have been acquitted, the court may quash the finding of unfitness and substitute a verdict of acquittal. In other cases where the appeal is allowed, the court makes such orders as are necessary to secure the appellant's attendance at the Crown Court to be tried.

An appellant against conviction may argue that he should have been found unfit to plead or **26.99** not guilty by reason of insanity instead of being convicted.

H   THE CRIMINAL CASES REVIEW COMMISSION

In response to the recommendation of the Royal Commission on Criminal Justice in 1993 **26.100** that a new body was needed to investigate and process allegations of miscarriages of justice, the Criminal Appeal Act 1995 set up the Criminal Cases Review Commission. It began to receive cases in April 1997.

26.101   The Commission took over the functions of the Home Secretary to refer cases to the Court of Appeal. Its remit is actually wider than that which the Home Secretary formerly possessed, since it covers not only convictions after trial on indictment, but referrals in respect of sentence, and it has power to deal with cases decided in the magistrates' courts as well as in the Crown Court.

26.102   Matters may be referred to the Commission by the Court of Appeal, which may direct it to investigate a particular matter in such manner as it thinks fit. The Commission must report to the Court of Appeal once it has investigated. In addition, the Secretary of State may seek assistance in relation to the prerogative of mercy.

26.103   Primarily, however, the machinery is intended to operate in such a way that the Commission refers cases to the Court of Appeal. The test which it must apply in deciding whether to do so is laid down by s 13 of the CAA 1995. It should not refer a case unless it considers that there is a real possibility that the conviction, verdict, finding, or sentence would not be upheld were the reference to be made. In the case of a conviction, the 'real possibility' must be judged, save in exceptional circumstances, on the strength of an argument or evidence not raised at trial or on appeal or on an application for leave to appeal. In the case of a sentence, the Commission must be able to identify a legal argument, or information, which was not raised at trial or in the course of an appeal. Any decision to refer a case to the Court of Appeal can only be made by a committee of at least 3 of the 14 Commissioners.

26.104   Once the Commission decides to refer a case which was dealt with in the Crown Court, it is treated as an appeal for the purposes of the CAA 1968. Similarly, if the case was originally dealt with in the magistrates' court, following a referral by the Commission it will be dealt with by the Crown Court. Once the case has been referred, the appeal may be on any ground relating to the conviction or sentence, whether or not the ground is related to the reason given by the Commission for making the reference. By s 315 of the CJA 2003, an appellant whose case is referred to the Court of Appeal by the Criminal Cases Review Commission requires leave before he can add grounds of appeal unrelated to the reasons which the Commission had for making the reference.

I   APPEALS TO THE HOUSE OF LORDS: CRIMINAL APPEAL ACT 1968, s 33

26.105   Either the prosecution or defence may appeal to the House of Lords from a decision of the Criminal Division of the Court of Appeal, but the appeal is subject to:

(a) the Court of Appeal certifying that the decision which it is sought to appeal involves a point of law of general public importance, and

(b) either the Court of Appeal or the House of Lords giving leave to appeal because it appears to them that the point of law is one which ought to be considered by the House.

26.106   An application to the Court of Appeal for leave to appeal to the House of Lords should either be made orally immediately after the court's decision, or it should be made within 14 days of the decision, notice of the application being served on the registrar in the prescribed form. There is no appeal against a refusal by the Court of Appeal to certify that a point of law of general public importance is involved (*Gelberg v Miller* [1961] 1 WLR 459). If the Court of Appeal is willing to certify that a point of law of general public importance is involved, but nevertheless refuses leave to appeal, an application may be made to the House of Lords within 14 days of the Court of Appeal's refusal. Such applications are referred to an appeal committee consisting of three Lords of Appeal. If leave to appeal is granted, at least three Law Lords must be present for the hearing (s 35) but it is usual to have five deciding the case. In disposing of the appeal, the House of Lords may exercise any powers of the Court of Appeal or remit the case to it: s 35(3).

The Court of Appeal may grant an appellant bail pending determination of his appeal to the House of Lords: s 36. If the prosecution are appealing to the House of Lords against the Court of Appeal's decision to allow an appeal and, but for his successful appeal, the appellant in the Court of Appeal would be liable to be detained in pursuance of a custodial sentence, the Court of Appeal may order that he be detained until the appeal is decided: s 37. **26.107**

J FREE PARDONS

Pardons have already been considered at 17.62 from the angle of a plea of pardon. As explained there, the modern practice is to grant pardons after conviction and sentence when it becomes tolerably plain that the convicted person was in fact innocent. The pardon is granted by the Crown, on the advice of the Home Secretary, in exercise of the royal prerogative of mercy. However, the effect of the pardon is *not* to quash the conviction or even expressly to acknowledge that the pardonee did not commit the crime. It merely, to use the words of the pardon itself, releases the recipient from 'all pains, penalties and punishments whatsoever that from the said conviction may ensue'. Since he still stands convicted, it is open to a pardoned offender to appeal to the Court of Appeal to have the conviction quashed: *Foster* [1985] QB 115. Indeed, in the eyes of the law, the pardonee's name is not cleared until that has happened. **26.108**

In cases where the Home Secretary is not prepared to recommend a pardon, but the doubts about a prisoner's conviction are too great for his continued detention to be justified, the intermediate solution of remitting the remainder of his sentence may be adopted. **26.109**

K EXAMPLE OF APPEAL

QUEEN

and

THOMAS JONES

26.110

The contents of a Notice of Application for Leave to Appeal and the drafting of Grounds of Appeal may be illustrated by the case of *Thomas Jones*. Jones, aged 18, was found guilty by a jury following his plea of not guilty to a charge of robbing Roger Thwaites of a brief-case, a wallet and £25 in cash. The case against him rested upon the evidence of the victim and P.C. Blewitt. Mr Thwaites, the headmaster of a secondary school, stated in evidence that he was walking home at about 10.30 p.m. on the night of January 26th 2008 after attending a parents' association meeting at his school. He was carrying a brief-case which happened to be empty—he had used it for taking exercise books to school in the morning. Going along a quiet residential street, he heard rapid footsteps behind him, then felt a sudden pull on his brief-case and, as he refused to let go, was pulled to the pavement, suffering scratches and bruising but no serious injury. His assailant bent over him on the pavement, and removed his wallet from his inside jacket pocket. Then the assailant ran off. Although the road was dimly lit, the incident happened near a street lamp, and Mr Thwaites said that the 'mugger' reminded him of a pupil who had left his school some two years earlier, and whom he had often had cause to reprimand. That pupil was Thomas Jones. Mr Thwaites went to the police, who arrested Jones and put him on an identification parade. Mr Thwaites picked him out as the person who had robbed him.

Jones was then taken back to his cell by P.C. Blewitt and another officer. According to the officers, Jones said: 'I suppose I might as well tell you what happened. I was hard up because I was out of work, and I saw this old geezer with a brief-case walking ahead of me. Well, I thought there might be something in the case, and the temptation was just too much for me. I grabbed the case, and when the bloke was on the ground took his wallet from his pocket. I'm sorry now for what I did. It was just my bad luck to pick on somebody who knew me. Mind you it makes up a bit for the way he used to bully me.' Jones refused to sign the contemporaneous record of the interview in the officer's notebook claiming that it did not correctly represent what he had said.

26.111   At the trial Jones gave evidence in his own defence, and stated that at the relevant time he was at a discotheque about a mile from the scene of the robbery. He had gone with a friend who had left earlier, but at around 10.30 he was dancing with a girl named Sophia, whom he had met at the disco. He took her telephone number with a view to meeting her again, but unfortunately he lost the piece of paper on which he had written it down and, as far as he could recall, she had not mentioned her surname. He had made efforts to trace her, but without success. Therefore, Jones had no witnesses to support his alibi. As to the remarks made to P.C. Blewitt, Jones denied saying that he had grabbed the case and taken the wallet. He had said, in response to the officer's questions, that he was hard up and that, if he had seen an old man with a brief-case walking by himself, he might have been tempted to commit an offence, but he also said that nothing of the sort had in fact happened. He said that he was sorry that Mr Thwaites had apparently been hurt by somebody. Prosecuting counsel in cross-examination asked Jones whether he was alleging that P.C. Blewitt was deliberately lying. Jones said: 'I don't know about that, but he has certainly got what I did say all twisted up.' His Honour Judge Allworthy, trying the case, ruled that Jones' evidence amounted to an assertion that Blewitt had deliberately fabricated his evidence. He therefore allowed Jones to be cross-examined about his two previous convictions, which had both been in 2005 and were for assault occasioning actual bodily harm and robbery. Jones was also asked about the way in which he had committed the previous offence of robbery, and the jury learnt that he had snatched a handbag from a woman walking by herself late at night.

In his summing-up Judge Allworthy said: **26.112**

> Members of the jury, you must approach the evidence of Mr Thwaites with special care. He picked out the defendant on an identification parade as the person who had taken his brief-case and wallet, but I must warn you that mistakes can easily be made when this type of evidence is given. Many people are prone to over-estimate the accuracy of their memory and powers of observation. So you must ask yourselves—could Mr Thwaites be making a mistake? Well, ladies and gentlemen, it is a matter for you, but remember that this is not a case where a witness has picked out a complete stranger on an identification parade. There is certainly ample room for mistake in that type of case, but this is a case where Mr Thwaites has told you that at the time of the attack he recognized his attacker as a former pupil, and then later he picked him out on a parade as well. You may feel—it's a matter for you, of course—that the chance of a mistake is considerably reduced. And remember that the whole incident happened near a street lamp, and that Mr Thwaites' attacker, whoever he was, must have bent over him to take his wallet from his pocket. Well, there it is. Perhaps these comments will help you decide where the truth lies in this case.

After the jury's verdict, antecedents evidence revealed that for his offence of assault Jones had been given a conditional discharge for two years, and that for the robbery he had been given a detention and training order of three months. Judge Allworthy adjourned for a pre-sentence report. He later passed a sentence of 18 months' detention in a young offender institution. He said:

> You are a young man who already has convictions for assault and robbery. Now you have injured and robbed an elderly, defenceless man. The streets must be made safe for decent, law-abiding people. I have come to the conclusion that this offence is so serious that a custodial sentence is the only answer. The sentence is therefore one of 18 months' detention in a young offender institution.

A week after Jones' conviction, a Miss Sophia Western contacted his solicitors, stating that she had read a report of the case in the local paper, and had realized that she was the girl Jones had been with at the discotheque. She could confirm everything that he had said, and remembered the date because it was the day before her birthday. She had been disappointed when Jones did not telephone her as promised, but now everything was explained.

The perfected Grounds of Appeal in Jones' case might read as follows: **26.113**

THE QUEEN

V

THOMAS JONES

———————————

GROUNDS OF APPEAL
AGAINST CONVICTION

———————————

Application is made for leave to appeal upon the ground that the conviction is unsafe for any or all of the following reasons, namely that the learned judge:

1. wrongly allowed Jones to be cross-examined about his previous convictions, whereas the Appellant had merely asserted his innocence of the charge;

2. wrongly failed to refuse to allow the prosecution leave to cross-examine the Appellant about his previous convictions, in accordance with s 100(3) of the Criminal Justice Act 2003. The Appellant only challenged a small part of P.C. Blewitt's evidence and did not suggest that the officer had been guilty of extensive fabrication;

3. wrongly allowed the cross-examination of the defendant about the way in which he committed the offence of robbery of which he had previously been convicted (p. 28A–C);

4. misdirected the jury in that:

    4.1 He reminded them of certain matters which tended to confirm the correctness of Roger Thwaites' identification of the appellant as the person who robbed him, but failed to remind them of other matters which cast doubt upon the identification. In particular, he failed to remind them that Mr Thwaites saw the person who robbed him at night, in a dimly lit road, for only a short time, in circumstances likely to occasion confusion and fear (p. 40A–C).

    4.2 He told them that Mr Thwaites 'recognized his attacker as a former pupil' whereas his evidence was that his attacker 'reminded' him of a former pupil (pp. 10D and 40B).

    4.3 He exaggerated the extent to which an identification of a person previously known to the witness is more likely to be reliable than an identification of a stranger, and thus he undermined the effectiveness of the warning he had earlier given about the dangers of identification evidence (p. 40B).

Further, the appellant wishes to call one Sophia Western to give evidence before the Court that at the time the offence occurred she was with the appellant at a distance of approximately one mile from the scene of the offence. The witness did not come forward until after the appellant's conviction. Her name and address could not with reasonable diligence have been discovered by the defence in time for her to be called at the trial.

GROUNDS OF APPEAL
AGAINST SENTENCE

Having regard to s 152 of the Criminal Justice Act 2003, the appellant should have been dealt with by non-custodial means. Contrary to the view expressed by the learned judge in passing sentence, the Appellant's offence was not so serious that only a custodial sentence could be justified for it; nor was it the case that such a sentence was required to protect the public from serious harm from the Appellant.

W. Partridge
Counsel for the Appellant

These Grounds of Appeal would be accompanied by an Advice on Appeal, the contents of which are beyond the scope of this work (for examples, see the Inns of Court School of Law, *Drafting Manual*, published by Oxford University Press).

KEY DOCUMENTS

Criminal Appeals Act 1968, as amended.

Criminal Justice Act 2003, ss 57 to 74 (to the extent it is in force).

Criminal Procedure Rules 2005, Parts 65 to 69 (available at <http://www.hmcourts-service.gov.uk/cms/pds.htm>).

Quashing Convictions by Prof J R Spencer [2007] Crim LR 835.

27

APPEALS FROM THE MAGISTRATES' COURTS

A decision by a magistrates' court can be challenged by: 27.01

(a) appeal to the Crown Court, or

(b) appeal to the High Court by way of a case stated by the magistrates for the High Court's opinion, or

(c) application to the High Court for judicial review of the magistrates' decision.

Appeal to the Crown Court is only by a person convicted. The other two procedures are available to any person aggrieved by a magistrates' court decision, which includes both a convicted accused and an unsuccessful prosecutor. Decisions of the Crown Court, not made in connection with its jurisdiction over trials on indictment, may also be challenged through a case stated for the opinion of the High Court or an application for review.

A   APPEALS TO THE CROWN COURT

27.02   Appeals to the Crown Court from a magistrates' court are governed by the Magistrates' Courts Act 1980 (MCA), ss 108 to 110, and CrimPR, Part 63.

The right of appeal

27.03   A person convicted by a magistrates' court following a plea of not guilty may appeal to the Crown Court against his conviction and/or his sentence. A person sentenced by the magistrates following a guilty plea may only appeal against his sentence: MCA, s 108(1).

27.04   An appeal to the Crown Court against sentence may be brought in respect of 'any order made on conviction by a magistrates' court': MCA, s 108(3). This is subject to an express prohibition on appealing an order to pay costs to the prosecution. Otherwise 'order made on conviction' appears to have the same wide meaning as 'order made when dealing with an offender', which is the phrase used in s 50 of the Criminal Appeal Act 1968 to define 'sentence' in the context of appeals from the Crown Court to the Court of Appeal (see 26.19). Thus, there is a right of appeal to the Crown Court against *inter alia* a magistrates' court's decision to conditionally or absolutely discharge an offender, to disqualify him from driving, to recommend him for deportation, or to make a hospital or compensation order.

27.05   Although a plea of guilty in the magistrates' court is generally a bar to appealing to the Crown Court against conviction, it is sometimes possible to argue that it should not have that consequence because it was not a genuine admission of guilt. If the Crown Court agrees, it remits the case to the magistrates with a direction that a not guilty plea be entered. Non-genuine pleas of guilty before the magistrates are usually referred to as 'equivocal pleas', but there is room for debate over the correct use of the terminology. Three main situations may be distinguished in which the Crown Court will remit for hearing on a not guilty plea following a guilty plea before the magistrates:

(a)   **Pleas equivocal when made.** If the accused says 'Guilty' when the information is put to him but he immediately adds words which show that he might have a defence, the plea is clearly equivocal. An example is the accused charged with assault who pleads, 'Guilty, but I only did it to defend myself'. The magistrates should explain to him the relevant law (i.e., that if he was acting in reasonable self-defence he is not guilty of the charge) and then ask the clerk to put the information again. If the accused then unambiguously pleads guilty, the magistrates will properly proceed to sentence, but if the plea remains equivocal they should enter a not guilty plea on the accused's behalf. Failure to do so (i.e., sentencing on a plea which remains equivocal) will, in the event of an appeal, lead to the case being remitted by the Crown Court for hearing on a not guilty plea.

(b)   **Pleas subsequently shown to be equivocal**. A plea which is unequivocally one of guilty when made may be rendered equivocal by information given to the magistrates before they pass sentence. In *Durham Quarter Sessions ex parte Virgo* [1952] 2 QB 1, for example, V, who was unrepresented, simply answered 'Guilty', when an information for stealing a motor cycle was put to him, but, when later asked if he had anything to say in mitigation, told the magistrates that he had taken the cycle by mistake believing that it was his friend's cycle and that the friend had given him permission to use it. Thus, his mitigation was inconsistent with the guilty plea. Similarly, in *Blandford Justices ex parte G* [1967] 1 QB 82, the prosecution brought to the juvenile court's attention, as part of their summary of the facts following G's plea of guilty to stealing jewellery from her employer, a statement to the police made by G in which she claimed that she had merely borrowed the jewellery intending to return it. Neither Virgo nor G were invited to change their pleas. In both cases, the High Court treated the matters subsequently put before the magistrates (Virgo's mitigation and G's written statement) as if they formed part of the plea to the respective charges. Their lordships therefore held that the Crown Court should have remitted the cases to the magistrates for trial since the pleas, although unequivocal when made, were rendered equivocal by the subsequent developments. However, it is important to note that, if a would-be appellant merely tells the Crown Court that he was mistaken as to the law when he entered his guilty plea but nothing emerged during the sentencing procedure that could have alerted the magistrates to his error, then he is bound by his plea and cannot have his conviction set aside.

An alternative analysis of the situations in *Ex parte Virgo* and *Ex parte G* is to say that the term 'equivocal plea' should be reserved for cases falling within (a) above. If something prior to the passing of sentence throws doubt on a plea of guilty which was unequivocal when made, the question is not strictly one of whether the plea should be treated as equivocal but whether the magistrates properly exercised the discretion which they undoubtedly have to allow a change of plea. If they failed to consider exercising their discretion or exercised it in a way which no reasonable tribunal would have done, the case should be remitted to them, but otherwise the accused is bound by his guilty plea. This analysis was adopted in *P. Foster (Haulage) Ltd v Roberts* [1978] 2 All ER 751. See *Bristol Justices ex parte Sawyers* [1988] Crim LR 754 and 10.53.

(c) **Pleas entered under duress.** Even if a plea of guilty was unequivocal when made and not put in doubt by any developments prior to the passing of sentence, the accused is not debarred from appealing his conviction to the Crown Court if the plea was entered under duress: *Huntingdon Crown Court ex parte Jordan* [1981] QB 857. *Ex parte Jordan* concerned a wife, jointly charged with her husband with shoplifting. The defence she would have run had she dared was that her husband forced her to commit the offences by threats of violence. Similar threats (so she alleged) prevented her from pleading not guilty. The High Court held that the Crown Court had jurisdiction to *remit* to the magistrates for hearing on a not guilty plea. Presumably the same would apply if a plea of guilty in the magistrates' court was induced by any of the forms of pressure which will lead the Court of Appeal to treat a plea of guilty entered on an indictment as a nullity (see 17.17 to 17.21).

In addition to the above situations, it seems that the Crown Court has power to consider a **27.06** plea of autrefois convict, even where the accused pleaded guilty without equivocation in the magistrates' court: *Cooper v New Forest DC* [1992] Crim LR 877.

Finally, the Criminal Cases Review Commission can refer a conviction in the magistrates' **27.07** court to the Crown Court even when based on a guilty plea (see 27.49). Despite the exceptional situations just described, the general rule is still that pleading guilty before the magistrates prevents one appealing against conviction to the Crown Court. If a plea was unequivocal when made, was not put into doubt by any subsequent developments prior to sentence and was not entered under duress or oppression, then MCA, s 108 permits an appeal against sentence but nothing more. There is no jurisdiction to set aside the conviction or remit to the magistrates simply on the basis that the accused now regrets pleading guilty and thinks that he might have an arguable defence (*Birmingham Crown Court ex parte Sharma* [1988] Crim LR 741). By contrast, if the accused pleaded guilty and was then committed for sentence, the Crown Court has a general discretion to remit to the lower court whenever that appears just (see *Camberwell Green Justices ex parte Sloper* (1978) 69 Cr App R 1). The reason for this prima facie anomalous distinction is that committing for sentence does not render the magistrates *functus officio*, whereas convicting and sentencing the accused does. In the former situation, therefore, the accused is not appealing against conviction but merely asking the Crown Court to refrain from sentencing him until proceedings have been properly completed in the lower court.

27.08   Crown Court directions that magistrates rehear a case on a not guilty plea can lead to unbecoming inter-court disputes, with the lower court indignantly protesting that the accused's plea was totally unequivocal and therefore refusing to comply with the Crown Court's wishes. Following some contradictory earlier decisions by the High Court, the rights and duties of the respective courts were finally established by Watkin LJ's judgment in *Plymouth Justices ex parte Hart* [1986] QB 950. Assuming that it conducted a proper inquiry into whether the accused's plea was equivocal and had sufficient evidence before it to come to the conclusion that it was, the Crown Court's direction that a not guilty plea be entered and a summary trial take place is binding on the magistrates and must be obeyed. Furthermore, the magistrates should assist the Crown Court in its inquiry into the equivocality of the plea by supplying affidavits (e.g., from the clerk in court or the chairman of the bench) dealing with what happened when the appellant appeared before them.

Procedure on appeal

27.09   Notice of appeal must be given in writing to the clerk of the relevant magistrates' court and to the prosecutor within 21 days of sentence being passed: CrimPR, r 63.2. The appellant has 21 days from the date of sentence or other disposal (e.g., committal for sentence) even if that is after the date of conviction and he is only appealing against conviction. The grounds of appeal should be stated. Provided notice is given within time, no leave to appeal is required. The Crown Court has a discretion to extend the time for giving notice, i.e., to give leave to appeal out of time: r 63.2(5).

27.10   If notice of appeal is given by an appellant upon whom the magistrates have passed an immediate custodial sentence, they may bail him to appear at the Crown Court at the time fixed for the hearing of the appeal: MCA, s 113(1). If the magistrates refuse to grant bail, application may be made to the Crown Court under the Supreme Court Act 1981, s 81(1)(b). Bail pending the appeal is particularly important because any custodial sentence imposed by a magistrates' court is necessarily short, so if not granted bail the appellant may have served much of his sentence by the time the appeal is heard.

27.11   An appeal is listed for hearing by a circuit judge or recorder who must normally sit with two lay magistrates (Supreme Court Act 1981, s 74). Prior to the hearing, the defence may request a copy of the clerk's notes of evidence of the summary trial. Any such request for a copy should be 'viewed sympathetically' (per Lord Lane CJ in *Clerk to the Highbury Corner*

Justices ex parte Hussein [1986] 1 WLR 1266). The appeal itself takes the form of a rehearing, exactly the same steps being gone through as were gone through at the summary trial. Thus, at an appeal against conviction, the prosecution makes an opening speech and calls his evidence, after which the defence may make a submission of no case to answer. If that fails, defence evidence is called, followed by closing speeches, and the court announces its decision. The parties are not limited to the evidence called at the summary trial, but may rely on material which has only become available to them since then, or which they simply chose not to use on the earlier occasion. The Crown Court itself, however, may neither amend the information on which the appellant was convicted (*Garfield v Maddocks* [1974] QB 7 and see *Swansea Crown Court ex parte Stacey* [1990] RTR 183) nor strike out an amendment made by the magistrates: *Fairgrieve v Newman* [1986] Crim LR 47. At an appeal against sentence, the prosecution simply outline the facts and call antecedents evidence, reports (if any) on the appellant are read, and the defence advocate mitigates.

Powers of the Crown Court

The decision of the Crown Court is announced by the judge, who should give reasons. These should be sufficient to demonstrate that the court has identified the main contentious issues in the case, and how it has resolved each of them. Failure to do so might amount to a denial of natural justice (*Harrow Crown Court ex parte Dave* [1994] 1 WLR 98). **27.12**

The powers of the Crown Court when disposing of an appeal are set out in s 48 of the Supreme Court Act 1981 as amended. Those powers are extensive. It may confirm, reverse or vary any part of the decision appealed against, it may remit the matter to the magistrates with its opinion thereon (e.g., where it considers the plea to be equivocal), or it may make such other order in the matter as it thinks just (e.g., in the case of a successful appeal, an order that the costs of the defence in the magistrates' court be paid by the prosecution or out of central funds). Varying the decision appealed against includes increasing the sentence imposed by the magistrates even in a case where the appeal is only against conviction, but the Crown Court sentence must not exceed that which the magistrates could have passed: s 48(4). In fact, it is unusual for the Crown Court to increase sentence, but the reason it, unlike the Court of Appeal on appeals from the Crown Court, has retained the power to do so may be that leave is never required for appeals to the Crown Court unless they are out of time. The possibility of an increase in sentence may therefore inhibit unmeritorious appeals. Furthermore, whenever an appeal fails, the appellant may be ordered to pay the prosecution's costs: Prosecution of Offences Act 1985, s 18(1)(b) and see CrimPR, r 78.1(2) which gives the Crown Court a general discretion to make such order for costs between the parties as appears just. A successful appellant may be awarded his costs out of central funds (i.e., out of government money): POA, s 16(3). This is known as a 'defendant's costs order' and it may include the appellant's costs in the magistrates' court. For general discussion of costs, see 29.12 to 29.18. **27.13**

Section 48 now enables the Crown Court to vary (e.g., by increasing sentence) *any part* of the magistrates' decision, even if the appellant chose not to appeal against that part. It also would seem to give the Crown Court power when a person appeals against his summary conviction for offence A to quash it and substitute a conviction for offence B of which the magistrates acquitted on the same occasion, since the acquittal is part of the decision against which the appellant is appealing. In theory, indeed, the Crown Court could even dismiss the **27.14** appeal against conviction for offence A and add a conviction for offence B. To avoid injustice to appellants, the Crown Court should, it is submitted, use its increased powers under s 48 sparingly. The appellant may abandon his appeal by giving notice in writing to that effect to the clerk of the magistrates' court, to the appropriate officer of the Crown Court and to the prosecution: CrimPR, r 63.5. The notice should be given at least three days before the hearing of the appeal. If notice to abandon an appeal is duly given, the Crown Court is thereby deprived of its power to order the appellant to pay costs but the magistrates may make an order in respect of expenses properly incurred by the prosecutor before he received the notice: MCA, s 109.

B   APPEALS TO THE HIGH COURT BY CASE STATED

27.15   An appeal by way of case stated is an appeal on a point or points of law, which are identified in a document (the case) drawn up by the clerk of the magistrates' court in conjunction with the magistrates whose decision is being questioned. The appeal is to the High Court.

27.16   Appeals by case stated are governed by the Magistrates' Courts Act 1980, s 111, CrimPR, Part 64 and Civiil Procedure Rules, Part 52.

The right of appeal

27.17   Section 111(1) of the MCA provides that '*any* person who was a party to any proceeding before a magistrates' court or is aggrieved by the conviction, order, determination or other proceeding of the court may question the proceeding on the ground that is *wrong in law* or *in excess of jurisdiction* by applying to the [magistrates] to state a case for the opinion of the High Court on the question of law or jurisdiction involved'. The following are the chief points to note:

(a)   Appeal by case stated is at the disposal of both the prosecution and the defence.

(b)   The appeal must be on one or other of the two grounds mentioned in s 111(1), namely that the decision complained of was wrong in law or in excess of jurisdiction. In his initial application to the magistrates to state a case a would-be appellant must specify the question of law or jurisdiction on which the High Court's opinion is sought, and if his application mentions only a question of fact the request for a case would be refused (see 27.18 to 27.23). The kind of issues which may properly be raised for the High Court's consideration are: whether the magistrates had power to try it, whether they were right to find that there was or (as the case may be) was not a case to answer, whether inadmissible evidence was received or admissible evidence excluded, and whether their verdict was the correct one in the light of the facts they found proved by the evidence. This last is perhaps the commonest argument put forward on a case stated. Either the prosecution says that the accused's acquittal should be reversed because on their stated view of the facts the magistrates clearly ought to have convicted, or the defence contend that the facts proved to the magistrates' satisfaction did not amount to the offence charged and so the conviction should be set aside. However, the lower court's decision as to what facts were established by the evidence cannot be appealed by case stated, save that a finding of fact which is totally unsupported by evidence or at which no reasonable tribunal properly directing itself could have arrived is treated as revealing an error of law and so may be taken to the High Court: *Bracegirdle v Oxley* [1947] KB 349. If the defence consider that the magistrates' decision on the facts was merely against the weight of the evidence, their only remedy is to go to the Crown Court for a rehearing of the evidence.

(c)   Most appeals by way of case stated are aimed at overturning either a summary conviction or a summary acquittal. They are not aimed at reducing or increasing a sentence passed after summary conviction, simply because it is rare for magistrates to pass a sentence which is wrong in law or in excess of jurisdiction. However, if they should happen to do so, the aggrieved party can ask them to state a case. Thus, on a number of occasions, the prosecution have obtained a ruling that magistrates sentencing for a drink/driving offence should have disqualified the offender, since the grounds he advanced for not being disqualified were incapable of being special reasons within the meaning of the Road Traffic Offenders Act 1988 (see *Haime v Walklett* (1983) 5 Cr App R (S) 165 for an example). In truly exceptional cases, the defence on an appeal by case stated may obtain a reduction in sentence by arguing that, although it was within the magistrates' statutory powers of punishment, it was outside the normal discretionary limits. (The approach is essentially the same as in appeals against sentence by way of judicial review: see 27.33 to 27.42.) The High Court will then presume that the magistrates in passing the sentence must have made some error in law, otherwise they would not have arrived at a decision so grossly out of line with good sentencing practice (see *Universal Salvage Ltd v Boothby* (1983) 5 Cr App R (S) 428).

(d)   On a correct interpretation of s 111(1), the right to ask the magistrates to state a case does not arise unless and until the proceedings in their court have resulted in a final determination of the would-be appellant's case (see dicta in *Atkinson v USA Government* [1971] AC 197). In the context of criminal proceedings, a final determination would be an acquittal, conviction or passing of sentence. It follows that neither errors of law during committal proceedings nor a decision to commit which was unjustified by the evidence can be challenged by case stated since a committal is not a final determination of a case: *Dewing v Cummings* [1972] Crim LR 38. The same reasoning would apply to a decision to commit for sentence, although the conviction which preceded the decision to commit could be appealed. The need for there to have been a final determination also means that if, during the course of a summary trial, the prosecution or defence consider that the magistrates have made a wrong decision in law, they must wait until the verdict has been pronounced before asking for a case to be stated—they may not seek an adjournment immediately after the decision complained of with a view to getting a ruling on the matter from the High Court during the period of the adjournment: *Streames v Copping* [1985] QB 920. Hence, in *Loade v DPP* [1990] 1 QB 1052, the High Court was asked to rule upon the validity of an information, referred to it by way of case stated from the Crown Court on appeal from the magistrates. Their lordships declined to answer the question formally, since there had been no final determination. In *Gillan v DPP* [2007] EWHC 380 (Admin), the Divisional Court dealt with an appeal by way of case stated against the refusal of the Crown Court to conduct a further *Newton hearing* (the magistrates had already conducted such a hearing prior to committal: see 22.30). Clearly, there had been no final decision by the Crown Court such as to ground an appeal by way of case stated. The Divisional Court decided to proceed by dealing with the matter as if it were an application for judicial review, and then coming to a decision on the merits.

Procedure on appeal

27.18   An application for the magistrates to state a case must be made within 21 days of acquittal or conviction, or, if the magistrates convicted an accused and adjourned before sentencing him, within 21 days of sentence: MCA, s 111(2) and (3). The application, should identify the question of law or jurisdiction on which the High Court's opinion is sought: CrimPR, r 64.1. If it is suggested that there was no evidence on which the magistrates could reasonably have come to a particular finding of fact, the fact in question should be specified. The application is sent to the clerk of the relevant magistrates' court. Where the magistrates consider that an application to state a case is frivolous they may refuse to comply with the application, but must give the applicant a certificate stating that his application has been refused: s 111(5). The applicant may then apply to the High Court for an order compelling the magistrates to state a case. Even if the application cannot be classed as frivolous, the magistrates may still doubt whether the applicant genuinely intends to go through with the appeal. To discourage money and time being wasted over appeals which are started and then abandoned, they may make their agreement to state a case conditional upon the applicant entering into a recognisance that he will 'prosecute the appeal without delay' and pay any costs which are ultimately awarded against him by the High Court: MCA, s 114.

27.19   A statement of case should set out the facts as found by the magistrates, but not the evidence which led them to those findings of fact (*Turtington v United Co-operatives Ltd* [1993] Crim LR 376). The only exception to the rule arises when the appellant contends that there was no evidence on which the magistrates could reasonably have reached a finding of fact, in which case a short statement of the relevant evidence must be included. The case also sets out the charge or charges heard by the magistrates, the contentions of the parties on the questions of law or jurisdiction raised, any authorities cited, the magistrates' decision, and the question for the High Court. The clerk to the magistrates is principally responsible for drafting the case. He consults with the magistrates, and takes into account any representations by the parties. After any necessary alterations have been made to the case as initially drafted by the clerk, it is signed by at least two of the magistrates whose decision is being appealed, or by the clerk on their behalf. It is then sent to the appellant or his solicitor (CrimPR, r 64.3), who, within ten days of receiving it, must deliver it to the Administrative Court Office at the Royal Courts of Justice.

27.20   Where magistrates have passed on an appellant an immediate custodial sentence, they may grant him bail pending the hearing of his appeal: MCA, s 113. The terms of bail are that, unless the appeal succeeds, he must appear at the magistrates' court within ten days of the High Court's judgment being given, the precise date being fixed by the magistrates after the appeal. If the magistrates refuse bail, an application for bail may be made to a High Court judge in chambers.

27.21   An example of a case stated is shown on pages 520 to 521.

27.22   After an application for the magistrates to state a case has been received, the clerk immediately prepares a draft case. The procedure is set out in detail in CrimPR, rr 64.2 and 64.3.

27.23   The time-limits mentioned in the Criminal Procedure Rules, part 64, can all be extended where necessary, but the 21 day period within which the initial application to the magistrates to state a case must be made is prescribed by statute, and cannot be varied even by the High Court: *Michael v Gowland* [1977] 1 WLR 296.

Hearing of the appeal

The appeal is heard by the Divisional Court of the Queen's Bench Division. The court consists **27.24** of at least two High Court judges, but sometimes three judges sit. If a two-judge court is equally divided, the opinion of the judge agreeing with the court below prevails and the appeal therefore fails: per Scrutton LJ at p. 107 in *Flannagan v Shaw* [1920] 3 KB 96. No evidence is called before the court. The appeal takes the form of legal argument for the appellant and respondent, based solely upon the facts stated in the case. If those facts give rise to a point of law not taken before the magistrates which might, if it had been taken, have provided the appellant with a good defence to the charge against him, the High Court will consider the point, so long as it does not depend upon any further findings of fact: *Whitehead v Haines* [1965] 1 QB 200. In disposing of the appeal, the High Court can 'reverse, affirm or amend' the magistrates' decision, or remit the matter to the magistrates with its opinion thereon, or make any other order it thinks fit in respect of the matter, including an order as to costs: Supreme Court Act 1981, s 28A. The powers of the High Court thus include both substituting for an appellant's conviction an acquittal, and, where the prosecution appeal following an acquittal, remitting the case to the magistrates with a direction that they convict and proceed to sentence. Alternatively, where it is plain what the sentence should be, the High Court may simply replace the acquittal with a conviction and impose the appropriate penalty themselves. If the appeal concerns a sentence which was allegedly beyond the magistrates' powers or 'harsh and oppressive', the Court on allowing the appeal may pass the sentence it considers right. Costs may be awarded to the accused out of central funds: Prosecution of Offences Act 1985, s 16(5). There is also power to order the unsuccessful party to pay his opponent's costs, but there is no power to grant the prosecution their costs out of central funds unless it is a private prosecution: Prosecution of Offences Act 1985, s 17(2).

It had been thought that, despite the wide powers given to the High Court by s 6 of the **27.25** Summary Jurisdiction Act 1857 (now the Supreme Court Act 1981, s 28A), their lordships were not permitted to order a retrial. Remitting to the magistrates covers sending a case back with a direction to convict if it is plain on the facts stated that that is the correct verdict. It also covers setting an acquittal aside and telling the magistrates to continue with the hearing if the acquittal followed the erroneous upholding of a submission of no case to answer at the end of the prosecution evidence. But, 'there is no power to order a retrial in the ordinary sense of the expression' (per Lord Goddard CJ in *Rigby v Woodward* [1957] 1 WLR 250).

In *Griffith v Jenkins* [1992] 2 AC 76, however, the House of Lords held that the High Court *did* **27.26** have power to order a rehearing, before the same or a different bench. In that case, the justices had dismissed charges of unlawful fishing and theft, acting of their own motion and without inviting representations from the parties. The prosecution appealed, and the High Court held that the justices had erred. Since two of the bench had retired, they could not remit to the same bench. Further, their lordships took the view they had no power under s 6 of the Summary Jurisdiction Act 1857 to remit the case for rehearing before a different bench. The House of Lords held that there was always power in the High Court, on hearing an appeal by case stated under s 6, to order a rehearing before the same or a different bench. A rehearing would only be ordered in circumstances where a fair trial was still possible. It was not appropriate to order a rehearing in the case in question.

Case stated under Magistrates' Courts Act 1980, s 111
(Criminal Procedure Rules, r 64.2)

In the High Court of Justice
  Queen's Bench Division

Between Mohammed KHAN Appellant
        and
        Peter CONSTABLE Respondent

Case stated by the justices for the county of Loamshire, in respect of their adjudication as a Magistrates' Court sitting at 1, High Street, Loamtown.

CASE

1. On the 25th day of July 2007 an information was preferred by the Respondent against the Appellant that he on the 11th day of July 2007 had with him in a public place namely Clay Road, Loamtown, an offensive weapon, namely a knuckleduster, without lawful authority or reasonable excuse, contrary to s 1(1) of the Prevention of Crime Act 1953.

2. We heard the information on the 5th day of September 2007, and found the following facts proved:

(a) On the 11th day of July 2007 the Respondent, who is a police officer, observed the Appellant and a white youth fighting in Clay Road, Loamtown. The Appellant is aged 19 and is of Asian origin. The white youth ran away, but the Respondent was able to arrest the Appellant on suspicion of having committed an offence contrary to s 4 of the Public Order Act 1986. The Respondent searched the Appellant, and found in his trouser pocket a knuckleduster. The knuckleduster was made for use for causing injury to the person.

(b) Clay Road, Loamtown is a public highway to which the public have access at all times.

(c) During a period of roughly a month before the day in question three Asian youths walking at night in the Clay Road area of Loamtown had, in separate incidents, been assaulted by white youths referred to as 'skinheads'. The last attack occurred on the 30th day of June 2007. The Appellant had never himself been assaulted prior to July 11th. He claimed that the white youth he was fighting when seen by the Respondent attacked him without cause. We made no finding on the point as the information we were trying did not directly concern the said fight.

(d) On Mondays and Wednesdays the Appellant attended evening classes which finished at approximately 10.00 p.m. His journey home necessitated his walking through the Clay Road area. After the first attack on an Asian youth he began to carry on the evenings when he attended evening classes the knuckleduster which the Respondent found in his possession. His reason for doing so was to protect himself should he be attacked, but he did not in fact use it during the fight on July 11th.

3. It was contended by the Appellant that he had a reasonable excuse for having a knuckleduster with him because, as a result of the attacks on Asian youths which had taken place, he was in immediate fear of attack on the occasions when he walked through the Clay Road area.

4. It was contended by the Respondent that the permanent carrying of weapons is prohibited by the Prevention of Crime Act 1953, and that, in the absence of any very recent attack upon the Appellant personally, he had no reasonable excuse for having a knuckleduster. Recent attacks upon persons belonging to the ethnic group to which the Appellant belongs could not be a reasonable excuse for the Appellant carrying an offensive weapon.

5. We were referred to the following cases —

Evan v Hughes [1972] 3 All ER 412

Peacock [1973] Crim LR 639

Bradley v Moss [1974] Crim LR 430

Southwell v Chadwick (1986) 85 Cr App R 235

Malnik v DPP [1989] Crim LR 451

6. We were of the opinion that the Appellant had the burden of proving that he had a reasonable excuse for having the knuckleduster with him in a public place. This he failed to do because he had never himself been attacked or put in fear of attack, and furthermore ten days had elapsed since the last attack on an Asian youth in the Clay Road area. Accordingly we convicted the Appellant and conditionally discharged him for 12 months.

QUESTION

7. The question for the opinion of the High Court is whether we were right in holding, as a point of law, that the Appellant's explanation for carrying the knuckleduster could not be a reasonable excuse within the meaning of s 1(1) of the Prevention of Crime Act 1953. If we were incorrect in so holding the Court is respectfully requested to reverse or amend our decision or remit the matter to us with the opinion of the Court thereon.

Dated the 2nd day of December 2007

J. Smith
R. Brown
*Justices of the Peace for Loamshire on behalf
of all the Justices adjudicating*

Appeal by case stated from the Crown Court

27.27   Appeal by way of case stated may be used not only to question the decisions of magistrates, but also to question the Crown Court's decisions in matters not relating to trial on indictment: Supreme Court Act 1981, s 28. The precise dividing line between decisions which do and those which do not relate to a trial on indictment is not easy to draw. Since the problem of drawing that line more commonly arises in the context of whether a Crown Court decision is subject to judicial review, detailed consideration of the question will be postponed until 27.44 (judicial review of Crown Court decisions). However, it is plain that the allowing or dismissal of an appeal from a magistrates' court is a decision totally unconnected with trial on indictment. Therefore, the unsuccessful party in the Crown Court (whether it be the prosecution who have seen a summary conviction overturned or the defence who have had the same result before the Crown Court as they had in the magistrates' court) may further appeal by case stated to the High Court. Of course, just as with an appeal direct from the magistrates to the High Court, the Crown Court decision may only be questioned on the ground that it was wrong in law or in excess of jurisdiction, not on the ground that it was against the weight of the evidence.

27.28   An application to the Crown Court to state a case should be made to the appropriate officer of the court within 21 days of the decision challenged being made: CrimPR, r 64.7(1). The rules make provision for this and other time limits for an appeal by way of case stated against a decision by the Crown Court to be extended, before or after expiry (r 64.7(14)). In this respect, the position differs from appeal from the magistrates, where the time limit is a statutory one, and cannot be extended (see 27.18). In *DPP v Coleman* [1998] 2 Cr App R 7, it was held that:

(a)   the decision whether to extend may be taken by the Crown Court judge alone;

(b)   in a case where the prosecution applied for the extension of time, the defendant must be given the right to make representations;

(c)   the application would normally be considered on the basis of written representations, without the need for an oral hearing.

The main difference between the procedure for magistrates stating a case and the procedure for the Crown Court doing so is that an appellant from the Crown Court has the responsibility for drawing up an initial draft case which is put before the judge who presided at the proceedings in which the disputed decision was made: r 64.7(8). The respondent to the appeal is also at liberty to submit a draft case to the judge. Having read the draft(s), the judge states and signs a case: r 64.7(12). It is sent to the appellant, who lodges it in the Crown Office, together with copies of the judgments or orders made both in the Crown Court and the magistrates' court: Rules of the Supreme Court, Ord 56, r 1. The appeal should normally be entered for hearing within six months of the Crown Court decision. Pending hearing of the appeal, the appellant may be granted bail by either the Crown Court or a High Court judge in chambers: Supreme Court Act 1981, s 81(1)(d) and Criminal Justice Act 1948, s 37. On disposing of the appeal, the High Court's powers are identical to those it possesses in disposing of an appeal from the magistrates.

27.29   Upon an application being made to magistrates to state a case for the opinion of the High Court, the applicant loses any right he had to appeal to the Crown Court: MCA, s 111(4). Therefore, if a person convicted by magistrates is dissatisfied both with the view of the facts they apparently took, and with their ruling on any question of law which arose, he is well advised to appeal to the Crown Court against conviction and refrain from asking the magistrates to state a case. At the rehearing in the Crown Court, the evidence is again called, and all questions of both fact and law may be fully ventilated. If the appeal fails, the appellant still has the right to ask the Crown Court to state a case for the High Court's opinion on the question of law. Had he appealed on the law direct from the magistrates' court to the High Court, he would have lost the chance of having the evidence reheard in the Crown Court.

C   APPLICATION FOR JUDICIAL REVIEW

One of the High Court's tasks is to supervise the work of inferior tribunals. The principal way **27.30** in which it does this is through issuing one or more of the three prerogative orders:

(a)   the quashing order (known until *Practice Direction: (Administrative Court: Establishment)* [2000] 1 WLR 1654, as *certiorari*), which quashes the decision of an inferior tribunal;

(b)   the mandatory order (formerly *mandamus*), which compels an inferior tribunal to carry out its duties; and

(c)   the prohibiting order (formerly the order for prohibition), which prevents an inferior tribunal acting unlawfully or in excess of jurisdiction.

The prerogative orders are only issued upon an application being made to the High Court for **27.31** judicial review of the inferior tribunal's decision. In the field of administrative law, judicial review is of great importance, being used to control the way in which a wide variety of tribunals and other persons under a duty to act judicially exercise their powers. It is also available in respect of decisions by magistrates (whether those decisions were made in the exercise of their civil or criminal jurisdiction), and in respect of decisions by the Crown Court when it is not exercising its jurisdiction in matters relating to trial on indictment: Supreme Court Act 1981, s 29(3). It is a useful supplement to appeal by case stated in that a person aggrieved by a decision of a magistrates' court or by a decision of the Crown Court on an appeal from the magistrates may sometimes be able to obtain judicial review when he could not have asked the magistrates or the Crown Court to state a case (see 27.45 for a comparison of the two remedies).

An applicant for judicial review must have a sufficient interest in questioning the decision **27.32** which it is sought to review. Whatever may be the precise meaning of 'sufficient interest'— and the concept has caused considerable difficulty in cases where the High Court has been asked to review the decision of an inferior tribunal in a civil matter—it is clear that the prosecution and defence each have a sufficient interest to apply for judicial review both of a magistrates' court's decision in a criminal case and of a Crown Court decision upon appeal from the magistrates. The application is made to the Divisional Court. The procedure is governed by s 31 of the Supreme Court Act 1981 and the Civil Procedure Rules, Part 54.

Scope of the orders

Broadly speaking, the purpose of judicial review is to prevent magistrates' courts and other **27.33** inferior tribunals exceeding their jurisdiction; to compel them to exercise the jurisdiction which is rightfully theirs, and to control the way they exercise that jurisdiction in the sense of correcting fundamental irregularities in their procedures. Errors of law made by magistrates when exercising their proper jurisdiction in the proper manner should be questioned by appealing by case stated, not by applying for judicial review.

27.34   The effect of a quashing order is to quash the inferior tribunal's decision. Until 2000, it was known as *certiorari*. When it grants the remedy, the High Court also has the supplementary powers of (a) remitting the case to the inferior tribunal with a direction to reconsider it and reach a decision in accordance with its (the High Court's) findings, and (b) replacing an unlawful sentence which it has quashed with the sentence it considers fit: Supreme Court Act 1981, ss 31(5) and 43. As regards criminal proceedings, its commonest use is to quash a summary conviction. It is also potentially available to quash any of the other orders or decisions which magistrates take in connection with the course of a prosecution, such as a decision to commit for trial or sentence, or to withhold representation by the Criminal Defence Service, or to refuse an application to withdraw an election for summary trial. However, the rule against double jeopardy (i.e., an acquitted accused should not be reprosecuted for the same offence) means that the order is rarely granted to quash an acquittal. If the magistrates pronounced their verdict after a genuine trial at which the accused was at risk of a valid conviction, the acquittal will not be reviewed, even if the prosecution were prejudiced by a gross breach of proper trial procedures which (had it happened in reverse) would have necessitated the quashing of a conviction. Although they thought it anomalous in view of the fact that summary acquittals can be reversed through appeal by case stated, this general principle was confirmed by the House of Lords in *Dorking Justices ex parte Harrington* [1984] AC 743. At the same time, they gave a generous interpretation to an exception to the principle. The exception is that, if magistrates purport to acquit when they have no jurisdiction to do so, the trial is treated as a nullity, the accused is regarded as not having been in genuine jeopardy, and a quashing order may be issued. Thus, a summary acquittal in respect of an offence triable on indictment only is quashable (*West* [1964] 1 QB 15), as is an acquittal for an offence triable either way if the correct procedures for determining mode of trial were not complied with: *Cardiff Magistrates' Court ex parte Cardiff City Council* (1987) *The Times*, 24 February 1987. Moreover, if magistrates pronounce an acquittal without listening to any prosecution evidence and without having good reason for refusing to hear witnesses whom the prosecution have available at court the verdict is similarly liable to be set aside (see *Hendon Justices ex parte DPP* [1994] QB 167). If a conviction is the subject of a quashing order, it would seem that the rule against double jeopardy does not prevent the accused later being reprosecuted for the same offence (*Kent Justices ex parte Machin* [1952] 2 QB 355), but that is most unlikely to happen in practice.

27.35   Subject to the restrictions on quashing an acquittal, a quashing order is issued in three main situations.

27.36   First, the order is made when the inferior tribunal acts in excess of jurisdiction. *Ex parte Machin* (above) provides an example. The magistrates tried M for offences triable either way without first explaining to him the possibility of being committed to Quarter Sessions for sentence. Since the procedure set out in the relevant statute, which alone could give them jurisdiction to try an indictable offence, had not been followed, the magistrates acted in excess of their powers in trying M, and accordingly issued an order to quash his convictions. A sentence passed by magistrates may also be in excess of jurisdiction. In *Llandrindod Wells Justices ex parte Gibson* [1968] 1 WLR 598 for example, G's disqualification from driving was quashed because, having pleaded guilty by post, he was disqualified in his absence without the magistrates first adjourning and notifying him of the reason for the adjournment. In those circumstances, the court had no power to disqualify him (see MCA, s 11(4) and 10.44). In *St Albans Crown Court ex parte Cinnamond* [1981] QB 480 the concept of a sentence in excess of jurisdiction was extended to cover a sentence which was so harsh and oppressive that no reasonable tribunal, properly understanding its powers, could have passed it. It would seem that the test which the High Court applies in appeals against sentence by way of judicial review is the same as that which is appropriate to such appeals which proceed by way of case stated (see 27.17(c)). The test suggested in *Tucker v DPP* [1992] 4 All ER 901 at 903 was: 'Is the sentence by any acceptable standard truly astonishing?' But in *Truro Crown Court ex parte Adair* [1997] COD 296, Lord Bingham CJ suggested that such a test was too subjective, and said that it would be more helpful to ask whether the sentence fell clearly outside the broad area of the lower court's sentencing discretion. However, the High Court clearly does not intend that an application for a quashing order should become a regular alternative to appealing against sentence to the Crown Court. An offender who feels that his sentence in the magistrates' court was harsh and oppressive should appeal in the normal way to the Crown Court, and only if that court refuses to reduce the sentence should he apply to the High Court for a quashing order: *Battle Justices ex parte Shepherd and another* (1983) 5 Cr App R (S) 124. *Ex parte Cinnamond* was a case where the Crown Court, far from reducing sentence, had unreasonably increased it to 18 months' disqualification for an offence of careless driving, so C's only possible remedy was to go to the High Court.

Secondly, a quashing order will be issued where the inferior tribunal acted in breach of the **27.37** rules of natural justice. The modern approach to alleged breaches of the rules of natural justice is to state, simply but vaguely, that a tribunal must act fairly having regard to the nature of the inquiry on which it is engaged. Traditionally, the rules of natural justice have been defined with a little more precision, and are said to involve two main principles—no man may be a judge in his own cause, and the tribunal must hear both sides of the case. Breaches of both so-called rules have led to convictions in the magistrates' courts being quashed. Numerous cases have concerned alleged breaches of the first rule through a magistrate or a clerk taking part in a case when he has a pecuniary interest in its outcome, or a non-pecuniary interest which is such as to give rise to a reasonable suspicion of bias (see 10.06). The second rule may be invoked where procedural irregularities have occurred which possibly prejudiced the applicant. Failure to give the accused reasonable time to prepare his defence (*Thames Magistrates' Court ex parte Polemis* [1974] 1 WLR 1371) refusing to issue witness warrants (*Bradford Justices ex parte Wilkinson* [1990] 1 WLR 692), failing to allow the defendant an adjournment where one of his witnesses was unavailable (*Bracknell Justices ex parte Hughes* [1990] Crim LR 266), announcing a verdict of guilty before hearing a closing speech by counsel on behalf of the accused (*Marylebone Justices ex parte Farrag* [1981] Crim LR 182), and not notifying the defence of witnesses who could support their case (*Leyland Justices ex parte Hawthorn* [1979] QB 283) have all been held to be breaches of the rules of natural justice. The last case is particularly interesting because a quashing order was issued even though the responsibility for not giving the defence the necessary information lay with the police not the court. Relying on that authority, the High Court has since been prepared to grant an order to quash whenever an error by the pro-secution seems seriously to have prejudiced the presentation of the defence case. Thus, in *Knightsbridge Crown Court ex parte Goonatilleke* [1986] QB 1 G's conviction for shoplifting was quashed because the store detective (who was treated by the High Court as being in effect the prosecutor) failed to tell the defence that he had a conviction for wasting police time arising out of his falsely informing the police while a serving officer that his warrant card had been stolen. The information would have been particularly useful as G's defence was that the store detective had 'planted' on him the items allegedly stolen so as to impress his superiors by the number of arrests he was making. Similarly, in *Liverpool Crown Court ex parte Roberts* [1986] Crim LR 622 failure to tell the defence that a police officer, the alleged victim of an assault by R, had made a statement to a superior officer soon after the event which suggested the incident might have amounted only to an accidental clash of heads was fatal to the conviction. However, in the absence of default by the prosecution, a conviction will not be quashed merely because fresh evidence favourable to the defence has come to light since the summary trial, unless the appellant can achieve the very difficult task of convincing the High Court that—in the light of the additional evidence—all the crucial evidence on which the magistrates convicted must have been perjured. In *Ex parte Roberts,* the police officer's failure to carry out his duty was regarded as a failure on the part of 'the total apparatus of the prosecution' (per Glidewell LJ).

27.38   The third situation in which a quashing order will be granted is where there is an error of law apparent on the face of the record of the inferior tribunal's proceedings—i.e., just by reading the record, and without receiving evidence on affidavit or otherwise as to what occurred in the court below, the High Court can tell that a mistake has been made. Historically, the quashing order was developed to correct such patent errors, the effect of the order (or writ as it then was) being to remove the record into the King's Bench where it would be rectified. Today, appeal by way of case stated provides a remedy for errors of law much broader in scope than the remedy provided by the quashing order. The problem in relying on judicial review when one wishes to have a magistrates' court decision quashed is that magistrates never give written reasons for their decisions, and such oral reasons as they may choose to give are usually brief. If the magistrates do give oral reasons, it has been held that they may be incorporated into the record of the court's proceedings (*Chertsey Justices ex parte Franks* [1961] 2 QB 152), but in the absence of such reasons the record will consist only of the charges against the accused, his pleas, the verdict and the sentence passed. The only errors likely to be revealed by such basic information are jurisdictional errors such as those already discussed (e.g., passing a sentence in excess of the statutory maximum for the offence of which, according to the record, the accused was convicted). One device by which the record can be augmented is illustrated by the case of *Southampton Justices ex parte Green* [1976] QB 11. G applied to the High Court to quash a decision by magistrates that she should forfeit the sum of £3,000, that being the amount in which she had stood surety for her husband who had 'jumped bail'. The record of the magistrates' court proceedings simply showed that they had made the order complained of. Since that order was undoubtedly within their powers, no error appeared, and the application for a quashing order failed. G appealed to the Court of Appeal against the High Court's decision. The Court of Appeal had before it affidavits sworn by the chairman of the magistrates and the clerk. They showed that the bench had approached its decision on whether to estreat the recognizance on a basis which was wrong in law. The affidavits were treated as part of the record (see Browne LJ's judgment at p 22), and therefore an error appeared on the face of the record, which enabled the Court of Appeal to issue a quashing order. However, there is no obligation on magistrates to make affidavits explaining the reasoning behind their decisions, and, if they do not, the problem remains that any errors of law they may have made are unlikely to be patent on the face of the record.

The position where the accused seeks an order quashing the rejection of an application to exclude evidence of a confession under ss 76 or 78 of the PACE 1984 was considered in *Re Proulx* [2001] 1 All ER 57. The High Court will only interfere with the magistrates' findings of fact, and assessment of their significance when ruling on the admissibility of the confession if they are outside the range of conclusions available to the reasonable magistrate (i.e., it will only grant such an order if the magistrates' findings are unreasonable in the light of the test in *Associated Picture Houses Ltd v Wednesbury Corporation* [1948] 1 KB 223). **27.39**

A mandatory order is used to compel an inferior tribunal to carry out its duties. Until 2000, it was known as *mandamus*. Thus, in *Brown* (1857) 7 E & B 757 magistrates who had refused to try an information on the plainly inadequate ground that, in their view, other persons should have been charged with the offence as well as the accused, were ordered to hear the case. Similarly, magistrates may be ordered to state a case for the opinion of the High Court if one has been properly requested under s 111 of the MCA and there are no reasons for regarding the application as frivolous. The scope of the mandatory order is, however, fairly limited. It is appropriate where jurisdiction is wrongly refused, but not where the inferior tribunal accepts jurisdiction and then allegedly makes a mistake in the exercise of that jurisdiction. It follows that if, during the course of a summary trial or committal proceedings, magistrates come to a seemingly erroneous decision (e.g., to exclude certain evidence or disallow a line of cross-examination), the aggrieved party may not there and then obtain an adjournment and go to the High Court for a mandatory order to compel reversal of the decision. All he can do is wait until the conclusion of the hearing, and then—if the ultimate decision goes against him—challenge that by appeal by case stated or an application for a quashing order as appropriate (see *Rochford Justices ex parte Buck* (1978) 68 Cr App R 114 and *Wells Street Stipendiary Magistrate ex parte Seillon* [1978] 1 WLR 1002). In brief, a mandatory order may be used to compel proper consideration of whether to exercise a discretionary power, but not, generally speaking, to compel the actual exercise of it. **27.40**

The prohibiting order is the reverse of the mandatory order. It prevents an inferior tribunal acting or continuing to act in excess of jurisdiction. Until 2000, it was known as an order for prohibition. It is, of course, unlikely that a magistrates' court would deliberately want to exceed its jurisdiction and act unlawfully, but occasionally there is genuine doubt about the limits of its powers. In that situation it is convenient to adjourn before the possibly *ultra vires* act is done, thus enabling the party who considers that what the magistrates propose is unlawful to apply to the High Court for a prohibiting order. One example of this happening is *Hatfield Justices ex parte Castle* [1981] 1 WLR 217, where the magistrates had announced their intention of holding committal proceedings in respect of a charge of criminal damage to a value of £23, believing that the special procedure whereby small-value criminal damage charges *must* be tried summarily did not apply. The High Court held that the magistrates' understanding of the law was wrong (i.e., the special procedure did apply), and they therefore granted a prohibiting order to prevent the committal proceedings taking place.

27.41   Finally, it is important to notice that quashing, mandatory and prohibiting orders are always discretionary. In cases where it is in law open to the High Court to grant the remedy, their lordships may nonetheless refuse it in the broader interests of fairness and the due administration of justice. Thus, in *Battle Justices ex parte Shepherd* (1983) 5 Cr App R (S) 124, an order to quash a sentence was refused because the applicant had ignored the more obvious and convenient remedy of appealing the magistrates' court's sentence to the Crown Court. Similarly, in *Birmingham Justices ex parte Lamb* [1983] 1 WLR 339 (see 10.26 for details) an application for a mandatory order to compel magistrates to try an information which they had wrongly dismissed without hearing any evidence failed on account of the undesirability of having the case heard long after the events in question, albeit that the delay was caused mainly by the prosecution having to make the application for judicial review to correct the magistrates' erroneous original decision. In *Bradford Justices ex parte Wilkinson* [1990] 1 WLR 692, on the other hand, Mann LJ said: 'I believe that a defendant is entitled to have a proper trial and a proper appeal. If he does not have a proper trial, he may…come to this court.' *Ex parte Wilkinson* was not followed in *Peterborough Justices ex parte Dowler* [1996] 2 Cr App R 561. In that case, the High Court took the view that a procedurally unfair conviction before the magistrates (which had been flawed by failure to disclose a potentially helpful witness statement to the defence) might be cured by a fair trial on appeal to the Crown Court. Judicial review, as a discretionary remedy, was refused to the applicant, who had an appeal pending before the Crown Court. Exceptional cases, where the court considered that judicial review should be granted since it might be determinative of the case as a whole, could still be heard by the High Court.

27.42   *Ex parte Dowler* was considered by the High Court in *Hereford Magistrates' Court ex parte Rowlands* [1998] QB 110, and was said not to be authority for the proposition that leave to apply for judicial review should be denied where there was a plausible complaint of procedural irregularity or unfairness. It was stressed that the defendant had the right to a proper trial before the magistrates, with a right of appeal to the Crown Court.

Procedure for an application

27.43   The procedure for applying for judicial review is contained in s 31 of the Supreme Court Act 1981 and the Civil Procedure Rules 1998, Part 54. It falls into two main stages. First, the applicant must obtain leave to apply for review. The application for leave is usually determined by a single judge on the basis of a private perusal of the grounds for review set out in a written statement filed by the applicant at the commencement of the proceedings. If leave to apply is granted, the application itself—the second stage in the procedure—is determined by the Divisional Court, which will hear argument from the applicant and anybody else who appears to have a sufficient interest in the outcome. Evidence may be received by the Court, but is usually in affidavit form, not oral. Details of the procedure are beyond the scope of this work, and reference should be made to *Blackstone's Criminal Practice 2008*, D28.28.

Judicial review of Crown Court decisions

27.44   Section 29(3) of the Supreme Court Act 1981 allows a decision of the Crown Court to be challenged through an application for judicial review, provided it was not a decision 'relating to a trial on indictment'. Precisely the same rule applies to appeals by way of case stated from the Crown Court (see 27.27 to 27.29). In *Re Smalley,* [1985] AC 622 the House of Lords considered what was meant by the phrase 'relating to a trial on indictment'. While not attempting a full definition, Lord Bridge said that it extended beyond decisions taken during the actual course of a trial on indictment and covered all decisions 'affecting the conduct of the trial', even if taken at a pre-trial stage. Applying the guidance, it has been held (or suggested in *obiter dicta*) that:

(a) forfeiting the recognizance of a person who stood surety for an accused who absconded;
(b) ordering the forfeiture of property belonging to a third party that had been used by an offender in connection with an offence of which he had been convicted;
(c) binding over an acquitted accused to keep the peace as a measure of preventative justice; and
(d) discharging a restriction on the publication of the identity of a juvenile,

could all have no bearing on the actual conduct of the accused's trial, and so were open to judicial review (see *Re Smalley* supra, *Maidstone Crown Court ex parte Gill* [1986] 1 WLR 1405, *Inner London Crown Court ex parte Benjamin* (1986) 85 Cr App R 267 and *Leicester Crown Court ex parte S* (1990) 94 Cr App R 153 respectively). On the other hand, the following have been held to relate to trial on indictment, with the result that they are not susceptible to judicial review:

(a) an order that counts should lie on the file marked not to be proceeded with without leave (*Central Criminal Court ex parte Raymond* [1986] 1 WLR 710);
(b) the decision by the Crown Court judge before arraignment not to dismiss a charge on grounds of alleged weaknesses in the Crown's evidence (*R (Snelgrove) v Crown Court at Woolwich* [2005] 1 WLR 3223);
(c) the decision by the trial judge whether or not the Crown Court has jurisdiction to try an indictment (*Manchester Crown Court ex parte DPP* (1993) *The Times,* 26 November 1993);
(d) the decision by the Crown Court judge that all or part of an indictment should be stayed as an abuse of process (*Re Ashton* [1994] 1 AC 9);
(e) an order from the trial judge that statements should be disclosed to the defence, despite the claim of the prosecution that they attracted public interest immunity (*Chelmsford Crown Court ex parte Chief Constable of Essex* [1994] 1 WLR 359);
(f) the decision by the Crown Court judge whether to hold a trial as to the defendant's fitness to plead (*Bradford Crown Court ex parte Bottomley* [1994] Crim LR 753);

The question of whether the decision of the Director of Public Prosecutions to consent to a prosecution is susceptible to judicial review arose in *DPP ex parte Kebilene* (1999) *The Times,* 2 November 1999. The *ratio decidendi* of the House of Lords in that case seems to be that, in the absence of dishonesty or *mala fides* or an exceptional circumstance, the DPP's decision to consent cannot be judicially reviewed.

A comparison of judicial review and appeal by case stated

The functions of mandatory and prohibiting orders on the one hand, and appeal by case stated **27.45** on the other are quite distinct. The appellant by case stated argues that the magistrates have made a mistake in exercising jurisdiction. The applicant for a mandatory prohibiting order argues either that the magistrates have failed to exercise their jurisdiction or that they should be prevented from exercising a jurisdiction which they do not lawfully have. The quashing order and appeal by case stated, on the other hand, serve similar purposes. The effect of both remedies is to set aside the decision of the court below, and the practitioner advising a person aggrieved by a decision of a magistrates' court or of the Crown Court on appeal from the magistrates may find the choice between the remedies difficult. Most of the points relevant to that choice have already been touched upon, but, in summary, the position is that:

(a) Where the magistrates or Crown Court have acted in excess of jurisdiction it is judicial review which should be pursued (*North Essex Justices, ex parte Lloyd* [2001] 2 Cr App R (S) 86.

(b) Where an error of law has been made, but the inferior tribunal was acting within its jurisdiction, appeal by case stated is the obvious remedy. If the error of law is patent on the face of the record of the inferior tribunal's proceedings, a quashing order could also be used, but, as explained at 27.33 to 27.44, most errors of law are latent rather than patent. Only through the statement of case will the latent error be revealed.

(c) If the rules of natural justice have been broken, the appropriate remedy is a quashing order. This is because the procedural irregularities which typically form the basis of an alleged breach of natural justice (e.g., a magistrate had an interest in the outcome of the proceedings or the defence was not given the opportunity to present its case properly) would not emerge from a case stated, which deals essentially with the facts the magistrates found proved and the legal issues arising from those facts (*R(P) v Liverpool City Magistrates* [2006] EWHC 887 (Admin)).

(d) A quashing order is again the only remedy where the defence wish to quash a committal for trial or sentence. Appeal by case stated will not lie because there has not been a final determination in the case (see 27.17). In fact, an application for an order to quash a committal for trial is almost certain to fail, but it is at least theoretically available. Applications to quash a committal for sentence on the basis that it was in excess of jurisdiction have a better chance of success.

(e) Where both a quashing order and appeal by case stated are available the latter is preferable because it enables the facts as found by the magistrates or the Crown Court to be placed clearly before the High Court, rather than relying on devices such as an affidavit from the chairman of the bench to supplement the court record (see *Ipswich Crown Court ex parte Baldwin* [1981] 1 All ER 596 where McNeill J said of a case which 'bristled with factual difficulties' that the only 'convenient and proper way' to have brought it before the High Court would have been to have appealed by case stated—B was criticised for applying for judicial review; see also *Morpeth Ward Justices ex parte Ward* (1992) 95 Cr App R 215).

D   APPEAL FROM THE HIGH COURT TO THE HOUSE OF LORDS

27.46 The decision of the High Court in a criminal cause or matter may be appealed to the House of Lords: Administration of Justice Act 1960, s 1(1)(a). The circumstances in which the appeal will lie are analogous to those in which an appeal lies from the Criminal Division of the Court of Appeal to the House of Lords—i.e., the High Court must certify that there is a point of law of general public importance involved, and either the High Court or the House of Lords must grant leave to appeal.

By contrast with the rule governing appeals against their civil decisions, the decision of the **27.47** High Court in a criminal case may only be appealed to the House of Lords—there is no intermediate right of appeal to the Court of Appeal: Supreme Court Act 1981, s 18(1). However, some decisions which are incidentally connected with criminal proceedings are nonetheless classified as being civil in nature so that s 18(1) does not apply. Thus, in *Southampton Justices ex parte Green* [1976] QB 11 the Court of Appeal held that it had jurisdiction to entertain an appeal against the High Court's refusal to quash an order by magistrates forfeiting a surety's recognizance. Although the order against G would not have been made if there had not been criminal proceedings against the person for whom she was a surety, the order in itself did not and could not result in her being prosecuted for a criminal offence. Therefore, any decisions by the High Court relating to that order were not in a criminal cause. For further discussion, see below.

E   THE CRIMINAL CASES REVIEW COMMISSION

The Criminal Cases Review Commission (see 26.100 to 26.104) has power to refer cases dealt **27.48** with in a magistrates' court to the Crown Court. The Crown Court may not, on a reference, impose any punishment more severe than that imposed by the court whose decision is being referred (Criminal Appeal Act 1995, ss 11 and 12).

KEY DOCUMENTS

Magistrates' Courts Act 1980.
Criminal Procedure Rules 2005, Part 63 (available at <http://www.hmcourts-service. gov.uk/cms/pds.htm>).

28

THE EUROPEAN DIMENSION

So far, we have concentrated almost entirely on English law as it affects criminal procedure.   **28.01**
Increasingly, however, there is a European dimension to the way in which the courts
interpret our law. There are two main ways in which European jurisprudence affects the
criminal courts. First, the United Kingdom, as a member of the European Union, is bound
by the Treaty of Rome. In effect, our domestic law is subject to the law of the European
Union, as interpreted by the European Court of Justice. This aspect of the European dimension is dealt with in 28.02. Second, as a member of the Council of Europe and a signatory of
the European Convention on Human Rights (ECHR), the United Kingdom has undertaken to
implement the rights contained in that Convention. These rights have acquired added
significance since the Human Rights Act 1998 (HRA) came into effect in October 2000. The
ECHR is dealt with at 28.05 to 28.33.

A   REFERENCES TO THE EUROPEAN COURT OF JUSTICE

Any English court, civil or criminal, may request a preliminary ruling on a point of European   **28.02**
Community law which arises before it. The point is then referred to the European Court of
Justice for a preliminary ruling under Art 234 (ex 177) of the EEC Treaty. Article 234 makes it
clear that the only court which is *obliged* to make such a reference in a criminal matter is the
House of Lords. Other courts have a *discretion* to make a reference.

In *Plymouth Justices ex parte Rogers* [1982] QB 863 (a case concerned with whether a fishing net   **28.03**
contravened EEC regulations) it was confirmed that magistrates have such a discretion, and
that the Divisional Court will not interfere with it unless the magistrates misdirect themselves
or act unreasonably. The Divisional Court said, however, that ordinarily:

> . . . justices should exercise considerable caution before referring [a case to the European Court]
> even after they have heard all the evidence. If they come to a wrong decision on Community law,

a higher court can make the reference and frequently the higher court would be the more suitable forum to do so. The higher court is as a rule in a better position to assess whether any reference is desirable. On references the form of the question referred is of importance and the higher court will normally be in a better position to assess the appropriateness of the question and to assist in formulating it clearly. Leaving it to the higher court will often also avoid delay.

28.04   *Henn v DPP* [1981] AC 850 examined the exercise of the same discretion by the Crown Court. Lord Diplock warned against any tendency to rush to Europe for a preliminary ruling:

> . . . in a criminal trial upon indictment it can seldom be a proper exercise of the presiding judge's discretion to seek a preliminary ruling before the facts of the alleged offence have been ascertained, with the result that the proceedings will be held up for nine months or more in order that at the end of the trial he may give to the jury an accurate instruction as to the relevant law, if the evidence turns out in the event to be as was anticipated at the time the reference was made—which may not always be the case. It is generally better, as the judge himself put it, that the question be decided by him in the first instance and reviewed thereafter if necessary through the hierarchy of the national courts.

As to the procedure for a preliminary ruling:

(a)   the national court makes the reference;
(b)   pending the ruling from the ECJ, the national proceedings are suspended;
(c)   after the ruling has been made, the national court applies it to the case and continues to judgment.

B   EUROPEAN CONVENTION ON HUMAN RIGHTS

28.05   The European Convention on Human Rights (ECHR) was signed in 1950, and came into force in 1953. It was produced by the Council of Europe, of which the United Kingdom was one of the original ten members (now considerably expanded), in the aftermath of the Second World War and the Nuremberg Trials. There is of course no direct connection between the Council of Europe and the European Community. Like the European Union, the Council of Europe has a Commission and a Court, which are based in Strasbourg. The European Court of Justice (see 28.02 to 28.04) has at times relied on the ECHR as an influence on the general principles of EU law, but the Convention has no formal role in determining EU law.

The legal status of the ECHR

28.06   The ECHR is an international treaty to which the United Kingdom is a signatory, and it is binding on all its signatories in international law. In most member countries of the Council of Europe, the ECHR has been made a directly enforceable part of the domestic legal system. Until the passage of the Human Rights Act 1998 (the HRA), the United Kingdom remained one of the few signatory countries which did not incorporate the Convention into its law in this way. Since the HRA was implemented in October 2000, however, the status of the ECHR in English courts has changed radically.

Position after the Human Rights Act 1998

28.07   The HRA 1998 aims to integrate the ECHR into our legal system, so that all courts have an obligation to consider arguments founded upon its provisions, and to act upon the rights which formerly could only be enforced in Strasbourg. The HRA came fully into force in October 2000. Section 2 places a duty upon any court, from the magistrates' court upwards, to take into account the decisions of the European Court of Human Rights, and the other bodies in Strasbourg which have interpreted the provisions of the ECHR. Section 3 lays down that primary and secondary legislation must be interpreted in a way consistent with Convention rights if that is possible. If it is impossible, the legislation will be valid and enforceable, but the higher courts (including the House of Lords, the Court of Appeal and the High Court—but not the Crown Court) may make a declaration of incompatibility (s 4). Section 6 makes it unlawful for a public authority (including a court) to act in a way which is incompatible with a Convention right, unless required to do so by provisions contained in, or made under, primary legislation. Where a court has declared that a statutory provision is incompatible with a Convention right, s 10 sets out a 'fast-track' procedure. This enables the government to produce legislation to remove the incompatibility speedily, using the affirmative resolution procedure.

Procedure of the European Court of Human Rights

Where an individual considers that the domestic courts have failed to protect a right enshrined in the ECHR, then the right of petition to Strasbourg remains available after incorporation, just as it was prior to the implementation of the HRA 1998. **28.08**

The aggrieved party sends a complaint to the Secretary to the Court of Human Rights at the Council of Europe in Strasbourg. The Secretary then forwards it to the Court for a decision on admissibility. Since November 1998, this preliminary issue has been considered by the Court itself. Prior to that date, admissibility was adjudicated upon by the Commission. The decision on whether the case should pass this first hurdle is an important one, and over 90 per cent of applications are rejected upon one of the bases set out in Art 35, which states that an application is inadmissible if: **28.09**

(a) it is anonymous;

(b) it concerns a matter already dealt with by the Court;

(c) it is incompatible with the ECHR, e.g., it deals with a right not contained in the ECHR;

(d) domestic remedies have not been exhausted (but there is no obligation to pursue remedies which offer no chance of success, e.g., because there is a binding domestic precedent);

(e) it was not made within six months of the date on which the decision allegedly in violation of the ECHR was made (but where the breach of the ECHR is a continuing one, time will not begin to run until the continuing state of affairs ceases to exist: *Temple v UK* (1985) 8 EHRR 319);

(f) the applicant was not a 'victim' in terms of Art 34, i.e., someone who has been, or will be, personally affected (if claiming on the basis of national law or policy, the applicant must show that he is affected to a greater extent than others);

(g) it is an abuse of the right of petition; or

(h) it is manifestly ill-founded. (This final condition is, in effect, a leave requirement which is based on a preliminary assessment of the merits.)

The decision that an application is inadmissible may be taken by a unanimous vote of a committee of three judges, acting under Art 28. If no decision is taken under Art 28, a chamber (usually consisting of seven judges) will decide on admissibility (Art 29). The Court will give its decision on admissibility in writing. There is no appeal against a decision that a case **28.10** is inadmissible, and such a decision precludes any further application based upon the same facts. If the Court decides that the application is admissible, it will try to reach a 'friendly settlement' (negotiated agreement) between the parties. This may involve the payment of compensation and/or a change in the law or administrative practice upon which the complaint is founded.

28.11   If there is no settlement, the parties (and individuals, organizations and other governments with the court's leave) may make further written and oral submissions. The oral hearing itself is very short, usually lasting a couple of hours, with speeches submitted in advance to allow for simultaneous translation to be as accurate as possible. The chamber at the oral hearing usually consists of seven judges, although in exceptional cases the more important issues will be decided by a grand chamber of 17 judges, provided that the parties consent.

28.12   If the Court considers that there has been a violation, it may also award 'just satisfaction'—damages and legal costs (Art 41). Each government is committed, as a signatory to the ECHR, to implementing the judgments of the Court, which includes amending the legislation or decision upon which the violation is based.

28.13   There is the prospect of an appeal to the grand chamber of 17 judges (Art 43). The parties have three months to seek leave for such an appeal from a panel of five judges, who must grant leave if 'the case raises a serious question affecting the interpretation or application of the ECHR or the protocols thereto, or a serious issue of general importance'. There is, however, no right of appeal against a decision that an application is inadmissible.

Principles operated by the European Court of Human Rights

28.14   There are certain features of the approach taken by the Court in Strasbourg which need emphasis for those accustomed to the practice of the courts in England and Wales:

(a) Its approach is *purposive*. The court searches for the aims underlying the broad statements of principle enshrined in the ECHR. Its purpose is to protect individual human rights (*Soering v UK* (1989) 11 EHRR 439), and is based upon the pluralism and tolerance contained in the preamble to the ECHR (*Handyslde v UK* (1976) 1 EHRR 737).

(b) Its approach is *evolutionary*, aiming at the adaptation of the ECHR in the light of the current social climate. In *Tyrer v UK* (1978) 2 EHRR 1, in holding that the use of corporal punishment as part of the criminal justice system on the Isle of Man was contrary to Art 3, the Court stated that 'the Convention is a living instrument which . . . must be interpreted in the light of present day conditions'.

(c) It produces decisions *based on specific sets of facts*, rather than laying down propositions of general applicability. Thus it is not really appropriate to suggest, for example, that 'the Court is likely to find that s 11 of the Criminal Procedure and Investigations Act 1996 is compatible with (or in violation of) Art 6 of the ECHR'. All that might be said is that a particular statutory provision will make it more (or less) likely that the rights of a defendant were violated in a particular case.

(d) It bases itself upon the *'margin of appreciation'*. Each country is permitted a certain tolerance in determining its own public policy, within the framework of review by the Court. The objective is to ensure that the political and cultural traditions of the signatory States are respected—they are given a 'margin of appreciation'.

Some of the rights in the ECHR are absolute, e.g., Art 3 prohibiting torture and inhuman or degrading treatment. Most of the rights, however, are subject to limitations. When the Court considers whether such qualifications constitute a violation, it will particularly look at:

(a) Whether the interference with the right is *prescribed by law*. If it is not, there will be a violation of the ECHR.
(b) Whether the limitation serves a *legitimate purpose*, e.g., national security, public safety.
(c) Whether it is necessary in a democratic society. This is sometimes framed in terms of a principle of *proportionality*. The interference will be 'disproportionate' if it is not necessary in a democratic society. Implicit in this test is the notion of balance. 'Inherent in the whole of the Convention is a search for the fair balance between the demands of the general interest of the Community and the requirements of the protection of the individual's human rights': *Soering v UK* (1989) 11 EHRR 439.

The rights contained in the ECHR

The content of the ECHR is largely concerned with basic personal freedoms. Cases in which **28.15** the UK has been involved in alleged breaches of this and other Articles of the ECHR relevant to criminal practice are detailed in specialist works on the ECHR, to which further reference should be made (see, for example, *Blackstone's Guide to the Human Rights Act 1998* (OUP 2003, 3rd edn). In addition, *Blackstone's Criminal Practice 2008* A7 summarizes the case law surrounding the ECHR. Three of the most important Articles of the ECHR are set out below, with a short commentary on each.

Article 3

No one shall be subjected to torture or to inhuman or degrading treatment or punishment. **28.16**

Article 3 is one of the few Articles in the ECHR where the right is guaranteed under all circumstances (the others are Arts 2, 4 and 7). In respect of the remaining articles, the governments which have ratified the ECHR have the right of derogation, i.e., to take measures required by war or other public emergencies (see Arts 15 and 16). No such right exists, however, in relation to the prohibition on torture and inhuman or degrading treatment.

Cases involving the United Kingdom in alleged violations of Art 3 have included:

(a) the use of corporal punishment as a criminal sanction (*Tyrer v UK* (1978) 2 EHRR 1);
(b) the treatment of terrorist suspects (*Republic of Ireland v UK* (1978) 2 EHRR 25);
(c) extradition, possibly to face the death penalty in the United States (*Soering v* UK (1989) 11 EHRR 439).

Article 5

(1) Everyone has the right to liberty and security of person. No one shall be deprived of his **28.17** liberty save in the following cases and in accordance with a procedure prescribed by law:
  (a) the lawful detention of a person after conviction by a competent court;
  (b) the lawful arrest or detention of a person for non-compliance with the lawful order of a court or in order to secure the fulfilment of any obligation prescribed by law;

(c) the lawful arrest or detention of a person effected for the purpose of bringing him before the competent legal authority on reasonable suspicion of having committed an offence or when it is reasonably considered necessary to prevent his committing an offence or fleeing after having done so;

(d) the detention of a minor by lawful order for the purpose of educational supervision or his lawful detention for the purpose of bringing him before the competent legal authority;

(e) the lawful detention of persons for the prevention of the spreading of infectious diseases, of persons of unsound mind, alcoholics or drug addicts or vagrants;

(f) the lawful arrest or detention of a person to prevent his effecting an unauthorised entry into the country or of a person against whom action is being taken with a view to deportation or extradition.

(2) Everyone who is arrested shall be informed promptly, in a language which he understands, of the reasons for his arrest and of any charge against him.

(3) Everyone arrested or detained in accordance with the provisions of paragraph (1) (c) of this article shall be brought promptly before a judge or other officer authorised by law to exercise judicial power and shall be entitled to trial within a reasonable time or to release pending trial. Release may be conditioned by guarantees to appear for trial.

(4) Everyone who is deprived of his liberty by arrest or detention shall be entitled to take proceedings by which the lawfulness of his detention shall be decided speedily by a court and his release ordered if the detention is not lawful.

(5) Everyone who has been the victim of arrest or detention in contravention of the provisions of this article shall have an enforceable right to compensation.

As can be seen from the text of Art 5, it has considerable relevance to criminal practice. It prohibits deprivation of liberty, save in the circumstances described in exceptions (1)(a) to (1)(f) (although, in common with most Articles, Art 5 is subject to the right of derogation laid down in Arts 15 and 16). The exceptions outlined in (a) to (f) cover, respectively, restrictions imposed as a result of:

(a) sentence after conviction;

(b) committal for contempt;

(c) remand in custody;

(d) the care of minors in specified circumstances;

(e) infectious illness, mental illness, and addiction;

(f) illegal immigrants.

There have been a number of cases brought against the UK, based upon Art 5, which involve the detention of suspected terrorists in the context of the situation in Northern Ireland (see, for example, *Brannigan and McBride v UK* (1993) 17 EHRR 539). Another issue which has arisen under Art 5 has been the direction for loss of time where the Court of Appeal believes that an appeal is totally without merit (see 26.58): *Monnell and Morris v UK* (1987) 7 EHRR 557. In an appropriate case, the refusal of bail by a domestic court could be challenged as contrary to Art 5(3). In *Wemhoff v FRG* (1968) 1 EHRR 55, it was stated that the government must show that there are 'relevant and sufficient' reasons to justify the applicant's continued detention. In a series of decisions, the European Court has upheld grounds for refusing bail which are similar to those in Sch 1 to the Bail Act 1976, i.e. the risk of the accused failing to surrender to custody, committing further offences or interfering with the course of justice (see Chapter 7 for the law on bail). This would not necessarily preclude the issue being canvassed in Strasbourg in appropriate circumstances, however, e.g., where the refusal of bail stemmed from a statutory prohibition upon grounds other than those which the European Court of Human Rights is prepared to hold acceptable.

Section 25 of the Criminal Justice and Public Order Act 1994, placed an absolute prohibition **28.18** on bail for anyone awaiting trial for murder, attempted murder, manslaughter, rape or attempted rape if he had a previous conviction for one of those offences (see 7.11). Its terms made the UK government vulnerable to complaints under Art 5, and a number of cases were pending when the statute was amended by s 56 of the Crime and Disorder Act 1998. This replaced the absolute prohibition with a presumption against bail which can be rebutted only if the court considers that there are exceptional circumstances justifying the grant of bail. The European Court of Human Rights has since indicated that a strong presumption against granting bail to those charged with very serious offences is not compatible with Art 5(3) or the presumption of innocence: *Iljikov v Bulgaria*, 26 July 2001, unreported; *Caballero v UK* [2000] Crim LR 587. The question whether s 25 is compatible with the ECHR was considered in *R (O) v Harrow Crown Court* (2003) *The Times*, 29 May 2003. In that case, the Divisional Court concluded that it was, although the two judges arrived at the same result by different paths. Kennedy LJ considered that s 25 imposed a neutral burden on the court, which had to be satisfied that there were exceptional circumstances. Hooper LJ took the view that the provision placed an evidential burden upon the defendant to point to material which supported the existence of exceptional circumstances. Once he had done so, it was for the prosecution to satisfy the court that bail should not be granted.

Article 6

(1) In the determination of his civil rights and obligations or of any criminal charge against **28.19** him, everyone is entitled to a fair and public hearing within a reasonable time by an independent and impartial tribunal established by law. Judgment shall be pronounced publicly but the press and public may be excluded from all or part of the trial in the interests of morals, public order or national security in a democratic society, where the interests of juveniles or the protection of the private life of the parties so require, or to the extent strictly necessary in the opinion of the court in special circumstances where publicity would prejudice the interests of justice.

(2) Everyone charged with a criminal offence shall be presumed innocent until proved guilty according to law.

(3) Everyone charged with a criminal offence has the following minimum rights:
   (a) to be informed promptly, in a language which he understands and in detail, of the nature and cause of the accusation against him;
   (b) to have adequate time and facilities for the preparation of his defence;
   (c) to defend himself in person or through legal assistance of his own choosing or, if he has not sufficient means to pay for legal assistance, to be given it free when the interests of justice so require;
   (d) to examine or have examined witnesses against him and to obtain the attendance and examination of witnesses on his behalf under the same conditions as witnesses against him;

(e) to have the free assistance of an interpreter if he cannot understand or speak the language used in court.

Article 6 is the most important for criminal practice. Article 6(1) deals with the general right to a fair trial in respect of both civil and criminal cases. It covers the principle of open justice, and the protection of the privacy of the parties, especially juveniles, in certain circumstances. It should be given a broad and purposive interpretation: *Moreiva de Azvedo v Portugal* (1990) 13 EHRR 721. It encompasses the principle of 'equality of arms', which is based on the right of the accused to procedural equality with the prosecution. To put it another way, the accused must have 'a reasonable opportunity of presenting his case to the court under conditions which do not place him at a substantial disadvantage *vis-a-vis* his opponent': *Kaufman v Belgium* (1986) 50 DR 98 at p 115. There are, however, limits to the reach of Art 6(1). The European Court of Human Rights will avoid substituting its view of the facts for that of the national court, unless the latter court has drawn unfair conclusions. In an exceptional case, however, they will be prepared to assess the evidence with which the domestic court was presented: *Barbera v Spain* (1988) 11 EHRR 360.

28.20 A violation of Art 6(1) was alleged in the case of *Saunders v UK* (1996) *The Times*, 18 December 1996. The applicant was the Chief Executive Officer of Guinness Plc, whose operations in the course of a take-over battle were investigated by the Department of Trade and Industry. S was interviewed by DTI inspectors on nine occasions, and required by law to answer the questions put to him, failing which he could face a prison sentence for contempt. The DTI transcripts and documents obtained as a result of interviews were passed to the Crown Prosecution Service. S was prosecuted for false accounting and theft. At the trial, the prosecution relied on the transcripts, which were read out to the jury. S was convicted, and appealed to the Court of Appeal. Although his sentence was reduced from five years to two and a half, and the appeal against conviction was upheld on one count, he was refused leave to appeal to the House of Lords against the remaining convictions. In due course, he appealed to the European Court of Human Rights, which held that S's right not to incriminate himself had been infringed, and there had consequently been a breach of Art 6(1) of the Convention. The right against self-incrimination was stated to have close links with the presumption of innocence contained in Art 6(2).

28.21 Another case brought against the United Kingdom under Art 6 was *Murray v UK* (1996) 22 EHRR 29. The government was alleged to have violated Art 6 in two ways:

(a) by denying M access to legal advice for the first 48 hours of detention; and

(b) by allowing inferences to be drawn from his silence (under the Northern Ireland predecessor of the provisions in ss 34 and 35 of the Criminal Justice and Public Order Act 1994).

The European Court of Human Rights upheld the complaint as far as (a) was concerned, but not with regard to (b). They emphasized that the other evidence of guilt was strong, and laid some store by the fact that the adverse inferences had been drawn by an experienced judge, sitting without a jury (a situation which differs from that in which ss 34 and 35 of the 1994 Act operate). In the circumstances, they refused to hold that the drawing of inferences from M's behaviour shifted the burden of proof from prosecution to defence so as to infringe the principle of the presumption of innocence. M had, however, also been denied access to a lawyer during the first 48 hours of his police detention. This was particularly important in view of the significance attached to his silence. It was therefore incompatible with the accused's rights under Art 6(1), taken in conjunction with Art 6(3)(c).

The failure on the part of the prosecution to disclose material relevant to credibility may con- **28.22** stitute a violation of Art 6(3)(d): *Edwards v UK* (1993) 96 Cr App R 1 (see also Field and Young, 'Disclosure, Appeals and Procedural Traditions: *Edwards v United Kingdom* [1994] Crim LR 264). In *Edwards*, material was discovered in time for the appeal, so that the Court of Appeal could assess its effect on the conviction's safety, and that was held by the European Court of Human Rights to have compensated for the defect in the original trial.

In *Rowe and Davis v UK* (2000) 30 EHRR 1, the European Court of Human Rights examined the **28.23** issue of the prosecution duty of disclosure, in particular as it relates to material for which immunity is claimed on the basis of sensitivity (for a description of the procedure, see 9.33 to 9.40). At the time of the trial of the applicants, the Criminal Procedure and Investigations Act 1996 was not yet in force, and the common law on disclosure was in a process of rapid development. The case does, however, have wider implications for the way in which the statutory procedure for disclosure is likely to be measured against the ECHR.

The Applicants, Rowe and Davis, were convicted (together with Johnson) in February 1990 of **28.24** murder, assault occasioning grievous bodily harm and three counts of robbery. Their appeal came before the Court of Appeal in October 1992. At the first hearing, counsel for the prosecution handed a document to the court, which was not shown to defence counsel, seeking a ruling on disclosure. He informed the court that the contents were sensitive, and that he should either be heard *ex parte* or if *inter partes*, only on an undertaking by defence counsel not to disclose what took place to their solicitors or clients. At that hearing, defence counsel indicated that they could not conscientiously give such an undertaking, and the prosecution in effect argued *ex parte* for non-disclosure. The Court of Appeal in its judgment:

(a)   stated that the procedure relating to material in the prosecution's possession which they sought to avoid disclosing had been changed by *Ward* [1993] 1 WLR 619. It was now for the court, not the prosecution, to decide whether disclosure should be made;
(b)   set out a series of procedural guidelines to be followed in such cases (summarized at 9.33 to 9.40); and
(c)   refused to order disclosure.

At the hearing of the substantive appeal, the convictions of Rowe and Davis, and their co-defendant Johnson, were upheld.

In due course, the case was referred to the Criminal Cases Review Commission (see 26.100 to **28.25** 26.104), which investigated the case in the period 1997–99. The investigation revealed that one of the leading prosecution witnesses was a long-standing police informant, who had approached the police and told them that the applicants Rowe and Davis were responsible for the crimes in question. He had received a reward of £10,300 and immunity from prosecution in relation to his admitted participation in the offences. He had never identified Johnson as one of the offenders. These facts had not previously been disclosed to the defence on grounds of public interest immunity. The CCRC commented that 'if the jury had been aware of this then the credibility of [the prosecution witnesses] might have been assessed in a more critical manner'. The case of the Applicants and Johnson was referred back to the Court of Appeal, which in due course upheld their appeal: *Davis* (2000) *The Times*, 25 July 2000.

Meanwhile, the Applicants sought a ruling from the European Court of Human Rights that **28.26** their trial violated Art 6(1) and (3)(a) and (b). The Applicants argued that the procedure at their trial, whereby the prosecution withheld evidence from the defence without consulting the judge, violated Art 6 of the ECHR. This defect was not rectified by the *ex parte* procedure before the Court of Appeal, which gave the defence no opportunity to put forward arguments on disclosure. It was argued on behalf of the Applicants that the exclusion of the accused from this procedure should have been counterbalanced by the introduction of a special independent counsel who could argue the relevance of the undisclosed evidence, test the strength of the prosecution claim to public interest immunity, and safeguard against the risk of judicial error or bias. A special counsel procedure has now been introduced in this country in respect of fair employment cases in Northern Ireland, certain immigration appeals, complaints relating to the interception of electronic communications, and cases where the trial judge prohibits an accused from cross-examining in person the complainant in a sexual offence.

28.27   The following points emerged from the decision of the full European Court of Human Rights:

(a)   The right to a fair trial means that the prosecution authorities should disclose to the defence all material evidence in their possession for and against the accused.

(b)   That duty of disclosure is not absolute, and 'in any criminal proceedings there may be competing interests, such as national security or the need to protect witnesses at risk of reprisals or keep secret police methods of investigation which must be weighed against the rights of the accused'.

(c)   Only such measures restricting the rights of the defence to disclosure as are strictly necessary are permissible under Art 6(1).

(d)   Any difficulties caused to the defence by a limitation on its rights must be sufficiently counterbalanced by the procedure followed by the court.

(e)   The procedure prior to the case of *Ward* [1993] 1 WLR 619, whereby the prosecution could decide to withhold relevant evidence without notifying the judge, was in violation of Art 6(1).

(f)   The procedure adopted by the Court of Appeal at the appeal of the Applicants in relation to disclosure did not remedy the unfair procedure adopted at trial. It was *ex parte* and the Court of Appeal was therefore reliant upon prosecution counsel and transcripts of the trial for an understanding of the possible relevance of the undisclosed material. In any event, if the trial judge had received the material, he could have monitored the importance of the undisclosed evidence at a stage when it could have affected the course of the trial. Further, the Court of Appeal, in considering the evidence *ex post facto* may have been unconsciously influenced by the jury's verdict of guilty into underestimating the significance of the undisclosed evidence.

The Applicants, therefore, did not get a fair trial. The case could be contrasted with that of *Edwards*. In that case, appeal proceedings were able to remedy defects in the trial because, by the time of the appeal the defence had received most of the missing information, and was able to argue in detail about the impact of the new material upon the tests for disclosure.

28.28   The European Court's decision cast doubt upon the ability of the Court of Appeal to remedy defective disclosure at trial. What it did not do, however, is to give a clear indication as to the fairness of *ex parte* procedure, insofar as that procedure is adopted at first instance (now embodied in the Crown Court (Criminal Procedure and Investigations Act 1996) (Disclosure) Rules

1997). The House of Lords looked at the fairness of the *ex parte* procedure, and the question of whether a special independent counsel should be appointed in *H* [2004] 2 WLR 335. Their Lordships declined to lay down a general principle that the appointment of special counsel was necessary wherever the *ex parte* procedure was adopted. Their guidance did, however state that:

> In appropriate cases the appointment of special counsel may be a necessary step to ensure that the contentions of the prosecution are tested and the interests of the defendant protected.

(See 9.33 to 9.47 for further detail on this area.)

In *V v UK* [2000] Crim LR 187, the European Court of Human Rights scrutinized England's **28.29** procedure adopted for the trial of juveniles in the Crown Court. T and V (both aged 10 at the time) abducted the two-year-old Jamie Bulger from a shopping precinct, took him on a two-mile journey, battered him to death, and left him on a railway line to be run over. The trial took place over a three-week period in November 1993, in public, at the Crown Court in Preston. It was preceded and accompanied by massive publicity. Throughout the proceedings, the arrival of the defendants was greeted by a hostile crowd. On occasion, attempts were made to attack the vehicles bringing the defendants to court. In the courtroom, the press benches and public gallery were full. At the opening of the trial, the judge made an order under CYPA 1933, s 39 that there should be no publication of the names, addresses or other identifying details of the Applicant (aged 11 at the time of trial) or V, or publication of their photographs. Nevertheless, the trial took place in the full glare of national and international publicity. At the end of the trial, the defendants were found guilty, and the judge modified the order under s 39 to allow publication of the names of T and V, but no other details. In due course, T appealed to the European Court of Human Rights, on the grounds *inter alia* that:

- his trial in the Crown Court amounted to inhuman and degrading treatment within the meaning of Art 3 of the ECHR;
- he had been denied a fair trial under Art 6(1).

The Court held (by 12 votes to five) that the applicant's trial did not amount to inhuman and degrading treatment contrary to Art 3. It did, however, violate his right to a fair trial under Art 6(1) (decision reached by 16 votes to one). The Court stated that it is essential that a young child charged with a grave offence attracting high levels of media interest should be tried in such a way as to reduce as far as possible any feelings of intimidation. It considered that the formality and ritual of the Crown Court must at times have seemed incomprehensible and intimidating for a child of 11. It noted that less serious crimes in England and Wales were dealt with in the youth courts, from which the general public is excluded and there are automatic reporting restrictions. It laid emphasis upon the blaze of publicity surrounding the trial, and the judge's comments on the effect which this must have had on witnesses. The implication was that this must have been even more traumatic for the defendants. There was evidence that certain of the modifications to the courtroom, in particular the raised dock which was designed to enable the defendants to see what was going on, had the effect of increasing the applicant's sense of discomfort during the trial, since he felt exposed to the scrutiny of the press and public. Further, there was evidence that the post-traumatic stress disorder suffered by the applicant, combined with the lack of any therapeutic work since the offence, had limited his ability to instruct his lawyers or testify in his own defence. He was unable to follow the trial or take decisions in his own best interests. He was unable to participate effectively in the criminal proceedings against him and was, in consequence, denied a fair hearing in breach of Art 6(1).

28.30 The decision was in the context of a particularly harrowing crime, and an unprecedented degree of media attention. In addition, the defendant was at the lower end of the range of criminal responsibility. Nevertheless, the remarks of the European Court of Human Rights about the effects of publicity upon a child defendant and the need to ensure that all defendants must be able to participate fully in the proceedings against them has undoubtedly had far-reaching implications for the trial of juveniles in the Crown Court (see 11.04 to 11.15).

28.31 One of the immediate results of the European Court's decision was the *Practice Direction (Crown Court: Trial of children and young persons)* (2000) *The Times*, 17 February 2000 which now forms para IV.39 of the *Practice Direction (Criminal Proceedings: Consolidation)* [2002] 1 WLR 2870. It stressed that the trial process should not itself expose the young defendant to avoidable intimidation, humiliation, or distress, and pointed out that all possible steps should be taken to assist him to understand and participate in the proceedings. Regard should be had to the welfare of the juvenile, as required by CYPA 1933, s 44. Where a juvenile was indicted jointly with an adult, the court should ordinarily order that the juvenile should be tried on his own unless a joint trial would be in the interests of justice and would not be unduly prejudicial to the welfare of the juvenile.

28.32 If a case against a juvenile might attract widespread public interest, the assistance of the police should be enlisted to ensure that the juvenile is not exposed to intimidation or abuse when attending for trial. The judge should be ready to impose such reporting restrictions as are within his powers.

28.33 The trial of a juvenile should, if practicable, be held in a courtroom in which all the participants are on the same, or almost the same, level. The juvenile should be free to sit with members of his family, in a place which permits easy, informal communication with his lawyers and others with whom he needs to communicate. Steps should be taken to ensure that each step of the trial is explained to him, and conducted in language which he can understand. Frequent and regular breaks would often be appropriate. Generally, robes and wigs should not be worn. Attendance at the trial should be restricted to a small number, perhaps limited to those with an immediate interest in its outcome. There should be no recognizable police presence in the courtroom save for good reason. The number of reporters might be restricted, subject to the public's right to be informed of the administration of justice in the Crown Court. If access by reporters is restricted, arrangements should be made for proceedings to be relayed to another room in the court complex if there is the need.

KEY DOCUMENTS

Human Rights Act 1998 (which contains all relevant provisions of the European Convention on Human Rights).

29

ANCILLARY FINANCIAL MATTERS

This Chapter deals with two ancillary financial matters which are of relevance to criminal   **29.01**
proceedings: public funding and costs.

A   PUBLIC FUNDING

The law on public funding in criminal matters is dealt with in the Access to Justice Act 1999   **29.02**
(AJA), and the Criminal Defence Service Act 2006, supplemented by various regulations.

The Criminal Defence Service (CDS) is the body which provides funding for defendants in   **29.03**
criminal proceedings—the system formerly known as legal aid. It began its operations in April
2001. It functions under the aegis of the Legal Services Commission, which also oversees funding for civil cases. The purpose of the CDS is 'securing that individuals involved in criminal
investigations or criminal proceedings have access to such advice, assistance and representation as the interests of justice require' (s 12(1) of the AJA 1999).

The CDS relies largely upon a system of contracting, based upon the 'General Criminal   **29.04**
Contract', which solicitors in private practice are required to obtain if they wish to carry out
publicly-funded criminal defence work. Once such a contract has been awarded, the firm is
monitored to ensure that it meets the necessary standards.

In addition, the Public Defender Scheme employs criminal defence solicitors who provide   **29.05**
advice, assistance, and representation to clients. The scheme was started as a pilot project in
seven centres, some of which are continuing in operation, whilst others are closing.

Advice and assistance

Prior to charge, there is a scheme under which a person who is under investigation can seek   **29.06**
legal advice from a solicitor. It is means tested, but recipients of certain welfare benefits
(notably income-based job seekers' allowance and income support) are deemed to qualify

automatically. Then, once a person has been charged or issued with a summons, the Post-Charge Advice and Assistance scheme is available. It is subject to the interests of justice test (see 29.08). In effect, if a solicitor believes that his client meets this test, he can undertake the initial preparatory work. He must, however, apply for a representation order as soon as is reasonably practicable. In practice, the Post-charge Advice and Assistance scheme is likely to be used to cover an initial interview, assistance in completing the application for a representation order, taking a proof of evidence, and any urgent preliminary correspondence, e.g., seeking to persuade the CPS to discontinue the prosecution. Thereafter, the cover provided by a representation order will be necessary (unless, of course, the defendant is able to pay privately).

The granting of representation

29.07   A representation order is required for a defendant to be represented at court on a publicly funded basis. For proceedings in the magistrates' court, the defendant must satisfy a means test and a merits test. In respect of cases to be tried on indictment, there is no means test, and representation will be granted if the merits test is satisfied (subject to the possibility of a recovery of defence costs order (see 29.11). The application must be made in writing on the relevant forms, and is processed administratively by the magistrates' court at which the defendant is due to appear.

29.08   As to the criteria on which the grant of a representation order is considered, these are set out in para 5 of Sch 3 to the AJA 1999. The overall decision is 'to be determined in accordance with the interests of justice'. The criteria for determining the interests of justice are:

(a)   whether, in the event of conviction, it is likely that the court would impose a sentence which would either deprive the accused of his liberty, or lead to loss of his livelihood, or seriously damage his reputation;
(b)   whether the case may involve consideration of a substantial question of law;
(c)   whether the accused may be unable to understand the proceedings or state his own case;
(d)   whether the nature of the defence is such as to involve the tracing and interviewing of potential defence witnesses or expert cross-examination of the prosecution witnesses; and
(e)   whether it is in the interests of a person other than the accused that the accused should be represented.

29.09   Some charges are so grave that, even though a grant of representation is not mandatory, it would in practice always be granted. Thus, no court would refuse one to a person charged with for example, manslaughter or causing grievous bodily harm with intent, or rape, or robbery. Other charges may or may not justify an order depending on the facts of the particular case. Thus, although the offence of assault occasioning actual bodily harm carries five years' imprisonment, magistrates are not obliged to make an order if the allegations against the accused are in fact of a trivial nature. They should consider how serious the charge really is, and, if they have done that and decide that an order is unnecessary, the High Court will not interfere with their decision unless it is plainly unreasonable: *Highgate Justices ex parte Lewis* [1977] Crim LR 611. The factors in para 5 illustrate how sometimes the granting of an order is as much an assistance to the court as it is to the accused. Where the accused would not be able to present his case adequately much time is saved by providing him with a lawyer. Similarly, where cross-examination of a witness by the accused personally would cause distress, the public interest is served by having the cross-examination carried out by a professional. But, however desirable it is that the accused be legally represented, he cannot be forced to have a lawyer—the court can do no more than offer him representation, it cannot make him accept. (There is something of an exception in respect of those cases where an unrepresented defendant is prohibited from cross examining a particular witness by the provisions of the Youth Justice and Criminal Evidence Act 1999: see 20.69 to 20.71.)

Appeals against refusal of representation

An accused who is refused the grant of a representation order because he has failed the interests of justice test is entitled to appeal to the court. **29.10**

Recovery of defence costs orders

The means test does not apply to cases which are to be tried on indictment. If the defendant is convicted, however, the Crown Court may make an order that he repay some or all of the cost of any such representation. Such an order is known as a Recovery of Defence Costs Order (RDCO). The procedure relating to the RDCO is set out in the Criminal Defence Service (Recovery of Defence Costs Orders) Regulations 2001 (SI 2001 No 856), as amended by the Criminal Defence Service (Recovery of Defence Costs Orders) (Amendment) Regulations 2004 (SI 2004 No 1195). **29.11**

B   COSTS

Depending on the precise nature and result of the proceedings, the court before which a case or appeal is concluded may make an order *either* that the loser pay the successful party his costs, *or* that costs be paid out of central funds (i.e., out of taxpayers' money). On the whole, the party in whose favour costs are to be ordered would prefer payment out of central funds as he is then sure of his money, whereas an order for *inter partes* costs may be difficult to enforce, especially if it is against the accused or an impecunious private prosecutor. The law on ordering costs is now contained in ss 16–21 of the Prosecution of Offences Act 1985 (POA). The main points are as follows: **29.12**

(i)   A *'defendant's costs order'* may be made by magistrates in favour of the accused if either they have found him not guilty following a summary trial, or they have discharged him following committal proceedings at which the prosecution were unable to establish a case to answer: POA 1985, s 16(1). The Crown Court may make a defendant's costs order whenever the accused in acquitted following a trial on indictment, even if he is acquitted on only one of several counts: s 16(2). It may also make such an order where it allows an appeal (whether against conviction or sentence) from the magistrates. The effect of an order is that the costs reasonably incurred by the accused in defending the proceedings are paid out of central funds. Provided the figure is agreed by the defence, the court may specify the amount the accused is to receive when it makes the order: s 16(9)(a). Otherwise, the costs are determined later by court officers in accordance with regulations made by the Lord Chancellor: s 16(9)(b). Where there are circumstances which make it inappropriate for the accused to receive his full costs, the court may assess what in its opinion would be 'just and reasonable' and specify that sum in the order, whether or not the accused agrees it: s 16(7).

(ii)   The court may order that the prosecution receive out of central funds the costs they incurred in connection with proceedings for an indictable offence: s 17(1). This applies even if the accused is acquitted, but is subject to the massive exception that a prosecuting authority which is publicly financed cannot have an order made in its favour: s 17(2) and (6). Thus, neither the police, the Crown Prosecution Service, government departments, nor local authorities can apply for an order under s 17(1). In practice, therefore, orders for prosecution costs out of central funds are rare. The reason why an order may not be made in favour of the CPS, etc. is that it would effectively result in the government paying its 'own' money to an organisation which it has to finance in any event.

(iii) Where the accused is convicted, he may be ordered to pay the prosecution such costs as the court considers 'just and reasonable': s 18(1). This applies both to trials on indictment and to summary trials, regardless of whether the offence charged is summary or triable either way. The amount to be paid must be specified in the order: s 18(3). Costs ordered against a juvenile may not exceed the amount of any fine imposed on him: s 18(5).

(iv)   Regardless of the nature of the offence charged or the result of the proceedings, the court may make an order that costs incurred by one party as a result of 'an unnecessary or improper act or omission' by another party shall be paid by that other party: s 19(1) and reg 3 of the Costs in Criminal Cases (General) Regulations 1986. Thus, if the prosecution were at fault in not having their witnesses at court on the day the case should have been tried, but the court none the less granted an adjournment, they may be ordered to pay the accused's costs of the day, even if he is ultimately convicted. In other words, the prosecution may be ordered to pay the costs which they have caused the defence to throw away and vice versa.

An order under s 19 is appropriate only where the default which caused costs to be thrown away is that of the accused or prosecutor personally.

(v)   Where the fault for the wasted costs lies with the legal representatives, then the court can order them to pay personally. The Courts and Legal Services Act 1990 inserted a new s 19A into the POA 1985. It gives the court power to order a solicitor or barrister to meet the whole or part of costs wasted 'as a result of any improper, unreasonable or negligent act or omission' by the representative or his staff.

(vi)   The 'proceedings' in respect of which costs may be ordered are defined so as to include proceedings in any court below the court which makes the order (see s 21). This means, *inter alia,* that when the Crown Court, following a trial on indictment, makes an order in favour of the accused, he will be entitled to his costs both of the Crown Court trial and of the committal proceedings. Similarly, if a conviction is set aside on appeal, the appellate court may extend its order for costs to cover the proceedings in which the appellant was convicted. As to the costs of appeals, see 26.74 and 26.75 (appeals to Court of Appeal), 27.13 (appeals to the Crown Court), and 27.24 (appeals to the High Court by case stated).

(vii) The magistrates' court, the Crown Court, and the Court of Appeal may make a 'third party costs order'. It will cover the payment of costs incurred by a party to proceedings by a person who was not a party to them ('the third party'). The order can only be made where there has been serious misconduct by the third party which the court considers ought to result in an award of costs: (s 19B, POA 1985).

The making of an order for costs is always discretionary. However, the approach the courts **29.13** should adopt is set out in the *Practice Direction (Costs in Criminal Proceedings)* [2004] 2 All ER 1070. A defendant's costs orders should normally be made where the defendant is acquitted, unless there are positive reasons for not doing so, e.g., where the defendant's own conduct has brought suspicion on himself and has misled the prosecution into thinking that the case against him was stronger than it actually was (para II.2.1). Where the defendant is convicted on some counts in the indictment and acquitted on others, the court may exercise its discretion to make a defendant's costs order, but may order that only part of the costs incurred be paid, taking into account what is just having regard to the relative importance of the charges in question and the conduct of the parties (para II.2.2).

After conviction or an unsuccessful appeal, some guidance on dealing with an application for **29.14** costs against the offender is provided in the *Practice Direction (Costs in Criminal Proceedings)* [2004] 2 All ER 1070. Paragraph VI.1.4 states: 'An order should be made where the court is satisfied that the offender or appellant has the means to pay.' Usually the costs are considerably less than the actual costs of the proceedings, since the court has to take into account the means of the offender and the effect of any other financial orders it is making (e.g., a fine or compensation order). A Crown Court judge should not use a high costs order as a means of 'punishing' an offender for electing trial on indictment in respect of a charge that could have been appropriately dealt with at the magistrates' court, but, on the other hand, any order made will inevitably reflect the fact that the defence did choose the more expensive mode of trial (see *Bushell* (1980) 2 Cr App R (S) 77).

Where a minor case is in the Crown Court through the prosecution's choice, by contrast, **29.15** they cannot expect to recover their full costs from the accused. In *Hall* [1989] Crim LR 228, H was willing to plead guilty to careless driving. The case went to the Crown Court because the prosecution insisted on a charge of reckless driving. In the Crown Court, H pleaded guilty to careless driving, and the Crown offered no evidence on the reckless driving charge. H was conditionally discharged and ordered to pay £372 prosecution costs. On appeal, the order was reduced to £25 (the amount appropriate to a guilty plea in the magistrates' court).

The defendant may appeal against a prosecution costs order made by the Crown Court, to the **29.16** Court of Appeal. There is, however, no appeal to the Crown Court against an order made by a magistrates' court against a defendant to pay prosecution costs, and the defendant's remedy in such a case is to appeal to the Divisional Court by way of case stated or judicial review as appropriate. In *Northallerton Magistrates' Court ex parte Dove* [1999] Crim LR 760, the Divisional Court said that the costs which the defendant was ordered to pay by the justices should not be grossly disproportionate to any fine imposed. They quashed an order that the defendant should pay costs four and a half times the amount of the fine, and remitted the matter to the magistrates for them to reconsider what costs if any should be paid to the prosecution.

In *Associated Octel Ltd* [1997] Crim LR 144, the Court of Appeal considered whether the defend- **29.17** ant can be ordered to pay costs incurred in the course of the investigation of the offence, as well as legal costs, and held that he could. The prosecution in this case, however, was the same as the investigatory body (the Health and Safety Executive acted in both capacities). It is submitted that the position would be different where the two functions are carried out by two distinct bodies. In such a case, it would not seem 'just and reasonable' (POA 1985, s 18(1)) for the judge or magistrates to order the defendant to pay to the CPS (for example) costs incurred by another body (the police).

29.18 Even where the court does not make a general order for payment of a party's costs, it may order that a witness called by that party shall be paid out of central funds such sum as is necessary to compensate him for the 'expense, trouble or loss of time properly incurred by him' through his attending court: POA, s 19(3). Furthermore, the Costs in Criminal Cases (General) Regulations 1986 state that defence witnesses and witnesses called by private prosecutors *shall* be allowed their expenses out of central funds, unless the court states to the contrary (reg 16). The regulations then specify how the expenses are to be calculated, breaking the sum up into a subsistence allowance, a loss of earnings allowance and travelling expenses. Special rules govern payments to interpreters, medical witnesses and other expert witnesses. The accused may claim a subsistence allowance and travelling expenses, but cannot recover for loss of earnings—see regs 17–23 for details.

30

YOUR PRACTICE

A INTRODUCTION

There was a time when crime was thought to be a relatively easy option for the practitioner. The **30.01** way in which it was perceived—particularly by those in the heady realms of Chancery or commercial practice—was as an area which was virtually devoid of law, and depended mainly upon a shrewd grasp of human foibles and an ability to present the facts attractively. The stereotype was perhaps best epitomized in John Mortimer's masterly creation, Rumpole of the Bailey.

For good or ill, the stereotype is totally at odds with the truth. If it ever had any credibility, it **30.02** has been buried in the avalanche of legislation and interpretative case law to which the criminal practitioner has been subjected in the past couple of decades. To practise conscientiously in the criminal courts at whatever level, it is necessary to keep up to date with the wide range of developments in the law which seems to be forever gathering momentum. In order to do so, we all need access to a range of library and research material—both in hard copy and online. In addition, it is necessary to keep our professional development up to date by attending courses, and participating fully in the appropriate professional organizations. This Chapter attempts to provide some guidance in these matters.

B PRACTITIONERS' WORKS

Blackstone's Criminal Practice (published annually by Oxford University Press) is an authoritat- **30.03** ive and readable text, much used by practitioners. It has the considerable advantage of being equally applicable to the magistrates' court and Crown Court. It has detailed explanation of the various subjects which crop up in criminal practice, including those which are not covered in this book. Hence, as well as covering procedure, it deals with substantive criminal offences, road traffic offences, sentencing, and evidence. It is also available on CD-ROM, and is updated on the OUP website (see 30.12).

30.04   *Archbold's Criminal Pleading and Practice* (published annually by Sweet and Maxwell) is a well-established and authoritative practitioner text, dedicated to dealing with practice and procedure in the Crown Court. There is now a separate companion volume which deals with the magistrates' court.

C   TEXTBOOKS

30.05   Throughout this book, the effects of the Criminal Justice Act 2003 loom large. There is an excellent guide to its impact, dealing with procedure, sentencing and evidence: *Blackstone's Guide to the Criminal Justice Act 2003* (OUP 2004) by Richard Taylor, Martin Wasik, and Roger Leng, which contains a lucid commentary and the text of the Act.

30.06   For a grasp of procedure, the consolidated Criminal Procedure Rules 2005 are crucial. They are reproduced in full as Appendix 1 in *Blackstone's Criminal Practice 2008*, and the text of that work contains commentary on the various rules at the appropriate points. The text of the *Consolidated Criminal Practice Direction* can also be found as Appendix 7 in *Blackstone's Criminal Practice 2008*.

D   LAW REPORTS AND JOURNALS

30.07   The Weekly Law Reports, All England Law Reports, and Times Law Reports should be available in any law library. The specialist criminal law reports the Criminal Appeal Reports and the Criminal Appeal (Sentencing) Reports are almost equally widely available, and they are the volumes to which criminal practitioners most frequently turn when in search of authority.

30.08   Among journals in the field, two are particularly worthy of mention. The Criminal Law Review (Sweet and Maxwell) is published monthly. Each issue contains three or four articles dealing with subjects of interest to the criminal practitioner. In addition, there is a very useful set of case reports in each issue, with a commentary on each case.

30.09   *Justice of the Peace* is published weekly, and contains articles of particular interest to the practitioner in the magistrates' court, together with notes on relevant cases.

30.10   General legal journals such as the *Solicitor's Journal, The Legal Executive, Counsel, Law Society Gazette, New Law Journal*, and *Legal Action Group* all contain a variety of articles and case reports of interest to the criminal practitioner.

E   ONLINE RESEARCH SITES

30.11   There are various resources available on a subscription basis, such as LAWTEL, JUSTIS, Westlaw, Criminal Law Week and the Crime Online service on <http://www.lexisnexis.com/uk/legal/>

which provides the LEXIS service. This incorporates a link to All England (Direct) Law Reports, and updated relevant statutory materials—useful for checking which amendments are in force.

A useful free website is provided for practitioners by Oxford University Press: <http://www. oup.co.uk/law/practitioner/cws/>. **30.12**

It contains links to *Blackstone's Criminal Practice*, giving regular updates from the authors.

The following free websites are worth marking for access when researching particular topics: **30.13**

- <http://www.ccrc.gov.uk> is the site of the Criminal Cases Review Commission, and gives information on the work carried out by this increasingly important body.
- <http://www.cps.gov.uk> provides access to research material, including reports of the Crown Prosecution Service. It is a valuable guide to their policy, charging standards, and the Codes which they apply.
- <http://www.opsi.gov.uk> is the website of The Stationery Office (formerly HMSO). It gives free access to the texts of statutes and statutory instruments. Note that what you will see is the original text of the Act or instrument, without any amendments, in respect of any legislation passed after 1988. However, legislation before that date is reproduced with revisions which have taken place since.
- <http://www.jsboard.co.uk> is the website of the Judicial Studies Board. It contains the Bench Book used by magistrates, and can be used to access specimen judicial directions on points of evidence (i.e., the formulae which are recommended for judges in summing up).
- <http://www.sentencing-guidelines.gov.uk> contains the various sentencing guidelines.
- <http://www.echr.coe.int/echr> contains general information and judgments, with a link to the searchable database for Strasbourg case law.
- <http://www.venables.co.uk> is a comprehensive free site providing links to many other sites in UK and abroad. It has a useful list of organizations providing continuous professional development.
- <http://www.lawcom.gov.uk> includes details of proposed reforms, law under review, and text of recent publications.
- <http://www.parliament.uk> includes *Hansard* for the House of Commons and the House of Lords, the text of Bills currently before Parliament, and judgments of the House of Lords in its judicial capacity.
- <http://www.hmcourts-service.gov.uk/cms/pds.htm> has the latest version of the *Consolidated Criminal Practice Direction*, and the Case Management Forms and accompanying guidance notes.
- <http://www.justice.gov.uk/criminal/procrules_fin/index.htm> for the latest version of the Criminal Procedure Rules 2005.
- <http://www.judiciary.gov.uk> is a useful source of information on the judiciary. It also contains various protocols used by the courts, e.g., in relation to disclosure.
- <http://www.bailii.org> covers British and Irish case law and legislation. It is a useful source for recent cases in particular.

F   PROFESSIONAL TRAINING

Each branch of the legal profession has its own requirements in relation to continuous professional development, and some information can be obtained from the Law Society, the **30.14**

Bar Council, the Institute of Legal Executives, and also the specialist bodies such as the Criminal Bar Association.

30.15   In addition, a number of organizations provide accredited professional development courses. Central Law Training, in particular, provide a wide range of courses in criminal procedure, evidence, substantive crime and sentencing. These are helpfully graded, e.g., 'intermediate', 'advanced', 'update' and are held at major cities throughout England and Wales (<http://www.clt.co.uk>). Other CPD providers can be accessed via <http://www.venables.co.uk/>.

30.16   Although some cost is involved, attendance at CPD courses provides a valuable means of keeping up to date while exchanging information and thoughts with other members of the profession. It is also a useful way of networking. The commercial providers (see 30.15) generally run courses which are attended by all branches of the legal profession.

APPENDIX 1

National Mode of Trial Guidelines

PRACTICE DIRECTION (CRIMINAL PROCEEDINGS: CONSOLIDATION) [2002] 1 WLR 2870, PARA. 51, MODE OF TRIAL

51.1 The purpose of these guidelines is to help magistrates decide whether or not to commit 'either way' offences for trial in the Crown Court. Their object is to provide guidance not direction. They are not intended to impinge upon a magistrate's duty to consider each case individually and on its own particular facts. These guidelines apply to all defendants aged 18 and above.

General mode of trial considerations

51.2 Section 19 of the Magistrates' Courts Act 1980 requires magistrates to have regard to the following matters in deciding whether an offence is more suitable for summary trial or trial on indictment: (a) the nature of the case; (b) whether the circumstances make the offence one of a serious character; (c) whether the punishment which a magistrates' court would have power to inflict for it would be adequate; (d) any other circumstances which appear to the court to make it suitable for the offence to be tried in one way rather than the other; (e) any representations made by the prosecution or the defence.

51.3 Certain general observations can be made: . . .(a) the court should never make its decision on the grounds of convenience or expedition; (b) the court should assume for the purpose of deciding mode of trial that the prosecution version of the facts is correct; (c) the fact that the offences are alleged to be specimens is a relevant consideration (although, it has to be borne in mind that difficulties can arise in sentencing in relation to specimen counts, see *Clark* [1996] 2 Cr App R (S) 351 and *Kidd* [1998] 1 Cr App R (S) 243); the fact that the defendant will be asking for other offences to be taken into consideration, if convicted, is not; (d) where cases involve complex questions of fact or difficult questions of law, including difficult issues of disclosure of sensitive material the court should consider committal for trial; (e) where two or more defendants are jointly charged with an offence each has an individual right to elect his mode of trial; (f) in general, except where otherwise stated, either-way offences should be tried summarily unless the court considers that the particular case has one or more of the features set out in paras. 51.4–51.18 and that its sentencing powers are insufficient; (g) the court should also consider its powers to commit an offender for sentence, under [the PCC(S)A 2000, ss. 3 and 4], if information emerges during the course of the hearing which leads them to conclude that the offence is so serious, or the offender such a risk to the public, that their powers to sentence him are inadequate. This means that committal for sentence is no longer determined by reference to the character and antecedents of the defendant.

Features relevant to the individual offences

51.4 Where reference is made in these guidelines to property or damage of 'high value' it means a figure equal to at least twice the amount of the limit (currently £5,000) imposed by statute on a magistrates' court when making a compensation order.

[*Note*: Each of the guidelines in respect of the individual offences set out below (except those relating to drugs offences) are prefaced by a reminder in the following terms 'cases should be tried summarily unless the court considers that one or more of the following features is present in the case *and* that its sentencing powers are insufficient. Magistrates should take account of the powers under [the PCC(S)A 2000, ss. 3 and 4] to commit for sentence'].

51.5 *Burglary: dwelling-house*

   (a)   Entry in the daytime when the occupier (or another) is present.

   (b)   Entry at night of a house which is normally occupied, whether or not the occupier (or another) is present.

   (c)   The offence is alleged to be one of a series of similar offences.

   (d)   When soiling, ransacking, damage or vandalism occurs.

   (e)   The offence has professional hallmarks.

   (f)   The unrecovered property is of high value: see para. 51.4 for definition of 'high value'.

   (g)   The offence is racially motivated.

Note: Attention is drawn to para. 28(c) of schedule 1 to the [MCA 1980], by which offences of burglary in a dwelling *cannot* be tried summarily if any person in the dwelling was subjected to violence or the threat of violence.

51.6 *Burglary: Non-dwellings*

   (a)   Entry of a pharmacy or doctor's surgery.

   (b)   Fear is caused or violence is done to anyone lawfully on the premises (e.g. nightwatchman, security guard).

   (c)   The offence has professional hallmarks.

   (d)   Vandalism on a substantial scale.

   (e)   The unrecovered property is of high value: see para. 51.4 for definition of 'high value'.

   (f)   The offence is racially motivated.

51.7 *Theft and fraud*

   (a)   Breach of trust by a person in a position of substantial authority, or in whom a high degree of trust is place.

   (b)   Theft or fraud which has been committed or disguised in a sophisticated manner.

   (c)   Theft or fraud committed by an organised gang.

   (d)   The victim is particularly vulnerable to theft or fraud (e.g. the elderly or infirm).

   (e)   The unrecovered property is of high value: see para. 51.4 for definition of 'high value'.

51.8 *Handling*

   (a)   Dishonest handling of stolen property by a receiver who has commissiond the theft.

   (b)   The offence has professional hallmarks.

   (c)   The property is of high value: see para. 51.4 for definition of 'high value'.

51.9 *Social security frauds*

   (a)   Organised fraud on a large scale.

   (b)   The frauds are subtantial and carried out over a long period of time.

51.10 *Violence (ss. 20 and 47 of the Offences against the Person Act 1861)*

   (a)   The use of a weapon of a kind likely to cause serious injury.

   (b)   A weapon is used and serious injury is caused

   (c)   More than minor injury is caused by kicking or head-butting.

   (d)   Serious violence is caused to those whose work has to be done in contact with the public or who are likely to face violence in the course of their work.

   (e)   Violence to vulnerable people (e.g. the elderly and infirm).

   (f)   The offence has clear racial motivation.

51.11 *Public Order Act Offences*

   (a)   Cases of violent disorder should generally be committed for trial.

   (b)   Affray.

   (i)   Organised violence or use of weapons.

   (ii)   Significant injury or substantial damage.

   (iii) The offence has clear racial motivation.

   (iv)   An attack on police officers, ambulance staff, firefighters and the like.

51.12 *Violence to and neglect of children*

   (a)   Substantial injury.

   (b)   Repeated violence or serious neglect, even if the physical harm is slight.

   (c)   Sadistic violence (e.g. deliberate burning or scalding).

51.13 *Indecent assault*

   (a)   Substantial disparity in age between victim and defendant, and a more serious assault.

   (b)   Violence or threats of violence.

   (c)   Relationship of trust or responsibility between defendant and victim.

   (d)   Several more serious similar offences.

   (e)   The victim is particularly vulnerable.

   (f)   Serious nature of the assault.

51.14 *Unlawful sexual intercourse*

   (a)   Wide disparity of age.

   (b)   Breach of position of trust.

   (c)   The victim is particularly vulnerable.

Note: Unlawful sexual intercourse with a girl *under* 13 is triable only on indictment.

Drugs

51.15 Class A

   (a)   Supply; possession with intent to supply: these cases should be committed for trial.

   (b)   Possession: should be committed for trial unless the amount is consistent only with personal use.

51.16 Class B

   (a)   Supply; possession with intent to supply: should be committed for trial unless there is only small scale supply for no payment.

   (b)   Possession: should be committed for trial when the quantity is substantial and not consistent only with personal use.

51.17 *Dangerous driving and aggravated vehicle taking*

   (a)   Alcohol or drugs contributing to dangerousness.

   (b)   Grossly excessive speed.

   (c)   Racing.

   (d)   Prolonged course of dangerous driving.

   (e)   Other related offences.

   (f)   Significant injury or damage sustained.

51.18 *Criminal damage*

   (a)   Deliberate fire-raising.

   (b)   Committed by a group.

   (c)   Damage of a high value.

   (d)   The offence has clear racial motivation.

Note: Offences set out schedule 2 to the Magistrates' Courts Act 1980 (which includes offences of criminal damage which do not amount to arson) *must* be tried summarily if the value of the property damaged or destroyed is £5,000 or less.

APPENDIX 2

Imaginary Brief

John Michael Smith has been charged with burglary from a sweet shop and, in the alternative, handling part of the proceeds of the burglary. He is to stand trial at Barchester Crown Court. The following pages represent the brief which might be sent to counsel instructed to defend Smith. The brief contains illustrations of some of the documents which have been referred to in the course of this book. In particular, it contains an indictment, statements tendered at committal proceedings under s 5B of the Magistrates' Courts Act 1980, a record of interview, and a proof of evidence from the defendant.

IN THE BARCHESTER CROWN COURT

BETWEEN

REGINA

and

John Michael SMITH

BRIEF TO COUNSEL TO APPEAR
ON BEHALF OF THE DEFENDANT

In this matter Instructing Solicitors act on behalf of the Defendant who was committed for trial from the Barchester Magistrates' Court on October 9th 2008 on charges of burglary of a sweet shop situated at 123, High Street, Barchester, and in the alternative, handling 5 boxes of chocolates, part of the proceeds of the burglary. He will plead not guilty to both charges.

Basically the prosecution will allege that the Defendant, together with two persons unknown, went to the aforesaid premises, broke in through a back door, and stole a quantity of sweets and cigarettes. The Defendant's van, according to the prosecution, was used in committing the burglary, and they will call a Mr Charles Watchman to state that he saw the burglars making their 'getaway' in a van number XYZ 999Y. That is the number of the Defendant's van. The Defendant will state that he was not involved in any way in the burglary. Either the witness made a mistake about the number of the van he saw, or the burglars, whoever they were, took the van without the Defendant's consent and returned it to where it had been parked, so that the Defendant did not know it had been taken. Unfortunately, the Defendant signed notes taken of an interview at the police station in which he admitted driving two persons, whom he does not name, to 123 High Street. These two persons broke into the shop, according to the Defendant, while he drove around in the van. At a pre-arranged time the Defendant drove back to the rear entrance of the shop, where the van was loaded with the stolen goods and then driven away. The Defendant will say that he only made these admissions because the police said he would not get bail unless he did so, and he was anxious about his wife, who was expecting a baby at the time.

As to the chocolates, these were found in the Defendant's sideboard. Apparently chocolates of this brand were stolen in the course of the burglary. The Defendant states that he bought the chocolates on the Saturday before the alleged offence. He bought them from a stall-holder in Barchester Market who was selling them cheaply. Counsel is asked to consider whether there is a case to answer as regards handling the chocolates, as there does not seem to be any evidence that they were stolen. The prosecution may try to rely on *Fuschillo* [1940] 2 All ER 489, but instructing solicitors suggest that the Defendant's case is clearly distinguishable from that of *Fuschillo*.

At the time of the alleged burglary, the Defendant was in bed with his wife.

Counsel is asked to advise generally, in conference if so desired, to draft a Defence Statement and thereafter appear on behalf of the Defendant.

No 081123

INDICTMENT

The Crown Court at BARCHESTER
THE QUEEN v JOHN MICHAEL SMITH

JOHN MICHAEL SMITH is CHARGED AS FOLLOWS:—

Count 1

Statement of Offence
Burglary contrary to section 9(1)(b) of the Theft Act 1968.

Particulars of Offence
JOHN MICHAEL SMITH, on the 9th day of July 2008, having entered as a trespasser a building known as 123 High Street, Barchester, stole therein 100 packets of Coffanchoke cigarettes, 100 packets of Coolsmoke cigarettes, 30 boxes of chocolates and 20 boxes of chocolate liqueurs.

Count 2

Statement of Offence
Handling stolen goods, contrary to section 22(1) of the Theft Act 1968.

Particulars of Offence
JOHN MICHAEL SMITH, on the 9th day of July 2008, dishonestly received stolen goods, namely 5 boxes of chocolates belonging to Stewart Salter, knowing or believing the same to be stolen goods.

R. D. Brown

Date: 3 December 2008

Officer of the Crown Court

STATEMENT OF WITNESS
(C.J. Act 1967 s 9; M.C. Act 1980 ss 5A(3)(a) and 5B; M.C. Rules 1981 r 70)

Statement of: Stewart SALTER
Age of Witness: Over 18
Occupation of Witness: Shop-owner

This statement consisting of 1 page, signed by me, is true to the best of my knowledge and belief and I make it knowing that, if it is tendered in evidence, I shall be liable to prosecution if I have wilfully stated in it anything which I know to be false or do not believe to be true.

Dated the 15th day of July 2008

Signed: S. Salter
Signature witnessed by: G. Regan

I am the owner of 'Sweet-tooth's', a tobacconist's and confectioner's of 123 High Street, Barchester. Last week, on the 8th July I think it was, I locked and made secure the premises of my shop before going home at about 6 p.m. The next morning, at about 8 a.m., I opened up the shop. As I went in I noticed the burglar alarm lying on the floor. There were no other signs of an intruder in the shop itself, but when I went through to my stockroom at the rear of the shop I noticed that the door to the yard was open and the lock had apparently been forced. I checked on my stock, and found that these items had been stolen

1 carton containing 100 packets of 'Coffanchoke' cigarettes, valued at £360—I produce the invoice No 2468, Exhibit SS/1

1 carton containing 100 packets of 'Coolsmoke' filter cigarettes, valued at £450—invoice No 987, Exhibit SS/2

1 case containing 30 boxes of 'Naughty but Nice' chocolates, valued at £180—invoice No 2992, Exhibit SS/3

1 case containing 20 boxes of 'Flavourful' chocolate liqueurs, valued at £200—Invoice No 5665, Exhibit SS/4

I have been shown 5 boxes of 'Naughty but Nice' chocolates (Exhibit No GR/1). They are like the chocolates which were stolen from my shop but I cannot positively identify them. I can say that my shop is the only one in Barchester which sells this brand of chocolates. I cannot remember selling 5 boxes to any one customer—if I had done I would remember.

I did not give anyone permission to enter my shop or take any property. I am willing to attend court and give evidence. I wish to claim compensation for all the property stolen from me, and also for the cost of repairing the alarm and the back door, which I estimate will come to £400.

Signed: S. Salter   Signature witnessed by: G. Regan

STATEMENT OF WITNESS
(C.J. Act 1967 s 9; M.C. Act 1980 ss 5A(3)(a) and 5B; M.C. Rules 1981 r 70)

Statement of: Charles WARING
Age of Witness: Over 18
Occupation of Witness: Fireman

This statement consisting of 1 page signed by me, is true to the best of my knowledge and belief and I make it knowing that, if it is tendered in evidence, I shall be liable to prosecution if I have wilfully stated in it anything which I know to be false or do not believe to be true.

Dated the 15th day of July 2008

Signed: C. Waring
Signature witnessed by: G. Regan

   I live at the above address. Opposite my house are the back entrances of a row of shops which face on to the High Street. One of the shops is a sweet shop called 'Sweet-tooth's'. About a week ago I remember getting up at about 1.30 in the morning. I had to get up at that time as I am a fireman, and that week I was on the early morning shift, so I had to be at the fire-station at 2 a.m. As I was getting dressed I noticed the sound of an alarm coming from across the road. I did not worry about it as the alarms are always going off for no reason, but I thought it went on for rather a long time. Then it stopped, and I forgot about it. I had a cup of tea, and left the house at roughly 1.45. As I opened the front gate I noticed a small, dark-coloured van parked about 20 yards down the road on the opposite side. It was parked just by the back entrance to 'Sweet-tooth's'. Two men seemed to be lifting something into the back of the van. Then one of the men climbed into the back of the van and the other got into the front passenger seat, and the van drove quickly off. When I first saw the van, I remembered the burglar alarm which had gone off earlier and that made me suspicious of what the men were doing. Just before the van drove off I was able to see clearly, in the light of a street lamp, what the number was. It was XYZ 999Y. I wrote the number down on the back of an envelope which I had in my pocket. I still have the envelope. Then I went back to my house and telephoned the police.
   I am willing to attend court and give evidence.
   The two men I saw seemed to be fairly young and above average height, but I would not be able to recognise them if I saw them again. It was dark and they had their backs to me.

Signed: C. Waring   Signature witnessed by: G. Regan

STATEMENT OF WITNESS

(C.J. Act 1967 s 9; M.C. Act 1980 ss 5A(3)(a) and 5B; M.C. Rules 1981 r 70)

Statement of: Brian BEATTY

Age of Witness: (Date of Birth) Over 18

Occupation of Witness: Police Constable

This statement, consisting of 1 page signed by me, is true to the best of my knowledge and belief and I make it knowing that, if it is tendered in evidence, I shall be liable to prosecution if I have wilfully stated in it anything which I know to be false or do not believe to be true.

Dated the 9th day of July 2008

Signed: B. Beatty

Signature witnessed by: J. Carter

On 9th July 2008 at 9 a.m. I attended at Barchester Fire Station where I saw a Mr Waring who lives at 10, Cathedral Street. As a result of what he told me I wrote an index mark, XYZ 999Y, on a piece of paper. I later transferred this number to crime sheet 1234. I did a vehicle check, and the vehicle owner came back as a Mr John Michael SMITH of 50 Fiddlers Lane, Barchester.

Signed: B. Beatty   Signature witnessed by: J. Carter

<u>STATEMENT OF WITNESS</u>
(C.J. Act 1967 s 9; M.C. Act 1980 ss 5A(3)(a) and 5B; M.C. Rules 1981 r 70)

<u>Statement of</u>: George REGAN
<u>Age of Witness</u>: (Date of Birth) Over 18
<u>Occupation of Witness</u>: Detective Sergeant
<u>Address and Telephone Number</u>: Barchester Police Station
1, Cooper Street,
Barchester

This statement, consisting of 2 pages, each signed by me, is true to the best of my knowledge and belief and I make it knowing that, if it is tendered in evidence, I shall be liable to prosecution if I have wilfully stated in it anything which I know to be false or do not believe to be true.

<u>Dated</u> the 9th day of July 2008

<u>Signed</u>: G. Regan
<u>Signature witnessed by</u>: J. Carter

On 9th July 2008 at about 10.30 a.m., in company with D.C. CARTER, I went to 50, Fiddlers Lane, Barchester where I saw John Michael SMITH. I told him we were police officers and showed him my warrant card. He invited us into his flat.

I said to him, 'I'm making enquiries into a burglary at a sweet shop and tobacconist's called "Sweet-tooth's" at 123, High Street, Barchester, which occurred last night. I believe you can help me with these enquiries.'

He said, 'I don't know what you're talking about.'

I said, 'Are you the owner of a van number XYZ 999Y?'

He said, 'Why are you asking?'

I said, 'Just answer the question please.'

He said, 'Well, I used to own it, but I sold it about a month ago, and I forgot to register the change of ownership.'

I said, 'Who did you sell it to?'

Before he could answer, the street door bell rang, and a woman I now know to be Mrs Janet SMITH walked into the room. In the presence and hearing of SMITH, I said to Mrs Smith, 'Does your husband own a van number XYZ 999Y?'

She said, 'Yes, I'm sure that's the number.'

I said, 'So he hasn't sold it recently.'

She said, 'No, of course not.'

Then SMITH said, 'All right, then, I do still own the van but I had nothing to do with the burglary you're asking about.'

<u>Signed</u>: G. Regan   <u>Signature witnessed by</u>: J. Carter

I said, 'That van was used in commission of the burglary, and I am arresting you on suspicion of being involved in the offence.' I cautioned him and he said 'It's got nothing to do with me.'

I said, 'Before we go to the police station, I am going to search the flat for any proceeds of the burglary.' In the sideboard in the back room I found 5 boxes of 'Naughty but Nice' chocolates (Exhibit GR/1). I said to SMITH, 'Where did you get these chocolates from? Chocolates like these were stolen in the burglary.'

He said, 'I'm not saying nothing until I've seen a solicitor. I know my rights.'

He was then taken to Barchester Police Station.

Later I interviewed SMITH at the police station in company with D.C. CARTER. At the conclusion of the interview the record of the interview was read through to SMITH by D.C. CARTER, and SMITH signed each page as being a correct record. The interview commenced at 1 p.m. and concluded at 1.30 p.m. It was tape recorded.

On 9th July 2008 at 2 p.m., SMITH was charged, the charge read over and cautioned and he made no reply.

<u>Signed</u>: G. Regan   <u>Signature witnessed by</u>: J. Carter

[There is also a statement from D.C. CARTER (not reproduced here) which is identical in all material respects to D.S. REGAN'S statement.

BARSETSHIRE CONSTABULARY
RECORD OF TAPE RECORDED INTERVIEW

Person interviewed	John Michael SMITH
Place of interview	Barchester Police Station
Date of interview	9.7.08

Time commenced	1300 hrs	**Time concluded**	1330 hours
Duration of interview	30 mins	**Tape Reference No**	12980

Interviewing Officer	DS Regan (J543)
Other persons present	DC Carter (J876)

Tape counter times	Person speaking	Text
001		INTRODUCTION TO INTERVIEW. CAUTION. OPTIONS UNDER PACE 1984 EXPLAINED
025		SMITH confirms he is willing to be interviewed without a solicitor.
0100	REGAN	I am going to ask you questions about your involvement in a burglary which occurred in the early hours of this morning at a shop called 'Sweet-tooth's' in Barchester High Street. Do you own a van number XYZ 999Y?
0175	SMITH	Yes.
	REGAN	Why did you say, when I asked you at your home, that you had sold the van?
	SMITH	Because you said that I was suspected of burglary.
0215	REGAN	But I had not said that the van was anything to do with the burglary. What made you think that the van might have been used in the burglary if you had nothing to do with it?
	SMITH	Well, I just sort of guessed. The van must have been used else you wouldn't have asked about it.
0280	REGAN	So, where was your van last night?
	SMITH`	Parked outside my house.
	REGAN	But I have a witness who lives at the back of 'Sweet-tooth's' who says that he saw your van at 1.30 this morning being loaded up with packages by two men and then driven away by a third man from 'Sweet-tooth's'. What do you say to that?

Tape counter times	Person speaking	Text
0360	SMITH	He must have made a mistake with the number, or perhaps somebody nicked the van.
	REGAN	When you went to the van this morning, had it been moved?
	SMITH	Not that I could see.
0400	REGAN	So, if it had been taken without your knowledge, the thieves had obligingly put it back in precisely the position it had been taken from. Did you leave the van locked last night?
	SMITH	I think so.
	REGAN	Was there any sign this morning that it had been broken into?
0450	SMITH	I didn't notice anything.
	REGAN	So there is no reason whatsoever to think that the van was taken without your knowledge?
		No answer
	REGAN	What about the 5 boxes of chocolates we found at your house? Boxes like those were stolen in the burglary at 'Sweet-tooth's'.
	SMITH	So what, I expect you can buy them in lots of places.
0500	REGAN	Where do you say you got them from?
	SMITH	[After a pause] Off a stall down Barchester Market last Saturday.
	REGAN	Why did you want 5 boxes? That's a lot to buy isn't it?
	SMITH	They were cheap. Why shouldn't I buy 5 boxes?
0575	REGAN	So what you are saying, John, is that either a mistake was made about the number of the van (even though the number the witness got matches the type of vehicle he described), or somebody unknown nicked your van and used it to commit a burglary without your knowledge. Then you tell us a lie about having sold the van, even though we hadn't even told you that the van was used in the burglary. And when we search your flat we find that chocolates like those stolen in the burglary are in your sideboard, but you say you bought them. If you weren't the driver of the van used in the burglary then a lot of strange coincidences link you to the crime. Why don't you think it over for a moment or two? [SMITH was silent for about a minute]

Tape counter times	Person speaking	Text
0715	SMITH	All right, I may as well tell you the truth. Last night I saw two mates in the pub. They said that there was a shop they could break into easy as falling off a log but they needed wheels to take the stuff away. I said, 'Why not nick a car?' They said they did not want to take the risk, and nobody would see my van so long as we were quick. They kept on pestering me, and eventually I said that I would drive for them. So, soon after midnight last night, I drove them to the back of this shop in the High Street and left them there. I then drove around for about ten minutes—I was nothing to do with the actual break-in. Then I came back, sat in the van while they loaded it up with what they had nicked, and drove us away. We unloaded the cigarettes and sweets and stuff at a lock-up garage. They said I would get my share once they had sold the goods. I asked if I could have some of the chocolates as they looked nice and I could give them to people for birthday presents. They said all right, which is how you came to find them in the sideboard.
0920	REGAN	So who are the two men you say you met in the pub?
	SMITH	I'm no grass. I've told you my part in it but you aren't getting any names out of me.
	REGAN	Is there anything else you want to say about this matter?
	SMITH	No, that's about everything.
		INTERVIEW CONCLUDED 1330 HOURS

JOHN MICHAEL SMITH
50, Fiddlers Lane,
Barchester.

d.o.b. 1 May 1978

will say

I have been charged with burglary and handling stolen goods and intend to plead not guilty to both charges.

The facts of the matter are as follows.

On July 8th 2008 I came home from work at about 6pm, and parked my van outside my flat as I usually do. I then had my dinner, and spent the evening watching television with my wife—I remember that the tennis was on in the early part of the evening. We went to bed at about 11pm, and got up at about 9am the next morning, which was a Wednesday. At no time during the night did I leave the house. My wife can confirm this because if I had done so I would have woken her up. I know nothing about the burglary.

Turning to the statements of the prosecution witnesses. It is true that when D.S. Regan asked me if I owned the van, I panicked, and said that I had sold it. It was a stupid thing to do, but I thought that he would never believe me if I just said I had nothing to do with the burglary. About the chocolates, I bought them from a stall in Barchester Market on the Saturday before all this happened. The man was selling them cheaply, and that is why I bought five boxes. I told the police that when they found the chocolates. It is not true that I said 'I'm not saying nothing until I've seen my solicitor'.

At the police station I was left for about an hour in a cell. I was getting very worried about my wife, because she was pregnant, and I knew she would be anxious about me. When the police questioned me in the interview room, I asked them when I could go home because I had to see my wife. They said I could go as soon as I told them everything that had happened. I thought that things looked so bad anyway that I might as well say anything they wanted me to say. The admissions I made at the end of my interview were not true. I only made them so as to get bail.

I work on the production line at 'Wellmade Engineering Works'. My normal take-home pay is about £260 per week, but I am presently on short time, so I only take home £135. I have several previous convictions, but since marrying in December last year I have settled down and gone straight. Two weeks ago my wife gave birth to a baby boy.

Signed: John Smith

PREVIOUS CONVICTIONS

Convictions Recorded Against:	John Michael SMITH	C.R.O. No 98765/89
Charged in name of	John Michael SMITH	

DATE	COURT	OFFENCES	SENTENCE	DATE OF RELEASE
8.10.92	Barchester Youth Court	Theft of a pedal cycle, value £30	Conditional discharge for 12 months	
25.11.93	Barchester Youth Court	(1) Burglary, (2) Criminal Damage (two cases t.i.c.)	Supervision Order for 2 years	
7.6.94	Fulchester Magistrates' Court	(1) and (2) Taking away m/v without lawful authority (3) and (4) Driving under age	3 months' detention in young offender institution (YO1)	2.8.94
1.12.97	Casterbridge Crown Court	(1) Robbery (2) Taking away m/v without lawful authority (3) No insurance (4 cases t.i.c.)	12 months' detention in YO1 On (2) and (3) l/e disqual. from driving for 12 months	1.7.98
24.12.01	Barchester Crown Court	(1) Assault occasioning ABH (2) Criminal Damage	2 years' probation on each	
15.10.04	Barchester Crown Court	(1) Burglary (2) Handling stolen goods	(1) 12 months' imprisonment (2) 6 months concurrent with (1) 6 months' imprisonment for concurrent ABH and criminal damage [the original offences for which SMITH was put on probation on 24.12.01].	15.4.05

NOTE ON CONTENTS OF THE BRIEF

In addition to the documents contained in this imaginary brief, there would, in real life, be a further witness statement from D.C. Carter, who accompanied D.S. Regan throughout his investigations. For all practical purposes, D.C. Carter's statement will be identical to Regan's. This is because both officers will have prepared their statements from notes written in their note-books soon after the conclusion of the interview with Smith. It is normal police practice for officers to confer together when writing their notes, and arrive at an agreed version of what took place. Since the statements repeat what is in the notes, they, like the notes, will be identical.

Defence solicitors, in addition to taking a statement from the accused, ought to have taken a statement from Mrs Smith confirming that on the night in question her husband did not leave the house. They may also have made efforts to trace the person who sold the accused the five boxes of chocolates. John Smith's proof of evidence will be in the possession of the defence, but the prosecution and the court will not see it.

APPENDIX 3

Trial Procedure in Outline

This Appendix sets out, in list form, the usual sequence of events which occur during a trial first in the magistrates' and then in the Crown Court. It is intended as an instant guide to and reminder of what has been described at length in the preceding pages.

A   SUMMARY TRIAL

1   The clerk puts the charge to the accused. If he pleads guilty, the prosecutor summarizes the facts of the offence, and then the case proceeds as at 7 below.
2   If the accused pleads not guilty, the prosecutor makes an opening speech.
3   The prosecutor calls his witnesses to give oral evidence and/or reads out written statements copies of which were served on the defence under Criminal Justice Act 1967, s 9, and not objected to within seven days.
4   Defence advocate may, if he wishes, submit that there is no case to answer. The prosecutor replies. If the submission succeeds, the accused is acquitted.
5   Whether or not he made a submission of no case, defence advocate may, if he wishes, call evidence from the accused and/or witnesses on his behalf. He may also read out written statements by virtue of s 9 of the Criminal Justice Act 1967 (see 3).
6   Defence advocate makes a closing speech.
7   The magistrates consider their verdict. If they convict the accused, they hear about his antecedents and character from the CPS representative. They may then adjourn for reports under MCA, s 10(3) (general power to adjourn for reports prior to sentencing), or under MCA, s 30 (power to adjourn for medical reports). The maximum period of the adjournment is three weeks in custody, four weeks on bail.
8   The magistrates read any reports on the accused, and defence advocate presents mitigation. If he wishes, he may call character evidence prior to mitigating.
9   The magistrates pass sentence (or commit for sentence under PCC(S)A 2000, s 3).

Notes
(a)   After the not guilty plea referred to in Step 2, the court would have to adjourn in order to find time to conduct the summary trial. On the date to which the trial had been adjourned, the prosecutor would make his opening speech.
(b)   The defence need not be represented at a summary trial. If they are represented, either counsel or solicitor may appear. If the accused is unrepresented he may conduct cross-examination, make speeches etc. on his own behalf.
(c)   The court may give either party leave to make a second speech, but if a second speech is granted to one party it must be granted to the other as well. A second speech for the prosecution is made before the second speech for the defence.

B   TRIAL ON INDICTMENT

1   The clerk puts the indictment to the accused. If he pleads guilty, the prosecutor summarizes the facts of the offence, and then the case proceeds as at 14 below.

2   If the accused pleads not guilty, the prosecution may offer no evidence (in which case the judge directs a verdict of not guilty to be recorded), or ask the judge to leave the indictment on the court file marked not to be proceeded with without leave. Otherwise the case proceeds as in 3 below.

3   A jury is empanelled.

4   The clerk puts the accused into the jury's charge.

5   Prosecutor makes his opening speech to the jury.

6   Prosecutor calls his witnesses to give oral evidence and/or reads written statements as evidence.

7   Defence advocate may, in the absence of the jury, submit to the judge that there is no case to answer. If the submission succeeds, the judge directs the jury to acquit.

8   Defence advocate makes his opening speech to the jury (but only if he is calling evidence as to the facts of the alleged offence apart from the evidence of the accused).

9   Defence advocate may, if he wishes, call the accused as a witness.

10 Whether or not he called the accused, defence advocate may call other witnesses to testify about the facts of the alleged offence and/or the character of the accused.

11 Prosecutor makes his closing speech to the jury.

12 Defence advocate makes his closing speech.

13 The judge sums up the case to the jury, and tells them to retire and seek to reach a unanimous verdict. If a period of at least 2 hours and 10 minutes has elapsed since the jury retired to consider their verdict, the judge may direct them that he will accept a majority verdict.

14 If the jury find the accused guilty (whether unanimously or by a majority) the court receives character and antecedents evidence about him. If necessary, the judge adjourns for reports, and remands the accused in custody or on bail for the period of the adjournment.

15 The judge reads the reports on the accused, listens to any character witnesses defence advocate wishes to call, listens to defence advocate's mitigation, and passes sentence.

Notes

(a) The accused need not be legally represented. If he is not, he conducts the cross-examination, makes speeches etc. on his own behalf. If he does not have the right to make an opening speech (and he is unrepresented) prosecutor loses the right to make a closing speech.

(b) If the defendant is represented, the prosecution has a statutory right to make a closing speech, but in practice should not exercise it if the defendant does not give or call evidence.

(c) If there are two or more accused separately represented, and each pleads not guilty, their defences are presented in the order in which their names appear on the indictment, i.e., Al's advocate makes an opening speech to the jury, calls Al and calls X on behalf of Al; A2's advocate makes an opening speech to the jury, calls A2 and calls Y on behalf of A2, and so forth. If Al and A2 are jointly represented, their advocate makes a single opening speech, calls Al, calls A2 and then calls their witnesses.

(d) Where there are two or more defendants separately represented, each may cross-examine prosecution witnesses, in the order in which they appear on the indictment. When it comes to the defence case, A1's witness is cross-examined by A2 first, and then by the prosecution; A2's witness is cross-examined by A1 first, and then by the prosecution, and so on.

(e) If there are two accused, and one pleads guilty and the other not guilty, the probability is that the former will not be sentenced until after the end of the trial of the latter.

(f) Where there is a submission of no case to answer, the judge, before upholding it, would call on prosecutor to present his counter-arguments, as with submissions of no case at committal proceedings and at summary trial.

INDEX